Hellenic Studies 57

HOMERIC DURABILITY

Recent Titles in the Hellenic Studies Series

Paideia and Cult
Christian Initiation in Theodore of Mopsuestia

Imperial Geographies in Byzantine and Ottoman Space

Loving Humanity, Learning, and Being Honored
The Foundations of Leadership in Xenophon's Education of Cyrus

The Theory and Practice of Life
Isocrates and the Philosophers

From Listeners to Viewers
Space in the Iliad

Aspects of History and Epic in Ancient Iran
From Gaumāta to Wahnām

Homer's Versicolored Fabric
The Evocative Power of Ancient Greek Epic Word-Making

Christianity and Hellenism in the Fifth-Century Greek East
Theodoret's Apologetics against the Greeks in Context

The Master of Signs
Signs and the Interpretation of Signs in Herodotus' Histories

Eve of the Festival
Making Myth in Odyssey 19

Kleos in a Minor Key
The Homeric Education of a Little Prince

Plato's Counterfeit Sophists

Multitextuality in Homer's Iliad
The Witness of the Ptolemaic Papyri

Tragedy, Authority, and Trickery
The Poetics of Embedded Letters in Josephus

A Californian Hymn to Homer

Pindar's Verbal Art
An Ethnographic Study of Epinician Style

http://chs.harvard.edu/chs/publications

HOMERIC DURABILITY

Telling Time in the Iliad

Lorenzo F. Garcia Jr.

CENTER FOR HELLENIC STUDIES
Trustees for Harvard University
Washington, DC
Distributed by Harvard University Press
Cambridge, Massachusetts, and London, England
2013

EDITORIAL TEAM
Senior Advisers: W. Robert Connor, Gloria Ferrari Pinney, Albert Henrichs,
    James O'Donnell, Bernd Seidensticker
Editorial Board: Gregory Nagy (Editor-in-Chief), Christopher Blackwell, Casey
    Dué (Executive Editor), Mary Ebbott (Executive Editor), Scott Johnson, Olga
    Levaniouk, Anne Mahoney, Leonard Muellner
Production Manager for Publications: Jill Curry Robbins
Web Producer: Mark Tomasko
Cover Design: Joni Godlove
Production: Kerri Cox Sullivan

Cataloging-in-Publication data available from the Library of Congress.
ISBN: 9780674073234

Contents

Acknowledgments. vii

Introduction. Homeric Durability: Time and Poetics in Homer's *Iliad*. 1

1. Decay, Disintegration, and Objectified Time: The Rhetoric of Time and Memory. 45

2. Men and Worms: Permanence and Organic Decay 65

3. Permanance and Non-Organic Structures: Walls in the *Iliad*. 95

4. Memorials, Tombs, and the γέρας θανόντων:
The (Im)Permanence of Mortuary Architecture in the *Iliad* 131

5. The Impermanence of the Permanent: The Death of the Gods? 159

Epilogue. Homeric Durability: Concluding Remarks 231

Appendix. The Semantic Field of "Decay" in Homeric Epic 239

Works Cited 273

Index Verborum 299

Index Locorum 303

General Index 317

Acknowledgments

T HE GROUNDWORK FOR THIS MANUSCRIPT began in 2005 while I was working on my doctoral thesis at UCLA and became intrigued with questions of architecture, particularly the permanence of monumental constructions and their status as material analogues to Homeric *kleos aphthiton*. Since then, the material that comprised but one part of my dissertation project has grown, with the assistance of many people, into a larger, self-contained work.

First, I wish to thank my former teachers, who inspired me with their work and passion, and continue to foster my ideas: Ann Bergren, Monica Cyrino, Robert Gurval, Michael Haslam, Katherine King, Kathryn Morgan, Sarah Morris, John Papadopoulos, and Alex Purves. My debt to these scholars and friends for their guidance and encouragement—especially Ann Bergren, the *sine qua non* of this project's original form—cannot be adequately stated.

I enjoyed opportunities to present material from this project at annual meetings of the American Philological Association (Chicago, 2008) and the Classical Association of the Middle West and South (Grand Rapids, 2011; Baton Rouge, 2012), and am thankful for the comments, questions, and suggestions from presiders, panelists, and audience members, including Egbert Bakker, Jenny Clay, Andromache Karanika, Andrew Lear, Bruce Louden, Melissa Mueller, Craig Russell, and Dan Turkeltaub.

I am grateful to Ann Bergren, Robert Gurval, Kathryn Morgan, and John Papadopoulos for creating opportunities for me to present my work to the UCLA Classics Department; to Monica Cyrino, Natasha Kolchevska, and Walter Putnam for the chance to speak at UNM's Department of Foreign Languages and Literatures; and to Philip Holt for invitations to participate in the Wyoming Humanities Council Summer Classics Institute at the University of Wyoming.

Acknowledgments

Ann Bergren, Monica Cyrino, Christopher Eckerman, Owen Goeslin, Karen Gunterman, Michael Haslam, Christopher Johanson, Katherine King, Alex Purves, Charles Stocking, and Lowry Sweeney read the manuscript (or portions thereof) at various stages of completion and offered valuable expertise and advice. Brent Vine and Tanya Ivanova-Sullivan helped me with questions about linguistics and provided me with bibliography; Katja Schroeter assisted me with translations of German; and Rajeshwari Vallury kindly looked over my translations of French. Emily Kratzer read more than one draft of the manuscript in its entirety and helped improve it immeasurably.

I extend thanks to my students, present and former, whose enthusiasm was sustaining: Scott Barnard, Daniel Bellum, Caley McGuill, Israel McMullin, Trigg Settle, and Jessica Wells.

I am deeply grateful to Casey Dué Hackney, Mary Ebbott, Jill Curry Robbins, and the entire editorial team at the Center for Hellenic Studies for their friendly guidance and commitment to seeing this project through to the end. In particular, two anonymous readers provided generous and keen observations that led me to rethink and reformulate several positions. My work is stronger and more original thanks to their criticisms and encouragements. Whatever shortcomings remain—alas!—are mine alone.

I thank my parents, Lorenzo F. Garcia and Lorraine Suazo-Garcia, for their support, encouragement, and love.

Finally, I wish to acknowledge Emily Kratzer, whose love, constant support, and ever-willingness to listen to my ramblings on Homer have sustained me these many years.

Introduction
Homeric Durability
Time and Poetics in Homer's *Iliad*

1. Iliadic Temporality: The "Still Perfectly" and the "Not Yet"

I begin not with Homer, but with David Finkel's recent book *The Good Soldiers* (2009). Finkel's book is an account of the U.S. army infantry soldiers of the 2nd Battalion, 16th infantry division (known as the "Rangers") out of Fort Riley, Kansas, under command of Lieutenant Colonel Ralph Kauzlarich. Finkel documents his observations as an embedded journalist with the 2-16 over an eight-month period in 2007 during the first year of "the surge" as the United States drastically increased the number of ground troops in Iraq. The first page of Finkel's book begins with a curious rhetorical strategy, narrating the past from a future-perfect perspective:

> His soldiers *weren't yet* calling him [= Lt. Col. Kauzlarich] the Lost Kauz behind his back, not when this began. The soldiers of his *who would be injured* were *still perfectly* healthy, and the soldiers of his *who would die* were *still perfectly* alive. A soldier who was a favorite of his, and who was often described as a younger version of him, *hadn't yet* written of the war in a letter to a friend, "I've had enough of this bullshit." Another soldier, one of his best, *hadn't yet* written in the journal he kept hidden, "I've lost all hope. I feel the end is near for me, very, very near." Another *hadn't yet* gotten angry enough to shoot a thirsty dog that was lapping up a puddle of human blood. Another, who at the end of all this would become the battalion's most decorated soldier, *hadn't yet* started dreaming about the people he had killed and wondering if God was going to ask him about the two who had been climbing a ladder. Another *hadn't yet* started seeing himself shooting a man in the head, and then seeing the little girl who had just watched him shoot the man in the head, every time he shut his eyes. For that matter, his own dream's *hadn't started yet*, either, at least the ones that he would

remember—the one in which his wife and friends were in a cemetery, surrounding a hole into which he was suddenly falling; or the one in which everything around him was exploding and he was trying to fight back with no weapon and no ammunition other than a bucket of old bullets. Those dreams *would be along soon enough*, but in early April 2007, Ralph Kauzlarich, a U.S. Army lieutenant colonel who had led a battalion of some eight hundred soldiers into Baghdad as part of George W. Bush's surge, was still finding a reason every day to say, "It's all good." (Finkel 2009:3–5; emphasis added)

Finkel's book has been hailed as perhaps being "the best book on war since the *Iliad*,"[1] and after reading it, I can attest to its manifold Iliadic qualities, but perhaps none so intriguing as the temporal strategy of its narration. At the beginning of Finkel's narrative Kauzlarich's soldiers were *not yet* unhappy, out of control, in pain, or dead. The very structure of the *not yet* indicates the present circumstance but contains the imminent future as well: though at the present moment Kauzlarich's men are "still perfectly healthy" and "still perfectly alive," they are not long to remain so, for the narrative marks soldiers as *not yet* injured, *not yet* dead, but soon to be. Kauzlarich's nightmares "hadn't yet started" but "would be along soon enough."

I begin with Finkel's "not yet," "still perfectly," and "would be" because I believe these temporal markers are authentically Homeric—more specifically, authentically Iliadic. The Iliadic quality of the *not yet* and the *would be* are at the heart of this study of the representation of time in Homer's *Iliad*. For Homer's *Iliad* represents its own poetic goals in temporal terms—namely, as the commemoration of its hero Achilles. As a memorial, a work that preserves the memory of its hero, I argue that the *Iliad* is caught between these temporal modes: it remembers the life of its hero who has *already died*, but preserves that memory as *not yet forgotten*. It projects a past into the future, and as such, the epic claims for itself a certain "durability": it endures beyond the life of its hero and aims to protect that memory for the future. It is the nature of this durability I want to investigate here. The epic's projected future, I aim to demonstrate, functions like Finkel's narrative "would be": the projected future is temporally bound,

---

[1] The promotional quote by author Geraldine Brooks, printed on the dust-jacket of Finkel's book, reads: "From a Pulitzer Prize-winning writer at the height of his powers comes an incandescent and profoundly moving book: powerful, intense, enraging. This may be the best book on war since the *Iliad*." Compare the review by David Holahan, "The Good Soldiers," in the 24 Sept. 2009 edition of the *Christian Science Monitor*, where Holahan writes: "Anyone who has read Homer's *Iliad* will have been struck by the graphic descriptions of war. Finkel vividly documents that it hasn't gotten more palatable over the centuries" (http://features.csmonitor.com/books/2009/09/24/the-good-soldiers/).

such that its end, though deferred for the moment, is essentially completed. It is the narrative of the future perfect.

The "not yet" of Homer's *Iliad* and the future-perfect of his narrative appears nowhere more clearly than in Achilles' κλέος ἄφθιτον "unwithered fame" which functions as the very poetic project of the *Iliad* itself. In the ninth book of the *Iliad*, Greek ambassadors approach Achilles' tent, sent to placate the young hero's anger at Agamemnon, the commander-in-chief of the Greek forces at Troy, and to convince him to return to the fight. Achilles had withdrawn from the war, after all, because Agamemnon publically insulted him when he took back the prize of honor distributed to him in recognition of his value to the army, namely Briseïs, a captive won by Achilles' own spear. The ambassadors— Odysseus, Phoenix, and Ajax—have come on behalf of Agamemnon to offer Achilles fabulous recompense, but Achilles will have none of it. He claims that he will not fight for Agamemnon again, "Not if he should give me ten times and twenty times that much, ... not if he should give me as many gifts as there are sand and dust" (IX 379, 385). Indeed, Achilles explains that he no longer holds possessions and their symbolic honor worth fighting for:

ληϊστοὶ μὲν γάρ τε βόες καὶ ἴφια μῆλα,
κτητοὶ δὲ τρίποδές τε καὶ ἵππων ξανθὰ κάρηνα,
ἀνδρὸς δὲ ψυχὴ πάλιν ἐλθεῖν οὔτε λεϊστὴ
οὔθ' ἑλετή, ἐπεὶ ἄρ κεν ἀμείψεται ἕρκος ὀδόντων.

Whereas both cattle and fat sheep can be carried off,
and both tripods and the tawny heads of horses can be acquired,
a man's life is neither able to be carried off nor captured so as to
make it come back,
once, whenever it should happen, it crosses over the teeth's barrier.

Iliad IX 406–409[2]

In the time he has sat by his ships while his companions were dying at Trojan hands, Achilles has come to reflect on the value of human life itself. Material goods can be acquired (κτητοί, IX 407) and taken by force (ληϊστοί, IX 406), but human life—one's *psychē*—cannot be conceived of in such terms. The basis for Achilles' radical revision of "why we fight," as it might be termed, is that, as he explains, he has a special fate:

---

[2] All citations of Homer's *Iliad* are from M. L. West's edition (1998–2000); those from Homer's *Odyssey* are from P. von der Mühl's edition (1984). Departures from the readings offered by these editors are signaled in the notes. All translations are mine.

μήτηρ γάρ τέ μέ φησι θεὰ Θέτις ἀργυρόπεζα
διχθαδίας κῆρας φερέμεν θανάτοιο τέλοσδε.
εἰ μέν κ' αὖθι μένων Τρώων πόλιν ἀμφιμάχωμαι,
<u>ὤλετο μέν μοι νόστος</u>, ἀτὰρ <u>κλέος ἄφθιτον ἔσται·</u>
εἰ δέ κεν οἴκαδ' ἵκωμι φίλην ἐς πατρίδα γαῖαν,
<u>ὤλετό μοι κλέος ἐσθλόν</u>, <u>ἐπὶ δηρὸν δέ μοι αἰὼν</u>
<u>ἔσσεται</u>, οὐδέ κέ μ' ὦκα τέλος θανάτοιο κιχείη.

For my mother, the goddess Thetis of the silver feet, ever says
that I bear a two-fold fate towards the final point of my death.
If, on the one hand, I remain here and fight around the city of the Trojans,
<u>my homecoming will be destroyed</u>, but <u>I will have unwithered fame</u>.[3]
But if, on the other hand, I go home to the dear land of my father,
<u>my good fame will be destroyed</u>, but <u>for a long time I will have vital force</u>,
nor will the final point of my death catch up to me quickly.

Iliad IX 410–416

Achilles has a choice between staying and fighting and dying young, but winning *kleos aphthiton* "unwithered fame" or returning home and having a long life (ἐπὶ δηρὸν … αἰών, IX 415) but no fame (ὤλετό μοι κλέος ἐσθλόν, IX 416). The circumstances that lead Achilles to stay and choose quick death instead of long life are the subject of the *Iliad's* narrative and are well known. What deserves note, however, is that the poetic project of the *Iliad* is to provide Achilles with *kleos* "fame," and that the project functions along temporal lines similar to Finkel's "still perfectly," "not yet," and "would be." The *Iliad* aims to preserve Achilles' fame such that it is "not yet" withered, but in so doing, the narrative opens a temporal perspective of the "no longer": at the end of the war, Achilles will "no longer" be alive; his homecoming will "no longer" be possible. The project of preserving Achilles' fame operates somewhere between the not yet and the no longer, for it unfolds within two temporal horizons: the "not yet" looks ahead to an as-yet uncompleted but eminently potential future (μοι .. κλέος ἄφθιτον ἔσται, "I will have unwithered fame"), while the "no longer" looks back to a completed and irrevocable past (ὤλετο μέν μοι νόστος, "my homecoming will be destroyed," IX 413).

---

3   There is some controversy regarding the translation of this line, whether one should read ἄφθιτον as an attributive or predicate adjective, and hence μοι as a "dative of interest" or a "possessive dative." See Volk 2002:62n6 for a full bibliography and history of the debate. I find Volk's arguments for reading ἄφθιτον as an attributive adjective convincing (in agreement with Nagy 2000:424–425, Watkins 1995:173–178), and hence translate: "I will have fame unwithering" (or more literally, "there will be for me fame unwithering"), as opposed to "my fame will be unwithering."

The Iliadic narrative, situated between past and future, tells of things done and those not yet done—of men still alive and those dead, of structures still intact and those destroyed, of traditions vital and those forgotten. The subject of the *Iliad*, I hope to show, is time itself and the durability of its objects to withstand time's withering flow. Much of my discussion about time and temporality—how time is experienced by characters—is influenced by the insights of twentieth-century phenomenology and the growing fields of phenomenological psychiatry and psychopathology, as I detail in the pages below. But to help demonstrate the importance of time and temporality for understanding the *Iliad*, I begin with a kind of linguistic analogy that has to do with the interpretation of Achilles' κλέος ἄφθιτον "unwithered fame" itself. In Greek, the noun κλέος means "fame." It is cognate with the verb κλύω "to hear," and indicates, literally, "what is heard" of someone, and hence, a person's "fame" or "reputation."[4] The second component ἄφθιτον is a compound verbal adjective in *-το- formed of the alpha-privative ἀ- added to the verbal root *φθι- whose original sense indicates the "decay" of vegetal life and the "failing" of streams of liquid.[5] The adjective has been translated as "imperishable,"[6] "undying forever,"[7] and "everlasting,"[8] to give only a handful of influential readings, all of which interpret ἄφθιτον as indicating the (im)possibility of decay. That is to say, Achilles' fame (κλέος) will not be able to wither away, but will be "imperishable," "everlasting," and "undying forever."

In our temporal interpretation of the *Iliad*, then, let us consider the significance of Achilles' κλέος ἄφθιτον "unwithered fame." The metaphorical application of ἄφθιτον to describe Achilles' fame is that the adjective emphasizes the disjunction between Achilles' own biological death and decay and the "unwithered" fate of his fame. Indeed, human life is often likened to plant life in the *Iliad* emphasizing that humans are temporal beings subject to death and decay, such as in the famous simile comparing men with leaves: "As indeed is the generation of leaves, just so is also that of men" (οἵη περ φύλλων γενεή, τοίη δὲ καὶ ἀνδρῶν, VI 146), or in the comparison of the vast size of the Greek army to the number of leaves and flowers that grow in season:

---

[4]   On the meaning and semantics of κλέος "fame, glory" especially as conferred by poetry, see Nagy 1999:15–18 (Ch.1§2–4).

[5]   On the meaning and semantics of ἄφθιτον and its cognate verbs φθίνω and φθινύθω, see Nagy 1974:229–261, esp. 240–255, Nagy 1999:174–189 (Ch.10§1–19), Floyd 1980, Steiner 1986:38, Risch 1987:4–5, Bakker 2002, Finkelberg 2007:346n19, and my Appendix below.

[6]   Lang, Leaf, and Myers 1950:158; Murray 1988:425.

[7]   Lombardo 1997:171. Compare Fagels 1990:265, "If I hold out here and I lay siege to Troy, | my journey home is gone, but my glory *never dies*" (emphasis added).

[8]   Lattimore 1951:209.

ἔσταν δ' ἐν λειμῶνι Σκαμανδρίῳ ἀνθεμόεντι
μυρίοι, ὅσσα τε φύλλα καὶ ἄνθεα γίνεται ὥρῃ.

They took their stand in the flowery Scamandrian meadow,
thousands of them, as many as the leaves and flowers that are born in
season.

Iliad II 467–468

Dying heroes are several times described as being cut down like trees, including Simoeisios (IV 482), the twins Krethon and Orsilokhos (V 560), Imbrios (XIII 178), Asios (XIII 389), Sarpedon (XVI 482), and—most fully—Euphorbos:[9]

οἷον δὲ τρέφει ἔρνος ἀνὴρ ἐριθηλὲς ἐλαίης
χώρῳ ἐν οἰοπόλῳ, ὅθ' ἅλις ἀναβέβροχεν ὕδωρ,
καλὸν τηλεθάον· τὸ δέ τε πνοιαὶ δονέουσι
παντοίων ἀνέμων, καί τε βρύει ἄνθεϊ λευκῷ·
ἐλθὼν δ' ἐξαπίνης ἄνεμος σὺν λαίλαπι πολλῇ
βόθρου τ' ἐξέστρεψε καὶ ἐξετάνυσσ' ἐπὶ γαίῃ·
τοῖον Πάνθου υἱὸν ἐϋμμελίην Εὔφορβον
Ἀτρεΐδης Μενέλαος ἐπεὶ κτάνε τεύχε' ἐσύλα.

As when a man raises <u>a vigorous young shoot of olive</u>
in a lonesome place, and when it has drunk down abundant
water,
<u>it blossoms beautifully</u>. And breezes of winds from
all directions
shake it, and <u>it teems with its white flower</u>.
But then suddenly a wind comes with many a storm
and wrenches it out of the ground and lays it out at length upon
the earth—
just so the son of Panthous, Euphorbos of the strong ash spear:
Menelaus, Atreus' son, killed him and stripped his armor.

Iliad XVII 53–60

Euphorbos is likened to a flourishing olive sapling (ἔρνος, XVII 53): like a tree, the young man blossoms in the flower of his youth. Death comes upon him like a storm and stretches his body out upon the ground like an uprooted tree.

---

[9]   Scott 1974:70–71 identifies fourteen "tree similes" in the *Iliad* and *Odyssey*, all in contexts describing heroes: "As trees either stand solidly or are cut down, so also there are warriors who remain unmoving or who fall dead on the battlefield" (70).

Significantly, Thetis likens Achilles to a sapling and a plant as she mourns his imminent death:

κλῦτε κασίγνηται Νηρηΐδες, ὄφρ' ἐῢ πᾶσαι
εἴδετ' ἀκούουσαι ὅσ' ἐμῷ ἔνι κήδεα θυμῷ.
ὤ μοι ἐγὼ δειλή, ὤ μοι δυσαριστοτόκεια,
ἥ τ' ἐπεὶ ἂρ τέκον υἱὸν ἀμύμονά τε κρατερόν τε
ἔξοχον ἡρώων· ὃ δ' ἀνέδραμεν <u>ἔρνεϊ ἶσος</u>·
τὸν μὲν ἐγὼ θρέψασα <u>φυτὸν</u> ὣς γουνῷ ἀλωῆς
νηυσὶν ἐπιπροέηκα κορωνίσιν Ἴλιον εἴσω
Τρωσὶ μαχησόμενον· τὸν δ' οὐχ ὑποδέξομαι αὖτις
οἴκαδε νοστήσαντα δόμον Πηλήϊον εἴσω.

Listen to me, you Nereïds, my sisters, so that you all
may know well when you have heard how many cares
      I have in my heart.
Oh alas, I am wretched, oh alas, I who bear of the best of children
      in vain,
since in truth I gave birth to a son both blameless and strong,
outstanding among heroes. He shot up <u>like a young tree</u>,
and I nurtured him, like <u>a plant</u> in the pride of the orchard,
and I sent him forth in curved ships to Ilion
to fight with the Trojans. But I will not receive him again
returned home to the house of Peleus.

Iliad XVIII 52–60

Mortals are like plants because we are short-lived.[10] From the perspective of both the immortal gods and even mankind itself, human life is utterly ephemeral.[11] It is against this background that the phrase κλέος ἄφθιτον has generally been interpreted to signify that through the cultural innovation of poetry, the natural cycle of death and decay incumbent upon all living things can be overcome: by choosing to stay and fight, Achilles himself perishes, but his fame (κλέος) ceases

---

[10] For further comparison of human life to the transient nature of vegetal life in Greek lyric poetry, see Mimnermus fr. 2 W with discussion and further bibliography at Griffith 1975 and Bakker 2002. Achilles' fate to be "short lived" is often noted in the *Iliad*, including I 352, where Thetis tells Achilles that he is to be "very short lived" (μινυνθάδιον), and I 416, where Thetis tells Achilles his life will be very short (ἐπεί νύ τοι αἶσα <u>μίνυνθά περ</u>, οὔτι μάλα <u>δήν</u> "since now your fate is <u>short lived</u>—no, <u>not very long at all</u>"). On references to Achilles' fate in the *Iliad*, see Burgess 2009 with bibliography.

[11] Consider, for instance, Pindar *Pythian* 8.95–96: <u>ἐπάμεροι</u>· τί δέ τις; τί δ' οὔ τις; σκιᾶς ὄναρ | ἄνθρωπος. "[Men are] <u>ephemeral beings</u>. What is a person? What is he not? Mankind is the dream of a shadow." On these verses, see Fränkel 1946.

to be part of the cycle of birth, growth, fading, and decay. Transformed into the cultural product of song, Achilles' κλέος remains pristine forevermore. In other words, within the poetics of Homeric epic Achilles has exchanged his life for a kind of poetic "immortality."[12]

I believe it is fair to say that this formulation represents the current *communis opinio* of Homeric studies. And while the idea that something permanent, immortal, and imperishable lives on after death makes this reading of the *Iliad* highly attractive, I believe it is ultimately problematic because it does not take into account the rich and complex nature of temporality in Homer's narrative—of what it means to exist within time.[13]

This poetics of Achilles' κλέος ἄφθιτον is clearly future-oriented from the standpoint of any given performance of the *Iliad*: in this aspect, commemoration is merely one of a collection of a culture's strategies for overcoming the

---

[12] I believe it is fair to say that the *communis opinio* of Homeric studies holds κλέος ἄφθιτον to be "immortal fame achieved through the cultural innovation of song," a gloss of Nagy's influential formulation (Nagy 1999:174–189 [Ch.10§1–18]), likening the poetic process to that of Hephaistos' material craftsmanship which produced Agamemnon's scepter:

> Let us begin with the *skēptron* "scepter" of Agamemnon (I 245–246), by which Achilles takes his mighty oath (I 234–244), and which is specifically described as "gold studded" (χρυσείοις ἥλοισι πεπαρμένον: I 246) and "golden" (χρυσέου: II 268). This *skēptron*, by which Agamemnon holds sway in Argos (II 108) and which an Achaean chieftain is bound by custom to hold in moments of solemn interchange (I 237–239, II 185–187), also qualifies specifically as *áphthiton aieí* "imperishable forever" (II 46, 186). It was made by the ultimate craftsman, Hephaistos (II 101), whose divine handicraft may be conventionally designated as both golden and *áphthito-* (e.g., XIV 238–239). ... Achilles is here swearing not only by the *skēptron* but also in terms of what the *skēptron* is—*a thing of nature that has been transformed into a thing of culture.* (Nagy 1999:179–180, ch. 10§7; emphasis added)

> In this light, let us reconsider the epithet *áphthito-*. We have already seen it conveys the *cultural* negation of a *natural* process, the growing and wilting of plants, and also, by extension, the life and the death of mortals. ... For both heroes [sc. Achilles and Demophoön], *the key to immortality is the permanence of the cultural institutions into which they are incorporated—cult for Demophoön, epic for the Achilles of our Iliad.* Both manifestations of both institutions qualify as *áphthito-.* (Nagy 1999:184, ch. 10§13; emphases added).

I cite Nagy (1999) here as the best and most complete formulation that poetry, as a cultural process, transforms what would be *naturally* susceptible to decay to something that will no longer rot (cf. Rubino 1979, Vernant 1981, Nagy 1981). However, I wish to note that in his extended argument, Nagy emphasizes *kleos* as an ongoing process: just as the rituals of hero cult must be performed on a recurring basis, so too must epic be performed, repeatedly, so that *kleos* does not wither away into oblivion. See Nagy 1999:94–117 (Ch. 6§1–30), esp. 116–117 (§30) for a claim that epic represses mention of the continual reperformance necessary for its survival: "What is recurrent in ritual is timeless in epic tradition, just like the *kléos áphthiton* of Achilles" (117). In other words, though Nagy provides the best formulation of the interpretation of κλέος ἄφθιτον I wish to challenge, our respective readings are actually much closer than they appear.

[13] On "temporality" as "what it means to exist within time," see my discussion below. On the connection between temporality and narrativity, see Paul Ricoeur 1979, 1980, and his three-volume opus *Time and Narrative* (1984–1988).

"restraints" of time, such as the development of technologies for storage and preservation.[14] However, future-orientation is not always to be associated with the concepts of eternity or infinity implied in translations of ἄφθιτον such as "imperishable," "undying forever," or "everlasting." As I will try to demonstrate, Homer does not present his project in terms of an unbound future horizon. Even those objects that would seem to entail a high degree of "durability" and "permanence" such as city walls, monuments, communal memory, and even the gods themselves, despite their "immortality" and "agelessness," are envisioned in the *Iliad* as temporal beings existing within time and subject to it.

One goal of my study of time and temporality in the *Iliad*, then, is to suggest a different interpretation of ἄφθιτον based on our examination of the temporality of the Iliadic narrative: instead of reading ἄφθιτον as indicating the non-possibility of the decay of Achilles' κλέος ("*imperishable* fame"), I wish to suggest that the adjective indicates a temporally-bound status—that is, that ἄφθιτον indicates not-yet-completed process ("*unwithered* fame"). The implication, as I will attempt to show in this study, is that Achilles' fame as represented within the Iliadic tradition is "not (yet) withered"; it occupies a temporal status like that of Finkel's narrative—between the "still perfectly"/"not yet" and the "would be"—as Achilles himself is represented as "still perfectly" alive and "not yet" dead at the end of the epic, though his death is guaranteed by the very tradition that aims to preserve his fame. As "not yet," the tradition imagines itself as enduring into the future, but as "no longer," it acknowledges both the demise of its hero and the potential of its own ultimate decay.

From a linguistic perspective, interpreting ἄφθιτον as implying a not-yet-completed action is formally possible. As I noted above, ἄφθιτον is a compound verbal adjective in *-το- formed of the alpha-privative ἀ- added to the verbal root *φθι-. Verbal adjectives in *-το- are, from a formal perspective, identical to the *-*tus* of the perfect passive participle in Latin, and the *-*ta-* of Vedic Sanskrit:

Gk. στατός	= Lat. *status*	= Ved. *sthitá*	"placed"
Gk. κλυτός	= Lat. *inclutus* (*inclitus*)	= Ved. *śrutá*	"heard, famous"[15]

These formal characteristics are to a certain degree matched by functional characteristics: as Andrew Sihler has argued, this formation of verbal adjectives in *-το- in Proto-Indo-European

---

[14] See, for instance, Purves 2004 for an association between the "storage" of food (placed in a pithos jar and buried underground) and concern for the "future" in Hesiod's *Works and Days*. On "storage capacity" as a cultural strategy to overcome the "restraints" of time, see Munn 1992: 106.

[15] Buck 1933:307–308, 335, Sihler 1995:621–622, Drinka 2009:143.

made a verbal adjective which construed with nouns that would stand in object relation to a transitive finite verb. Nouns that would have been in subject relation are either absent or are marked with some case other than nom[inative] or acc[usative]. There was in effect no tense to start with, but as such forms refer to states, they inevitably imply something like the completed past tense (once such a category became established in IE languages). (Sihler 1995:622)[16]

Sihler cites forms such as γραπτός "marked with letters" (cognate with the verb γράφω "scratch, write"), γνωτός "understood" (cognate with the verb γιγνώσκω "come to know"), and δρατός "flayed" (cognate with the verb δέρω "skin") as evidence of adjectives in *-το- functioning to mark a "completed past tense." In an important paper published in 1929, Antoine Meillet argued that Indo-European verbal adjectives in *-to- indicate "a process reaching its end."[17] For my purposes of interpreting ἄφθιτον as implying completed action, I wish to note merely that the process of decay, designated by the categories "withered" and "unwithered," does indeed have to do with a process reaching its end.

The same suffix *-το- also appears in the formation of Greek ordinal numbers and superlative adjectives; these forms in *-το- indicate an ending or completion of a process, series, or continuum.[18] Ordinal numbers often appear in Homeric epic to mark the last number of a series:

ἔνθεν δ' ἐννῆμαρ φερόμην ὀλοοῖσ' ἀνέμοισι
πόντον ἐπ' ἰχθυόεντα· ἀτὰρ δεκάτῃ ἐπέβημεν
γαίης Λωτοφάγων.

From there for nine days I was carried by destructive
       winds
upon the fishy sea; but on the tenth day I set foot upon
the land of the Lotus-eaters.

Odyssey ix 82–84

---

[16] On stative verbs, see further Sihler 1995:564–568 and Buck 1933:308.

[17] Meillet 1929:638, "Le rôle de l'adjectif en –τος est d'indiquer un procès aboutissant à son terme."

[18] On the suffix *-to- and the formation of the ordinal and superlative, see Benveniste 1975:144–168 with bibliography. Chantraine 1961:283 observes, "This suffix *-to- is originally the same that we see in the superlatives and ordinals, and expresses, as a rule, the accomplishment of a verbal process." ["Ce suffixe *-to- est le même originellement que l'on observe dans les superlatifs et les ordinaux et exprime, en principe, l'accomplissement du procès verbal."] See also Meier-Brüger 2003:219–223 (§F325) and 285 (§W203) with bibliography.

The ordinal δέκατος "tenth" in Odysseus' narrative marks the last day in a series and thereby completes the numeric series.[19] Likewise, when the Achaean assembly praises Odysseus' chastisement of Thersites, the superlative adjective ἄριστος "best" marks the end of a continuum of "good" deeds (ἐσθλά) that Odysseus has accomplished:

ὦ πόποι, ἦ δὴ μυρί' Ὀδυσσεὺς <u>ἐσθλὰ</u> ἔοργεν
βουλάς τ' ἐξάρχων ἀγαθὰς πόλεμόν τε κορύσσων,
νῦν δὲ τόδε μέγ' <u>ἄριστον</u> ἐν Ἀργείοισιν ἔρεξεν.

Oh man, truly Odysseus has done <u>good deeds</u> beyond counting
both while bringing forward good counsels and marshalling battle,
but now this great thing is <u>the best deed</u> he accomplished among the
      Argives.

Iliad II 272–274

Like the ordinal, the superlative marks the end of a series or continuum. As Benveniste explains, "The ordinal indicates the last term which completes a series, whether by adding to a number or to a list. In the same way, the superlative indicates the final term that brings to its completion a quality that other terms indicate" (Benveniste 1975:162).[20]

My suggestion, then, is that we read ἄφθιτον as implying the completion of the verbal idea of "decaying, failing, withering." The alpha privative prefix (ἀ-) does not necessarily imply the "impossibility" of the verbal process, but rather can indicate its particular temporal quality of "not yet" being complete. I adduce as a parallel Ann Bergren's keen analysis of the adjective ἀδμήτη in the *Homeric Hymn to Aphrodite* 81–83. Aphrodite stands before Anchises "like an untamed virgin" (ὁμοίη παρθένῳ ἀδμήτῃ, 82); her status as a παρθένος "virgin" is designated by the adjective ἀδμήτη "un-tamed," formed with the alpha-privative added to the zero-grade of the verbal root *δαμ- "tame, break, conquer" (ἀ-δμή-τη) and yet, the alpha-privative does not point to the impossibility of taming (here, and emphatically, equivalent to sexual penetration by the *membrum virile*), but rather to a temporal status of not yet being tamed. Bergren writes,

---

[19] Benveniste (1975:145) notes, "the ordinal properly designates the element in a numeric series which ends and 'completes' it, and therefore is the *last* term" ['l'ordinal désigne proprement l'élément d'une série numérique qui la termine et la 'remplit', donc le dernier terme"].

[20] "L'ordinal indique le terme *dernier* qui complète un ensemble, en s'ajoutant soit à nombre soit à une énumération. De même le superlatif dénote le terme ultime qui porte à son point final une qualité que d'autres termes manifestent."

To forestall the realistic reaction of the male, the goddess disguises herself as her opposite. But her opposite is not—as the alpha-privative, ἀ + δμήτη, and the principled, perpetual virginity of Athena, Artemis, and Hestia might suggest—a true absence of sexuality. The opposite of female sexuality is not "female non-sexuality," for any female old enough to be called παρθένος "virgin" is always "tame-able," always potentially sexual. Even virgin goddesses can be made pregnant. In the logic of heterosexuality, *the opposite of female sexuality is only a temporal, temporary precondition*. The only real absence marked by the alpha-privative here is that of the phallus, for the virgin has *not yet* experienced the instrument by which the female is "tamed." No wonder, then, that an "untamed virgin," this absence heretofore of "Aphrodite" as sexual experience, is so attractive to Anchises, for it incites the presence of what is always only temporarily lacking. (Bergren 1989:10, rpt. Bergren 2008:196; emphases added).

In other words, the alpha-privative negative compound does not necessarily indicate "impossibility" but rather a temporary "absence" or "separation" of the completion of a process.[21] Such absences can always be recuperated, and such separations can be bridged. In short, I wish to suggest ἄφθιτον indicates a state absent and separate from the completion of the verbal idea expressed by *φθι- "decaying, failing," but that such separation is temporally conditioned. That which is not yet decayed exists only within the temporality of the "not yet" and the "still perfectly": it remains subject to potential decay.

While my suggested interpretation of ἄφθιτον as "unwithered" is formally possible and can be paralleled by such terms as ἀδμήτη (*Homeric Hymn to Aphrodite* 82) in early Greek poetry, I must acknowledge that an interpretation indicating "non-possibility" cannot be ruled out. Greek verbal adjectives in *-το- are formally different than the perfect passive participial system, and do not always indicate completed action.[22] For instance, alongside the active intransitive ῥυτός "flowing," we find its Vedic counterpart srutá "having flowed."[23] Further, the Greek verbal adjective in *-το- can indeed express possibility, as in

---

[21] See the dense and rewarding discussion of the semantics of the alpha privative at Puhvel 1953.

[22] Indeed, Meillet (1929:636) argues that adjectives in *-to- in Greek did not develop into perfect passive participles specifically because Greek already had a fully developed participial system; instead, Greek verbal adjectives in *-to- were used as perfect passive participles only for compound adjectives.

[23] Liddell, Scott, and Jones 1996:1578, s.v., Sihler 1995:622, Drinka 2009:143. Compare also Greek ἔμετος "vomiting" with Vedic vamitá- "made to vomit," both traceable to PIE *wemh₁-to- (Sihler 1995:622; Liddell, Scott, Jones 1996:541, s.v.).

φατός "utterable,"[24] and βρωτός "edible," though Sihler considers this a "chiefly post-Homeric" development (Sihler 1995:622–623). Chantraine suggests that negative compound adjectives in *-το- played a role in the development of this very *"valeur de possibilité"*:

> The adjective in –τός originally expressed a passive state, but has taken on the value of possibility: a compound like ἄμβροτος "that which does not die" means as well "that which cannot die," where for the simple βρότος the sense is "that which can die." (Chantraine 1961:284)[25]

In other words, the force of a compound adjective like ἄμβροτος shifts from a perfect passive sense of "not (yet) dead" to one connoting passive (im)possibility, "unable to die, immortal." Benveniste goes further in ascribing *"l'origine de valeur de 'possibilité passive'"* to negative compounds in *-το-:

> This creation of compound negatives is also the source of the value of "passive possibility" that adjectives in *-to- often carry, especially, though not exclusively, in Greek. The development of this value comes from one of these unformulated principles, formulated only with difficulty, which underlie many a semantic category and which specifically determine, according to one's "mental framework," noun classifications; we could express it like this: what has never been done once cannot be done. So ἄβατος "not crossed" > "impassable"; ἄρρηκτος "unbroken" > "unbreakable." This sense can always develop in negative forms, as in Latin *invictus* ["invincible"], and it could occur from the beginning. One sees it in the parallel expression in Vedic *ákṣiti śrávaḥ* (*RV* 1.40.4) and Homeric κλέος ἄφθιτον (*Iliad* IX 413) "imperishable fame," inherited from Indo-European poetic phraseology. (Benveniste 1975:166)[26]

---

[24] See Liddell, Scott, and Jones 1996:1919, s.v., for citations; however, contrast Hesiod *Works and Days* 3, ἄνδρες ἄφατοι τε φατοί τε "men both not famous and famous": here the adjective ἄφατος indicates men who are not famous—i.e. "not (yet) spoken about." See West 1978:139 *ad loc.*

[25] "L'adjectif en –τός exprimait à l'origine un état passif, mais a pris la valeur de possibilité: un composé comme ἄμβροτος 'qui ne meurt pas' signifie aussi bien 'qui ne peut pas mourir', d'où pour le simple βρότος le sens de 'qui peut mourir' ..."

[26] "Cette création des composés négatifs est en outre à l'origine de la valeur de 'possibilité passive' que portent fréquemment, surtout—mais non exclusivement—en grec, les adjectifs en *-to-. Le développement de cette valeur tient à un de ces principes non formulés, difficilement formulables, sous-jacents à mainte catégorie sémantique et qui orientent spécifiquement, selon les 'mentalités', les classifications nominales; on pourrait l'exprimer ainsi: ce qui n'a pas été fait une fois ne peut pas l'être. Ainsi ἄβατος 'non franchi > infranchissable'; ἄρρηκτος 'non brisé > infrangible'. Ce sens peut toujours se développer dans des formes négatives, cf. lat. *invictus*, et il a pu se manifester dès l'origine. On le voit dans l'expression concordante véd. *ákṣiti śrávaḥ*

Like Chantraine, Benveniste argues that compound adjectives in *-to-*, like ἄ-φθι-τον, are perhaps the origin of expressions of "passive possibility": as Benveniste formulates it, "what has never been done once cannot be done." An adjective like ἄρρηκτος, a negative compound in *-το- formed on the verbal root *ϝρηγ- (cf. ῥήγνυμμι) "break," therefore means not merely "unbroken" but "unbreakable."[27] But Benveniste goes further than Chantraine in implying that such a transformation from perfect passive participle to "passive possibility" had already occurred in Indo-European, as implied by the cognate phraseology of Homeric κλέος ἄφθιτον and the Vedic *śrávas ... ákṣitam* (RV I.9.7bc) and *ákṣiti śrávas* (RV 1.40.4b, 8.103.5b, 9.66.7c).[28]

As I noted above, I am interested in the linguistic features of verbal adjectives in *-το- because interpreting these adjectives helps us approach questions of narrative temporality. To take Benveniste's example, when Homer calls the Trojan wall ἄρρηκτος (e.g. XXI 447), we are faced with an interpretative question: the epic tradition of the Trojan War is itself predicated on the destruction of Troy, such that its "unbreakable" wall is in fact "broken" at some point, though beyond the narrative scope of the *Iliad*; the tradition of the Trojan War rests on the fact of Troy's destruction. To render ἄρρηκτος as "unbreakable" is to translate the affective, not the literal meaning: when a character hopes the Achaeans' defensive wall "will be an unbreakable protection of the ships and the men" (ἄρρηκτον νηῶν τε καὶ αὐτῶν εἶλαρ ἔσεσθαι, XIV 56), he is projecting a present wish into the future that is in fact not tenable; the defensive wall will in fact be broken (cf. XII 10–18). In a similar way, I argue that through its representation of the experience of human time, the *Iliad* represents itself as time-bound as any of its characters. In other words, I wish to suggest that Homer likewise comprehends the "imperishable" fame of Achilles as "unwithered."

(RV. I.40. 4) et hom. κλέϝος ἄφθιτον (I 413) 'gloire impérissable', héritée de la phraséologie poétique indo-européenne."

[27] On ἄρρηκτος, see Liddell, Scott, and Jones 1996:247, Frisk 1973–1979:II.652–653, Chantraine 1968–1980:971–972, and my discussion in chapter 3 below.

[28] The connection between κλέος ἄφθιτον and *śrávas ... ákṣitam* was first drawn by Adalbert Kuhn, "Über die durch Nasale erweiterten Verbalstämme," *Zeitschrift für Vergleichende Sprachforschung* 2 (1853) 455–471. As Clackson (2007:180) summarizes, "In both traditions, the phrase means 'imperishable fame,' and since the words for 'fame' (Greek κλέος and Sanskrit *śrávas*) and 'imperishable' (Greek ἄφθιτον, Sanskrit *ákṣitam*) are exactly cognate, it appears possible to reconstruct a PIE phrase *kléwos n-dʰgʷʰitom*." For discussion of Indo-European phraseology and poetics, see Wackernagel 1943, Schmitt 1967:61–102, esp. 66–67, Nagy 1974, and 1999:102 (Ch. 6§11–12), 117–119 (Ch. 7§1–2), 135 (Ch. 7§21n6), 184–185 (Ch. 10§13–14), Watkins 1995, and Katz 2005.

2. Homer and His Traditions

In the course of this study, I speak of Homer as a traditional poet, yet one who innovates within his tradition so as to produce specific narrative effects. I draw on specific features of his language, such as the negative compound verbal adjective in *-to-, that mark temporal features, such as the "unwithered" character of Achilles' fame. In other words, I will have occasion to use the construction "Homer + verb" in discussion of the narrative and poetics of the *Iliad* ("Homer innovates"; "Homer uses"; "Homer presents" etc.), and so I should clarify my position on Homer as poet of the *Iliad*. As Gregory Nagy has pointed out in his fundamental *Homeric Questions* (1996), it is potentially misleading to speak of "Homer" as an individual poet divorced from a poetic tradition:

> The usage of saying that "Homer does this" or "the poet intends that" may become risky for modern experts if they start thinking of "Homer" in overly personalized terms, without regard for the traditional dynamics of composition and performance, *and* without regard for synchrony and diachrony. (Nagy 1996:21)

Homer, the poet of the *Iliad*, is not to be separated from the tradition of epic poetry—indeed, Nagy compares how diachronic institutions were often attributed, as if synchronic entities, to a single figure such as a legendary lawgiver like Solon or Lycurgus (Nagy 1996:20–21). Moreover, the name "Homer" may itself indicate the poetic process of "joining" verses "together," thereby implying an inseparable bond between poet and tradition.[29] Certainly, after the works of Milman Parry, Albert Lord, and their students, we know that Homer was an oral poet working within a tradition of epic poetry, perhaps dating back to Mycenaean days, as suggested both by the mention of Bronze Age military equip-

---

[29] The etymology of Ὅμηρος "Homer" from ὁμοῦ + ἀρ- (< ἀραρίσκω "join together") was first proposed by Welker 1835–1847:128; while the ὁμοῦ ("in the same place") element has been questioned, a derivation from *ὁμ(o)- ("together, in agreement") + *ἀρ- ("join together") has been largely accepted, although not without dissenting voices. In approval, see Boisacq 1950:700, Chantraine 1968–1980:797, and Frisk 1973–1979:II.386, s.v. ὅμηρος, Nagy 1999:296–300 (Ch. 17§10), 1990b:372–373, 1996:89–91, and West 1999:374–376. The most extensive treatments are Thesleff 1985 and Markwald's article at *LfgrE* III (2004):678–680, s.v. Ὅμηρος. Both provide a concise history of the question and discuss various alternative interpretations offered by scholars. Thesleff concludes (a) that although it is not possible definitively to rule out a foreign origin for the word, a Greek origin is certainly possible and even likely, and (b) that a derivation from ἀραρίσκω poses no problems (299–300). Of particular importance is Thesleff's note that ὅμηρος and ῥαψῳδός ("he who stitches together songs" < ῥάπτω "stitch together" + ᾠδή "song") represent related concepts: "And the same idea of ἀραρίσκειν is also present in the term ῥαψῳδός where ῥάπτειν apparently refers to the 'stitching together' of the ἔπη (oral epic formulae)" (307).

ment (e.g., silver-studded swords, tower shields, boar-tusk helmets)[30] and by the preservation of ancient dialectical features by the conservative force of the hexameter verse.[31]

I follow the conception of Homer as an oral poet fully involved in a living oral tradition handed down from Mycenaean times. As such, my arguments rely on the traditional character of both Homer's language and narrative. And yet, Homer's narrative does have a distinct quality unlike other traditional epic poetry—particularly the so-called "epic cycle" poems about the Trojan War. Although Homer's *Iliad* is part of the tradition of the Trojan War, and often refers to other parts of the war that were part of the cycle poems (e.g., Paris' abduction of Helen, the gathering of the Greeks at Aulis, the early years of the war, the Amazonomachy and Achilles' battle with Memnon, the death and after-life of Achilles, the role of Philoctetes, Neoptolemos, and the Palladium in the destruction of Troy, the sack of Troy, the returns of the Greek heroes, etc.),[32] it ultimately deviates from those other poems, particularly in its tragic tone.[33] For instance, Jasper Griffin (1977) has demonstrated that the *Iliad* tends to suppress the "magical" or "supernatural" features seemingly common in the epic cycle poems.[34] Those supernatural features which do remain—such as Achilles' divine horses who predict his death (XIX 404–423) or Zeus' tears of blood shed in sorrow over the imminent death of his son Sarpedon (XVI 458–461)—add to the general pathos of the narrative.[35]

[30] The tower shield especially associated with Ajax (cf. *Iliad* VII 219) seems to have gone out of use before the end of the fourteenth century BCE. Consider likewise the Homeric φάσγανα "swords" paralleled by Mycenaean *pa-ka-na* (KN Ra 1540: cf. Ventris and Chadwick 1953:92, Horrocks 1997:197). On the boar's tusk helmet in use before the fifteenth century BCE, see Janko 1994:179–180, with bibliography. On Homeric references to Bronze Age military equipment more gener-ally, see Lorimer 1950:152–153, 212–219, 273–274, Page 1959:232–235, Luce 1975:101–107, 119, and M. West 1988:156–159, with bibliography.

[31] See Janko 1982 for a list of old linguistic features that may provide relative dates between Homer, Hesiod, and the poet of the *Homeric Hymns* based on the frequency of their observance: e.g., the observance of digamma; masculine ᾱ- stem genitive singular in –ᾱο vs. –εω; α- stem genitive plural in –ᾱων vs. -έων or -ῶν; o- stem genitive singular in –οιο vs. –ου; and the oblique case ending –φι. See further West 1988 and Horrocks 1997:196–199.

[32] See Clark 1986 for a review of earlier neoanalytic approaches to Homer, and the more recent discussions of Willcock 1997 and Burgess 2001, 2009.

[33] See, for instance, Redfield 1975, Griffin 1976, 1980, Rutherford 1982, and Schein 1984.

[34] See already Paton 1912 and 1913 on the suppressed themes of the hero's spear that once thrown, magically returns to his hand (and cf. *Iliad* XXII 273–277 where Athena returns Achilles' spear without Hektor noticing), and of marching around a city's walls as a magical ritual designed to destroy those very walls (and compare XXII 208 where Achilles chases Hektor three times around Troy with the Biblical account of the battle of Jericho where soldiers march around the city seven times: *Joshua* 6:1–27).

[35] On the tragic elements in the Iliadic depiction of "supernatural" features, such as Achilles' horses, see Schein 2002; on Zeus' tears of blood, see Lateiner 2002.

Some scholars have taken these distinct features as a sign that Homeric poetry is of a different kind than other oral epic poetry, that Homer stands outside of his tradition in some fundamental way. For instance, Joseph Russo powerfully argued that

> In trying to estimate the relation between Homer and his tradition, I think it more likely that Homer was not the Mozart but the *Beethoven* of the heroic epic tradition; that he represents not the perfection of all that went before him but the eruption of a mighty and singular talent into wholly new realms of expression. My thesis is that although Homer conspicuously carries with him many features of his tradition, there are many examples in the two poems of the kind of creative departure from the tradition, or innovative playing with the tradition, that point to the kind of freedom not found in the tradition-bound oral poet. (Russo 1968:278)

Russo's image of a figure struggling against convention to express something new—indeed, something even *non-traditional*—recalls Adam Parry's thesis in his influential article on "The Language of Achilles" (1956) that when Achilles criticizes the heroic conventions of fair exchange and honor that have led to his alienation from his fellow Greeks, he comes up against the very poetic tradition of the genre of epic heroic poetry:

> Homer in fact, has no language, no terms, in which to express this kind of basic disillusionment with society and the external world. ... The poet does not make a language of his own; he draws from a common store of poetic diction. This store is a product of bards and a reflection of society: for epic song had a clear social function. ... Achilles has no language with which to express his disillusionment. Yet he expresses it, and in a remarkable way. He does it by misusing the language he disposes of. ... He uses conventional expressions where we least expect him to ... All this is done with wonderful subtlety: most readers feel it when they read the *Iliad*; few understand how the poet is doing it. (Parry 1956:6–7)

Neither Homer nor Achilles has a way to speak against the tradition, since the very diction and formulae that make up the epic are part of the tradition itself. And so, Parry argues, Homer and Achilles must "misuse" the tradition; it is only through coming in conflict with the tradition that Achilles—and Homer—can say something new.

I am sympathetic with this reading of *Iliad* IX, yet I do not believe we need to think of Homer as a poet at odds with his tradition in the terms Adam Parry suggests. The careful work of many scholars following Milman Parry and Albert Lord has shown that Homer was not constrained by his medium—indeed, we may think of the formality of the hexameter crystallizing around poetic diction instead of acting like a pre-fabricated mold into which diction must be fitted;[36] in other words, the hexameter does not hinder, but rather helps the poet in his oral recomposition-in-performance.[37] Further, the fact that Homer can transform the very formulaic system that shapes the hexameter,[38] including the variation and expansion of preexisting diction and motifs (e.g. type scenes),[39] indicates that he can transform narrative elements as well.[40] And yet, even these transformations are themselves traditional. Consider, for instance, Richard Martin's remarkable demonstration that the very lines of Achilles' speech in *Iliad* IX that Adam Parry took as evidence of the poet inventing against his tradition, are themselves made up of other formulae and modified formulaic phrases (Martin 1989:146–205). Martin summarizes,

> almost all of Achilles' great speech consists of formulas, either paradigmatic or syntagmatic. That is, the speech is traditional, in terms of the *Iliad* itself. But, more important, the number of paradigmatic formulas far outweighs the number of syntagmatic; Achilles as a speaker (which is to say Homer when imagining how he speaks) chooses to use very small, unconnected bricks for his edifice: only occasionally can he rely on the ready-made longer phrase. Each choice of word in a given place in the line is one that can be paralleled elsewhere, but the effect of this method of composing in discrete units is one of tone: we seem to hear a man searching laboriously for the right word at every turn. (Martin 1989:166)

[36] See the discussion in Nagy 1974:140–149 and 1999:1–5 (Introduction §2–9), 78–79 (Ch. 5§19). Watkins (1995:17) stresses that formulae should be viewed as the surface expressions of underlying *themes*—namely the network of myth, culture, and poetic diction.

[37] See especially John Miles Foley's work on oral poetic composition (1988, 1991, 1995, 1999).

[38] On the "flexibility" and "modification" of formulaic lines in the Homeric hexameter and the construction of "analogical" formulae, see Parry 1971:68–74, 175–180, Russo 1963, 1966, and 1997, Hoekstra 1964, Hainsworth 1968, Ingalls 1970 and 1976, Janko 1981, and M. Edwards 1986 and 1988.

[39] On type scenes and their variation and expansion, see Lord 2000:25–27, 68–98, Fenik 1968 and 1978, Edwards 1980, Martin 1989:206–230. See Hainsworth 1970 for further examples of Homeric "innovation," and more generally Nagy 1999 on the interplay between meter, diction, and theme.

[40] See Willcock 1964, 1977 and Braswell 1971 on Homer's "*ad hoc* inventions"—that is, the creation of stories told by one character to another for a specific purpose, such as to exhort someone to do something, to console them, or to provide motivation for a someone's actions by referring to past services rendered to that person.

Homer's traditional language can be reconfigured; instead of working in larger structural units, the poet substitutes other words or small semantic units—each one itself traditional in its specific metrical position—into those structures, thereby creating "new" formulaic language by analogical formation (Martin 1989:164–166). The result seems strange and new, but at heart is in every way traditional.

I imagine, then, Homer as a thoroughly traditional poet, and yet, like Russo's "*Beethoven* of the heroic epic tradition," less "the perfection of all that went before him" than "the eruption of a mighty and singular talent,"[41] a *creative* poet whose every creation is itself wholly constructed of the tradition, modified for the specific purpose of enhancing the narrative at a given point.[42] When I argue in my investigation below that Homer employs traditional terms in a specific way that brings out their inherent temporal dimensions—such as ἄφθιτος "unwithered," ἄρρηκτος "unbroken," or ἄσβεστος "unquenched"—I believe that the poet is exploiting potentialities already available within the tradition, but with an eye towards the expression of specific significance within the context of the *Iliad*. In a concrete example, the shared Indo-European phraseology of κλέος ἄφθιτον (attested in Homer and later Greek poetry)[43] and the Vedic Sanskrit and śrávas ... ákṣitam "fame imperishing" (*RV* I.9.7bc) and ákṣiti śrávas (*RV* 1.40.4b, 8.103.5b, 9.66.7c) suggests a shared Indo-European poetics.[44] Yet, in the Vedic texts śrávas ... ákṣitam appears in context of long life and prosperity given by the gods, as does κλέος ἄφθιτον in its non-Homeric uses, both of which suggest a tension with the specific deployment of the formula in the *Iliad*.[45] Indo-European linguist James Clackson summarizes the evidence:

[41] Russo 1968:278, cited above.

[42] Consider, for instance, the instances in which the poet introduces possible narrative events that are ὑπὲρ μοῖραν / ὑπὲρ μόρον / ὑπὲρ αἶσαν "beyond destiny," such as the premature death of Aeneas (XX 336) and the premature sack of Troy at Achilles' hands (XX 30, XXI 517). In such instances Homer appears to challenge the very tradition in which he is working—which we may think of as a kind of "destiny" for the narrative in its own right, as Morrison 1997:284 argues—and asserts his own authority for the direction the narrative takes. On these scenes and other "contrafactual narratives," see Nagy 1999:81–82 (Ch. 5§25n2), Lang 1989, Morrison 1992, 1997 (esp. 283–285), Louden 1993, and Garcia Jr. 2007:51–53 with bibliography. On the possibility of Homer revising or working against a traditional plot of the *Iliad*, consider further the analogue of Hera's deception of Zeus which essentially hijacks Zeus' "plan" for how events will turn out: see my discussion in chapter 3 below with further bibliography.

[43] See the evidence collected in Floyd 1980.

[44] On κλέος ἄφθιτον and śrávas ... ákṣitam indicating a shared Indo-European poetic tradition, see the works cited above. For a dissenting view, see Finkelberg 1986 and 2007 who argues that the Homeric κλέος ἄφθιτον is not a "traditional formula," but rather "a formulaic modification created by analogy with formulae and formulaic patterns available to the poet" (Finkelberg 2007:342).

[45] Edwin Floyd (1980) challenged the idea that the Vedic uses of śrávas ... ákṣitam / ákṣiti śrávas imply a fame that will last forever (*pace* Nagy 1974). Instead, Floyd argued that the śrávas "fame"

If Achilles chooses to have *kléos áphthiton*, the glory will be given to him after his death, and his fame will come from the tales and songs of poets. Elsewhere in early Greek the phrase is used slightly differently. In an early dedicatory inscription from Delphi, the phrase is used by the donor in an address to the gods, in the hope that his gifts might bring him imperishable fame. In a fragment of Pseudo-Hesiod, Zeus "called her [reference uncertain] Leukothea, so that she might have unfading fame." In both these passages it appears that the gods are able to grant fame, and that fame is compatible with a long life or prosperity. The Vedic formula is used similarly: mortals request imperishable fame from the gods, together with material benefits. *Achilles' use of the formula is innovative, in that it specifically rejects the associations of life and prosperity and a divine origin.* (Clackson 2007:181–182; emphasis added)

Once again, the *Iliad* appears as innovative within its tradition—here, by making use of perhaps the oldest and most traditional material of the epic, namely the

---

in these texts is only *ákṣitam* "imperishing" within a bound temporal extent (Floyd 1980:135–139). That is to say, in Indic poetry the concept of fame (*śrávas ... ákṣitam*) privileges material possessions which are to be understood as lasting a lifetime, not eternally. Much of the debate between Floyd and Nagy depends on the analysis of one of the three epithets besides *ákṣitam* that qualify *śrávas* "fame" at RV 1.9.7bc: *viśváyur* "everlasting" (Nagy 1974:110) vs. "lasting our life-time" (Floyd 1980:136n6). Nagy responded to Floyd's argument in an important and dense article (Nagy 1981, recast as 1990a:122–127) in which he looks at the etymology of *viśváyur*—in particular its element *-áyu-/-áyus* "vital force," cognate with Avestan *āyu-* "span of life," Greek αἰών "vital force" and αἰεί "continually, ever," Latin *aeuum* "lifespan, eternity" and *aeternus* "long lasting, eternal," and the related Indo-European words for "young": Sanskrit *yuvan-*, Avestan *yava-*, Latin *iuuenis*, which seem to be connected with a root sense of "vital force" as denoting the period of one's life when one is at the acme of his or her physical vitality (Nagy 1981:114–115; on the etymologies, see Benveniste 1937, Puhvel 1954, Chantraine 1968–1980, and Frisk 1973–1979). Nagy concludes, "from the standpoint of the Indo-European language-family the notion of material security is not incompatible with the notion of eternity. To put it another way: the notion of eternity is actually visualized in terms of material security. Thus for example the word *aión*, which is to be realized for Achilles in his possession of material wealth after a safe homecoming, has a built-in temporal sense by virtue of designating the vital force that keeps one alive and without which one would not be alive. The notion of 'duration' extends to 'age,' 'generation,' with an open-ended perspective on the future ... Homeric poetry has separated not so much the theme of material wealth from the theme of perpetuity but rather the theme of personal immortalization from the theme of immortalization by poetry. Achilles is in effect saying that he chooses immortality as conferred by the *Iliad* over immortality as conveyed by the material visualizations of *aión* and *nóstos*" (Nagy 1981:115–116). I interpret Nagy as suggesting that Homeric poetry presents an innovation in the conception of durability: the "immortality" conveyed by return and material goods in the Vedic tradition has become the "immortality" of poetic commemoration (*kleos aphthiton*). My goal in these pages is both to emphasize the innovative feature of the Homeric attestation of κλέος ἄφθιτον and to refine the concept of its implied "durability" in terms of the temporal status and experiences of the characters and objects represented within the narrative.

hero's fame that constituted part of a shared Indo-European poetic tradition[46]—by removing certain features (long life, divine favor) in order to set a specific "mood" for the epic. Against this background, then, I speak of an innovative yet thoroughly traditional poet in terms of the construction "Homer + verb," and focus my arguments on how specific diction and formulae work specifically within the narrative of the *Iliad*.

3. Homeric Durability: Telling Time in the *Iliad*

3.1. Durability and Decay

I have titled my study of the temporal dimensions of the poetics of the *Iliad* "Homeric Durability," and defined "durability" in terms of the *long lasting status* the tradition claims for itself in the description of Achilles' κλέος "fame" as ἄφθιτον "unwithered" (IX 413). In other words, the *Iliad* represents itself as withstanding the destructive influence of time. Chapters 1 through 4 are devoted to the study of this destructive influence—namely decay. Decay is but one of the natural rhythms that appear throughout the *Iliad* as physical bodies exist within time. After nine long years of fruitless battle on Trojan shores, the timbers and ropes of the Achaeans' ships have begun to rot (II 135): time has influenced—literally *flowed into*—the compound bodies of the ships and their rigging, and it has weakened these bodies at their joints, the points where plank meets plank and plait meets plait. Elsewhere throughout the epic characters feel anxiety over the condition of their dead comrades, lest time flow into those bodies as well, and cause decay through liquefying putrescence and the destruction of flies and worms. Nevertheless, decay is still a more fundamental principle for defining the narrative world of the *Iliad*. Consider, for instance, the rhythms of the human body, especially as opposed to those of the gods: human life is caught up in an economic cycle of consuming food and expending energy.[47] Thomas

---

[46] See Risch's discussion of compound names in -*kleos* in Linear B, including, perhaps, a woman's name *a-qi-ti-ta* (MY Oe 103, KN Ap 639.12) which Risch interprets as **Ak^ʷhthitā* (Risch 1987:9). Risch explores the possibility that *Ak^ʷhthitā* may be a hypocorism for a name like **Ak^ʷhthitoklewejja*, a name compounded of ἄφθιτον and κλέος, just as *e-te-wa* / *Etewās* (PY An 657.3) appears hypocoristic for *Etewoklewēs* (Risch 1987:10–11). In other words, we may have an attestation of *kleos aphthiton* in Mycenaean Greek, strengthening the belief in a continuous Indo-European poetic tradition. For the use of proper names in reconstructing traditional epic phraseology, compare Schmitt's argument that the Vedic Sanskrit formula *śrávas pr̥thú* "broad fame" must have replaced an earlier (and no longer attested) phrase *śrávas urú "wide fame," based on the evidence of the Sanskrit proper name *Uruśravās* and the cognate Greek phrase *kléos eurú* (1967:73–74).

[47] See Vernant 1991:33–36, and Sissa and Detienne 2000 on the economy of food/energy as distinguishing mortals and immortals in Greek mythology; Bachelard 2000:140 makes the same point from a perspective influenced by Bergson's *durée*. Boisvert 2006 discusses the temporality of hunger (represented by Boisvert's term "stomach time").

Fuchs, a researcher in phenomenological psychology, speaks of the temporality of the biological organism's need to re-fill, re-fuel, and re-store specifically in terms of the "rhythm" of shortage and satisfaction.

> Rhythm is the way the organism maintains its inner order against the decaying processes of anorganic nature. Homeostasis is not a "static" state, but is marked by a periodical alternation of intake and excretion, exhaustion and regeneration, wake and sleep, ergotropic and trophotropic phases; marked also by disturbances, shortages and corresponding counterregulations. These periodical discrepancies or imbalances become apparent in subjective experiences of urge or unpleasant feelings; as drive needs in hunger or sexuality; as sleepiness, exhaustion, pain or illness—states which all press for their own abolition by a suitable behavior towards the environment. Shortage and need, labor and pain are the price life pays for its inner order to be maintained against the physical world.
>
> This is connected with the primordial experience of time which is always directed toward the future. Plants live in immediate exchange with their environment, without temporal discrepancies. Animals, however, experience time lags, i.e., feel shortages as "not yet." Animals suffer the separation of drive needs and satisfaction. With this discrepancy arises an appetitive tension, a "being after something" (e.g., the prey not yet grasped, the sexual partner not yet met). ... Lived time thus results from periodical asynchronies or discrepancies. It is characterized by the cyclical repetition of drive needs or interests and their orientation toward a compensation in the future. Time experience arises with want and suffering. (Fuchs 2001a:180)[48]

According to Fuchs, our very concept of time itself is first felt in the "asynchrony" or "discrepancy" between our appetites for food, sleep, sex, and the like and their fulfillment. In the nineteenth book of the *Iliad*, Odysseus makes a strong argument against Achilles' desire that the Achaeans return to battle immediately so he may avenge Patroklos' death, for, Odysseus explains, men need to eat and drink to maintain the strength to do battle (XIX 155–170, 225–233). Achilles refuses to eat, so Athena descends from heaven, unseen, and pours *nektar* and *ambrosia* inside Achilles (XIX 352–354). Filled with *ambrosia* and *nektar*, Achilles is temporarily situated in a temporality of a timeless duration; he is, for a short while, at least, freed from the biological economy of human life, namely that we

---

[48] For further analysis of chronobiology from a phenomenological perspective, see Fuchs 2005a:114–115, Fuchs 2005b:196, and Wyllie 2005a, esp. 175–176.

must constantly replenish our bodies with food and rest so that we can continue to exert ourselves. Unlike the gods who seem to have super-bodies that do not need to be re-filled, re-fueled, and re-stored, our mortal bodies always run down: we diminish, we fade, we decay.[49] And so, when Achilles is removed from the temporal cycle of re-filling, re-fueling, and re-storing—the very process by which we feel the "asynchrony" and "discrepancy" between need and fulfillment and which produces our experience of time—, he is like nothing so much as the pristine corpses of Sarpedon, Patroklos, or Hektor temporarily preserved by *nektar* and *ambrosia* against the forces of decay and the corruption of flies and worms, no longer alive, but not yet dead, occupying a temporality between "not yet" dead but "no longer" fully alive.

I hope to demonstrate, then, that temporal complexity is not merely a feature of the narrative's structure, but is, in fact, a major theme within the narrative itself.[50] When Homer's characters speak and act within the world of the *Iliad*, they are acutely aware of time as both an abstract concept as well as a force that produces great change. Physical objects within the Homeric world provide a record of the past that continues to exert force upon the present.[51] The *Iliad* is full of such material records of time, each of which functions essentially as a "clock," an objective record by which characters—both mortal and divine—measure the passage of time through its physical effects. The duration of time itself has left certain traces which can be read as inscriptions upon a pliant surface: the organic decay of ship timbers and of mortal flesh as well as the eventual disintegration of non-organic physical structures, including the defensive walls built around the Trojan city and Achaean camp and the σήματα "tombs" erected to commemorate the dead. These "clocks" each measure the durability of time for men and gods; physical structures decay and disintegrate, and the event of this physical deterioration indicates the otherwise indeterminable passage of time.

---

[49] On the contrast between the "superbody" of the gods and that of mankind, see Vernant 1986, in English translation at Vernant 1991:27–49, and consider Thomas Fuchs' remarks on "optimal synchronization" of the organism and its biological needs (Fuchs 2005b:196).

[50] Consider, for instance, Sinos 1980:14 with nn8–14 on the etymological and thematic relationship between ἥρως "hero" and ὥρα "season": "Both words involve the notion of being *in season*: coming to maturity, ripeness or seed-time" (14). In other words, the epic, as a commemoration of the famous deeds (κλέα) of heroes, must deal intimately with issues of time and temporality—namely, the processes of death and decay each hero must undergo.

[51] See the recent work by Bassi 2005 and Grethlein 2008 on objects as indicators of the "past" in Greek literature.

3.2. Telling Time: Clocks and Objective Time

The subtitle of my study is "Telling Time in the *Iliad*," which I mean in three different senses. In the first sense, I refer to time in an "ordinary" or "objective" sense: that it is like a line stretching from past to future, made up of a series of instants of "not yets" that pass into "now" to be immediately succeeded by still more "nows." The former "nows" recede into the past and become "no longers."[52] The value of this systematic image of time is that it essentially spatializes time and allows us to mark a specific instant; it allows us to speak of a "time when." We can measure this objective time by a clock—the constant and regular movement of the hands of our wrist watch allows us to measure time both at an instance and in its expanse. If an event occurs while the hands of my watch move a given distance, I can say that the event took so long: I have "timed" it.[53] One element of my investigation, then, deals with the question of how one "tells time" in the *Iliad*.

Indeed, Homer makes use of several expressions that indicate "time when." As the German Classicist Hermann Fränkel argued, Homer generally uses ἦμαρ "day" to indicate time when: ἤματι τῷ ὅτε ... "on the day when ..."[54] In this sense, ἦμαρ "day" can be used as the subject of a clause: "the day will come when ..." (ἔσσεται ἦμαρ, ὅτ᾽ ἄν). Homer also uses adverbial phrases with ἦμος "when," which, as Alice Radin (1988) demonstrated, locate human activities within natural "cyclical" (that is, repeated and repeatable) events, such as the movement or position of the sun in the sky. For example, Homer locates the time when the tide of a battle changes by associating it with an ἦμος clause describing the movement of the sun βουλυτόνδε, which we can roughly translate as "to the position of the sun in the sky at which herders generally loosen their oxen."[55]

---

[52] Martin Heidegger calls this the "ordinary conception of time." See his analysis at Heidegger 1962:472–480 (§81).

[53] For a description of time in these terms, see Einstein *et al.* 1952:38–40, Einstein 1961:10–12, 25–31, and Heidegger's definition of a clock, which relies on the concept of time in physics: "*How does the physicist encounter time?* His grasping and determining of time have the character of measuring. Measuring indicates the how-long and the when, the from-when-till-when. A clock shows the time. A clock is a physical system in which an identical temporal sequence is constantly repeated, with the provision that this physical system is not subject to change through any external influence. The repetition is cyclical. Each period has identical temporal duration. ... The way in which the stretch of this duration is divided up is arbitrary" (Heidegger 1992:4, emphasis added). This "ordinary" conception of time as held by "the physicist" is essentially that expressed at Aristotle *Physics* IV 10–14: see Coope 2005 for discussion with bibliography.

[54] Fränkel 1968:2–5. See further Fränkel 1975, esp. 516–520, and the short discussions at Vivante 1970:141–146 and Kullmann 2001:385. For ἤματι τῷ ὅτε "on the day when," see *Iliad* II 351, 743, III 189, V 210, VI 345, VIII 475, IX 253, 439, XI 766, XIII 355, XIV 250, XV 76, XVIII 85, XIX 60, 89, 98, XXI 77, XXII 359, 471, XXIII 87; *Odyssey* v 309, xx 19, xxiii 252.

[55] *Odyssey* ix 58–59: ἦμος δ᾽ ἠέλιος μετενίσετο βουλυτόνδε, | καὶ τότε δὴ Κίκονες κλῖναν δαμάσαντες Ἀχαιούς. "But when the sun moved to *boulutonde*, that's indeed when the Kikonians turned

As Radin explains, βουλυτόνδε is a reference to "the visual, spatial nature of the description of the sun's path. The sun moves toward the ox-unyoking place: that is, the position in the sky associated with the human activity."[56] In other words, Homer does know of and represents specific temporal events, including ritualized human actions that occur at regular intervals or in conjunction with specific solar or celestial phenomena: sunrise and sunset, seasons, the revolution of a year.[57] Furthermore, Homer several times refers to situations that entail a sophisticated concept of time, such as wage labor contracted by time, not task (e.g. XXI 441–452);[58] the recording of history in terms of genealogical tales (e.g., Glaukos' story at VI 145–211);[59] the use of historical or mythological *paradeigmata* in speeches to shape the future response of an audience;[60] and the representation of simultaneous actions, especially when one action occurs at a different *velocity*, such that we can speak of one character or event "catching up with" another character or event "from behind" (κιχάνω, καταμάρπτω).[61] It appears clear that Homer has both a conception of abstract time and a means to measure it.[62] The decaying ships of the Achaeans and the bodies of fallen heroes

---

the tide of battle by conquering the Achaeans." Scholia QV at *Odyssey* ix 58 (Dindorf) glosses βουλυτόνδε as τὸν καιρὸν ἐν ᾧ οἱ βόες λύονται τῶν ἔργων, "The specific time at which oxen are loosened from their labors," measuring specific time (τὸν καιρόν) in terms of position of the sun in the sky. On the semantic difference between χρόνος and καιρός, see Smith 1969.

[56] See Radin 1988:299. See further Radin 1988:299n18 for an argument that the –δε of βουλοντόνδε, when interpreted as referring to a *spatial* position of the sun in its course across the sky as opposed to a *temporal* concept, fits the regular understanding of the directional adverb –δε (so Frame 1978:164, cited by Radin). Radin compares μέσον οὐρανόν "to the middle of the sky" as another expression that indicates *spatial* position of the sun and not simply *temporal* meaning.

[57] On ἦμος clauses indicating repeated "cyclical" time, see Radin 1988:298n16 citing Leach 1961:124–136 ("Two Essays Concerning the Symbolic Representation of Time"). Radin is especially concerned with "sunrises" and "sunsets" as locations of events in time in Homeric epic.

[58] See especially *Iliad* XXI 443–445 where Poseidon and Apollo were once wage-laborers for the Trojan king Laomedon: ὅτ' ἀγήνορι Λαομέδοντι | πὰρ Διὸς ἐλθόντες θητεύσαμεν εἰς ἐνιαυτὸν | μισθῷ ἔπι ῥητῷ "when to proud Laomedon we came from Zeus to be servants for a year for a specified wage-contract," and XXI 450–451: ἀλλ' ὅτε δὴ μισθοῖο τέλος πολυγηθέες ὧραι | ἐξέφερον. "But when indeed the very gladdening seasons brought the end of our wage-contract." See Whorf 1956b:153–154 on the temporal structure of time-wages specific to Western languages and thought, including specifically "the building up of a commercial structure based on time-pro-rata values: time wages (time work constantly supersedes piece work), rent, credit, interest, depreciation charges, and insurance premiums."

[59] On the temporal significance of genealogical tales, see Munn 1992:101–102 and Whorf 1956b:153.

[60] On the rhetorical use of *paradeigmata*, see Nagy 1992, Howie 1995, and Alden 2000 with further bibliography.

[61] See Garcia Jr. 2007:54–61, discussing Paris catching up with Hektor in *Iliad* VI.

[62] One could make further mention of the tense system of the Indo-European verb, which generally divides actions into present, past, and future time, with further distinctions of aspect (ongoing, simple, and complete). Moods like the subjunctive and optative show conditionality—that something may occur, given certain circumstances. Further, adverbs such as ὀπίσω "back, behind, hereafter, in the future" indicate a spatial location of different temporal relations (see Dunkel

in danger of decay are examples of such clocks that provide objective measure of the flow of time.

3.3. Telling Time: Temporality, a Phenomenological Approach

The second implication of "Telling Time in the *Iliad*" is how time is narrated— that is, how does Homer *tell us* about time? How does Homer describe his characters' experiences of time? As the Achaean ships lie decaying on Trojan shores, the Achaeans have lived through those same nine years of frustration, and their moral resolve and sense of social responsibility have likewise decayed. From Patroklos' death in the sixteenth book of the *Iliad* until his burial in the twenty-third, Achilles is aware of the fact of his dead companion as a body and of the danger of its unseemly decay. Achilles' own concern over his friend involves him in a specific experience of time that Homer aims to reproduce for us. The gods themselves, when caught up in their care for mortals, come to experience time like humans do. I borrow the term "temporality," which designates the human experience of time, from the philosophical phenomenology of Edmund Husserl[63] and Martin Heidegger,[64] and use it to mark the difference of the experience of time (= temporality) from objective time itself (= ordinary time, as discussed in section 3.2 above).

Husserl's phenomenological analysis marks a radical distinction between an objective time, which can be measured with clocks, and a subjective time constituted by the ongoing stream of consciousness of being in the world. Husserl describes how the perception of an object in the world implies an internal consciousness of temporal succession, such that we can observe continuity of an object through change.[65] But objects we perceive in time are themselves temporalized by the very fact of our perceiving them: they are "temporal objects" in

---

1982–1983 and Bettini 1991 on the spatialization of temporal relations through adverbs, and Purves 2004 on image of the pithos jar used to store food *beneath* the ground as a spatialization of the "future").

63 I refer specifically to Husserl 1962 (original edition 1913), 1991 (original edition 1928), and his 1905 lecture notes on "internal time consciousness" published in translation as Husserl 1981.

64 The works I draw on here are Heidegger's *Being and Time* (1927, rpt. 2006, trans. 1962), and two lectures that led up to that work: (1) Heidegger's *"Der Begriff der Zeit"* ("The Concept of Time") delivered to the Marburg Theological Society in July, 1924 (available in English translation with the original German on facing-pages as Heidegger 1992); and (2) his 1925 lecture series *"Geschichte des Zeitbegriffs"* ("History of the Concept of Time") published in 1979 as volume 20 of Heidegger's *Gesamtausgabe* and translated into English as Heidegger 1985.

65 "Duration, succession, changes *appear*. What is implied in this appearing? In a succession, for example, a 'now' appears and, in union with it, a 'past.' The unity of the consciousness that encompasses intentionally what is present and what is past is a phenomenological datum" (Husserl 1991:16, §6)

Husserl's terminology.[66] A temporal object is an object, like a tone, or a melody, or even an architectural construction, which is temporally extended in our perception, and yet is still experienced as a whole or a unity. In our perception of the first tone of a melody or the front façade of a building, the objects remain in our consciousness as we hear the subsequent tones or see the other elements of the construction. The temporal object is not experienced as a succession of discrete "now"-points along a time-line, but rather as a continuum which incorporates a present "now"-point with the "now"-point that has become "just-past." I hear a present tone not as a "now" divorced from what came before, but as succeeding a tone just-past which is still retained in my present consciousness: Husserl calls this hold-over of the past continuing into the present a *retention* (Husserl 1991:32–36). Furthermore, as we hear a few notes of a melody or see a few elements of a building, we begin to anticipate the rest: though we have not yet perceived these elements, they too exist in the present moment as a *protension* of our present act of perception (Husserl 1991:40, cf. 54–59). The entire phenomenon of our perception, then, is temporally conditioned, since we experience objects (at least certain objects) as temporal entities: from this perspective, the time in which the Achaeans' ships rot can be differentiated from the temporality of the men who watch them deteriorate, day after day. Further, the very perception or experience of temporal objects is itself a temporalizing act: through perceiving and experiencing, we are ourselves drawn into an experience of time—we feel its duration.

Husserl's concept of temporal objects and the experience of time as duration will prove useful for our analysis of a specific kind of temporal event, namely the experience of pain and sorrow. Researchers in phenomenology, psychiatry, psychopathology, and neuroscience have distinguished two different temporal modes experienced by patients suffering pain and sorrow: "implicit" and "explicit" temporality. Implicit temporality is the "lived time" we experience when we are engaged in a given task and seem to forget about time or the outside world altogether.[67] Explicit temporality is precisely the opposite: we are unable to engage in our tasks because something is constantly distracting us and dragging us back into the world—namely our own physical body experienced

---

[66] "By *temporal objects in the specific sense* we understand objects that are not only unities in time but that also contain temporal extension in themselves. When a tone sounds, my objectivating apprehension can make the tone itself, which endures and fades away, into an object and yet not make the duration of the tone or the tone in its duration into an object. The latter—the tone in its duration—is a temporal object. The same is true of a melody, of any change whatsoever, but also of any persistence without change, considered as such" (Husserl 1991:24).

[67] Fuchs 2005b:195. On "lived time," see Minkowski 1970, Fuchs 2001a, Wyllie 2005a, 2005b.

as a distraction, hindrance, or obstacle to our activities.[68] Explicit temporality is the experience of our corporal body "turning into the object of attention" (Fuchs 2005b:196).[69] As Thomas Fuchs explains,

> Lived time may be regarded as a function of the lived body, opened up by its potentiality and capability. The more we are engaged in our tasks, the more we forget about time as well as the body; we are, as it were, "inside time." On the other hand, in explicit temporality the body often appears in the corporal or explicit mode as well. For example, when falling ill, we experience the body no more as a tacit medium but rather as an object or obstacle, while we notice the slowing down of time and may even feel excluded from the movement of life. Thus, embodiment and temporality have a parallel background-foreground structure. (Fuchs 2005b:196)

We come to experience time when we are in moments of crisis when we are in need, pain, or shame, and our attention is drawn from our task at hand, our living and acting in the world, to our own physicality. Temporality is constructed, first and foremost, then, as explicit self-consciousness as a body in the world. We

---

[68] Fuchs speaks of disturbances of lived time in terms of "synchrony" and "desynchronization." When we are "in synch" with the "manifold ways of timing" that constitute our participation in the social world we share with others (including the rhythms of sleeping, eating, working, and so on), we are caught up in "lived time"; we are "synchronized" with the world. However, we become "desynchronized" from the world on both biological and social levels through the experience of loss (e.g., hunger = biological loss; grief = social loss); these experiences of loss "entangle the person in his/her past, and he/she temporarily loses the lived synchrony with others" (Fuchs 2001a:181). Compare Minkowski's distinction between "syntony" and "schizoidism" which he calls a "functional asymmetry": Minkowski's terms capture the same basic structure as Fuchs, though from a perspective of personal "*élan vital*" rather than of shared "social time" or "world time" (Minkowski 1970:xxv, 73–76, 291–294; cf. Fuchs 2001a:180). See further Toombs 1992:62–70 on "the lived body in illness."

[69] On the distinction between the "lived body" and "corporal body," see Fuchs 2001b, esp. 224–225: "The *lived body* means not only the felt body, the subjective space of bodily sensations, but comprises my prereflective experience as a whole, insofar as it is conveyed by the medium of the body, by its senses and limbs. I act through my body, perceive and exist through it, without explicitly reflecting on it. ... [T]he corporeal body appears whenever a reaction or resistance arises to the primary performance of the lived-body; when the body loses its prereflective, automatic coherence with the surrounding world; when our spontaneous bodily expressions are disturbed, blocked, or objectified by an inversion of our attention upon ourselves. The corporeal body is the obstinate or heavy body that eludes my disposal; the body as shown or exposed to others; the body that I am bound to, or that I reflect upon." In other words, the corporeal body is the body as such that is now object of our thought because it has been brought to our attention in moments of need (hunger, sleep, sexual desire, etc.), pain, or shame. See Fuchs 2001b, 2003, 2005a. On the body becoming the whole of our attention in moments of pain, see Scarry 1985; on the experience of the body in illness, see Toombs 1992.

feel time when we are in pain. Accordingly, several recent studies on illness, pain, and medical ethics have utilized Husserl's phenomenology to analyze the temporal experience of suffering physical pain.[70] Calvin Schrag argues that pain is a lived experience, and, as such, the patient is drawn into the temporality of duration as he or she must endure the pains:

> Being in pain, as an undivided process and structure of configurative behavior, is that which one *lives through. Pain has a durational dimension. Pains endure*, even if only for a moment—which is never an abstracted, discrete atomic instant. ... The moments of pain are subject to the variability and intensity of concerns within its time span. They do not follow the regular and ordered sequence of seconds and minutes that are marked off by the swing of a pendulum or the ticking of a clock. Clock time is isotropic. The values of its units are uniform. The time of one's being in pain is anisotropic. Its values vary with the intensity of the pain. (Schrag 1982:122; emphasis added)

Pains endure; feeling pain is a temporal experience. We suffer it through a temporal experience incommensurate with objective clock-time: in its intensity minutes may seem like hours.[71] We do not experience pain as a series of "atomic instants"—we experience it as one of Husserl's temporal objects, as S. Kay Toombs explains: "the person in pain experiences his pain as a continuum. ... [P]ains just-past are retained in consciousness, along with the present now-pain, and future pains are anticipated as part of the present experience" (Toombs 1990:132).[72] The temporality of being in pain consists of the retention of pains just-passed and the protension of pains yet-to-come: the experience, measured by its own rhythm of throbs and aches, enfolds us in a temporal experience of duration.

In chapter 5, I demonstrate that when Homer's gods are forced to suffer physical pain, they become enmeshed in human temporality: no longer outside of time, they feel their pain as duration. Homer uses the verb *τλάω to mark a god (or a mortal) "enduring" pain through time, as when Dione consoles Aphrodite, wounded by Diomedes' spear, with stories of other gods who have "endured" pains at mortal hands: τλῆμεν ... ἐξ ἀνδρῶν χαλέπ' ἄλγε' "we endured difficult pains at the hands of men" (V 383–384). Ares, Hera, and Hades all "endure" (τλῆ μὲν Ἄρης ... τλῆ δ' Ἥρα ... τλῆ δ' Ἀΐδης ..., V 385, 392, 395) pains.

---

[70] See, for instance, Kestenbaum 1982, Schrag 1982, Leder 1984–1985, 1992, Scarry 1985, and Toombs 1990, 1992.

[71] Kestenbaum 1982:13–16, Toombs 1990:237, 1992:62–70, 90–98.

[72] See further Toombs 1992:15 on "temporality," and 51–80 on "the lived body."

Indeed, the most basic sense of the very rich and complex verb *τλάω and its cognates seems to be "to hold up," as in the nouns τελαμών which indicates the "strap" which holds up a sword or shield or the "base" that holds up a *stēlē*,[73] and τάλαντον, which Homer uses in the plural to denote "scales" which hold up and measure the relative weight of two things.[74] When someone "holds up" and "endures," they experience time as duration, as Homer indicates by using the adverbs δηρόν and δήν "for a long time" in conjunction with a god's experience of pain, as when Ares, wounded by Diomedes' spear, lies suffering "for a long time" (δηρόν, V 885), or when the Achaeans experience the many years waiting on Trojan shores without taking the city (δηρόν, II 298; cf. τλῆτε, II 299 and my discussion in chapter 1 below). The second major use of *τλάω as "to dare to do something"[75] seems to follow from the sense of holding up and enduring through time: while enduring, one develops a kind of future orientation—an anticipation of the day when one will no longer be under duress. As Fuchs argues, while in pain, the temporality we experience is a future-oriented "not yet": I am not yet out of pain, but am driven forward to try to alleviate or escape it (Fuchs 2003:71–72). Compare, for instance, Archilochus fr. 13 W where "the gods placed in addition powerful endurance (κρατερὴν τλημοσύνην) as an antidote (φάρμακον) for incurable evils (ἀνηκέστοισι κακοῖσιν)" (5–6). In the context of providing a consolation for people mourning those lost at sea, the poet suggests that "endurance" may—in time—provide a cure against even those evils that now seem "incurable," for, as he explains, fortune changes in time, such that though we now suffer, at some later time someone other than us will suffer (7–9). Indeed, the very rhetoric of a *consolatio*, as in Archilochus 13 W or in Dione's speech to Aphrodite, is that pain will eventually subside over time if one endures. Through sustained endurance what is "incurable" (ἀνήκεστος)[76] can eventually come to be cured: what is affectively incurable is literally merely that which has not yet been cured. Temporally speaking, as long as a possible future lies open, the unaccomplished may still be accomplished.

The durability of characters or structures in the *Iliad*—including the poetics of the *Iliad* itself—relies on that character's or structure's ability to *endure*. The very fact that gods can be made to endure—that is, to suffer and experience time the way a mortal does—suggests that gods and men, in temporal terms, are not necessarily that different.

---

[73] See Liddell, Scott, and Jones 1996:1769, s.v. τελαμών.

[74] See *Iliad* XII 433 for a simile of a woman weighing out wool with scales, and VIII 69, XXII 209 for the scales Zeus uses to weigh out human destinies (and cf. XIX 223 and *Homeric Hymn to Hermes* 324).

[75] Compare the uses at *Iliad* I 228, VII 480, XXI 150, XXIV 35, 505, 519.

[76] ἀνήκεστος is the negative compound adjective (ἀ- "not (yet)") in *-το- built on the nominal stem *ηκεσ- "cure" (< ἄκος "cure"; cf. the denominative ἀκέομαι "to cure").

3.4. Telling Time: The Narrative Temporality of the *Iliad*

The final significance of my subtitle "Telling Time" is that the very representation of time and temporality in the *Iliad* tells us something about the epic. The representation of time itself is telling: it teaches us about the tragic dimensions of mortal temporality, and locates the poetics of the *Iliad* within this same temporality. Here I turn to Martin Heidegger, Husserl's student, who took the concept of temporality even further than his teacher, associating temporality not merely with human perception, but with our very being:[77] "What is this now (*diese Jetzt*), the time now as I look at my watch? ... Am I the now (*Bin ich das Jetzt*)? Is every other person the now? Then time would indeed be I myself, and every other person would be time. And in our being with one another we would be time—everyone and no one" (Heidegger 1992:5).[78]

Heidegger envisions temporality in broader terms than Husserl: it is our very condition of existing in the world among other beings; our existence is defined as a "Being-there" (*Da-sein*) in the world with other beings,[79] before and about whom we feel anxiety (*Angst*).[80] Our "care" (*Sorge*) for ourselves, for being in the world (*Besorgen*), and for other beings (*Fürsorge*), constitutes our very being-in-the-world: through our concern for other beings, we become "entangled" (*verfängt*) in our care for them.[81] We feel anxiety not over any particular

---

[77] In his summer semester course of 1928 titled "Metaphysical Foundations of Logic," Heidegger noted, "That which Husserl still calls time-consciousness, i.e., consciousness of time, is precisely time, itself, in the primordial sense" (cited at Dastur 1998:9).

[78] For further differentiation between "clock time" and Heidegger's temporality as being itself, see Dastur 1998:3–4.

[79] On *Dasein*, see Heidegger 1962:150 (= 2006:114), "Dasein is an entity which is in each case I myself; its Being is in each case mine (*Dasein ist Seiendes, das je ich selbst bin, das Sein ist je meines*)." On Dasein's being-in-the-world, see Heidegger 1992:7, "Dasein is that entity which is characterized as *being-in-the-world* (*In-der-Welt-sein*)." See also Heidegger 1962:225 (= 2006:114) on being-in-the-world consisting of a "Being-there with others" (*das Mitdasein der Anderen*): "By reason of this *with-like* (*mithaften*) Being-in-the-world (*In-der-Welt-seins*), the world is always the one that I share with Others. The world of Dasein is a *with-world* (*Die Welt des Daseins ist Mitwelt*). Being-in is *Being-with Others* (*Das In-Sein ist Mitsein mit Anderen*). Their Being-in-themselves within-the-world is *Dasein-with* (*Mitdasein*)" (1962:155 = 2006:118).

[80] On Heidegger's use of "anxiety" (*Angst*), see Heidegger 1962:227–235 (= 2006:182–191), especially pp. 231–232 where he defines the source of anxiety as "Being-in-the world itself." Dastur (1998:25) observes, "'that' which makes us anxious is already there, at once nowhere and yet so close that it takes our breath away, literally choking us (*Angst* has the same root as the Latin *angustus*, which means narrow)." On Heidegger's *Angst*, see further Inwood 1999:16–18.

[81] On Heidegger's *Sorge*, *Besorgen*, and *Fürsorge*, see Inwood 1999:35–37. Heidegger uses the term "care" (*Sorge*) "in a purely ontologico-existential manner" (1962:237 = 2006:193), such that "This expression [= *Sorge* "care"] too is to be taken as an ontological structural concept. It has nothing to do with 'tribulation,' 'melancholy,' or the 'cares of life,' though ontically one can come across these in every Dasein" (1962:84 = 2006:57). Nevertheless, as Heidegger points out in the following sentence, "These—like their opposites, 'gaiety' and 'freedom from care'—are ontically possible

danger, but over possibility itself, which is to say the possibility of our actions.[82] Heidegger takes this concern over our possibility as an indication that our being is temporally conditioned: existence is oriented toward the future, and the ultimate limit of our future possibility is death.[83] Like Solon's proclamation in Herodotus' account of his visit to the Lydian king Croesus (*Histories* 1.29–33), death, for Heidegger, defines our being by providing its end: "how is this entity to be apprehended in its Being before it has reached its end? After all, I am still underway with my Dasein. It is still something that is not yet at an end" (Heidegger 1992:10).[84] The implication—clearer in his earlier work of 1924 and 1925 than in his *Being in Time* of 1927—is that death provides a kind of narrative

---

only because Dasein, when understood *ontologically*, is care" (Ibid.). In other words, even though Heidegger's concern is with the ontological structure of being, his analysis still holds true for the specific "ontic" phenomena of feeling care for oneself or another—tribulation, melancholy, gaiety, and even freedom from care—since they are possible through the ontological structure of care. On this point, see Hubert Dreyfus's analysis of "the care-structure" in Heidegger's *Being and Time*: "In a conversation with Heidegger I pointed out that 'care' in English has connotations of love and caring. He responded that that was fortunate since with the term 'care' he wanted to name the very general fact that '*Sein geht mich an*,' roughly, that being gets to me. *Thus all ontic senses of caring are to be included as modes of ontological caring*" (Dreyfus 1991:239, emphasis added).

[82] See Heidegger 1962:401–418 (= 2006:350–366) on the temporal structure of the "in-order-to" (*das Um-zu*) and the "towards-which" (*das Wozu*) of intentionality. See further Heidegger 1985:303–304 on the connection between intentionality and "care."

[83] Heidegger 1962:285–311 (= 2006:241–267). Cf. Heidegger 1992:11, "The end of my Dasein, my death (*Das Ende meines Daseins, mein Tod*), is not some point at which a sequence of events suddenly breaks off, but a possibility (*eine Möglichkeit*) which Dasein knows of in this or that way: the most extreme possibility of itself (*die äußerste Möglichkeit seiner selbst*), which it can seize and appropriate as standing before it. Dasein has in itself the possibility of meeting with its death as the most extreme possibility of itself." This possibility is precisely "*its ownmost possibility of being at an end (Zu-Ende-seins)*."

[84] Note that Heidegger indicates a difference between biological death, which he terms "demise" (*Ableben*), and "dying" (*Sterben*) which does not refer to the physical death of Dasein, but rather its end in a different sense—namely, as the possibility of its no longer existing in the world: "Let the term '*dying*' stand for that *way of Being* in which Dasein is *toward* its death (*Sterben aber gelte als Titel für die Seinsweise, in der das Dasein zu seinem Tode ist*)" (1962:291 = 2006:247); "With death, Dasein stands before its *ownmost* potentiality-for-Being (*Seinkönnen*). This is a possibility in which the issue is nothing less than Dasein's Being-in-the-world. Its death is the possibility of no-longer being-able-to-be-there (*Sein Tod ist dei Möglichkeit des Nicht-mehr-dasein-könnens*). If Dasein stands before itself as this possibility, it has been *fully* assigned to its ownmost potentiality-for-Being" (1962:294 = 2006:250).

On the theme of the "end" of life giving definition to that life—and, significantly, to the narrative about that life, see Dunn 1996 (esp. 3–6 with n5) on "endings" in Greek tragedy, citing Aeschylus *Agamemnon* 928–929, Sophocles *Women of Trachis* 1–5, *Oedipus the King* 1528–1530, *Tyndareus* (F 646 TrGF), *Tyro* (F 662 TrGF), Euripides *Andromache* 100–102, *Children of Herakles* 865–866, *Electra* 954–956, and *Trojan Women* 509–510 in which one cannot be judged happy until one's life is at an end. As Dunn observes, the actual "end" for Herodotus' Croesus as well as the "end" for the tragedians' various tragic heroes is not "death" *per se*, but rather a significant event (Herodotus' Croesus is defeated by Cyrus, Sophocles' Oedipus learns of his transgressions, Aeschylus' Xerxes survives if only to comprehend the magnitude of his loss) that gives shape to

structure to a life; it turns it into a *biography*, as Hubert Dreyfus explains in his summary of scholarship on Heidegger's concept of death: "*dying* is a way of life that takes account of the certainty of that final event. Thus, dying, or being-towards-death, as a way of life gives life seriousness, and a narrative structure, and so makes possible a life that makes sense in terms of a beginning, middle, and end" (Dreyfus 2005:xxxi).[85] Heidegger's clearest explanation of death can be found in his 1925 lecture series (Heidegger 1985:307–318 = 1979:424–440). In those pages Heidegger elaborates a phenomenological analysis of death, explaining that,

> Death does not stand out in Dasein, but *stands before* (*bevorsteht*) Dasein in its being, and constantly at that, as long as it is Dasein. In other words, death is always impending (*immer schon bevorstehend*). As such, death belongs to Dasein itself even when it is not yet whole and not yet finished, even when it is not dying. Death is not a missing part of a whole taken as composite. Rather it *constitutes the totality of Dasein from the start* (*konstituiert die Ganzheit des Daseins von vornherein*), so that it is only on the basis of this totality that Dasein has the being of temporally particular parts, that is, of possible ways to be (*möglicher Weisen zu sein*). (Heidegger 1985:313 = 1979:432)

It is only through the fact that death is *before* us and always already *impending* as our ownmost possibility of ceasing-to-be that Dasein can conceive of itself as a whole, and thereby reflect upon its "possible ways of being" in terms of particular choices, attitudes, and actions. In other words, Being-towards-death provides the possibility of a kind of self-narrativizing.

Heidegger's more refined sense of temporality as the condition of our existing in the world with other beings and entangled in our care for them will prove useful to our reading of temporality in the *Iliad*, in particular in terms of "emotional" pain. The care that a character has for another entangles that character in a temporal experience that is wholly human, insofar as it is entailed in the very experience of Being-in-the-world. In other words, care—the experience of emotional anxiety or pain for oneself or for another—is a temporalizing experience that constitutes the very essence of what it means to be human. When Homer's gods care for other characters in the epic, they become like humans through their experience of time. For instance, Achilles' immortal horses become caught up in human temporality when they separate

---

the character's experience: through the "end," that character's life becomes a narrative to the character him- or herself.

[85] On this interpretation of Heideggerian "authenticity," see Guignon 1984, 1993, 2000.

themselves from the battle to mourn the death of Patroklos. They seem to have become something less than divine—they are no longer self-sufficient because of their "longing" for Patroklos, and their sorrow over his death has tainted their immortal beauty:

ἵπποι δ' Αἰακίδαο <u>μάχης ἀπάνευθεν ἐόντες</u>
<u>κλαῖον</u>, ἐπεὶ δὴ πρῶτα πυθέσθην ἡνιόχοιο
ἐν κονίῃσι πεσόντος ὑφ' Ἕκτορος ἀνδροφόνοιο.
[...]
<u>ἀλλ' ὥς τε στήλη μένει ἔμπεδον</u>, ἥ τ' <u>ἐπὶ τύμβῳ</u>
ἀνέρος ἑστήκῃ τεθνηότος ἠὲ γυναικός,
ὣς μένον ἀσφαλέως περικαλλέα δίφρον ἔχοντες
οὔδει ἐνισκίμψαντε καρήατα· <u>δάκρυα</u> δέ σφι
<u>θερμὰ</u> κατὰ βλεφάρων χαμάδις ῥέε <u>μυρομένοισιν</u>
<u>ἡνιόχοιο πόθῳ·</u> θαλερὴ δ' ἐμιαίνετο χαίτη
ζεύγλης ἐξεριποῦσα παρὰ ζυγὸν ἀμφοτέρωθεν.
Μυρομένω δ' ἄρα τώ γε ἰδὼν ἐλέησε Κρονίων,
κινήσας δὲ κάρη προτὶ ὃν μυθήσατο θυμόν·
"ἂ δειλώ, τί σφῶϊ δόμεν Πηλῆϊ ἄνακτι
<u>θνητῷ</u>, ὑμεῖς δ' ἐστὸν <u>ἀγήρω τ' ἀθανάτω τε</u>;
ἦ ἵνα <u>δυστήνοισι μετ' ἀνδράσιν ἄλγε'</u> ἔχητον;
οὐ μὲν γάρ τί πού ἐστιν ὀϊζυρώτερον ἀνδρὸς
πάντων, ὅσσά τε γαῖαν ἔπι πνείει τε καὶ ἕρπει."

But the horses of Aiakides, <u>standing apart from the battle</u>,
<u>wept</u>, since indeed they first learned that their charioteer
had fallen in the dust at the hands of man-slaying Hektor.
[...]
But <u>like a grave marker that remains secure in the ground</u>, one that has
        been stood up
<u>upon the tomb</u> of a man or woman who has died,
just so they remained, holding the very beautiful chariot motionless,
and they leaned their heads upon the ground. <u>Warm tears</u>
flowed down from their eyelids as the horses <u>cried</u>
<u>out of longing for their charioteer. And their luxurious hair was stained</u>
as it streamed out from the yoke-pad along either side of the yoke.
Indeed, when he saw these two crying, the son of Kronos pitied them,
and moved his head and spoke to his own spirit:
"Alas, miserable ones, why did we give you two to lord Peleus,
<u>a mortal</u>, when you are <u>both ageless and immortal</u>?
Was it indeed so that you would have <u>grief among wretched men</u>?

For there is nothing anywhere more miserable than man
of all things, however many that breathe and creep upon the earth."

Iliad XVII 426–428, 434–447

Achilles' horses are "ageless" and "immortal" (ἀγήρω τ' ἀθανάτω τε, XVII 444), and yet, in their care for wretched human creatures to whom they have been given, they feel pains (ἄλγε' ἔχητον, XVII 445). They are no longer complete in their being, for they now feel "longing" (πόθῳ, XVII 439) for Patroklos. Suffering and pain entangle them in human temporality—though not only a future-oriented "not yet." Phenomenological psychology explains that in extreme grief, we can lose sight of any possible future such that our typical future-orientation reverses and we become fixated on the irretrievable past; our "not yet" becomes a "no longer."[86] In such circumstances, patients can experience a "retardation" of time, felt as an "eternity" in the most extreme cases of depression: they experience themselves as slowing down while the world passes them by; they feel hindered from their actions by sluggishness, loss of energy, and rigidity.[87] Achilles' horses seem to suffer in this way: Patroklos is "no longer" with them; they are "no longer" as they were before. Their experience of mortal temporality has tainted them: their hair is now stained (ἐμιαίνετο, XVII 439), and their swift movement is now halted (ἀσφαλέως περικαλλέα δίφρον ἔχοντες, XVII 436), such that they remain in place (μένει ἔμπεδον, XVII 434; μένον, XVII 436)—as if once given to the world of mortals, they can never quite return.[88] These swift creatures have indeed become rigid, as they give over

---

[86] Fuchs (2003:72) notes, "Suffering and pain, by their dialectical nature, open up the dimensions of the no-more and the not-yet, of the time gone by and the time to come." When we periodically experience suffering in the case of physical shortages or losses such as hunger, sleepiness, sexual desire, we can generally satisfy and fill these gaps; the drive to re-fill, re-fuel, and re-store keep us active within the world and oriented toward the future. But emotional losses—as when a friend or loved one dies—can disrupt our temporal experience of the "not yet": "Hence, in loss or guilt, a new time experience arises: It is not the time of 'not yet,' the time of desires and wishes directed toward the future, but the time of 'no more,' the time of irrevocable past" (Fuchs 2001a:181).

[87] Retardation of time: Straus 1960, Straus 1966:292–294, Wyllie 2005a:178–183, Fuchs 2005a:116–117, Fuchs 2005b:196; the corporeal body experienced as sluggish, heavy, and rigid to the point of resembling a corpse: Fuchs 2001a:183–184, Fuchs 2001b:231, 235, 237, 239, Fuchs 2005a:109–112, Fuchs 2005b:196–97, and compare Minkowski 1970:187–188 on the loss of "personal *élan*"; time felt as glutinous, heavy: Fuchs 2003:70; time experienced like "eternity" without the possibility of future change: Straus 1960:137, 1966:291–294, Minkowski 1970:190, Fuchs 2001a:184, 2001b:231, 239, 2003:73–74, 2005a:113–118, 2005b:196–197, Wyllie 2005a:176, 178–183. These characterizations of the temporal experience of patients suffering severe pain, grief, and depression have been experimentally verified: see Minkowski 1970:186–193, Wyllie 2005a:180, Fuchs 2005a:117 for bibliography.

[88] On Achilles' horses as indicating human temporality, see Schein 2002 and Lynn-George 1996:2. See further Krell 1993 for an analysis of Heideggerian ethics via this Homeric passage.

their vitality to a pure static mourning and stand like funerary monuments to Patroklos.

Thetis, too, experiences human temporality as she is burdened by grief over the imminent death of her son Achilles. Like the immortal horses, her experience of grief likewise separates her from the world of the gods, as she states: αἰδέομαι δέ | μίσγεσθ' ἀθανάτοισιν, ἔχω δ' ἄχε' ἄκριτα θυμῷ "I feel shame to mingle with the immortals, since I have sorrows that cannot be separated in my heart" (XXIV 90–91). Thetis' grief prevents her from willingly returning to Olympos, as if her entanglement in the affairs of mortals has forced her to absent herself from the world of gods. Her care for Achilles enmeshes her in mortal time: her sorrows lead her to separate herself from the other gods, as Zeus acknowledges in his reply: ἤλυθες Οὔλυμπόνδε ... <u>κηδομένη περ</u>, | <u>πένθος ἄλαστον</u> ἔχουσα μεγὰ φρεσίν "You have come to Olympos <u>even though you are filled with care</u>, since you have <u>unforgettable grief</u> in your heart" (XXIV 104–105). Thetis' pains are designated as "unable to be separated from one another" (ἄχε' ἄκριτα, XXIV 91), and her grief is described as "unforgettable" (πένθος ἄλαστον, XXIV 105): both adjectives are compound verbal adjectives in *-το-, ἄκριτα from the verb κρίνω "to separate, decide," and ἄλαστον from the verb λανθάνω "forget," both formally equivalent with ἄφθιτον "unwithered."[89] I suggest that how we translate these adjectives depends on our interpretation of Thetis' temporal experience within the *Iliad*. If Thetis is trapped in the past without a foreseeable future in which her pains may be eased, her temporal "not yet" can only appear as a "no longer": her pains appear "inseparable" and her grief "unforgettable." Inseparable pains and unforgettable grief indicate the degree to which Thetis has become enmeshed in the human temporality of her son as she mourns his death; in this temporal mode she appears no longer fully divine, as though she lost something that can never be recovered. But given time, endurance, and the temporal recuperation of the grieving process, Thetis' temporal structure may open up to a future possibility of being pain-free once again: if she comes to endure her suffering within the future-oriented temporal structure of the "not yet," her pains will appear "unforgotten" for the present moment only. Though currently entangled in the world of men and their experience of time, she may one day return to the world of gods.

[89] For ἄκριτος, see Chantraine 1968–1980:585–585, Frisk 1973–1979:II.20–21, and Beekes 2010:I.780–781, s.v. κρίνω. For ἄλαστος, see Chantraine 1968–1980:54, s.v. ἀλάστωρ, Frisk 1973–1979:I.64–65, and Beekes 2010:I.61–62, s.v. ἄλαστος. Although the derivation of ἄλαστος from λανθάνω is formally impeccable, all three scholars note some reservation because of the sense, especially when one takes into account the mythological figure Ἀλάστωρ, a vengeance demon who appears frequently in the tragedians, and whose name, following this etymology, would have to be understood as "he who cannot forget or be forgotten."

Within the narrative scope of the *Iliad*, Thetis is most certainly entangled in human temporality, both as a goddess forced to marry a mortal man, and as a mother of a doomed son whom she cannot protect. When she visits Hephaistos to acquire new armor for her son, Thetis laments over her own status:

Τὸν δ' ἠμείβετ' ἔπειτα Θέτις <u>κατὰ δάκρυ χέουσα·</u>
Ἥφαιστ', ἦ ἄρα δή τις, ὅσαι θεαί εἰσ' ἐν Ὀλύμπῳ,
τοσσάδ' ἐνὶ φρεσὶν ᾗσιν <u>ἀνέσχετο κήδεα λυγρά,</u>
ὅσσ' ἐμοὶ ἐκ πασέων Κρονίδης Ζεὺς <u>ἄλγε'</u> ἔδωκεν;
ἐκ μέν μ' ἀλλάων ἁλιάων <u>ἀνδρὶ δάμασσεν,</u>
Αἰακίδῃ Πηλῆϊ, καὶ <u>ἔτλην</u> ἀνέρος εὐνήν
πολλὰ μάλ' οὐκ ἐθέλουσα. ὃ μὲν δὴ γήραϊ λυγρῷ
κεῖται ἐνὶ μεγάροις ἀρημένος, ἄλλα δέ μοι νῦν·
υἱὸν ἐπεί μοι δῶκε γενέσθαί τε τραφέμεν τε
ἔξοχον ἡρώων, ὃ δ' ἀνέδραμεν ἔρνεϊ ἶσος,
τὸν μὲν ἐγὼ θρέψασα φυτὸν ὣς γουνῷ ἀλωῆς
νηυσὶν ἐπιπροέηκα κορωνίσιν Ἴλιον εἴσω
Τρωσὶ μαχησόμενον· τὸν δ' οὐχ ὑποδέξομαι αὖτις
οἴκαδε νοστήσαντα δόμον Πηλήϊον εἴσω.
ὄφρα δέ μοι ζώει καὶ ὁρᾷ φάος ἠελίοιο,
<u>ἄχνυται,</u> <u>οὐδέ τί οἱ δύναμαι χραισμῆσαι ἰοῦσα.</u>

Then Thetis replied to him <u>as she shed a tear</u>:
"Hephaistos, in truth who is there—however many goddesses
          there are on Olympos—
who <u>suffers</u> in her heart as many <u>grievous cares</u>
as Zeus, Kronos' son, has given <u>pains</u> to me out of all the other
          goddesses?
Out of the other women of the sea, <u>he made me subject to
          a man</u>,
Peleus, son of Aiakos, and <u>I endured</u> the marriage with a man,
though it was very much against my will. Indeed, he lies
in his great halls, destroyed by grievous old age, but now I have
          other concerns,
since he gave me a son both to bear and to raise up
outstanding among heroes. And he shot up like a young tree,
and I nurtured him, like a plant in the pride of the orchard,
and I sent him forth in curved ships into Ilion
to fight with the Trojans. But I will not receive him again
returned home into the house of Peleus.

Yet while he is still alive and sees the light of the sun,
he grieves, and though I go to him, I am not able to protect
      him at all.

Iliad XVIII 428–443

Thetis has been subjected to the mortal world both through her marriage to Peleus, a union forced upon her by Zeus, and by the birth of a mortal son. Both husband and son exist within mortal temporality: Peleus is now himself ruined by old age (γήραϊ λυγρῷ ... ἀρημένος, XVIII 434-435), and Achilles' death is imminent,[90] while the goddess herself is powerless to protect him from death (οὐδέ τί οἱ δύναμαι χραισμῆσαι ἰοῦσα, XVIII 443).[91] Even her love isn't sufficient to preserve her son, as Achilles explains: "Don't hold me back from battle, even though you love me; you won't persuade me" (μηδέ μ' ἔρυκε μάχης φιλέουσά περ· οὐδέ με πείσεις, XVIII 126). Although a goddess, Thetis mourns like a mortal mother (XXIV 104-105; cf. XXII 405-407, XXIV 747-760). Perhaps along with her grief Thetis is also caught up in human temporality in the experience of great anger, as Laura Slatkin (1986, 1991) has reconstructed it: Zeus forced the goddess to marry a mortal husband and bear a mortal child to protect his own hegemony—the price of Zeus' rule is no less than Achilles' death and Thetis' grief.[92] Thetis' self-imposed separation from Olympos (XXIV 90–91) is a sign of both her grief and anger: both emotions signal her status as caught up in the world of mortals and human time.

These examples of immortals caught up in human temporality suggest that Homer's gods are normally quite beyond the world of mortals, apart in their own world and unburdened by the experiences that make us human: they are free from pain, sorrow, old age, illness, hunger, labor, death, and generally speaking, care. Indeed, Achilles certainly views the gods as uncaring or forgetful as he speaks to Priam in Book XXIV of the *Iliad*; in his view, mankind is subject to grief (ἀχεύω), whereas the gods themselves are "carefree" (ἀκηδέες):

ἀλλ' ἄγε δὴ κατ' ἄρ' ἕζευ ἐπὶ θρόνου, ἄλγεα δ' ἔμπης
ἐν θυμῷ κατακεῖσθαι ἐάσομεν ἀχνύμενοί περ·
οὐ γάρ τις πρῆξις πέλεται κρυεροῖο γόοιο·

---

[90] For Thetis' and Achilles' acknowledgments of his impending demise, see XVIII 95-96, 98-103, 115-116, 120-121.

[91] On Thetis' representation as a mother in the *Iliad*, compare the descriptions of her taking both Dionysus (Θέτις θ' ὑπεδέξατο κόλπῳ, VI 136) and Hephaistos (Θέτις δ' ὑπεδέξατο κόλπῳ, XVIII 398) to her breast when those gods were in pain. While Thetis could nurse these gods back to health, she can do nothing to help Achilles.

[92] See Slatkin 1986, esp. 22, and Loraux 1998:49. See further Loraux 1998:43-49 on Demeter and her grief for her daughter, Persephone.

ὡς γὰρ ἐπεκλώσαντο θεοὶ δειλοῖσι βροτοῖσι
ζώειν ἀχνυμένοις· αὐτοὶ δέ τ’ ἀκηδέες εἰσί.

But come now and sit down on the chair, and our <u>pains</u>,
          in any case,
let’s let them lie still in our spirit, <u>though we are mourning</u>.
For there is no practical advantage from cold lamentation,
for the gods have spun it out for wretched mortals
<u>that we live in grief</u>. But they themselves are <u>without a care</u>.

Iliad XXIV 522–526

In Achilles’ expressed world-view, there is nothing to be gained, no real advantage (πρῆξις, XXIV 524), from grief, for the entire mortal experience of Being-in-the-world is “to live in grief” (ζώειν ἀχνυμένοις, XXIV 526); human temporality is based in care—pain (ἄλγεα, XXIV 522), grief (ἀχνύμενοί, XXIV 523; ἀχνυμένοις, XXIV 526), and lamentation (γόοιο, XXIV 524). It is this very experience of care that defines the difference between mortals and immortals—the gods create the world, and in it, we mortals are entangled in care; but the gods are outside and apart, unaffected by care (ἀκηδέες, XXIV 526), and therefore outside of all human experience.[93] However, the epic reveals this is not so: the gods do care, as their very involvement in the world of mortals indicates, especially the concern they show over the bodies of the dead (e.g. Sarpedon, Hektor); they feel sorrow over the fate of humans that matter to them.[94] As Zeus explains

---

[93] This view has been taken up by various scholars. For instance, Griffin (1980:199) notes, “Men are of enough importance to make Zeus incur trouble for their disputes; at the same time they are beneath the serious notice of the gods, who apply to them the words which the haughty Suitors use when their princely banquet is disturbed by the quarrel of the beggars”; Rinon (2008:134) argues that “from the point of view of eternity, which is literally the divine point of view, all such phenomena [i.e. the world of humans] are no more than trifles. Hera’s relation to time, which is also that of her fellow gods, is therefore one of serene indifference.”

[94] Sarpedon: As Patroklos is about to kill Zeus’ son Sarpedon, Zeus is distressed (ᾤ μοι ἐγών, XVI 433) and considers violating Sarpedon’s fated death by rescuing him (XVI 435–438). Hera dissuades Zeus, noting that the best way to honor the memory of his son is to mourn him and let (τεὸν δ’ ὀλοφύρεται ἦτορ, XVI 450), let him die, and see to it that he receives heroic honors and proper burial (XVI 440–442, 450–457). Zeus, at one of his most paternal moments, invoked in these verses by his title of “father of both men and gods,” obeys Hera’s behest and sheds bloody tears in honor of his son (οὐδ’ ἀπίθησε πατὴρ ἀνδρῶν τε θεῶν τε. | αἱματοέσσας δὲ ψιάδας κατέχευεν ἔραζε | παῖδα φίλον τιμῶν, τόν οἱ Πάτροκλος ἔμελλεν | φθείσειν ἐν Τροίῃ ἐριβώλακι, τηλόθι πάτρης, XVI 458–461). In a remarkable study of this passage, Lateiner (2002) notes that throughout the epic “bereaved parents’ tears and laments compose a Homeric motif” (60), and argues that the image of Zeus’ bloody tears illustrates Zeus’ “‘humanity’ and connectedness to the mortals of the Trojan war” (42). Lateiner speaks of “Zeus’ human-like affect” (43), and notes that “the unnatural event humanizes Zeus and displays his helplessness” (43n5); the bloody tears “express anthropomorphic parental agony” (47). Lateiner concludes: “The distinction

to Poseidon, "they are a care to me, even though they are dying" (μέλουσί μοι ὀλλύμενοί περ, XX 21).

Homer's gods also feel anxiety over the stability their current situation (as exemplified in the constant threat of battle and strife implied in the Anatolian "succession" motif that runs throughout Homer's representation of the gods), as well as distress over the physical pains they suffer at the hands of men and one another.[95] These experiences of time lead gods to the threshold of death itself, as if the gods, once enmeshed in mortal temporality through care, anxiety, and pain, are no longer fully "immortal," as if they can never quite recover from the mortal stain of human temporality. To judge by later criticism of Homer—specifically that of the second-century CE Christian writer Tertullian—these very scenes in which Homer's gods suffer emotional or physical pains were read

---

between unaging gods and miserable humans collapses in [*Iliad*] 16.459 to enhance Zeus' intermittent 'humanity.' He sorrows like a human" (49).

Hektor: Zeus mourns at heart over Hektor's death ("My heart is in mourning for Hektor," ἐμὸν δ' ὀλοφύρεται ἦτορ | Ἕκτορος, XXII 169–170). Hecuba acknowledges that the gods loved Hektor while he was alive, and continued to care for him in his death ("Truly while you were still alive for me, you were dear to the gods, and even in your decree of death, they still care about you," ἦ μέν μοι ζωός περ ἐὼν φίλος ἦσθα θεοῖσιν, | οἳ δ' ἄρα σεο κήδοντο καὶ ἐν θανάτοιό περ αἴσῃ, XXIV 749–750). At XXIV 134–135, the gods are "angry" (σκύζεσθαι), and Zeus, beyond all the others, is "enraged" (κεχολῶσθαι) because Achilles has not yet given back Hektor's body. At XXIV 152 Zeus sends Iris to inform Priam that the gods will protect him as he makes his way to Achilles' tent to ransom back Hektor's body: μὴ δέ τί οἱ θάνατος μελέτω φρεσὶ μὴ δέ τι τάρβος "Let death not be a care to him at all, nor a source of fear." Priam does not need to be *concerned* or *anxious* about the possibility of death (μὴ ... οἱ θάνατος μελέτω) because the gods will take care of him. On the similarity between Zeus' sorrow for Sarpedon and Hektor, compare XVI 440–449 with XX 168–181.

95 Hephaistos suffers crippling pain when Zeus hurls him from Olympos and he falls for an entire day (I 591–593, XVIII 395–399). Aphrodite screams in pain (V 343); she and Ares bleed *ikhōr* when they are wounded (V 339–343, 855–862, 870); she falls to her knees (V 357), and Ares collapses when struck (V 391, 886). Artemis likewise feels pain and weeps as Hera beats her (XXI 489–496). In her plight, the goddess can only think of escape: she twists about (ἐντροπαλιζομένην, XXI 492) and finally breaks free (ὕπαιθα θεὰ φύγεν, XXI 493), but not without suffering loss—her divine accoutrements (ὡς ἢ δακρυόεσσα φύγεν, λίπε δ' αὐτόθι τόξα, "thus she fled weeping, and left her bow and arrows there," XXI 496). Gods can also feel fear, like Dionysus who trembled in fear before the mortal Lycurgus (VI 137). When involving themselves in human affairs, gods seem to feel the drag of human temporality in their physical exertions: Hephaistos bustles about (I 600, XVIII 472), and perspires (XVIII 372) as he works, as does Hera (IV 27). Levy (1979:215, 217) reads such scenes as proof of an earlier theology in which the gods themselves were not immortal; Andersen (1981:324) reads them as *ad hoc* additions to the plot and never constitutive of any kind of "religion." Whether representative of belief or literary feeling, however, the scenes serve to make gods like humans in their experience of time. See, for instance, Rinon 2008:127–144, 188–193, who focuses on Hephaistos as a "humanized god" set apart from other gods in the *Iliad* with "a difference closely associated with the god's exceptional conception of time and pain" (134). Rinon emphasizes Hephaistos' human traits as he is "afflicted in body and limited in movement, suffering pain and humiliation, and constricted by human institutions such as marriage and divorce" (143).

in antiquity as "degrading" the concept of divinity by entangling gods within human temporality: "[Homer] dragged down divine majesty with the human condition, when he imbued his gods with human sufferings and passions" (*diuinam maiestatem humana condicione tractauit, casibus et passionibus humanis deos imbuens* [*Ad nationes* 1.10.38]).[96]

In a remarkable article, Michael Lynn-George (1996) investigates "structures of care" in the *Iliad* and applies a Heideggerian analysis to investigate the ways in which "care" motivates the narrative. The most striking instance of "care," Lynn-George argues, is the commemorative project of the *Iliad* itself:

> And the poetics of the *Iliad* itself is in a fundamental sense that of being mindful, thoughtful, constructing a work from care and respect. The great force opposed to λήθη ["forgetfulness"] is not simply (or only) "memory," but μνημοσύνη with its important sense of "a bearing in mind, thought or care for something." μιμνήσκω and μνάομαι have the meaning of "bethinking oneself of; not to neglect, turn one's mind to." These verbs are related in this sense to μέδομαι "to observe, watch (over); to take thought (for something); remember, care for," from which we have the Latin *meditare*, *medeor*, English "meditate" and "many words expressing the notion of thought or care." ... In the Homeric undertaking, to "remember" is to care and to take care of. This coupling of memory and care, of recollection and thoughtful reflection, is of major significance for the epic poetics of memory itself, in so far as poetry actively strives to overcome forgetfulness, neglect, indifference, and disappearance without a trace. ... [I]t is the epic itself *which emerges finally as the ultimate structure of care*. In this relation the *Iliad* initiates a significant poetic concern—and a definition of poetry *as concern* ... (Lynn-George 1996:20; emphases added)

The epic poetic tradition is itself a structure of care: it aims to preserve the memory of its hero against "forgetfulness, neglect, indifference, and disappearance without a trace." Heideggerian care, then, is itself at the heart of the epic tradition, and from this perspective, is concerned with the preservation of Achilles' κλέος ἄφθιτον. Here, too, Heidegger's sense of temporality helps us read the *Iliad* (and, correspondingly, the *Iliad* enriches our reading of Heidegger).

---

[96] Tertullian (*Ad nationes* 1.10.39) draws attention both the physical pains that Homer's gods suffer, such as Aphrodite's wound (*Iliad* V 330–343: see chapter 5 below) or Ares' long incarceration in a bronze jar (V 382–391: see chapter 5 below), as well as the emotional pains they suffer over mortals, such as Zeus' tears for Sarpedon (see the previous note). On Tertullian and the Christian critique of "weeping gods," see Corbeill 2009:305–307.

Both Achilles' decision to stay in Troy and fight and die, as well as the tradition's understanding of its own end revealed in its claim to preserve Achilles' κλέος ἄφθιτον, call to mind Heidegger's "Being-toward-death" (*das Sein zum Tode*) and "Being-toward-the-end" (*das Zu-Ende-sein*). Achilles' Being-toward-death takes the form of an acknowledgment and acceptance of his impending fate, as he expresses to his mother Thetis at *Iliad* XVIII 98–116. Now that Patroklos is dead and Achilles has accepted his fate, he can become what he is meant to be—the hero of the war epic: "But now I wish to take up noble fame" (νῦν δὲ κλέος ἐσθλὸν ἀροίμην, XVIII 121). As for the tradition itself, its claim to preserve Achilles' κλέος ἄφθιτον—specifically as understood as a "fame" that is "not (yet) withered"—is likewise oriented toward the future possibility of its own end. This Being-toward-the-end is determined as its ownmost Being-toward-decay. The implicit acknowledgment by the tradition of its own end is signaled in the form and semantics of the adjective ἄφθιτον: its end is entailed in its very being. But it is this Being-toward-its-end that enables the tradition to flourish, and like Achilles, it becomes what it is meant to be—beautiful, precious, and a true testament of care—through the fragility of its being.

3.5. Overview

In chapters 1 and 2, I address the theme of "decay" of organic bodies. In chapter 1, I look at how the timbers of the Achaeans' ships, along with the bodies of dead Greeks and Trojans, act as "clocks" by measuring the duration of time; bodies rot and lose their physical integrity within time. In chapter 2, I study how the bodies of Sarpedon, Patroklos, and Hektor are all linked by the anxiety that is shown over their potential decomposition; the gods intervene to prevent the bodies from rotting before they can be buried. This motif of the temporarily-preserved body is a figure for the epic tradition of *kleos aphthiton* which seeks to preserve the memory of those heroes.

In chapters 3 and 4, I deal with the decay of more stable, non-organic bodies—the *sēmata* of heroes and the walls of the Trojans and Achaeans. In these instances, the material objects are architectural edifices built to last; the Trojan Wall, in particular, was traditionally considered to be the craft of the gods (Poseidon and Apollo) and as such, was to be thought of as permanent and ἄρρηκτος "unbreakable" (XXI 447). Nevertheless, all these architectural structures are in fact destroyed, though, like Achilles himself, their "death" does not occur within the narrative confines of the *Iliad*. Indeed, the very tradition of the *Iliad* relies on the destruction of Troy and its defensive wall, such that what was ἄρρηκτος "unbreakable" turns out to be a temporally conditioned "not (yet) broken." I argue that this representation of structures that are temporarily permanent function as tropes for poetic κλέος ἄφθιτον.

In chapter 5, I argue that Homer's gods in the *Iliad*—although the very embodiment of permanence—do themselves experience time through pain and confinement; in extreme circumstances, they even experience something rather like death.[97] Moreover, the theogonic tales of succession and transgenerational strife paint a picture that is anything but stable.

In short, I try to offer a view of the *Iliad* as something more fragile and perhaps stranger than is commonly held. Its poetics preserve its hero for a time against death, occupying a gray area between the living and the dead; Achilles' life is put on pause before death sets back in, before decay begins, before time—like a dog—devours his body. This gray area is the location of ἄφθιτος "unwithered" and ἀθάνατος "immortal, undying." Achilles' fame is not "immortal" in our understanding of the word—it is never meant to last "forever" and to be "everlasting," but is temporarily sheltered from time, even though its end is entailed in its existence. While Achilles is "still perfectly" healthy and alive in the *Iliad*, even in the final verses of the poem that end with the burial of Hektor, the very tradition that preserves the *Iliad* for us guarantees his death. There is a critical shift that we should make, then, from ἄφθιτον "unwithered" to the process of the poetic tradition itself as indicated by κλέος "epic fame," which is literally "that which we hear." The poetics of the *Iliad* remains durable so long as it retains κλέος—that is, only so long as we continue to read and teach it.

---

[97] See, for instance, Cassin 1981 and Wexler 1993 on the death of the gods in Sumerian and Hittite mytho-poetic traditions; Burton 2001 on the death of the gods in the succession-motifs of Greek mythology; Loraux 1986 on the impossible possibility of death for Ares in *Iliad* V; and Purves 2006a on the "falling" of Hephaistos and Ares in the *Iliad*, a headlong pitch that replicates the mortal fall of heroes on the battlefield. See further Levy 1979 and Andersen 1981 debating the "mortality" of gods; Clay 1982 on the gods' immortality as partly dependant upon the constant renewal of their immortality through the consumption of *ambrosia* and *nektar* (on which, see my discussion in chapter 2 below); Slatkin 1986, 1991, Faraone 1992, and Purves 2004:160–164 on the "binding" of gods as a kind of death, which should be compared with Walcot 1961, 1966:61 and Johnson 1999 on the representation of Tartaros, the containment cell where rebellious gods are held, as a "bronze jar." See Astour 1980:229 and Poljakov 1982 for comparative evidence that the underworld in Near Eastern mythology was also viewed as a "bronze jar," and my discussion in chapter 5.

Chapter 1

Decay, Disintegration, and Objectified Time
The Rhetoric of Time and Memory

THE TERMS THAT FRAME THE DISCUSSION OF κλέος ἄφθιτον and the durability of the poetic tradition as conceived by the tradition itself are *time* and *memory*. Time has disintegrating effects—physical objects and social obligations both decay over time; what is cohesive, whole, and pristine wears down, falls apart, and fades away over time. Memory in a pure or ideal form, on the other hand, preserves its object against time; it maintains or even re-presents, holding in an unadulterated state what is not to remain cohesive, whole, and pristine for long, or bringing what is no longer so back to mind in all its vitality. The very project of epic commemoration is an attempt to preserve the memory of the hero and his deeds, to render them free of the effects of time and to recreate them again in the present with each performance of the story.

In this chapter, I argue that this play between time and memory within the oral epic tradition operates within the narrative of the *Iliad* itself. Achilles' withdrawal from the war signals a crisis in the Achaean effort beginning in the second book of the *Iliad*: Zeus sends Agamemnon a deceptive dream indicating that *now* the Greeks may be victorious over the Trojans; and in a speech structured by a kind of rhetoric of time, Agamemnon likewise presents the Achaeans with a notion of a decisive present *now* that will break with a static past of so many years of fruitless war. The very plot of the *Iliad* as represented in the actions and speeches of its characters, therefore, indicates a sense of time as a disintegrating force. The Greeks' will to fight has rotted away like their ships lying still on Trojan shores. Odysseus counters this representation of decaying time with a rhetoric of memory in which the distance between past and present is partially elided. He recalls the past so vividly that events that took place nine or more years previously now seem like they happened "yesterday or the day before." In other words, his memory recalls the past into the present while still acknowledging its pastness.

These mutually opposed views of time as decaying or proximal designate the parameters of epic commemoration. On one extreme, time destroys all; on the other, memory resuscitates the past, bringing it to view in a way that is never quite present, but only nearly so. The degree to which memory falls short helps us measure the durability of the Homeric epic tradition. In other words, Odysseus' speech will fail to recoup the past in its completeness, just as all monuments—including epic itself—fail to preserve the memory of their hero permanently.

1. Agamemnon and Temporal Disintegration

At the opening of the second book of the *Iliad*, Zeus can't sleep. He is too filled with care and concern over how he is to bring about the ruin of the Achaean army that he promised to Thetis in order that Achilles may be honored by the Greeks.

> ἄλλοι μέν ῥα θεοί τε καὶ ἀνέρες ἱπποκορυσταί
> ηὗδον παννύχιοι, Δία δ' οὐκ ἔχε νήδυμος ὕπνος,
> ἀλλ' ὅ γε μερμήριζε κατὰ φρένα, ὡς Ἀχιλῆα
> τιμήσῃ, ὀλέσῃ δὲ πολὺς ἐπὶ νηυσὶν Ἀχαιῶν.

The rest of the gods and men, too, armed fighters from chariots,
were sleeping all through the night, but sweet sleep[1] was not
>> holding Zeus;
he, on the contrary, was pondering in his heart how he would honor
>> Achilles,
and how he would destroy a great number of men at the
>> Achaeans' ships.

Iliad II 1–4

In these opening verses of *Iliad* II, the poet subtly emphasizes the temporal complexity that encompasses the plot of the *Iliad* set in motion here. While all

---

[1] See Leumann 1950:44–45 and Reece 2009 (*passim*) for discussion and bibliography on ἔχε νήδυμος ὕπνος as a variant interpretation of *ἔχεν ἥδυμος ὕπνος (cf. *Iliad* II 2, XIV 242, *Odyssey* iv 793, xii 311). This reinterpretation of *ἔχεν ἥδυμος occurred as aural features of the language, such as the disappearance of the digamma (*ἔχε [f]ἥδυμος ὕπνος), led to innovations, such as the use of a "moveable *nu*" suffix to prevent hiatus (*ἔχεν ἥδυμος ὕπνος); over time, the *nu* came to be understood differently, in this case as an *n*-privative prefix of ἥδυμος (*ἔχε ṇ-ἥδυμος ὕπνος = ἔχε νήδυμος ὕπνος). These new words formed through "junctural metanalysis," in Reece's terminology, could themselves then became productive, such that we find νήδυμος deployed in situations where there is no issue of hiatus, as at *Iliad* X 187 (τῶν νήδυμος ὕπνος) and XIV 354 (Ἀχαιῶν νήδυμος ὕπνος).

others sleep, Zeus is awake. The formulaic ηὗδον παννύχιοι "they were sleeping all through the night" (cf. X 2 = XXIV 678)[2] indicates an extended period of time during which the backdrop of the comparison takes place: everyone goes to bed and remains asleep, except for Zeus. Zeus continues to be preoccupied; the two verbal phrases οὐκ ἔχε "(sleep) was not holding" and μερμήριζε "(Zeus) was pondering," both in the imperfect tense like ηὗδον "they were sleeping," suggest that his wakeful thinking occupies the same extent of time: παννύχιος "all night long." What Zeus is pondering is the future, namely how he is to honor Achilles and destroy the lives of many men beside the ships of the Achaeans. His purpose is at once double and singular, for by destroying Achaeans, Zeus will honor Achilles, according to the terrible logic of Achilles' request at *Iliad* I 407–412, 505–510. In those passages Achilles requests that Zeus allow the Trojans to be victorious until the Achaeans realize the error they made in disrespecting him, their best fighter, by taking from him Briseïs, his prize of honor. Zeus' plan for the future is to be set in motion by a decisive action in the present: *now* is the critical moment, for it both links and separates extended past from what is yet to come.

Zeus' plan, shaped in a static and extended past with an eye to the future, forms a specific temporal pattern that runs throughout the opening of the action. The durative past gives way to a new and different future by means of a dramatic action in the present.[3] This movement from static past to intended future through dramatic present figured in Zeus' plan of how he will affect the war and its outcome is the very structure of a narrative plot; it is no coincidence then that the Διὸς βουλή "the plan of Zeus" is the epic's term for its own "plot."[4]

To this end Zeus puts the "plot" in motion by sending a "destructive dream" (οὖλον ὄνειρον, II 6) to (mis)inform Agamemnon that the gods will *now* allow him to capture Troy:

νῦν γάρ κεν ἔλοις πόλιν εὐρυάγυιαν
Τρώων· οὐ γὰρ ἔτ' ἀμφὶς Ὀλύμπια δώματ' ἔχοντες

---

[2] At *Iliad* II 2, X 2, and XXIV 678 ηὗδον παννύχιοι occurs in the same metrical (line-initial) position. The formula is highly flexible for, though it describes the same situation in each instance—everyone is sleeping except for one character—the wakeful character is different on each occasion: Zeus, Agamemnon, and Hermes (who rouses Priam and drives him home from Achilles' tent while the Greeks are still asleep).

[3] Here my formulation differs slightly from Wolfgang Kullmann's assessment in his penetrating essay "Past and Future in the *Iliad*" where he concludes: "Thus the present event is not experienced in the present and as a fact: it becomes a confirmation of something that has already announced itself in the past, and a sign of the future" (2001:407).

[4] *Iliad* I 5 posits the Διὸς βουλή as the name for the epic's plot: Διὸς δ' ἐτελείτο βουλή "the plan of Zeus was accomplished." For further discussion, see Bassett 1922, Redfield 1979, Murnaghan 1997, and Clay 1999 with further bibliography.

ἀθάνατοι φράζονται (ἐπέγναμψεν γὰρ ἅπαντας
Ἥρη λισσομένη), Τρώεσσι δὲ κήδε' ἐφῆπται
ἐκ Διός.

For now you could capture the wide-wayed city
of the Trojans, for no longer are they who have homes about Olympos,
the immortals, thinking about it (for she bent all of them to her purpose,
Hera did, through her supplication), and cares are in store for the Trojans
from Zeus.

Iliad II 29–33

These words are reported three times to emphasize their importance: first
in Zeus' command to the messenger Dream (II 12–15); again during Dream's
announcement to Agamemnon of Zeus' promise (II 29–33); and finally during
Agamemnon's conference with the Achaean leaders (II 66–70).[5] This emphatic
development is marked by the temporal adverb νῦν "now" which indicates a
narrative disjunction: events at Troy—referred to, though not directly narrated
within the scope of the *Iliad* itself[6]—are about to change. The "new" future

---

[5] The triple repetition of the command within such a short space has drawn much criticism, dating back at least as far as Zenodotus, who is said to have "condensed" (συντέτμηκεν) *Iliad* II
60–71 to a two-verse summary: ἠνώγει σε πατὴρ ὑψίζυγος, αἰθέρι ναίων, | Τρωσὶ μαχήσασθαι
προτὶ Ἴλιον. ὣς ὁ μὲν εἰπών | ᾦχετ' ἀποπτάμενος. "Father Zeus, who sits on high and dwells in
the ether, commands you | to make war with the Trojans at the gates of Ilion. Thus speaking |
[Dream] flew off and departed" (Scholia A at *Iliad* II 60–71, Erbse). In his edition of the *Iliad*, Leaf
felt that "the third repetition of the message is really too much" and approved of Zenodotus'
more concise version (1990–1902:53). Kirk offers useful analysis, noting both that the repetition is appropriate to the "oral style" and more importantly, that the repetition of these verses
is particularly appropriate, "since they are part of an emphatic development in the action"
(1985:121–122).

[6] Homer's references to events of the Trojan War that fall outside of the narrative scope of the
Iliad were controversial even in antiquity. Readers have long argued that certain features of the
text, such as the Catalogue of Ships, the *Teikhoskopia*, and the duel between Menelaus and Paris,
refer more properly to the beginning of the conflict than its tenth year. For instance, Aristotle
criticized the chronological verisimilitude of the *Teikhoskopia* as "illogical" (ἄλογον), because he
found it unlikely that after ten years of war Helen would not yet know the whereabouts of her
brothers (Aristotle fr. 147, Rose; cf. *Iliad* III 236–244). Likewise, Heraclides Ponticus called the
episode and Helen's ignorance of Castor's and Pollux's deaths "unbelievable" (ἀπίθανον εἶναι
δοκεῖ ἐννέα ἐτῶν διελθόντων τοῖς Ἕλλησιν ἐν Ἰλίῳ μηδένα τῶν βαρβάρων ἀπαγγεῖλαι τῇ Ἑλένῃ
περὶ τῶν ἀδελφῶν, "It seems to be unbelievable that nine years have passed for the Greeks in
Ilion without anyone of the foreigners announcing to Helen about her brothers," fr. 172, Wehrli).
More generally, Aristotle describes how Homer introduces material from beyond the scope of
the *Iliad* to break up the narrative into episodes: "And now taking up one part, [Homer] makes
use of many episodes [of other parts of the war], such as the catalogue of ships and other episodes with which he breaks up his poem" (νῦν δ' ἓν μέρος ἀπολαβὼν ἐπεισοδίοις κέχρηται αὐτῶν
πολλοῖς οἷον νεῶν καταλόγῳ καὶ ἄλλοις ἐπεισοδίοις [δὶς] διαλαμβάνει τὴν ποίησιν, *Poetics* XXIII
1459a35–37, Kassel). Modern scholars have likewise been troubled over temporal verisimilitude

direction, indicated by the potential optative ἕλοις ("for now you <u>could capture</u>," νῦν γὰρ <u>κεν ἕλοις</u>, II 9)[7] is set against a now ruptured static past marked by the adverbial "no longer" (οὐ γὰρ ἔτ', II 30). *No longer* do the gods debate the issue, for Hera has persuaded them all with her appeals. The adverbs νῦν "now" and οὐκ ἔτι "no longer" both emphasize the extent of time that has elapsed before this moment and indicate that Agamemnon's forthcoming efforts will prove different.

Inspired by the dream, Agamemnon decides to "test the Achaeans with words" (πρῶτα δ' ἐγὼν ἔπεσιν πειρήσομαι, II 73) in order to provoke them into redoubling their efforts. He lectures the men that their mission has failed, both to his disgrace and theirs, since so great an Achaean host failed to take a city defended by so many fewer men.[8] His speech, we note, is marked by the same kind of temporal pattern we saw above as Zeus pondered the future and set the plot of the *Iliad* into action, for Agamemnon also speaks of a temporal shift from durative past situation to a decisive new action for the future.

> ὦ φίλοι, ἥρωες Δαναοί, θεράποντες Ἄρηος,
> Ζεύς με μέγα Κρονίδης <u>ἄτῃ</u> <u>ἐνέδησε βαρείῃ</u>,
> σχέτλιος, ὃς <u>πρὶν</u> μέν μοι ὑπέσχετο καὶ κατένευσεν
> Ἴλιον ἐκπέρσαντ' εὐτείχεον ἀπονέεσθαι,
> <u>νῦν δὲ</u> κακὴν ἀπάτην βουλεύσατο, καί <u>με κελεύει</u>
> <u>δυσκλέα</u> Ἄργος ἱκέσθαι, ἐπεὶ πολὺν ὤλεσα λαόν.
> οὕτω που Διὶ <u>μέλλει</u> ὑπερμενεΐ φίλον <u>εἶναι</u>,
> ὃς δὴ πολλάων πολίων <u>κατέλυσε</u> κάρηνα
> <u>ἠδ' ἔτι καὶ λύσει</u>· τοῦ γὰρ κράτος <u>ἐστὶ</u> μέγιστον.
> αἰσχρὸν γὰρ τόδε γ' ἐστὶ <u>καὶ ἐσσομένοισι</u> πυθέσθαι,
> μὰψ οὕτω τοιόνδε τοσόνδε τε λαὸν Ἀχαιῶν
> <u>ἄπρηκτον</u> πόλεμον πολεμίζειν ἠδὲ μάχεσθαι
> ἀνδράσι παυροτέροισι, <u>τέλος δ' οὔ πώ τι πέφανται</u>.

---

of the events narrated in the *Iliad*. For instance, van Leeuwen 1911 argued that the entire war could have taken place in a few months, and the "original" version of the *Iliad* told the story of this short war—however, later interpolations falsified the original into a ten-year war (discussion at Scott 1913, Foster 1914). For other scholars, Homer makes "allusions" to the entire war, thereby introducing anachronistic moments into his narrative of the tenth-year of fighting: see, for instance, Whitman 1958:39–45, Reckford 1964:7–9, Kakridis 1971:32, Bergren 1980:19–20, Schein 1984:19–25, Edwards 1987:188–197, Taplin 1992:83–109, 257–284, Dué 2002:39–40, and Dowden 2004:201–202.

[7] Goodwin 1893:77–78 (§232–234).

[8] Indeed, Agamemnon calculates that the Achaean army outnumbers the Trojan men at a ratio of greater than ten to one (*Iliad* II 123–128), a fact that cannot but bring shame to the Achaeans, as Rabel 1997 points out: "Thinking that he will conclude the war by taking Troy on the very day that begins in Book 2 (*Iliad* II 37), Agamemnon tries to shame the Argives into renewing their commitment to the war" (61).

O my friends, Danaän heroes, servants of Ares,
Zeus the great son of Kronos <u>bound me with heavy self-deception</u>,
wretched god that he is, who <u>before</u> promised to me and consented
     with his nod
that I might sack Ilion with its good walls and sail away back home.
<u>But now</u> he has plotted evil deception, and <u>orders me</u>
<u>to return to Argos in dishonor</u>, since I lost a great number of people.
Thus, I suppose, <u>it will be</u> a dear thing to Zeus who is overly powerful,
who indeed <u>has broken down</u> the crowns of many cities
and <u>will even break more later on</u>, for his power <u>is</u> the greatest.
This is a shameful thing <u>even for the men of the future</u> to learn
     about,
that in vain so great and so large a host of Achaeans
waged a war <u>not yet brought to completion</u> and fought
against far fewer men, but <u>an end has not yet appeared at all</u>.

Iliad II 110–122

Agamemnon's test provides a richly textured study of temporal relations connecting the durative past (up to now) to the future (after now) through a present decisive moment. For up to now, Agamemnon claims that he was "bound with heavy self-deception" (II 111); the implication is one of stasis without change. The war the Achaeans have been waging has *not yet* been brought to completion (ἄ-πρηκτον, II 121, from *ἄ-πραγ-το-, the negative compound adjective in *-το- of the verb πράσσω "to do, accomplish"),[9] and its end has *not yet* been made manifest (τέλος δ' οὔ πώ τι πέφανται, II 122). The temporal implications of the alpha-privative prefix ἀ- and the adverb οὔ πω "not yet" both contribute to the image of a static past, yet one oriented toward the future: up to now the army has not yet been able to accomplish its goals, but the possibility of it doing so remained. A new event, however, changes that temporal orientation as Agamemnon states "but now" (νῦν δὲ, II 114) and shifts into the present tense: "Zeus <u>commands</u> me to return home to Argos in dishonor" (με κελεύει | δυσκλέα Ἄργος ἱκέσθαι, II 114–115). The present moment, determined by Zeus' command, produces a break from the static past; the Greeks will *no longer* continue their fruitless efforts to take the city, but will turn their attentions toward home: in Agamemnon's rhetoric, the future possibility of successful war has closed and the "not yet" has become a "no longer." Indeed, when the Achaeans hear Agamemnon's speech they rush (ἐσσεύοντο, II 150) to their ships with a shout of joy and begin preparations for the flight home. This "rushing"

---

9   On interpreting verbal adjectives in *-το- of compound verbs (here a negative compound of ἀ-πράσσω), see my discussion in the Introduction above with examples and bibliography.

marks a shift in the temporality of the episode; they *no longer* sit inactive at the shore, but *now* spring into action. The dynamic present threatens to bring an end to the static past as men and ships are about to return to motion and life.

Agamemnon claims that the return home is to be one of "dishonor" (δυσκλέα, II 115) because such a premature return home can only mark the expedition to Troy as a failure. Though Agamemnon could lead men to war, he could not achieve the victory he sought. The years spent waging war in vain (μάψ, II 20) against Troy are experienced as unfulfilled opportunity; time appears as a *not yet* when Agamemnon claims he is fighting a "war <u>not yet brought to completion</u>" (<u>ἄπρηκτον</u> πόλεμον, II 121) for which "an end has <u>not yet</u> appeared" (τέλος δ' <u>οὔ πώ</u> τι πέφανται, II 122). A few lines later in his speech, he speaks in the same terms: "but for us, the task for the sake of which we came here remains <u>not yet fulfilled</u>" (ἄμμι δὲ ἔργον | αὔτως <u>ἀκράαντον</u>, οὗ εἵνεκα δεῦρ' ἱκόμεσθα, II 137–138); the Achaeans' purpose, that for which they came to accomplish (οὗ εἵνεκα δεῦρ' ἱκόμεσθα), is left without completion (ἀκράαντον). Hence, a return home now without capturing the city can only signal a change in temporality from a *not yet* to a *no longer*:

> ἀλλ' ἄγεθ', ὡς ἂν ἐγὼ εἴπω, πειθώμεθα πάντες·
> φεύγωμεν σὺν νηυσὶ φίλην ἐς πατρίδα γαῖαν,
> <u>οὐ γὰρ ἔτι</u> Τροίην <u>αἱρήσομεν</u> εὐρυάγυιαν.

> But come, let us all be won over to what I say:
> let us flee with our ships to the dear land of our fathers,
> <u>for no longer will we capture</u> Troy of the wide ways.

Iliad II 139–141

The very definition of failure is to pass from a *not yet* to a *no longer*: an opportunity has passed, and one was not able to seize it. The combination of adverbial "no longer" (οὐκ ἔτι) and future verb (αἱρήσομεν) indicates a future not to come; no longer will X be the case, but rather Y will happen. Agamemnon speaks of a different, unintended future projected from a present in which the Achaeans quit fighting. The consequences of such an action in the present—going home in dishonor after having failed to conquer a city defended by many fewer men—are twofold: it *will be* a dear thing to Zeus (Διὶ <u>μέλλει</u> ὑπερμενέϊ φίλον <u>εἶναι</u>, II 116) and a shameful thing *even for men of the future* to learn about (αἰσχρὸν γὰρ τόδε γ' ἐστὶ <u>καὶ ἐσσομένοισι</u> πυθέσθαι, II 119). The future constructions of verb (μέλλει ... εἶναι) and participle (ἐσσομένοισι) help reveal the thrust of Agamemnon's temporal rhetoric: he is signaling to his men that *if* they go home now with the task unfinished, they will return home in shame (αἰσχρὸν γὰρ τόδε, II 119) and dishonor (δυσκλέα, II 115), and their failure *will* only be dear to a wicked god (σχέτλιος, II 112).[10]

Explicit in Agamemnon's speech is a sharp contrast between Zeus and the Achaeans posed in temporal terms. Whereas Agamemnon has not been able to achieve victory at Troy and his *not yet* is about to become a *no longer*, he envisions Zeus as experiencing a different sort of temporality altogether defined by sheer *continuity*. Zeus *has destroyed* cities in the past (πολλάων πολίων κατέλυσε κάρηνα, II 117) and *will continue* to do so in the future (ἠδ' ἔτι καὶ λύσει, II 118), specifically because he *is* the strongest (τοῦ γὰρ κράτος ἐστὶ μέγιστον, II 118). Agamemnon pictures a temporally continuous Zeus: his enduring status as "the strongest" insures that what took place in his past will continue into his future. But such temporal continuity is out of reach for humans, as Agamemnon seems to see it; indeed, from Agamemnon's perspective Zeus' continuing victories are due to an overabundance: his might is not only the greatest (τοῦ γὰρ κράτος ἐστὶ μέγιστον, II 118), but is even excessive (Διὶ μέλλει ὑπερμενέϊ φίλον εἶναι, "it will be a dear thing to Zeus who is overly powerful," II 116). From Agamemnon's perspective, we humans are not like the gods; our future is not entailed in our enduring present status, but must be continually renegotiated one decisive moment at a time.

The concluding lines of Agamemnon's speech continue his rhetoric of separating past and future through a decisive present. He makes explicit mention of the nine years that have passed while the Achaeans have been waiting on the shores of Troy. The effects of time's passage over the past many years are palpable. The Greeks have been engaged in an inconclusive war now for a long time, far from their wives and children back home. The effects of time are objectively measured through the physical decay of the ships' timbers and rigging cables, and in turn through the moral degeneration of the men themselves.

ἐννέα δὴ βεβάασι Διὸς μεγάλου ἐνιαυτοί,
καὶ δὴ δοῦρα σέσηπε νεῶν, καὶ σπάρτα λέλυνται,
αἳ δέ που ἡμέτεραί τ' ἄλοχοι καὶ νήπια τέκνα
εἵατ' ἐνὶ μεγάροις ποτιδέγμεναι· ἄμμι δὲ ἔργον

---

[10] Agamemnon's leadership has long been the source of debate, especially since his rhetoric produces a different effect than he anticipated. Whitman 1982 perceptively observed, "The troops do not know what [Agamemnon] is up to—and neither do most of the commentators" (73). Similarly, Heiden 1991 states, "the precise motives of this plan remain somewhat obscure despite much scholarly discussion" (4). A sample of the interpretations of Agamemnon's speech Whitman and Heiden have in mind includes: Leaf 1900–1902:46–47 (at *Iliad* II 73), Sheppard 1922:26, Dodds 1968:16 (who speaks of a "conflation of variants, as in the Diapeira"), Beye 1966:123 and 1993:117–118, Willcock 1976:18 (at *Iliad* II 73–74), and Kirk 1985:122–123 (at *Iliad* II 73–75). For a survey of literature on this scene, see Knox and Russo 1989.

αὔτως ἀκράαντον, οὗ εἵνεκα δεῦρ' ἱκόμεσθα.
ἀλλ' ἄγεθ', ὡς ἂν ἐγὼ εἴπω, πειθώμεθα πάντες·
φεύγωμεν σὺν νηυσὶ φίλην ἐς πατρίδα γαῖαν,
οὐ γὰρ ἔτι Τροίην αἱρήσομεν εὐρυάγυιαν.

Now nine full years of great Zeus have gone by,
and indeed the wood of our ships <u>has rotted</u>, and the ropes <u>have been
        destroyed</u>;
and I suppose <u>both our wives and helpless children</u>
sit within our halls, <u>waiting for us</u>. But for us the task
for the sake of which we came here is unaccomplished as ever.
But come, let us all be won over to what I say:
let us flee with our ships to the dear land of our fathers,
for no longer will we capture Troy of the wide ways.

Iliad II 134–141

The Greek verb σήπω "to cause to rot" (here in the perfect σέσηπε with an intransitive sense "[the wood] has rotted")[11] is used three times in Homer, twice to
describe the physical decay of corpses over an extended period of time, and once,
here, to describe the decay of another organic material—the wood composing
the Achaeans' ships.[12] It is the most restricted of the three verbs in Homeric epic
which define the semantic field of "decay": σήπω, πύθω, and φθί(ν)ω/φθινύθω,
each providing specific shades of meaning ranging from *rot*, *decay*, *wither*, *waste
away*, to the colorless *perish*. Here, it denotes the specific biological process
of organic decay effected through time. Note that the verb σήπω "to cause to
rot" is coordinated with λύω "to loosen, destroy": time weakens the integrity
of material structures. An ancient Homeric scholiast commented on the line,
explaining that the decay of the wood and rope is a result of time: σέσηπε·
διασέσηπται <u>ἐκ τοῦ χρόνου</u>, "It has rotted: it has completely rotted <u>under the
influence of time</u>" (Scholia D at *Iliad* II 135, van Thiel).[13] The Homeric scholia find
verse II 135 to be an appropriate and realistic detail, noting that Theopompus of
Chios (*FGrHist* 115 F 351) cited this line with its explicit mention of decay as the
real cause behind the various shipwrecks during the Greeks' voyages home after
Troy was finally sacked (Scholia bT at *Iliad* II 135, Erbse). Modern scholars have
also approved of the detail, such as Kirk who writes, "Nothing is said elsewhere

---

[11]   Liddell, Scott, and Jones 1996:1594, s.v. σήπω II.
[12]   See *Iliad* XIX 27: κατὰ δὲ χρόα πάντα σαπήη; *Iliad* XXIV 414: χρὼς σήπεται. See my Appendix
       below for a study of the semantic field of "decay" in early Greek poetry.
[13]   For van Thiel's edition of the Homeric D Scholia, see van Thiel 2000b. For a thorough discussion
       of the sources of the D Scholia, see van Thiel 2000a.

about the poor condition of the ships; it is a well-observed detail which might be distracting in other contexts but is *a forceful illustration here of the lapse of time* with nothing accomplished" (Kirk 1985:131, emphasis added).

Agamemnon's speech does not achieve his apparent desired effect of rousing the men to action in a renewed war effort. Instead, at the close of Agamemnon's speech, the men return to action in a different way altogether as they rush joyously to their ships to undertake their shameful return home.

> τοὶ δ' ἀλαλητῷ
> νῆας ἔπ' ἐσσεύοντο, ποδῶν δ' ὑπένερθε κονίη
> ἵστατ' ἀειρομένη. τοὶ δ' ἀλλήλοισι κέλευον
> ἅπτεσθαι νηῶν ἠδ' ἑλκέμεν εἰς ἅλα δῖαν,
> <u>οὐρούς τ' ἐξεκάθαιρον·</u> <u>ἀϋτὴ δ' οὐρανὸν ἷκεν</u>
> οἴκαδε ἱεμένων· ὑπὸ δ' ᾔρεον ἔρματα νηῶν.

> And these men with a shout
> rushed to the ships, and the dust from beneath their feet
> stood in a raised cloud; and these men were calling to one another
> to grab hold of the ships and to drag them to the brilliant salt sea,
> <u>and they cleaned out the launching channels</u>; and <u>a shout reached heaven</u>
> of the men hastening home; and they grabbed the props from beneath the
> ships.

Iliad II 149–154

The men begin to drag their ships to the sea, but before they can do so, they need to clean out (ἐξεκάθαιρον, from ἐξ "out" + καθαίρω "clean, purify") the launching channels (οὐρούς).[14] The channels, dug into the seashore, have apparently long since been filled with sand or vegetation that needs to be removed so the ships can be dragged back into the sea. The detail indicates the passage of time, a point well noted by the ancient scholiast who observed that "there was a great deal of wood around them [i.e. the channels] <u>because of the extent of time</u>" (τῷ δὲ χρόνῳ πολλή τις ὕλη περὶ αὐτοὺς ἦν, Scholia bT at *Iliad* II 153b, Erbse).

The dual image of Achaean ships rotting on Trojan shores with their clotted canals, overgrown, perhaps, with brush or wood, makes it abundantly clear that both the Homeric narrator and the characters themselves are fully cognizant of

---

[14] The noun οὐρός "launching channel" in this verse (οὐρούς, *Iliad* II 153) is a Homeric *hapax legomenon*, but is cognate with the verb ὀρύσσω "to dig, dig up" (compare Chantraine 1968–1980 and Frisk 1973–1979, s.v. οὐρός). Scholia D *ad loc.* (van Thiel) defines οὐροί as "dug-out trenches by means of which ships are dragged down to the sea" (ταφροειδῆ ὀρύγματα δι' ὧν αἱ νῆες καθέλκονται εἰς τὴν θάλασσαν). See further Ebeling 1963:II.113, s.v. οὐρός.

the duration of time. Time has not passed unnoticed, for its effects are palpable in the state of the ships' timber and their launching channels. These objects act like clocks, devices that provide an objective means by which to measure the flow of time, for both the decay of organic matter and the growth of vegetable life are not instantaneous events; they occur within time. Moreover, time has brought about the same effect on the Achaean men and their resolve as it has to the ships. It has worn down the cohesive forces of social obligation and the desire to win glory, such that the army is reduced to a multiplicity of individuals—or at best, separate collectives of men from the same town—each pining for his own wife and children, each wanting to return to his own home and have nothing more to do with the Achaeans or their war.[15] In other words, the dual image of decay and disorder serves a symbolic function within the action.

The fundamental message of the image of rotting ships is one of loss of cohesion through waiting. The Achaeans and their ships have waited long on the shore; their wives and children have likewise remained waiting for their return, as Agamemnon notes: "They sit within our halls, <u>waiting</u> for us" (εἵατ' ἐνὶ μεγάροις <u>ποτιδέγμεναι</u>, II 137). Like the organic matter of the ships, the men's resolve has deteriorated; they choose to return prematurely over staying and completing their task, the opposite of the heroic model established by the epic's vision of Achilles. In other words, the tension here between decaying ships on the one hand and a disintegrating army on the other functions as a thematic analogue for Achilles' own mutually exclusive options: to lose his νόστος "return home" but gain κλέος "fame" through death in battle, or to gain νόστος "return home" but lose κλέος "fame" (IX 410–416). That is, within the *Iliad* "fame" and "a return home" are incompatible. The Achaeans here choose to return home with bad reputation (*duskleos*) over renown (*kleos*). As they fly to their ships after Agamemnon's speech, "a shout reached the sky" (ἀϋτὴ δ' οὐρανὸν ἷκεν), not because the men have been roused to battle, but because they were hastening home (οἴκαδε ἱεμένων, II 153–154).[16] The formulaic οὐρανὸν ἷκεν "it reaches heaven" in line final position (cf. *Iliad* II 458, XII 338, *Homeric Hymn to Apollo* 442) in the context of men rushing home in dishonor is in ironic relation with *Odyssey* ix 20 where Odysseus speaks of his "fame" as so great that it reaches heaven itself:

---

[15] On this point, see Cook 2003 on the pain of separation from family as driving the Achaeans to abandon the war.

[16] Shouting is regularly used as an indication of a warrior's eagerness for battle: compare *Iliad* XI 10–14 where the goddess Eris shouts (ἤϋσε, XI 10) and when the Achaeans hear it, "for them war became sweeter than to return in their hollow ships to the dear land of their fathers" (XI 13–14).

εἴμ' Ὀδυσεὺς Λαερτιάδης, ὃς πᾶσι δόλοισιν
ἀνθρώποισι μέλω, καί μευ <u>κλέος οὐρανὸν ἵκει</u>.

I am Odysseus, son of Laertes, who for all my tricks
am an object of concern to men, and <u>my fame reaches heaven</u>.

Odyssey ix 19–20

The Achaeans' resolve and emotional state register the long years they have waited on the shore; they, too, record time through their attitude toward Agamemnon and their mission to take Troy. Their desire to return the ships to the water and to sail home must be read as an attempt to recoup temporality, but a failed one at best. They hope to exchange the possibility of winning κλέος "fame" for a long life at home—the reversal of Achilles' ultimate choice. But in fleeing the decay of waiting on Trojan shores, their move threatens to decay their very existence in the poetic tradition.

2. Odysseus and Mnemonic Reintegration

Time is a disintegrating force. It causes objects and collectives to weaken at their joints. The ships and their ropes are both compound objects, after all. That is to say, they are literally *composed* (from the Latin *com-pono* "place together") of smaller parts bound together at their point of juncture. The ship is made of multiple planks, each fixed one to an other by some kind of joint. Ropes, too, are woven out of multiple fibers plaited together into a larger and stronger combination. The cohesion of the composition relies on the joint or the plait which binds each constituent element, each wooden plank, each fibrous thread, together. For composed objects must be held together against the force that tends to drive its constitutive individual elements to split off on their own. Without the joint, the ship's planks separate as they are freed from the tension of the binding that held them in place; so too do the fibers of ropes unwind as the plait which kept them together under tension breaks down. Time affects bodies at the joints; joints weaken and the objects literally *de-compose*. The unity of the object *dis-integrates* back into its constitutive elements. The whole splits into individuals once again.[17]

The wood joined together to make the Achaeans' ships solid has come undone; in this light, it is instructive to note that Leaf, relying on a passage in Varro, argues that σπάρτα may mean the ropes which tie a ship's planks together

---

[17] See Dougherty 2001:19–37, 189–192 for a comparison between the composition of Achaean ships and the composition of Homeric poetry, both of which are described as *stitched together*. See further my discussion on the temporal significance of joints enabling an object to remain standing "upright" (ἔμπεδος) in chapter 2 below.

rather than a ship's cables or rigging, suggesting even more strongly the disintegrating force of time and the metaphorical equation between rotting ships and the Greek army.[18] As for the men, the cohesion as a group under the leadership of Agamemnon has similarly become loosened to the point that each man thinks only of his own home, wife, and children. The oaths and promises the Achaeans made at the outset of the trip which bound them to the common goal of sacking Troy no longer hold them together. Without the binding joint of social obligation, the army is in danger of falling apart.

It is Odysseus who saves the day by stopping the men from boarding their ships and reintegrating them into a single army, specifically by reminding them of their obligations to stay and fight, for they "promised" to fight until Troy was sacked.

---

[18] Leaf 1900–1902:I.58, quoting Varro: "Varro, perhaps rightly, took the word [sc. σπάρτα] to mean *thongs* used to bind the timbers together: *Liburni plerasque naves loris* <u>suebant</u>: *Graeci magis cannabo et stupa, caeterisque sativis rebus, a quibus* σπάρτα *appellabant* ["The Liburnians <u>used to sew together</u> the greater number of their ships by means of leather thongs: the Greeks more often used hemp and flax, and other cultivated materials, from which they were called σπάρτα," (my translation-LG)] (Varro *apud* Aulus Gellius *Attic Nights* 17.3). This suits the context better than to take σπάρτα = *cables*, a less vital matter." Varro's point is that the σπάρτα are ropes made from cultivated plants, whether hemp or flax or broom; he hints at an etymological connection between σπάρτα "ropes" and σπαρτά "plants cultivated from seed." More important for our purpose, however, is the fact that he speaks of these σπάρτα as being used to <u>sew together</u> a ships' timbers (*naves ... suebant*). On this point, compare Pliny *Natural History* 24.65: *dubito an haec [sc. genista] sit quam Graeci auctores sparton appellavere ... et numquid hanc designaverit Homerus, cum dixit navium sparta dissoluta. nondum enim fuisse Hispanum Africanumve spartum in usu certum est et, cum fierent sutiles naves, lino tamen, non sparto umquam sutas*, "I have my doubts whether this plant [sc. broom] is what the Greek writers have called *sparton*, ... I also doubt whether Homer has alluded to this plant, when he said that the *sparta* of the ships disintegrated. For it is certain that in those times the *spartum* of Spain or Africa was not yet in use, and that when <u>vessels were sewn together, they were stitched with flax, never with *spartum*</u>." Here, too, what is important is the note that ships are constructed through sewing together their constituent parts. See further Aeschylus *Suppliants* 134–135 and its metaphorical description of a ship as "a linen-stitched house of wood that keeps out the salt sea" (λινορραφής τε | δόμος ἅλα στέγων δορός). An ancient scholia at Aeschylus' *Suppliants* (134–135, Smith) explains: "linen-sewn house of wood—i.e. a ship. They used to drill ships and <u>sew them together</u> with <u>cords of sparta</u>. And the phrase in Homer 'fixing ships' indicates the <u>sewing them together</u>" (λινορραφὰς δόμος δορός· ἡ ναῦς, παρόσον τρυπῶντες τὰς ναῦς <u>σπάρτοις</u> αὐτὰς <u>συνέρραπτον</u>. καὶ τὸ παρ' Ὁμήρῳ νῆας ἀκειόμενον τὸ <u>συρράπτοντα</u> δηλοῖ). Dougherty 2001:19–37, 189–192 draws similarities between the composition of *ships* and the composition of *poetry* in early Greek poetry. Her argument relies on the comparison between the "sewing together" of component parts in compositions. I find Dougherty's comparison of great interest, and—though she does not carry the analogy so far—the questions her analogy raises: namely, what "shipwreck"—so common a theme, especially in the *Odyssey* and the *Nostoi* tradition at large—might mean for the early Greek concept of poetry. In other words, can we think of a poem that becomes unstitched over time, or one that is no longer "sea-worthy" or can no longer effectively carry its cargo? Can a poem or perhaps an entire poetic tradition be conceived of as becoming disarticulated over time?

Ἀτρείδη, νῦν δή σε, ἄναξ, ἐθέλουσιν Ἀχαιοί
πᾶσιν ἐλέγχιστον θέμεναι μερόπεσσι βροτοῖσιν,
<u>οὐδέ τοι ἐκτελέουσιν ὑπόσχεσιν ἥν περ ὑπέσταν</u>
ἐνθάδ' ἔτι στείχοντες ἀπ' Ἄργεος ἱπποβότοιο,
<u>Ἴλιον ἐκπέρσαντ'</u> εὐτείχεον ἀπονέεσθαι.
<u>ὥς τε γὰρ ἢ παῖδες νεαροὶ χῆραί τε γυναῖκες</u>
ἀλλήλοισιν ὀδύρονται οἰκόνδε νέεσθαι.

Son of Atreus, now indeed, O king, the Achaeans are willing
to make you the most contemptible among all mortal men,
<u>and they will not bring to completion the promise, the very one</u>
        <u>they undertook</u>
while still making their way to this place from Argos, land of
        horse-pastures,
namely to return home <u>after they sacked Ilion</u>, the well-walled
        city.
<u>For always either like young children or widowed women</u>
they cry out and complain to one another about returning home.

Iliad II 284–290

Odysseus reminds the men of the promise (ὑπόσχεσιν, II 285) they made (ἥν περ ὑπέσταν, II 285): the ὑπο- prefix in both noun (ὑπόσχεσις "a promise, under-taking") and verb (ὑφίστημι "to promise, place oneself under engagement") marks the obligation each one has placed himself under, as if the promise itself were a yoke and the promiser a beast of burden duty-bound to see the project through to the end. But the Achaeans are no longer faithful to their word and no longer willing to see the project through to its end (οὐδέ τοι ἐκτελέουσιν, II 286). Instead, Odysseus accuses the Achaeans of acting like women and children, classes of people whose speech is not dependable.[19] The Achaeans are neglecting their duty towards Agamemnon and the world of men, since they are thinking only of themselves and their return home. Their failure to carry through on their promise essentially alienates them from society; they are no longer part of a corps dedicated to keeping promises and making war, but have

---

[19]   In her penetrating study of the term νήπιος in Greek epic diction, Edmunds 1990 cites this passage (*Iliad* II 289–290) and notes that "children are grouped with women to form a class of those who are ineffectual. To compare a warrior to a woman is an insult. ... men are called 'like women and children' because they are behaving in an unwarriorlike fashion" (4). Scott 1974 notes several passages (*Iliad* II 289, 337–341, XI 389, 560–561, XIII 470, *Odyssey* iv 32, xxi 282) in which warriors are likened to children, and argues that "in each case a character is doing something which is odd, inept, or unbefitting the person" (74).

marginalized themselves as women and children—ineffective speakers and actors.[20]

Odysseus does acknowledge the Achaeans' eagerness to be done with their task—nine years is a long time to be separated from one's home and family, after all. But, he argues, to return home prematurely is a shameful thing.

ἦ μὴν καὶ πόνος ἐστὶν ἀνιηθέντα <u>νέεσθαι</u>·
καὶ γάρ τίς θ' ἕνα μῆνα <u>μένων</u> ἀπὸ ἧς ἀλόχοιο
<u>ἀσχαλάᾳ</u> σὺν νηΐ πολυζύγῳ, ὅν περ ἄελλαι
χειμέριαι εἰλέωσιν ὀρινομένη τε θάλασσα·
ἡμῖν δ' εἴνατός ἐστι περιτροπέων ἐνιαυτός
<u>ἐνθάδε μιμνόντεσσι</u>. τῶ οὐ νεμεσίζομ' Ἀχαιούς
<u>ἀσχαλάαν</u> παρὰ νηυσὶ κορωνίσιν· ἀλλὰ καὶ ἔμπης
<u>αἰσχρόν</u> τοι <u>δηρόν τε μένειν κενεόν τε νέεσθαι</u>.

Truly it is also labor <u>to return home</u> while distressed;[21]
for someone who <u>remains away from his wife</u> for even a single
　　　　month
in a many-benched ship <u>grows impatient</u>, especially one whom the
　　　　storm winds
of winter and the agitated sea thwart his progress;
whereas for us it is the ninth year of [the years] which turn about
<u>while we remain in this place</u>. Accordingly, I don't blame the Achaeans
for <u>growing impatient</u> beside the curved ships; but nevertheless,
I tell you, <u>it is a shameful thing both to remain so long and to return
　　　　home empty-handed</u>.

　　　　　　　　　　　　　　　　　　　　　　　　Iliad II 291–298

---

[20] On the connection between those who cannot speak or communicate ineffectively and the social outcast, Edmunds 1990 notes: "The typically νήπιος figure lives in a fragmented and dangerous world, in danger of becoming an orphan and consequently a social outcast, or failing to observe the laws of hospitality; he or she is outside the web of human interconnections. Furthermore, the νήπιος person is unable to put together inferences from the past or signs that reveal the future and is thus trapped in the ephemera" (98).

[21] The interpretation of this line is difficult. Leaf 1900–1902:I.70, following K. Lehrs *De Aristarchi studiis Homericis* (Leipzig, 1865) 74, took the line to mean "truly here is toil to make a man return disheartened," and argued that the ἦ μὴν καί "introduces an excuse" why the men are no longer willing to fight. This reading seems to fit with the sense of the following verses (II 292–297). However, as Kirk 1985:147 points out, Leaf's interpretation creates problems with II 297–298 where Odysseus argues why the men should *not* return home. It seems better, therefore, to translate *Iliad* II 291 as I have here, and understand ἦ μὴν καὶ πόνος as indicating that although it is difficult work (πόνος) to stay and fight, it is equally difficult to return home empty-handed (κενεόν, II 298) after waiting so long (δηρόν τε μένειν, II 298).

Odysseus' speech focuses on three terms, each repeated within the passage: waiting (μένων, II 292; μιμνόντεσσι, II 296), feeling impatient (ἀσχαλάᾳ, II 293; ἀσχαλάαν, II 297), and returning home (νέεσθαι, II 291, 298; cf. II 290). These are the terms which frame the Achaeans' state of mind: after so long a time (δηρόν, II 298)—a period of no less than nine years (εἴνατός ... ἐνιαυτὸς, II 295)— the men are impatient and eager to return home. This impatience is the force that threatens to tear the Greek army asunder against the cohesive social bond of oaths to fight to the end—it is the psychological measure of the extent of empty time felt only as a separation from what one wants: waiting <u>here</u> (ἐνθάδε μιμνόντεσσι, II 296), waiting far <u>away from</u> one's wife (μένων ἀπὸ ἧς ἀλόχοιο, II 292). Such a reaction, Odysseus notes, is perfectly natural—this is the experience of temporality as duration: as Martin Wyllie, a researcher in phenomenology and psychiatry notes, "inactivity makes one aware of the 'passage of time' and this can manifest itself as 'boredom.' When bored, one begins to sense the stagnation of one's personal lived time against the dynamic background of intersubjective time" (Wyllie 2005a:178). The Achaeans have come to feel the drag of time through their own inactivity: time has grown stagnant, and they feel impatient (ἀσχαλάᾳ, II 293; ἀσχαλάαν, II 297), wanting to go forward, to get on with their lives, but unable to do so.[22] Odysseus cannot blame the Achaeans for feeling impatient and disheartened beside their curved ships (τῷ οὐ νεμεσίζομ' Ἀχαιοὺς | ἀσχαλάαν παρὰ νηυσὶ κορωνίσιν, II 296–297) that sit ever ready to carry them home again.

Odysseus counters the disintegrating effect of time by once again reminding the Achaeans of their social responsibilities: to return home now without having carried through the war to its completion would be αἰσχρόν "an ugly, shameful thing." In his work on Greek ethical concepts, Arthur Adkins has demonstrated that within the context of Greek society where one was expected to produce "results" for the benefit of one's friends and relations, the adjective αἰσχρός "ugly, shameful" indicates that one has failed or fallen short of accomplishing what was deemed necessary for society.[23] In our passage, then, Odysseus initially

---

[22] See Fuchs 2005b:196 on the experience of temporal "acceleration" as a cause of impatience: "While implicit temporality is characterized by synchronization with others, explicit temporality arises in states of desynchronization (acceleration or retardation): It is mainly by discrepancies or separations from others to whom our lived time is primarily related that we experience the irreversibility and the rule of time. ... Acceleration of one's time in relation to the environment may be experienced as impatience, pressure, or dysphoric agitation." On implicit and explicit temporality, see my discussion in the Introduction above.

[23] Adkins views αἰσχρός as an indication of failure within a context of a culture that values "results": see Adkins 1960, 1971, 1972, 1982 (esp. p313). See further Long 1970, esp. 124n9, arguing that "intention," though denied by Adkins, must be considered a constitutive element in shame, especially in Odysseus' speech here at *Iliad* II 284–332 where he exhorts the Achaeans not to give up and go home. On the conception of ancient Greece as a "shame culture," see Dodds

responds by trying to shame the Greeks into fulfilling their promise in terms similar to Agamemnon's rhetorical use of *duskleos* "bad reputation" above: to fail to see the war through to its end will be only αἰσχρόν, an ugly and shameful thing. However, Odysseus' rhetoric counters Agamemnon's earlier speech, for Odysseus employs a different rhetorical strategy of representing time. First, he notes that it is the very extent of time that has made the soldiers so impatient which will bring them shame should they return home now without having accomplished their goals: shame lies in the conjunction of waiting so long (δηρόν τε μένειν) and returning home empty-handed (κενεόν τε νέεσθαι, II 298). Had the Achaeans decided to quit after only a single year of unsuccessful fighting, it would not be so shameful; but as it is, the greater extent of time and their greater ineffective effort work in concert to produce a still greater shame. The very extent of the nine years, Odysseus suggests, should not weaken the men's resolve to carry out their promises; if anything, the long time should bind them all the more to the task at hand. This argument is an implicit rejection of Agamemnon's temporal rhetoric of a decisive present that breaks with a static past. Instead of introducing change through a decisive present, Odysseus suggests that the extent of the past itself is the strongest reason to continue waiting; change now, with nothing accomplished, would only be failure. In other words, Odysseus is rejecting the transformation of a "not yet" into a "no longer": the city not yet taken is not one that cannot be taken. By rejecting Agamemnon's "no longer" Odysseus opens up again a possible future for the Achaeans, one in which their efforts may be rewarded.

Yet, Odysseus does not win the men over merely by appealing to their sense of social responsibility made even more important through the length of time they have been waging war. Instead, he employs a second rhetorical strategy to overcome the disintegrating effect of the passage of time and reintegrate the men. Once again, like Agamemnon's testing speech, Odysseus' rhetoric makes use of temporal relations; however, unlike Agamemnon's speech, Odysseus does not follow a narrative of static past giving way to projected future through dramatic present. Instead, he employs a rhetoric in which the immediacy of lively memory trumps the pastness of the past. Specifically, Odysseus reminds the Achaeans of the prophetic sign (Odysseus calls it a μέγα σῆμα "great sign" at *Iliad* II 308) they received at Aulis before they sailed to Troy. On that occasion some ten years before, a snake devoured a mother-bird and her eight chicks before being turned to stone by Zeus (II 308–320). The seer Calchas interpreted the sight to mean that the Greeks would fight nine inconclusive years in Troy, but

---

1951 and Williams 1993. For a different perspective, see Hooker 1987 who argues that *aidōs* originally indicated "respect" instead of "shame."

would take the city in the tenth (II 322–329). Odysseus calls upon the Achaeans to wait a little longer to see whether Calchas' prophecy will come true, and then seeks to charm them with the absolute *immediacy* of the prophetic event:

τλῆτε φίλοι, καὶ μείνατ' ἐπὶ χρόνον, ὄφρα δαῶμεν
ἤ' ἐτεὸν Κάλχας μαντεύεται ἦε καὶ οὐκί.
εὖ γὰρ δὴ τόδε ἴδμεν ἐνὶ φρεσίν, ἐστὲ δὲ πάντες
μάρτυροι, οὓς μὴ κῆρες ἔβαν θανάτοιο φέρουσαι·
χθιζά τε καὶ πρωΐζ' ὅτ' ἐς Αὐλίδα νῆες Ἀχαιῶν
ἠγερέθοντο κακὰ Πριάμῳ καὶ Τρωσὶ φέρουσαι ...
ἔνθ' ἐφάνη μέγα σῆμα.

Be patient, my friends, and stay a little while yet until we know
whether Calchas prophesied truly or not.
For in truth, I know this thing well in my heart, and you all are
witnesses, whomever the spirits of death have not come to carry away.
It was either yesterday or the day before when at Aulis the ships of the
        Achaeans
were gathered to bring evils to Priam and to the Trojans ...
Then a great sign was made manifest.

Iliad II 299–304, 308[24]

Odysseus, the hero who most embodies patience, asks the men to wait just a little longer: τλῆτε "be patient, endure," μείνατ' ἐπὶ χρόνον "stay a little while yet" (II 299). His use of χρόνος "time" (II 299) makes explicit the temporal element in his speech. He recalls to their attention an event long past (ten years previous at Aulis), yet full of such importance that the elapsed time seems like "yesterday or the day before" (χθιζά τε καὶ πρωΐζ', II 303). Through lively memory, the past almost becomes present once again as implied by the visual terms Odysseus uses τόδε ἴδμεν "I have seen/know this thing here" (II 301) and ἐστὲ δὲ πάντες | μάρτυροι "you all are witnesses" (II 301–302).[25] Consider further the deictic

---

[24] I punctuate this text after Allen (1931) instead of following West (1998–2000), who seems to want to read χθιζά τε καὶ πρωΐζ' with φέρουσαι: "whomever the spirits of death have not come to carry away yesterday or the day before." In support of my reading, see Leaf 1900–1902:I.71 (comment at *Iliad* II 303): "the principle verb is ἔφανη (308) ... In this case, the phrase is used to make light of the long duration of the war, 'it is as it were but yesterday, when,' etc."

[25] The perfect οἶδα "I know" (ἴδμεν = first person plural perfect active indicative, with poetic use of the plural) and aorist εἶδον "I saw" are both from the same root verb unattested in the present tense in Greek (*εἴδω: compare Latin *video*). The perfect οἶδα retains a sense of visual basis, as knowledge itself is based on vision. Compare *Iliad* II 484–486 where the poet notes the Muses' knowledge based on their omnipresence and vision (πάρεστέ τε, ἴστέ τε πάντα "you are present

force of the demonstrative τόδε "this thing here" (II 301) which implies the immediacy and proximity of the memory itself.[26]

Odysseus essentially recasts Agamemnon's description of the preceding nine years: his version offers the immediacy of memory as an antidote for the long period of elapsed time. Wolfgang Kullmann speaks of Odysseus as bridging "distance in time" in such a way that he recreates the future for the Achaeans:

> Odysseus thus, fully cognizant of objective time (nine years), *brings the past so close to the present* that for him and his hearers it is like something that happened yesterday or the day before. From this *proximity* of favorable omens in the past *he creates confidence for the future*. (Kullmann 2001:393; emphases added)

Odysseus seeks to undo the disintegration of the Achaeans' emotional resolve, deteriorated by the long years of waiting, by eliding that very temporal expanse. He reduces the nine-years to a day or two in the context of the vividness of memory (εὖ γὰρ δὴ τόδε ἴδμεν ἐνὶ φρεσίν, II 301), and thereby reconstitutes the men's resolve. My interpretation here is in agreement with the work of Egbert Bakker (1993, 1997, 1999) who has argued how the "performance" of a past event in epic functions to bring that memory to the present. In this case, Odysseus literally re-presents the past—the prophetic sign observed so many years before at Aulis—through his narrative description; he recreates the event for his audience and essentially makes the past present once again. In his study of Odysseus' speech, Bakker notes in particular how the use of the particle ἄρα (cf. II 310) in his recollection of the portent "marks Odysseus's speech as the description of what he sees and of his involvement therewith. But as a narrator ... his narrative is directed at recreating a shared experience from the past as a shared reality in the here and now of the present" (Bakker 1993:18). Odysseus' mnemonics bridge the distance between past and present, spatializing time and drawing it *near*.

Nevertheless, Odysseus' χθιζά τε καὶ πρωΐζ' "yesterday or the day before" (II 303) does not fully elide the distance between past event and present moment. Whereas Odysseus recalls the great sign and makes it vivid for his audience, it remains in the past. The past never quite becomes a here and now. That is to say, Odysseus' vivid narrative recalls the past while at the same time acknowledging

---

and know all things") as opposed to human knowledge, which is based entirely on hearing second-hand report (ἡμεῖς δὲ κλέος οἶον ἀκούομεν, οὐδέ τε ἴδμεν "but we hear only report, and do not know").

[26] On deixis in Homeric poetry as signaling "immediacy," see Bakker 1999 and 2005 (especially chapter 5), with bibliography.

its very pastness. The distance separating Odysseus' vivid past from his fully present moment points to memory's inability to fully re-present the past in perfect temporal proximity. For the epic tradition, the claim to preserve Achilles' κλέος ἄφθιτον would seem to be predicated upon the possibility of perfect recall; perfect durability—were it possible—would mean freeing the subject from decaying time altogether. Memory, as an act of care (as discussed in the Introduction above), aims to preserve the cohesive against disintegrating decay. Nevertheless, a re-presentation which is not fully present, one which produced a vividness not of "here and now" but of "yesterday or the day before," leaves a gap—however small—into which time can creep and work its ruin.

Chapter 2

Men and Worms

Permanence and Organic Decay

TIME LEAVES INDELIBLE TRACES. All organic material, like a ship's timber, eventually rots. The Greek verb used to describe this process, σήπεσθαι, occurs twice in the context of the decay of mortal flesh. Like the ship wood, heroes' bodies mark time through their own internal cycles of growth and deterioration.

Not all bodies are equal, however. The *Iliad* gives special attention to three bodies above and beyond all others: the corpses of Sarpedon, Patroklos, and Hektor. These three figures function as links in a larger chain—the bond of fate that links the destruction of Troy inevitably with the death of Achilles, the best of the Achaeans. According to the logic of the *aristeia* in the *Iliad*, a man can be *aristos* "the best of his kind" only temporarily, for by becoming victor over another, he marks himself as the potential victim of a still greater foe. So Sarpedon is killed by Patroklos (XVI 479–491), who in turn is killed by Hektor (XVI 818–829), and Hektor falls to Achilles (XXII 325–363). The chain of victor and victim, although left incomplete within the scope of the narration of the *Iliad*, leaves it virtually accomplished that Achilles himself will fall at the hands of another, as Hektor prophesies with the clarity of a man near death's door:[1]

---

[1] Heyne observes, "*Animae morientium sunt μαντικαί*" ("The souls of men who are about to die are 'prophetic,'" Heyne 1821:385, comment at *Iliad* XXII 358). Consider Patroklos' prophetic dying words spoken to Hektor at *Iliad* XVI 851–854: ἄλλο δέ τοι ἐρέω, σὺ δ᾽ ἐνὶ φρεσὶ βάλλεο σῇσιν· | οὔ θην οὐδ᾽ αὐτὸς δηρὸν βέε᾽, ἀλλά τοι ἤδη | ἄγχι παρέστηκεν Θάνατος καὶ Μοῖρα κραταιή, | χερσὶ δαμέντ᾽ Ἀχιλῆος ἀμύμονος Αἰκίδαο, "But I will tell you another thing, and do you cast it into your heart: you yourself will certainly not live long, but already for you Death and strong Fate are standing at hand, to be subdued at the hands of blameless Achilles, Aeacus' son." See further Heyne 1821:184 (comment at *Iliad* XVI 842–854), Rohde 1925:36, 52n69, and Burgess 2009:45.

φράζεο νῦν, μή τοί τι θεῶν μήνιμα γένωμαι
ἤματι τῷ, ὅτε κέν σε Πάρις καὶ Φοῖβος Ἀπόλλων
ἐσθλὸν ἐόντ᾽ ὀλέσωσιν ἐνὶ Σκαιῇσι πύλῃσιν.

Consider this now, lest I become some cause of the gods' wrath for you
on that day, whenever it is, when Paris and Phoibos Apollo
will destroy you, although you are strong, at the Skaian gates.

Iliad XXII 358–360

With the death of Hektor, Achilles' death is a foregone conclusion.[2] His death
is guaranteed by the inexorable logic that links Hektor's death with those of
Patroklos and Sarpedon. The fates of these men's corpses are also linked by the
same logic: special cares given to Sarpedon, Patroklos, and Hektor are anticipations for the ritual care that will be extended to Achilles' body, though his death
is not recorded within the narrative of the *Iliad* itself.

In this chapter, I argue that the anticipatory care given to Achilles' corpse,
as foreshadowed in the way the gods treat Sarpedon, Patroklos, and Hektor,
is itself an analogy for the epic tradition's goal of preserving Achilles' κλέος
ἄφθιτον "unwithered fame." The *Iliad* emphatically describes the corpses of
Sarpedon, Patroklos, and Hektor, each linked with Achilles' own death, as being
in danger of rotting (σήπεσθαι). Yet, the gods intervene to prevent the decay
of these bodies through the application of special substances (*ambrosia, nektar*)
applied to their flesh such that their bodies are for a short while removed from
the progression of time and its powers of decay. Apollo, Thetis, and Aphrodite
each act to delay the process of decay for a short while, until proper burial
rituals can be carried out for the dead.

I argue that the preservation of these exquisite corpses serves as an
analogue within the poem for the very project of the epic commemoration of
Achilles—as if the epic were a "freezing" of temporal flow against the ravages
of time. The tradition aims to preserve Achilles' fame like *ambrosia* and *nektar*
would his body: epic commemoration tries to remove the hero and his "fame"
(κλέος) from the decaying progression of time and hence render it "unwithered" (ἄφθιτον). Yet, by this very analogy of modes of preservation, the temporally conditioned nature of the preservation implied by the tradition's κλέος
ἄφθιτον becomes clear, for, as I demonstrate below, the application of *ambrosia*

---

[2]   References to Achilles' death occur several times throughout the *Iliad*: I 352, 416, IX 410–416,
XVII 401–409, XVIII 37–60, XVIII 95–99, 329–332, XIX 416–417, XXI 108–113, 277–278, XXII 359–
360, XXIII 80–81. See Burgess 2009:41–55 for discussion and further bibliography. Achilles is the
only major character in the *Iliad* to have foreknowledge of his fate; some minor characters, such
as Euchenor (XIII 663–670), possess such knowledge: see King 1987:237n14 and Burgess 2009:43.

and *nektar* (and whatever process is to be understood by the verb *tarkhuein*) to mortal bodies is necessarily conditioned by time: the gods can only temporarily remove a body from time. By analogy, then, the preservation implied by the κλέος ἄφθιτον of the tradition is itself conceived of as only a temporary preservation from the forces of time—Achilles' fame can only be "not (yet) withered" (ἀ-φθι-τον).

1. Sarpedon: *Tarkhuein, Ambrosia,* and the Temporality of Preservation

Let us begin with Sarpedon, son of Zeus and lord of the Lycians. In Book XVI of the *Iliad* Zeus ponders rescuing Sarpedon from his fated death. Hera dissuades him from doing so—not because it is beyond his power, but because it will create hard feelings among the other gods who have mortal children likewise fated to die in war. If Zeus really cares for his son, she argues, he will allow him to die and then see to the proper care of his mortal remains by sending Sarpedon's corpse home so that his people can provide him fitting funerary rites.

ἀλλ᾽ <u>εἴ τοι φίλος ἐστί, τεὸν δ᾽ ὀλοφύρεται ἦτορ,</u>
ἤτοι μέν μιν ἔασον ἐνὶ κρατερῇ ὑσμίνῃ
χέρσ᾽ ὑπὸ Πατρόκλοιο Μενοιτιάδαο δαμῆναι,
αὐτὰρ ἐπὴν δὴ τόν γε λίπῃ ψυχή τε καὶ αἰών,
πέμπειν μιν Θάνατόν τε φέρειν καὶ νήδυμον Ὕπνον,
εἰς ὅ κε δὴ Λυκίης εὐρείης δῆμον ἵκωνται,
<u>ἔνθά ἑ ταρχύσουσι κασίγνητοί τε ἔται τε</u>
<u>τύμβῳ τε στήλῃ τε· τὸ γὰρ γέρας ἐστὶ θανόντων.</u>

But <u>if he is dear to you</u>, and <u>your heart mourns for him</u>,
in truth, I tell you, let him in the strong encounter
be subdued under the hands of Patroklos, Menoitios' son,
but whenever his soul and life-force leave him,
send both Death and sweet Sleep to carry him
until they reach the people of wide Lycia,
<u>where both his brothers and countrymen will pay him funeral rites,</u>
<u>with a burial mound and gravestone. For this is the privilege of those</u>
<u>who have died.</u>

Iliad XVI 450–457

Sarpedon is dear (φίλος) to Zeus, and Zeus' heart mourns for him (τεὸν δ᾽ ὀλοφύρεται ἦτορ, XVI 450). But divine care does not entail preservation from death; rather, Zeus' care is to take the form of grief coupled with concern that

Sarpedon receive proper ritualized care in burial. In death, care for a loved one takes the form of preserving that loved one's honor through providing all due ritual cares—what Homer calls the γέρας θανόντων. One's γέρας is the manifestation of his or her honor; it is the indication of the degree of respect others feel for him or her made visible for all to see.[3] The γέρας of a dead man, Hera explains, consists of the proper treatment of his mortal remains: the practice of funeral rites (ταρχύειν), followed by the heaping up of a burial mound (τύμβος) and erection of a gravestone (στήλη).[4]

The treatment provided to the dead is of interest for our investigation, for it forms part of a ritual analogue to the commemorative epic itself that aims to preserve the memory of the fallen hero. As Hera notes, part of that ritual includes the burial of the dead, heaping up a burial mound, and erecting a gravestone. I look at the procedure of Homeric burial at length in chapter 4 below. In this chapter, I am interested in the period of time between death and before burial when characters express anxiety over the possible fate of the corpse of a loved one. This anxiety, I argue, is partly expressed through the verb ταρχύειν. The verb ταρχύειν presents special difficulty for interpretation because the question remains yet unresolved whether it is a term borrowed from an Anatolian source, or whether it is an inherited Proto-Indo-European word. In the former case, the exact meaning of the borrowed term is difficult to determine with certainty; in the latter case, cognates in other Indo-European languages may help us interpret the precise meaning of the verb.[5] Scholars have traced the verb back to a Lycian root *tarχu and indicated possible Indo-European cognates, citing Lycian *Trqqñt- (attested in the nominative singular Trqqas/Trqqiz and dative singular Trqqñti), an adjective designating a god who overcomes the wicked, and the related Luvian Tarḫunna/Tarḫunta/Tarḫunza, the name of the storm god and head of the Luvian pantheon;[6] further apparent cognates are the Hittite verbal

---

[3] Benveniste 1969:II.43–50, Adkins 1972, Garland 1982, Staten 1993:342–343, 347, 354, 360n14, Antonaccio 1994:397 with nn42–44, and Finkelberg 1998. See Garland 1982 on the association of γέρας with γῆρας "old age": Garland argues that the original sense of γέρας was "that which is due to a person in respect to his age," and was later generalized to denote any honorific portion or visible manifestation of one's honor. Beekes 2010:I.267–268, 271, s.vv. γέρας, γῆρας notes the etymological connection between the two words, but cannot explain "the remarkable long vowel" of γῆρας.

[4] In general, γέρας is the exactly measured physical manifestation of one's honor (τιμή) within a community: see citations in the preceding note, but esp. Nagy 1990a:137–138 and Antonaccio 1994:397 with nn42–44. On the γέρας θανόντων, see Garland 1982 and Sourvinou-Inwood 1995:130–131. In an archaic epitaph, a σῆμα "tomb" is said to be the γέρας θανόντος (Hansen 1983:40 and Peek 1955:156, cited in Sourvinou-Inwood 1995:130n60).

[5] I wish to thank Professor Brent Vine for his assistance with these interpretative problems surrounding ταρχύω.

[6] Blümel 1927:82–83, Kretschmer 1940:104, Nagy 1983:196, 212nn28–29, 2010:337, Bryce 1986:177, Janda 1996:80, Tsymbursky 2007:155–156, and West 2007:247 with further bibliography.

stem *tarḫzi* and *tarḫuzi/taruḫzi* "to overcome" with derivative adjective *tarḫu-* which means "conquering, victorious."[7] The associations between the Greek ταρχύω and cognate Lycian, Luvian, and Hittite terms suggest a reconstructed Indo-European verbal root $*trh_2$- with the sense of "overcome, vanquish."[8] The implication—if the theory of a Proto-Indo-European origin holds true—is that the rites provided to Sarpedon somehow "preserve" him and help him "overcome" or "vanquish" death, perhaps through Lycian cult where he will be treated "like a god."[9] Françoise Bader has suggested that the collocation of νέκυς "corpse" and ταρχύω in *Iliad* VII 84–85 (τὸν δὲ <u>νέκυν</u> ἐπὶ νῆας ἐϋσσέλμους ἀποδώσω, | ὄφρά ἑ <u>ταρχύσωσι</u> κάρη κομόωντες Ἀχαιοί) points to an actively felt relationship between *νεκ-* and $*trh_2$ that appears most clearly in the etymology and semantics of νέκταρ (as we will discuss below), a substance applied to the corpses of Patroklos and Hektor to help them temporarily "overcome death" through preserving them against the temporal force of decay—perhaps through some form of embalming (Bader 2002:11–12).[10] As Blümel stated, "In any case, *tarχu describes a man who is preserved far beyond his appointed death."[11]

The etymology of ταρχύω is obscure and controversial, and it is surely unwise to base an interpretation of the text solely on it. However, it is possible to strengthen the claim that the verb ταρχύω implies "temporary preservation" by investigating the specific details that appear in the context of Sarpedon's death

---

[7] Kretschmer 1940:104, 112–114, Pugliese Carratelli 1954, Nagy 1983:196–197, 213nn30–31, Heubeck 1984:110–111, and Janda 1996:80. For a concise history of scholarship on ταρχύω, see Janda 1996:79–81 and Tsymbursky 2007:152–158.

[8] Nagy 1983:196, 213n31, 1990a:131–139, 190, 1990b:270n102, 2010:337, Schein 1984:48, Watkins 1995:351–356, 391–397, 443–446, and Bader 2002:11–12. For a different view, see Janda 1996:82–86 who argues that ταρχύω is based on an Indo-European root *dherĝh- attested in the Hittite *tuḫš-*, *tuḫḫušta* "it is finished," the Celtic root *dūnom* "come full circle," and Latin *fūnus* "funeral."

[9] Blümel 1927:84, Kretschmer 1940:103–104, Nagy 1983 *passim*, 1990a:132, 2010:337; for a dissenting view, see Clarke 1999:187n61.

[10] For an interpretation of ταρχύω as implying the "embalming" of a corpse, see Blümel 1927:81, Myloans 1948:57–58 with nn8–9, and Janda 1996:79–80, who propose a relationship with ταριχεύω "to preserve a body by artificial means: embalming, salting, pickling" (used by Herodotus 2.86 and Plato *Phaedrus* 80c to describe Egyptian mummies, and by Xenophon *Anabasis* 5.4.28 to describe preserved meat), and τάρῑχος "a body preserved by artificial means: embalming, mummification, pickling, salting, smoking, drying" (cf. Herodotus 9.120 of the hero Protesilaus "dead or preserved like a salted fish"). Chantraine seems to vacillate on a connection between ταρχύω and ταρῑχεύω/τάρῑχος, raising the possibility on one page (Chantraine 1968–1980:1094, s.v. τάρῑχος: "Y a-t-il un rappor avec ταρχύω?"), only to deny it on the next (Chantraine 1968–1980:1095, s.v. ταρχύω: "*La form et le sens excluent tout raprochment avec ταριχεύω, τάρῐχος*"). See further Bernal 2006:370 who argues that "The slight phonetic distinction between *tarikheuō* and *tarkhuō* disappears completely if they are both borrowings from a third language," namely (for Bernal) Egyptian; and West 1997:386 who denies any connection between ταρχύω and ταρῑχεύω.

[11] Blümel 1927:83.

which point to the phenomenon of Sarpedon's body "temporarily overcoming" decomposition and decay. For, in addition to the funeral rites with burial mound and gravestone, Zeus requests special treatment for his son's body before it is transported to Sarpedon's homeland, where his people will see to his proper funeral.

εἰ δ' ἄγε νῦν, φίλε Φοῖβε, κελαινεφὲς αἷμα <u>κάθηρον</u>
ἐλθὼν ἐκ βελέων Σαρπηδόνα, καί μιν ἔπειτα
πολλὸν ἄποπρο φέρων <u>λοῦσον</u> ποταμοῖο ῥοῇσιν
<u>χρῖσόν τ' ἀμβροσίῃ, περὶ δ' ἄμβροτα εἵματα ἕσσον.</u>
πέμπε δέ μιν πομποῖσιν ἅμα κραιπνοῖσι φέρεσθαι,
Ὕπνῳ καὶ Θανάτῳ διδυμάοσιν, οἵ ῥά μιν ὦκα
θήσουσ' ἐν Λυκίης εὐρείης πίονι δήμῳ·
<u>ἔνθά ἑ ταρχύσουσι χασίγνητοί τε ἔται τε</u>
<u>τύμβῳ τε στήλῃ τε· τὸ γὰρ γέρας ἐστὶ θανόντων.</u>

But come now, if you will, dear Phoibos, go and <u>clean</u> the dark blood
[caused] by the missiles from Sarpedon,[12] and then
carry him far away; <u>bathe</u> him in the running water of a river,
<u>and anoint him with ambrosia, and clothe him all around in ambrosial</u>
      <u>clothing.</u>
Then send to him the nimble messengers to carry him together,
Sleep and Death, twin brothers; they will swiftly
place him in the rich *deme* of wide Lycia.
<u>There both his brothers and countrymen will pay him funeral rites,</u>
<u>with a burial mound and gravestone. For this is the privilege of those who</u>
      <u>have died.</u>

Iliad XVI 667–675

Apollo is to remove the body some distance from the fighting, to separate him from the battle (πολλὸν ἄποπρο φέρων, XVI 669).[13] Then he is to wash (λοῦσον,

---

[12] I follow Heyne's interpretation in translating this line: "ἐλθὼν κάθηρον—h[oc] e[st] ἐλθὲ καὶ κάθαιρε Σαρπηδόνα (κατὰ τὸ) αἷμα ἐκ βελέων (*purga Sarpedonis corpus a sanguine e uulneribus*) ..." (Heyne 1821:175).

[13] On the idea of Sarpedon being *snatched* away from the fray, see Vermeule 1979:169 who notes the possible linguistic connection between the name of Sarpedon and that of the Harpes (*σαρπ- > ἁρπ-), and suggests that Death and Sleep have been substituted for the more traditional "lady birds ... to match more familiar configurations of epic mortality." Sarpedon is associated with myths of people being snatched away by storm winds: the North Wind (Boreas), who revives Sarpedon at *Iliad* V 697, is said to have snatched the maiden Orithuia away to a rock named *Sarpēdōn* (Scholia to Apollonius of Rhodes *Argonautica* I 211c = Pherecydes of Athens *FGrHist* 3 F 145). See further Vermeule 1979:242n36 with bibliography.

XVI 669) and clean (κάθηρον, XVI 667) Sarpedon's body of blood and gore (αἷμα, XVI 667) with fresh-running water and anoint his mortal flesh with immortal ointment, *ambrosia* (χρῖσόν τ' ἀμβροσίη, XVI 670). Then he is to dress him in ambrosial clothing (περὶ δ' ἄμβροτα εἵματα ἕσσον, XVI 670). The verb ταρχύω appears in this context: through Apollo's application of *ambrosia*, the body may receive ritual care (ταρχύειν). For our argument, then, the meaning of ταρχύειν may be ascertained more securely through a study of the semantics of *ambrosia*.

Just what is this *ambrosia* used to anoint Sarpedon's body and define his clothing, what does it have to do with the special treatment of the dead, and what does it tell us about the Greek experience of human temporality? An investigation of the etymology of the word "*ambrosia*" and its use in Greek myth will assist in our understanding of the scene. *Ambrosia* is closely associated with the gods' immortality. The word ἀμβροσίη is related (an abstract noun built on an adjectival stem) to ἄμβροτος, a compound adjective consisting of alpha-privative (ἀ- "not") plus the adjective "mortal" (βροτός).[14] The Greek word family has been demonstrated to have secure foundations in the Indo-European root *ṇ-mṛto-, the privative form of the root indicating *mortal*; the well-attested Vedic cognate *amŕtam* denotes the food or drink of the gods which bestows immortality upon them.[15] The special property of *ambrosia* (and of *nektar*, the divine substance with which *ambrosia* is most frequently paired)[16] of bestowing immortality upon its recipient appears throughout early Greek mythic thought and literature.[17] In Homer, *ambrosia* sometimes appears as the food of the gods or

---

[14] The formation of ἀμβροσία from ἄμβροτος follows the regular rules for noun formation of abstract feminine nouns in –σιᾱ/-σιη, added directly onto τ- stem adjectives (ἀμβροτ-). See Schwyzer 1950–1971:I.469, Leumann 1950:125 with n95, 127, and Risch 1974:124–125 (§44a).

[15] Watkins 1995:392. See Leumann 1950:127 and Chantraine 1958:24, 1968–1980:197–198, s.v. βροτός, who suggest an Indo-European root *mer which figures in Latin *morior*, Sanskrit *mriyáte*, old Slavic *mìrǫ*, Lithuanian *mìrštu*, Armenian *meṙanim*. On Vedic *amŕtam*, see Grassmann 1964, s.v., "*das Unsterbliche als Gesamtheit der Götter; das Unsterbliche als Götterwelt; der Unsterblichkeitstrank, ἀμβροσία*" (quoted at Watkins 1995:392n1). The derivation is, of course, not without controversy; see Leaf 1900–1902:I.50–51 (comment at *Iliad* I 19), Wright 1917:6, and Haupt 1922:231–234 on the theory that *ambrosia* is derived from the Semitic *armara* "fragrant," and hence is related to the word "ambergris," suggesting that *ambrosia* is some kind of fragrant oil. See Hocart 1922, esp. 57–63 for a lively refutation of this view (*contra* Leaf *et al.*). See Onians 1954:292 for a brief summary of the earlier alternative interpretations of Bergk, Roscher, and Gruppe.

[16] On *nektar*, see my discussion below.

[17] See Hesiod *Catalogue* fr. 23a on the Achaeans' sacrifice of Agamemnon's daughter (Iphimede in the epic tradition) before setting sail to Ilion: "But [Artemis], the deer-shooter who delights in arrows, very easily sent [Iphimede] away, and infused pleasant ambrosia down upon her head, so that her flesh might be *empedos*, and she made her immortal and ageless for all days" (αὐτὴν δ' ἐλαφηβόλος ἰοχέαιρα | ῥεῖα μάλ' ἐξεσάωσε, καὶ ἀμβροσίην ἐρατεινὴν | στάξε κατὰ κρῆθεν, ἵνα οἱ χρὼς ἔμπεδος εἴη | θῆκεν δ' ἀθάνατον καὶ ἀγήραον ἤματα πάντα [Hesiod fr. 23a.21–24 M-W]). On *empedos*, see my discussion below. In the *Homeric Hymn to Demeter*, the child Demophoön is

of their immortal horses;[18] it is also described as an applied hygienic or beautifying agent, used especially for its fragrant aroma.[19] Its adjectival form describes Night[20] and Sleep[21] as well as the gods' hands,[22] hair,[23] sandals,[24] and clothing.[25] Each of these uses indicates that *ambrosia* truly defines that which is more than mortal, what is proper to the gods and their possessions. *Ambrosia* is given to mortals only in very select instances. Only the clothes of Sarpedon and Achilles

---

nursed by the goddess Demeter; she anoints him with ambrosia during the day, and at night places him in the fire to burn away his mortality: χρίεσκ' ἀμβροσίῃ ὡς εἰ θεοῦ ἐκγεγαῶτα, | ἡδὺ καταπνείουσα καὶ ἐν κόλποισιν ἔχουσα, "she anointed him with *ambrosia* as if he had been born a god and she breathed down sweetly upon him and held him in her lap" (237–238). The child grows at an astounding rate due to the special treatment; it is only his mother, Metanaera, who unwittingly prevents Demeter from making him immortal. On the concept of "burning off" mortality in fire, see Iamblichus *De mysteriis* 5.12: "fire ... destroys all of the material part in sacrifices; it purifies the things that are brought near it and releases them from the bonds of matter, and through its purifying nature, it makes them fit for communion with the gods" (πῦρ ... ἀναιρεῖ τὸ ὑλικὸν πᾶν ἐν ταῖς θυσίαις, τά τε προσαγόμενα τῷ πυρὶ καθαίρει καὶ ἀπολύει τῶν ἐν τῇ ὕλῃ δεσμῶν, ἐπιτήδειά τε διὰ καθαρότητα φύσεως πρὸς τὴν τῶν θεῶν κοινωνίαν ἀπεργάζεται). Compare the Greek tradition of Thetis attempting to make her son Achilles immortal through anointing him with *ambrosia* and either burning him in fire, boiling him in a cauldron, or dipping him in the river Styx. On the tradition and its traces in the *Iliad*, see Mackie 1998 and Curry 2005:383–385. See further Aristotle *Metaphysics* III 4.12, 1000a5–17 who attributes to "the school of Hesiod and all the theologians" (οἱ μὲν οὖν περὶ Ἡσίοδον καὶ πάντες ὅσοι θεολόγοι) the belief "that whatever did not taste of the *nektar* and *ambrosia* became mortal" (τὰ μὴ γευσάμενα τοῦ νέκταρος καὶ τῆς ἀμβροσίας θνητὰ γενέσθαι φασίν). Although Aristotle treats the idea with scorn, his testimony indicates that the belief was in circulation.

18 For *ambrosia* as the food of the gods, see *Odyssey* v 93, 199, *Homeric Hymn to Demeter* 49, and compare the rationalization offered at *Iliad* V 341 for why gods lack "blood." At *Iliad* II 755, *Odyssey* ix 359 and x 514, it seems to refer to wine. For further citations, see Monro *LfgrE* I (1955) [rpt. 1979]:617, s.v. ἀμβρόσιος II.1 and Risch *LfgrE* I (1955) [rpt. 1979]:617–618, s.v. ἄμβροτος. For *ambrosia* as food for immortal horses (ἀμβρόσιον ... εἶδαρ), see *Iliad* V 369, 777, XIII 35. Similar may be the *ambrosial* mangers of the divine horses (ἀμβροσίῃσι κάπῃσιν, *Iliad* VIII 434). Compare *nektar* which is also either a food or a drink of the gods (Hesiod *Theogony* 642 uses *nektar* as the object of the verb πατέομαι "partake of," and *Theogony* 640 uses *nektar* as the object of the verb ἔδω "eat"). On the indifference in early Greek poetry of whether *ambrosia* and *nektar* are solid food or drink, see West 1966:342, comment at *Theogony* 640 with further citations.

19 Hera uses *ambrosia* to clean up and beautify herself as part of *Dios apatē* narrative (*Iliad* XIV 170). At *Odyssey* xviii 193 Athena beautifies Penelope with *ambrosia*. Its fragrance is noted at *Odyssey* iv 445, where *ambrosia* is used to protect Menelaus and his henchmen against the strong odor of the sea-lion skins in which they must disguise themselves. *Homeric Hymn* 7.37 describes the odor emanating during Dionysus' epiphany as "ambrosial"; cf. *Homeric Hymn to Demeter* 237. See further Monro *LfgrE* I (1955) [rpt. 1979]:617, s.v. ἀμβρόσιος II.2.

20 *Iliad* II 57, X 41, 142, XVIII 267–268, *Odyssey* iv 427 = v 574, vii 283, ix 199, xv 8.

21 *Iliad* II 19.

22 *Homeric Hymn to Demeter* 41.

23 Zeus' hair at *Iliad* I 529; Hera's hair at XIV 177.

24 Hermes' sandals at *Iliad* XXIV 340–341 = *Odyssey* I 97 = v 45.

25 For the *ambrosial* clothes of the gods, see *Iliad* V 338, XIV 172, 178; *Homeric Hymn to Aphrodite* 63. The clothes of the gods are perfumed (τεθυωμένον) and of divine craft, made by Athena (cf. *Iliad* XIX 178) or the Graces (V 338). Compare Artemis' veil at XXI 507.

are called "ambrosial";[26] only Achilles is fed *ambrosia* to allow him to continue his fast without growing weary on the battlefield;[27] and it is used to anoint the flesh of Sarpedon, Patroklos, and Hektor alone.[28] In the case of its application to mortal flesh, it seems to act as a means to preserve that flesh—even if only temporarily—from the cycle of organic decay. We may compare Pindar *Olympian* 1.59–63 where Tantalus is given *nektar* and *ambrosia* by the gods, "by means of which they made him *aphthiton*" (νέκταρ ἀμβροσίαν τε ... οἷσιν ἄφθιτον | θέν νιν). For Homer, the application of *ambrosia* to a corpse likewise appears to render it ἄφθιτον—and yet, the body does not remain "unwithered" forever; rather, the body is preserved until it can be returned to its homeland where it will be given proper funerary rites, including burial with a tomb and gravestone. In other words, *ambrosia* and *nektar*, as immortal and immortalizing substances,[29] achieve for the hero's body what epic claims to do for his fame: to render it ἄφθιτον "unwithered."

Zeus, then, both does and does not follow Hera's advice; he allows Sarpedon to die, but asks Apollo to "immortalize" him for a short time, to allay the decomposition of his corpse until proper funeral rites can be conducted among the people of Lycia. The care of the gods reveals itself as concern over the state of Sarpedon's mortal remains: the respect due the dead (γέρας θανόντων) and the "overcoming" function of ταρχύειν can only be offered to the dead whose body has been lovingly preserved against decay. There is some reason to think that the "preserving" features of ταρχύειν may even include a kind of epic commemoration—the fixation of a pristine memory of the fallen—as we find in the third and final attestation of the verb in Homer where Hektor challenges the best of

---

[26] As noted by Janko 1994:396; cf. *Iliad* XVI 670, 680, *Odyssey* xxiv 59; otherwise, only gods have "ambrosial" clothing: cf. *Odyssey* vii 260, *Homeric Hymn* 6.6. Add to Janko's list Achilles' "immortal" cloak at *Iliad* XVIII 25: νεκταρέῳ δὲ χιτῶνι (and see my discussion on νέκταρ below).

[27] *Iliad* XIX 347, 353. See XIX 160–170 on Odysseus' argument on the importance of food for a warrior to keep up strength in battle, and XIX 205–214 for Achilles' refusal to eat out of mourning for Patroklos. See Vernant 1991:31–33 for a very rich treatment of the constantly waning human strength which must be replenished by food: "the vital energies [the human body] deploys and the psychological and physical forces it puts into play can remain only for a brief moment in a state of plentitude" (32). It would seem, then, that by providing Achilles with *ambrosia*, Athena is temporarily excusing Achilles from the constant cycle of re-filling, re-fueling, and re-storing incumbent upon mortals.

[28] *Iliad* XVI 670, 680, XIX 38, XXIII 187. In the *Homeric Hymn to Demeter* 237, Demeter "repeatedly anointed [Demophoön] as if he had been born from a god" (χρίεσκ' ἀμβροσίη ὡς εἰ θεοῦ ἐκγεγαῶτα, 237); in the *Homeric Hymn to Demeter*, anointing Demophoön with *ambrosia* is paired with placing the child in the fire at night to make him ageless and immortal (καί κέν μιν πρίησεν ἀγήρων τ' ἀθάνατόν τε "and she would have made him ageless and immortal," 242). In other words, applying *ambrosia* is part of a strategy for immortalizing human flesh.

[29] See Thieme 1952 on the use of *ṇ-mṛto-* derivative words as indicating not merely "immortal" but also "immortalizing," a claim accepted by Nagy 1990a:141n81. See further Clay 1982 and Sissa and Detienne 2000:77–80 on the immortalizing powers of *nektar* and *ambrosia*.

the Greeks to single-combat, and promises that he will return the corpse of his victim to his people,

ὄφρα ἑ ταρχύσωσι κάρη κομόωντες Ἀχαιοί
σῆμά τε οἱ χεύωσιν ἐπὶ πλατεῖ Ἑλλησπόντῳ.

so that the long-haired Achaeans may pay him funeral rites
and heap up a tomb for him upon the broad Hellespont.

Iliad VII 85–86

Placing a tomb on the Hellespont is a strategy for preserving the memory and fame of the dead, as the tomb is set in a highly conspicuous location and will be looked upon by travelers who are envisioned as telling the tale of the dead as they pass by.[30] The rituals given to Sarpedon, then, whether cult or epic, are associated with the temporary preservation of the body through the immortalizing substance *ambrosia* and its power to remove the corpse from the cycle of decomposition; the corpse becomes ἄφθιτον, at least temporarily.

The application of *ambrosia* marks a violation of human temporal experience. The natural processes of decomposition and decay are halted and held in reserve. This disturbance of human temporal verisimilitude will become clearer as we look at the next two examples of Patroklos and Hektor. Divine intervention, like Apollo's special treatment of Sarpedon, may slow the process of decomposition. But, as we will see, mortal corruption cannot be (or at least *is not*) permanently prevented; what we are left with is a temporality of the "not yet."

2. Patroklos: *Empedos, Nektar,* and the Temporality of Duration

The *ambrosia* used to preserve Sarpedon's mortal remains serves as a thematic link to the other important dead in the *Iliad*. Patroklos, Achilles' nearest and dearest companion, likewise receives special treatment upon his death: his body is preserved by the application of *ambrosia* and *nektar* in an attempt to retard the process of decay.

Patroklos is slain by Hektor at the end of Book XVI of the *Iliad*. A long battle ensues over the body, the narration of which spans more than one-thousand verses[31]—Hektor and the Trojans attempt to capture the body and defile it, and

---

[30] Compare *Odyssey* xi 71–78, xii 8–15, xxiv 80–84, and my discussion in chapter 4 below.
[31] See *Iliad* XVII 1–XVIII 313, totaling 1074 verses, after which the Achaeans recover the body and begin to mourn the fallen Patroklos.

the Achaeans strive to recover the body for proper burial.[32] Achilles single-handedly puts the Trojans to flight upon his return to the battlefield in an otherworldly, epiphanic appearance: he steps onto the battlefield dressed in the *aegis* (XVIII 203–204), his head is encircled with a flaming, golden cloud (XVIII 205–214), and he emits a terrifying, more-than-human shout (XVIII 217–221).[33] When the Greeks finally do recover the body, Achilles states that the body cannot yet be buried:

νῦν δ᾽ ἐπεὶ οὖν, Πάτροκλε, σέ᾽ ὕστερος εἶμ᾽ ὑπὸ γαῖαν,
<u>οὔ σε πρὶν κτεριῶ, πρίν γ᾽ Ἕκτορος ἐνθάδ᾽ ἐνεῖκαι</u>
τεύχεα καὶ κεφαλήν, μεγαθύμου σοῖο φονῆος.

But now since I will go under the earth later than you, Patroklos,
<u>I will not bury you with honors until</u> I have brought here Hektor's
armor and head, since he was your great-hearted killer.

Iliad XVIII 333–335[34]

The dramatic situation, in which Achilles seeks death as the blood-price for his fallen companion, entails another long delay before Patroklos can be buried.[35] The sheer delay itself becomes thematized within the narrative, such that Achilles stops himself from continuing his assault against the Trojans after Hektor's death and recalls Patroklos still unburied body (XXII 378–394);[36] even

---

[32] See *Iliad* XVII 125–127, XVIII 175–177 for Hektor's desire to decapitate Patroklos, drag the body back to Troy and feed it to the dogs, and impale the head on a pike. On the abuse of dead bodies, see Friedrich 2003 and Segal 1971, who notes that the theme of mutilation only appears in emotionally or dramatically charged contexts. Compare the tradition of μασχαλισμός, in which a murderer cuts off the extremities (μασχαλίσματα or ἐξάργματα) of his victim and ties them around the victim's neck, apparently as a precaution against the victim's vengeful spirit, found at Aeschylus *Libation Bearers* 439, Sophocles *Electra* 445 and fr. 623, and discussed by Rohde 1925:Appendix II and Garland 2001:94, 196n94. See further Liddell, Scott, and Jones 1996:1084, s.v. μασχαλίζω, μασχαλίσματα, μασχαλισμός and 587, s.v. ἐξάργματα.

[33] Even Achilles' shout seems to be invested with supernatural quality; the text seems to say that it frightened twelve Trojans to death: τρὶς μὲν ὑπὲρ τάφρου μεγάλ᾽ ἴαχε δῖος Ἀχιλλεύς, | τρὶς δὲ κυκήθησαν Τρῶες κλειτοί τ᾽ ἐπίκουροι. | ἔνθα δὲ καὶ τότ᾽ ὄλοντο δυώδεκα φῶτες ἄριστοι | ἀμφὶ σφοῖς ὀχέεσσι καὶ ἔγχεσιν, "three times brilliant Achilles shouted loudly over the ditch, and three times the Trojans and their renowned companions were routed. And there even at that time twelve of the best men among them perished upon their own chariots and spears" (*Iliad* XVIII 228–231).

[34] I read πρίν γ᾽ Ἕκτορος at XVIII 334 instead of West's πρὶν Ἕκτορος (1998–2000:II.184), both for metrical purposes (πρίν is guaranteed long by the meter), and to afford better contrast with the previous πρίν: "I won't bury you beforehand (πρίν)—not before I kill Hektor, that is (πρίν γ᾽)."

[35] Hektor dies at *Iliad* XXII 361, approximately 2172 verses after Achilles' claim that Patroklos cannot be buried until Achilles avenges his death by killing Hektor.

[36] Richardson 1993:145 notes that "Achilles' first suggestion ... appears to be that they should attack the city immediately," and argues that here Homer is referring to later events in the

more emphatically, the ghost of Patroklos visits Achilles to request that his burial not be delayed any further (XXIII 65–76).[37] It is within this context that we must consider the special treatment given to Patroklos' corpse, which includes anointing with *ambrosia* and *nektar* so as to preserve his body from decay.

Book XIX of the *Iliad* opens with Thetis delivering the armor, newly fashioned by Hephaistos, to her son. Achilles accepts the weapons, but hesitates to arm himself and enter the fray, for he fears that "in the meantime" (τόφρα) Patroklos' corpse will suffer corruption and begin to rot:

μῆτερ ἐμή, τὰ μὲν ὅπλα θεὸς πόρεν οἷ' ἐπιεικές
ἔργ' ἔμεν ἀθανάτων, μηδὲ βροτὸν ἄνδρα τελέσσαι.
νῦν δ' ἤτοι μὲν ἐγὼ θωρήξομαι· ἀλλὰ μάλ' αἰνῶς
δείδω, μή μοι τόφρα Μενοιτίου ἄλκιμον υἱόν
μυῖαι καδδῦσαι κατὰ χαλκοτύπους ὠτειλὰς
εὐλὰς ἐγγείνωνται, ἀεικίσσωσι δὲ νεκρόν—
ἐκ δ' αἰὼν πέφαται—κατὰ δὲ χρόα πάντα σαπήῃ.
Τὸν δ' ἠμείβετ' ἔπειτα θεὰ Θέτις ἀργυρόπεζα·
τέκνον, μή τοι ταῦτα μετὰ φρεσὶ σῇσι μελόντων.
τῷ μὲν ἐγὼ πειρήσω ἀλαλκεῖν ἄγρια φῦλα
μυίας, αἵ ῥά τε φῶτας ἀρηϊφάτους κατέδουσιν.
ἤν περ γὰρ κεῖταί γε τελεσφόρον εἰς ἐνιαυτόν,
αἰεὶ τῷ γ' ἔσται χρὼς ἔμπεδος, ἢ καὶ ἀρείων.
[...]
ὣς ἄρα φωνήσασα μένος πολυθαρσὲς ἐνῆκε·
Πατρόκλῳ δ' αὖτ' ἀμβροσίην καὶ νέκταρ ἐρυθρόν
στάξε κατὰ ῥινῶν, ἵνα οἱ χρὼς ἔμπεδος εἴη.

"Mother of mine, a god has bestowed these weapons—they are
     the sort
of work that is <u>befitting</u> of the immortals—not for a mortal man to
     complete.
And now, in truth, I tell you, I will arm myself. But very terribly
am I afraid lest in the meantime <u>the flies enter</u>

Trojan Cycle, namely the attack on the city walls after the death of Memnon (as related in the *Aethiopis*: cf. Proclus' summary at Davies 1988:47, *Proculi Aethiopidos ennarratio*, 18–21). However, Richardson does not comment on the fact that Achilles' first suggestion is explicitly postponed by his recollection that Patroklos has not yet been buried.

37 The literature on Achilles' dream-visitation by Patroklos is large, and mostly deals with issues concerning the archaic conception of the soul, underworld, afterlife, etc. See, for instance, Rohde 1925, Vermeule 1979, I. Morris 1989, Sourvinou-Inwood 1995, Clarke 1999, Garland 2001, all with further bibliography. My interest in Patroklos' ghost is the emphasis on the characters' experience of time as duration, a point generally ignored by the works cited above.

Menoitios' strong son, <u>down through the wounds beaten into him by bronze</u>,
  <u>and breed maggots, and do unbefitting things to the corpse</u>—
now that his life has been slain out of him—and that <u>all his flesh may completely rot</u>."
And then she answered him, the goddess Thetis of the silver feet:
"My child, may these things not be a cause of care to you in your mind.
I will attempt to <u>ward off</u> from him the swarming race
of <u>flies</u>, which always devour men slain in war.
<u>For even if he lies until a year has brought its completion</u>,
<u>his flesh will always be *empedos*</u>, or even better."
[...]
After she spoke to him thus, she sent very courageous might into him,
and in turn for Patroklos *ambrosia* and red *nektar*
she instilled through his nose, <u>so that his flesh might be *empedos*</u>.

Iliad XIX 21–33, 37–39

Achilles praises the armor his mother has brought him from Hephaistos, master craftsman of the gods. It is work "befitting" (ἐπιεικές, XIX 21) the gods themselves. And yet, at the same time that he praises the handiwork that will protect his body in battle, he is worried that flies and worms "may do unbefitting things" (ἀεικίσσωσι, XIX 26) to Patroklos' body. Unlike Achilles' body, still supple and intact and soon to be covered with metallic armor, Patroklos' body is open and vulnerable, stripped of his armor by Hektor and punctured by "bronze-beaten wounds" (χαλκοτύπους ὠτειλάς, XIX 25), into which corruption may enter the corpse and cause it to rot away entirely (κατὰ δὲ χρόα πάντα σαπήη, XIX 27). Achilles has failed to defend his friend in life and fears he will be unable to do so again in death;[38] he expresses the poignant awareness that his promise not to bury Patroklos until he has killed Hektor entails certain consequences. Time truly is of the essence.[39]

It is Thetis who will defend Patroklos in death by "warding off" (ἀλαλκεῖν, XIX 30) the flies from his corpse, a claim that colors the goddess as a warrior in

---

[38] See Achilles' words at *Iliad* XVIII 98–100: "I must die soon, then, since I was not to stand by my companion when he was killed. And now, far from the land of his fathers, he has perished, and lacked my fighting strength to defend him."

[39] Odysseus advises that mourning should be kept within the practical bound of a single day: "But we must bury that man, whoever is dead, with a pitiless heart, weeping for a single day" (ἀλλὰ χρὴ τὸν μὲν καταθάπτειν ὅς κε θάνῃσιν | νηλέα θυμὸν ἔχοντας, ἐπ' ἤματι δακρύσαντας, *Iliad* XIX 228–229). He does not mention physical decay of the corpse as the impetus behind the speedy funeral, however, but the necessity for the men to return to their responsibilities of fighting.

battle, defending her people against the foemen.[40] Importantly, the verb ἀλέξω is used repeatedly to indicate not only the defense of one's companions or city from the enemy, but quite specifically, the defense of the hero's body from mutilation by dogs or flies.[41] Thetis says she will defend Patroklos' body by anointing it with *ambrosia* and red *nektar* in order to preserve his flesh "so that it may be *empedos*." There are two key terms here we need to examine in order to grasp the temporal implications of the episode: *empedos* and *nektar*.

The adjective *empedos* appears to be formed from the compound ἐν "on, in" plus πέδον "ground"; its most basic sense is "in place," with extended meanings of "unchanged, undisturbed, still present," as well as the metaphorical "firm, reliable, continuous."[42] In his comprehensive study of the uses of the adjective in early Greek epic, M. A. Harder emphasizes that *empedos* does not indicate a permanent quality, but rather the absence of change—for the time being—of place, activity, intention, or quality.[43] I append a few important examples for our study:

[A] τὸ καὶ <u>οὔ τι πολύν χρόνον ἔμπεδον</u> ἦεν (*Iliad* XII 9)

[sc. The Achaean wall] was <u>not</u> to be <u>in place for a very long time at all</u>

---

[40] The verb ἀλαλκεῖν (the reduplicated thematic aorist of the *alek- verbal root appearing as ἀλέξω in the present tense: see Chantraine 1968–1980:57–58 and Irigoin *LfgrE* I (1955) [rpt. 1979]:472–474, s.v. ἀλέξω) is used in a variety of battle contexts in the *Iliad*, usually indicating a god or hero "warding off" destruction from companions, city, ships, and the like: e.g. I 590, III 9, V 779, IX 605, XVII 356, XXII 196 (defend companions); XXI 138, 150, 539, 548 (defend the city); IX 347, 670 (defend the ships); XIII 475 (defend oneself , in a simile); XVIII 365, XV 565 = XVI 562, XX 369 (to be or become good at "defending"); IX 251, XX 315 = XXI 374 (defend against the evil day); IV 8 = V 908 (an epithet of Athena as "defender," Ἀλαλκομενηῒς Ἀθήνη).

[41] At *Iliad* XVII 153 Glaukos blames Hektor for failing to protect Sarpedon's body and "to ward off" the dogs who will devour it (νῦν δ' οὔ οἱ <u>ἀλαλκέμεναι</u> κύνας ἔτλης); at XIX 30 Thetis "wards off" flies from Patroklos' corpse (τῷ μὲν ἐγὼ πειρήσω <u>ἀλαλκεῖν</u> ἄγρια φῦλα μυίας); at XXII 348 Achilles tells Hektor that now there is no one who can "ward off" the dogs from his head (ὡς οὐκ ἔσθ' ὃς σῆς γε κύνας κεφαλῆς <u>ἀπαλάλκοι</u>); at XXIII 185 Aphrodite "wards off" dogs from devouring Hektor's corpse (ἀλλὰ κύνας μὲν <u>ἄλακε</u>).

[42] See the excellent treatments by Ebeling 1963:400–401 and Harder in *LfgrE* II (1991) 565–566, s.v. ἔμπεδος.

[43] Harder *LfgrE* II (1991) 565–566: "from the lit[eral] meaning 'standing firmly on (in?) the ground' (πέδον) developed on the one hand to *unchanged, undisturbed*, (still) *present* (1a), on the other to (metaph[orical]) *firm, reliable* (1b); sometimes w[ith] a temp[oral] connot[ation]: *continuous* (1c) ... The adv[erb appears] 2x (*Il.* 17.434, *Od.* 17.464) applied in the lit[eral] sense of standing (upright and immovably) *in* the ground." Further discussion can be found at Vernant 1991:39–41; however, Vernant does not discuss the temporal element built into the concept of *empedos*. The most recent study of *empedos* is Purves 2006a which contrasts the status of *standing in place* against that of *falling* which essentially mark the two possible states for mankind in life and in death: "Aging, then, is just another way of being unstrung, of having one's limbs loosened and thereby losing the grounded, upright position of being *empedos*" (191).

[B] ἤ μοι ἔτ᾽ ἔμπεδόν ἐστι ... λέχος (*Odyssey* xxiii 203)

or is my bed <u>still in place</u>?

[C] ἔτι μοι μένος ἔμπεδόν ἐστιν (*Iliad* V 254)

my might is <u>still in place</u>

[D] εἴθ᾽ ὣς ἡβώοιμι, βίη δέ μοι ἔμπεδος εἴη (*Iliad* VII 157)

<u>if only I were as I was in my youth</u> and my strength were <u>in place</u> ...

Example [A] is the Iliadic narrator's comment on the Achaean defensive wall erected in Book VII of the *Iliad*. Although it is "in place" *for the moment*, it will not long remain so; its present quality of stability, indicated by the adjective *empedos*, is not permanent. Likewise, in example [B] we find Odysseus questioning Penelope whether the wedding bed he constructed out of a live tree, around which he built his entire household, is *still* "in place" and attached to the roots of the tree, or has been undercut and moved elsewhere.[44] Odysseus' very question indicates the temporal status of his bed's proper placement: its displacement is always possible, such that its status as *empedos* is temporally conditioned. In example [C] Diomedes rejects Sthenelus' advice to give way before Pandarus and Aeneas, for, he claims, his might is *still* "in place." A warrior's *menos* is not a permanent and stable quality, as indicated by the adverbial ἔτι "still": Diomedes can stand against Aeneas and Pandarus now, but at another time, when his resources have dwindled, he will have to retire. And finally, in example [D] Nestor expresses the impossible wish that he still had his youthful vigor—for then his strength would be "*in place*." Unlike Diomedes, Nestor is no longer in possession of a *menos* that is *empedos*: old age has sapped his strength. Examples [C] and [D] both concern the warrior's *menos* "might" as a property of the "organic continuity" of the young warrior which must continually be replenished through rest and the consumption of food.[45]

In each of these examples we see *empedos* used to describe a transitory state of being. Let us return to our passage. Thetis promises that she will defend Patroklos' corpse from decay with *nektar* which will keep his flesh *empedos*:

ἤν περ γὰρ κεῖταί γε <u>τελεσφόρον εἰς ἐνιαυτόν</u>,
<u>αἰεὶ τῷ γ᾽ ἔσται χρὼς ἔμπεδος</u>, ἤ καὶ ἀρείων.

---

[44] On the importance of the bed as an architectural symbol of the couple's relationship, see Bergren 1995, and compare the *empeda sēmata* of *Odyssey* xxiii 206. On the *empedon sēma* (gravestone) of the fallen warrior, see Redfield 1975:180, Purves 2006a:191–192, and chapter 4 below.

[45] Redfield 1975:172–173 and Vernant 1991:39–41; see further the discussion and bibliography in the Introduction above on the experience of time felt in moments of biological "lack" of food, sleep, sex, etc.

> For even if he lies <u>until a year has brought its</u>
> <u>completion,</u>
> his flesh will <u>continually</u> be *empedos*, or even better.

Iliad XIX 32–33

Thetis promises that Patroklos' flesh will be held in a state of uprightness: it will remain stable, more alive than dead, more like a young man full of *menos* "might" than an old man whose prime has passed. And yet, the very temporal terms that Thetis introduces into her promise, that Patroklos' flesh will "always/ continually" (αἰεί, XIX 33) remain "in place" even as long as a year (τελεσφόρον εἰς ἐνιαυτόν, XIX 32), indicate that the period of being and remaining *empedos* is always bounded by temporal limits for mortals and their bodies. As Alex Purves has noted, "To be *empedos* is thus briefly to achieve an ideal of the human body that cannot be upheld in practice—to be secure on the feet and lasting throughout time" (Purves 2006a:191). In other words, the adverb *aiei* "always" in Thetis' promise must not be understood as an offer to keep Patroklos *empedos* for an unbounded "forever," but rather as referring to a *continuous* state within the bounds of a specified period of time. That is to say, Thetis' promise is not one of permanence, but only of long duration—the body will rot eventually; she merely buys Achilles some time to complete his promise of slaying Hektor before he buries his companion.

This reading of the passage is further supported by an examination of the etymology and semantics of *nektar*. *Nektar* is most often paired with *ambrosia* in early Greek poetry (cf. ἀμβροσίην καὶ νέκταρ, *Iliad* XIX 38; νέκταρ τε καὶ ἀμβροσίην, *Iliad* XIX 347), and like *ambrosia*, it is closely associated with the immortal gods; it is their food or drink, or their perfumed ointment or oil. In every instance, it plays a constructive role in the gods' identity as gods. *Nektar* acts, in Greek thought, as one of the devices by which the gods are marked as separate and different than mortals (Clay 1982). The etymology of the word is difficult and remains in contentious debate. The initial element *νεκ- provides little difficulty: it is the Indo-European radical theme II*$ə_2$nek- "death" (according to Benveniste's terminology: Benveniste 1935:18), as found in Greek νεκ-ρός, νέκ-υς, νέκ-ες (= νεκροί "the dead," according to Hesychius); Latin *nex*, *ēnectus*, *noxa*, and *noceō* (Householder Jr. and Nagy 1972:52). The difficulty arises with the second element *–ταρ. Benveniste explained it in terms of a nominal suffix formation (Benveniste 1935:18); however, the semantic pairing of νέκταρ with ἀμβροσίη (i.e. "death" with "immortal/immortalizing substance") creates a problem with this analysis. In recent work on the subject Calvert Watkins argues for an analysis of *$nek̑$-trh_2-, in which the Indo-European verbal root *trh_2- "to overcome (temporarily)" is reflected back to the nominal root *$nek̑$- (Watkins

1995:391–393, West 2007:158).[46] In other words, *nektar* is "[that which] overcomes death" at least temporarily.[47] I wish to emphasize the "temporary" quality noted by Watkins and others. The significance of this interpretation for our reading is that the "victory" over the further "death" of Patroklos—the legions of flies, maggots, and rot—is only temporary. The status of the body is held in static reserve.[48]

When Thetis promises Achilles that she will defend Patroklos' body from the corruption of flies, maggots, and decay through *ambrosia* and *nektar*, her promise is not that she will "immortalize" the corpse and entirely remove it from the destructive forces of time forever. Rather, her protection is a temporary and temporally conditioned aid granted to Achilles to give him time to complete his own heroic endeavor of killing Hektor before he has to worry about Patroklos' funeral.

τῷ μὲν ἐγὼ πειρήσω ἀλαλκεῖν ἄγρια φῦλα
μυίας, αἵ ῥά τε φῶτας ἀρηϊφάτους κατέδουσιν.
ἤν περ γὰρ κεῖταί γε τελεσφόρον εἰς ἐνιαυτόν,
αἰεὶ τῷ γ᾽ ἔσται χρὼς ἔμπεδος, ἢ καὶ ἀρείων.
[…]
ὣς ἄρα φωνήσασα μένος πολυθαρσὲς ἐνῆκε·
Πατρόκλῳ δ᾽ αὖτ᾽ ἀμβροσίην καὶ νέκταρ ἐρυθρόν
στάξε κατὰ ῥινῶν, ἵνα οἱ χρὼς ἔμπεδος εἴη.

[46] The derivation *nek̑-trh₂- was first proposed by Thieme 1952:5–15, and in his articles on "Nektar" and "Ambrosia" (reprinted in Schmitt 1968:102–112, 113–132). Thieme's proposal has been championed by Schmitt 1961, who found corroborative evidence for Thieme's theory in Vedic Sanskrit (cf. Schmitt 1967:190 §384), and acknowledged by Householder Jr. and Nagy 1972:52–53. The noun *nektar* has also been analyzed as *ne-* "not" + *ktr-* "death," suggested as early as Wheeler 1889:130; compare Güntert 1919:158–163 and Kretschmer 1947. However, attempts have been made to derive *nektar* from Semitic (see Haupt 1922 and Levin 1971, tentatively followed by Morris 1997:618 with n67) or even Egyptian roots (Griffith 1994, Bernal 2006:287). For a review of the controversy, see Markwald's excellent entry in *LfgrE* III (2004) 312–314, s.v. νέκταρ. For citations of scholarship prior to 1885, see Ebeling 1963:I.1135–1136, s.v. νέκταρ.

[47] Consider the cautious assessment of Clay 1982, who notes that "Attempts to draw any significant distinctions between the functions of nectar and ambrosia have failed, nor have etymological speculations … produced scholarly consensus," but goes on to emphasize "what matters to us here and deserves emphasis is that, in Homer, nectar and ambrosia do not by themselves make the gods immortal, but they prevent them from aging and exempt them from the natural cycle of death and decay" (114–115).

[48] Compare the analysis of *nektar* and *ambrosia* by Sissa and Detienne 2000:77–80; their study draws similar conclusions, though without the linguistic and etymological arguments I provide above: "Ambrosia and nectar could thus be said to be a treatment for immortality, substances that give a body the ability to resist time and defy death. On immortal bodies, a regular application of them sustains beauty, brilliance, and energy" (80). The very fact that *nektar* and *ambrosia* must be continually reapplied indicates their temporary status.

I will attempt to ward off from him the swarming race
of flies, which always devour men slain in war.
For even if he lies until a year has brought its completion,
his flesh will always be *empedos*, or even better."
[...]
And so after she spoke to him thus, she sent very courageous might into
       him,
and in turn for Patroklos *ambrosia* and red *nektar*
she instilled through his nose, so that his flesh might be *empedos*.

Iliad XIX 30–33, 37–39

Thetis makes Patroklos' flesh *empedos*—temporarily "in place"—by applying *ambrosia* and *nektar*, two substances that temporarily "immortalize" his body by removing it from the passage of time. Thetis preserves Patroklos continuously (αἰεί, XIX 33), but not eternally: the reference to the passing of a year in a conditional temporal expression ("even if it takes a full year": cf. XIX 32) indicates a limit to Thetis' protection. Sooner or later the body will return to mortal time, and only funeral rites can prevent the body's disintegration by decay and predation.

I wish to make one final note about the scene where Thetis delivers Achilles' new armor to her son, who is caught up in his concern over the durability of Patroklos' mortal remains. The armor is the work of Hephaistos,[49] and like all divine craft, it is marked as possessing special qualities: beauty,[50] elaborate detail,[51] and extreme durability.[52] The scene presents us with a striking contrast: on the one hand lies the immortal armor of Hephaistos, and on the other, the all-too-mortal corpse of Patroklos, which cannot be buried until Hektor, his

---

[49] The divine work is emphasized in two passages: ἣ δ' ἐς νῆας ἵκανε θεοῦ πάρα δῶρα φέρουσα, "And she arrived beside the ships bearing the gifts of the god" (*Iliad* XIX 3); τύνη δ' Ἡφαίστοιο πάρα κλυτὰ τεύχε' δέξο, | καλὰ μάλ', οἷ' οὔ πώ τις ἀνὴρ ὤμοισι φόρησεν, "But now accept the glorious armor from Hephaistos, exceedingly beautiful and of a sort that no mortal yet has ever worn on his shoulders" (XIX 10–11).

[50] The armor is described as καλά at *Iliad* XVIII 466, XIX 11. Note that it is described as shimmering in the light (XVIII 618: τεύχεα μαρμαίροντα, XIX 18: θεοῦ ἀγλαὰ δῶρα), a quality that emphasizes its metallic construction. Also, note that its beauty instills *thauma* "wonder" in those who see it: τεύχεα καλά ... οἷά τις αὖτε | ἀνθρώπων πολέων θαυμάσσεται, ὅς κεν ἴδηται, "beautiful armor ... the sort that now one, now another of many men will wonder at, whoever catches sight of it" (XVIII 466–467).

[51] The armor is described as δαίδαλα at *Iliad* XIX 13 and 19. On the adjective *daidalos* and its relation with divine craftsmanship, see Morris 1992.

[52] Compare the ἄμβροτα τεύχεα "immortal armor" (*Iliad* XVII 194, 202) describing Achilles' first set of armor, a wedding-gift to Achilles' father Peleus, and, significantly, also made by Hephaistos (cf. XVIII 83–85). Other gifts of the gods, such as Achilles' horses (XVI 381 = XVI 867) and Penelope's cosmetics (*Odyssey* xviii 191) are called *ambrota* as well.

killer, has paid the blood price for his death. The difference between flesh and metal, between mortal and immortal material, stands out clearly—one will last, the other will not. Thetis' intervention is meant to provide a temporary protection for Patroklos' body; the *nektar* and *ambrosia* will keep away decay for an unspecified amount of time, but one with definite limits. It is most instructive to learn, then, that the new armor Hephaistos makes for Achilles, presumably as "immortal" as the earlier set of arms stripped from Patroklos' body and now worn by Hektor,[53] will not prevent Achilles from dying altogether, but only keep him safe for a while. Hephaistos says to Thetis upon her request for the armor:

αἲ γάρ μιν θανάτοιο δυσηχέος ὧδε δυναίμην
νόσφιν ἀποκρύψαι, ὅτε μιν μόρος αἰνὸς ἱκάνοι,
ὥς οἱ τεύχεα καλὰ παρέσσεται, οἷά τις αὖτε
ἀνθρώπων πολέων θαυμάσσεται, ὅς κεν ἴδηται.

If only I were thus able to hide him far away
from terrible sounding death, whenever awful fate catches up with him,
as surely as beautiful armor will be provided for him, the sort that now
     one,
now another out of many men will wonder at, whoever catches sight of it.

Iliad XVIII 464–467

Hephaistos expresses the impossible wish that he could save Achilles, hide him away from his fate; but he cannot.[54] The best he can do is provide beautiful, glorious, god-made armor.[55] Can we not say that Achilles' ἄμβροτα τεύχεα

---

[53] See the ἄμβροτα τεύχεα "immortal armor" (*Iliad* XVII 194, 202), cited in the preceding note. The text notes a certain tension in describing a mortal wearing immortal armor; Zeus seems to feel disturbed that Hektor donned Achilles' immortal armor: cf. XVII 205–206, and Zeus' pronouncement that the action was οὐ κατὰ κόσμον "inappropriate." Edwards 1991:81 suggests that "Probably only sons of divinities like Achilles and Memnon, and perhaps marriage-connexions like Peleus ... may properly wear armor made by Hephaistos."

[54] See Leaf 1900–1902:II.301 for an explanation of the syntactical construction: "This is the not uncommon formula where the certainty of one event is affirmed by contrasting it with the impossibility of another." Other examples in the *Iliad* include IV 178–179, 313–314, VIII 538–541, XIII 825–828, XVI 722, and XXII 346–348. See also Sheppard's brief comments (1922:1), Combellack 1981, and the excellent discussion at Edwards 1991:199.

[55] Rinon 2008:136–137 draws a connection between Hephaistos' own experience of pain and human temporality on the one hand and his skilled craftwork on the other as a "palliative" against the tragedy of mortal death itself: "And it is here that Hephaestus, who acknowledges Thetis' agonizing situation by referring to the unavoidable death of her son, binds once again deep pain and helplessness with the palliative power of his art: he explicitly juxtaposes his inability to protect her son from woeful death and his ability to create beautiful armor ... The armor might be limited in its power to protect its bearer, but it is powerful enough to strongly affect its beholder ..." (137).

functions like the *nektar* and *ambrosia*, acting to preserve the hero, to keep him *empedos* "in place" for a short time only, but then no more?

3. Hektor: The Temporality of Delay

It would be easy to think that the death of Hektor marks the climax of the action of the *Iliad*. After all, Achilles promised that he would not bury his companion Patroklos until he avenged his death. Moreover, the death scene itself is literally spectacular—Achilles cuts down his opponent as the helpless Trojans look on from the battlements of the city wall (Griffin 1978, 1980:179–204). Achilles drags the body back to the Achaean camp, and afterwards conducts funeral rites and celebratory games for his dead companion. However, the very fact of Patroklos' burial reveals a sharp contrast between the treatment of the two corpses: Patroklos is given proper rites, whereas Hektor is left to rot and be devoured by birds and dogs (Macleod 1982:18, Richardson 1993:272). The contrast is invested with emotional tension by the very lavish nature of Patroklos' burial and games. Meanwhile, Hektor's abused and unburied body becomes an image of duration itself; Achilles will not submit to its burial, but through divine agency it will neither rot nor be devoured. The gods themselves feel the force of time weighing down on the impossible situation of what to do about the body. The status of Hektor's body is held in reserve until the time when Achilles finally submits to let go of his anger and to release the body to Priam. The body, preserved by the gods, is allowed to be buried and to re-enter the scale of human temporality once again.

In short, the *Iliad* contains another narrative climax, a more subtle one, in which human temporality, left in disarray by the multiple supernatural violations of the mortal cycle of death and decay, must be put on track once again. The issue of human temporality raised in the final books of the *Iliad* focuses on the status of Hektor's body; the two subjects, mortal time and the human body, are inseparably bound in their resolutions.[56] The restoration of mortal time constitutes the emotional climax of the *Iliad*.

Achilles leaves Hektor to rot and be eaten by birds and dogs—in a heated moment Achilles wishes he could eat Hektor's flesh himself (XXII 345–354).[57]

---

[56] On the connection between time and the human body, understood as a "body-subject-in-the-world," see Wyllie 2005b.

[57] The expression of a desire to eat an enemy's flesh marks the extremity of passion driven to savagery: compare Hecuba's desire to eat Achilles' liver in revenge for Hektor's murder (*Iliad* XXIV 212–214), and Zeus' comment to Hera that perhaps her anger towards the Trojans would be satiated if she ate them raw (IV 34–36). See Griffin 1980:19–21 who compares the representation of cannibals in the *Odyssey*—the Lastrygonians at x 114, and the Cyclops at ix 289—and the epic cycle, including Tydeus who gnaws on the skull of his enemy Melanippus (*Thebaid* fr. 5 Davies

Andromache imagines the pitiful treatment of Hektor's body as she watches Achilles drag it away from the city:

νῦν δὲ σὲ μὲν παρὰ νηυσὶ κορωνίσι νόσφι τοκήων
αἰόλαι <u>εὐλαὶ ἔδονται</u>, ἐπεί κε <u>κύνες</u> κορέσωνται,
γυμνόν.

But now beside the curving ships, far away from your parents,
wriggling <u>maggots will eat</u> you, whenever the <u>dogs</u> have had their fill,
[as you lie] naked.

Iliad XXII 508–510

The image of Hektor being eaten by dogs, birds, and worms weighs heavily on the minds of the Trojans (cf. XXIV 210–211). They express the same fear of the forces of decay that Achilles feels regarding Patroklos' remains, as indicated by Andromache's mention of αἰόλαι εὐλαί, a phrase whose play between vowels and liquid consonants matches the very "wriggling" these "maggots" will do in their host's flesh (Richardson 1993:162). But worse than the fear of decay is that of dogs who will devour Hektor's body, as they eat the nameless, unburied dead on the battlefield.[58] The possibility is explicitly noted by Achilles, as he speaks to the shade of Patroklos now in Hades, once again emphasizing the difference between proper and improper treatment of the hero's body:

χαῖρέ μοι, ὦ Πάτροκλε, καὶ εἰν Ἀΐδαο δόμοισιν·
πάντα γὰρ ἤδη τοι τετελεσμένα, ὥς περ ὑπέστην,

= Scholia Gen. at *Iliad* V 126, Nicole). See further Mark Buchan's thoughtful analysis of the cannibalistic desire of Polyphemus and Achilles (Buchan 2001:11–34).

[58] For Hektor's body left for the dogs and birds to eat, see *Iliad* XXIII 182–187, cited below. Being eaten by dogs and birds is the sad fate common to warriors in general, as stated programmatically in the *Iliad*'s proem (I 4–5): cf. II 393; XI 818; XVII 241, 558; XVIII 271; XXII 89, 509. It is common to taunt one's enemy with the prospect of death without burial: cf. IV 2237; VIII 379–380; XI 395, 453–454; XIII 831–832; XVI 836; XXII 335–356, 354. Perhaps most horribly, at XI 394–395 Diomedes boasts that if he strikes a man with his spear, "that man <u>putrefies</u> as he stains the earth red with his blood, and there are <u>more birds around him than women</u>" (ὃ δέ θ' αἵματι γαῖαν ἐρεύθων | <u>πύθεται</u>, οἰωνοὶ δὲ περὶ πλέες ἠὲ γυναῖκες). Vermeule 1979 draws our attention to the "ceremonial" aspect of this boast which "mingles the sex life of the warrior with the role of the women of his household, in tending, cleaning, and loving his body in the ceremonies of death" (105), for instead of these women who will beautify the hero's body for proper burial, there will be only birds to devour his carcass, as at *Iliad* XI 162 where fallen warriors become "dearer to vultures than to their wives" (γύπεσσιν πολὺ φίλτεροι ἢ ἀλόχοισιν). See Bassett 1933 for a defense of Achilles' violent treatment of Hektor's corpse: "It was entirely in accord with the Homeric code of honor to outrage the body of a foeman ... in order to avenge the death of a dear friend or kinsman" (54). Segal 1971 emphasizes the theme of the "excess" of Achilles' behavior not noted by Bassett. In general, see the good discussion at Macleod 1982.

δώδεκα μὲν Τρώων μεγαθύμων υἱέας ἐσθλοὺς
τοὺς ἅμα σοὶ πάντας πῦρ ἐσθίει· Ἕκτορα δ᾽ οὔ τι
δώσω Πριαμίδην πυρὶ δαπτέμεν, ἀλλὰ κύνεσσιν.
Ὣς φάτ᾽ ἀπειλήσας· τὸν δ᾽ οὐ κύνες ἀμφεπένοντο,
ἀλλὰ κύνας μὲν ἄλαλκε Διὸς θυγάτηρ Ἀφροδίτη
ἤματα καὶ νύκτας, ῥοδόεντι δὲ χρῖεν ἐλαίῳ
ἀμβροσίῳ, ἵνα μή μιν ἀποδρύφοι ἑλκυστάζων.
τῷ δ᾽ ἐπὶ κυάνεον νέφος ἤγαγε Φοῖβος Ἀπόλλων
οὐρανόθεν πεδίονδε, κάλυψε δὲ χῶρον ἅπαντα
ὅσσον ἐπεῖχε νέκυς, μὴ πρὶν μένος ἠελίοιο
σκήλει᾽ ἀμφὶ περὶ χρόα ἴνεσιν ἠδὲ μέλεσσιν.

"Hail, my friend Patroklos, even in the house of Hades—
for everything has been accomplished for you, just as I promised
            before:
twelve noble sons of the great-hearted Trojans
all of whom the fire will devour along with you. But Hektor,
son of Priam, I will not at all give to the fire to eat, but to the dogs."
Thus he spoke, threatening. But the dogs did not gather about him,
but rather Aphrodite, Zeus' daughter, warded off the dogs
throughout days and nights, and she anointed him with a rosy,
ambrosial oil, so [Achilles] might not tear his flesh by continually
            dragging it.
And upon him Phoibos Apollo led a dark cloud
from heaven to the ground, and covered the entire space,
however much the corpse was taking up, lest too soon the might of
            the sun
might wither his flesh all around on his sinews and limbs.

Iliad XXIII 179–191

At the very moment when Achilles offers Patroklos funeral rites, he excludes
Hektor from the possibility of such rites.[59] Instead of giving the body "to the fire
to eat," Achilles gives him "to the dogs [to eat]." And yet, the mutilation of the
corpse feared by Andromache and desired by Achilles does not occur.

---

[59] Achilles' speech here is an echo of an earlier speech at *Iliad* XXIII 19–23. Note especially Achilles'
      claim that he has dragged Hektor to the Achaean camp to feed to the dogs: πάντα γὰρ ἤδη τοι
      τελέω τὰ πάροιθεν ὑπέστην, | Ἕκτορα δεῦρ᾽ ἐρύσας δώσειν κυσὶν ὠμὰ δάσασθαι, "for I am now
      accomplishing everything I promised before: after having dragged Hektor here to give him to
      dogs to tear up" (XXIII 20–21). Both speeches recall his earlier promises (XVIII 333–337 and XXII
      354 with XXI 27–32).

The pattern of care extended to Hektor's body is already familiar from our study of Sarpedon's and Patroklos' remarkable bodies.[60] Like those two warriors before him, Hektor is anointed with ambrosial oil that serves to prevent bodily deterioration for an indeterminate period of time. In this passage the deterioration is concretized in the figure of the dogs that Aphrodite "wards off," just as Thetis promised to "ward off" the flies from Patroklos' corpse (XIX 30–31). The dogs function as a strong transition between Achilles' threatening speech at Patroklos' burial and the divine protection of Hektor—note the triple repetition of "dogs" used in three successive verses: κύνεσσιν, κύνες, κύνας (XXIII 183–185). Meanwhile, Apollo repeats his role as a caretaker of bodies—he protects the body from the harsh rays of the sun by enshrouding (κάλυψε, XXIII 189) its entire volume in a dark cloud (κυάνεον νέφος, XXIII 188). The cloud provides shade and moisture, a defense against premature drying.[61] I emphasize "premature" here, for the text provides clear evidence that once again, these procedures of preservation are merely temporary: the πρίν of XXIII 190 which I translate here as "too soon" indicates that the body will eventually decay. Apollo's task is to ensure it does not happen before the body has been returned to the Trojans to bury it properly.[62]

There is a third destructive force in the preceding passage, though it is merely alluded to. Aphrodite wards off dogs and then anoints the body with ambrosial oil "so that [Achilles] might not tear his flesh by <u>continually dragging</u> it" (ἵνα μή μιν ἀποδρύφοι ἑλκυστάζων, XXIII 187). The shift to the third-person singular in the Greek after the text's insistence on the distinctly plural dogs is jarring. The reference looks forward to Book XXIV when we learn that Achilles regularly drags Hektor's corpse around Patroklos' tomb (XXIV 14–18, cited below);[63] the juxtaposition creates a virtual simile, suggesting that Achilles

---

[60] See Lynn-George's rich study of "structures of care" in the *Iliad*, particularly in the form of the burial rites given to the dead: "Humans attempt to cope with sorrow and cares *through care*, care of the κηδεμόνες, of the living for the dead, care exercised in Homer without *fear* of the dead" (1996:21).

[61] On the verb σκέλλω "to dry up" and its connection with the semantic field of "decay" in Homer, see the Appendix below.

[62] On the "elliptical" use of πρίν which looks forward to a as-yet-unspecified event, compare *Iliad* XXIV 800 (Trojan guards posted during Hektor's funeral μὴ πρὶν ἐφορμηθεῖεν ... Ἀχαιοί) and Macleod 1982:17 with n1. Macleod notes "the 'before' of line 190 must imply 'before Hektor was buried' and thus points forward to Book 24" (17). See further Richardson 1993:190.

[63] Leaf 1900–1902:II.484–485 (comment at *Iliad* XXIII 184–191) notes that Fäsi and Düntzer rejected XXIII 184–191 precisely because they anticipate events in Book XXIV; Leaf generally rejects their claim, though he finds verse 187 with its reference to Achilles dragging the corpse as "indefensible ... [T]he lines, with their unexplained anticipations [of Book XXIV], rather interrupt than help the narrative and would be better away." I disagree that the lines do not belong here; rather, it is the very unexpectedness of their appearance that makes them effective. See

is himself like one of the dogs he wishes would rend Hektor's flesh. We find the description of Achilles dragging Hektor's corpse around the tomb of Patroklos at the very opening of Book XXIV, a passage worth reading in full for its many interesting observations regarding human and divine temporality:

αὐτὰρ Ἀχιλλεύς
κλαῖε φίλου ἑτάρου μεμνημένος, οὐδέ μιν ὕπνος
ᾕρει πανδαμάτωρ, ἀλλ' ἐστρέφετ' ἔνθα καὶ ἔνθα,
Πατρόκλου ποθέων ἀνδροτῆτά τε καὶ μένος ἠΰ,
ἠδ' ὁπόσα τολύπευσε σὺν αὐτῷ καὶ πάθεν ἄλγεα,
ἀνδρῶν τε πτολέμους ἀλεγεινά τε κύματα πείρων·
τῶν μιμνησκόμενος θαλερὸν κατὰ δάκρυον εἶβεν,
ἄλλοτ' ἐπὶ πλευρὰς κατακείμενος, ἄλλοτε δ' αὖτε
ὕπτιος, ἄλλοτε δὲ πρηνής· τοτὲ δ' ὀρθὸς ἀναστὰς
δινεύεσκ' ἀλύων παρὰ θῖν' ἁλός. οὐδέ μιν Ἠώς
φαινομένη λήθεσκεν ὑπεὶρ ἅλα τ' ἠϊόνας τε.
ἀλλ' ὅ γ' ἐπεὶ ζεύξειεν ὑφ' ἅρμασιν ὠκέας ἵππους,
Ἕκτορα δ' <u>ἕλκεσθαι</u> δησάσκετο δίφρου ὄπισθεν·
τρὶς δ' ἐρύσας περὶ σῆμα Μενοιτιάδαο θανόντος
αὖτις ἐνὶ κλισίῃ παυέσκετο, τὸν δέ τ' ἔασκεν
ἐν κόνι ἐκτανύσας προπρηνέα. τοῖο δ' Ἀπόλλων
πᾶσαν ἀεικείην ἄπεχε χροΐ, φῶτ' ἐλεαίρων
καὶ τεθνηότα περ, περὶ δ' αἰγίδι πάντα <u>κάλυπτεν</u>
χρυσείῃ, ἵνα μή μιν ἀποδρύφοι <u>ἑλκυστάζων</u>.

But Achilles
wept as he remembered his dear companion, nor did Sleep
seize him, who subdues all, but he tossed and turned here and there,
longing for Patroklos and his manhood and goodly might
and all the things which he accomplished with him and the pains he
        suffered,
getting through both the wars of men and difficult waters.[64]
Continually remembering these things, he shed down swelling tears,
at one time lying down upon his side, and at another again
on his back, and still another face-down. Then standing straight up

---

Macleod 1982:17–19 for an argument on the important anticipations of Book XXIV in Book XXIII which deal with "the contrast between the burial [of Patroklos] accomplished and the burial [of Hektor] withheld ..." (18).

[64] On the zeugma between πτολέμους and κύματα, both objects of πείρων, see Macleod 1982:86 and Richardson 1993:274–275.

he continually circled about in distraction beside the sea's shore. Nor did
      dawn
ever escape his notice as she appeared over the sea and the sea-banks.
But he, whenever he would yoke his swift horses beneath the chariot,
he would bind Hektor behind the carriage <u>to drag</u> him,
and after pulling him three times around the tomb of Menoitios' dead son,
he would continually pause once again in his shelter, but would continu-
      ally leave
him stretched out, face-down in the dust. But Apollo
took pity on the mortal and held away everything unseemly from his flesh,
even though he was only a dead man. And he <u>covered</u> him all around
with the golden aegis, so that [Achilles] might not tear his flesh <u>by</u>
      <u>continually dragging</u> it.

Iliad XXIV 3–21

Achilles abuses Hektor's corpse out of longing (ποθέων, XXIV 6) for Patroklos. As we noted in the Introduction above while discussing the temporality of "no longer" that attends the experience of extreme loss, here signaled by Achilles' *pothos* for Patroklos, phenomenological psychology describes how the melancholic patient experiences time slowing down as the horizons of the future itself seem to close off: "The loss of goal-oriented capacities of the body, of drive, appetite and desire are equivalent to a slowing-down and finally standstill of lived time. Thus the past, the guilt, the losses and failures gain dominance over the future and its possibilities" (Fuchs 2005a:119). Time indeed seems to slow for Achilles in the repetitive nature of his dragging Hektor's body: the use of imperfect verbs (ἤρει, XXIV 5; ἐστρέφετο, XXIV 5; εἶβεν, XXIV 9), iterative verbs and participles (μιμνησκόμενος, XXIV 9; δινεύεσκε, XXIV 12; λήθεσκεν, XXIV 13; δησάσκετο, XXIV 15; παυέσκετο, XXIV 17; ἔασκεν, XXIV 17), generalizing optatives (ζεύξειεν, XXIV 14), and spatial-temporal adverbs (ἔνθα καὶ ἔνθα, XXIV 5; ἄλλοτε, XXIV 20–22 [three times] ; αὖτε, XXIV 10; αὖτις, XXIV 17) all indicate that the forward progress of time has collapsed for Achilles. Colin Macleod has well described the effect created by the multiple frequentative verbs in the passage: "the description of one night merges into a series of nights" (Macleod 1982:86).[65] The single event becomes serialized, and each action takes on the

---

[65] The force of λήθεσκεν in verse XXIV 13 is particularly effective; it implies that Achilles has spent several wakeful nights on the shore and not once has he missed dawn's rising. See also Richardson 1993:275. Neither scholar notes the importance of the spatial adverbs in the passage that serve to "spatialize" the narrative and effectively freeze the forward progression of the narrative into a static tableau, in the terms of literary critic Robert Frank (1963, 1977, 1978, 1981). See further Spanos 1970, Smitten 1981, and Mitchell 1980, 1984, 1989 on "spatialization"

weight of its repeated predecessor. The effect is vertiginous; time is lost in the transition from the single night following the funeral games to the present. It is not until verse XXIV 31 that the elapsed time is measured out: "but truly when it was the twelfth dawn from that day [sc. when Hektor died]" (ἀλλ' ὅτε δή ῥ' ἐκ τοῖο δυωδεκάτη γένετ' ἠώς, XXIV 31).[66] Yet, in the midst of Achilles' serial abuse of Hektor's body in which time expands continually outward from singular instance to serial repetition, we find Apollo working against that time, seeking to diminish its ravages through the application of yet another magical substance, the golden *aegis* wrapped around Hektor's body. Note that XXIV 21 is a formulaic repetition of XXIII 187 with analogical substitution of χρυσείη for the metrically equivalent ἀμβροσίῳ in the same position (allowing spondaic substitution, i.e. - - - for - u u -).[67] That is to say, the *aegis* functions within the metrical, semantic, and mythological registers as an equivalent substitution for the *ambrosial oil* Aphrodite applies to the corpse as a means of preserving it from the rending of the flesh by dogs and Achilles.[68]

The gods themselves experience the weight and depth of the twelve days since Hektor's death. Zeus explains to Thetis when he summons her in Book XXIV,

ἐννῆμαρ δὴ νεῖκος ἐν ἀθανάτοισιν ὄρωρεν
Ἕκτορος ἀμφὶ νέκυι καὶ Ἀχιλλῆϊ πτολιπόρθῳ.

Indeed, for nine days a quarrel has arisen among the immortals
about Hektor's corpse and Achilles, sacker of cities.

Iliad XXIV 107–108

Time is out of joint; both the human and divine worlds are at an impasse. Achilles' repetition of abuse is countered by Apollo and Aphrodite applying divine preservatives. Time has become a vicious circle as Achilles seeks psychological closure through the image of the rotting body of Hektor: the decay of flesh mimics the healing of self-inflicted wounds to one's face and body in

---

in literature. For an application of Robert Frank's work to the analysis of Classical texts, see Andersen 1987.

[66] The twelve day period is to be understood as counting from Hektor's death, as confirmed by *Iliad* XXIV 413–414. The twelve days consist of a three-day period for Patroklos' funeral, followed by nine days of continual abuse of the corpse during which, we later read, the gods quarrel with one another over what should be done with Hektor's body (cf. XXIV 107–116).

[67] On formulaic analogy in Homeric hexameter, see Parry 1971:68–74, 175–180, Russo 1963, 1966, and 1997, Hoekstra 1964, Hainsworth 1968, M. Edwards 1986, 1988, and the particularly enlightening Ingalls 1970 and 1976.

[68] On the connection between *Iliad* XXIII 187 and XXIV 21, see Macleod 1982:17.

traditional Greek funeral rites;[69] time's effects on a body measure the limits of one's own mourning.[70] But since Hektor's body will not decay, Achilles is himself caught up in the non-human temporality of delay: time has slowed for him as his repetitive action can produce no resolution. Achilles is himself like the corpses of Sarpedon, Patroklos, and Hektor—he is in a kind of suspended animation between life and death, vitality and decay.[71]

It is up to Zeus to restore proper temporality to men and gods. This restoration is accomplished over and through the body of Hektor; Achilles must be persuaded to let go of his anger and return the body to Priam so that it may be burned and buried. Zeus sends Hermes, the god of crossing boundaries, to broker the exchange; the body is moved from Achilles' tent where it lingers in an unstable and timeless situation, neither decaying nor yet able to remain intact for very long, to the city of Hektor's people. Hermes, disguised as a henchman of Achilles, approaches Priam as he makes his way to ransom back the body of Hektor, and describes the as-yet-uncorrupted state of the corpse:

> ὦ γέρον, οὔ πω τόν γε κύνες φάγον οὐδ' οἰωνοί,
> ἀλλ' ἔτι κεῖνος κεῖται Ἀχιλλῆος παρὰ νηΐ
> αὔτως ἐν κλισίῃσι· δυωδεκάτη δέ οἱ ἤδη
> κειμένῳ, οὐδέ τί οἱ χρὼς σήπεται, οὐδέ μιν εὐλαὶ
> ἔσθουσ', αἵ ῥά τε φῶτας ἀρηϊφάτους κατέδουσιν.
> ἦ μέν μιν περὶ σῆμα ἑοῦ ἑτάροιο φίλοιο
> ἕλκει ἀκηδέστως, ἠὼς ὅτε δῖα φανήῃ,
> οὐδέ μιν αἰσχύνει· θηοῖό κεν αὐτὸς ἐπελθών,
> οἷον ἐερσήεις κεῖται, περὶ δ' αἷμα νένιπται,
> οὐδέ ποθι μιαρός· σὺν δ' ἕλκεα πάντα μέμυκεν,
> ὅσσ' ἐτύπη· πολέες γὰρ ἐν αὐτῷ χαλκὸν ἔλασσαν.
> ὥς τοι κήδονται μάκαρες θεοὶ υἷος ἑῆος
> καὶ νέκυός περ ἐόντος, ἐπεί σφι φίλος περὶ κῆρι.

---

[69] On self-mutilation (beating one's breast, lacerating one's cheeks, tearing one's hair) in ancient Greek funerary rites, see *Iliad* X 78, 406, XIX 284–285, XXIV 711, Sappho 140a L-P, Aeschylus *Libation Bearers* 23–31, 423–428, *Persians* 1054–1065, Sophocles *Electra* 89–91, Euripides *Suppliant Women* 71, 826–827, 977–979, 1160, *Alcestis* 86–92, 98–104, *Phoenician Women* 1485–1492, *Andromache* 825–835, and Plato *Phaedo* 89b. See further Alexiou 1974:6, 8, 10, 18, 21, 28–29, 32–33, 41, 55–56, 68–69, 207n27. Alexiou notes the specifically rhythmic aspect of these mourning gestures, as "the women ... beat their breasts, tear their cheeks and pull at their loosened hair or at a black scarf, in time to the singing" (41).

[70] On the temporally bounded nature of mourning, see Wyllie 2005a:182.

[71] On extreme cases of grief producing "a corporealization, namely in the sense of coming nearer to the corpse, the dead body" in the melancholic patient, see Fuchs 2001a:183–184, 2001b:231, 235, 237, 239, 2005a:109–112, 2005b:196–197, Wyllie 2005b:213.

Old man, <u>not yet</u> have the dogs eaten him, nor the birds,
but that man <u>still</u> lies beside Achilles' ship
among the encampments as before. But it is <u>already</u> the twelfth day for
      him
lying there, <u>but neither is his flesh rotten at all, nor do maggots</u>
<u>eat him, which indeed always devour mortals slain in battle</u>.
True, around the tomb of his dear companion
he drags him without offering funeral rites, whenever brilliant dawn
      appears
<u>but he does not mutilate him</u>. You yourself can look in wonder when you
      go there
how he lies fresh with dew, and the blood all around has been washed
      from him,
nor is he defiled anywhere. All the wounds have closed up,
all the ones that were struck; for many drove bronze into him.
So, I tell you, the blessed gods <u>care</u> for your son,
even though he is but a corpse, since <u>he was dear to them at heart</u>.

Iliad XXIV 411–423

Hermes' description of Hektor's body is at once both graphic and tender, for, as Hermes explains, though he is but a corpse, the gods hold him dear to their hearts. The care they render (κήδονται, XXIV 422) is represented as a delaying of natural processes, as the stark "not yet" (οὔ πω, XXIV 411) at the beginning of the speech emphasizes.[72] These natural processes include decay (σήπεται, XXIV 414) and the onset of maggots (εὐλαί, XXIV 414), whose inevitable invasion has been forestalled by the magical closing of Hektor's wounds (σὺν δ' ἔλκεα πάντα μέμυκεν, XXIV 420),[73] virtually creating a hermetic seal against decay.[74] Achilles

---

[72] See further *Iliad* XXIII 184–191 where Aphrodite and Apollo protect Hektor's corpse by annointing it with immortal oil to keep him safe from dogs and birds of prey, and covering it with a dark cloud to ward off the sun's rays. At XXIV 18–21 Apollo guards Hektor's body with the golden aegis to protect it from lacerations while being dragged behind Achilles' chariot.

[73] Besides the "closing" of wounds, the verb μύω is used to describe the "closing" of eyes, as Priam requests a bed to be made for him after his meeting with Achilles, "A bed for me now, most quickly, O Zeus-reared one, so that even now we may take our pleasure in sweet sleep as we go to bed. For my eyes have <u>not yet closed</u> (οὐ γάρ πω μύσαν ὄσσε) beneath my lids since that time when my son lost his life beneath your hands, but I have always been grieving ... Now I have tasted food again and have let the gleaming wine go down my throat. Before, I had tasted nothing" (*Iliad* XXIV 635–642).

[74] The ancient Homeric scholia record some difficulty in believing how Hektor's wounds could have closed: παράδοξον· τὰ μὲν γὰρ τῶν ζώντων ἕλκη μετὰ θάνατον μύει, τὰ δὲ μετὰ θάνατον γινόμενα (Χ 371, 375, Ω 421) σήπεται. ἀδύνατον νεκρῶν τραύματα μύειν, "This is miraculous, for the wounds of living men close after death, but those occurring after death (cf. *Iliad* XXII 371, 375; XXIV 421) rot. It's not possible for the wounds of corpses to close up" (Scholia T at *Iliad* XXIV

himself has not mutilated (αἰσχύνει, XXIV 418) the corpse, but only drags it around Patroklos' grave in the morning. After twelve days, Hektor lies clean and dewy fresh (ἐερσήεις, XXIV 419)—the sight is indeed a wonder for Priam to behold (θηοῖό, XXIV 418).[75]

The "not yet" (οὔ πω) of Hektor's body indicates a body at the boundaries of mortal and immortal time. It has not been allowed to rot or to be buried; life has been held in check. The events of a single day, exemplified by Achilles' insomnia and ritual abuse of the corpse, have expanded to fill the entire narrative—until now. Once the exchange of Hektor's corpse is completed, life begins to flow once again, and those who refused to take part in its activities begin to participate once more. Priam, who had formerly not eaten nor slept, now eats and sleeps, and Achilles once again sleeps with Briseïs at his side.[76] The Trojans are finally able to grieve over the loss of their husband, son, friend, and protector: through mourning Hektor, the city prepares for its own forthcoming demise. Lastly, the world of action is returned to human time, where the only delays are those imposed through the agreement of men, such as Achilles' promise to hold off the Achaeans for twelve days to allow Priam time to bury Hektor (XXIV 656–672, 779–781). This twelve-day period is not the product of divine intervention, but of a pact made between human adversaries brought together, however temporarily, by the bonds of χάρις "kindness, goodwill, and, in response, a profound

---

420b, Erbse). The debate over the issue appears to go back at least as early as Aristotle (fr. 167, Rose), whom Scholia T cites in connection with the point.

[75] Hecuba also calls Hektor's body "dewy" (ἐερσήεις, *Iliad* XXIV 757) as she laments over it upon Priam's return. "Dewy" is used to describe the λωτός flower that springs up beneath Zeus and Hera during the *Dios apatē* as he, bewitched by Aphrodite's *zōnē*, takes Hera in his arms and covers the two of them with a golden cloud raining dew on the grass below (*Iliad* XIV 346–351). The dew on Hektor's body accords with the cloud cover provided by Apollo to safeguard the body from decay (XXIII 184–191), as Richardson notes (1993:315). See Boedeker 1984:73–79 on dew used in extended metaphors for blood, esp. 77–78 where she analyzes our passage (XXIV 416–420) and points to "the differences between the expected and real appearance of Hector" as articulated by Hermes' claim that the body is covered with *dew* instead of *blood*.

[76] At *Iliad* XXIV 635–642, Priam has now eaten and is drowsy, though he had neither eaten nor slept since Hektor's death. Achilles has already slept, albeit briefly during Patroklos' burial rites (XXIII 231–234), and eaten before he meets with Priam (XXIV 475–476), but now he sleeps with Briseïs at his side (XXIV 675–676). The description fulfills Thetis' earlier plea that he keep his sorrow within bounds and return to the cycle of mortal life by eating and sleeping with a woman (XXIV 128–132). On the return to human rituals of food, sleep, and sex, see Macleod 1982:142, King 1987:44, and Lynn-George 1996:14. See also Fuchs 2001a:185 and 2005a:118–120 on "resynchronization therapy" for melancholic patients who have in their extreme grief lost the ability to complete the natural process of mourning: these therapies aim "to give rhythm to everyday life," which includes an attempt to return to the human rituals shared with others (termed "intersubjective" or "social" time: Fuchs 2001a:180–184, 2005a:115, Wyllie 2005:177–180), which include eating, sleeping, and engaging in sexual activity.

gratitude,"[77] and as such is subject to vicissitude and uncertainty. Trojan guards stand watch during the burial "lest the well-greaved Achaeans attack too soon" (μὴ πρὶν ἐφορμηθεῖεν ἐϋκνήμιδες Ἀχαιοί, XXIV 800).

The time set aside for Hektor's funeral, though extended and filled with ritual care for Hektor's mortal remains, will eventually come to an end.[78] The χάρις "kindness, goodwill, and, in response, a profound gratitude" between enemies will eventually also come to an end with the resumption of hostilities between Trojans and Achaeans. At some unspecified point after Hektor's funeral, Achilles himself is to make his return to battle, where death will eventually catch up with him. The *Iliad* has virtually narrated these events, though not directly within the limits of the poem itself. The *Iliad* claims for itself the duty of preserving the κλέος ἄφθιτον "unwithered fame" of its hero, and accomplishes this feat by drawing to a close while its hero is "still perfectly" alive and "not yet" dead. Nevertheless, as we have traced through the preceding chapters, the logic of the "still perfectly" and the "not yet" always operates within a bounded temporal system. One can be "still perfectly" and "not yet" only from a future-perfect perspective which acknowledges an end. The "still perfectly" and "not yet" of both Achilles and his epic tradition can exist and thrive only insofar as they are oriented toward their own future and the possibility of their respective ends.

---

[77] See Priam's response when Achilles asks how long the Trojans will need to provide Hektor with proper funeral rites: ὧδέ κέ μοι ῥέζων, Ἀχιλεῦ, κεχαρισμένα θείης "by acting for me in this way, Achilles, you would render me obligated in *kharis*" (*Iliad* XXIV 661). Michael Lynn-George observes in his analysis of this scene, from which I cite his rendering of χάρις in the text above: "The sense of the term κεχαρισμένα, and its implications, are far stronger than are conveyed by the conventional renderings 'acceptable, welcome, pleasing' (LSJ). The word acknowledges *the force of χάρις: kindness, good will, and, in response, a profound sense of gratitude.* It is easy to overlook that the final eleven days of the epic are made possible by χάρις. In the dark and bleak setting of a doomed world, in which the future of both Troy and Achilles are limited, this is the enduring achievement: not only that it is still possible to do something, but that it should be χάρις that prevails at the end" (Lynn-George 1996:14, emphasis added).

[78] Note that Fuchs 2005a also indicates the importance of establishing a "spatial and temporal frame creating a definite and legitimate recovery period for the patient, a 'time out' so-to-speak" as part of "resynchronization therapy" for melancholic patients who have become completely "desynchronized" from their environment (119).

Chapter 3

Permanence and Non-Organic Structures
Walls in the *Iliad*

IN THE LAST CHAPTER, WE INVESTIGATED the theme of the decomposition of human remains and the special preservation of the bodies of certain figures. The corpses of Sarpedon, Patroklos, and Hektor are all in danger of suffering unseemly decay or worse; yet, the process of decomposition, though ultimately inevitable, is held in reserve until each hero can receive proper commemoration through the cultural institution of burial rites and the architectural constructions of σήματα "tombs." The process of temporarily preserving heroes' bodies, I suggested, is a figure for the role the epic tradition posits for itself of (temporarily) preserving the memory of heroes. In this chapter, I wish to turn our attention to other material objects that undergo the same process of temporary preservation—I am specifically referring to the defensive walls that surround the city of Troy and the military camp of the Achaeans. As we will see, both of these walls are constructed for the purpose of defense, and each wall in fact functions as a substitute for a great hero, since Achilles and Hektor, among others, are likened to defensive walls. I argue, accordingly, that the walls participate in the same temporal economy as the heroes themselves. Both walls remain standing throughout the *Iliad*, but their eventual destructions are prefigured within that work. I wish to investigate the status of these temporary structures, and once again suggest their importance for viewing the function of the epic tradition as conceived within the tradition itself.

To begin with, then, it is necessary to establish the importance of "walls." The action of the *Iliad* takes place largely on the battlefield that lies between the extreme points of the Greek camp on the one hand and the Trojan city on the other. The Greek camp consists of rows of ships dragged onto the shore and the soldiers' wooden huts. The Achaean camp is a temporary structure; whatever amenities the soldiers have provided for themselves in the duration of the nine years of the Trojan War, the camp is never intended to supply permanent housing. The Achaeans are to remain there until they sack Troy, and then they will abandon the camp and return home. On the other side, meanwhile, stands the Trojan city of Ilion, surrounded with a great wall and made to last. Oliver Taplin has emphasized the contrast between the two spaces:

> Troy is a great *stone-built city, many generations old,* with many *well-known permanent* features and landmarks. The Achaean camp could hardly be in greater contrast. It is an *improvised, wooden world,* peopled by soldiers and their captured women. *The camp does not even have a wall (and that built later in the poem will be obliterated after the war ...).* It has no temples, no *long-term* landmarks or formalized social spaces. It is not a proper place. (Taplin 1992:94; emphasis added)

Taplin finds the contrast between the Achaean and Trojan structures so great that he denies the Greek camp is "a proper place." It is made of wood instead of stone; it is temporary and not permanent; it lacks landmarks, familiar topographical features, or any sort of formalized space for cultural exchange; and its population consists only of soldiers and slaves temporarily located there. In short, according to Taplin, it is a camp and not a city.

Taplin's characterization of the site is instructive. In his desire to establish as strong a contrast as possible between the two spaces, he denies the Achaean camp any indication of durable structure. Taplin opposes the Trojan "stone-built" city to the "wooden world" of the Achaeans, and the "well-known" and "permanent" features of Troy with the "improvised" newness of the Greek camp. Perhaps the clearest example of his contrasting rhetoric appears in his initial denial that the Achaeans have a defensive wall, followed immediately by a correction, stating that the wall they do have "will be obliterated after the war."

Taplin's characterization of the differences between the Achaean and Trojan fortifications is elegant—yet, like most elegant encapsulations, it simplifies a more complex issue. For Taplin's temporary/permanent dichotomy fails to account for the fundamental similarity between the two structures: *both* sites have defensive walls, *neither* of which will long survive the war. As I will seek to demonstrate in this chapter, the narrative achieves a sense of temporal depth through the representation of the two walls that, though integral and intact at present, are fated to be overthrown. The present is burdened with impending destruction; each wall undergoes a virtual death in which the future, though not yet complete, is already virtually so.

1. The Achaean Wall: The Temporality of Mortal Artifact

The narrative of the Achaean wall and its construction in Book VII of the *Iliad* follows the lengthy description of the first day's battle, spanning Books III through VII. General battle breaks out after the inconclusive duel between Menelaus and Paris in Book III. The scenes of Helen being led by Aphrodite to Paris' bed (III 383–447) and Pandarus' bowshot (IV 105–126),[1] fired in violation of the great oath that the armies would cease fighting,[2] replicate the original violations carried out by the Trojans against the Greeks: the rape of Helen and the violation of sacred bonds established through exchange of friendship and oaths (Reckford 1964:10).

This first day of fighting is carried largely by the Greeks, following Diomedes' *aristeia* in Book V; however, the Greek side is not without heavy losses of its own. According to J. A. Davison's count, "In these few hours eighteen Achaeans 'of name' (even if we know no more of them than that) have died at the enemy hands, and the troops have perished in uncounted heaps" (Davison 1965:19). Hera complains to Zeus, asking why he is not indignant with Ares for destroying so great a number of Achaean fighters (V 757–759). Athena and Apollo finally allow the fighting to stop, as they set up a single duel between champions: Hektor and Ajax (VII 17–42). The day ends indecisively, and the combatants exchange gifts as a sign of their mutual respect.[3]

---

[1] The momentousness of the shot is emphasized by the extended description of Pandarus' bow (IV 105–111) and the actions of stringing the weapon (IV 112–113), opening his quiver and selecting an arrow (IV 116–117), fitting the arrow on the string (IV 118), praying to Apollo (IV119–121), drawing the string (IV 122–125), and finally, letting the arrow fly (IV 125–126). See Austin 1966 on the poetic device of marking the importance of a scene through retarding its narration.

[2] The oath is first mentioned by Paris-Alexander (III 74), and formally offered by Hektor (III 94), both variations of the same line: οἱ δ' ἄλλοι φιλότητα καὶ ὅρκια πιστὰ τάμωμεν, "But as for the rest of us—let's cut a deal of friendship and trustworthy oaths." The explicit *cutting* imagery of the oath, expressed in the verb τάμειν, indicates the slaughter of sacrificial victims (cf. III 103–104), whose blood is poured on the ground, along with wine, as an indication of the deadly implications of violating the oath. See especially III 298–301 for the ritual prayer uttered by someone of the Achaeans or the Trojans: "Most glorious and greatest Zeus, and you other immortal gods, whichever of the two groups should first do harm in transgression of the oaths (ὑπὲρ ὅρκια πημήνειαν), may their brains be made to pour on the ground just as this wine, their own and their children's, and their wives have sexual intercourse with others." The seriousness of the oath is emphasized by the number of references to it both by Achaeans (IV 157–168, 234–239, VII 400–402) and Trojans (VII 351–353). See Kitts 2005 for a recent account of how the narrative theme of the violated oath both as a presages and justifies further violence.

[3] On the duel between Hektor and Ajax as motivating the construction of the Achaean defensive wall, see Bassett 1927:154–155, who argues that the duel is represented to make Hektor appear "as a very dangerous antagonist ... Without Hector there need have been no [Achaean] Wall; without the distinct impression that Hector was a very dangerous antagonist there would have been an equal lack of any reasonable excuse for building it."

It is in this context that Nestor advises the Achaeans to negotiate a cease-fire to collect bodies, conduct burial rites for them, and to build a defensive wall out of the series of tombs erected for the dead.

Ἀτρεΐδη τε καὶ ἄλλοι ἀριστῆες Παναχαιῶν,
πολλοὶ γὰρ τεθνᾶσι κάρη κομόωντες Ἀχαιοί,
τῶν νῦν αἷμα κελαινὸν ἐΰρροον ἀμφὶ Σκάμανδρον
ἐσκέδασ' ὀξὺς Ἄρης, ψυχαὶ δ' Ἀϊδόσδε κατῆλθον·
τώ σε χρὴ πόλεμον μὲν ἅμ' ἠοῖ παῦσαι Ἀχαιῶν,
αὐτοὶ δ' ἀγρόμενοι κυκλήσομεν ἐνθάδε νεκροὺς
βουσὶ καὶ ἡμιόνοισιν· ἀτὰρ κατακήομεν αὐτούς
τυτθὸν ἄποπρο νεῶν, ὥς κ' ὀστέα παισὶν ἕκαστος
οἴκαδ' ἄγῃ, ὅτ' ἂν αὖτε νεώμεθα πατρίδα γαῖαν.
τύμβόν τ' ἀμφὶ πυρὴν ἕνα χεύομεν ἐξαγαγόντες
ἄκριτον ἐκ πεδίου· ποτὶ δ' αὐτὸν δείμομεν ὦκα
πύργους ὑψηλούς, εἶλαρ νηῶν τε καὶ αὐτῶν.
ἐν δ' αὐτοῖσι πύλας ποιήσομεν εὖ ἀραρυίας,
ὄφρα δι' αὐτάων ἱππηλασίη ὁδὸς εἴη.
ἔκτοσθεν δὲ βαθεῖαν ὀρύξομεν ἐγγύθι τάφρον,
ἥ χ' ἵππον καὶ λαὸν ἐρυκάκοι ἀμφὶς ἐοῦσα,
μή ποτ' ἐπιβρίσῃ πόλεμος Τρώων ἀγερώχων.

Both you sons of Atreus and you other chiefs of all the Achaeans:
[Heed my words:] for many long-haired Achaeans have died,
whose dark blood now around fair-flowing Scamander
keen Ares spilt, and their souls went down to the house of Hades.
Accordingly you must put a stop to the battle of the Achaeans
        at dawn,
and we ourselves will gather up the corpses and wheel them
        here
with oxen and mules. But let us burn them
a short distance away from the ships, so each man may take
        the bones
back home to the children, whenever we return to our native land
        again.
And about the pyre let's heap up a single burial mound, having drawn it
from the plain, without separation [between mounds]; and quickly let's
        build against it
lofty towers, a defense for both the ships and for ourselves.
And in them we will make well-fitted gates,
so that there may be road for chariots through them.

And outside, let's dig a deep ditch nearby,
which, since it is about [the wall], would hold off both horses
      and people,
lest battle of the brave Trojans ever fall heavily upon us.

Iliad VII 327–343

Agamemnon accepts Nestor's advice; he tells the Trojan herald Idaeus that he grants a cease-fire to bury the dead, but withholds Nestor's wall-building wisdom (VII 408–411).[4] The entire scene is meant to be surprising; even the gods are in the dark about Nestor's plans, as Poseidon notes as he complains to Zeus about the unexpected construction:

Ζεῦ πάτερ, ἦ ῥά τίς ἐστι βροτῶν ἐπ᾽ ἀπείρονα γαῖαν
ὅς τις ἔτ᾽ ἀθανάτοισι <u>νόον</u> καὶ <u>μῆτιν</u> ἐνίψει;
οὐχ ὁράᾳς, ὅτι δ᾽ αὖτε κάρη κομόωντες Ἀχαιοὶ
τεῖχος ἐτειχίσσαντο νεῶν ὕπερ, ἀμφὶ δὲ τάφρον
ἤλασαν, οὐδὲ θεοῖσι δόσαν κλειτὰς ἑκατόμβας;

Father Zeus, truly, who is there among mortals upon
      the limitless earth
who will still tell his <u>mind</u> and <u>cunning intelligence</u>
      to the immortals?
Do you not see how now the long-haired Achaeans
have built a wall in defense of the ships, and have driven
a trench around it, but did not give famed hecatombs to the gods?

Iliad VII 446–450[5]

The Achaean wall is specifically represented as a mortal artifact; the gods were given no prior indication of its construction nor offered any sacrifices (κλειτὰς ἑκατόμβας, VII 450).

But just what constitutes Nestor's "mind and cunning intelligence" (νόον καὶ μῆτιν) here? Let us examine the construction closely.

---

4   Shive 1996:191 puns instructively on this scene: "[Agamemnon] withholds Nestor's wisdom from unwitting *Widaios*, the Trojan herald" (emphasis added). Idaios' name is apparently related to the verbal root *ϝιδ- (as Shive indicates by his "*Widaios*") which denotes both "seeing" and "knowing." The fact that Idaios *cannot see* what the Achaeans are up do is an indication of Nestor's cunning intelligence here. See *Iliad* VII 447 for Nestor's plan called *mētis* (cited below). Nestor's own name indicates his intellectual prowess: see Frame 1978:82–85 for the derivation of Nestor from the Indo-European root *nes-, the verbal root of the cognate words *noos* "mind, intelligence," *nostos* "a return home," and *neomai* "to achieve a return (home)."

5   At VII 448, I read ὅτι δ᾽ with Allen (1931) instead of West's (1998–2000) ὅ τε δή.

ἦμος δ' οὔτ' ἄρ πω ἠώς, ἔτι δ' ἀμφιλύκη νύξ,
τῆμος ἄρ' ἀμφὶ πυρὴν κριτὸς ἤγρετο λαὸς Ἀχαιῶν,
τύμβον δ' ἀμφ' αὐτὴν ἕνα ποίεον ἐξαγαγόντες
ἄκριτον ἐκ πεδίου· ποτὶ δ' αὐτὸν τεῖχος ἔδειμαν,
πύργους ὑψηλούς, εἶλαρ νηῶν τε καὶ αὐτῶν.
ἐν δ' αὐτοῖσι πύλας ἐνεποίεον εὖ ἀραρυίας,
ὄφρα δι' αὐτάων ἱππηλασίη ὁδὸς εἴη,
ἔκτοσθεν δὲ βαθεῖαν ἐπ' αὐτῷ τάφρον ὄρυξαν,
εὐρεῖαν μεγάλην, ἐν δὲ σκόλοπας κατέπηξαν.

But when it was not yet dawn, but still crepuscular night,
then a chosen body of Achaeans gathered about the pyre,
and about it they made a single burial mound, having drawn it
from the plain without separation; and they built against it a wall
and lofty towers, a defense for both the ships and themselves.
And they made in them well-fitted gates,
so that there would be road for chariots through them;
and outside they dug a deep trench hard upon it,
a wide and great one, and in it they fastened palisades.

Iliad VII 433–441

A selected group (κριτὸς ... λαός, VII 433) of Achaeans gather *at night*; the time is emphasized by the *hapax legomenon* ἀμφιλύκη (VII 433), which seems to indicate the twilight period "on either side (ἀπφι-) of the light (λύκη)." Like the night-time spy mission of the *Doloneia* in *Iliad* X, the temporal setting marks the construction as an occulted activity. There is a dissonance between the *select* men (κριτὸς ... λαός, VII 433) men who draw together a *single* burial mound (τύμβον ... ἕνα, VII 435) out of the multiple burials into an undifferentiated mass *without separation* (ἄκριτον, VII 436). The wall, therefore, is to be envisioned as formed from the extension of each individual warrior's tomb into the other.[6] The actual construction of the wall (VII 433–439) follows Nestor's instructions closely (cf. VII 336–343), with formulaic repetition, as is regular practice in scenes where previously narrated instructions are carried out. At *Iliad* VII 436, however, the Achaeans "build a <u>wall</u> up against the burial mound" (ποτὶ δ' αὐτὸν [sc. τύμβον]

---

6   See Shive's convincing analysis of the "logistics" of Nestor's plan: "Scholars fail to appreciate Nestor's logical logistics. They visualize the cremation of all the corpses on one spot and then on that spot the incorporation of the single pyre into a wall built around the camp. This would be impractical, if not impracticable, within the constraints of the situation. Nestor rather envisions a series of cremations on the perimeter of the camp, each a little off from their own ships so that each can recover bones for his children back home and *each extend their own pyre-tumulus to join one continuous tumulus-wall*" (Shive 1996:191, emphasis added).

τεῖχος ἔδειμαν).[7] They build gates into the wall, dig a ditch all around it, and—another new detail—they fasten palisades inside the new deep and wide trench (VII 441). The trench and wall function together to limit access to the camp.

The appearance of this wall in Book VII has long been considered a controversial passage for two reasons. First, the detail that the Achaeans are to gather the bones of the dead and convey them back to the dead men's families has been felt to be a late interpolation, deriving from the historically based practice in fifth century Athens of collecting and carrying bones back home.[8] I am unconvinced that one needs to hang Homeric detail on historic practice, however.[9] Furthermore, as I will demonstrate in the next chapter (chapter 4), it is difficult to determine a "norm" for burial customs from the evidence of the *Iliad* and *Odyssey*, so that any argument based on claims of "un-Homeric" practice must be treated with caution. Finally, as we will see, Homer elsewhere speaks of *kenotaphs* "empty tombs," such that the tombs in Book VII piled up without human remains inside them need not be taken as anomalous.

The second and more significant source of controversy over the authenticity of this passage is due to a failure to understand the purpose of the wall and an inability to account for its construction now in the tenth year of the war. Much of the scholarly debate has centered on a passage in the "Archaeology" of Thucydides' *History of the Peloponnesian War* (1.11.1). As part of his strategy to emphasize the unprecedented magnitude and importance of the war he is about to narrate, Thucydides attempts to degrade the importance of the Trojan War. His general argument runs as follows: the Trojan War lasted ten years only because so few Greeks participated in it, and their number was further reduced by lack of sufficient supplies; a large contingent of the army was forced to conduct raids for supplies or even farm the coastline; otherwise, the war would

---

[7] The Achaean defensive wall is consistently referred to as a τεῖχος in the *Iliad*: see VII 436, 449, 461, 463; VIII 177; IX 67, 87, 232, 349; XII 4, 12, 18, 25, 26, 32, 36, 64, 90, 137, 143, 177, 198, 223, 257, 261, 264, 289, 291, 308, 352, 374, 380, 388, 390, 399, 416, 420, 438, 440, 443, 468, 469; XIII 50, 87, 679, 683; 14.15, 32, 55, 66; 15.345, 361, 384, 391, 395, 736; XVI 397, 512, 558; XVIII 215; XXI 49. A study of the distribution of τεῖχος in reference to the Achaean wall demonstrates the word's great frequency during the *teikhomakhia* spanning from Book XII through Book XV of the *Iliad*. Beginning in Book XVI, once Patroklos dons Achilles' armor and leads the Myrmidons into battle, the tide of the battle shifts, and attention turns from the Achaean wall to the Trojan wall.

[8] The view that the description of the gathering of bones for transfer home represents a custom instituted in Athens in 464 BCE originates with Jacoby 1944:44n30, followed by Page 1959:323, Kirk 1962:195, 1964:180, 1985:10, 1990:279, West 1969:259, Kurtz and Boardman 1971:187. An earlier critical tradition, beginning with Aristarchus (Scholia A at *Iliad* VII 334; compare Scholia T at *Odyssey* xxiv 80–81), objected to the description as different than other "normal" burials in Homer where the bones are buried in the ground. In general, see Shive 1996 for a review of scholarship on this issue.

[9] On this point I find myself in agreement with van der Valk 1963–1964:I.423, Willcock 1978–1984:I.256, and Shive 1996.

have been decided far sooner. The problematic line explains that the Greeks "won an initial victory when they arrived—this is obvious, for they wouldn't have built up a defensive wall for their camp" (ἀφικόμενοι ... ἐνίκησαν· δῆλον δέ· τὸ γὰρ ἔρυμα τῷ στρατοπέδῳ οὐκ ἂν ἐτειχίσαντο). The implication is that the Greeks drove the Trojan defenders back from the shore and built a defensive wall upon taking the beach when they first landed. The debate, then, runs that Thucydides must be talking about a different wall than the one in Book VII of the *Iliad*, since Thucydides clearly—if the text is sound—is describing a wall built *upon arrival*, i.e. in the first year of the Trojan War.[10]

Regarding the specific details of Thucydides' *eruma*, I have nothing to add; the debate has little value for our investigation here, whether or not the text of Thucydides 1.11.1 is sound. After all, it has long been noted that several details in the early books of the *Iliad* seem to make better sense within a first-year scenario than within a tenth-year scenario.[11] What I am more interested in is the narrative logic of the *Iliad* itself: Why represent the construction of the wall *now*? The answer, I suggest, is an obvious one: the Achaeans need a wall *now* because Achilles, thanks to his quarrel with Agamemnon, is no longer on the battlefield. Previously, the Achaeans needed no wall, no "defense both of their

---

[10] The debate is an ancient one, as the scholia to Thucydides reveal; the scholiast concluded that Thucydides' wall was a different one than Homer's: it was "an earlier and smaller one" (ἔρυμα νῦν λέγει οὐχ ὅπερ ἐν τῇ η΄ λέγει Ὅμηρος γενέσθαι, ἀλλὰ πρότερον μικρότερον, "The wall now does not mean the one which Homer talks about in *Iliad* VII, but an earlier and smaller one" [Scholia at Thucydides 1.11.1]). Page 1959:Appendix II, following G. Hermann *Philologus* 1 (1846) 367–372, argued that Thucydides did not know about the wall in *Iliad* VII; hence, the entire episode must have been interpolated sometime after Thucydides' death, but before the period of Alexandrian scholarship. Tsagarakis 1969 and West 1969 independently argued against Page's stance, Tsagarakis arguing the difference in nuance between ἔρυμα and τεῖχος in Thucydides, and West demonstrating the extent to which the Achaean wall is integrated into the text of the *Iliad*. Other scholars have taken a different approach, arguing that the text of Thucydides is unsound, finding a basic illogic in the combination of "being victorious" and "building defensive walls" (see esp. Davison 1965 and Morrison 1994); instead, they offer various emendations to solve problems of logical consistency and to bring the text into closer agreement with Homer. See in particular the ingenious suggestions of Dittrich 1895, Robertson 1924, and Cook 1954–1955. In general, see the comprehensive study of earlier work by Dolin 1983, who concludes after a very cautious and detailed review of the evidence and scholarship, "In my view, unless there are arguments which I have overlooked, to conclude after a review of the evidence that the manuscript text is authentic would be a last resort" (147). More recently, important articles by Davies 1986, Singor 1992, and Morrison 1994 also suggest textual difficulty in Thucydides. Nevertheless, the question is still vexed, for although it is generally true (as noted by Scodel 1982:33) that few scholars are willing to argue that the wall scene in Book VII of the *Iliad* contains large scale interpolations, one of the more recent articles on the subject does just that: Maitland 1999 finds inconsistencies in the various passages describing the Achaean wall throughout the *Iliad* and concludes "if there was ever a case for multiple authorship, this is one" (8).

[11] See van Leeuwen 1911 for a catalogue of such details, with a convenient summary by Foster 1914. See more recently Reckford 1964:9n11, and Bergren 1980 with bibliography.

ships and of themselves" (εἶλαρ νηῶν τε καὶ αὐτῶν, VII 338), for Achilles was that defense—he was their wall.[12] Achilles makes the point explicitly during the Embassy scene when he tells Odysseus,

> ἦ μὲν δὴ μάλα πολλὰ πονήσατο <u>νόσφιν ἐμεῖο</u>·
> καὶ δὴ <u>τεῖχος ἔδειμε</u>, καὶ ἤλασε τάφρον ἐπ' αὐτῷ
> εὐρεῖαν μεγάλην, ἐν δὲ σκόλοπας κατέπηξεν·
> ἀλλ' οὐδ' ὣς δύναται σθένος Ἕκτορος ἀνδροφόνοιο
> ἴσχειν. <u>ὄφρα δ' ἐγὼ</u> μετ' Ἀχαιοῖσιν <u>πολέμιζον</u>,
> <u>οὐκ ἐθέλεσκε</u> μάχην <u>ἀπὸ τείχεος</u> ὀρνύμεν Ἕκτωρ,
> ἀλλ' ὅσον ἐς Σκαιάς τε πύλας καὶ φηγὸν ἵκανεν.

> Yes, in truth, very many things have been labored over <u>while I have been
>   away</u>—
> indeed, he [*sc.* Agamemnon] even <u>built a wall</u>, and drove a ditch up to it,
> a great and wide one, and he fixed stakes down inside it.
> But not even so is he able to hold back the strength of man-slaughtering
> Hektor. Yet <u>while I was fighting</u> among the Achaeans
> Hektor <u>was never willing</u> to stir up battle <u>away from the [Trojan] wall</u>,
> but would reach only as far as the Scean gates and the fig tree.

> *Iliad* IX 348–354

As long as (ὄφρα, IX 352) Achilles used to fight (πολέμιζον, IX 352), the Achaeans had no need for a defensive wall, for Hektor was unwilling (οὐκ ἐθέλεσκε, IX 353) to venture far from his own city's defenses (ἀπὸ τείχεος, IX 353); the imperfect and iterative verb tenses (πολέμιζον, IX 352; οὐκ ἐθέλεσκε, IX 353) and temporal clause (ὄφρα ... πολέμιζον, κτλ., IX 352–354) all point to the enduring state of affairs before Achilles separated himself from the battle (νόσφιν ἐμεῖο, IX 348).[13] The ancient scholia to these verses describe Achilles as μείζων τείχους

---

[12]   Scodel 1982:33 found the description of the wall's construction "poetically simple and coherent, even though it may be preposterous in practical terms that the Achaean camp should have lacked such a protection for so long." My claim is the episode is in fact motivated within the Iliadic narrative by the absence of the hero Achilles; hence, the wall could *only* be built here and not earlier.

[13]   Hektor claims at *Iliad* XV 721–723 that he had previously been prevented from attacking the Achaean ships by the cowardice of the Trojan elders; the claim appears to contradict Achilles' assessment in *Iliad* IX that Hektor was "unwilling" to meet him in battle. Willcock 1977:48 and Andersen 1990:33–34 have noted that Hektor makes his claim while he is in fact attacking the ships, such that the immediate context colors his words (see further Willcock 1964 and Braswell 1971 on "*ad hoc*" inventions in the *Iliad*). What is more important for our analysis, however, is the fact that Achilles is associated with the Achaean defensive wall, and both are compared in terms of their effectiveness of protecting the Achaeans from Hektor. The *Iliad* repeatedly notes Hektor's absence during the time before Achilles' quarrel with Agamemnon: see V 788–791,

"mightier than a wall" (Scholia bT at *Iliad* IX 352–353, Erbse), and at another point, describe Achilles as a "living wall" (τεῖχος ἔμψυχον) for the Achaeans (Scholia T at *Iliad* XII 29d1, Erbse). Another scholion posits Achilles' absence from the field of battle as the reason why the Trojans are only now daring to leave the city and fight the Achaeans: οἱ γὰρ Τρῶες Ἀχιλλέως παρόντος οὐδέποτε ἐξήεσαν τῶν πυλῶν, "for the Trojans never went out of their gates when Achilles was present" (Scholia bT at *Iliad* I 1b, Erbse).[14] In short, the defensive wall (τεῖχος) of the Achaeans is a mere substitute for the now absent Achilles.[15] Furthermore, like Achilles, the Achaean wall remains standing within the *Iliad* itself, but is fated to fall beyond the scope of the epic.

The opening verses of *Iliad* XII offer a remarkable description of the fate of the Achaean wall. The narrative perspective shifts from the description of battle and offers a retrospective on the wall's destruction years later. I cite the passage at length:

οἳ δὲ μάχοντο
Ἀργεῖοι καὶ Τρῶες ὁμιλαδόν· οὐδ' ἄρ' ἔμελλεν
τάφρος ἔτι σχήσειν Δαναῶν καὶ τεῖχος ὕπερθεν
εὐρύ, τὸ ποιήσαντο νεῶν ὕπερ, ἀμφὶ δὲ τάφρον,
ἤλασαν· οὐδὲ θεοῖσι δόσαν κλειτὰς ἑκατόμβας·
ὄφρά σφιν νῆάς τε θοὰς καὶ ληΐδα πολλὴν
ἐντὸς ἔχον ῥύοιτο· θεῶν δ' ἀέκητι τέτυκτο
ἀθανάτων· τὸ καὶ οὔ τι πολὺν χρόνον ἔμπεδον ἦεν.
ὄφρα μὲν Ἕκτωρ ζωὸς ἔην καὶ μήνι' Ἀχιλλεύς
καὶ Πριάμοιο ἄνακτος ἀπόρθητος πόλις ἔπλεν,
τόφρα δὲ καὶ μέγα τεῖχος Ἀχαιῶν ἔμπεδον ἦεν.

XIII 105–110, and compare the situation with Meleager in Phoenix's rhetorical myth at IX 550–552.

[14] See Davison 1965:11, 19–20. Davison's thesis essentially follows that expressed by the bT scholia, although he does not cite it. Morrison 1994 demonstrates that the construction of the Achaean wall is of utmost importance, for it marks a turn of the battle's tide: the Greeks' camp, once walled, becomes likened to a city itself under siege: "Once the Greeks are under attack, the defense of their wall evokes images of a city under siege" (214). See further Singor 1992:402. A study of the distribution of the word τεῖχος in the *Iliad* confirms Morrison's suggestion: the word is used to refer to the Trojan wall exclusively in those books where the city is under siege; likewise, the Achaean wall is called a τεῖχος in the books when the Trojans attack the Greek camp.

[15] As a substitute for the fighter, the wall participates in the economy of the *therapōn* "ritual substitute" like Patroklos. On the connection between Greek *therapōn* and Hittite *tarpašša-/tarp(an)alli-* "ritual substitute," see Van Brock 1959 (esp. 125–126), who argues that the Hittite reflects an older Anatolian word borrowed by Bronze-Age Greek which survived as θέραψ/θεράπων (cf. Van Brock 1959:143n27); on Patroklos as a "ritual substitute" for Achilles, see Householder Jr. and Nagy 1972, Nagy 1999, Sinos 1980, and Lowenstam 1981. On the wall as a substitute for Achilles, see Edwards 1987:239.

αὐτὰρ ἐπεὶ κατὰ μὲν Τρώων θάνον ὅσσοι ἄριστοι,
πολλοὶ δ᾽ Ἀργείων οἳ μὲν δάμεν, οἳ δὲ λίποντο,
πέρθετο δὲ Πριάμοιο πόλις δεκάτῳ ἐνιαυτῷ,
Ἀργεῖοι δ᾽ ἐν νηυσὶ φίλην ἐς πατρίδ᾽ ἔβησαν,
δὴ τότε μητιόωντο Ποσειδάων καὶ Ἀπόλλων
τεῖχος ἀμαλδῦναι, ποταμῶν μένος εἰσαγαγόντες,
ὅσσοι ἀπ᾽ Ἰδαίων ὀρέων ἅλα δὲ προρέουσι,
Ῥῆσός θ᾽ Ἑπτάπορός τε Κάρησός τε Ῥοδίος τε
Γρήνικός τε καὶ Αἴσηπος δῖός τε Σκάμανδρος
καὶ Σιμόεις, ὅθι πολλὰ βοάγρια καὶ τρυφάλειαι
κάππεσον ἐν κονίῃσι καὶ ἡμιθέων γένος ἀνδρῶν·
τῶν πάντων ὁμόσε στόματ᾽ ἔτραπε Φοῖβος Ἀπόλλων,
ἐννῆμαρ δ᾽ ἐς τεῖχος ἵει ῥόον· ὗε δ᾽ ἄρα Ζεὺς
συνεχές, ὄφρά κε θᾶσσον ἁλίπλοα τείχεα θείη.
αὐτὸς δ᾽ Ἐννοσίγαιος ἔχων χείρεσσι τρίαιναν
ἡγεῖτ᾽, ἐκ δ᾽ ἄρα πάντα θεμείλια κύμασι πέμπεν
φιτρῶν καὶ λάων, τὰ θέσαν μογέοντες Ἀχαιοί.
λεῖα δ᾽ ἐποίησεν παρ᾽ ἀγάρροον Ἑλλήσποντον,
αὖτις δ᾽ ἠϊόνα μεγάλην ψαμάθοισι κάλυψεν,
τεῖχος ἀμαλδύνας· ποταμοὺς δ᾽ ἔτρεψε νέεσθαι
κὰρ ῥόον, ᾗ περ πρόσθεν ἵεν καλλίρροον ὕδωρ.
ὣς ἄρ᾽ ἔμελλον ὄπισθε Ποσειδάων καὶ Ἀπόλλων
θησέμεναι· τότε δ᾽ ἀμφὶ μάχη ἐνοπή τε δεδήει
τεῖχος ἐΰδμητον, κανάχιζε δὲ δούρατα πύργων
βαλλόμεν᾽.

> They were fighting,
the Argives and Trojans, in a crowd. Nor was the ditch
of the Danaäns any longer going to hold them back, nor the wide wall
above it, which they had built in defense of their ships, and around it
drove a ditch. They did not give famed hecatombs to the gods,
so that it might protect for them both the swift ships and the plentiful
> booty
they had inside. But it was built against the will of the immortal gods.
And so it was not to remain in place for a long time at all.
As long as Hektor was alive and Achilles was angry
and the city of King Priam was unsacked,
for so long also the great wall of the Achaeans was in place.
But when as many as were the best men of the Trojans died,
and of the Argives, many were beaten down, but some survived,

105

and the city of Priam <u>was sacked in the tenth year</u>,
and the Argives <u>went</u> in their ships to the dear land of their fathers,
<u>then indeed</u> Poseidon and Apollo took counsel
to overpower the wall by leading against it the force of rivers.
As many [rivers] as flow forth to the sea from the mountains of Ida—
Rhesus and Heptaporus and Caresus and Rhodius
and Grenicus and Aesepus and brilliant Scamander
and Simoeis, where many ox-hide shields and helmets
fell down in the dust along with the race of half-god men—
Phoibos Apollo turned the mouths of all of these together,
<u>and he cast the flow against the wall for nine days. And Zeus rained
continuously</u>, so as to set it more quickly under the sea.
And the earth-shaker himself while holding in his hands the trident
guided them, and he sent out to the waves all the foundations
of wooden blocks and stones, which the toiling Achaeans had set up,
<u>and he made it smooth beside the great-flowing Hellespont
and once again covered the great shore with sand
after he overpowered the wall</u>. Then he turned the rivers to return,
each one to its respective flow, in the very place where formerly the very
        beautiful water went.
Thus <u>afterward</u> Poseidon and Apollo <u>would
set things</u>. <u>But for the time being</u>, battle and shouting were blazing
about the well-built wall, and the timbers of the towers crashed
when they were struck.

Iliad XII 2–37

The passage presents a complex image of the fate of the wall. It is in danger in the present moment and will not last long; its destruction is guaranteed, though its durability is preserved within the narrative scope of the *Iliad* itself. Only in the future, after Hektor has been killed and Troy has been sacked, after the surviving Achaeans have returned to their homelands, then the wall will be wiped out and completely obliterated, and the shore wiped clean of any traces of its existence. The wall—itself a stand-in for Achilles, as I argued above—here functions as an image of the tradition itself and its view of its own temporal durability.

    The passage begins by implying the destruction of the Achaean wall during the present skirmish: "the ditch was not going to hold them back any longer" (οὐδ' ἄρ' ἔμελλεν | τάφρος ἔτι σχήσειν, XII 3–4). The verb οὐδ' ... ἔμελλε plus the future infinitive σχήσειν and the adverb ἔτι all work to shape a temporal perspective of the Achaean wall in terms of "no longer" (οὐδ' ... ἔτι, XII 3–4): the Achaeans' hope about their wall's continued protection ceases to be projected into an open future as a "not yet," as in a wall "not yet broken." Instead, the narrative speaks of the wall as lacking a future—it will not remain in place for very long (τὸ καὶ οὔ τι πολὺν χρόνον ἔμπεδον ἦεν, XII 9)—such that the temporal perspective has shifted to the "no longer," indicating a failure: it will no longer perform the task it was meant to do. Such a temporal shift creates a kind of narrative expectation in which one of the great Trojan fighters or their allies—Hektor or Sarpedon—will come crashing through the wall.

Nevertheless, the passage goes on to refine the precise temporal boundaries in of the wall's durability. With the temporal markers "as long as" (ὄφρα μὲν, XII 10), "for so long" (τόφρα δέ, XII 12), "but when" (αὐτὰρ ἐπεί, XII 13), and "then indeed" (δὴ τότε, XII 17), Homer locates the destruction of the Achaean wall far in the future, after Troy has been sacked, its heroes killed, and the surviving Achaeans departed homeward. Imperfect verbs (ἔην καὶ μήνι', XII 10; ἀπόρθητος ... ἔλπεν, XII 11; ἔμπεδον ἦεν, XII 12) paint a static picture of the wall's endurance against which aorist verbs (θάνον, XII 13; δάμεν ... λίποντο, XII 14; ἔβησαν, XII 16) mark key events in its history. When these events have been accomplished, then (δὴ τότε, XII 17), we are told, Poseidon, Apollo, and Zeus act in concert to wipe out the wall and erase all traces of its existence: Apollo drives rivers against the wall, Zeus pours rain, and Poseidon smooths out all the traces of the former Achaean presence (λεῖα δ' ἐποίησεν, XII 30), and once again he covers up the beach with sand (αὖτις δ' ἠϊόνα μεγάλην ψαμάθοισι κάλυψεν, XII 31). The very foundations of the wall are undermined under the gods' liquid onslaught.

Indeed, later in the narrative during the "Great Day" of fighting, the wall's watery demise is recalled as the Trojans at least partially breach its defenses. Apollo leads the Trojans against the Achaean wall; their rush is described as a metaphorical flood:

προπάροιθε δὲ Φοῖβος Ἀπόλλων
ῥεῖ' ὄχθας καπέτοιο βαθείης ποσσὶν <u>ἐρείπων</u>
ἐς μέσσον κατέβαλλε, γεφύρωσεν δὲ κέλευθον
μακρὴν ἠδ' εὐρεῖαν, ὅσον τ' ἐπὶ δουρὸς ἐρωή
γίγνεται, ὁππότ' ἀνὴρ σθένεος πειρώμενος ᾖσιν.
τῇ ῥ' οἵ γε προχέοντο φαλαγγηδόν, πρὸ δ' Ἀπόλλων
αἰγίδ' ἔχων ἐρίτιμον· <u>ἔρειπε δὲ τεῖχος Ἀχαιῶν</u>
ῥεῖα μάλ', ὡς ὅτε τις <u>ψάμαθον</u> πάϊς ἄγχι θαλάσσης,
ὅς τ' ἐπεὶ οὖν ποιήσῃ ἀθύρματα νηπιέῃσιν,
<u>ἂψ αὖτις συνέχευε</u> ποσὶν καὶ χερσὶν ἀθύρων·
ὣς ῥα σύ, ἤϊε Φοῖβε, πολὺν κάματον καὶ ὀϊζὺν
<u>σύγχεας</u> Ἀργείων, αὐτοῖσι δὲ φύζαν ἐνῶρσας.

> And before them Phoibos Apollo
> easily <u>threw down</u> the banks of the deep trench with his feet
> and cast them [i.e. the banks] down into the middle, and he bridged a path
> long and broad, as far as a spear is cast,
> whenever a man making trial of his strength hurls it.
> By means of this they [i.e. the Trojans] <u>poured forward in ranks</u>, and
> > Apollo was before them
> holding the highly-prized aegis. <u>He threw down the wall of the Achaeans</u>
> very easily, as when a child near the sea,
> one who when he makes playthings in his childishness,
> <u>pours the sand back together again</u> with his feet and hands while playing.
> So indeed, darter Phoibos, you <u>pour together</u> the great toil and misery
> of the Argives, and you roused flight in them.

Iliad XV 355–366

Apollo throws down (ἐρείπων, XV 356; ἔρειπε, XV 361)[16] the banks of the Achaeans' defensive trench (ὄχθας καπέτοιο, XV 356)[17] and their wall (τεῖχος, XV 361). The Trojans "pour forward in ranks" (προχέοντο φαλαγγηδόν, XV 360); the verb χέω "to pour" implies liquid motion, especially in this context where we find Apollo "pouring together" (XV 366) the Achaean works as easily as a child "pours together" (συνέχευε, XV 364) sand-castles he has built on the shore.[18] In short, the passage in *Iliad* XII would appear to be a proleptic announcement of the destruction of the Achaean wall by Trojan forces literally "flooding" over it.[19] The imagery of Trojans "pouring forth" against the wall and Apollo

---

[16] The verb ἐρείπω is regularly used to describe the act of "throwing down" walls (*Iliad* XIV 15, XV 356, 361) or palisades (XII 258); it is also used intransitively to describe a soldier "falling" to the ground (V 47, 57) or "falling" to his knees (V 309).

[17] The word κάπετος here, as at XVIII 564 (Hephaistos depicts a κάπετος and ἕρκος around a vineyard on Achilles shield), is the "trench" drawn alongside a wall; however, at XXIV 797–798 Hektor's cremated remains are set within a "trench" and covered with a cairn of stones (αἶψα δ' ἄρ' ἐς κοίλην κάπετον θέσαν, αὐτὰρ ὕπερθε | πυκνοῖσιν λάεσσι κατεστόρεσαν μεγλαοισι, "swiftly they placed it [*sc.* the urn containing Hektor's bones] inside a hollow trench-grave, but above it they packed it tightly with great stones"). When Apollo throws down the banks of the κάπετος and flings Achaeans inside, their death recalls funereal ritual.

[18] See Fenno 2005 for an in-depth study of water imagery in Homeric battle scenes. Fenno notes that "verbs such as *seuō*, *kheō*, and *rheō* commonly show extended meanings that do not necessarily evoke the idea of water in motion. But within the *Iliad*, where troops will be likened to water over and over again, the latent image seems to acquire a more persistent evocative power" (478). See especially Fenno's discussion of the associations between the Greeks and the sea (476–482) and the Trojans and rivers (482–487).

[19] The Trojans "rush" from the city gates with a "rumble" (II 809–810 = VIII 58–59; cf. Paris "rushing" out of the city gates at VII 1); later they "pour into" the Greek wall (ἐσέχυντο, XII 470) like waves, rank after rank (XV 360); in flight from Achilles some "pour forth" toward the city

smashing it like a child "pours back together again" (ἄψ αὖτις συνέχευε, XV 364) the sand he has temporarily made into a plaything recalls the image of the Achaean wall's destruction under the flood of Apollo, Zeus, and Poseidon, and the sand that buries the remnants of the Achaean labors (ψαμάθοισι, XII 31; cf. ψάμαθον, XV 362).

In an influential and often-cited article, Ruth Scodel (1982) has studied the destruction of the Achaean wall in light of other "flood" narratives familiar from the Semitic, Sumerian, Hittite, and Greek traditions. Scodel notes the general character of these narratives as marking a greater separation between gods and men; the former race of demigods (ἡμιθέων γένος ἀνδρῶν, XII 23)[20] is wiped out in a massive destructive event that brings the entire age to a decisive end.[21] What I wish to emphasize is the implication that in *Iliad* XII the Achaean wall is linked not merely with the figure of Achilles, for whom it functions as substitute, but with the entire heroic age which is to come to an end.[22] The wall, built out of the joined tombs of the Achaean fighters, is to be utterly wiped out; without funeral marker, the very κλέος "fame" of the men is in danger of perishing forever in the depths of time. This image of the concomitant loss of a hero's tomb and his κλέος becomes particularly significant when we recall the river Scamander's threat to bury Achilles under a mound of silt so the Achaeans will not be able to find his bones nor erect a σῆμα for him (XXI 316–323). Gregory Nagy has read the description of Poseidon and Apollo covering the entire beach with sand to be "consciously offered as a variant of the tradition that tells how the Achaeans had made a funeral mound for the dead Achilles by the Hellespont

---

(προχέοντο, XXI 6) while others "pool together" into the river (εἰλεῦντο, XXI 8: for εἴλω with water imagery, cf. ἀλὲν ὕδωρ, XXIII 420); Achilles is compared to an irrigator (ἀνὴρ ὀχετηγὸς, XXI 257–264) who reverses the stream of Trojan warriors back into their city, where they "pour into" the city "in a rush" (ἐσσυμένως ἐσέχυντο, XXI 610); there they collect behind the walls like a pool of water (εἰς ἄστυ ἄλεν, XXII 12, κατὰ ἄστυ ἐέλμεθα, XXIV 662; cf. ἀλὲν ὕδωρ, XXIII 420). See Fenno 2005:485 for discussion of these passages.

20 Compare the account in *Genesis* 6:1–4 of the Nephilim (rendered as γίγαντες "giants" in the Septuagint), the offspring of the "sons of God" and the "daughters of men": "The Nephilim were on earth at that time (and even afterwards) when the sons of God resorted to the daughters of man and had children by them. These are the heroes of days gone by, the famous men" (*The Jerusalem Bible* [Garden City, NY, 1966]). These Nephilim perish along with all humanity in the great flood—save for Noah and his family and reproducing pairs of every species of animal. Scodel 1982 notes, "The analogy between these 'giants,' children of divine beings and mortal women, and the Greek demigods is obvious" (42). See Scodel 1982:42nn22–23 for bibliography.

21 Scodel (1982) argues, "The Trojan War thus functions as a myth of destruction, in which Zeus brings about the catastrophe in order to remove the demigods from the world and separate men from gods, to relieve the earth of the burden caused by overpopulation, or to punish impiety" (40).

22 Compare Hesiod's narrative of the five ages in *Works and Days* 106–201. Each age is brought to utter extinction before the next is born, marking further and further separation from the gods. Note that Hesiod calls the fourth race, the race of heroes, ἡμίθεοι "half-gods."

(xxiv 80–84)" (Nagy 1999:160n1, Ch. 9§16n1). In other words, the epic knows a future fate for Achilles' tomb as well: his σῆμα upon the Hellespont (*Odyssey* xxiv 80–84) is imagined as erased in the flood that wipes out all material traces of the heroic age.

At its very center, the *Iliad* foresees its own end.[23] The men who fought at Troy and the material traces of their existence will all someday be utterly wiped out. And along with those men and their walls will perish their κλέος "fame" and their very names. Yet, the future destruction is held in deferment by the epic tradition itself; though fragile, the epic will strive to maintain the status of its heroes and their walls frozen in time. The effect is a kind of double-vision representing the temporal depth of Achilles himself—the ultimate "dead man walking"—for both man and structure, while here now, are doomed to be destroyed later. In other words, they are both here and gone at once.

In the next section we will see how Poseidon calls for the destruction of the Achaean wall because he is afraid that the κλέος of the Greeks and their wall will outlast the wall he built himself for the Trojans. In this context, the image of the wall erased from the shore implies the erasure of Greek κλέος as well.[24]

2. The Trojan Wall: The Temporality of Divine Artifact

In the *Iliad* the city of Troy is consistently described as being surrounded by a massive wall built around it (τεῖχος).[25] The wall is of great height, as indicated by the adjectives which describe it: αἰπύς "sheer, steep" (VI 327, XI 181: αἰπύ τε τεῖχος) and ὑψηλός "high, lofty" (XVI 702: τείχεος ὑψηλοῖο). The wall has towers (πύργοι),[26] described once as "well built" (ἐϋδμήτους ὑπὸ πύργους, XXII 195), and "beautiful" battlements (ἐπάλξεις: cf. καλῇσιν ἐπάλξεσιν, XXII 3).[27] It

---

[23] Compare Scodel 1982:48, "At its very center, the poem places its events far away in a past which becomes remote and fated not only to end, but to vanish."

[24] See Scodel 1982:48 with n38. The Greek mytho-poetic tradition preserves the concept of the utter eradication of all the remnants of the Trojan war: compare Euripides *Helen* 108, ὥστ' οὐδ' ἴχνος γε τειχέων εἶναι σαφές, "... that the traces of the walls not be visible."

[25] A complete tabulation of τεῖχος (in its various nominal cases) in the *Iliad* referring to the Trojan wall includes: IV 34; VI 327, 388, 434, 436; VIII 533; IX 353; XI 181; XIII 764; XVI 702, 714; XVII 404, 558; XVIII 256, 279; XX 30, 145; XXI 277, 295, 299, 446, 463, 516, 530, 534, 536, 540, 557, 608; XXII 4, 16, 56, 85, 99, 112, 144, 146, 168, 237, 507; XXIII 81. Study of the use of the word τεῖχος clearly indicates a pattern of frequency both during the "domestic" scenes of Book VI and the battle scenes that take place around the city, spanning Books XVI through XXII.

[26] *Iliad* III 153–154; VI 386, 431; VIII 164–166, 518–519; XVI 700; XVIII 274; XXI 526; XXII 195.

[27] *Iliad* XXII 3 is the only use of ἐπάλξεις in the *Iliad* used to describe the Trojan wall. Compare XII 258, 263, 308, 375, 381, 397, 406, 424, 430 for the term describing the Achaean wall (see further discussion below). The adjective καλός in Homer indicates, in its primary sense, the beauty achieved through the perfection of material craftsmanship (I owe this observation to Ann Bergren); hence, the "beautiful battlements" work in concert with the "well-built towers,"

has a number of gates (πύλαι) once called "lofty" (ὑψηλαί τε πύλαι, XVIII 275),[28] "tightly fitted" double-doors (σάνιδες: cf. σανίδας πυκινῶς ἀραρυίας, XXI 535; cf. σανίδες τ' ἐπὶ τῆς ἀραρυῖαι, XVIII 275),[29] and bolts to hold the doors shut (ὀχῆες, XXI 537). The wall is the *sine qua non* of the city of Troy; more than just their defense against invaders, it is the very means by which the *polis* defines itself as separate from everything else (cf. Scully 1990). The architecture of the wall delimits inside from outside, creating relationships of identity and alterity.[30]

The Trojan wall is well constructed. Its "well built towers" (XXII 195), "beautiful battlements" (XXII 3), and "tightly fitted" double-doors (XVIII 275, XXI 535) all designate it as the product of master craftsmanship. In fact, the epic tradition knows the city wall to be the product of the gods, built by Poseidon and Apollo while they were working under the employment of Laomedon, the king of Troy in the generation before Priam's rule.[31] The story appears in two separate passages, the first mentioned in reference to the construction of the Achaean wall in Book VII, and second during the *Theomakhia* in Book XXI. In

---

[28] both indicating the expert craftsmanship of the wall. See further the discussion on Poseidon as builder of the Trojan wall below.

Iliad III 145; VI 237, 307, 392; VIII 58; IX 354; XVI 712; XVIII 275; XXI 537; XXII 99.

[29] Compare the three other uses of σάνιδες in the *Iliad* used to describe the Achaean wall: XII 121, 453, 461. The "double doors" of the Achaean wall are never described as "fitted, joined" or given any attributes suggesting superior craftsmanship.

[30] Compare Gottfried Semper's theory of architecture as vertical space enclosures: "As *the first partition wall* made with hands, *the first vertical division of space invented by man*, we would like to recognize the screen, the fence made of plaited and tied sticks and branches, whose making requires a technique which nature hands to man, as it were. The passage from the plaiting of branches to the plaiting of hemp for similar domestic purposes is easy and natural" (G. Semper *Der Stil in den technischen und tektonischen Kunsten oder praktische Aesthetik*, 2nd ed. [Frankfurt 1861–1863] 212, cited in Rykwert 1981:30; emphasis added). See further Bergren 1992:38–39n41 and Bergren 1995:218n43 for a discussion of the role of the female as architect *par excellence*, noting the ability to weave attributed especially to the female both in early Greek thought and in Freudian analytic theory, and the identification by Vitruvius and Semper of hanging textiles serving as the first and most fundamental of architectural edifices—the wall.

[31] There seems to be some question as to whether Laomedon is Priam's father or not; Priam's regular patronymic associates Priam with Dardanus (10 times in the *Iliad*, occurring in all grammatical cases: e.g. Δαρδανίδης Πρίαμος: III 303, VII 366, XXII 352, XXIV 629; Πριάμοιο ... Δαρδανίδαο: V 159, XXI 34; Δαρδανίδη Πρίαμῳ: XIII 376; Δαρδανίδην Πρίαμον: XXIV 631; Δαρδινίδη Πρίαμε: XXIV 171 [cf. XXIV 354]). He is identified as the son of Laomedon at XX 236 as part of Aeneas' genealogical history, but is given the patronymic Λαομεδοντιάδη only once (III 250). Andrews 1965:35 notes the unusualness of Priam's patronymic derived neither from his father nor grandfather: "This is the only exception to the Homeric rule of practice that the patronymic is derived only from the father, or very rarely from the grandfather; Priam is the fifth generation from Dardanos." He goes on to suggest that "at some earlier stage in the tradition Priam really was son of Dardanos," but Andrew's reconstruction of pre-Homeric myth, while suggestive, can only remain non-probative.

Book VII, Poseidon expresses anger over the construction of the Achaean wall, for it threatens to deprive him of *kleos* for the construction of the Trojan wall.[32]

τοῦ δ᾽ ἤτοι κλέος ἔσται, ὅσσον τ᾽ ἐπικίδναται ἠώς,
τοῦ δ᾽ ἐπιλήσονται, ὅ τ᾽ ἐγὼ καὶ Φοῖβος Ἀπόλλων
ἥρῳ Λαομέδοντι πολίσσαμεν ἀθλήσαντε.

In truth, I tell you, there will be *kleos* of it, as far as the dawn spreads,
and they will forget about the one, which I and Phoibos Apollo
built for the hero Laomedon through our toil.

Iliad VII 451–453

It is unseemly that mortal architecture should outlast immortal architecture; the craftwork of the immortals is itself immortal, after all. And yet, since the Achaeans are bound to sack Troy and overthrow its wall, their own wall will outlive Poseidon's wall—a wall meant to last forever. The point is made explicit in the second passage. In Book XXI, Poseidon chides Apollo for siding with the Trojans despite the rough treatment they received in recompense for their labor:

νηπύτι᾽, ὡς ἄνοον κραδίην ἔχες· οὐδέ νυ τῶν περ
μέμνηαι, ὅσα δὴ πάθομεν κακὰ Ἴλιον ἀμφί
μοῦνοι νῶϊ θεῶν, ὅτ᾽ ἀγήνορι Λαομέδοντι
πὰρ Διὸς ἐλθόντες θητεύσαμεν εἰς ἐνιαυτόν
μισθῷ ἔπι ῥητῷ, ὃ δὲ σημαίνων ἐπέτελλεν.
<u>ἤτοι ἐγὼ Τρώεσσι πόλιν πέρι τεῖχος ἔδειμα</u>
εὐρύ τε καὶ <u>μάλα καλόν</u>, <u>ἵν᾽</u> ἄρρηκτος πόλις εἴη·
Φοῖβε, σὺ δ᾽ εἰλίποδας ἕλικας βοῦς βουκολέεσκες
Ἴδης ἐν κνημοῖσι πολυπτύχου ὑληέσσης.
ἀλλ᾽ ὅτε δὴ μισθοῖο τέλος πολυγηθέες ὧραι
ἐξέφερον, τότε νῶϊ βιήσατο μισθὸν ἅπαντα
Λαομέδων ἔκπαγλος, ἀπειλήσας δ᾽ ἀπέπεμπεν·

---

[32] Commentators have long held this passage suspect; Zenodotus, Aristophanes, and Aristarchus all found the scene to be an interpolation (see Scholia A at *Iliad* VII 443–464), and recently Kirk 1985:289 agreed, largely because the scene "interrupts a generally workmanlike narrative and is anticlimactic in itself, while the new Achaean wall can hardly be seen as a serious rival to the huge enceinte of Troy (452f.)." I cannot agree with Kirk's assessment of the passage. First, passages athetized by Zenodotus, Aristophanes, and Aristarchus on the grounds that they repeat information given elsewhere in the epic can have no validity in light of the *Iliad*'s oral composition; moreover, the passage poses no interruption to the scene, but follows naturally after the description of its construction; and finally, as for the degree to which the Achaean wall constitutes a threat to Poseidon's *kleos*, see my discussion below.

σὺν μὲν ὅ γ᾽ ἠπείλησε πόδας καὶ χεῖρας ὕπερθεν
δήσειν, καὶ περάαν νήσων ἔπι τηλεδαπάων,
στεῦτο δ᾽ ὅ γ᾽ ἀμφοτέρων ἀπολεψέμεν οὔατα χαλκῷ.
νῶϊ δὲ ἄψορροι κίομεν κεκοτηότι θυμῷ,
μισθοῦ χωόμενοι, τὸν ὑποστὰς οὐκ ἐτέλεσσεν.

Foolish boy, do you have a thoughtless heart? Don't you remember the
      things,
the very many evil ones we suffered around Ilion,
we two alone of the gods, when to haughty Laomedon
from Zeus we came to be servants for a year
for an arranged wage, and he commanded us, acting like a master.
<u>Yes, I tell you, I built a wall around the city for the Trojans</u>,
a wide and <u>exceedingly beautiful</u> one, <u>so the city would be unbreakable</u>.
And you, Phoibos, tended the curved-horned cattle
in the mountain valleys of many-furrowed, wooded Ida.
But when the much-rejoiced season brought about the end of our hire,
then he forcefully withheld all our wages from us,
outrageous Laomedon did, and he sent us away with a threat.
This man threatened to bind our feet together and our hands above,
and sell us off to far-lying islands,
and he gestured as if he would cut off both of our ears with bronze.
And we two went back, wroth at heart
and angry over the wage which he promised but did not fulfill.

Iliad XXI 441–457

Poseidon's wall, like all divine works, is emphasized as being both "exceedingly beautiful" (μάλα καλόν, XXI 447) and "unbreakable" (ἄρρηκτος, XXI 447), a term formally equivalent with the adjective "imperishable" (ἄφθιτον) said of Hephaistos' craft.[33] The verbal adjective ἄρ(ρ)ηκτος is formed from the alpha-privative plus adjectival stem in *-το- from the root *ϝρηγ- (cf. ῥήγνυμι) "break," and hence indicates the wall's "unbroken" status.[34] The privative force of the prefix denotes a temporal element to the concept: Poseidon's wall is "unbreakable" only because it has not yet been broken (cf. Benveniste 1975:166). Homer is silent about the reason why the two gods served the Trojan king. Later sources supplement the myth, explaining that Poseidon and Apollo were forced to

---

[33] In this passage the wall is attributed to Poseidon alone, while Apollo tended Laomedon's flocks; at *Iliad* VII 452–453, however, Poseidon said that both he and Apollo built the walls. I agree with Richardson (1993) that this is "hardly a serious contradiction" (91).

[34] On the form, see Chantraine 1968–1980:972, s.v. ῥήγνυμι, and Ebeling 1963:I.171, s.v. ἄρρηκτος.

work for Laomedon either as punishment for their rebellion against Zeus,[35] or perhaps in order to "test" Laomedon to determine whether he is righteous or not.[36] Our concern here is merely the fact that the Trojan wall is identified as the work of the gods (Poseidon and Apollo), and is characterized as beautiful and unbroken.[37]

[35] Various sources explain that Poseidon was punished for being party to the *coup d' état* referred to at *Iliad* I 395–406, when Thetis freed Zeus from his bonds and led Briareos to quash the rebellion. Apollo may have been punished for killing the Cyclopes, ostensibly in anger over the death of his son Asclepius (killed by Zeus), but presumably in a rebellious attempt to deprive Zeus of the source of his lightning bolts (see my discussion of this motif in chapter 5 below). Otherwise, Apollo may have been part of the "binding" at *Iliad* I 400 (with some commentators following Zenodotus' reading of Apollo for Athena in that line: see Scholia A at *Iliad* I 400, Erbse). The principle sources are: Pindar *Olympian* 8.30–46 with scholia at *Olympian* 8.31/41; Hellanicus (*FGrHist* 4 F 26a) *apud* the scholia of the Geneva manuscript of *Iliad* XXI 444c, Nicole; Hellanicus (*FGrHist* 4 F 26b) *apud* Scholia A at *Iliad* XX 146, Erbse; Ovid *Metamorphoses* XI 194–210; ps.-Apollodorus 2.5.9; Lucian *On Sacrifices* 4; Hyginus *Fabulae* 89.1–2; *Mythographi Vatacani* I 136, II 193. For the labor as punishment, see: Lucian *On Sacrifices* 4, *Jupiter confutatus* 8; Scholia T at *Iliad* XXI 444d, Erbse; Scholia vetera at Pindar *Olympian* 8.31/41; J. Tzetzes, scholion on Lycrophon 34. For modern critical work, see Fontenrose 1983, Lang 1983, Caldwell 1987, Slatkin 1986 and 1991. Especially useful are Lang's (1983) reconstruction of the myth from its scattered references throughout the *Iliad*, and Slatkin's (1986, 1991) analysis of the inter-traditional references in the *Iliad* activated by the character of Thetis.

[36] See, for instance, Eustathius 1245, 49: οἱ μὲν αἰτίαν τῆς ῥηθείσης θητείας ἀπέδωκαν τὴν ἐκ τοῦ Διὸς ποινήν, ὅτι συνδῆσαι αὐτὸν ἐβουλεύσαντο. ἕτεροι δέ φασιν, ὅτι οὐχὶ ἄκοντες, ἀλλ' ἑκόντες ἐθήτευσαν ξένοις ἐοικότες, ἵνα τὴν Λαομέδοντος ὕβριν πειράσωσιν, "Some attributed the cause of the indentured servitude to Zeus' punishment, because they had wanted to bind him. But others say that they weren't unwilling, but were willing to be servants, and they made themselves look like strangers in order to test Laomedon's hubris." See further Metrodorus (*FGrHist* 43 F 2 = 70 B 4 DK) *apud* the scholia of the Geneva manuscript of *Iliad* XXI 444c, Nicole, and Scholia T at *Iliad* XXI 444d, Erbse. The concept of gods visiting men in disguise in order to "test" them appears in the *Odyssey*, where the other suitors warn Antinous not to abuse the disguised Odysseus, lest he be "some god come down from heaven, since the gods liken themselves to strangers from far away, put on all manner of shapes, and visit cities to behold both the hubris and righteousness of men" (*Odyssey* xvii 484–487).

[37] There does appear to be some confusion regarding which Trojan walls Poseidon and Apollo actually built: was it the walls of Priam's Troy, to be sacked by the Greeks, or the walls of King Laomedon's Troy, previously sacked by Herakles in anger over Laomedon's failure to pay the hero the horses promised for the rescue of his daughter Hesione? The *Iliad* does refer to Laomedon's agreement with Herakles, his failure to pay, and the subsequent sack of the city (V 640–642, 648–651; and perhaps XIV 250–256 and XX 145–148, on which see Lang 1983 *passim* and Kirk 1990 *ad loc.*). The issue is more complex than I can deal with adequately here, but I wish to suggest that the *Iliad* elides any distinction between the two walls. Poseidon's anger at the Achaean wall and the *kleos* it will have makes no sense if the wall Poseidon built had *already* been sacked by Herakles; the force of Poseidon's complaint must lie in the fact that a hastily-built wall of mortal manufacture—i.e. the Achaean defensive wall—will outlive the "unbreakable" wall built by Poseidon himself. Scodel (1982) has shown that the narrative of the destruction of the Achaean wall has incorporated other traditional "destruction" stories and motifs, including the story of a great "flood." It may be that the Trojan wall was similarly a locus of destruction stories, in which the invasions of Herakles and the Achaeans fuse into a single event. For a different view, see Fehling 1991.

The "unbreakable" quality of the divinely-crafted Trojan wall sets it apart from the mortal-made Achaean wall.[38] During the fierce fighting about the Greek wall during the "Great Day" of fighting which spans from Books XI through XVIII, Sarpedon and Hektor penetrate the Achaean wall. Although the Achaeans had hoped to build a wall that would last, as Nestor explains to Agamemnon, it has failed to do so:

τεῖχος μὲν γὰρ δὴ κατερήριπεν, ᾧ ἐπέπιθμεν
ἄρρηκτον νηῶν τε καὶ αὐτῶν εἶλαρ ἔσεσθαι.

For indeed, the wall has gone down which we trusted would be an unbreakable protection for both our ships and us.

Iliad XIV 55–56

The Achaeans trusted in the wall (τεῖχος ... ᾧ ἐπέπιθμεν, XIV 54), believing that it would be an unbreakable protection (ἄρρηκτον ... εἶλαρ, XIV 55), but in vain: the wall has fallen (τεῖχος ... κατερήριπεν, XIV 55). Agamemnon's response to Nestor touches on the same themes of hope frustrated by the ultimate inability of the wall to hold off the Trojans:

τεῖχος δ᾽ οὐκ ἔχραισμε τετυγμένον, οὐδέ τι τάφρος,
ᾗ ἔπι πολλὰ πάθον Δαναοί, ἔλποντο δὲ θυμῷ
ἄρρηκτον νηῶν τε καὶ αὐτῶν εἶλαρ ἔσεσθαι.

The wall we built didn't keep us safe, nor at all did the trench,
over which the Danaäns suffered many things, but they were hopeful at
      heart
that it would be an unbreakable protection to their ships and to them.

Iliad XIV 66–68

In both passages, the Greeks express hope that the protection provided by the defensive wall would last. The use of verbs of "trusting" (πείθω, XIV 55) and "hoping" (ἐλπίζω, XIV 67) with the future infinitive ἔσεσθαι (XIV 56, 68) note the future projection of the wall's "unbroken" status. They hoped it would be "unbreakable," but the wall has failed to keep the Achaeans safe (κατερήριπεν, XIV 55; οὐκ ἔχραισμε, XIV 66). It is instructive to note the Greek wall is called "unbreakable" only in contrary-to-fact scenarios; the Achaeans trusted and hoped it would remain unbreakable (ἄρρηκτον ... ἔσεσθαι, XIV 55, 68), but events have proven otherwise. The implication is that man-made craft cannot match

---

[38] See S. Morris 1997:617–618 for Near Eastern parallels of gods building cities for men (e.g. Uruk in the Mesopotamian epic of Gilgamesh) and then destroying them in anger or divine retribution.

divine craft. Only the Trojan wall can be truly ἄρρηκτον "unbreakable" in a durable way, as if the divine origin of the Trojan wall guarantees its impregnability. While inside their wall, the Trojans cannot be taken by force.[39] And yet, the epic tradition relates that this unbreakable wall does in fact fall—although not within the scope of the *Iliad*.

In Homer, then, we find that divine craftwork itself exists within human temporality: although it is durable, it is not eternally enduring. The concept of the god-made wall of the Trojans broken by mortal forces does not appear as such elsewhere in the tradition, and the very problem of the necessarily broken Trojan wall prompts a narrative *aition* in extra-Homeric folktale, in circulation from at least Pindar's time. The contradictory logic of the divine craftwork breached by mortals finds apology in the non-Homeric tradition that Aiakos, father of Peleus and Telamon, worked as an assistant to Poseidon and Apollo while they built the wall.[40] For, as the ancient scholiast to Pindar's *Olympian Odes* explains, the section of the wall built by the mortal builder *was* vulnerable:

οὗτοι [δὲ] συνεργὸν εἵλοντο τὸν Αἰακόν, ἐπειδὴ ἦν αὐτῷ πεπρωμένον, τῷ τείχει, πολέμου γενομένου πυρὶ καταφλεχθῆναι πολλῷ. οὐ γὰρ ἦν δυνατὸν ἁλῶναι αὐτό, εἰ τὸ πᾶν ἔργον ἦν θεῶν.

---

[39] There are three passages in the *Iliad*, however, which seem to allude to attempts to storm the city walls: (1) Andromache tries to convince Hektor to stay near the city instead of taking the field around the Achaean ships by noting a single structural weakness in the wall at VI 433–439, esp. 433–434, stating "there [sc. near the fig tree] most of all the city is mountable and the wall open to attack" (ἔνθα μάλιστα | ἀμβατός ἐστι πόλις καὶ ἐπίδρομον ἔπλετο τεῖχος). (2) Patroklos attempts to climb the wall and is prevented by Apollo: "Three times Patroklos tried to mount upon the bend of the lofty wall and three times Apollo drove him back away by thrusting at the bright shield with his immortal hands" (τρὶς μὲν ἐπ᾽ ἀγκῶνος βῆ τείχεος ὑψηλοῖο | Πάτροκλος, τρὶς δ᾽ αὐτὸν ἀπεστυφέλιξεν Ἀπόλλων | χείρεσσ᾽ ἀθανάτῃσι φαεινὴν ἀσπίδα νύσσων, XVI 702–704). (3) Priam expresses fear that Achilles might leap the wall in his destructive fury: "I am afraid lest this destructive man leap inside the wall" (δείδα γὰρ μὴ οὖλος ἀνὴρ ἐς τεῖχος ἅληται, XXI 536). Note the important role of the *vertical* component of the wall and its vulnerability to attack. On ἀμβατός "mountable" and ἐπίδρομον "open to attack" in VI 433–434, see Scully 1990:50. Compare *Iliad* XIII 683–684 where one portion of the Achaean wall is described as "built closest to the ground" (τεῖχος ἐδέδμητο χθαμαλώτατον, XIII 683) and therefore most vulnerable to the Trojans. The description of Patroklos attempting to "mount the slope of the lofty wall" (ἐπ᾽ ἀγκῶνος βῆ τείχεος ὑψηλοῖο, XVI 702) emphasizes the fighter's strength and fury as he attempts to scale the wall. On Andromache's tactical advice to Hektor, see the sensitive reading of Schadewaldt 1965:219 (translated at Jones and Wright 1997:134).

[40] See Fontenrose 1983:55, 62n5. In his very interesting study, Fontenrose adduces parallels between the story of the construction of the walls of Troy with the building of Asgard's walls in Snorri Sturlson's Icelandic Prose Edda; he concludes that the two stories are possibly derived from an Indo-European story-type of "an employer cheating a workman of the pay he has promised him, when the workman either has completed the task or is kept by trickery from its certain completion" (61). For further discussion, see Stubbs 1959.

They [i.e. Poseidon and Apollo] chose Aiakos to be their co-worker, since it was fated for it—i.e. for the wall—to be completely burned down in a great fire during the coming war. For it would not be able to be captured, if it were entirely the work of gods.[41]

Scholia vetera at Pindar *Olympian* 8.33/44b, Drachmann

The fact that the wall does break is blamed on structural weakness at the point where the mortal architect worked, for this would not have been possible had the wall been *entirely* the work of the gods (εἰ τὸ π̱α̱ν̱ ἔργον ἦν θεῶν).

An earlier attested alternate tradition is recorded in the epic Cycle poems, especially the *Little Iliad* and the *Sack of Troy*.[42] Both texts—surviving only in fragmentary form—apparently described the breach of the city wall as a direct result of the "Trojan Horse" which was built too large to fit inside the city gates, thereby necessitating the partial destruction of the city wall by the Trojans themselves. Proclus summarizes the plot of the *Little Iliad* (*Ilias Parua*):

οἱ δὲ Τρῶες τῶν κακῶν ὑπολαβόντες ἀπηλλάχθαι, τόν τε δούρειον ἵππον εἰς τὴν πόλιν εἰσδέχονται, <u>διελόντες μέρος τι τοῦ τείχους</u>, καὶ εὐωχοῦνται ὡς νενικηκότες τοὺς Ἕλληνας.

The Trojans, for their part, supposing they had been delivered from evils, both received the wooden horse into the city <u>by destroying a certain portion of the wall</u>, and feasted sumptuously as though they had conquered the Greeks.

Davies 1998:53 = Bernabé 1987:75

---

[41] See further Euphorion (fr. 58 M) *apud* Scholia at Pindar *Olympian* 8.31/41a, Drachmann. Pindar himself (*Olympian* 8.32–36) is more elliptical, claiming that the gods chose Aiakos as their συνεργόν τείχεος, since "it had been fated that in the city-sacking battles of the rising wars, it would breathe forth ravenous smoke" (ἦν ὅτι νιν πεπρωμένον | ὀρνυμένων πολέμων | πτολιπόρθοις ἐν μάχαις | λάβρον ἀμπνεῦσαι καπνόν).

[42] On the Cycle poem fragments, see Huxley 1969, Davies 1989, Burgess 1996, 2001, 2004, 2009. The *Ilias Parua* and *Ilioupersis*—separate poems attributed to Lesches of Pyrrha or perhaps Mytilene and Arctinus of Miletus, respectively (cf. Huxley 1969)—both deal with the events of the Trojan War that take place after the events narrated in the *Iliad*. The two poems apparently overlapped in some details, particularly how the Trojans led the wooden horse into the city. Proclus' summary of the two poems attempts, artificially, "to produce the impression of a single coherent narrative" (Davies 1989:60; cf. Huxley 1969:144, 147). According to Lesbian tradition, Lesches pre-dated Terpander (*flourit* 676 BCE: cf. Hellanicus *FGrHist* 4 F 32a), whereas Arctinus was Homer's pupil, born in the ninth Olympiad (744/741 BCE: cf. Artemon *FGrHist* 443 F 2). Huxley (1969) thinks "Lesches and Arktinos, then, can reasonably be supposed to have competed about 700 B.C." (144). The relationship between Homer and the Epic Cycle poems remains a controversial issue, and the scholarly bibliography is vast. A select list of works on the topic I have found useful include Kullmann 1960, 1984, Griffin 1977, Clark 1986, Slatkin 1991, Dowden 1996, Willcock 1997, Burgess 2001, and West 2002, 2003, all with further bibliography.

Virgil also incorporates this detail in his description of the sack of Troy, for his Sinon explains how Calchas ordered the wooden horse to be constructed *too large* to be taken in through the city gates (*Aeneid* 2.185–187),[43] so that the Trojans tore down their own wall. Aeneas narrates at *Aeneid* 2.234, "We breached the outer-walls and layed open the inner-walls of the city" (*diuidimus muros et moenia pandimus urbis*).[44] According to this version of the tradition, the Greeks are unable to breach the wall; it can only be broken by the Trojans themselves. Hence, the deception of the wooden horse (narrated at *Odyssey* viii 492–495, 511–515, cf. *Odyssey* iv 271–289, xi 523–537, xv 71) is designed to induce the Trojans to take the horse inside the city.[45]

In short, the impregnable wall of Troy does indeed fall within the epic tradition. Homer does not narrate the breach of the city's wall and its ultimate

---

[43] Virgil *Aeneid* 2.185–187: *Hanc tamen immensam Calchas attollere molem | roboribus textis caeloque edu-cere iussit | ne recipi portis aut duci in moenia posset*: "Nonetheless, Calchas commanded that they raise up this immense structure out of woven oak-wood and build it up to the sky, that it could not be received by the gates or led into the walls."

[44] See Williams 1972:I.230 on the difference between Virgil's *muros*—"the city walls which they breach by the gate"—and *moenia*—"the buildings within."

[45] The "Trojan Horse" is first represented on a fragment of a Boeotian bronze fibula (London, British Museum 3205; see Hampe 1936:plates 2–3) offering a literal depiction of a wooden horse on wheels and small hatches around its belly; a second representation appears on the Cycladic relief pithos discovered in Mykonos in 1961 (first and definitively published by Ervin 1963:37–75, plates 17–28); see also the colossal sized horse on wheels with hatches on its side and neck in which are seen the heads and arms of soldiers (Friis Johansen 1967:26–28 with figures 1–2); the Late Corinthian aryballos in Paris depicting a large horse with hatches and fighters emerging from the horse and engaging with the enemy (de Ridder *Catalogue des vases peints de la Bibliothèque Nationale* [Paris, 1902] No. 186; *CVA*, pl. 18); and a fragment of an Attic vase showing men climbing down the leg of a large horse (Berlin F 1723; see *Jahrbuch des Deutschen Archäologischen Instituts* 1931:51 fig. 5; *Mitteilungen des Deutschen Archäologischen Instituts: Athenische Abteilung* 1962:54 fig. 1). See Sparkes 1975 on the Trojan Horse in Classical art.

In later writers the "horse" was understood to be a kind of "battering ram" used to force entry into a fortified town: see Pliny *Natural History* 7.202, Servius at Virgil *Aeneid* 2.15, and Pausanius 1.23.8. Hainsworth (1988) attributes the notion of the "horse" as a battering ram to anachronistic "rationalism"; instead, he suggests instead that it is "the elaboration of a motif of myth or folk-tale" and compares the tale of the Egyptian capture of Joppa by concealing men in pithoi (379, citing Pritchard 1969:22–23). However, Anderson 1970–1971, Rouman and Held 1972, and S. Morris 1995 (esp. 227–229, 232–235 with figures 15.12A–D, 15.14, and 15.15) have con-vincingly argued that far from being a late "rationalization," the Greek tradition of the "Trojan Horse" may well be a distorted memory of battering-ram devices used in Near Eastern town-sieges. Two Assyrian relief carvings depicting an assault on Upa by Tiglath-Pileser III (745–727 BCE) and a campaign against Gezer led by Esarhaddon (681–669 BCE) reveal wheeled siege-engines equipped with hatches (S. Morris 1995:234–235, figures 15.13–14). The siege-engines were covered with hides and had "tusk-like" protrusions, hence motivating the visual metaphor (Anderson 1970–1971:24). For our purposes, it is important to note the association between the horse and the breaching of the city walls—an association made all the more strongly if the tradi-tion of the Trojan Horse rests upon memory of a pre-Homeric Assyrian siege-engine.

destruction in the *Iliad*; however, he does allude to these events several times.[46] The sheer number of passages alluding to the sack of Troy creates the sensation for the audience that the wall has indeed already been breached and the city already been taken, since Homer's audience would have been able to supplement non-narrated elements from their familiarity with the entire story arc.[47] I wish to emphasize this image of a wall that is *temporarily* still standing, for it functions within the system of *objective duration* we have identified and been discussing in this section of my study. The Trojan wall, like the wooden ships of the Achaeans, will be affected by the passage of time, for in time the wall will be breached and the city will perish in flames. And yet, like the bodies of Sarpedon, Patroklos, and Hektor, the wall is preserved for the time being; its disintegration is guaranteed, but is only *virtually* narrated by the *Iliad*. In order to apprehend this structure more clearly, I wish to study in brief the system of allusions Homer makes to the future downfall of Troy.

---

[46] See Duckworth 1933 on Homer's practice of "foreshadowing," including events that are not narrated within the epics themselves. Moore 1921 offers a more specialized study of the use of "prophecy" to foreshadow events in the epic. For more recent work on foreshadowing ("prolepsis") in Homeric epic, see de Jong 1985, 1987, 1997, 2001, 2002, and Richardson 1990. See Dickson 1992 for a fascinating study that explicates the narratological strategies of prolepsis (foreshadowing) and analepsis (flashback) through reference to the epic figures of the prophet Calchas and the aged advisor Nestor.

[47] See Nagler's discussion of Lord's work on South-Slavic oral poetry: "according to Professor Lord, a South-Slavic singer will occasionally omit a structurally significant portion from one of his songs. When confronted with such an omission, his first reaction will be to deny it outright, 'Of course I sang that part'" (Nagler 1967:308). Nagler explains that his own field work in Crete corroborates Lord's findings: "Cretan singers often break off a performance of a song, not only long before the end of the piece, but even in the middle of a sentence, with resulting loss of intelligibility. Of course, their concentration on the music partially explains this catalexis of the words, but it is also to be explained *by the presence of the omitted portion in the memory of the hearers*" (308n70; emphasis added). In other words, the entire story or story arc (Nagler's "Gestalt") exists in the memory of both the singer and audience, such that references to one part of the story may well activate memory of another element of the story, even though that element is not narrated in full.

Ruth Scodel (1997) has recently argued that the assumption that "poet and audience both knew the entire tradition extremely well" is problematic (202). In an insightful close-reading of the openings of the *Iliad* and *Odyssey*, including how characters are first introduced, Scodel demonstrates that the works themselves do not require their audiences to know "the entire tradition" beforehand, but rather supplies whatever information it needs at the appropriate time (Scodel 1997, *passim*). I accept Scodel's argument here, but wish to note that even in her minimal-familiarity theory, certain information must be assumed to be known by the audience, which Scodel herself notes: "If we look at the opening of the *Iliad*, we can again see immediately that the Trojan War itself is taken for granted: there is no explanation of the setting at all" (206). The multiple presages of the city's future destruction from the *Iliad*'s perspective, along with the scattered references to the Trojan Horse from the *Odyssey*'s perspective indicate that the Greek sack of Troy by means of stratagem forms part of the prerequisite knowledge of the Homeric audience.

3. The Fall of Troy and the Future-Perfect in Homeric Epic

The Homeric allusions to the sack of Troy take several forms, including prophetic speeches by the gods themselves—particularly Zeus—as well as prophetic interpretations by the mortal seers within the poem. Hence, Zeus foretells Hektor's *aristeia* and Patroklos' death:

οὐ γὰρ πρὶν πολέμου ἀποπαύσεται ὄβριμος Ἕκτωρ,
πρὶν ὄρθαι παρὰ ναῦφι ποδώκεα Πηλεΐωνα
ἤματι τῷ, ὅτ’ ἂν οἳ μὲν ἐπὶ πρύμνῃσι μάχωνται
στείνει ἐν αἰνοτάτῳ περὶ Πατρόκλοιο θανόντος·
ὣς γὰρ θέσφατόν ἐστι.

For not sooner will stout Hektor be stayed from war
until he stirs up beside the ships the swift-footed son of Peleus
on that day—whenever it is—when they will fight by the beached
        ships
in the most dreadful, narrow place around the fallen Patroklos.
For so it is fated to be.

Iliad VIII 473–477

Zeus speaks this early prophecy to Hera, accompanied by a threat lest she interfere with his plans any further. The details are not yet clearly delineated. We are told that Hektor will be unstoppable until he stirs up Achilles, and that the two will fight over Patroklos' corpse; Zeus remains silent on *how* all of this is to come about, however. He is merely insistent on the fact that it is a "fated"—literally "god-spoken"—outcome (ὣς γὰρ θέσφατόν ἐστι, VIII 477). In Book XV, Zeus supplies a more detailed outline for the rest of the *Iliad* including the eventual fall of Troy:

Ἕκτορα δ’ ὀτρύνῃσι μάχην ἐς Φοῖβος Ἀπόλλων,
αὖτις δ’ ἐμπνεύσῃσι μένος, λελάθῃ δ’ ὀδυνάων
αἵ νῦν μιν τείρουσι κατὰ φρένας, αὐτὰρ Ἀχαιούς
αὖτις ἀποστρέψῃσιν ἀνάλκιδα φύζαν ἐνόρσας,
φεύγοντες δ’ ἐν νηυσὶ πολυκλήϊσι πέσωσιν
Πηλεΐδεω Ἀχιλῆος. ὃ δ’ ἀνστήσει ὃν ἑταῖρον
Πάτροκλον· τὸν δὲ κτενεῖ ἔγχεϊ φαίδιμος Ἕκτωρ
Ἰλίου προπάροιθε, πολεῖς ὀλέσαντ’ αἰζηούς
τοὺς ἄλλους, μετὰ δ’ υἱὸν ἐμὸν Σαρπηδόνα δῖον·
τοῦ δὲ χολωσάμενος κτενεῖ Ἕκτορα δῖος Ἀχιλλεύς.
ἐκ τοῦ δ’ ἄν τοι ἔπειτα παλίωξιν παρὰ νηῶν

αἰὲν ἐγὼ τεύχοιμι διαμπερές, εἰς ὅ κ' Ἀχαιοί
Ἴλιον αἰπὺ ἕλοιεν Ἀθηναίης διὰ βουλάς.

Let Phoibos Apollo rouse Hektor to battle,
and let him breathe might into him once again, that he may forget
        the pains
which now wear him down in his heart, but the Achaeans—
let him stir up strengthless panic into them and turn them back once
        more;
let them in their flight fall among the well-benched ships
of Peleus' son Achilles. He will stand up his companion,
Patroklos, and glorious Hektor will kill that man with his spear
before Ilion, after he has destroyed many other young men
among them my own son, brilliant Sarpedon.
In anger over him brilliant Achilles will kill Hektor.
And from that point then, I tell you, I will bring to pass ever
        continuously
that the Achaeans turn around from their flight, until they
should capture lofty Ilion through the plan of Athena.

Iliad XV 59–71

Zeus' speech here fills in the details left unspecified in his earlier pronounce-ment; he projects the plot of the remainder of the *Iliad* and beyond. Hektor will return and shift the tide of the battle; Achilles will send Patroklos into battle, where Patroklos will fight, kill Sarpedon, and be killed in turn; Achilles will kill Hektor out of anger for his fallen companion; Troy will eventually fall. The means by which the Achaeans will sack Troy—the Trojan Horse, ambiguously called the "plan of Athena" (Ἀθηναίης διὰ βουλάς, XV 71) here—is to be spelled out only in the Cycle tradition. Its occurrence, however, is guaranteed as part of the *Dios boulē*, the "plan of Zeus," which governs the events of the epic itself.[48]

---

[48] *Iliad* I 5 posits the *Dios boulē* as the name for the epic's plot: Διὸς δ' ἐτελείτο βουλή "the plan of Zeus was accomplished." Scholia bT at *Iliad* I 5c (Erbse) indicates an ancient debate whether *Dios boulē* refers only to his promise to Thetis to honor Achilles (as held by Aristarchus) or whether it refers to the entire trajectory of the Trojan War. Indeed, the poet of the *Kypria* (*Kypria* fr. 1, Davies 1988:34–36) uses the same formula (Διὸς δ' ἐτελείτο βουλή) refer to his decision to bring an end to the heroic age, thereby relieving the earth of its excess human population. It is the particular characteristic of the Iliadic representation of the *Dios boulē* that Zeus' promise to Thetis and his plans for the entire Trojan War coincide. For further discussion, see Bassett 1922, Redfield 1979, Murnaghan 1997, and Clay 1999, with further bibliography.

    The poet also "foreshadows" events in his own voice. At *Iliad* XVI 46–47, 249–252, and 684–693, Homer points to Patroklos' imminent death; the passages reach a crescendo in the narration of the death itself. On the poet's own voice as functionally similar to Zeus'—and hence the poet's

121

The fall of Troy is further predicted by the interpretations of mantic priests. Both Calchas and Polydamas offer glimpses of future events, including the ultimate destruction of the city. As part of his rhetorical strategy to convince the troops to stay and fight a while longer, Odysseus reminds the Achaeans of the portents they witnessed at Aulis. Calchas interpreted the foreboding vision of a snake devouring eight chicks and their mother before being turned into stone as an indication that the Achaeans would take Troy in the tenth year of the war (II 303–332, esp. 328–329). Nestor likewise offers his own vision of the prophecy, ending with the certainty that the Achaeans should not cease fighting until they sack the city and capture Trojan women (II 350–353). Similarly, Polydamas advises Hektor to order the Trojans to retreat from battle, for he saw an unfavorable bird-sign that presaged the rout of the Trojans (XII 216–229). Hektor, flush with his temporary victory, chooses to ignore the warning.[49]

We may consider as typologically similar the "oath" sworn by both parties and violated by Pandarus in *Iliad* III.[50] The violated oath is recalled by Agamemnon on the Greek side as a means to inspire the troops to battle (IV 157–168, 235–239); Diomedes, too, feels the Greek victory is certain:

> γνωτὸν δὲ, καὶ ὃς μάλα νήπιός ἐστιν,
> <u>ὡς ἤδη</u> Τρώεσσιν ὀλέθρου πείρατ᾽ ἐφῆπται.

> It is known, even for one who is a great simpleton,
> <u>how already</u> the ends of destruction are hanging over the
> Trojans.

> *Iliad* VII 401–402

From Diomedes' perspective, Troy is as good as sacked already. On the Trojan side, Hektor mentions the broken oath in his challenge to single-combat with the best fighter of the Achaeans:

> ὅρκια μὲν Κρονίδης ὑψίζυγος οὐκ ἐτέλεσσεν,
> ἀλλὰ κακὰ φρονέων τεκμαίρεται ἀμφοτέροισιν,

---

organization of the plot as the *Dios boulē*—see Moore 1921:111, "Strictly speaking his words are not prophecy, but they are used by him to produce in us the same effects as the utterances of a god or seer would do."

[49] Consider the analogous predictions made by characters close to their own death; Patroklos and Hektor both foretell the death of their murderers (XVI 851–854, XXII 358–360). Similarly, the ghost of Patroklos visits Achilles from the dead and foretells his death (XXIII 80–81).

[50] The oath called for violence upon the party responsible for first breaking it: "Let those, whichever side they may be, who first do wrong to the oaths sworn, let their brains be spilled on the ground as this wine is spilled now, theirs and their sons' and let their wives be the spoil of others" (*Iliad* II 299–301).

εἰς ὅ κεν ἢ ὑμεῖς Τροίην εὔπυργον ἕλητε,
ἢ’ αὐτοὶ παρὰ νηυσὶ δαμείετε ποντοπόροισιν.

The son of Kronos on-high did not fulfill the oaths,
but by design he fashioned evil things for both sides,
until the time when either you should capture well-towered Troy
or are yourselves beaten down beside your ships before the sea.[51]

Iliad VII 69–72

He does not accept blame for the Trojan violation of the oath, but attributes it to Zeus' plan to bring evils upon both Trojans and Achaeans.[52] Antenor, however, does acknowledge Trojan blame for the broken oath—it is an indication, he argues, that the Trojans are now fighting without hope; the best course of action, he argues, is to give back Helen and her possessions at once:

δεῦτ’ ἄγετ’, Ἀργείην Ἑλένην καὶ κτήμαθ’ ἅμ’ αὐτῇ
δώομεν Ἀτρεΐδησιν ἄγειν. νῦν δ’ ὅρκια πιστὰ
ψευσάμενοι μαχόμεσθα· τῶ οὔ νύ τι κέρδιον ἥμιν
ἔλπομαι ἐκτελέεσθαι, ἵνα μὴ ῥέξομεν ὧδε.

Come on now, let us give back Argive Helen and her possessions along
             with her
to the sons of Atreus to lead away. <u>Now we are fighting</u>
<u>after being false to the oaths of trust;</u> <u>accordingly, I expect nothing</u>
             <u>profitable</u>
<u>will come out if it for us</u>, unless we do this.

Iliad VII 350–353

Nothing good can come of the Trojan's efforts now that they have violated the sacred oath. In all four examples, the broken oath entails destruction of the Trojans. As Margo Kitts (2005) has recently shown, the narrative theme of the violated oath both prefigures and justifies violence.

---

[51] These four verses have been considered corrupt by critics of the analyst school: see Bassett 1927:148–150 for a defense of their textual authenticity.

[52] Hektor's words here may reflect the tradition noted in the opening verses of the *Kypria* that Zeus brought about the Trojan War in order to depopulate the earth: see *Kypria* fr. 1. However, Bassett 1927:149 sees Hektor's silence about actual responsibility of the violation of the oath a mark of tact: "before the beginning of his success on the field, when he is still the faultless knight, it is unthinkable that he should have made no reference to the violation of the truce, although he cannot excuse it. There is a lacuna in the thought at [verse] 72, but *this must be put down to the embarrassment of the speaker*. He can say no more about the violation of the truce, and of course cannot refer to his own views about it" (emphasis added).

Furthermore, Hektor is repeatedly called the lone defender of Troy (VI 403, XXII 507).[53] His name is derived from the verb ἔχω, itself from the Indo-European root *segh- which means "to hold," and in Homeric Greek "to protect."[54] The *Iliad* puns on this etymological meaning when Sarpedon chides Hektor for holding back from the fight:[55]

φῆς που ἄτερ λαῶν <u>πόλιν ἐξέμεν</u> ἠδ' ἐπικούρων
<u>οἶος</u>, σὺν γαμβροῖσι κασιγνήτοισί τε σοῖσιν.

I suppose you say <u>you will hold the city</u> without men and allies,
<u>you alone</u>, with your brothers-in-law and your own brothers.

Iliad V 473–474

In the later tradition about the Trojan War Hektor will be called "he who <u>holds</u> the city" (πολίοχος: Euripides *Rhesus* 166, 821). His fate and the fate of the city are inextricably linked. Hektor foresees his own death during his final meeting with Andromache and imagines it in connection with the sack of the city and the enslavement of his wife (VI 457–465). Andromache sees his death coming, too—she begs him not to return to the field, but stay near the city wall (VI 431–432), and leads her women in a threnody for Hektor while he is still alive, afraid that he will not return from battle (VI 500–502). For Andromache, Hektor's death will bring about her own downfall as well as the certain enslavement or murder of their son Astyanax.[56] Priam foresees the destruction of the city and his own pitiful demise, cut down in his own halls and fed to his own dogs (XXII 59–76)—an image he relates to Hektor to convince him to stay within the city wall and not try to face Achilles in battle.[57] Hecuba likewise foresees Hektor's death at the hands of Achilles, and explains that she will be unable to mourn him, for his body will be fed to the dogs and worms by the Achaean ships (XXII 85–89). When Hektor does die, the entire city wails; a simile compares the crying over

---

[53] Compare Andromache's words to Hektor at VI 403: οἶος γὰρ ἐρύετο Ἴλιον Ἕκτωρ "For Hektor alone defends Ilion"; and Andromache's words about Hektor after his death at XXII 507: οἶος γάρ σφιν ἔρυσο πύλας καὶ τείχεα μακρά "For Hektor alone defended the gates and long walls for them."

[54] On ἔχω as "to protect," see Cunliffe 1963:174, s.v. ἔχω (12).

[55] See further Watkins 1998:206–211.

[56] For a sensitive treatment of the death of Astyanax in the Greek epic and artistic traditions, see Lorimer 1950 and Morris 1995. Morris demonstrates that the theme of the murder of the young prince appears to be a motif inherited from city-siege sagas from the Bronze Age Near East.

[57] See Rinon 2008:130–132 on the network of concepts at play in Priam's vision of being devoured by his own dogs: "The description could not be more terse: the same dogs that were nourished by Priam as warders of the gates (22.69) will savagely drag his corpse to the portals (22.66–67) and then drink his blood (22.70). Thus, those who were fed will feed on their feeder at the very site that symbolizes their former protective function" (132).

his death as if over the burning of the city: "and the people all about him were taken with wailing and lamentation throughout the city; it was most similar to this—as if all of Ilion on its hilltop were burning with fire down from its height" (XXII 408–411).[58] Now that Hektor is dead, Priam tells his other children, the city will all the more easily fall:

ῥηΐτεροι γὰρ μᾶλλον Ἀχαιοῖσιν δὴ ἔσεσθε
κείνου τεθνηῶτος ἐναιρέμεν. αὐτὰρ ἐγώ γε,
πρὶν ἀλαπαζομένην τε πόλιν κεραϊζομένην τε
ὀφθαλμοῖσιν ἰδεῖν, βαίην δόμον Ἄϊδος εἴσω.

For you all will be <u>much easier</u> for the Achaeans
to slay, <u>now that he</u> [sc. Hektor] <u>is dead</u>. But
<u>before</u> I see with my own eyes my city both ruined
and laid to waste, <u>I wish to go</u> to the house of Hades.

Iliad XXII 243–246

The association between Hektor's death and the fall of the city is explicit; now that Hektor is dead (κείνου τεθνηῶτος, XXIV 244), the city and its inhabitants are "much easier" (ῥηΐτεροι γὰρ μᾶλλον, XXIV 243) for the Achaeans to slay. The destruction of the city is imminent, such that Priam can speak of seeing the destruction "with his own eyes."

And finally, certain events take on a symbolic force, such as when Andromache's "diadem" slips from her head upon seeing the death of her husband.

τῆλε δ' ἀπὸ κρατὸς βάλε δέσματα σιγαλόεντα,
ἄμπυκα κεκρύφαλόν τε ἰδὲ πλεκτὴν ἀναδέσμην
<u>κρήδεμνόν</u> θ', ὅ ῥά οἱ δῶκε χρυσῆ Ἀφροδίτη
ἤματι τῷ, ὅτε μιν κορυθαίολος ἠγάγεθ' Ἕκτωρ
ἐκ δόμου Ἠετίωνος, ἐπεὶ πόρε μυρία ἔδνα.

And far from her head she threw the shining band,
the headband and hair net and pleated hair-binder
and <u>diadem</u>, which golden Aphrodite gave her
on that day when Hektor of the shining-helm led her
from the house of Eëtion after he gave countless bride-gifts.

Iliad XXII 468–472

---

[58] ἀμφὶ δὲ λαοὶ | κωκυτῷ τ' εἴχοντο καὶ οἰμωγῇ κατὰ ἄστυ | τῷ δὲ μάλιστ' ἄρ' ἔην ἐναλίγκιον ὡς εἰ ἅπασα | Ἴλιος ὀφρυόεσσα πυρὶ σμύχοιτο κατ' ἄρκης (XXII 408–411). In his comment on the passage, Richardson 1993:150 notes, "For the Trojans Hektor's death means the end of Troy."

The noun κρήδεμνον has ambiguous force in early Greek hexameter poetry; although it has but a single etymological sense—a "head (or top) binder" (< κάρα + δέω)[59]—it has three distinct denotative meanings as a woman's headdress,[60] a kind of wine-stopper,[61] or the battlements of a city.[62] The metaphorical association between headdress and city wall raises the possibility of reading into the image of Andromache's falling veil a suggestion of the overthrow of the Trojan wall.[63] In fact, epic diction twice speaks of "sacking a city" in terms of "loosening" the city's κρήδεμνον, both in reference to the breach of the Trojan wall. In *Odyssey* xiii, Odysseus calls upon Athena for help devising a scheme by which he can punish the suitors:

ἀλλ' ἄγε μῆτιν ὕφηνον, ὅπως ἀποτείσομαι αὐτούς·
πὰρ δέ μοι αὐτὴ στῆθι μένος πολυθαρσὲς ἐνεῖσα,
οἷον ὅτε <u>Τροίης λύομεν λιπαρὰ κρήδεμνα</u>.

---

[59] See Chantraine 1968–1980:581, s.v. κρήδεμνον, Nagler 1967:298, 1974:44–45, and Hokestra 1989: 187–188.

[60] *Iliad* VIII 184, XVIII 382, XXII 470; *Odyssey* iv 623, v 346, 351, 373, 459, vi 100; *Hymn to Demeter* 25, 41, 438, 459; *Kypria* fr. 1.3. See Nagler 1967:279–280 for a different arrangement of the verses that illustrates their metrical and phraseological flexibility. Nagler 1974:44–63 offers a much expanded treatment of the occurrences. On what kind of headgear is to be envisioned by the term, see Leaf 1900–1902:II.596 fig. 3 and Lorimer 1950:386 who both think it was a kind of veil or shawl; see further the excellent discussion at Bergren 1989:11n58 and Hokestra 1989: 187–188.

[61] *Odyssey* iii 392.

[62] *Iliad* XVI 100; *Odyssey* xiii 388; *Hymn to Demeter* 151–152; *Hymn to Aphrodite* 6.2; ps.-Hesiod *Shield of Herakles* 105. Leumann 1950:296n60 identifies this meaning as a metaphorical usage ("Übertragener Gebrauch"). On the association between city walls and headgear, consider the frequent association in Greek poetry between city walls and "crowns": ἐυστεφάνῳ ἐνὶ Θήβῃ "in well-<u>crowned</u> Thebe" (*Iliad* XIX 99, Hesiod *Theogony* 978); ἀνδρὸς μὲν <u>στέφανος</u> παῖδες, πύργοι δὲ πόληος "children are the <u>crown</u> of a man, towers of a city" (Homer *Epigram* 13.1); νῦν δ' ἀπὸ μὲν <u>στέφανος</u> πόλεως ὄλωλεν "and now he perished away from the <u>crown</u> of the city" (Anacreon fr. 46 PMG); Ἰλίῳ μέλλοντες ἐπὶ <u>στέφανον</u> τεῦξαι "as they were about to fashion a <u>crown</u> for Ilion" (Pindar *Olympian* 8.32); <u>στεφάνωμα</u> πύργων "the <u>crownings</u> of towers" (Sophocles *Antigone* 122); <u>στεφάναν</u> πύργων "<u>crown</u> of towers" (Euripides *Hecuba* 910); πύργων ἐπ' ἄκρας <u>στεφάνας</u> "upon the high <u>crowns</u> of towers" (Euripides *Trojan Women* 784). See West 1966:425 (comment at Hesiod *Theogony* 978) for further citations, and Hokestra 1989:187–188 (comment at *Odyssey* xiii 388) for discussion.

[63] The association between κρήδεμνον as "diadem" and κρήδεμνον as "battlement" is most fully argued by Nagler 1974:44–63; Fenik 1977:63 cautiously accepts Nagler's arguments here: "We are perhaps willing to believe that the word κρήδεμνα, in the sense of 'battlements,' conjures up the outrage and violation of the city's capture ..." Richardson 1974:194 (comment at *Hymn to Demeter* 151–152) notes that the Iliadic Τροίης ἱερὰ κρήδεμνα λύωμεν "may have been suggested by the idea of a captive woman whose veil is torn off." Compare Foley 1994:44, "The Iliad deliberately links the fall of Hector, the fall of Andromache's veil, and the fall of Troy." See also Nagler 1967:298–307 and Schein 1984:9.

But come, weave a strategy how I may take vengeance on them [*sc.* the
      suitors];
and you yourself, stand beside me, casting very courageous might
      into me,
as when <u>we loosed the shining battlements of Troy</u>.

Odyssey xiii 386–388

Athena and Odysseus together loosed (λύομεν, xiii 388) Troy's battlement—its
"diadem." The ancient scholiast called the use of κρήδεμνα here a "metaphorical" expression for "wall": μεταφορικῶς τὸ τεῖχος (Scholia H at *Odyssey* xiii 388,
Dindorf). Likewise, in the *Iliad* we find Achilles expressing the impossible wish
that all the Achaeans and all the Trojans might perish, save for Patroklos and
Achilles alone, and that they might "loosen" Troy's κρήδεμνον:

αἲ γὰρ, Ζεῦ τε πάτερ καὶ Ἀθηναίη καὶ Ἄπολλον,
μήτέ τις οὖν Τρώων θάνατον φύγοι, ὅσσοι ἔασιν,
μήτέ τις Ἀργείων, νῶϊν δ' ἐκδῦμεν ὄλεθρον,
ὄφρ' <u>οἶοι Τροίης ἱερὰ κρήδεμνα λύωμεν</u>.

If only, father Zeus and Athena and Apollo,
no one then of the Trojans might escape death, as many as
      they are,
no one of the Argives, but we two might avoid[64] destruction,
so that <u>we alone could loosen the holy battlements of Troy</u>.

Iliad XVI 97–100

Achilles wishes to be left alone with Patroklos to seek glory through "loosening" its holy battlements.[65] Once again, the ancient scholiastic tradition read
κρήδεμνα as a "metaphor" for the Trojan wall: νῦν τὰ τείχη, μεταφορικῶς· ἰδίως
γὰρ κρήδεμνον τὸ τῆς κεφαλῆς κάλυμμα "Now it means 'the walls' metaphorically, for κρήδεμνον properly means a head-covering" (Scholia A at *Iliad* XVI
100, Erbse).

    The metaphorical link between Andromache's diadem and the battle-
ments of Troy is further charged by the use of the verb λύω "loosen" in the
passages cited above. In ancient Greek wedding custom, especially as depicted
in Athenian black and red figure vases, the veiled bride was ritually revealed

---

[64] On the form of ἐκδῦμεν (optative with *-υι- contracted to *-ῡ-), compare δαίνῦτο at *Iliad* XXIV
    665 and see Chantraine 1958:51 and Janko 1994:329.

[65] Achilles' wish reveals the contradictory logic of wanting glory while at the same time rejecting
    the heroic society which alone can grant it, as noted by King 1987:35–36. On the adjective "holy"
    (ἱερός) applied to cities and city walls, see Scully 1990.

to her groom during the *anakalupteria* or "unveiling" as the bride's attendant, the *numpheutria*, raised her veil before her new bridegroom.[66] The *anakalupteria* offered the bridegroom his first view of his bride's face (Mayo 1973, Oakley 1982, Oakley and Sinos 1993:136n50, and Reeder 1995:170); scholars generally agree that the gesture "was an actual and symbolic beginning to the disrobing of the bride," and hence metonymically joined with the sex act that follows the procession leading the bride to her new home (Reeder 1995:127). To "loosen" a veil, then, is euphemistic terminology for sexual intercourse, since the bride wears a κρήδεμνον on her wedding day which her husband removes; one may compare the formulaic λύω "loosen" + ζωνήν "girdle" which likewise serves as a euphemism for sexual intercourse.[67] In the context of capturing a city, however, the act of "loosening" a woman's veil, symbol of her chastity, takes on the sinister implications of rape.[68] Michael Nagler (1974) notes, "Throughout the ancient world the idea of seizure and violation of the women would follow all too naturally on that of the ἁρπαγή 'taking' of a city" (Nagler 1974:53). The plot of the *Iliad* is itself motivated by the rape of women (Helen, Chryseïs, and Briseïs),[69] and the characters are all clear on the fact that the capture of Troy will end with the rape of its women.[70] Hence, Andromache's κρήδεμνον signifies the dual

[66] Mayo 1973, Oakley 1982, Bergren 1989:25, Richardson 1993:157, Reeder 1995:166, 170. See For representations of this gesture, see the Attic loutrophoroi published by Reeder 1995:163–165 fig. 23 (= *ARV*[2] 1127.13), 165–168 fig. 24 (= Boston, Museum of Fine Arts *Annual Report* 1 [1903] 62, 71), 169–171 fig. 26 (= *ARV*[2] 1017.44), and the detailed discussion of marriage-scenes in Athenian red figure pottery in Oakley 1995, esp. 64–69.

[67] See *Odyssey* xi 245 where Poseidon "loosed the maiden girdle" of Tyro (λῦσε δὲ παρθενίην ζώνην), the beginning of what are called "acts of love" in the following verse (φιλοτήσια ἔργα); see also *Hymn to Aphrodite* 164 for the disrobing of Aphrodite by Anchises: "he loosed her girdle" (λῦσε δέ οἱ ζώνην), with discussion at Smith 1981:60 with further bibliography.

[68] See Schein 1984:77, 87n24 for discussion and bibliography. The "rape of Troy" was a favorite topic of Attic red figure vase painters; see esp. the cup signed by Euphronius as potter and Onesimus as painter ca. 490 BCE (Malibu, J. Paul Getty Museum, inv. no. 83.AE.362) featuring Locrian Ajax dragging a nude Cassandra away from the altar of Athena. Stewart (1995) suggests Cassandra's nudity in this depiction is a proleptic figure of her rape (83). See Stewart 1995, esp. 77, 83, 89n23, 89n71, 90n72 more generally on the rape of women captured in war.

[69] See *Iliad* IX 327 where Achilles states that he "used to fight men for the sake of their [i.e. Agamemnon's and Menelaus'] women" (ἀνδράσι μαρνάμενος ὀάρων ἕνεκα σφετεράων); at XVIII 265 Polydamas warns Hektor that Achilles will soon rejoin the battle and "he will fight over our city and women" (περὶ πτόλιός τε μαχήσεται ἠδὲ γυναικῶν). See Gottschall 2001 for an argument that the male desire to rape women stems from an evolutionary biological drive to reproduce. Gottschall argues that heroes prized women as war booty, driven by a biological imperative to produce as great a progeny as possible.

[70] See Nestor's attempt to motivate the soldiers by speaking of sexual violence against the Trojan women (II 354–356). Similarly, Agamemnon imagines the aftermath of the war by speaking of dead men left as food for scavenger birds while women and children are dragged off to the ships (IV 237–239). In a moment of bleak foresight, Hektor speaks of the rape Andromache will endure after his death (VI 454–465).

violence to come; as the "diadem" falls from her head, so the city's "diadem"—its battlements—will fall, and the storming Greeks will penetrate the city and seize its women.[71]

To conclude this discussion, I wish to cite George Duckworth's insightful study of narrative foreshadowing in Greek and Latin epic. He describes the effects of Homer's multiple indications of the future fall of the city:

> [T]he reader has a vivid picture of the events which are to happen after the close of the *Iliad*. The poem ends on a quiet note, the funeral of Hector, but the later events—the death of Achilles and the fall of the fated city—have impressed themselves upon the consciousness of the reader *almost as vividly as if the poet had extended his epic to include them.* (Duckworth 1933:32; emphasis added)

The effect of the numerous proleptic images of the sack of Troy create a kind of double-vision of the city for the audience: Troy as already in ruins, still standing in the present, but with its fate hanging over it (cf. VII 402: ὡς ἤδη Τρώεσσιν ὀλέθρου πείρατ᾽ ἐφῆπται). The superimposition of the Troy still in place (ἔμπεδος) with that of the Troy in ruins creates the effect of virtual death. Both here and not here, both intact and decomposed, the city wall is part of the same temporal economy that governs the organic materials of wood and flesh we saw above. Though the product of divine craft, the wall exists within human temporality and is therefore temporally bound: its end is there from its beginning, such that it can never be "unbreakable" but only "unbroken."

---

[71] Athena as the maiden goddess who guards the city of Athens belongs to the same conceptual framework: as Athena is herself a perpetual "maiden," so too the city of Athens would remain "un-penetrated" by invading forces. Consider further the verb δαμάζω (root *δαμ-) used both in contexts of "marrying a woman," "conquering an enemy," and "taming a wild animal." Another verb used commonly to denote sexual intercourse, μίγνυμι "to mix," also appears in battle contexts in the sense "to mix it up (with an enemy)." Vermeule 1979:101 argues that "The aim [of a warrior's taunts] is to turn the opposing soldier into a female, or into the weaker animal role." In other words, the taunts used to describe warfare are closely associated with the practice of sexual aggression carried out against a weaker party.

The metaphor of invading a city as sexual violence against a female continues throughout the Classical tradition. I cite as an example Livy's narrative of the rape of Lucretia, conceived as part of a larger narrative about siege operations against the town of Ardea. Livy uses military metaphors to describe Tarquin's rape (see Philippides 1983 on Livy's military metaphors). The tradition continues into William Shakespeare's *The Rape of Lucrece* 463–469: "His hand that yet remains upon her breast | (Rude ram, to batter such an ivory wall!) | May feel her heart (poor citizen!) distress'd, | Wounding itself to death, rise up and fall, | Beating her bulk, that his hand shakes withal. | This moves in him more rage and lesser pity | To make the breach and enter this sweet city" (ed., Evans 1997).

Both walls then, Achaean and Trojan, belong to the temporal order of specific heroes (Achilles, Hektor) as well as that of the entire age of heroes. They are represented as remaining in place (ἔμπεδος) within the time frame of the *Iliad* itself, but their unbroken status (ἄρρηκτος) is bound to fail. They will each fall to ruins, and be covered over by the sands of time and forgetfulness. Only within the epic themselves are they granted temporary respite from the ravages of time.

Chapter 4

Memorials, Tombs, and the γέρας θανόντων

The (Im)Permanence of Mortuary Architecture in the *Iliad*

What is he that builds stronger than either the mason, the shipwright, or the carpenter? ... say a "grave-maker": the house that he makes lasts till doomsday.

—Shakespeare *Hamlet* V, i.41–59

PHYSICAL OBJECTS PLAY AN IMPORTANT ROLE in determining the narrative temporality of the *Iliad*. For instance, the wooden timbers of the Achaean ships slowly rotting on Trojan shores, the bodies of Sarpedon, Patroklos, and Hektor in danger of decaying and requiring divine preservatives (*ambrosia* and *nektar*) until they can be offered funeral rites, and the defensive walls of the Greeks and Trojans are all invested with a certain degree of temporal durability within the epic. Each object, whether made of flesh, wood, or stone, has an inherent lifespan which cannot be exceeded; it undergoes a natural process of degradation. Wood and flesh rot; architectural constructions and human bodies weaken at the joints and finally disintegrate. The rate of this decay marks time, and the objects themselves function like windows to the past and future.[1]

In this chapter, I discuss a particular set of objects that also participates in this cycle of temporal durability—the burial mounds (τύμβοι) and grave markers (σήματα) that dot the Trojan landscape. Troy abounds with markers of its former rulers—Ilos, Dardanus, and Aisuetes—which feature as landmarks and give shape and meaning to the space in which they are situated. These examples of mortuary architecture indicate the past within the present, as the traces of the dead still exist among and for the living. In a very tangible way

---

[1] On the temporal dimensions of physical objects in Greek literature, see Bassi 2005 and Grethlein 2008.

tombs contribute to the epic project of preserving the *kleos* of the dead. The tomb offers a visual counterpart of the verbal account of epic poetry; the two supplement each other in the common cause of remembering the deeds of men.

And yet, this very intersection between tombs and epic helps reveal the temporal nature of poetic *kleos* itself. For, as the *Iliad* demonstrates, tombs, though made to be long-lasting and stable reminders of the fallen, are every bit as mortal as the human bodies they cover. Tombs fade over time; they can be worn down by time or torn down by human hands; and eventually, they will be forgotten and become indistinguishable from the land itself. What is implicit in this slow disintegration of the physical monument is the concurrent demise of its verbal counterpart, epic poetry.

My argument in this chapter is broadly similar to Andrew Ford's analysis of physical objects in the *Iliad* in his perceptive *Homer: The Poetry of the Past* (Ford 1992:131–146). We are both concerned with the status of *sēmata* in the Homeric poems, both adduce much of the same textual evidence, and both find that commemorative architecture is represented in the *Iliad* as temporary. However, we differ in aim; Ford uses the impermanence of physical signs as evidence for a general theory that Homer—the poet coming at the end of the oral and beginning of the textual tradition of the *Iliad* and the *Odyssey*[2]—felt a genuine distrust for the commemorative powers of writing.[3] Hence, Ford privileges the *kleos aphthiton* of the oral tradition above any and all physical manifestations of that *kleos*, such as a warrior's τύμβος and στήλη. In contrast, it is my contention that the *Iliad* conceives of even oral *kleos aphthiton* as a kind of "mortal" architecture. As tombs and grave markers, the material counterpart of *kleos aphthiton*, eventually fade, so too is the epic itself temporally conditioned. The adjective *aphthiton* designates a temporality which does not last "forever" but rather endures a temporally bound though indefinite period; *aphthiton* specifies the temporality of the "not yet decayed."

The *Iliad* represents the tomb as an object fated to suffer the ravages of time and as a figure for its own status as verbal monument. Like the wood, flesh, and stone noted above, these graves and their markers are presented as mortal objects within the narrative so as to indicate the mortal temporality the epic lays claim to for itself. Towards this end, we will begin by looking at the ritual practices

---

[2] Ford (1992) notes, "If we think of Homer as the 'great master' at the end of the tradition who fixed the poems, by definition he had come across the fact of alphabetic writing" (132).

[3] At the outset of his discussion Ford (1992) asks, "What was it for a poet descended from an oral tradition to meet writing? Would he have immediately perceived and embraced its potential to fix his songs in a stable and enduring form?" (135). By the end of his analysis of *sēmata* in the poems, he concludes, "Homer seems to go beyond self-assertion here to undertake an aggressive war on the visible; he seems determined to show that *no tangible, visible thing can be trusted to mark the fames of men accurately and enduringly*" (146, emphasis added).

associated with burial and tombstones, namely the γέρας θανόντων "the honorable portion due to the dead" which consists of rites and practices designed to achieve a more permanent status for the mortal body of the hero. As we progress, it will become apparent how the construction of the tomb is an extension of the funerary ritual, for both function to preserve the physical remains and the memory of the fallen. Then we will turn our attention to those passages within the *Iliad* that posit a problematic permanence for *sēmata* and the *kleos* of heroes.

1. Burial Rites, Purifying Fire, and the State of Mortal Permanence

In the sixteenth book of the *Iliad*, as Zeus contemplates rescuing his son Sarpedon from his appointed death, Hera dissuades him by saying that it would be a violation of natural law to do so. Instead, she consoles, he should allow Sarpedon to die and be carried off by the gods Sleep and Death to his home in Lycia,

> ἔνθά ἑ ταρχύσουσι κασίγνατοί τε ἔται τε
> τύμβῳ τε στήλῃ τε· τὸ γὰρ γέρας ἐστὶ θανόντων.

> where his brothers and countrymen will perform burial rites for him
> with both tomb and gravestone—for this is the honorable portion due to
> the dead.

Iliad XVI 456–457 = XVI 674–675

I isolate the phrase γέρας θανόντων "the honorable portion due to the dead" because of its implication that certain activities performed for the dead fall within the nexus of obligations implied by the Homeric term γέρας.

The Greek noun γέρας, appearing already in Mycenaean Linear B,[4] appears related to γῆρας "old age" and γέρων "old man," but achieved independence of its linguistic roots early in its history.[5] Literally, *geras* is that which is due to a person in respect to his age, but comes to designate a gift, service, or reward given as an index of one's social status. *Geras* is a key term in the social contexts: meat is divided (δαίομαι "to divide") for the feast (δαίς "a feast," a nominal derivative from the verbal root of δαίομαι) and apportioned to each member of the feast as a γέρας—the cut and amount of meat is a manifest token of the feaster's public value.[6] As such, one's γέρας is the physical manifestation of his or her τιμή, the

---

[4]   Morpurgo 1963 identifies γέρας with *ke-ra* of Linear B, as does Palmer 1963:199, 211, 426, s.v. *ke-ra*, citing PY Eb 416.1: *i-je-re-ja ke-ra* "the γέρας (*ke-ra*) of the priestess," where *ke-ra* (γέρας) is used to designate land-holdings.

[5]   See Chantraine 1968–1980:216, s.v. γέρας, and Garland 1982:69 with nn3–4.

[6]   For the etymological relationship between δαίομαι and δαίς, see Chantraine 1968–1980:247–248, s.v. δαίομαι. On "division" as the paramount principle in the Homeric feast, see Saïd 1979 and

term that designates the degree of esteem and value a person has in the eyes of his or her peers, and correspondingly, the self-image one possesses from how he or she is treated by others.[7] It is Agamemnon's act of dishonorable distribution, taking Achilles' γέρας—the girl Briseïs—for himself, which precipitates Achilles' withdrawal from battle and the destruction of so many Achaean fighters.

Social worth must be scrupulously respected in the distribution of gifts, services, and rewards, since violations in distribution entail disastrous consequences.[8] Appropriate honors must be accorded to a hero even in death—proper treatment of the hero's corpse is first and foremost among the services that must be rendered to the dead. The failure to provide such γέρας for the dead results in shame for the living, as Sarpedon warns his compatriot Glaukos in his dying moment:

σοὶ γὰρ ἐγὼ καὶ ἔπειτα <u>κατηφείη</u> καὶ <u>ὄνειδος</u>
ἔσσομαι <u>ἤματα πάντα διαμπερές</u>, εἴ κέ μ' Ἀχαιοὶ
τεύχεα συλήσωσι νεῶν ἐν ἀγῶνι πεσόντα.
ἀλλ' ἔχεο κρατερῶς, ὄτρυνε δὲ λαὸν ἅπαντα.

For I will be <u>a cause of shame and reproach</u> even for you hereafter
<u>for all days continuously</u>, if the Achaeans ever
strip me of my armor now that I have fallen in the gathering of the ships.
But hold on strongly, and stir up all our people.

Iliad XVI 498–501

Rundin 1996. Clay 1994 investigates how seating arrangement and order at the symposium function as a spatial manifestation of the principles of division in accordance with social hierarchy. The division of goods and services can be expressed in one of two models. In a democratic model, all parties receive "equal" shares. In contrast, the Homeric *isē dais* appears to follow what Saïd 1979:18–19 and Rundin 1996:196 have identified as a "proportional," "geometric," or even "virtually equal" model of division, "whereby some are more equal than others; that is, a proportional or virtually equal distribution is a distribution of shares that are not equal in the strict sense we are accustomed to, but rather weighted according to their recipients' varied social statuses" (Rundin 1996:196). On the Homeric *isē dais*, see further Motto and Clark 1969.

[7]   Aristotle (*Nicomachean Ethics* I 5, 1095b23–24) claims that ἀρετή "personal excellence, virtue" is superior to τιμή "honor, status" precisely because "τιμή is thought to depend on those who bestow honor rather than on him who receives it" (δοκεῖ γὰρ ἐν τοῖς τιμῶσι μᾶλλον εἶναι ἢ ἐν τῷ τιμωμένῳ). Finkelberg (1998) notes that ἔμμορε τιμῆς "he or she has been allotted *timē*" is "the only Homeric formula in which the word *timē* occurs ... This seems to indicate that *timē* should be regarded not as a competitive but as what can be called a 'distributive' value" (16).

[8]   Motto and Clark 1969 demonstrate that Achilles is primarily concerned with the *fairness* of the distribution of γέρας in accordance with τιμή. See also Muellner 1996 who reveals the connection between Achilles' μῆνις "rage" and social disequilibrium.

If Glaukos abandons his friend Sarpedon and allows the Achaeans to strip him of his armor and to deny him cremation and burial rites,[9] he will suffer shame and reproach, two terms designating the inner dynamics of blame poetry, the doublet of Homeric *epos*. As Marcel Detienne (1996) and Gregory Nagy (1999) have demonstrated, blame poetry is the functional opposite of epic praise; it shrouds its subject in darkness and forgetfulness, casting its subject into oblivion, devouring him like the dogs that feast upon the unburied corpses of the dead.[10] The blame for failing to protect Sarpedon's corpse will itself dog Glaukos "for all days, continuously" (ἤματα πάντα διαμπερές, XVI 499), functioning as the negative equivalent of Achilles' "unwithered fame" (κλέος ἄφθιτον, IX 413). The connection between blame and the failure to protect a comrade's corpse from disgrace is proved by the identical collocation of terms in a passage where Menelaus speaks to himself of the blame he will incur if he fails to defend the fallen fighter Patroklos:

σοὶ μὲν δὴ Μενέλαε <u>κατηφείη καὶ ὄνειδος</u>
ἔσσεται <u>εἴ κ</u>’ Ἀχιλῆος ἀγαυοῦ πιστὸν ἑταῖρον
τείχει ὕπο Τρώων <u>ταχέες κύνες ἑλκήσουσιν.</u>
ἀλλ’ ἔχεο κρατερῶς, ὄτρυνε δὲ λαὸν ἅπαντα.

For you indeed, Menelaus, this will be <u>a cause of shame and reproach</u>
<u>if ever</u> the <u>swift dogs drag</u> the trustworthy companion
of haughty Achilles beneath the walls of Troy.
But hold on strongly, and stir up all our people.

Iliad XVII 556–559

The formulaic repetitions (σοὶ … κατηφείη καὶ ὄνειδος | ἔσσεται, XVI 498, cf. XVII 556; ἀλλ’ ἔχεο κρατερῶς, ὄτρυνε δὲ λαὸν ἅπαντα, XVI 501 = XVII 559) in an analogous situation—namely that a hero must defend the corpse of a companion from the opposing army—indicates the necessity implicit in carrying out those activities which constitute the γέρας θανόντων, the rites and practices due to

---

[9]   A dead hero is usually—though not always—cremated in his armor. Compare *Iliad* VI 416–419 (Eëtion), *Odyssey* xi 72–76 (Elpenor). Only Achilles' second set of armor is specifically *not* cremated with the hero; it becomes the source of contention between Odysseus and Ajax during the funeral games held in honor of Achilles, and motivates Ajax' enduring hatred of Odysseus.

[10] Detienne 1996, esp. 39–52 identifies "blame" as the opposite of "praise," the poetic manifestations of the opposed pair of concepts "memory" and "forgetfulness." Nagy's analysis (1999:222–227, Ch. 12§1–6) complements Detienne's study by tracing the use of particular diction associated with each category of poetic speech. On blaming speech "devouring" (δάπτω) its victim like a dog devours a corpse and the blame-poet "fattening himself" (παίνομαι) upon the object of his blame, see Nagy 1999:225–226, Ch. 12§5 with n8. Nagy concludes, "In effect, then, the language of praise poetry presents the language of unjustified blame as parallel to the eating of heroes' corpses by dogs" (226, Ch. 12§5).

the dead as an indication of their status. Further, the image of Patroklos torn apart by dogs is a concrete image of the blame Menelaus will suffer, as reproach will figuratively bite and devour him. That is to say, the fate of the hero's body has repercussions on the honor of his surviving *philoi*: the destruction of the hero's physical body is intimately tied with the metaphorical devouring of the social body of his *philoi*.

Besides the passages referring to the rites due to Sarpedon, the term γέρας appears four more times in Homer in association with what is due to the dead.[11] First, it is used to describe the procession of Myrmidons with their horses and chariots during Patroklos' funeral (XXIII 9). In the fourth book of the *Odyssey*, Pisistratus calls the practice of cutting one's hair in mourning and shedding tears "the γέρας for miserable mortals" (iv 197–198).[12] Toward the end of the *Odyssey*, the souls of the dead suitors complain that their bodies have been left unburied, and that since their friends do not know about their death, they cannot clean their wounds, lay out their bodies, and bury them, "which is the γέρας of the dead" (xxiv 190). And finally, Laertes, thinking his son Odysseus is dead, laments that he did not have the chance to close his son's eyes in death—an action which he calls the γέρας of the dead (xxiv 292–296). These passages do not describe any single activity that might be considered the γέρας θανοντῶν, but rather point to an entire range of activities that are performed as part of the funeral rituals for the fallen hero. The range of activities listed above is confirmed in the descriptions of the funerals of the principal characters in the *Iliad*: Patroklos (funeral: XXIII 108–227; games: XXIII 229–897), Hektor (funeral: XXIV 719–804), and Achilles, whose funeral is described at length in the *Odyssey* (funeral: xxiv 43–84; games: xxiv 85–93).[13] These passages describe how the hero's body is washed and anointed (Patroklos, Hektor, Achilles); the dead man is lamented (Patroklos, Hektor, Achilles); participants cut their hair in sign of mourning (Patroklos, Achilles); the corpse is circled by a procession of armed warriors (Patroklos, Achilles); sheep and cattle are slaughtered over the pyre (Patroklos, Achilles); honey and

[11] There may be a further association between γέρας and θάνατος: Lincoln 1991:62–75 has demonstrated that Charon, the figure who ferries souls across the river Styx to the land of the dead in Greek mythology, is a personification of old age. Lincoln notes the regular description of Charon as an "old man" in Greek, Old Norse, Germanic, Celtic and other Indo-European traditions (Greek γέρων; Old Norse *karl*; Anglo-Saxon *ceorl*); this repeated adjective suggests a link between age and death, represented by a single Proto-Indo-European verbal root (*ǵer-) indicating the verbal idea "to age, mature, ripen," and in its oldest sense "to rub away, erode, become worn down" (Lincoln 1991:64, 73n14, citing Pokorny 1989:390–391).

[12] Although this passage does not contain the exact phrase γέρας θανόντων, it does refer to γέρας in a funerary context as what is due to "mortals" when they have died.

[13] On these burials and ancient burial rites in general as described in Homer, see Garland 1982, Kurtz and Boardman 1971, Lorimer 1950, Mylonas 1948, Petropoulou 1988, Sourvinou-Inwood 1981, 1995, and Whitehead 1984.

oil are placed in jars around the pyre (Patroklos, Achilles); the pyre's flames are quenched with wine (Patroklos, Hektor); the cremated remains are placed in a golden urn which is then buried (Patroklos, Hektor, Achilles); and the rite is accompanied by a banquet (Patroklos, Hektor) and celebratory games (Patroklos, Achilles).[14]

One feature not overtly mentioned in the list of actions judged part of what is due to the dead but assumed within the entire ritual is the cremation of the corpse. Cremation is the *sine qua non* of Homeric funerary ritual. Even Homer's use of the Greek verb θάπτω "to bury," which would seem to imply inhumation, in fact is always used in contexts in which the hero's body is cremated (Mylonas 1948:62, Garland 1982:73, 2001:34–37). For instance, Patroklos' ghost visits Achilles to request a speedy burial once he has been cremated: "Bury me (θάπτέ με) as quickly as possible, that I may pass through the gates of Hades … no longer will I come back from Hades, once you give me my allotment of fire (ἐπήν με πυρὸς λελάχητε)" (XXIII 71, 75–76).[15] The act of offering the dead "his share of fire" is a clear euphemism for cremation.[16] In the *Odyssey*, the ghost of Elpenor—who, like Patroklos, had not yet been buried—approaches Odysseus and begs Odysseus not to leave him "unburied," but to "burn" him:

μή μ' ἄκλαυτον <u>ἄθαπτον</u> ἰὼν ὄπιθεν καταλείπειν
νοσφισθείς, μή τοί τι θεῶν μήνιμα γένωμαι,
ἀλλά με <u>κακκῆαι</u>.

---

[14] Patroklos' lavish funeral may borrow some of its details from a second millennium BCE funeral for Hittite royalty known as the *Šalliš waštaiš* ritual, a multi-day funeral on the third day of which the following details are mentioned: "When it dawns on the third day, women go to the p[yr]e, to the bones to gather (them). | They extinguish the fire with ten vessels of beer, te[n vessels of wine] <and> ten vessels of w.-beverage. | <They take> a silver h.-vessel (weighing) twenty minae and a half (?), filled with fine oil. | They tak[e] (out) the bones with silver tongs? and put them (i.e. the bones) into the fine oil in the silver h.-vessel. | They take them out of the fine oil and lay them down on the linen g.-cloth. A fine cloth is laid under the linen cloth. | When they finish to gather the bones, they wrap them | in the linen and fine cloths. They put them on the š.-chair for sittin[g | But if it is a woman (i.e. if the queen has died), they put them on the h.-benches" (Kassian, Korolëv, and Sidel'tsev 2002:261). For text and commentary on the Hittite ritual, see Otten 1958 and Kassian, Korolëv, and Sidel'tsev 2002; for discussion and bibliography, see van den Hout 1994 and Rutherford 2007. On Homeric reflections of Hittite language and culture, see Puhvel 1991, Watkins 1998. See, in general, the excellent and concise treatment on the subject of burial and the cult of the dead in Burkert 1985:190–194, 424–426.

[15] The verb λελάχητε is the reduplicated causal aorist subjunctive of λαγχάνω "to make to obtain, to give one his due": on the reduplicated causal aorist, compare λελάθη "make him forget" at *Iliad* XV 60 and ἐκλέλαθον "they made him forget" at II 600 with discussion at Risch 1974:243 (§87c) and Janko 1994:235, 265.

[16] See *Iliad* VII 79–80 = XXII 342–343, XV 350 with Kirk 1990:244 and Janko 1994:265. See further Hesychius' gloss of λελαχεῖν as θάψαι "to bury" which he supports by citing *Iliad* VII 80.

Don't leave me behind you unwept, <u>unburied</u>, as you go
after you've turned away, lest for you I become some source of the gods'
    anger,
but rather, <u>burn me up completely</u>.

Odyssey xi 72–74

The scene with its collocation of ἄθαπτον "unburied, not yet buried" (xi 72) and κακκῆαι "burn" (xi 74) blurs the distinction between burial and cremation. We must conclude that in Homer, the verb θάπτω indicates burial as part of a tradition of a funeral ritual in which the deceased is mourned, cremated, and the remains are then interred.[17]

In Greek epic poetry, cremation followed by burial represents the normal custom; any deviation from that norm is marked as such. For instance, the now fragmentary epic cycle poem *The Little Iliad*, according to Porphyry's epitome, described how the Achaean warrior Ajax was not cremated according to the standard epic custom, but was simply buried:

ὁ τὴν μικρὰν Ἰλιάδα γράψας ἱστορεῖ <u>μηδὲ καυθῆναι συνήθως τὸν Αἴαντα, τεθῆναι δὲ οὕτως ἐν σορῷ</u> διὰ τὴν ὀργὴν τοῦ βασιλέως.

The [poet] who wrote the "Little Iliad" narrated that <u>Ajax was not burned in the usual way</u>, but <u>was simply placed in a coffin</u> because of the anger of the king.

Little Iliad fr. 3, Davies 1988:54 = Bernabé 1987:77

The myth, as preserved by fragments of *The Little Iliad*, Sophocles' *Ajax*, and ps.-Apollodorus' *Library* (5.7), explain how Ajax flew into a blind rage at being judged second to Odysseus during the funeral games held in celebration of Achilles' death; Ajax went mad and attacked the Achaeans' sheep and cattle, mistaking them for the Achaean leaders. When he came to his senses, he was so ashamed that he threw himself on his own sword. Ajax' funeral, specifically noted as unusual (μηδὲ ... συνήθως), seems to be due to Agamemnon's anger at Ajax' behavior.[18] The norm is here subverted, and Ajax' body is treated as a special case.

---

[17]   Clarke 1999:186 argues that θάπτω refers "to the whole process of committing the corpse to the earth, not specifically to burning." Sourvinou-Inwood 1995:110 notes that Achilles himself seems to think of the act of "burying Patroklos" as consisting of multiple parts: cremation of the corpse, followed by erection of a σῆμα, and finally, the cutting of mourners' hair. See further Burkert 1985:190–194 on the multiplicity of ritualized events that constitute the ancient funeral.

[18]   The observation that Ajax' interment without cremation is exceptional may go back to Aristarchus: see Severyns 1928:331–332. On the entire issue of Ajax' burial, see Holt 1992. I read διὰ τὴν ὀργὴν τοῦ βασιλέως with Holt as referring to Agamemnon's anger at Ajax; for a different

It is my claim that the funerary rituals described in the *Iliad* and *Odyssey*, those performed as the γέρας θανοντῶν, operate within the general economy of permanence and decay. Ritual cremation aims to reduce the corpse of the hero to a more permanent form; it burns away the flesh to leave the relatively more stable bones, which are in turn covered with still more permanent structures of earth and stone: the τύμβος and στήλη.[19] To analyze the body's role in this process, it is most convenient to digress briefly to the work of the French anthropologist Robert Hertz (1960) and his work on the social dimensions of burial practices. Hertz' theory of the function of burial has been adopted by recent and influential scholars in anthropology, archaeology, and cultural anthropology: in particular, Maurice Bloch (1982), Sally Humphreys (1981), and Jean-Pierre Vernant (1981).

In his seminal work on burial practices among the people of Borneo, Hertz identified two distinct stages of the burial process. First, after the death of the individual, the corpse is deposited in a temporary burial situation for a length of time.[20] The corpse is left to decompose for a given time, spanning from the usual period of two years to an exceptional one-hundred years in the case of certain chieftains (Hertz 1960:31, 118n18). Hertz interprets the process of decomposition as a kind of "purification"—"it is only when the decomposition of the corpse is completed that the newcomer among the dead is thought to be rid of his impurity and deemed worthy of admittance to the company of his ancestors" (35). Once the flesh has entirely decayed and left behind a bare skeleton, the remains are exhumed and transferred from their isolated spot to a communal burial site, which is seen as the symbolic reintegration of the dead with his or her ancestors (53–55). Once established within the communal burial

---

view, see Holt 1992:319n1, explaining an alternate interpretation suggested by an anonymous referee for the *American Journal of Philology*.

[19] I wish to emphasize that the burial customs I describe here are those found in Greek epic poetry. I do not attempt to make any claims about actual funerary practices in Greece or elsewhere. The relationship between Homer's burials and what might be considered to be contemporary burials on the Greek mainland or in Ionia—that is, burials discovered by archaeologists and analyzed as belonging to the late Bronze or early Iron ages—is notoriously vexed. Aegean archaeologists have long noted that the ubiquitous cremations in the epic poems appear to be at odds with the actual practice among the Greeks, for whom cremation is rare during the Bronze and Iron ages: for discussion see Kurtz and Boardman 1971, I. Morris 1987, Mylonas 1948, Sourvinou-Inwood 1995, Vermeule 1979, and compare the comment by Janko 1994:165. Coldstream 1976 and Whitley 1988 discuss the possible impact Homeric epic made on funerary practices in Greece in the eighth century BCE. A treatment of the funerary practices is beyond the scope of my investigation—I am interested in establishing the practice of funerary ritual and its ideology as expressed within epic itself.

[20] See Hertz 1960:30, "Whatever the variety of these customs, which often co-exist in one place and are substituted one for the other, the rite, in its essence, is constant; the body of the deceased, while awaiting the second burial, is temporarily deposited in a burial-place distinct from the final one; it is almost invariably isolated."

grounds, the person essentially ceases to be an individual, becoming instead one of the beneficent "ancestors."[21]

Hertz distinguishes, therefore, two different stages in the burial process: a primary and secondary burial. The purpose of the primary burial appears to be the "purification" of the corpse by setting it aside and allowing time for the flesh to decay completely from the bones. The secondary burial, then, entails moving the "purified" bones to a centralized location where they will be placed alongside the bones of the ancestors. French anthropologist Arnold van Gennep saw this phenomenon of secondary burial as evidence of a structural binary distinction between two social classes (alive, dead) with an intermediary "liminal" phase (dying); the movement between classes across the liminal phase constitutes a "rite of passage" (Van Gennep 1960, Huntington and Metcalf 1991:29–37). According to van Gennep, mortuary practices universally treat the dying man as undergoing a transformation from *living* to *dead*, between which the person is *dying*. Applying the model to Hertz's primary and secondary burial produces some startling insights, including the observation that while a corpse's flesh is left to decay, he or she is in a sense *not yet dead*, but still *dying*; death represents the more stable status of secondary burial when the bones are enshrined in a more permanent repository.

Van Gennep's model was taken up in a modified form by Richard Huntington and Peter Metcalf, who emphasize the role of van Gennep's "liminal" phase. They recast the "rite of passage" as something closer to a material dialectic, in which we find "the three stages of preparation, decomposition, and extraction" (Huntington and Metcalf 1991:73). According to Huntington and Metcalf, funerary rituals are more *product*-driven than *procedure*-driven; through the process of primary followed by secondary burials with intervening period of organic decomposition, the corpse is manufactured into something useful.

> From something perishable, inconveniently bulky, and useless in its present form, something long lasting, compact, and useful is obtained. The bones of the deceased partake of this nature, so that it is logical to take the time to recover them and store them with the other ancestors, from where they may exercise a benign influence upon their descendants. (Huntington and Metcalf 1991:74)

---

[21] Hertz's major contribution was the observation that the multiple stages of death—exclusion, purification, reintegration—essentially mirrors the spiritual journey of the dead person's soul from the land of the living to limbo and on to the land of the ancestral dead. In depth discussions of Hertz's work and influence can be found at Huntington and Metcalf 1991:33–38, 79–107, Parker Pearson 2000:45–56.

Huntington and Metcalf compare the manufacture of permanent and useful "bones of the deceased" out of his or her "perishable [and] inconveniently bulky [body]" with other manufacturing techniques that employ rotting and fermentation to create a more stable and "useful" product, such as the production of indigo dye out of rotting vegetal matter; the production of hemp for textiles by leaving the stalks to rot in water some weeks so as to allow the fibers to be separated more easily; the production of wine and other spirits through the distilling of liquids running off of decaying organic matter; and the production of certain food products, such as pickled vegetables or meats, through the partial anaerobic rotting of food items in tightly sealed containers.[22] In each of these examples, rotting appears to have a positive value insofar as it produces useful, refined products from organic matter.

These anthropological models regarding the treatment of the dead are applicable to the Homeric poems, for in Homer we find a similar situation of double burial: the cremation of the hero's body is followed by the interment of his bones.[23] As noted above, cremation is the *sine qua non* of Homeric funerary ritual. In a highly elaborate ritual, the hero's body is burned on a pyre; once the flesh is all burned off, his bones are collected to be buried elsewhere. In an influential essay on the social implications of funerary practices in ancient Greece, Sally Humphreys (1981), Classicist and distinguished scholar in social anthropology,[24] has noted that the cremation of the body and collection of bones in Homeric epic point to a process in line with the observations of Hertz:

> Seen in a wider context, both the collection of bones for secondary burial after the flesh has decayed and the belief that at death a spiritual part of the person leaves the body to become established in some new form of existence form part of the tendency to try to transform what was a living person and is now a decaying cadaver into something permanent and stable—mummy, monument or memory, ash, ancestor or angel. ... [A]llowing the bones of the dead to become separated from the flesh which once encased them is only one of a number of ways of representing the separation of a part of the person which is capable of

---

[22] See Huntington and Metcalf 1991:72–74, drawing on the work of Adams 1977.

[23] Williams (2004) notes how cremation is not at odds with Hertz' "primary burial," for both operations serve a similar function of transforming the cadaver into a more stable form (267). Indeed, Williams details how the performance of cremation can work as a "technology of remembrance" by creating "such a unique and powerful impact on the senses that it can form the very basis of the way the dead person is remembered" (267).

[24] For a useful discussion and critique of Humphreys' application of theories of social anthropology to the study of Classical antiquity, see Hunter 1981.

achieving immortality from the parts which are subject to destruction by time. (Humphreys 1981:268–269)

Bone is more stable than flesh; it is a stronger material and less susceptible to decay. Following Huntington and Metcalf's concept of productive death and decay, we may view Homeric funerary practice as a system for creating something more permanent out of what is wholly transitory. The cremating fire, then, is an accelerated version of the processes of natural organic decay; it produces the transformation from instable to stable more quickly, if not quite immediately, thereby shielding the grisly aspect of death from the celebrants, allowing them to maintain in their memories an image of the youthful fighter with flesh still supple. As anthropologist Maurice Bloch explains,

> The ideal is ... for the body to be immediately cremated so that disfiguration and decay do not occur. The image of the uncorrupted youth continues and maintains the undiminished life of the ideal society. The perfect body is in itself the source of the timelessness of the second side of the funeral, in that it represents an unchangingly vigorous martial order of society composed forever of incorruptible heroes. (Bloch 1982:228)[25]

Humphreys notes three main ways of accomplishing this transformation of the instable body into something more permanent: (1) "The deceased may become identified with some stable material object, usually a part of, receptacle for, or representation of his or her own body"; (2) "he or she may be reincorporated into society as an ancestor or by reincarnation"; and (3) "he or she may start a new life in the world of the dead" (Humphreys 1981:268). The second possibility points to the practice of preservation of the memory of the dead through cultic worship; the third, to preservation of the soul of the dead as guaranteed by a particular culture's eschatology. I leave these topics aside because my analysis of Homer is not concerned with the historical worship of heroes or religious cults; instead, I pursue the first possibility, the identification of the mortal body with something durable within the *Iliad* itself. For Homer this "stable material object" is indeed the "receptacle for" and "representation of" the deceased

---

[25] See Williams 2004 on the cremation process itself creating a powerful "memory" of the event through the sights, sounds, smells, and length of time for the corpse to be reduced to bone and ash (upwards of ten hours). In other words, the corpse acts as an agent in creating its own memory of the deceased and the experience of the funeral. For a similar argument, see Robb 2007 on the agency of bodies (vs. "mourner active models"), culturally embedded death, and biographical narratives reflected in funerary rituals.

man's body, to use Humphrey's terms: it is the very tombstone and grave marker erected in honor of the dead.

2. The Homeric σῆμα and Achilles' κλέος ἄφθιτον

The tomb (σῆμα) in Homeric epic consists of a mound (τύμβος) and grave marker (στήλη).[26] The tomb has three essential functions in Homeric epic: it indicates the location of the hero's grave; it serves to indicate a hero's identity; and it lends a sense of durability to the hero's memory. These functions of indication, identification, and durability constitute a shared field between the tomb and heroic poetry itself. In this section I draw parallels between the commemoration of the hero by means of the architectural σῆμα "tomb" and the preservation of the hero's name and a narrative of his deeds in epic poetry. Both the σῆμα "tomb" and κλέος ἄφθιτον "unwithered fame" aim to preserve the hero against the oblivion of death; neither, I argue, can be perfectly successful.

The Greek noun σῆμα, which usually bears the general meaning "sign," is regularly used with a specialized meaning "tomb." The overlap of meaning between these two uses is remarkable and suggests that the function of the "tomb" is to serve as a "sign" for the dead person buried there. The "tomb" consists of a burial mound—the τύμβος—and a vertical marker or column placed on top of the mound—the στήλη—which points to the fact that a hero is buried at the spot; its function is, in part, "indexical" (Sourvinou-Inwood 1995:113–118). The mound and column mark the spot as a landmark; the place itself becomes invested with meaning as the repository of a dead hero.

The long survivial of Ilos' tomb (XI 166–168, 369–372, X 415, XXIII 349) and those of other long gone ancestors (Aiputos of Arcadia at II 604 and "old man Aisuetes" at II 793) points to the fact that tombs are built to last (cf. McGowan 1995:620). Tombs are more stable than human flesh. They aim to provide the kind of permanence the human body can never achieve. The concept of the permanence of the tomb is closely associated with other means of preserving the hero's memory—namely, the poetic tradition of κλέος ἄφθιτον. We see in the very choice of location for the tomb—namely, that it is set up in a conspicuous location—indicates that the dead person buried there has a claim to fame. For example, Odysseus' companion Elpenor requests that he be buried in a manner that "men of the future may come to know of me":

ἔνθα σ' ἔπειτα, ἄναξ, κέλομαι μνήσασθαι ἐμεῖο.

[26] On the τύμβος "grave mound" in Homeric epic, see *Iliad* II 604, 793, IV 177, VII 336, 435, XI 371, XVI 457 = XVI 675, XVII 434, XXIII 245, XXIV 666; *Odyssey* I 239 = xiv 369, iv 584, xi 77, xii 14, 15, xxiv 32, 80. Compare the verb τυμβοχοέω "to heap up a tomb" at *Iliad* XXI 323. On the στήλη "grave marker" in Homeric epic, see *Iliad* XI 371, XIII 437, XVI 457, 675, XVII 434; *Odyssey* xiii 14.

μή μ' ἄκλαυτον ἄθαπτον ἰὼν ὄπιθεν καταλείπειν
νοσφισθείς, μή τοί τι θεῶν μήνιμα γένωμαι,
ἀλλά <u>με κακκῆαι</u> σὺν τεύχεσιν, ἄσσα μοί ἐστι,
<u>σῆμά τέ μοι χεῦαι</u> πολιῆς ἐπὶ θινὶ θαλάσσης,
ἀνδρὸς δυστήνοιο, <u>καὶ ἐσσομένοισι πυθέσθαι·</u>
ταῦτά τέ μοι τελέσαι <u>πῆξαί τ' ἐπὶ τύμβῳ ἐρετμόν,</u>
τῷ καὶ ζωὸς ἔρεσσον ἐὼν μετ' ἐμοῖσ' ἑτάροισιν.

There, then, my lord, I bid you to remember me.
Don't leave me behind you unwept, unburied, as you go
after you've turned away, lest for you I become some source of the
        gods' anger,
but rather, <u>burn me</u> with my armor, as much as belongs to me,
and <u>heap up a tomb for me</u> upon the shore of the grey sea
and <u>for men-to-come to know of me</u>, an unhappy man.
Fulfill these things for me, and <u>fix upon the burial mound my oar</u>
with which I rowed while I was alive among my comrades.

Odyssey xi 71–78

The shade of Elpenor addresses Odysseus in the underworld and asks to be cremated and buried in a conspicuous location so that men of the future may learn about him. In other words, Elpenor asks for a tomb that will help preserve his memory—the tomb's function is essentially to maintain his κλέος.[27] In fact, after Odysseus completes the goal of his mission to the underworld (his conversation with the prophet Tiresias), he sails back to Kirke's island to see to Elpenor's requested burial:

ἦμος δ' ἠριγένεια φάνη ῥοδοδάκτυλος Ἠώς,
δὴ τότ' ἐγὼν ἑτάρους προΐην ἐς δώματα Κίρκης
οἰσέμεναι νεκρὸν Ἐλπήνορα τεθνηῶτα.
φιτροὺς δ' αἶψα ταμόντες, <u>ὅθ' ἀκροτάτη πρόεχ' ἀκτή,</u>
<u>θάπτομεν</u> ἀχνύμενοι, θαλερὸν κατὰ δάκρυ χέοντες.
αὐτὰρ ἐπεὶ <u>νεκρός τ' ἐκάη</u> καὶ τεύχεα νεκροῦ,
<u>τύμβον χεύαντες</u> καὶ ἐπὶ στήλην ἐρύσαντες
πήξαμεν <u>ἀκροτάτῳ τύμβῳ</u> εὐῆρες ἐρετμόν.

---

[27] On the association between πυνθάνομαι/πεύθομαι and κλέος, cf. *Iliad* IX 524: οὕτω καὶ τῶν πρόσθεν <u>ἐπευθόμεθα κλέα ἀνδρῶν</u> | ἡρώων ..., "thus also we <u>used to learn of the famous deeds</u> of men who were heroes in former times ..." On κλέα ἀνδρῶν used to indicate epic poetry, see *Iliad* IX 186-189 where the Achaean ambassadors find Achilles "delighting his heart with a clear-toned lyre" as "he was singing the famous deeds of men" (ἄειδε δ' ἄρα κλέα ἀνδρῶν).

When early-born, rosy-fingered Dawn appeared,
then I sent forth my companions to Kirke's house
to fetch the corpse of Elpenor who had died.
Straightway then we cut wood logs, and, <u>in the place where the headland
  lies furthest out to sea,</u>
<u>we buried him</u>, sorrowing and shedding big tears.
But when <u>the corpse was burned</u>, and the dead man's armor,
<u>we heaped up a mound</u> and <u>dragged a column upon it</u>,
and <u>on the topmost part of the mound</u> we planted his shapely oar.

Odyssey xii 8–15

Odysseus and his companions bury Elpenor as he requested, cremating his body and heaping up a mound. On the top of that mound they drag a στήλη, which is apparently to be identified with Elpenor's "shapely oar" (Heubeck 1989:117, Sourvinou-Inwood 1995:116). The oar is a personal touch; it suggests to the observer that the person buried there was a sailor (Heubeck 1989:82). Odysseus and his companions bury Elpenor in the most conspicuous possible location—"in the place where the headland lies furthest out to sea" (ὅθ' ἀκροτάτη πρόεχ' ἀκτή, xii 11).[28] Located at the strand of the shore lying furthest out to sea, Elpenor's tomb will attract the attention of those who pass by, and hence, his fame will survive.[29]

In the *Odyssey*, Telemachus indicates that the absence of a τύμβος actually brings about the consequent loss of fame for the deceased and his kin—for had Odysseus perished while fighting in Troy, he would have been given proper burial and won κλέος for himself and his family; as it is, however, since he is presumably lost at sea and dead without proper burial, there is no fame (ἀκλειῶς):

[28] See Stanford 1967:I.406–406 on the conspicuousness of the location of the σῆμα as an indication of the hero's esteem.

[29] However, see Kahane 2005:112–113 for an interesting argument that the epic suggests that even Elpenor's oar is not guaranteed to remain a stable signifier of a dead sailor. Kahane compares Tiresias' prophecy to Odysseus and the instructions pertaining to how he may win favor at last with Poseidon, by carrying an oar far inland until someone from the mainland mistakes it for a winnowing fan (*Odyssey* xi 127). The mistaken identification will be a "very clear sign" (σῆμα ... μάλ' ἀριφραδές, xi 126) for Odysseus and an indication of where he is to plant that oar and establish a center of worship for the god far from the sea. The key issue here is the fact that the oar Odysseus is to establish far inland will always be misread as a winnowing fan; Kahane observes, "The force of the oar's misreading is underscored by the fact that it is perfectly reasonable for a landlocked observer to interpret an oar as a winnowing fan" (113). The implication is that even Elpenor's oar can be read correctly only under a set of rather specific circumstances—though the oar's location on the sea shore would seem to satisfy Kahane's requirements. See further Purves 2006b:11–18 on the σῆμα that Odysseus carries inland, and 2006b:14–15 on the connection between oar/winnowing fan as a σῆμα for Elpenor on the shore and for Odysseus while inland.

τῷ κέν οἱ <u>τύμβον</u> μὲν ἐποίησαν Παναχαιοί,
ἠδέ κε καὶ <u>ᾧ παιδὶ μέγα κλέος</u> ἤρατ' <u>ὀπίσσω</u>.
νῦν δέ μιν <u>ἀκλειῶς</u> ἅρπυιαι ἀνηρέψαντο.

In that case, all the Achaeans would have made a <u>tomb</u> for him,
and he would have won <u>great fame</u> <u>even for his son hereafter</u>.
But now stormwinds carried him off <u>without fame</u>.

Odyssey I 239–241

Because Odysseus is apparently lost at sea, there was no opportunity for the Greeks to honor him with a tomb (κέν οἱ τύμβον μὲν ἐποίησαν, I 239), and as a consequence, there is neither any κλέος for Odysseus himself or for Telemachus.[30]

The association between tomb and fame is drawn even more securely in Menelaus' description of the tomb he constructed in memory of Agamemnon in the fourth book of the *Odyssey*. He explains how while shipwrecked on Egypt, he learned of his brother's fate and erected a monument to him.

αὐτὰρ ἐπεὶ κατέπαυσα θεῶν χόλον αἰὲν ἐόντων,
<u>χεῦ'</u> Ἀγαμέμνονι <u>τύμβον</u>, ἵν' <u>ἄσβεστον κλέος</u> εἴη.

But when I had stayed the wrath of the gods who always are,
<u>I heaped up</u> <u>a burial mound</u> for Agamemnon, that his <u>fame might be
       unquenchable</u>.

Odyssey iv 583–584

Menelaus, while still in Egypt, heaps up a cenotaph for his dead brother Agamemnon, specifically so that Agamemnon's κλέος may be preserved. The association between a person's "fame" and the physical marker of his death is clear. The adjective ἄσβεστος can be analyzed as the compound verbal adjective in *-το- of the verb *σβέννυμι "to put out, quench," and is a formal equivalent of Achilles' κλέος ἄφθιτον (IX 413) In Homer the adjective ἄσβεστος is used to describe fire (φλόξ: XVI 123, XVII 89), laughter (γέλως: I 599, viii 326, xx 346), might (μένος: XXII 96), the cry of battle (βοή: XI 50, XIII 169 = XIII 540), and finally, a person's fame (κλέος: iv 584 of Agamemnon, vii 333 of Alkinoos). Although Menelaus claims that Agamemnon's fame will be "unquenchable," a study of

---

[30] See Sinos 1980:47 who cites this passage to argue that "In Epic, we find that the τύμβος 'tomb' of a hero is closely connected with his κλέος and that of his descendants." For similar passages connecting fame with one's τύμβος, see *Iliad* VII 86–91; *Odyssey* iv 584, xi 72–76, xiv 369–370, xxiv 80–94; and compare descriptions of the preservation of *kleos* through song: *Odyssey* iii 203–204, xxiv 196–202.

the other uses of ἄσβεστος suggests otherwise, for each activity described as "unquenchable," although long lasting, does in fact eventually come to an end. The fire set upon the Achaeans' ships is extinguished (XVI 123, XVII 89); the gods eventually cease laughing at Hephaistos' lame foot (I 599); Hektor's μένος is eventually extinguished when he is killed by Achilles (XXII 96); and the βοή that continually punctuates the great day of battle is finally silenced with the death of Hektor and the end of battle narrative in the *Iliad*. So too, I submit, is the κλέος associated with the construction of tombs only temporarily "unquenchable"—sooner or later it is put out like a flame doused in gleaming wine: compare *Iliad* XXIII 250 where Achilles "quenches" (σβέσαν) the fires of Patroklos' pyre; the verb used here (σβέσαν "they quenched" < σβέννυμι) is the root of ἄσβεστος.

The preservation of the hero's κλέος, then, is a key element in the ideology of the funeral monument. The most magnificent burial throughout the Homeric corpus is that of Achilles himself, narrated in the twenty-fourth book of the *Odyssey*. Agamemnon explains how the Achaeans treated their dead hero:

> ἀμφ' αὐτοῖσι δ' ἔπειτα <u>μέγαν καὶ ἀμύμονα τύμβον</u>
> χεύαμεν Ἀργείων ἱερὸς στρατὸς αἰχμητάων
> <u>ἀκτῇ ἔπι προὐχούσῃ</u>, ἐπὶ πλατεῖ Ἑλλησπόντῳ,
> ὥς κεν <u>τηλεφανὴς</u> ἐκ πόντοφιν ἀνδράσιν εἴη
> <u>τοῖσ', οἳ νῦν γεγάασι καὶ οἳ μετόπισθεν ἔσονται.</u>

> Then, we piled up <u>a great and blameless grave mound</u> about them,
> we the sacred army of Argive spearmen,
> <u>upon the headland furthest out to sea</u> on the broad Hellespont,
> so that it might be <u>visible from far off</u> from the sea for men,
> <u>both for those who are now living and those who will be in the</u>
>   <u>hereafter.</u>

> *Odyssey* xxiv 80–84

The tomb heaped up for Achilles is specified as "great and blameless," and its location is specified as a prominent and conspicuous location—on the headland jutting out to sea, much like Elpenor's tomb discussed above. The location is selected so as to be seen from far away (τηλεφανής, xxiv 83). The spectators who are to look upon Achilles' tomb are both those contemporary with the tomb—the men who live "now"—and those who will be "in the hereafter." The orientation of the tomb is specifically toward the future, the "men in the hereafter." I argue in the remainder of this chapter that this sense of futurity does not necessarily imply "eternity" or an unbound extent of time, but firmly locates funerary architecture within a temporally bound status.

3. The (Im)Permanence of the Hero's σῆμα in the *Iliad*

As we have seen, σῆμα indicates the location of the hero's mortal remains by means of a mound and column; moreover, it implies temporal durability insofar as its structures are relatively stable and can better withstand the ravages of time than the organic body of the dead man. And yet, this stability is itself several times demonstrated to be impermanent in the *Iliad*: the marker may fail to denote location, or it may be moved; the memory associated with the dead man can fail and be corrupted or fade entirely. Homeric epic even demonstrates a problematic view of the tomb of Achilles himself—though built in a prominent place and meant to preserve his memory, the texts seem to raise the possibility of the eventual destruction or disintegration of the tomb itself. The problematic status of material objects, I argue, functions to foreshadow the potential demise of the oral epic tradition itself and the κλέος ἄφθιτον it seeks to preserve and disseminate.

Let us begin with two striking passages that point to the failure of the "indexical" function of the σῆμα. The first passage comes from the *theomakhia* of the twenty-first book of the *Iliad*, when Athena defends herself against Ares.

> ἣ δ' ἀναχασσαμένη λίθον εἵλετο χειρὶ παχείῃ
> κείμενον ἐν πεδίῳ, μέλανα τρηχύν τε μέγαν τε,
> τόν ῥ' ἄνδρες πρότεροι θέσαν ἔμμεναι <u>οὖρον</u> ἀρούρης·
> τῷ βάλε θοῦρον Ἄρηα κατ' αὐχένα, λῦσε δὲ γυῖα.

> But [Athena] drew back and with her stout hand seized a stone
> lying in the plain, black, jagged, and huge,
> which earlier men had placed to be <u>a boundary marker</u> of a
>   plow-field.
> With it she struck furious Ares in his neck and loosened his
>   limbs.

> *Iliad* XXI 403–406

Athena picks up a great stone and uses it as a weapon, as is common for Greek and Trojan warriors.[31] What is remarkable here, however, is that this stone has a history—men of old (ἄνδρες πρότεροι, XXI 405) used it to mark the physical boundary (οὖρον, XXI 405) between shares of land that would otherwise be

---

[31] For instance, Tydeus picks up and hurls a boulder described as "a great work (μέγα ἔργον) such as no two men, such as they are now, could lift" (*Iliad* V 302–304). Compare VII 264–265 (~ XXI 403–404) where Hektor strikes Ajax's shield with a "stone lying in the plain, black, jagged, and huge"; and see further XII 380–383, 445–449, XX 285–287.

indistinguishable from one another.[32] The stone's location is significant; it has been placed at an exact spot as a stable marker of property division. It is the tangible sign of the mutual agreement between men, a symbol of the cultural institution of legal negotiation that guided its placement. When Athena picks up the stone and casts it at Ares, then, she disturbs the boundary marker, and thereby destroys its referential force. As Andrew Ford (1992) notes in his analysis of the passage, "the goddess has erased the border; wherever it lands it will have lost its original significance" (147). Athena's act demonstrates the fundamental failure of the indexical sign—once it is moved, it no longer fulfills the function for which it was established.

The second passage which points to the failure of the indexical σῆμα occurs in the twenty-third book of the *Iliad* during the funeral games held in honor of Patroklos. Nestor gives his son Antilochus advice about how to compensate for his slower horses by means of careful observation and well-timed steering.

σῆμα δέ τοι ἐρέω μάλ' ἀριφραδές, οὐδέ σε λήσει·
ἕστηκε ξύλον αὖον ὅσον τ' ὄργυι' ὑπὲρ αἴης,
ἢ δρυὸς ἢ πεύκης· τὸ μὲν οὐ καταπύθεται ὄμβρῳ·
λᾶε δὲ τοῦ ἑκάτερθεν ἐρηρέδαται δύο λευκὼ
ἐν ξυνοχῇσιν ὁδοῦ, λεῖος δ' ἱππόδρομος ἀμφὶς·
ἤ τευ σῆμα βροτοῖο πάλαι κατατεθνηῶτος,
ἢ τό γε νύσσα τέτυκτο ἐπὶ προτέρων ἀνθρώπων,
καὶ νῦν τέρματ' ἔθηκε ποδάρκης δῖος Ἀχιλλεύς.

---

[32] On the importance of boundary divisions, compare XII 421–423, a simile in which the Lycians and Danaäns face off at close quarters and fight like men fighting over the proper placement of a boundary marker between fields: "as when about boundary markers (ἀμφ' οὔροισι) two men fight while they hold measuring-cords (μέτρα) in their hands at the place where fields join together (ἐπιξύνῳ), and the two of them in a small area (ὀλίγῳ ἐνὶ χώρῳ) contend over the equal division, just so did the battlements hold them [sc. Lycians and Danaäns] apart." On this simile, see Elmer 2008 who compares the boundary dispute represented here with the ancient ball game known as *episkuros* as both feature "a territorial conflict in which one side seeks to dispossess the other of the area it occupies" (416). Hence, the game *episkuros* functions as "a symbolization of a boundary dispute," whereas the Iliadic simile of XII 417–424 is, "from the point of view of the audience, ... a stylization of the 'real-life' situation of boundary disputes. That is, epic narrative and game occupy analogous positions as images of an archetypical conflict over boundaries" (420). On the importance of the οὖρος "boundary marker" (ὅρος in Attic) as a landmark, it is interesting to note that the noun can be used with the sense of a "memorial stone" or "pillar" (e.g. Herodotus 1.93), especially one set up on mortgaged property to indicate the terms of debt (see Solon fr. 36.6 W: ὅρους ἀνεῖλον). The eradication of such markers is nothing short of revolutionary, as we read in Solon fr. 36 W: see Almeida 2003:8–9 (with nn40–41), 27–28, 34, 40, 95, 223–224 for discussion and further bibliography.

But I will tell you a very clear sign [σῆμα], and it will not escape your
    notice.
There is a dry stump standing as much as six feet above the ground,[33]
either of oak or of pine, which is not completely rotted away by
    rain-water.
And two white stones leaning on either side of it,
at the joining place of the road, and there is a smooth race-course around
    it.
Either it is the tomb (σῆμα) of a man who died long ago,
or it was set up as a turning-post by men of former times,
but now swift-footed, brilliant Achilles has made it the goal.

                                Iliad XXIII 326–333

Nestor begins his advice by pointing out what he calls "a very clear sign" (σῆμα
... μάλ' ἀριφραδές, XXIII 326), a tree stump with two white stones leaning against
it. However, as Nestor goes on to describe the σῆμα more completely, we find
it to be anything but "very clear." The stump has indeed weathered the ages;
Nestor specifies that it has not completely "rotted" (οὐ καταπύθεται, XXIII 328)
in the rain. Nevertheless, he is not able to identify what kind of tree it is: it might
be oak, or it might be pine. The coordinating conjunctions ἤ ... ἤ "whether ...
or" point to the indefiniteness inherent in the σῆμα. More important for our
purposes, however, is the fact that Nestor is further unable to tell whether the
stump and white stones is a "tomb of a man who died long ago" (τευ σῆμα βροτοῖο
πάλαι κατατεθνηῶτος, XXIII 331), or was a turning-post (νύσσα, XXIII 332) for
a race-course set up by men long ago (προτέρων ἀνθρώπων, XXIII 332).[34] Once
again, the two options are presented as coordinate pairs following the conjunctions ἤ ... ἤ "either ... or." In other words, Homer is offering us an example of
a sign which has lost its referent; if the stump and stones were at one point a
hero's tomb and the tangible sign of his κλέος, that sign is no longer legible—
significantly, not even by Nestor himself, that great repository of ancient lore.[35]
Whatever oral tradition was once connected to that σῆμα, it has faded beyond
the reaches of living memory.

[33] The unit of measure indicated by ὄργυια—traditionally rendered as "a fathom"—implies the
distance measured out by a man's outstretched arms. Stanford 1967:I.383 draws our attention
to its cognate verb ὀρέγω "to stretch out," and notes that "the length across an average man's
outstretched arms and shoulders" is approximately six feet. The phrase ὅσον τ' ὄργυιαν appears
twice in the *Odyssey* (ix 325, x 167; cf. xi 25), though only here in the *Iliad*.

[34] See McGowan 1995 on the use of funerary markers as turning posts in funeral games.

[35] On Nestor's authoritative memory spanning three generations, see *Iliad* I 250–252. On Nestor
and memory, see especially Dickson 1992, 1995. On the ambiguities in Nestor's speech here, see
Dickson 1995:216–219, 224n8, Ford 1992:144–145, Kahane 2005:114, Lynn-George 1988:265–266,
and Peradotto 1990:159–160.

The first two examples we have surveyed, then, demonstrate the problem of the stability of the σῆμα in two diametrically opposed senses. First, the σῆμα itself might be destroyed or moved from its proper location. This dislocation is a failure of the σῆμα to remain fixed; its status as ἔμπεδος "fixed in/on the ground" is of necessity temporally bound, for every structure is eventually destroyed. Second, even when the σῆμα should outlast the disintegrating effects of time, such as Nestor's σῆμα which has not rotted in the rain, it still may lose its referentiality if the supplemental oral tradition that specifies the object as the tomb of a specific warrior or even as a tomb at all fades away beyond all recovery. That is to say, the σῆμα can only function as a "sign" which conveys meaning as long as it is connected to a living memory or tradition of memory. Once that tradition has died out, the σῆμα is no longer stable.[36] Sourvinou-Inwood explains,

> As long as the deceased's memory lived on in the community, and the grave monument was identified as the index of his burial, its physical presence inevitably activated the memory of the deceased, in those who perceived it, and in this way it also fed the memory and contributed to its preservation. (Sourvinou-Inwood 1995:118)[37]

A more extreme example of this outright forgetfulness of the tradition supporting the σῆμα is the description of the "tomb of Myrina," a landmark in the Trojan plain known to the Trojans as a "hill," but known only to the gods (and to the narrator) as a "tomb":

ἔστι δέ τις προπάροιθε πόλιος αἰπεῖα κολώνη
ἐν πεδίῳ ἀπάνευθε περίδρομος ἔνθα καὶ ἔνθα,
τὴν ἤτοι ἄνδρες Βατίειαν κικλήσκουσιν,
ἀθάνατοι δέ τε σῆμα πολυσκάρθμοιο Μυρίνης.

There is a certain steep hill in front of the city
in the plain, far off, with passage around on one side and
      the other,
which, truly, I tell you, men regularly call "Bramble Hill,"
but the immortals "The Tomb of Much-Leaping Myrina."

Iliad II 811–814

---

36 Compare Ford 1992:144, who also notes the necessity of a continuous tradition to "supplement" the identity of the person buried in a given tomb.

37 In his discussion of *Iliad* XXIII 326–333 and Nestor's inability to tell whether the turning post is the tomb of a long-dead hero or not, Dickson (1995) notes, "At this ultimate limit, once memory has failed and all narrative and naming along with it, *kleos* surely must fail as well" (219).

An ancient scholiast identifies this Myrina as one of the Amazons who invaded Phrygia in prehistoric times.[38] The *Iliad* offers us a brief glimpse of a mis-read sign; the large τύμβος "grave mound" piled over the Amazonian fighter has been mistaken for a natural feature of the landscape.

Regarding the destruction of the σῆμα or outright oblivion of its supporting oral tradition, what are we to make of situations in which the supplementary oral tradition remains intact? It has often been claimed that traditional epic poetry goes further than material structures in preserving the memory of the dead. For instance, Jean-Pierre Vernant has claimed,

> There is a parallelism or continuity between Greek funeral rituals and epic verse. Both are directed to the same end, but *the epic goes a step further than the funeral ritual.* The funeral rites aim to procure for the person who has lost his life access to a new state of social existence, to transform the absence of the lost person into a more or less stable positive social status, that of "one of the dead." *Epic goes further: through glorifying praise, indefinitely repeated*, it ensures for a small minority of the chosen—who thus stand out from the ordinary mass of the deceased, defined as the crowd of "nameless ones"—*the permanence of their name, their fame, and the exploits they have accomplished. In this way it completes and crowns the process that the funeral rites have already set in motion*: the transformation of an individual who has ceased to be into a figure whose presence, as one of the dead, is forever a part of the existence of the group. (Vernant 1981:285, emphases added)

Epic poetry "goes a step further" than funerary ritual and its material constructions; it establishes for the select few "the permanence of their name, their fame, their exploits" and "crowns" the process of preservation set in motion by the funeral ritual with its substitution of increasingly more durable material representations for the human body. That is to say, epic poetry is thought to provide a "permanent" status to a dead person's name and deeds. Note that Vernant's terms function as near translation for the terms we have been engaged with so far, ἄφθιτον "unwithered" and ἔμπεδος "in place." Epic aims to create a state of non-decay for the dead, to elevate the dead to the status of

---

[38] Myrina is identified as an Amazon by Scholia D at *Iliad* II 814. A tradition regarding an Amazonian invasion is attested at *Iliad* III 189 where Priam recalls how he helped fight the Amazons at the river Sangarius off to the east (cf. Leaf 1900–1902:I.111 and Kirk 1985:247). There is some historic evidence of an Aeolic town named "Myrina," and Strabo claims that Cyme and Smyrna were also named after Amazons (11.5.4, 12.8.6, 13.3.6, 14.1.4).

immortality, as Gregory Nagy has argued, through the fixation of the dead in the cultural medium of poetry and art.[39]

Yet, I maintain that the indefinite in Homer is always conditioned by the logical structure of the "not yet": at best, the κλέος achieved through poetry is only as durable as the tradition in which it flourishes. There is enduring danger, therefore, that κλέος will fade or fail, as Vernant himself indicates in his observation that the epic tradition functions only under the condition of its being "indefinitely repeated." The possibility remains open that a tradition can *cease* to be repeated, or that a specific monument can be *reprogrammed* to accommodate a different memory. Indeed, the *Iliad* itself represents an imagined scenario in which the σῆμα and its associated oral tradition meant to commemorate a fallen hero's life can be re-programmed to indicate something else entirely once the living oral tradition that would support its original significance no longer exists. In particular, in the seventh book of the *Iliad* Hektor challenges the best of the Achaeans to single-combat with him in order to settle the battle once and for all. His offer is nothing short of a threat, for it hints at the loss of his victim's reputation.

> ὑμῖν δ' ἐν γὰρ ἔασιν ἀριστῆες Παναχαιῶν,
> τῶν νῦν ὅν τινα θυμὸς ἐμοὶ μαχέσασθαι ἀνώγῃ,
> δεῦρ' ἴτω ἐκ πάντων πρόμος ἔμμεναι Ἕκτορι δίῳ.
> ὧδε δὲ μυθέομαι, Ζεὺς δ' ἄμμ' ἐπὶ μάρτυρος ἔστω·
> εἰ μέν κεν ἐμὲ κεῖνος ἕλῃ ταναήκεϊ χαλκῷ,
> τεύχεα συλήσας φερέτω κοίλας ἐπὶ νῆας,
> σῶμα δὲ οἴκαδ' ἐμὸν δόμεναι πάλιν, ὄφρα πυρός με
> Τρῶες καὶ Τρώων ἄλοχοι λελάχωσι θανόντα·
> εἰ δέ κ' ἐγὼ τὸν ἕλω, δώῃ δέ μοι εὖχος Ἀπόλλων,
> τεύχεα συλήσας οἴσω προτὶ Ἴλιον ἱρὴν
> καὶ κρεμόω ποτὶ νηὸν Ἀπόλλωνος ἑκάτοιο,
> τὸν δὲ νέκυν ἐπὶ νῆας ἐϋσσέλμους ἀποδώσω,
> ὄφρα ἑ ταρχύσωσι κάρη κομόωντες Ἀχαιοὶ
> <u>σῆμά</u> τέ οἱ χεύωσιν ἐπὶ πλατεῖ Ἑλλησπόντῳ.
> καί <u>ποτέ</u> τις εἴπῃσι καὶ ὀψιγόνων ἀνθρώπων,
> νηΐ πολυκλήϊδι πλέων ἐπὶ οἴνοπα πόντον·
> "<u>ἀνδρὸς μὲν τόδε σῆμα πάλαι κατατεθνηῶτος</u>,
> ὅν <u>ποτ</u>' ἀριστεύοντα κατέκτανε φαίδιμος Ἕκτωρ."
> ὣς <u>ποτέ</u> τις ἐρέει, <u>τὸ δ' ἐμὸν κλέος οὔ ποτ' ὀλεῖται</u>.

---

[39]   See Nagy 1974:229–261, more forcefully formulated at Nagy 1999:179–181 (Ch. 10§7–9), analyzing Agamemnon's scepter.

Since among you are the best of all the Achaeans,
let one of you, whomever his passion drives him on to fight with me,
come here now from all the others to be in the front against brilliant
      Hektor.
I make the following claim, and may Zeus be witness upon it:
if, on the one hand, that man should take my life with thin-edged
      bronze,
let him strip my armor and carry it to the hollow ships,
but give my body back home, so that the Trojans
and the wives of the Trojans may give me my share of fire, when I am
      dead.
But if, on the other hand, I shall kill him—may Apollo grant me the
      prayer!—
I shall strip his armor and carry it toward holy Ilion
and I will hang it up in the shrine of Apollo the far-shooter,
but I will give back the corpse to the well-benched ships,
so that the long-haired Achaeans may offer him proper funeral rites
and heap up a tomb (σῆμα) for him upon the broad Hellespont.
And someday someone will say, even among late-born men,
as he is sailing with his ship with many oar-locks upon the wine-
      dark sea,
"This here is the tomb (σῆμα) of a man who died long ago,
who was once one of the best—glorious Hektor killed him."
So someday someone will speak, and my fame (κλέος) will never perish.

Iliad VII 73–91

Hektor's challenge points to an ethics underlying heroic combat, for even though one may kill the other, the victor will not defile the corpse of his victim, but return it to friends and family so it may be fittingly cremated and buried. Here, the burial is envisioned as taking place in a conspicuous location, upon the shore overlooking the Hellespont. What is remarkable here, however, is that Hektor imagines a long-lasting tomb that is not forgotten; in Hektor's vision, the tomb remains connected to an active oral tradition that preserves memory of past events. Note especially Hektor's claim that "someday someone will say, even among late-born men" (ποτέ τις εἴπῃσι καὶ ὀψιγόνων ἀνθρώπων, VII 87). The implications of the indefinite temporal adverbs καί ποτέ "even someday" (VII 87, 91), the future orientation of the verbs εἴπῃσι (VII 87)[40] and ἐρέει (VII

---

40 Although εἴπῃσι, strictly speaking, is an aorist subjunctive verb, the subjunctive mood shows expectation about the future. See Goodwin 1893:97–98; Willcock 1978–1984:I.252. For the pattern

91), and the temporal adverb ὀψέ "late" (in the compound ὀψιγόνων "of late-born men," VII 87), all point to the idea that the σῆμα and its supplementary oral tradition may survive far into the future.[41] However, what we must notice is that the σῆμα is here imagined to preserve the κλέος not of the victim, but of the victor—Hektor's hypothetical observer from the future will say, "This here is the tomb (σῆμα) of a man who died long ago, who was once one of the best—glorious Hektor killed him." There is no mention of the fallen man's name nor any of the circumstances of his life; of course Hektor is speaking generally, since no Greek fighter has risen to fight him yet, but the generic identification—"whomever the spirit moves to fight me" (ὅν τινα θυμὸς ἐμοὶ μαχέσασθαι ἀνώγῃ, VII 74)—sits uneasily with the emphasis on remembering the hero's name in the epic tradition. The single fact remembered, so far as Hektor is concerned, about the fallen is that Hektor killed him. Only the victor's fame will survive: "So someday someone will speak, and my fame (τὸ δ' ἐμὸν κλέος) will never perish (οὔ ποτ' ὀλεῖται)" (VII 91). Like the *sēma* that Nestor identifies during the chariot race at Patroklos' funeral games, the *sēma* in Hektor's speech will have lost its referent: instead of marking the tomb and *kleos* of the dead who lies there, it commemorates that of his killer.[42] This passage gives us a model for what happens when a supplementary oral tradition fails to function: the monument loses its mnemonic force, and comes to mean something else altogether.

In conclusion to this investigation of mortuary architecture and its association with the hero's κλέος ἄφθιτον, I wish to draw our attention to two final passages which present the strong exception taken by the sixth-century BCE Greek lyric poet Simonides to an epigram attributed by him to Cleobulus, supposedly inscribed upon the funeral marker for Midas. The funerary epigram reads:

---

of aorist subjunctive εἴπῃσι followed by future indicative ἐρέει, compare Hektor at *Iliad* VI 459–462, a passage speculating about future events.

[41] See, for instance, Kirk 1990:246, "The second καί in 87 could mean either 'even' or 'also,' the point being that *the mound will last long into the future*" (emphasis added).

[42] Hektor's claim that his fame will never perish (κλέος οὔ ποτ' ὀλεῖται#, VII 91) makes use of a formulaic variation of Achilles' own "fame unwithered" (κλέος ἄφθιτον ἔσται#, IX 413) found elsewhere in early Greek poetry at *Iliad* II 325 (on the fame of the great portent Zeus showed the Achaeans at Aulis before they sailed to Troy), *Odyssey* xxiv 196 (on Penelope's fame for remaining faithful to Odysseus), Hesiod fr. 70.5 M-W = fr. 41 Most (on Ino nursing Dionysus [?] so his fame would never perish), *Homeric Hymn to Apollo* 156, and Theognis 867. See Finkelberg 2007 for an argument that the two phrases are genetically connected. The fact that Hektor's κλέος οὔ ποτ' ὀλεῖται is an analogical formulaic substitution for Achilles' κλέος ἄφθιτον ἔσται is further confirmed in terms of the similar status of temporality in each construction, since Hektor essentially posits his "fame that will not perish" upon the enduring status of the tomb of his victim (σῆμα, VII 86, 89); yet, as I have established in this chapter, the status of the material monument of the dead is itself of temporary durability.

155

χαλκῆ παρθένος εἰμί, Μίδου δ' ἐπὶ σήματος ἧμαι.
ἔς τ' ἂν ὕδωρ τε νάῃ καὶ δένδρεα μακρὰ τεθήλῃ
ἠέλιος δ' ἀνιὼν φαίνῃ λαμπρά τε σελήνη,
καὶ ποταμοί γε ῥέωσιν, ἀνακλύζῃ δὲ θάλασσα,
αὐτοῦ τῇδε μένουσα πολυκλαύτῳ ἐπὶ τύμβῳ
σημανέω παριοῦσι Μίδης ὅτι τῇδε τέθαπται.[43]

I am a bronze maiden, and am set upon the tomb of Midas.
As long as both water flows and tall trees flourish,
and the sun shines when it rises as does the shining moon,
and the rivers run and the sea breaks upon the shore,
I, all the while remaining here upon this much-lamented tomb,
will announce to those who pass by that Midas has been buried
      here.

The epigram claims to be an inscription upon a funerary monument which here takes the form of a bronze maiden (χαλκῆ παρθένος εἰμί, 1). The text claims to represent the voice of the maiden herself, set upon Midas' tomb to proclaim to all who pass by that Midas is buried here. Most striking, however, is the text's claim to extreme durability—it will last "as long as" (ἔς τ' ἂν, literally rendered "up to whenever," 2) the natural world continues. As long as rivers flow, trees flourish, and the sun rises, so too will the monument "remain" (μένουσα, 5) in place and will "speak" (σημανέω, 6) to passers by. The tomb's durability is emphasized by pairing the future tense σημανέω with a string of subjunctive verbs (νάῃ ... τεθήλῃ, 2; φαίνῃ, 3; ῥέωσιν ... ἀνακλύζῃ, 4) in a future-more-vivid temporal construction. Simonides' response attacks this claim:

τίς κεν αἰνήσειε νόῳ πίσυνος Λίνδου ναέταν Κλεόβουλον,
ἀενάοις ποταμοῖσ' ἄνθεσί τ' εἰαρινοῖς
ἀελίου τε φλογὶ χρυσέας τε σελάνας
καὶ θαλασσαίαισι δίναισ' ἀντία θέντα μένος στάλας;
ἅπαντα γάρ ἐστι θεῶν ἥσσω· λίθον δὲ
καὶ βρότεοι παλάμαι θραύοντι· μωροῦ
φωτὸς ἅδε βούλα.

---

[43] One tradition attributes this epigram to Homer: *Vita Homeri Herodotea* 135–140 (ed. Allen *Homeri Opera, Vol. V*, p. 198–199), *Certamen Homeri et Hesiodi* 265–270 (ed. Allen *Homeri Opera, Vol. V*, p. 235–236), Homer *Epigram* 3 (West). An alternate tradition attributes it to Cleobulus, the tyrant of Lindos in Rhodes around 600 BCE, considered by some to be one of the "Seven Sages" (cf. Plutarch *de E Delphico* 3): Simonides fr. 581 PMG, Diogenes Laertes 1.6, and the *Palatine Anthology* 7.153. Plato *Phaedrus* 264c–d also preserves the poem, with variant reading: ὄφρ' ἂν for ἔς τ' ἂν in verse 2.

Who is there who is sound in mind who could approve of Cleobulus, who
      lives in Lindos,
who against ever-flowing rivers and springtime flowers,
and against the blaze of the sun and of the golden moon,
and against the eddying of the seas, sets the might of a tomb?
For all these things are lesser than gods; but stone
even mortal hands can shatter. This is the opinion
of a stupid man.

Simonides fr. 76 PMG

Only a fool, Simonides argues, would set a stone up in competition against the
sun, the moon, rivers, and trees, for all these things are gods and therefore
(presumably) immortal, whereas a tomb is truly mortal architecture: anyone
can destroy it with his or her own hands.

    This controversy points to a deep-seated ambivalence inherent in the
ideology of monumental architecture and the epic tradition already apparent
in Homer. The funerary practices of cremation followed by burial indicate a
desire to preserve the body beyond the capacity of its own material substance.
The tomb and marker serve such a function, but never in an unambiguous way.
Tombs may be destroyed or forgotten; the stories attached to them may be
corrupted or entirely forgotten. What is significant about all this is that these
funeral monuments are deeply connected with the epic tradition of κλέος
ἄφθιτον. Like its verbal counterpart, the funerary monument is a durable but,
ultimately, temporally bound construction.

Chapter 5

The Impermanence of the Permanent
The Death of the Gods?

Philology, like philosophy, begins in wonder. Surprise should be taken seriously,
for it has an important hermeneutic function: it signals a lack of correspondence
between our horizon of expectations and some new object and thus suggests that,
if we have not radically misunderstood that object, then our prior expectations
must be significantly revised.

—Glenn W. Most[1]

THROUGHOUT THE PRECEDING CHAPTERS, I have attempted to demonstrate the temporal dimensions of the Iliadic narrative by analyzing images of decaying ships and human bodies along with the more durable yet still mortal structures of defensive walls and tombs. The temporal structure of the people and objects of the Iliadic world is conditioned by the state of constant degeneration: everything tends towards decay, though it may "not yet" (οὔ πω) have achieved that status.

In this chapter, I argue that the very concept of "permanence" in the Homeric epics, the near contemporary work by Hesiod, and the corpus of poems known as the *Homeric Hymns*, is more complex than is generally assumed.[2] Men and gods occupy what can be thought of as two different "worlds," each governed by its own temporality. The mortal world and mortal time are filled with labor, pain, grief, and death. The world of gods is free from such experiences; gods live easily and spend their time feasting and enjoying the divine music of the Muses. And yet, when we look at the way these two "worlds" are situated, we find that although separate, they are not mutually exclusive. That is to say, it is possible for a member

---

[1] Most 1987:3.
[2] I follow the relative dating of Homer, Hesiod, and the *Homeric Hymns* established by Janko 1982.

of one of the "worlds" to become *distant* from his own world and its accompanying temporality and therefore to become *close* to the world and temporality of the other. Within this framework we may situate the tradition of a pre-historic race of men who do not work, do not grow old, do not get sick, and essentially do not experience death; they are characterized as occupying a space *far away* and *apart* from the world of men, a space which is correspondingly *close* to the world of the gods. In a reciprocal move, then, it is possible for gods to undergo certain experiences that make them *distant* from the space proper to gods and that bring them *close* to the mortal world and the wasting effects of mortal time.

From this perspective, we may examine those moments within the narrative of the *Iliad* and its contemporary texts where gods come to experience mortal time—becoming enmeshed in human temporality—through the experience of pain, anxiety, grief. Here we examine the physical sufferings of Aphrodite, Hera, Hades, and Ares. Furthermore, we look at a series of interrelated stories that constitute a traditional "motif" which deals with one god challenging the chief divinity and either overthrowing him or being overthrown by him. These stories representing the "succession motif" are significant for our study because they contain clear instances of gods forced to experience mortal temporality, wherein the defeated challenger is made to feel physical pain by being struck with Zeus' lightning bolt, and is then quite literally made *distant* from the world of the gods: he is "hurled" out of heaven itself and into the murky depths of Tartaros, the underground containment cell for defeated gods and their analogical "Hades." Here we compare the Homeric narrative of the fall of Hephaistos with the Hesiodic narrative of the fall of Typhoeus/Typhaon, along with the Iliadic descriptions of Atē, the goddess of "delusion," and Hupnos, the god of "sleep," who are cast or nearly cast from heaven never to return.[3]

Let me be forthright: no god actually "dies" in the *Iliad*. Yet, several divinities experience something very similar to "death."[4] Being caught up in mortal time through pain and suffering, being struck by lightning, or being thrown into Tartaros are essentially as close as any god comes to "death." And yet, once a god experiences mortal time, he or she is deeply affected—he or she comes to experience a virtual death. As we will see, Hephaistos once wounded never quite regains his original status, but remains marked by the lasting effects of

---

[3] Purves 2006a has discussed Hephaistos' and Ares' experience of mortal time through their respective "falls" to earth. My analysis locates those "falls" within a larger context of gods who suffer the effects of mortal time. Hence, it is important to note that Hephaistos does not merely fall, but is thrown: he suffers as the Titans and Typhoeus before him, and as Atē ("Delusion"), Hupnos ("Sleep"), and Hera *nearly* do in *Iliad* XIV.

[4] Consider other possible scenarios raised by the Iliadic narrative though not actually carried out, such as actions carried out ὑπὲρ μοῖραν "beyond destiny" with Willcock's observation that it is "theoretically possible to frustrate [fate], but in practice this does not happen" (1976:19). Like actions that violate fate, the death of the gods is represented as a *possible* outcome.

his "mortal" experiences. In a less marked way, Hera is also drawn into mortal temporality through her suffering of a an "incurable pain" (ἀνήκεστον ... ἄλγος, V 394) at Herakles' hands, and Ares is brought to the very threshold of death in his thirteen month long captivity in a bronze jar (καί νύ κεν ἔνθ' ἀπόλοιτο "and now he might have died," V 388).

In short, then, I aim to show that Homer's gods themselves come to be conditioned by time. That is to say, Homer presents his gods as experiencing the world the way humans experience it when they feel sorrow, loss, and pain. The death of their loved ones cuts them metaphorically, and weapons can cut them quite literally. They weep, bleed, endure physical pain, and in certain circumstances, even seem to undergo something strikingly similar to death.[5] They may lose their powers and prerogatives through binding and imprisonment;[6] they can be physically incapacitated through loss of breath or blood; and they can be subdued with Zeus' lightning bolt or even human weapons. Finally, they can be cast into Tartaros, a prison for Zeus' enemies, which contains these "dead" gods just as Hades contains the souls of dead mortals.

What does it mean for the gods of Greek epic, by definition the very personification of permanence, to be subject to time and perhaps even to "die"? Such a question is deeply connected with the concepts of temporality and durability, for, I believe, the image of a dying god necessarily forces us to revise our notion of permanence itself. I argue that this question informs our understanding of Homer's epic project—the preservation and dissemination of Achilles κλέος ἄφθιτον "unwithered fame."

1. Immortal and Ageless Forever? The Spatial and Temporal Dimensions of Immortality

At first glance, the gods in Greek epic appear to be outside of time and immune to its withering effects.[7] They are regularly called "immortal and ageless" (ἀθάνατος καὶ ἀγήρως) in a collection of formulaic phrases in Greek hexameter

---

[5]   On the question of the "death" of gods in Homer, see Willcock 1964, 1970, 1977, Braswell 1971, Levy 1979, Vermeule 1979:118–144, Andersen 1981, Loraux 1986, Harrell 1991, Sissa and Detienne 2000, Burton 2001, and Purves 2006a.

[6]   See Detienne and Vernant 1978:115–116 on binding as a form of "death" for gods (cited below). In this context, we may consider the "binding" of Zeus (cf. *Iliad* I 396–404) as an instance of the mythical succession-motif in which a challenger seeks to overthrow and permanently incapacitate the king of the gods so that he may rule in his place: see Lang 1983, Slatkin 1986, 1991:66–69, and Alden 2000:38–39.

[7]   The topic of the nature of the gods as represented in Homeric epic is vast, but a selection of important discussions must include Bowra 1930:215–233, Dodds 1951, Lesky 1996:65–73, Willcock 1970, Fränkel 1975:53–93, Dietrich 1967, 1979, Vermeule 1979:118–144, Griffin 1980:144–204, Clay 1982, Schein 1984, Thalmann 1984:78–112, Edwards 1987:124–142, Vernant 1991:27–49, and Sissa and Detienne 2000.

poetry which point to the structural opposition underlying the distinction between gods and human beings.[8] Unlike "mortals" (θνητοί or καταθνητοί), the gods are "immortal" (ἀθάνατοι): they do not experience death, that biological event which defines the human condition. What is more, Greek gods do not undergo the process of physical decomposition brought upon mortals by time and age—they are ἀγήρως "ageless." They are not part of the temporal cycle of growth and decay.[9] Unlike mortals who exist only for a short time, gods are beings who "always are" (αἰεὶ ὄντες).[10] They are distinguished from mortals in terms of what they eat. Man eats the fruits of the earth: compare *Iliad* XXI 465: ἀρούρης καρπὸν ἔδοντες "[men] eating the fruit of the plowed field"; VI 142: εἰ δέ τίς ἐσσι βροτῶν οἳ ἀρούρης καρπὸν ἔδουσιν, "if you are someone of mortals, men who eat the fruit of the plowed field"; and the formula ἐπὶ χθονὶ σῖτον ἔδοντες "[men] eating food upon the earth" (*Odyssey* viii 222, ix 89, x 101). Gods,

---

[8]   "Immortal and ageless" constitutes a very common formula in Greek hexameter poetry, found in line initial position (ἀθάνατος καὶ ἄγηρος) [#–uu–uu–u], as at Hesiod fr. 25.28 and 229.8 M-W, with a variation extending the line initial formula to the Adonic segment (ἀθανάτους ὄντας καὶ ἀγήρως, *vel sim.*) [#–uu––‖ uu–uu], as at *Odyssey* vii 94, Hesiod *Theogony* 305, and *Hymn to Demeter* 260; a similar variant extends from line initial position to Adonic segment [#–uu ἀθάνατος καὶ ἀγήρως –uu–x#] at *Iliad* VIII 539, *Odyssey* v 136 = vii 257 = xxiii 336, Hesiod *Theogony* 949, Hesiod fr. 23a.12 and 23a.24 M-W, *Hymn to Apollo* 151, *Hymn to Aphrodite* 214 (compare also Hesiod *Theogony* 955 with ἀπήμαντος "without suffering" substituted for ἀθάνατος "immortal": ναίει <u>ἀπήμαντος καὶ ἀγήραος ἤματα πάντα</u> [#–u u–––uu –uu–x#]); and lastly, we find a version extending from the feminine caesura to the end of the verse (ἀγήρω τ᾽ ἀθανάτω τε) [u–––uu–x#], as at *Iliad* II 447, XII 323, XVII 444, *Hymn to Demeter* 242 (compare *Odyssey* v 218 and Hesiod *Theogony* 277). I emphasize the metrical flexibility and variability of the phraseology for "immortal and ageless" as an indication both of the traditionality of the concept and of its functionality: on the traditionality and functionality of the formula "immortal and ageless," see Janko 1981. On the gods as defined in structural opposition to man, see Vermeule 1979:118–144, Clay 1982, Vernant 1991:27–49, and Sissa and Detienne 2000.

[9]   Purves 2006a:190–191 analyzes the connection between death in battle and old age, both of which cause mortals to fall with weakened knees: "Aging, then, is just another way of being unstrung, of having one's limbs loosened and thereby losing the grounded, upright position of being *empedos*" (191). The adjective ἀγήρως "ageless" is always used in conjunction with ἀθάνατος "immortal" in epic diction: compare Ebeling 1963:13, s.v. ἀγήραος.

[10] The traditionality of the expression "the gods who always are" (θεοὶ αἰὲν ἐόντες) is guaranteed by the formulaic status and metrical/phraseological flexibility. We find the formulaic expression θεοὶ αἰὲν ἐόντες [uu–uu–x#] some 10 times in Greek epic poetry: *Iliad* I 290, 494, XXI 518, XXIV 99, *Odyssey* v 7, viii 306, xii 371, 377, Hesiod fr. 296.2 M-W, and compare *Hymn to Demeter* 325 θεοὺς αἰὲν ἐόνας [––uu–x#] with θεοὺς in synizesis (on which, see Allen, Halliday, and Sikes 1980:166–167 with n325 and n345). The formula also appears in the accusative with different metrical shape: θεοὺς uu–uu αἰὲν ἐόντας [u– uu–uu <u>–uu–x</u>#]: *Odyssey* I 263, 378, ii 143, viii 635, *Hymn to Aphrodite* 62, and compare *Odyssey* iii 147 and Hesiod *Theogony* 801. Further, the formula appears in the genitive case as well: θεῶν uu αἰὲν ἐόντων [u– uu <u>–uu––</u>#]: *Odyssey* iv 583, *Hymn to Hermes* 548, and compare Hesiod *Theogony* 33 and *Works and Days* 718 for μακάρων uu αἰὲν ἐόντων and *Theogony* 21 and 105 for ἀθανάτων uu-uu αἰὲν ἐόντων. On the flexibility of the Homeric formula, see esp. Hainsworth 1968, 1993:1–31 and Russo 1997.

on the other hand, eat *nektar* and *ambrosia*.[11] Gods and humans are further distinguished by where they live, for human beings dwell on the earth (οἱ ... ἐπὶ χθονὶ ναιετάουσιν "men who dwell upon the earth," *Odyssey* vi 153;[12] ἐπιχθονίων ἀνθρώπων "men upon the earth," *Iliad* IV 45, *Odyssey* I 167, xviii 136, xxii 65, 414;[13] θνητοῖσι βροτοῖσιν ἐπὶ ζείδωρον ἄρουραν "mortals liable to death upon the life-giving ploughland," *Odyssey* iii 3, xii 386, *Homeric Hymn to Apollo* 69, and cf. *Odyssey* xix 593), whereas gods dwell high above, on the peak of Mt. Olympos or in heaven itself (οἳ Ὄλυμπον ἔχουσιν "[the gods] who hold Olympos," *Iliad* V 890, *Odyssey* vi 240, xii 337, xiv 394, xviii 180, xix 43, *Homeric Hymn to Apollo* 498, 512; τοὶ Οὐρανὸν εὐρὺν ἔχουσιν "[the gods,] those who hold wide heaven," *Iliad* XX 299, *Odyssey* I 67, iv 378, v 167, vi 50, 243, vii 209, xii 344, xiii 55, xvi 183, 211, xxii 39). And perhaps most tellingly, whereas men are "unhappy" (δύστηνος: cf. *Iliad* XVII 445) and "very wretched" (ὀϊζυρώτερος: cf. *Iliad* XVII 446) because they must toil ceaselessly for their sustenance, the gods are "blessed" (μάκαρες: *Iliad* I 406, IV 127, XIV 143, XX 54, XXIV 23, 99, 422) and "live easily" (ῥεία ζώοντες: *Iliad* VI 138, *Odyssey* iv 805, v 122).

The distinction between mortals and gods is emphatically foregrounded in the *Iliad* during the occasional encounters between mortals and divinities on the battlefield, such as Apollo's warnings to Diomedes, Patroklos, and Achilles, who in the midst of their *aristeiai*, strive to be something more than human.[14] Leonard Muellner's analysis of formulaic phraseology equating the mortal hero to his divine counterpart/nemesis during his *aristeia* is especially instructive:

> Antagonism and, paradoxically, heroic glory itself arise when the hero tries to reach and surpass the god with whom he identifies and against

---

[11] See Clay 1982 and my discussion in chapter 2 above. According to Nicholas Richardson (1993), the difference between mortal and immortal food "emphasizes the earthbound, temporal character of men, as compared with the gods (οὐ γὰρ σῖτον ἔδουσ' ... [*Iliad*] 5.431)" (93). I treat this point below. Distinctions in selection of food items divides not only man from god, but even one group of men from another. For instance, we see a distinction between those mortals who are closely related to gods (e.g. Achilles) versus those who are not (e.g. Hektor): Achilles may have been raised on *ambrosia* (cf. *Iliad* XIX 347–348, 352–354, Apollonius of Rhodes *Argonautica* IV 869–872, and the discussion by Gantz 1993:I.230–231, Mackie 1998, Burgess 2009:9–13), whereas Hektor was raised on *milk* (cf. *Iliad* XXII 79–83, XXIV 58, and the discussion by Kitts 1994). Kitts (1994) further demonstrates distinctions between *drinkers-of-milk* on the one hand and *eaters-of-grain* on the other.

[12] Compare οἱ ... ἐπὶ χθονὶ ναιετάασκεν "those who continually dwell upon the earth" at *Hymn to Apollo* 279.

[13] Compare the related ἐπιχθονίων ... ἀνδρῶν "men upon the earth," *Iliad* I 266, IX 558; ἄνδρας ἐπιχθονίους, *Homeric Hymn to Aphrodite* 12; and the substantive use of the adjective ἐπιχθονίος to indicate "men upon the earth": *Iliad* XXIV 220, *Odyssey* xvii 115, xxiv 197.

[14] On the components of the Homeric *aristeia*, see Fenik 1968:9–77, Krischer 1971:13–85, and Muellner 1996:10–18.

whom he struggles. In the case of a warrior in his *aristeía*, the diction and themes of battle narrative make it plain that the god whom the warrior incarnates and competes with is Ares himself. Thus the formula *daímoni îsos*, "equal to the god," which occurs nine times in the *Iliad*, is always and only used of a hero in his *aristeía*, whether it be Diomedes, Patroklos, or Achilles himself. (Muellner 1996:12)

The phrase δαίμονι ἶσος "equal to a god," occurs nine times in Homeric epic, describing Diomedes (*Iliad* V 438, 459, 884), Patroklos (XVI 705, 786), and Achilles (XX 447, 493, XXI 18, 227) at the height of their respective *aristeiai*. Most remarkable about the passages describing Diomedes and Patroklos is the theme of "counting" that appears as Diomedes and Patroklos each strive in turn against a god three times, but on the fourth time they are beaten back.[15] For instance, during his *aristeia* Diomedes attacks Aeneas three times, even though the Trojan is protected by Apollo himself; the god repulses Diomedes three times in silence, but when the hero makes a fourth attempt, the god issues a stern warning:

γιγνώσκων ὅ οἱ αὐτὸς ὑπείρεχε χεῖρας Ἀπόλλων,
ἀλλ᾽ ὅ γ᾽ ἄρ᾽ οὐδὲ θεὸν μέγαν ἅζετο, ἵετο δ᾽ αἰεί
Αἰνείαν κτεῖναι καὶ ἀπὸ κλυτὰ τεύχεα δῦσαι.
<u>τρὶς</u> μὲν ἔπειτ᾽ ἐπόρουσε κατακτάμεναι μενεαίνων,
<u>τρὶς</u> δέ οἱ ἐστυφέλιξε φαεινὴν ἀσπίδ᾽ Ἀπόλλων·
ἀλλ᾽ ὅτε δὴ <u>τὸ τέταρτον</u> ἐπέσσυτο <u>δαίμονι ἶσος</u>,
δεινὰ δ᾽ ὁμοκλήσας προσέφη ἑκάεργος Ἀπόλλων.
φράζεο, Τυδεΐδη, καὶ χάζεο, μηδὲ θεοῖσιν
ἶσ᾽ ἔθελε φρονέειν, <u>ἐπεὶ οὔ ποτε φῦλον ὁμοῖον</u>
<u>ἀθανάτων τε θεῶν χαμαὶ ἐρχομένων τ᾽ ἀνθρώπων.</u>

Although [Diomedes] recognized that Apollo himself was holding his
       hands over him,
nevertheless he at least did not shrink even from the great god, but was
       going ever onward
to kill Aeneas and to strip away his glorious armor.
Then <u>three times</u> he drove forward in a fury to cut him down,
and <u>three times</u> Apollo battered aside his bright shield;
but indeed when he rushed on <u>for the fourth time equal to a divinity</u>,

---

[15] On the theme of "three times" in Greek literature, see Göbel 1935, Perry 1972, Bell Jr. 1975, and Hansen 1976. Göbel's study of "threes" includes threefold anaphora and alliteration as well as uses of τρίς and τρείς in Homer. However, only Perry notes—though he does not analyze—the role of "the fourth time" in Homer. On the significance of heroes making a "fourth" attempt, see Muellner 1996:12–18 and Buchan 2004:50–56.

Apollo who strikes from afar cried aloud terribly and addressed him:
"Watch out, son of Tydeus, and give way; don't
be wanting to think like the gods, <u>since never is the breed the
      same,</u>
<u>that of the immortal gods and that of men who walk upon the ground."</u>

Iliad V 433–442

The "breed" (φῦλον, V 441) of men and that of the gods are not the same, Apollo claims; men cannot hope to compete with the gods, so they should give up any attempt to do so. Even the hero, the great figure who is something more than an ordinary man through his willingness to die in battle while still in the prime of his life,[16] can only draw near to the gods, but without ever actually succeeding in crossing that boundary. He may attempt the superhuman three times (τρίς), but no more. The fourth attempt (τὸ τέταρτον) appears to carry him to the very edge of divinity itself; on the fourth attempt, the hero becomes more like a god than a man—he becomes δαίμονι ἶσος "equal to a god."[17] In his study of the "limits" of heroism, Mark Buchan perceptively analyzes the significance of *counting* (three-four-five) as marking the distance between mortals and immortals. He analyzes the passages in which Patroklos also rushes three times and then a fourth time against Apollo:

> To try and fail to do something three times remains a normal, human pattern for failure; to make a fourth attempt is to move into a shady realm between god and man. … The [fourth] attack is therefore a fundamental challenge to the order that guarantees the separation of men from gods … If Patroklos becomes equal to the god on the fourth attempt, he is clearly not yet a god; he temporarily takes a god's place, but this is not yet permanent identity with a god. The narrative establishes an order through prohibition: no humans are allowed beyond

---

[16] On this formulation of the "hero," see Vernant 1981, 1991, and Rubino 1979.

[17] On δαίμονι ἶσος and its significance in the hero's attempt to become a god during his *aristeia*, see Muellner 1996:12–14 with n19. Nagy 1999:143–144 (Ch. 8§3–4) argues that the phrase δαίμονι ἶσος points to a ritual antagonism between hero and god. Collins 1998:15–45 demonstrates how during a warrior's *aristeia*, he is filled with ἀλκή "battle strength," a strength or power regularly associated with the war god Ares; during battle, then, Ares "enters" (δύειν) the warrior and "possesses" him (κατέχειν), effectively turning the warrior into Ares himself (cf. Collins 1998:41–43). One may compare the antagonism between a warrior who has become δαίμονι ἶσος and a god with those other mortals unfortunate enough to challenge a god, such as Thamyris who is blinded for wishing to compete with the Muses (II 594–600), Niobe who is destroyed for comparing her children with Leto's (XXIV 602–609), or Eurytus who is killed by Apollo for challenging him in archery (viii 224–227).

165

three assaults, and if any should go as far as a fourth, they will be punished. (Buchan 2004:51)[18]

The punishment, as Apollo warns, is μῆνις "divine rage," which, as Leonard Muellner (1996) has demonstrated, is conceived of as a response to social and/or cosmic disequilibrium in Homeric epic. For a mortal to contend with a god a fourth time poses a threat to the cosmic order which relies on the stable and defining difference between mortals and immortals.

Perhaps the distance between gods and men appears most clearly in those episodes when gods confront one another over the fate of mortals. For instance, Apollo acknowledges to Poseidon that the miserable brevity of mortal life is not worth troubling themselves over:

Ἐννοσίγαι', οὐκ ἄν με σαόφρονα μυθήσαιο
ἔμμεναι, εἰ δὴ σοί γε βροτῶν ἕνεκα πτολεμίξω
δειλῶν, οἳ φύλλοισιν ἐοικότες ἄλλοτε μέν τε
ζαφλεγέες τελέθουσιν, ἀρούρης καρπὸν ἔδοντες,
ἄλλοτε δὲ φθινύθουσιν ἀκήριοι. ἀλλὰ τάχιστα
παυώμεσθα μάχης· οἳ δ' αὐτοὶ δηριαάσθων.

Shaker of the earth, you would say I am one without prudence
if indeed I am to make war with you for the sake of wretched
mortals, who, like leaves, ever at one time
flourish and grow warm as they feed upon the fruit of plowed field,
and at another time wither, deprived of life. But rather with all speed
let us cease our battle; let them fight on their own.

Iliad XXI 462–467

---

[18] See Buchan's argument in full at Buchan 2004:50–56, and see also Muellner 1996:12–18 on the significance of counting "three times ... but on the fourth time" in Homeric epic. It is significant to note that of the four passages in which Achilles is said to be δαίμονι ἶσος "equal to a god" (XX 447, 493, XXI 18, 227), only one appears in the formulaic line ἀλλ' ὅτε δὴ τὸ τέταρτον ἐπέσσυτο δαίμονι ἶσος "but indeed when for the fourth time he rushed against [him/them], equal to a god" (XX 447 = V 438 = XVI 705 = XVI 786, and compare the variant αὐτὰρ ἔπειτ' αὐτῷ μοι ἐπέσσυτο δαίμονι ἶσος "but when he rushed against me myself, equal to a god" at V 459 = V 884). In that passage (XX 447)—which West in fact excises from his edition of the *Iliad*—Achilles attacks Hektor, whom Apollo protects by covering him in a thick mist (τὸν δ' ἐξήρπαξεν Ἀπόλλων | ῥεῖα μάλ' ὥς τε θεός, ἐκάλυψε δ' ἄρ' ἠέρι πολλῇ "But Apollo seized him away very easily, since he is a god, and covered him up in a thick mist," XX 443–444). Although Achilles leaps against the mist three and then four times, he is not rebuffed by the god; instead, Achilles shouts after Hektor that the gods have saved him but he will not be so lucky if they meet again, after which he then turns his attention to killing other Trojans. It would seem that Achilles alone can be δαίμονι ἶσος with impunity in the *Iliad*, for he does not strive against the gods nor try to press forward beyond what is fated, but checks his activity within certain bounds.

Mortals flourish in one season only to wither and perish in another like the leaves of trees and the fruit of the field upon which they feed—the consumption of food which itself grows and rots guarantees man's participation in the same temporal economy.[19] It is always the case—note the "epic" or "generalizing" τε at XXI 464[20]—that at one time (ἄλλοτε μέν, XXI 464) he flourishes, and at another (ἄλλοτε δὲ, XXI 466), he dies (ἀκήριοι, XXI 466)[21] and withers away (φθινύθουσιν, XXI 466).[22]

Not even that most extraordinary of mortals, the hero, can escape the clutches of time. There is the possibility—though insecure and contested—that the very term ἥρως "hero" may be etymologically related to the word ὥρη "season."[23] If true, the implication, according to Dale Sinos, is that the hero is "one who is *in time*, or one who passes through successive stages of life exhibiting the ideal characteristics of each. He is ὡραῖος 'seasonal' in a vegetal sense, passing from immaturity to ripeness" (Sinos 1980:14).[24] In other words, since mortal temporality is inherently and inextricably bound with the concept of seasonality, even the hero is none other than he who participates in the vegetal cycle of growth and decay incumbent on human life. According to Seth Schein, "a 'hero' is 'seasonal' in that he comes into his prime, like flowers in

---

[19] On the relationship between mortality and eating food, as opposed to enjoying the savor of sacrificial offerings or imbibing *nektar* and *ambrosia*, see *Hymn to Hermes* 130–136 where Hermes refuses to eat sacrificial meat, thereby guaranteeing himself a place among the Olympian gods, on which, see Kahn-Lyotard 1977 and Kahn 1978. See further Vernant 1977 and 1989 for an analysis of the consumption of sacrificial meat in Hesiod's *Theogony* and *Works and Days* and its function as the mythological *aition* for why man dies. For gods and the savor of sacrifice understood in its widest connotations, including perfume and incense that emit their smoke and odor upward along a vertical axis, see Detienne 1994.

[20] On epic τε as expressing a *fait permanent* "permanent fact" linking two ideas in a particular context (here leaves that flourish and then wither in context of a discussion of the ephemeral nature of human life), see Ruijgh 1971:15–18, Davies 1977, and Bakker 2002:77.

[21] On ἀκήριος "without life, spirit" (from ἀ- + κῆρ "without heart"), compare *Iliad* V 812, 817, VI 100, XI 392, XIII 224, and see Eustathius' definition as ἴσος τῷ νεκρῷ "[one who is] equal to a corpse" (852.35). See further Ebeling 1963:63, s.v. ἀκήιος, Monro 1893:382, and Kirk 1990:144.

[22] On φθινύθω, other cognate *φθι- "decay" root words, and their temporal implications, see the Appendix below.

[23] See Pötscher 1961, Householder Jr. and Nagy 1972:50–52, and O'Brien 1993:5, 113–117, 137–139. These studies indicate the formulaic, contextual, and mythological associations between ἥρως and Ἥρη/Ἥρᾱ "Hera," not least of which is that the hero *par excellence* is none other than Herakles whose very name is a compound of Hera + *kleos* "the glory of Hera" (Ἡρα-κλῆς). Note further Chantraine's cautious assessment that, although the etymology of ἥρως is unknown, a relationship with Ἥρη/Ἥρᾱ "Hera" is possible (Chantraine 1968–1980:417, s.v. ἥρως). However, Chantraine finds arguments positing a relationship between Ἥρη/Ἥρᾱ and ὥρα "season" as very doubtful ["*ces hypothèses sont fort douteuses*"] (415–416, s.v. Ἥρᾱ). See Adams 1987 for a different attempt to associate ἥρως and Ἥρᾱ with a posited root indicating "youthful vitality."

[24] Sinos here draws on the work of Pötscher 1961. See also Schein 1984:69, 85n8.

the spring, only to be cut down once and for all" (Schein 1984:69). Whether a secure etymological connection can be drawn between ἥρως "hero" and ὥρη "season" or not, we find the concept of the hero intimately associated with the vegetable imagery throughout the *Iliad*, as in Homer's comparison of the vast size of the Greek army to the number of leaves and flowers that grow "in season" (ὥρῃ, II 468),[25] or Glaukos' famous comparison of the generations of men to those of leaves that flourish "in season" (ὥρῃ, VI 146–149),[26] recalled in Apollo's conversation with Poseidon as he speaks of "mortals, who like leaves, ever at one time flourish and grow warm as they feed upon the fruit of plowed field, and at another time wither, deprived of life" (XXI 464–466). From the perspective of both the immortal gods and even mankind itself, human life is utterly ephemeral; man is "in season" because he cannot exist outside of time.

Nevertheless, although gods are consistently represented as "immortal and ageless" and as those who "always are" in early Greek poetry, Homer and Hesiod both posit a time when things may have not always been so. In his second creation story—the so-called "Myth of the Ages" (*Works and Days* 106–201)—Hesiod claims that men and gods have a common origin: ὡς ὁμόθεν γεγάασι θεοὶ θνητοί τ' ἄνθρωποι, "so from the same place were born gods and mortal men" (*Works and Days* 108).[27] The phrase ὁμόθεν + γίγνεσθαι "to be born from the same place" is properly used in Greek epic to denote blood relationship: for instance, at *Hymn to Aphrodite* 135, Aphrodite, disguised as a mortal maiden, seduces Anchises by telling him to "[Show me] to your brothers who were born from the same place as you" (σοῖς τε κασιγνήτοις, οἵ τοι ὁμόθεν γεγάασιν). Similarly, in Book IV of the *Iliad*, Hera explains to Zeus that they are born of the same race: "For I am also a god, and the race from which I come is that from which you come" (καὶ γὰρ ἐγὼ θεός εἰμι, γένος δέ μοι ἔνθεν ὅθεν σοι, IV 58).[28] The implication of Hesiod's claim that men and gods are born "from the same place" (ὁμόθεν), according to

---

[25] ὅσσα τε φύλλα καὶ ἄνθεα γίνεται ὥρῃ "as many leaves and flowers are born in season" (*Iliad* II 468).

[26] ὅη περ φύλλων γενεή, τοίη δὲ καὶ ἀνδρῶν. | φύλλα τὰ μέν τ' ἄνεμος χαμάδις χέει, ἄλλα δέ θ' ὕλη | τηλεθόωσα φύει, ἔαρος δ' ἐπιγίνεται ὥρῃ "Just as the generations of leaves, so also are the generations of men. The wind sheds the leaves upon the ground, but the tree, ever burgeoning grows, and [the leaves] come in the season of spring" (*Iliad* VI 146–148). On the vegetal imagery implied by the verb τελεθόωσα (< θάλλω), see Lowenstam 1979.

[27] On Hesiod's ἕτερος λόγος "second story" and the narrative inconsistencies it raises in terms of his earlier account of Prometheus and Pandora, see West 1978:172–177 and Verdenius 1985:77–79. Verdenius argues that ὁμόθεν places "special perspective" on the "estrangement of men from gods" (78). Rowe (1983) argues convincingly that Hesiod is offering not opposing but complementary narratives to address the same problem of the origin and nature of human mortality.

[28] For further citations, see West 1978:178.

Martin West, is that "they started on the same terms" (West 1978:178).[29] Indeed, Hesiod describes these early men as "living like the gods":

ὥστε θεοὶ δ' ἔξωον, <u>ἀκηδέα θυμὸν</u> ἔχοντες,
<u>νόσφιν ἄτερ τε πόνου καὶ ὀϊξύος</u>· οὐδέ τι δειλόν
γῆρας ἐπῆν, αἰεὶ δὲ πόδας καὶ χεῖρας ὁμοῖοι
τέρποντ' ἐν θαλίῃσι, <u>κακῶν ἔκτοσθεν ἀπάντων</u>.

They used to live like gods, with <u>a care-free heart</u>,
<u>far away and apart from toil and misery</u>. Nor at all was wretched
old age upon them, but always the same with respect to their feet and
      hands
they took pleasure in feasts, <u>outside of all evils</u>.

Works and Days 112–115

Here we find a race of men who, like the gods, appear to be ἀγηρώς "ageless," for Hesiod specifies that "not at all was cruel old age upon them" (οὐδέ τι δειλόν | γῆρας ἐπῆν, 113–114) and that their bodies never diminished with the passing of time: their bodies remain "always the same" (αἰεὶ ... ὁμοῖοι, 114). Notice, in particular, the spatial dimensions of man's privileged position "far away" (νόσφιν, 113) and "apart" (ἄτερ, 113) from toil and misery; old age is not "upon" (οὐδέ τι ... ἐπῆν, 113–114) him, but he is "outside" (ἔκτοσθεν, 115) of all evils. Hesiod's men of the "golden age" inhabit a space literally "outside" of time and "far away" from its degenerative effects. The spatial concepts of separation—away, apart, outside—define the utopian status of this early race of men. Instead of living in a world in which pain, suffering, and even death are inescapable experiences, these men live elsewhere. Hence, we may compare also the utopian vision of mankind before Promethean sacrifice in Hesiod's *Works and Days*:

<u>πρὶν</u> μὲν γὰρ ζώεσκον ἐπὶ χθονὶ φῦλ' ἀνθρώπων
<u>νόσφιν ἄτερ τε κακῶν καὶ ἄτερ χαλεποῖο πόνοιο</u>
<u>νούσων τ' ἀργαλέων</u>, αἵ τ' ἀνδράσι κῆρας ἔδωκαν.

For <u>before this</u>, the races of men used to live on earth
<u>far away and apart from evils and apart from hard toil</u>
<u>and painful diseases</u>, which gave death to men.

Works and Days 90–92

[29] For a similar representation of gods and men as born "from a single mother" (ἐκ μιᾶς δὲ ... ματρός), see Pindar *Nemian* 6.1–6 with discussion by Hogan and Schenker 2001.

We find the same vocabulary of distance (νόσφιν ἄτερ ... καὶ ἄτερ, 91) indicating man's prior (πρίν, 90) and ongoing status (note especially the iterative imperfective ζώεσκον at verse 90, indicating continual and repeated action). They inhabit the same mythic space occupied by the gods, for, as the tradition explains, they are ἐγγὺς θεῶν γεγονότας "born near to the gods" (Dicaearchus fr. 49.3 Wehrli, *apud* Porphyry *De abstinentia* 4.2). Their "nearness" to the gods (ἐγγὺς θεῶν) implies a similarity both in terms of spatial position and ontological status.

An important fragment of Hesiod's *Catalogue of Women* further defines the characteristic "closeness" between men and gods of old. For they were not always differentiated in terms of their diet and spatial dwelling; instead, they enjoyed commensal relations, sharing the same foods, as they also, apparently, shared the same sexual partners:[30]

Νῦν δὲ γυναικῶν φῦλον ἀείσατε, ἡδυέπειαι
Μοῦσαι Ὀλυμπιάδες, κοῦραι Διὸς αἰγιόχοιο,
αἳ πότ' ἄρισται ἔσαν[
μίτρας τ' ἀλλύσαντο [
μισγόμεναι θεοῖσ[ιν
ξυναὶ γὰρ τότε δαῖτες ἔσαν, ξυνοὶ δὲ θόωκοι
ἀθανάτοις τε θεοῖσι καταθνητοῖς τ' ἀνθρώποις.

And now of the race of women sing, sweet-speaking
Olympian Muses, daughters of aegis-bearing Zeus,
the women who were once the best [
and who loosened their waistbands [
as they had sexual intercourse with gods [
For at that time feasts were in common, and common were seats
for both the immortal gods and mortal men.

Hesiod fr. 1.1–7 M-W

At some unspecified point in the past, mankind shared common meals with the gods, and the gods took mortal women as sexual consorts.[31] Commensality

---

30 Consider, for instance, the motif of "divine twins" born with two fathers, one mortal and one divine: Herakles and Iphicles, sired by Zeus and Amphitryon; Kastor and Polydeuces, sired by Zeus and Tyndareus; and Amphion and Zethos, sired by Zeus and Epopeus. On "divine twins" and the theme of dual paternity, see Ward 1968:3–4, 10–14.

31 Reference to a pre-historical time when men and gods were closer to one another, including intermarriage between the two races and the birth of semi-divine offspring may also be found in the Biblical references to the Nephilim in *Genesis* 6:1–4: "When men had begun to be plentiful on the earth, and daughters had been born to them, the sons of God, looking at the daughters of men, saw they were pleasing, so they married as many as they chose. Yahweh said, 'My spirit

implies equality, as is suggested by the "common seats" (ξυνοὶ δὲ θόωκοι) for men and gods.[32] Homer uses the word θόωκος/θῶκος to mean both the physical seat upon which one sits (e.g. ἕζετο ἐν πατρὸς θώκῳ "he sat in his father's chair," *Odyssey* ii 14) as well as the seated assembly where men or gods speak publicly and make decisions (e.g. θεῶν δ᾽ ἐξίκετο θώκους "[Zeus] arrived at the seated assembly of the gods," *Iliad* VIII 439; οὔτε ποθ᾽ ἡμετέρη ἀγορὴ γένετ᾽ οὔτε θόωκος "not yet has our meeting nor our seated assembly been held," *Odyssey* ii 26).[33] The implication, then, is that men once shared even in divine council. The image of men and gods eating together further recalls those most pious races of men in Homeric epic: the Aethiopians, with whom the gods dine and participate in sacrificial feasts,[34] and the Phaeacians, who are close relatives of the gods and called ἀγχίθεοι "near to the gods."[35] Alkinoos, king of the Phaeacians, explains to Odysseus,

> αἰεὶ γὰρ τὸ πάρος γε θεοὶ φαίνονται ἐναργεῖς
> ἡμῖν, εὖθ᾽ ἔρδωμεν ἀγακλειτὰς ἑκατόμβας,

---

must not for ever be disgraced in man, for he is but flesh; his life shall last no more than a hundred and twenty years.' The Nephalim were on the earth at that time (and even afterwards) when the sons of God resorted to the daughters of man, and had children by them. These are the heroes of days gone by, the famous men" (*The Jerusalem Bible* [New York, 1966]). See Scodel 1982:41–43 and Hendel 1987 for discussion and bibliography.

Commensality with the gods is relegated to the period perhaps shortly before the appearance of the heroic age of Achilles and Hektor. At *Iliad* IX 535 the gods are said to feast on the hecatombs, but this meal (as noted by Griffin 1980:187n22) belongs to the past, before the coming of the Calydonian boar and the aftermath of the famed hunt. Men and gods both participated in the wedding feast of Peleus and Thetis, but again, this event marks the pre-history of the Iliadic heroes. On the participation of gods at the wedding of Peleus and Thetis, see *Kypria* fr. 3 Davies 1988 = fr. 3 Bernabé 1987, Pindar *Pythian* 3.86–96, *Nemian* 4.65–68, 5.22–39, *Isthmian* 8.46–47. Gods are depicted at the wedding feast on the François Vase. See further Lesky 1956.

32 See Hogan and Schenker 2001 (no pagination): "Particularly suggestive are hints of common dining and amicable gathering. Far from focusing on basic antagonisms in the cosmos, this perspective suggests a social unity symbolized by the shared meal. Mortals dined with the gods, enjoyed their company, received favors from them and put them under social obligation; there was a time, in this mythical perspective, when hospitality was indifferent to boundaries between mortal and immortal."

33 See Cunliffe 1963:194 and Ebeling 1963:I.579, s.v. θῶκος.

34 On gods feasting with the Aethiopians, see *Iliad* I 423–424, XXIII 205–207. In *Odyssey* i 22–26, Poseidon is described as particularly close with the Aethiopians; he participates in the sacrificial offering of bulls and rams (ἀντιόων ταύρων τε καὶ ἀρνειῶν ἑκατόμβης, i 25) and takes pleasure in being present at the feast (ἔνθ᾽ ὅ γε τέρπετο δαιτὶ παρήμενος, i 26). On the Aethiopians, see the excellent, concise account by S. West 1988:75–76.

35 See *Odyssey* v 35 = xix 279: Φαιήκων ἐς γαῖαν, οἳ ἀγχίθεοι γεγάασιν "to the land of the Phaeacians, who have been born near to the gods." Hainsworth (1988) believes that ἀγχίθεοι refers to the "Phaeacians' special relationship with the gods rather than their kinship" (258, and compare his comment at p. 334 on vii 205). What is important is to note that the relationship is marked by an adverb of spatial proximity.

δαίνυνταί τε παρ' ἄμμι καθήμενοι ἔνθα περ ἡμεῖς.
εἰ δ' ἄρα τις καὶ μοῦνος ἰὼν ξύμβληται ὁδίτης,
οὔ τι κατακρύπτουσιν, ἐπεί σφισιν ἐγγύθεν εἰμέν,
ὥς περ Κύκλωπές τε καὶ ἄγρια φῦλα Γιγάντων.

For <u>always</u> in the past at least the gods <u>used to appear clearly</u>
<u>to us</u>, whenever we conducted famous hecatombs,
<u>and they would feast beside us, sitting down here in the very place</u>
      <u>where we do.</u>
And indeed, even if some traveler while going alone meets up with them,
they do not at all conceal it, <u>since we are near to them</u>,
as indeed are both the Cyclopes and the wild tribes of Giants.

Odyssey vii 201–206.[35]

The Phaeacians enjoyed commensal relations with the gods in which equality between the parties is suggested by the equality of seating arrangements: the gods used to sit "here in the very place where we [sit]" (ἔνθα περ ἡμεῖς, vii 203). The privilege of such close relations with the gods is an index of being "near" (σφισιν ἐγγύθεν, vii 205) to them.[36]

In Hesiod's *Theogony*, the pre-historical period in which men and gods ate together has ended, and now men and gods are separated (ἐκρίνοντο, 535).[37]

---

[36]   See citations in the preceding note for the Phaeacians as ἀγχίθεοι "near to the gods." Compare *Hymn to Aphrodite* 200–201 for ἀγχίθεοι indicating a close relationship or similarity in appearance or size: ἀγχίθεοι δὲ μάλιστα καταθνητῶν ἀνθρώπων | αἰεὶ ἀφ' ὑμετέρης γενεῆς εἶδός τε φυήν τε, "Those especially <u>close to gods</u> among mortal men <u>in both look and size</u> are always from your family." In addition to the Aethiopians and Phaeacians, one may also cite the Hyperboreans, the mythical people imagined to live far to the north, who, like the men of Hesiod's "golden age," enjoy freedom from sickness and old age: according to Pindar *Pythian* 10.41–44, "Neither sickness nor destructive old age is mixed with this holy race; they dwell <u>apart</u> <u>from toils and</u> <u>battles</u>, as they avoid the just retribution of Nemesis" (νόσοι δ' οὔτε γῆρας οὐλόμενον κέκραται | ἱερᾷ γενεᾷ· <u>πόνων δὲ καὶ μαχᾶν ἄτερ</u> | οἰκέοισι φυγόντες | ὑπέρδικον Νέμεσιν). They are regularly depicted as favored by the gods—especially Apollo—who is himself sometimes given the epithet "the Hyperborean" (e.g. Claudius Aelianus *Varia historia* 2.26); Leto, Apollo's mother, is said to come from the land of the Hyperboreans (Aristotle *History of Animals* 580a18, Diodorus Siculus 2.47, Pausanius 1.18.5, Cicero *On the Nature of Gods* 3.57)—though Kirk (1990) cautions that Apollo more likely came to Greek mythico-religious traditions from south-west Asia Minor (witness his epithet *Lukeios*, possibly indicating connection with Lycia) and that his "Hyperborean associations seem to be secondary" (6). The Hyperboreans feast with the gods (Pindar *Pythian* 10.34–40, *Isthmian* 6.23, *Paean* 8.63). Although not quite immortal, they are said to live up to a thousand years (Simonides fr. 570 PMG, Megasthenes *FHG* 30.30, Strabo 15.57). Homer is silent about the Hyperboreans; Herodotus 4.32 (= Allen 1912:115–116, *Testemonium* 3) notes that the Hyperboreans figure in the epic poem *Epigonoi*, but doubts whether the poem was really composed by Homer.

[37]   Note that Hesiod's narrative suggests that before this "separation" at Mekone, there was *no* difference in diet between men and gods: see Kirk 1990:10, "Indeed the Hesiodic tale of the division

Prometheus' sacrifice marks a new relationship between men and gods, one marked first and foremost by distance.[38] As a consequence of the Promethean sacrifice, a chain of events is set in motion—the concealment of the meat and the theft of fire, the fabrication and acceptance of Pandora—which constrains mankind to toil, illness, old age, and death. Now men and gods inhabit different spaces, each of which is characterized by specific temporal qualities. Whereas gods continue to occupy that same space where, in the fleeting days before the onset of evils, man knew neither labor nor illness nor even old age,[39] men now dwell in a world defined by the ravages of time: labor, illness, old age, and death.

There is a kind of nostalgia, then, in the representation of the gods in early Greek poetry. What is important for our study here is the fact that stories of the god-like origins of man indicate that the difference between men and gods is conceived of more as a difference in degree rather than a difference in kind. That is to say, gods are essentially "men" who do not age, who do not eat corruptible food, and who do not die; they are like the pre-historical men who lived "apart" and "far away from" mortal temporality. Further, the stories of pre-historical "golden age" men who lived "like gods" function to create a model of transferability between the temporally disjunctive worlds of men and gods. For if mankind can somehow participate in divine temporality, if it can

---

at Mekone showed that until the end of that golden age of commensality gods and men had eaten, on special occasions at least, the same food: the best cuts, that is, of oxen." See further Hogan and Schenker 2001:(no pagination) n20. Note also that though Hesiod descibes these pre-"separation" men as dying, their death is like sleep: θνῆσκον δ' ὥσθ' ὕπνῳ δεδμημένοι, "they died as if overcome by sleep" (*Works and Days* 116). In an important passage dealing with what the death of a god might be like, Detienne and Vernant 1978:115–116 (= 1974:113–114) argue that, "A divine being cannot die; it can only be bound. What does this binding mean? First, that the god loses one of his principle prerogatives: the power of instantaneous movement ... Even when a god is chained up somewhere within the organized universe, his immobility so utterly reduces his sphere of activity, and his power and being are thus so diminished, that he appears as an enfeebled, impotent, exhausted figure, *existing only in that state of quasi-death which sleep represents for the gods*" (emphasis added). In other words even though Hesiod's pre-historical man is mortal, even his death is strikingly like the "death" of a god.

[38] The separation between men and gods is also represented in the Greek mythological tradition in terms of former friendships between gods and humans that have soured, such as between Leto and Niobe at Sappho fr. 142 L-P (Λάτω καὶ Νιόβα μάλα μὲν φίλαι ἦσαν ἕταιραι, "Leto and Niobe were very dear companions"); compare Sophocles *Antigone* 832 and see the discussion by Hogan and Schenker 2001.

[39] See Vernant 1977:96, "Auparavant la vie des hommes ne connaissait pas le mal: ni travail, ni maladie, ni vieillesse" ["Formerly, the life of man knew no evil: no work, no sickness, no old age"]. See further Arthur 1982, 1983, and Vernant 1989 on Hesiod's concept of a world before sacrifice and the separation of men and gods. In spite of the shared tables and sexual consorts, however, Hesiod does suggest that the relative length of lifespan for men and for gods remained different: see Hesiod fr. 1.8–13 M-W, with discussion at West 1985:122–124.

somehow be outside of the withering effects of mortal time, then by analogy, gods too must be able to become caught up in that mortal time. We now turn our attention to the temporally conditioned experiences the gods do undergo in Homer's *Iliad*—namely, physical pain and suffering.[40]

2. Pathetic Temporality: The Physical Pain of Gods in the *Iliad*

ἀθάνατοι θνητοί, θνητοὶ ἀθάνατοι,
ζῶντες τὸν ἐκείνων θάνατον, τὸν δὲ ἐκείνων βίον τεθνεῶτες.

Immortals are mortal, mortals immortal,
one living the others' death, and one dying the others' life.

—Heraclitus B 62 D-K

Although no god is explicitly said to "die" in the *Iliad*, we do read that gods can feel physical pain. In a few extreme circumstances, they can even be wounded by human weapons and bleed. In Book V of the *Iliad*, Diomedes is granted the special ability to recognize the gods operating behind the scenes,[41] and he stabs Aphrodite in the hand with a spear thrust as she strives to rescue her son Aeneas from battle.

ἔνθ' ἐπορεξάμενος μεγαθύμου Τυδέος υἱός
ἄκρην οὔτασε χεῖρα μετάλμενος ὀξέι δουρί
ἀβληχρήν· εἶθαρ δὲ δόρυ χροὸς ἀντετόρησεν
ἀμβροσίου διὰ πέπλου, ὅν οἱ χάριτες κάμον αὐταί,
πρυμνὸν ὕπερ θέναρος.

---

[40] I leave aside here the role of emotional pain suffered by gods—though see my discussion in the Introduction above—most especially by goddesses over the fate of their mortal children and/or lovers: Thetis (Achilles, Peleus), Eos (Tithonus, Memnon), Aphrodite (Aeneas, Anchises, Adonis), Kalypso (Odysseus), and Hera, who suffers from envy and hatred of her husband's many lovers and of at least some of the children born of those illicit unions. However, gods too suffer over the death or suffering of their mortal children: Apollo (for Asklepios), Ares (for Askalaphos), and Zeus (for Sarpedon and Herakles). On the suffering of the goddesses and their relationship to human temporality, see Slatkin 1986, 1991, and Murnaghan 1992 who notes that "Thetis is several times seen grieving in advance over the inevitable death of Achilles, through her shameful and wrenching situation *as the mother of a mortal coming as close as any god can to a direct awareness of what it is like to be human*" (260–261, emphasis added). See also Bergren 1989 for an analysis of the temporal dimensions of the "blame" Aphrodite suffers through her sexual relations with a mortal and birth of a mortal child. On the death of Ares' son Askalaphos and Ares' violent reaction (*Iliad* XIII 518–525, XV 100–148), see Lowenstam 1981:119–125, and my discussion below.

[41] See *Iliad* V 127–128: Athena clears the mist away which hides the gods from mortal view. Virgil copies this motif brilliantly, as he depicts Venus removing the mist from Aeneas' eyes, revealing the gods dismantling the city (*Aeneid* 2.604–606).

Then reaching out against [Aphrodite], the son of great-hearted Tydeus
<u>wounded</u> the top part of her delicate hand as he leapt after her with his
        sharp spear.
The spear <u>tore straight through</u> her flesh,
<u>through her immortal robe</u>, which the Graces themselves made for her,
above the hollow of her hand.

Iliad V 335–339

The goddess is not impervious to Diomedes' spear; the language describing
Diomedes' attack against the goddess is entirely typical of the diction and syntax
of human-vs.-human battle scenes. As Bernard Fenik has noted, "Aphrodite's
disastrous attempt to rescue her son *is* a battle scene, and is typical in the
same way as encounters between mortals. ... The wounding of Aphrodite, then,
as unusual as it is, turns out to be constructed according to a typical pattern
with an almost entirely typical set of details" (Fenik 1968:40–41).[42] The weapon
pierces (note the *τορ- root in ἀντετόρησεν, V 337)[43] straight through (εἶθαρ, V
337) Aphrodite's hand and ambrosial clothing (ἀμβροσίου διὰ πέπλου, V 338).
The goddess cries out in pain (ἰάχουσα, V 343) and withdraws from the battle,
taunted by Diomedes as she retreats.

    More remarkable even than Diomedes' audacity to attack a god, however, is
the fact that he actually injures one. For when he stabs at Aphrodite, his spear
penetrates through her robe—which, like Achilles' armor is called "immortal"

---

[42] Note especially the close parallels Fenik (1968) draws between Aphrodite's wounding and that of
     Deiphobos at *Iliad* XIII 527–539: both are wounded in the arm, both drop what they were holding
     (Aeneas, Askalaphos' helmet), both are led away from the battlefield on chariots, and both are
     described as bleeding and in pain (40). Kirk (1990) sees the wounding of Aphrodite as a "parody"
     of typical battlefield encounters between men (96).

[43] The verb ἀντιτορέω is used primarily to describe the act of a burglar "breaking into" a house by
     gouging his way through a wall: compare *Iliad* X 267 (πυκινὸν δόμον ἀντετόρησας "he gouged
     his way into a compact house"), *Hymn to Hermes* 178 (μέγαν δόμον ἀντετορήσων "I will gouge my
     way into his great house"), and 283 (ἀντιτοροῦντα δόμους εὖ ναιετάοντας "gouging your way
     into well-dwelled houses"). What is essential here is the sense of penetrating *through* an object
     from one side to the other. The verbal root *τορ- can also be used to describe the "piercing" act
     of stabbing *through* other objects, including shields or flesh—consider especially the compound
     adjective <u>ῥινο</u>τόρος at *Iliad* XXI 392, an epithet of Ares. Scholia D at *Iliad* XXI 392 thinks the term
     refers to the fighter who pierces *shields*, which are called ῥινοί because they are made out of ox-
     hide; Scholia A, b, and T at *Iliad* XXI 392, however, think the term refers not to shields made of
     ox hide, but to human flesh itself, and hence interpret the epithet as "he who pierces through
     human flesh" (ὁ τιτρώσκων τὸ τῶν ἀνθρώπων δέρμα, Scholia A at *Iliad* XXI 392). Compare also
     Iliad XI 236 for a spear thrust that "did not pierce through a belt" (οὐδ' ἔτορε ζωστῆρα), and *Hymn
     to Hermes* 119 where the god "pierced through the marrow" (δι' αἰῶνας τετορήσας) of cattle he
     sacrifices, stabbing them with a sharp instrument. See Ebeling 1963:I.138, s.v. ἀντιτορέω, II.264,
     s.v. ῥινοτόρος, II.340, s.v. τορέω.

(ἀμβροσίου διὰ πέπλου, V 338)[44]—and through her hand (εἶθαρ δὲ δόρυ χροὸς ἀντετόρησεν, V 337). Once she is cut, the goddess' immortal "blood" begins to flow from the wound:

> ῥέε δ' ἄμβροτον αἷμα θεοῖο,
> ἰχώρ, οἷός πέρ τε ῥέει μακάρεσσι θεοῖσιν.
> οὐ γὰρ σῖτον ἔδουσ', οὐ πίνουσ' αἴθοπα οἶνον·
> τούνεκ' ἀναίμονές εἰσι καὶ ἀθάνατοι καλέονται.

> And the immortal blood of the goddess was flowing,
> *ikhōr*, the very sort that always flows for the blessed gods.
> For they do not eat food, they do not drink gleaming wine;
> for this reason they are without blood and are called "immortals."

Iliad V 339–342

The goddess can be said to "bleed," but only by analogy, for what flows from her wound is not blood, but *ikhōr*, a substance which functions for gods as blood does for humans. The text explains *ikhōr* as both blood and not blood, for the gods are "without blood" (ἀναίμονες, V 342), and yet, *ikhōr* is the "immortal blood of a god, the sort that always flows for gods" (ἄμβροτον αἷμα θεοῖο | ἰχώρ, οἷος πέρ τε ῥέει ... θεοῖσιν, V 339–340). The word *ikhōr* appears once more in the *Iliad* when Dione, Aphrodite's mother in the Iliadic tradition, cleans off the blood from her daughter's wound:

> ἦ ῥά, καὶ ἀμφοτέρῃσιν ἀπ' ἰχῶ χειρὸς ὀμόργνυ·
> ἄλθετο χείρ, ὀδύναι δὲ κατηπιόωντο βαρεῖαι.

> Thus she spoke, and with both hands wiped away the *ikhōr* from her hand;
> the hand was healed, and the heavy pains were lightened.

Iliad V 416–417

Later in the same Book, Diomedes wounds the war god himself (V 855–859), and Ares also bleeds ἄμβροτον αἷμα "immortal blood" (V 870), but it is not specifically called *ikhōr* in the text.

---

[44] For Achilles' "immortal armor" (ἄμβροτα τεύχεα), see *Iliad* XVII 194, 202. Achilles' armor, a wedding-gift made by Hephaistos (XVIII 83–85) and presented to Achilles' father Peleus when he married Thetis, is one of several gifts of the gods, such as Achilles' horses (XVI 381 = XVI 867) and Penelope's cosmetics (*Odyssey* xviii 191), which are likewise specified as *ambrota* "immortal." What is significant, however, is that neither Achilles' "immortal" armor nor Aphrodite's "immortal" robe are able to render their wearers impervious to weapons; note further that Patroklos and Hektor both die while wearing Achilles' first set of armor, and Achilles will die while wearing his second set god-made of armor.

Ikhōr is a strange and problematic substance. The word's etymology is unknown (Chantraine 1968–1980 and Frisk 1973–1979, s.v. ἰχώρ, Bolling 1945, Kleinlogel 1981), and in later usage (especially in the Hippocratic corpus) the term does not mean "the blood of gods," but rather "the watery part" or "serum" of human and animal blood (Liddell, Scott, and Jones 1996, s.v. ἰχώρ II, Jouanna and Demont 1981, Kleinlogel 1981). It has been argued that the change in semantics is a "degradation" from the older Homeric usage (Leumann 1950:310), or conversely, that the Homeric use distorts the meaning of an old Ionian technical term (Jouanna and Demont 1981:197–199).[45] We will not concern ourselves with these issues, but rather focus on what the text does tell us, however—namely that *ikhōr* and "blood" (αἷμα) are not the same thing. Gods are ἀναίμονές, literally "without αἷμα." The adjective ἀναίμων "without αἷμα" occurs only here in Homer with the sense of "without blood"; all other uses describe human conflicts as "without bloodshed" (*Iliad* XVII 497–498, *Odyssey* xviii 149–150, xxiv 531–532).[46] The difference between gods "without αἷμα" and men who do possess αἷμα is specifically posited upon the difference in their food and drink: because the gods do not eat food nor drink wine as humans do, they cannot have the same blood coursing through their veins. Instead, the divine food and drink of the gods—*ambrosia* and *nektar*—imply a different biology for gods and for men.[47] *Ikhōr* functions as blood for gods by "always flowing" for them; yet, it is not blood, for blood is, by definition, *human* blood, a substance made of the very food and liquors we mortals ingest. It is a bloodless blood, then; the text itself points to this interpretation by describing *ikhōr* as ἄμβροτον αἷμα (V 339),

---

[45]   In the conclusion of their argument, Jouanna and Demont (1981) argue that *Iliad* V 340 is either an ancient interpolation (202) or at very least should not be taken to mean that all *ikhōr* is "gods' blood" but rather, that god's blood is a species of *ikhōr* which must be understood to mean "serum." Their analysis is in line with that of Wilamowitz-Moellendorf, who argued that "ἰχώρ cannot be a foreign word for blood; discussion must not start with the well-known Homeric passage but with Hippocrates and the later physicians" (*Litteris*, Vol. I [Lund 1924] 4, cited and translated at Fraenkel 1962:702). See Heubeck 1984:109–111 for discussion. However, the materials collected by Zannini Quirini (1983) support reading ἰχώρ as the god's blood: Prometheus, the Giants, the monster Talon, and even the line of Tantalos are all described as bleeding *ikhōr* (see Zannini Quirini 1983:355–357 for citations and discussion; further citations at Kleinlogel 1981:264–265 with nn37–38).

[46]   The conflicts are described as "bloodless, without bloodshed" in litotes—i.e. a battle was not without bloodshed. See Koller 1967:149–150 for further discussion.

[47]   On the difference in "dietary rules" implying a difference in the "anatomo-physiology" between men and gods, see Sissa and Detienne 2000:29–30. However, Sissa and Detienne go on to argue that even if men and gods are marked as different in kind because of the substance that runs in their veins, "*haima* constitutes an exception" for "Apart from the matter of blood, everything in the bodies of mortals and in those of the Immortals corresponds perfectly" (30–31). See also the association between diet and blood in King 1986, esp. 25–26, who analyzes the myth of how Tithonos became a cicada—a creature said to live without food but only on dew—in the context of Aristotle's theories of blood in the *History of Animals* and *Parts of Animals*.

as if Homer himself were offering a play on words, inviting us to understand ἄμβροτον as derived at once from two different stems: ἀ + βροτός "im-mortal"[48] and ἀ + βρότος "without blood/gore."[49] It has often been suggested that the rare Homeric βρότος came to mean "blood" precisely through the juxtaposition of ἄμβροτον αἷμα and the discussion of gods and men eating different foods (V 339–342).[50] If that is the case, then we may suggest a certain inference: if gods who are bloodless—that is to say, if they bleed "a αἷμα which is not blood" (ἀ + βρότον αἷμα)—nevertheless bleed *ikhōr*, blood's functional equivalent, then perhaps a god whose veins course with "αἷμα that does not die" (ἀ + βροτόν αἷμα) can nonetheless die a death which, though not the same as human death, is its functional equivalent. In short, a god who bleeds something much like blood suggests a god who can die something much like death.

The immortal's experience of this "something much like death" is nothing other than pain, for pain enmeshes its victim in mortal temporality. The physical experience of time measured by throbs and aches constitutes a rhythm of lived experience: a body in pain is a body in time, a body caught up not in objective "clock" time, but in an internal "durational" time of something that must be lived through.[51] After Diomedes wounds Aphrodite and taunts her, the goddess makes her way from the battlefield, burdened with her experience of mortal temporality:

---

[48] βροτός has been demonstrated to be related to the Indo-European root *mr̥to-, the root indicating *mortal*; the Greek term *ambrosia* "not mortal" is supported by the well-attested Vedic cognate *amŕ̥tam* which denotes the food or drink of the gods which bestows immortality upon them. See Chantraine 1958:24 and 1968–1980:197–198, s.v. βροτός, who suggests an Indo-European root *mer* which figures in Latin *morior*, Sanskrit *mriyáte*, old Slavic *mĭrǫ*, Lithuanian *mìrštu*, Armenian *meṙanim*; see Leumann 1950:127 for the same derivation. See further Watkins 1995:392 with n1, and my discussion in chapter 2 above.

[49] The Homeric noun βρότος "blood, gore" is without secure etymology (Chantraine 1968–1980:198, s.v. βρότος); it appears in only two phrases: βρότον αἱματόεντα "bloody blood/gore" (*Iliad* VII 425, XIV 7, XVIII 345, XXIII 41) and ἀπονίψοντες μέλανα βρότον ἐξ ὠτειλέων "washing dark blood/gore from wounds" (*Odyssey* xxiv 189). See Ebeling 1963:241, s.v. βρότος for citations of pertinent scholia. See also the related participle βροτόεις in the form ἔναρα βροτόεντα "bloodied spoil" (*Iliad* VI 480; cf. XIV 509, ps.-Hesiod *Shield of Herakles* 367) and βεβροτωμένα τεύχεα "blood-stained armor" (*Odyssey* xi 41).

[50] Leumann 1950:124–127, Onians 1954:506–507, Vermeule 1979:124, Kleinlogel 1981:270–273, Clay 1983:143–145, Loraux 1986:489–491. See Louden 1995 for an analysis of modes of Homeric "word-play" including *figura etymologica* as here with βροτός, βρότος, and ἄμβροτον αἷμα.

[51] On the temporality of physical pain, see the important work of Toombs (1990, 1992), who builds on Sartre's and Merleau-Ponty's phenomenological analyses of "the lived body." See further Schrag 1982 and Leder 1984–1985, 1992, Fuchs 2003, 2005b, Wyllie 2005a. On the "rhythm" of pain, consider Sartre's (1956) comparison of pain with melody as objects experienced through time: "each concrete pain is like a note in a melody: it is at once the whole melody and a 'moment' in the melody. Across each pain I apprehend the entire illness and yet it transcends them all, for it is the synthetic totality of all pains, the theme which is developed by them and through them" (336).

ὣς ἔφαθ'· ἣ δ' ἀλύουσ' ἀπεβήσετο, τείρετο δ' αἰνῶς.
τὴν μὲν ἄρ' Ἶρις ἑλοῦσα ποδήνεμος ἔξαγ' ὁμίλου
ἀχθομένην ὀδύνῃσι, μελαίνετο δὲ χρόα καλόν.

So he spoke. She took her leave and departed, <u>and was terribly worn down</u>.
Iris <u>the wind-footed</u> took her and led her out of the battle-throng
<u>burdened with pains</u>, and her beautiful skin was dark with blood.

Iliad V 352–354

The verb τείρω "to wear down, use up" entails mortal temporality, for the very
act of "wearing down" occurs within time, and further, implies limited resources
which diminish over time. The verb τείρω is used to describe how a person is
"worn down" by physical pain[52] (including pain from wounds),[53] emotional pain
or anxiety[54] (or other strong feelings, like *erōs* "desire"),[55] or even physical exer-
tion[56] and old age.[57] Aphrodite is here worn down such that her typical divine
facility of movement is lost; instead of darting or flying off "like a shooting star"
(IV 75–77), or "as swift as thought" (XV 80–83), or "as rapid as snow or hail"
(XV 170–173) as Homeric goddesses typically move,[58] the goddess is "weighed
down" by her pains (ἀχθομένην ὀδύνῃσι, V 354). Her physical pains have literally made her body into a burden: the denominative verb ἄχθομαι is related to
ἄχθος "burden, load," a noun that regularly construes with the verb φέρω "to
bear, endure."[59] The contrast between the burdened Aphrodite is emphasized in
contrast with Iris who grabs her and leads her from the fight, for Iris appears
here with her epithet ποδήνεμος "wind-footed": the unwounded Iris appears in
her immortal glory, neither burdened nor worn out, but able to move "like the
wind."

---

[52] Compare XV 16: ὀδυνάων αἳ νῦν μιν τείρουσι κατὰ φρένας "pains which now wear him down in
his wits."

[53] Compare XVI 510: τεῖρε γὰρ αὐτὸν ἕλκος "for the wound was wearing him down."

[54] Compare XXII 242: ἔνδοθι θυμὸς ἐτείρετο πένθεϊ λυγρῷ, "his heart within him was being worn
down by heavy sorrow."

[55] Compare Hesiod fr. 298 M-W: δεινὸς γάρ μιν ἔτειρεν ἔρως Πανοπηίδος Αἴγλης, "for a terrible
desire for Aiglē, daughter of Panopeus, was wearing him [sc. Theseus] down."

[56] Compare V 796: ἱδρὼς γάρ μιν ἔτειρεν "for the sweat was wearing him down"; XVII 745: ἐν δὲ
θυμός | τείρεθ' ὁμοῦ καμάτῳ τε καὶ ἱδρῷ σπευδόντεσσιν, "and in them the heart is being worn
down at the same time by hard work and by sweat as they work on in seriousness."

[57] Compare *Iliad* IV 315: ἀλλά σε γῆρας τείρει, "but old age is wearing you down."

[58] On the typical representation of the movement of gods and goddesses—especially Thetis,
Aphrodite, and Hera—who "dart" (ἀίσσω) or "fly" (πέτομαι) and are described as moving
"swiftly" (with the adverb καρπαλίμως and adjective ὠκύς), see Purves 2006a:194–195 with
bibliography.

[59] See the citations at Liddell, Scott, and Jones 1996:296, s.v. ἄχθος, and consider the cognate compounds ἀχθοφορέω, ἀχθοφορία, and ἀχθοφόρος.

Once pained, Aphrodite's very status as an "immortal" is called into question. She apparently lacks the ability to return to Olympos by herself, for she supplicates her brother Ares to loan her his chariot:

φίλε κασίγνητε, κόμισαί τέ με δὸς δέ μοι ἵππους,
ὄφρ' ἐς Ὄλυμπον ἵκωμαι, ἵν' ἀθανάτων ἕδος ἐστίν.
λίην ἄχθομαι ἕλκος, ὅ με βροτὸς οὔτασεν ἀνήρ,
Τυδεΐδης, ὃς νῦν γε καὶ ἂν Διὶ πατρὶ μάχοιτο.

Dear brother, save me and grant me your horses,
so that I may return to Olympos, where the seat of the <u>immortals</u>
      is.
<u>I am weighed down too much by my wound</u>, which a <u>mortal</u> man
      stabbed,
Tydeus' son, who now, at any rate, would even fight with father Zeus.

Iliad V 359–362

The ὄφρα clause with subjunctive verb ἵκωμαι indicates that the use of Ares' horses is the condition upon which Aphrodite may return to Olympos. Without his horses, she could not return, for, as she explains, she is "weighed down too much" (λίην ἄχθομαι, V 361) by her wound. The adverbial λίην "too much" emphasizes the unexpressed statement, powerful in its absence, that without Ares' assistance Aphrodite's body has become "too much" of a burden to return to Olympos at all. Instead of returning to the place defined here as "where the seat of the immortals is," Aphrodite would be trapped on the earth, the realm of "mortal" mankind. The implication of "weight" expressed in Aphrodite's ἄχθομαι "I am weighed down" (V 361, cf. ἀχθομένην, V 354) maps out the distinction between gods, who dwell high above on Olympos, and men who dwell below; weight is the property of mortality; it is the experience of what it means to experience "lived in," bodily time (Fuchs 2001b, 2003, 2005a, Wyllie 2005a, 2005b). Aphrodite's wound (ἕλκος, V 361), then, makes her mortal; she lives in mortal time, the time experienced by a body in pain.

Nevertheless, Aphrodite, though she experiences mortal time, does not remain "mortal." Ares gives her his chariot team, and Iris drives the goddess back to Olympos where her mother Dione comforts the wounded Aphrodite and wipes the *ikhōr* from her hand. As a rhetorical *consolatio*, Dione explains that Aphrodite is not the only god to have been injured by mortals (Willcock 1964). She relates a series of stories about other gods who have suffered at the hands of mortals, and like Aphrodite, those gods also experienced mortal time through their pains.

τέτλαθι, τέκνον ἐμόν, καὶ <u>ἀνάσχεο</u> κηδομένη περ.
πολλοὶ γὰρ δὴ <u>τλῆμεν</u> Ὀλύμπια δώματ' ἔχοντες
ἐξ ἀνδρῶν <u>χαλέπ' ἄλγε'</u> ἐπ' ἀλλήλοισι τιθέντες.

<u>Endure</u>, my child, and <u>bear it</u>, although you are troubled.
For many [of us gods] who have Olympian homes have <u>endured
terrible pains</u> at the hands of men, when gods set them against one
                     another.

Iliad V 382–384

Dione's stories begin with an admonition that Aphrodite endure (τέτλαθι) and
hold up (ἀνάσχεο) under her suffering (κηδομένη περ, V 382). The verb *τλάω
"endure, suffer" plus an object—implied or otherwise—denoting suffering (here
κηδομένη, V 382; cf. the cognate κῆδος "care, distress") marks the connection
between Aphrodite's current pain and the various stories Dione relates. As she
explains, many gods have endured pains (τλῆμεν ... ἄλγε', V 383–384) at the
hands of mortals. First, she tells of how Ares endured pains (τλῆ μὲν Ἄρης, V
385) when Otus and Ephialtes locked him in a bronze jar for thirteen months (V
385–391)—we will return to this scene below. Then, Dione tells how Hera and
Hades suffered when Herakles shot them with arrows:

<u>τλῆ</u> δ' Ἥρα, ὅτε μιν κρατερὸς πάις Ἀμφιτρύωνος
δεξιτερὸν κατὰ μαζὸν ὀιστῷ τριγλώχινι
βεβλήκει· τότε καί <u>μιν ἀνήκεστον λάβεν ἄλγος</u>.
<u>τλῆ</u> δ' Ἀίδης ἐν τοῖσι πελώριος ὠκὺν ὀϊστόν,
εὖτέ μιν ωὑτὸς ἀνήρ, υἱὸς Διὸς αἰγιόχοιο,
ἐν Πύλῳ ἐν νεκύεσσι βαλὼν <u>ὀδύνῃσιν ἔδωκεν·</u>
αὐτὰρ ὃ βῆ πρὸς δῶμα Διὸς καὶ μακρὸν Ὄλυμπον
<u>κῆρ ἀχέων</u>, ὀδύνῃσι πεπαρμένος, αὐτὰρ ὀϊστός
ὤμῳ ἔνι στιβαρῷ ἠλήλατο, <u>κῆδε δὲ θυμόν</u>.

And Hera <u>endured</u> it, when the mighty son of Amphitryon
struck her in her right breast with a triple-barbed arrow.
Even then an <u>incurable pain seized her</u>.
And Hades the huge <u>endured</u> a flying-arrow among them,
when the same man, the son of aegis-bearing Zeus,
<u>gave him over to pains</u> when he shot him among the dead in
                 Pylos.
But he went to the houses of Zeus and to tall Olympos

grieved at heart because he had been driven through with pains. For an
  arrow
had been driven within his powerful shoulder, and he was suffering at
  heart.

Iliad V 392–400

Hera and Hades, among unknown others (note ἐν τοῖσι "among them," V 395)
suffered on one or more than one occasion when they were shot by Herakles.[60]
The text does not provide any further details about the event(s), although we find
various references elsewhere to a tradition in which Herakles made war against
Nestor's father, Neleus, and the Pylians because they supported Orchomenus or
Elis against Herakles' hometown of Thebes (Scholia T at *Iliad* XI 690, Pausanias
5.3.1), or because Neleus refused to purify Herakles of the murder of Iphitus (ps.-
Apollodorus 2.6.2), or because of a dispute over cattle (Scholia bT at *Iliad* XI 690,
Isocrates *Archidamus* 19, and see Hainsworth 1993:300). Elsewhere in the *Iliad*
Nestor refers to an incident when Herakles once killed all of Neleus' sons—save
Nestor himself—at Pylos (*Iliad* XI 690–693; cf. Hesiod fr. 35.6–9 M-W, Pausanias
3.26.8). It is possible that this battle was where Herakles wounded Hera and
Hades (Scholia bT at *Iliad* V 392–394, and see Fontenrose 1974:327–330). Pindar's
Olympian 9 speaks of Herakles fighting Poseidon, Apollo, and Hades—apparently
on a single occasion:[61]

---

[60] See Kirk 1985:101, "Hades himself is wounded ἐν τοῖσι, i.e. as one of those divine victims, again
by arrow-shot."

[61] See Molyneux 1972, esp. 303–313, and Pavlou 2008:545–554, both of whom note specific stylistic
features in Pindar that suggest a single occurence: e.g. the identification of ἀμφὶ Πύλον σταθείς
(31) without mention of other location, emphatic repetition of ἤριδεν (31, 32), the lack of any
phrase like δ' αὖ to mark a new theme, and the apparent three-fold ἀνίκα clause governing ἤριδε
(31), ἤριδεν δέ (32), and οὐδ' ... ἔχε (33) which would indicate a single occasion ("when X and Y
and Z happened"). However, it is possible that Pindar has conflated separate incidents, since
the mythological biography of Herakles includes separate conflicts with various gods, including Ares (ps.-Hesiod *Shield of Herakles* 359–367), Hera (Lycophron *Alexandria* 39–40 with scholia),
Apollo who refused to give Herakles an oracle because of *miasma* (Scholia at Pindar *Olympian*
9.43, 44a, 48, ps.-Apollodorus 2.6.2, Cicero *On the Nature of the Gods* 3.42, Plutarch *Moralia* 378d,
Pausanius 3.21.8, 10.13.7), and Hades who refused to allow Herakles to take Kerberos (Scholia bT
at *Iliad* V 395–397; compare Scholia at Pindar *Olympian* 9.43, 44a, 48). See also Gantz 1993:413–414
for a description of a now lost Corinthian cotyle of the early 6th century BCE which depicted
Herakles menacing Hades with his bow in one hand and a stone raised in the other. See further
the series of 5th century vases collected by John Boardman under "Heracles" no. 3488–3497
in *Lexicon Iconographicum Mythologiae Classicae* depicting Herakles with, shaking hands with, or
carrying a man with a cornucopia, identified by Boardman as "Palaimon," though Gantz suggests the figure is a representation of Hades. Gantz interprets the iconography: "not impossibly
Herakles, after wounding the lord of the Underworld, takes him up to the earth or Olympos to be
cured" (456), or following Lactantius' claim that Herakles took the cornucopia—which he broke
off of Achelous' head—with him when he went to Hades (Scholia at Statius *Thebaid* 4.106), Gantz

ἀγαθοὶ
δὲ καὶ σοφοὶ κατὰ δαίμον᾽ ἄνδρες
ἐγένοντ᾽· ἐπεὶ ἀντίον
πῶς ἂν τριόδοντος Ἡ-
ρακλέης σκύταλον τίναξε χερσίν,
ἀνίκ᾽ ἀμφὶ Πύλον σταθεὶς ἤρειδε Ποσειδάν,
ἤρειδεν δέ νιν ἀργυρ<έῳ> τόξῳ πολεμίζων
Φοῖβος, οὐδ᾽ Ἀΐδας ἀκινήταν ἔχε ῥάβδον,
βρότεα σώμαθ᾽ ᾇ κατάγει κοίλαν πρὸς ἄγυιαν
θνᾳσκόντων;

But men become brave and wise as divinity determines: for how else could Heracles have brandished his club in his hands against the trident when Poseidon stood before Pylos and pressed him hard and Phoibos pressed him while battling with his silver bow, nor did Hades keep still his staff, with which he leads down to his hollow abode the mortal bodies of those who die?

Pindar Olympian 9.28–35 (ed. and trans. Race 1997)

Pindar's narrative is in many ways strikingly similar to Dione's account: we are given a list of gods wounded by Herakles; Hades is mentioned last and is given greater treatment than the preceding gods; and the stylistic repetition of ἤρειδε ... ἤρειδε δ᾽ is reminiscent of Homer's τλῆ μέν ... τλῆ δ᾽ ... τλῆ δ᾽ ... at *Iliad* V 392–400.[62] Panyassis' fifth-century epic about Herakles also seems to have included an account of a conflict "in sandy Pylos" (ἐν Πύλῳ ἠμαθόεντι, fr. 24 Davies) where—according to Arnobius—Herakles wounded Hera and Hades (fr. 25 Davies).[63] The location of a conflict between Herakles and Hera (or Apollo), Hades, and Poseidon at Messenian Pylos is explained by saying that Poseidon and his allies came to assist Neleus, but Herakles was aided by Zeus and Athena.[64]

---

notes "we might also ask if in some sources Herakles did not present the cornucopia to Hades as a gift or compensation for his wound, thus serving to justify the god's possession of this familiar attribute in fifth-century art" (456).

[62] See Pavlou 2008:551n68. Pavlou finds the parallels between Homer and Pindar striking enough to suggest that "Pindar might have had [*Iliad*] Book 5 and Dione's narrative in mind while composing his poem." Molyneux (1972) also notes the similarities, and tries to account for the anomolous appearance of Apollo as "an imperfect reminiscence" of V 401–404 and the appearance in Dione's narrative of Paieon as he heals Hades' wound (310n23).

[63] In ps.-Hesiod's *Shield of Herakles* 359–367, Herakles wounds Ares "above sandy Pylos" (ὑπὲρ Πύλου ἠμαθόεντος).

[64] Scholia A at *Iliad* XI 690, Erbse: συνεμάχουν δὲ τῷ μὲν Νηλεῖ τρεῖς Θεοί, Ποσειδῶν Ἥρα Ἀιδωνεύς, ὡς καὶ ἐν τῇ Ε φησί, τῷ δὲ Ἡρακλεῖ δύο, Ἀθηνᾶ καὶ Ζεύς "Three gods were fighting alongside Neleus—Poseidon, Hera, and Hades—as also [Homer] says in Book V, and two were fighting

The precise details of this myth are complex and contradictory, but surely point to a traditional account in Herakles' mythological biography.[65] For our purposes, the precise episode need not concern us here; what is important for our discussion is the description of gods suffering pain when shot by Herakles' arrows. When Hera is wounded (ὅτε μιν … βεβλήκει "when [he] struck her," V 392–394), "even then an incurable pain seized her" (τότε καί μιν ἀνήκεστον λάβεν ἄλγος, V 394).[66] The only other use of the adjective ἀνήκεστος "incurable" in Homer is *Iliad* XV 217 where Poseidon claims that if Zeus should decide to save Troy and rob the Achaeans of the glory of sacking the city, Poseidon's anger at him will be without cure: "there will be an incurable anger for us two" (νῶϊν ἀνήκεστος χόλος ἔσται, XV 217). The adjective ἀνήκεστος (cf. νήκεστος at Hesiod *Works and Days* 283) is the negative compound verbal adjective (ἀ- "not") in *-το- built on stem *ηκεσ- (< ἀκέομαι "to cure," itself a denominative formation from the noun ἄκος "cure"),[67] and can indicate either complete action ("uncured, not yet cured") or possibility ("incurable"). In these passages, "uncured" captures the literal meaning whereas "incurable" captures affective meaning: "incurable" indicates that the pain is particularly intense. Poetic exaggeration emphasizes the temporal aspect of the pain itself.

Although age-less (ἀ-γήρως) and im-mortal (ἀ-θάνατος), Hera comes to experience human time through the physical pain of her wound, for she must endure (τλῆ) incurable (ἀν-ήκεστον) pain when she is shot by Herakles (V 392–394). The experience of physical pain ensnares Hera in mortal time. Hesiod characterizes the divine realm as one without pain when he describes the apotheosis of Herakles upon the completion of his labors: ναίει ἀπήμαντος καὶ ἀγήραος ἤματα πάντα, "he dwells without pain and unaging throughout all

---

alongside Herakles—Athena and Zeus." Scholia bT at *Iliad* V 392–394a1–2 and Scholia A at *Iliad* XI 690 provide the only evidence regarding Hera's participation in the battle with Herakles at Pylos (as noted by Willcock 1978–1984:I.236; cf. *Iliad* V 392–400 for Herakles wounding Hera), but various other sources provide corroboration of Herakles' fight with Hades: see Pindar *Olympian* 9.33 with scholia, ps.-Apollodorus 2.7.3, and Pausanias 6.25.2 in addition to the Homeric scholia cited above. It appears that Aristarchus (Scholia T at *Iliad* V 397) took ἐν Πύλῳ ἐν νεκύεσσι to refer to the "gate" of the land of the dead, as if ἐν Πύλῳ = ἐν πύλῃ [sc. Ἀΐδαο]; for the "gates of Hades," see *Iliad* V 646, XXIII 71 and compare IX 312. The reference to "Pylos" (or "the gate [of the underworld]") remains unclear; Pausanias 6.25.2 suggests a third possibility, the Eleian Pylos where Hades had a temple.

65 On the concept of traditional "mythological biographies" of heroes, see most recently Burgess 2009 with bibliography.

66 I follow Ameis, Hentze, and Cauer 1965:69n394 in reading καί here as adverbial. Compare further the numerous Homeric examples of ὅτε "when" paired with καὶ τότε "even then" or "then also" at Kühner and Gerth 1963:255–256.

67 On the form, see Chantraine 1968–1980:49, s.v. ἄκος, and on s-stem nouns more generally, Meissner 2006. On the temporal aspects of the privative prefix ἀ-, see my discussion in the Introduction above (with bibliography).

days" (Hesiod *Theogony* 955).[68] If divine temporality is to be characterized by *lack* of toil, pain, and physical degeneration and disintegration,[69] then when Hera comes to suffer physical pain, she must be experiencing mortal time.[70] The experience of this mortal time, of the body in pain, is one of pure duration: the verb *τλάω "endure, suffer" marks the mortal experiences of the gods. Indeed, it is significant that the semantics of the *τλάω family includes both "enduring" (cf. ἔτλη "he endured," πολύτλας "much enduring") as well as a technical term for a unit of weight (τάλαντον):[71] as we saw in the case of Aphrodite, enduring pain entails being "weighed down."

[68] Note that in this passage (Hesiod *Theogony* 955), the adjective ἀπήμαντος is an analogical variation for ἀθάνατος in the formula ἀθάνατος καὶ ἄγηρος: see West 1966:419.

[69] For this characterization of the body of the gods, see Clay 1982, Vernant 1991:27–49, and Sissa and Detienne 2000.

[70] See Scarry 1985:22 on the connection between physical pain and human sentience, "the felt-fact of aliveness." Note that—at least from a Heideggerian viewpoint—sentience is nothing other than the experience of finite human temporality, that is, of being-in-the-world (cf. Heidegger 1962:38–40, 45–49, 277–278, 374–382, 418–423). Significantly, Scarry (citing Deuteronomy 4:28, Habukkuk 2:18, 19, Hosea 11:8, and Jeremiah 8:21, 9:1, 9:17, 18, 10:14, 19, 20, 42:12, 15, 17, 51:17) goes on to discuss the representation of God in Christian religious texts as possessing sentience, which entails the suffering of physical pain: "He [sc. God] now not only reminds his people that he is alive, that he sees, moves, hears, breathes (and by implication, even eats, for the absence of this attribute is included in his denunciation of wooden and stone objects), *but even that he experiences the most passive, extreme, and unselfobjectifying form of sentience, physical pain*" (Scarry 1985:230–231, emphasis added).

Emotional suffering produces the same effect of drawing a divinity into human temporality. See especially Schein's analysis of Achilles' immortal horses as they mourn over the fallen Patroklos (*Iliad* XVII 432–440): "Although as immortals the horses should be immune to death and the ravages of time, their tears and the language in which they are described make them seem virtually human in their suffering" (Schein 2002:197). Schein argues persuasively that the image of Achilles' immortal horses with their beautiful manes "stained" (ἐμιαίνετο, XVII 439) with dust are an image of "the contradiction between this immortality and their participation in the sorrows of human existence" (198). On this interpretation, see also Thalmann 1984:48–49, Purves 2006a:187–188, and my discussion in the Introduction above. Note that although "the two [horses] away from their manes cast the dust to the ground" (τὼ δ' ἀπὸ χαιτάων κονίην οὐδάσδε βαλόντε, XVII 457), they do not quite recover from being tainted with mortal pain and suffering, for we hear later that the horses cannot compete in Patroklos' funeral games because "the two stand grieving for him, and their manes have reached down to rest on the ground, and the two of them stand with sorrow in their hearts" (τὸν τώ γ' ἑσταότες πενθείετον, οὐδεΐ δέ σφιν | χαῖται ἐρηρέδαται, τὼ δ' ἕστατον ἀχνυμέω κῆρ, XXIII 283–284). Once "stained" with mortal time through mourning for the accomplished death of Patroklos and the forthcoming death of Achilles, the immortal horses never quite recover (cf. Schein 2002:200).

[71] *Τλάω is a rich verbal stem that appears in root theme I (*telh₂) expressed as τελα- (e.g. τελαμών "strap, belt"), root theme II (*tleh₂) expressed as τλᾱ-/τλη- (e.g. ἔτλη "he endured," the athematic root aorist, πολύ-τλητος "much enduring"), root theme III (*tlh₂) expressed as ταλα- (e.g. τάλας "suffering, wretched" and ἀταλός "tender, delicate"), and even an o-grade (cf. τολμάω "undertake, endure, submit, dare" and τολμά "courage, daring"); the semantics of the word family suggest a basic meaning of "bear up." See Beekes 1969:200–201, Palmer 1996:219–220, and my discussion in the Introduction.

Like Hera, Hades also comes to experience mortal time as he "endures" (τλῆ δ' Ἀΐδης, V 395) pains when injured by Herakles. Herakles "gave him over to pains when he shot him" (βαλὼν ὀδύνῃσιν ἔδωκεν, V 397). He was "grieving at heart" (κῆρ ἀχέων, V 399), "pierced through with pains" (ὀδύνῃσι πεπαρμένος, V 399), and "suffering in spirit" (κῆδε δὲ θυμόν, V 400). Nevertheless, unlike Hera's "incurable" pains, Hades' pains do find a cure, for he makes his way to Olympos where he, like Aphrodite, is freed from the pains inflicted by a mortal. There Paieon, the divine healer, "cures" Hades of his pains:

τῷ δ' ἐπὶ Παιήων ὀδυνήφατα φάρμακα πάσσων
ἠκέσατ'· οὐ μὲν γάρ τι καταθνητός γ' ἐτέτυκτο.

But Paieon by sprinkling pain-killing drugs upon him
cured him. For he was in no way made to be mortal.

Iliad V 401–402

Paieon (only here at *Iliad* IV 401, V 899, and *Odyssey* iv 232) is the doctor of the gods; here, he "cures" Hades. The verb ἠκέσατε, the aorist indicative of ἀκέεσθαι "to cure," is from the same root (ἄκος "cure") at the adjective ἀν-ήκεσ-τος "without a cure" which described Hera's "not yet cured" pains.[72] Like Hera, Hades becomes enmeshed in mortal time through suffering physical pains—note that they both "endure" pains (τλῆ: Ares, V 385; Hera, V 392; Hades, V 395; cf. τέτλαθι, V 382 and τλῆμεν, V 383); yet, unlike Hera, Hades is rescued from human temporality through the removal of his pains. Note, however, that Hades' cure comes at considerable cost—it requires two unprecedented actions: Hades must leave the underworld and ascend to Olympos,[73] and he must be plied with magical "pain-killing drugs" (ὀδυνήφατα φάρμακα, V 401) of divine origin.[74]

---

[72] See Ebeling 1963:61–62, s.v. ἀκέομαι and 126, s.v. ἀνήκεστος; Chantraine 1968–1980:49–50, s.v. ἄκος; on the form of the verbal adjective in –τος, see Risch 1974:19–25 (§10).

[73] See West 2001:192, "indeed, the idea of his [sc. Hades'] ever entering Olympus is startling." Nevertheless, West defends *Iliad* V 398–402 against Koechly's condemnation of these verses by noting the general concord with the "rhetorical structure" of the surrounding context, since after Dione tells Aphrodite how Paieon healed Hades, Dione herself goes on to heal Aphrodite. See also Gantz 1993:70–71 on the rape of Persephone as the only "certain appearance" of Hades outside of the underworld. The *Iliad* itself indicates the unusual appearance of Hades outside of the underworld, as at the beginning of the *Theomakhia* of the gods (*Iliad* XX 54–66) Hades is afraid (ἔδεισεν, XX 61) that Poseidon might break open the earth (γαῖαν ἀναρρήξειε, XX 63) and the terrible, mouldering homes of the dead (οἰκία ... σμερδαλέ' εὐρώεντα, XX 64–65)—a sight ever hateful to the gods (τά τε στυγέουσι θεοί περ, XX 65)—might become visible (φανείη, XX 64) to humans on earth and gods in heaven.

[74] The adjective ὀδυνήφατα occurs only two more times in Homer: once at *Iliad* V 900 (= V 401) where Paieon "cures" the pain of another god, Ares, when he is wounded by Diomedes, and again

At *Iliad* V 901 Paieon heals Ares as he did Hades before, "for he was not at all made to be mortal" (οὐ μὲν γάρ τι καταθνητός γε τέτυκτο, V 901 = V 402). This "typically emphatic generalization," as Kirk (1985:103) terms it, serves to reassert the divine nature of gods at the very moment when they are wounded, bleeding, and in pain. That is to say, Homer seems to reassure his audience of the gods' immortality at those very moments when they appear most mortal. And yet, as Nicole Loraux (1986) has elegantly argued, the very act of reasserting the immortality of the gods serves rather to emphasize the fact that their wounds would otherwise be mortal (469). That is, at the very moment that the text affirms Hades and Ares as immortal, it raises the specter of their virtual deaths (Loraux 1986:649n3).

3. Punitive Temporality: Succession, Repression, Incarceration

The images of carnal gods who are wounded, bleed, feel pain, and narrowly avoid death, are not confined to Book V of the *Iliad*, nor only to circumstances in which a hero at the height of his *aristeia* becomes more god than man—δαίμονι ἶσος "equal to a god"—and injures a god with weapons. Indeed, divinities frequently threaten or carry out violence against one another, invoking the theme of *theomakhia* "battle of the gods." They "endure" pain at the hands of other gods.

One context in which we find *theomakhia* "battle of the gods" involves the cosmic instability when one order is displaced by another. Such are the narratives of the succession of rule as Kronos overthrows Ouranos and Zeus overthrows Kronos, for during Zeus' campaign against his father and the older gods, the Titans, violence is carried out on a grand scale—the victorious Olympian gods seize control of the cosmos, whereas the vanquished Titans are bound and incarcerated in Tartaros. Although the *Iliad* locates itself in a period after Zeus and the Olympians have come into power, Zeus' power is not stable. The *Iliad*

---

at *Iliad* XI 847 where Patroklos cures Eurypylus' pains with a special root: "And he cast a bitter root upon him, a pain-killer (ὀδυνήφατον), and rubbed it in thoroughly with his hand; it held back all his pains (ἔσχ' ὀδύνας); the wound dried, and the blood stopped (παύσατο δ' αἷμα)" (XI 846–848). Patroklos' pain-killing drugs are themselves from a divine source, for, we are told, he learned about these "gentle drugs" (ἤπια φάρμακα, XI 830) from Achilles (XI 831), who, in turn, learned them from the immortal centaur Chiron, the venerable trainer of heroes (on Chiron and the education of Achilles, see Hesiod fr. 204.87–89 M-W, Pindar *Pythian* 6.21–23, *Nemian* 3.43–53, Hainsworth 1993:310, and Mackie 1997). These drugs, then—both the φάρμακα Paieon sprinkles on Hades and again later on Ares and the ῥίζα πικρή "bitter root" Patroklos rubs into Eurypylus' wound—are special, something more than mortal. They and they alone have the power to "cure" Hades' pains and to "hold back the pains" and stanch the blood-flow of the injured Eurypylus. It requires divine force to rescue the wounded god from mortal temporality, just as the same "pain-killing drugs" rescue humans from death itself.

often insinuates violence between gods within the context of rebellion in which dire consequences await those who are vanquished: the possibility of death for the rebellious gods takes the form of being "hurled" out of Olympos by Zeus and bound within Tartaros.[75] In this section, we examine four passages from the *Iliad* in which Zeus hurls enemies to earth, or threatens to do so. In each instance (Hephaistos, Atē, Hupnos, and Hera), I will argue, Homer introduces the possibility of the rebellious god's "death."

3.1. Oedipal Criminals: Hephaistos, Typhoeus, Apollo

A prime example of a god injured while in conflict with Zeus appears in Book I of the *Iliad* as Hephaistos begs his mother to cede to Zeus' will. He apologizes that he cannot do more to help her, but claims that he is powerless against Zeus. He recalls a time when once before he tried to stand up against Zeus and rescue Hera from his clutches, only to be thrown from Olympos to crash painfully on the earth far below:

ἤδη γάρ με καὶ ἄλλοτ' ἀλεξέμεναι μεμαῶτα
ῥῖψε ποδὸς τεταγὼν ἀπὸ βηλοῦ θεσπεσίοιο·
πᾶν δ' ἦμαρ φερόμην, ἅμα δ' ἠελίῳ καταδύντι
κάππεσον ἐν Λήμνῳ, ὀλίγος δ' ἔτι θυμὸς ἐνῆεν.

For even at another time once before when I was eager to help you,
[Zeus] grabbed hold of my foot and hurled me from the threshold of
    heaven;
for an entire day I was carried along, and at the same time as the sun was
    setting
I fell down in Lemnos, and there was not much life left in me.

Iliad I 590–593

Hephaistos' fall nearly kills him—he had little life or breath (ὀλίγος ... θυμός, I 593) left in him afterward.[76] As Robert Garland (1981) has demonstrated in

---

[75] Compare the discussion by Eliade 1969:92–124 on the sovereign god in Indo-European mythology who "punishes by 'bondage' (that is, by illness or impotence) anyone who infringes the law, and is guardian of the universal order" (97). For further associations between "binding" and death, see Eliade 1969:99, 101, 105, 107, 109–110.

[76] For an interpretation of θυμός as "breath, breath-soul or spirit," see Onians 1954:44–45, Caswell 1990:7–8, 12–16, and Clarke 1999:75–83. Clarke cites *Iliad* I 593 (ὀλίγος ... θυμὸς ἐνῆεν) as evidence of how "an exhausted man has little breath" and compares *Odyssey* v 456–458 where Odysseus lies breathless with exhaustion (ὁ δ' ἄρ' ἄπνευστος καὶ ἄναυδος "So he lay breathless and speechless") but then recovers his breath (ἀλλ' ὅτε δή ῥ' ἄμπνυτο καὶ ἐς φρένα θυμὸς ἀγέρθη "but when he indeed returned to consciousness and his breath was gathered into his lungs") (Clarke 1999:78). Scholia D at *Iliad* I 593 (van Thiel) points to a similar association between θυμός

his study of descriptions of death in the *Iliad*, the loss of θυμός is the most frequently cited cause of biological death in Homeric narrative—that is to say, the most common way to express a character's death in the *Iliad* is to describe the loss of his or her θυμός.[77] Although the god survives the fall, his recovery is not perfect—it leaves its permanent trace in the god's legs.[78] After the fall he is regularly called ἀμφιγυήεις "with crooked limbs on both sides" (*Iliad* I 607, XIV 239, XVIII 383, 393, 462, 587, 590, 614; *Odyssey* viii 300, 349, 357), an epithet which appears to be related to the verb γυιώσω which is used at *Iliad* VIII 402 and 416 to mean "make lame."[79] In the eighteenth and twentieth Books of the *Iliad* he is given the epithet κυλλοποδίων "little twisted-foot" (XVIII 371, XX 270); once in Book XXI he is addressed by the same epithet in the vocative case as Hera rouses him to action (ὄρσεο, κυλλοπόδιον, ἐμὸν τέκος "get up, little club-foot, my child," XXI 331).[80] Further, at *Iliad* XVIII 397 the god describes himself as χωλός "lame."[81] Hephaistos' injury is his identifying mark: his twisted feet or legs are

---

and life/breath when it glosses ὀλίγος δ' ἔτι θυμὸς ἐνῆεν "and there was little θυμός still in me" as ἀντὶ τοῦ ἐλειποψύχουν "[Homer says this] instead of 'I was losing my breath [*psukhē*].'" See Nehring 1947 for an analysis of how one's θυμός only leaves one's body in death; when one is knocked unconscious, the θυμός is not lost, but merely weakened or dulled. When one recovers, his θυμός is likewise "gathered up" again: cf. θυμὸς ἀγέρθη (*Iliad* IV 152, XXII 475; *Odyssey* v 458, xxiv 349), ἐσαγείρετο θυμόν (*Iliad* XV 240, XXI 417), θυμηγερέων (*Odyssey* vii 283).

[77] Garland 1981, esp. 47 with Figure 2 and 56 with Tables 7–8. By Garland's count, the loss of θυμός figures in 40 out of a total 88 passages describing "biological death" in the *Iliad*; a glance at Garland's Figure 2 (47) shows that the loss of θυμός is by far the most common way to express death in the *Iliad*.

[78] See Edwards 1991:192, "At 1.590–4 Hephaistos tells how Zeus (his father, *Odyssey* 8.312) hurled him from Olympos when he tried to help Hera, and the Sinties took care of him on Lemnos; in this version *the fall must have caused his lameness*" (emphasis added). See also Purves 2006a:197–200.

[79] At *Iliad* VIII 402 and 416 Zeus threatens to "make lame" the horses drawing Hera and Athena to the Trojan plain as they ride to bring help to the Achaeans. Kirk 1985:114 ponders whether the verb is "itself perhaps derived from the assumption that the ancient description of Hephaistos ἀμφιγυήεις, must mean 'crippled' in some sense." The exact meaning of ἀμφιγυήεις remains disputed: see Hainsworth 1988:366–367 at *Odyssey* viii 300 for bibliography. However, the other evidence which points to a lame Hephaistos (which I discuss below) is compelling.

[80] κυλλοποδίων is the diminutive form of the compound κυλλός "crooked" + ποδ- (πούς). See Ebeling 1963:I.938–939, s.v. κυλλοποδίων and Chantraine 1968–1980:598–599, s.v. κυλλός. On the formation of the denominative in -ων, see Risch 1974:56–57 (§24c).

[81] See also *Odyssey* viii 308, 332. The same adjective is used to describe Thersites who is "lame in one foot" (χωλὸς ἕτερον πόδα, *Iliad* II 217). See further *Hymn to Apollo* 315–316 where Hephaistos is described by Hera as ῥικνὸς πόδας "shriveled up in his feet"; although the hymn claims Hephaistos' lameness to be a birth-defect rather than the result of his fall, the image of the damaged god remains consistent with that of a god wounded from falling to earth. In *Hymn to Apollo* 316 Hephaistos is also called ἠπεδανός "weak." Cunliffe 1963:126, 182, s.vv., ἔμπεδος, ἠπεδανός, suggests a connection with ἔμπεδος "in place, steady," implying something like "not firm on one's feet." However, see Risch 1974:106 on the formation of adjectives in -εδανός (as ῥῑγ-εδανή "horrible, something to shudder at" at *Iliad* XIX 325 next to ῥῖγος "cold" and ῥῑγέω "to shudder at in cold or fear"), and the assumption of a root *ἧπος, perhaps cognate with Lithuanian *opus*

often represented on vase paintings depicting the "Return of Hephaistos" story, beginning with the representation of the scene on the François Vase which shows a mounted Hephaistos with his right foot twisted to face the opposite direction.[82] Alex Purves has noted of Hephaistos' injury,

> As an after-effect of falling, Hephaestus displays his strained relation-ship to time through his body. The dragging of his foot lingers on as a physical trace of his encounter with human temporality. Through his limp, the god will always carry with him the sign of a specific event that took place in the past. (Purves 2006a:200)

The god's feet are enduring reminders of the pain he experienced at the hands of Zeus.[83] His fall, although not fatal, has marked him for life; he is now the object of laughter among the gods because of his injury: at *Iliad* I 600 the gods laugh as they watch Hephaistos bustle about, pouring wine for the others,[84] and Scholia bT at *Iliad* I 584b1 (Erbse) interprets Hephaistos' movement here as ridiculous because of his lame leg (γέλωτα κινεῖ τὸ ἀναΐξας ἐπὶ τοῦ χωλοῦ τιθέμενον), yet pairs the laughter with the remembrance of the fall he suffered at Zeus' hands (καὶ μεμνημένος, πῶς ὁ Ζεὺς τοῦ ποδὸς λαβόμενος ἔρριψεν αὐτὸν οὐρανόθεν).

Hephaistos' fall and injury at Zeus' hands is not a singular event. Rather, it is part of a traditional "succession motif" narrative pattern in which a challenger struggles against the reigning king of the gods. If successful, the challenger

---

"soft, receptive, invalid" and Sanskrit *ap$_u$vā́* "mortal fear" (cf. Beekes 2010:522, s.v. ἠπεδανός with bibliography). See my discussion below on the close association between Hephaistos and Typhoeus/Typhaon who was also injured through falling; *Hymn to Apollo* pairs the two gods func-tionally as children born to Hera in response to Zeus' delivery of Athena from his head.

[82] On the François Vase, see Boardman 1974:44 plate 46.7, discussion at 218. See also the representa-tion of Hephaistos' crippled feet on a Laconian cup from Ialysus by the Boreads Painter (Rhodes 10711, at Boardman 1998:207 plate 419) and a Caeretan hydria by the Eagle Painter (Vienna 3577, at Boardman 1998:252 plate 495.11). See further Brommer 1978:11, 16, Himmelmann 1998:58–59, 129n5, and most recently, Fineberg 2009.

[83] Detienne and Vernant 1978:259–275, 300 offer a different explanation for Hephaistos' curved feet. According to their analysis, "The peculiar shape of his feet is the visible symbol of his *mētis*, his wise thoughts and his craftsman's intelligence. ... In order to dominate shifting, fluid powers such as fire, winds and minerals which the blacksmith must cope with, the intelligence and *mētis* of Hephaestus must be even more mobile and polymorphic than these" (272–273). I do not disagree with this analysis, but merely wish to emphasize that within the *Iliad*, Hephaistos' lame feet are closely linked with his fall. There is not necessarily any real dissonance between these two readings, since gods in Greek mythology who bring the craft of divine fire to man-kind—including Prometheus in addition to Hephaistos, both culture gods in this respect (see Detienne and Vernant 1978:280)—are depicted as enemies of Zeus. Part of the craft-god's *mētis*, then, appears to be the dissemination of an illicit knowledge to mankind.

[84] Hephaistos' lameness is also emphasized throughout *Iliad* XVIII as he bustles about to make new armor for Achilles: see XVIII 387, 411, 417–421. On Hephaistos' energetic hustling about as an index of his involvement with human temporality, see Purves 2006a:200 with nn63–65.

becomes the new king; if unsuccessful, he is cast to the ground and banished forever. In this way Zeus, as he rises to power, wages war against the rulers of the former generation—the Titans—and defeats them.[85] Zeus "drove the Titans away from heaven" (Τιτῆνας ἀπ' οὐρανοῦ ἐξέλασεν Ζεύς, Hesiod *Theogony* 820); then he and his allies bound the Titans and sent them beneath the earth forever to be imprisoned in Tartaros:[86]

> καὶ τοὺς μὲν ὑπὸ χθονὸς εὐρυοδείης
> πέμψαν καὶ <u>δεσμοῖσιν</u> ἐν ἀργαλέοισιν <u>ἔδησαν</u>,
> νικήσαντες χερσὶν ὑπερθύμους περ ἐόντας.

> And they sent them [sc. the Titans] beneath the wide-wayed earth
> and <u>bound them up</u> in grievous <u>bonds</u>,
> after they defeated them with their hands, although [the Titans] were
> excessively spirited.

> *Theogony* 717–719

After defeating, binding, and imprisoning the Titans, Zeus must face one more challenger, Typhoeus (called Typhaon in the *Homeric Hymn to Apollo*). After a great struggle,[87] Zeus eventually defeats his foe with repeated blows and casts him down to earth:

> αὐτὰρ ἐπεὶ δή μιν δάμασε πληγῆσιν ἱμάσσας,
> <u>ἤριπε</u> <u>γυιωθείς</u>, στονάχιζε δὲ γαῖα πελώρη.

---

[85] On the Titans, see esp. West 1966:200–201, where he explains: "The essential characteristics of the Titans are that they represent an older generation of gods, 'the former gods' ([*Theogony*] 424, 486), and that they are no longer active in the world, but dwell in Tartarus ([*Theogony*] 729ff., 814)" (200). The Iliadic tradition also places the Titans underground and within Tartarus: θεοὺς ... τοὺς ὑποταρταρίους, οἳ Τιτῆνες καλέονται "the gods below in Tartarus, who are called 'Titans'" (*Iliad* XIV 279). For discussion, see Janko 1994:195–196. On Zeus' battle with the Titans, see West 1966:336–338, who notes that "A war of gods ... marks the end of an age: the old gods are killed, or imprisoned, and a new régime begins" (337).

[86] On Tartaros as prison, see West 1966:357–358. Caldwell 1987:105 calls it "a prison for oedipal criminals." See further Northrup 1979, Harrell 1991, Johnson 1999, and my discussion of Tartaros and Ares' bronze jar below.

[87] According to ps.-Apollodorus 1.6.3, Typhoeus temporarily overcomes Zeus and removes the sinews from his body and places them in a container. Hermes steals the sinews and returns them to Zeus' body. According to Nonnus *Dionysiaca* 1.481–512, Kadmos disguised himself as a shepherd and won back Zeus' sinews from Typhoeus under the pretext of needing them for the strings of a lyre with which he could play for the monster. Caldwell 1978:46 offers a convincing psychological reading of the succession motif in Typhoeus' temporary defeat of Zeus and argues "the theft by Typhoeus of Zeus' sinews" is "a sexual crime, an attack on the father's sexual prerogatives," especially when we consider the uses of νεῦρον "sinew" as a metaphor for "phallos" (cf. Henderson 1991:116 with n47–49 and Nonnos *Dionysiaca* 493 for νεῦρα ... σφριγόωντα "swelling sinew").

But indeed when [Zeus] conquered him by lashing him with strokes,
[Typhoeus] <u>fell down</u> and <u>was crippled</u>, and huge earth groaned.

Theogony 857–858

Note the similarities between Typhoeus' defeat here and our earlier discussion of
Hephaistos' fall from heaven. In both cases the gods endure a "fall" at the hands
of Zeus (Hephaistos: κάππεσον; Typhoeus: ἤριπε),[88] and both are "crippled" from
the impact of the blow (Hephaistos: ἀμφιγυήεις; Typhoeus: γυιωθείς).

The similarities between Typhoeus/Typhaon and Hephaistos are more
than coincidental. The birth of Hephaistos as related both in Hesiod's *Theogony*
(924–929) and the *Homeric Hymn to Apollo* (305–358) is represented as a response
to Zeus' delivery of Athena from his head. Hera is angered that Zeus produced a
child without her, and in retaliation, gives birth to Hephaistos herself "without
mixing in love" (οὐ φιλότητι μιγεῖσα, *Theogony* 927) with any god.[89] According to
the *Hymn to Apollo*, however, Hephaistos turns out to be a disappointment:

αὐτὰρ ὅ γ' ἠπεδανὸς γέγονεν μετὰ πᾶσι θεοῖσι
παῖς ἐμὸς Ἥφαιστος ῥικνὸς πόδας ὃν τέκον αὐτὴ
ῥίψ' ἀνὰ χερσὶν ἑλοῦσα καὶ ἔμβαλον εὐρέϊ πόντῳ.

But he, at any rate, was born a weakling among all the gods,
my son Hephaistos, shriveled up in his feet, whom I bore by
myself—

---

[88] ἤριπε is the aorist indicative active of ἐρείπειν "to fall" often used to indicate the moment when
a dead body falls in combat: *Iliad* IV 493; V 47, 58, 68, 75, 294, 357; VIII 122, 260, 314; XI 743; XV
452; XVI 319, 344; XVII 619; XXII 330. It can be used for non-fatal blows in combat as when warriors fall only to one knee (IV 309, VIII 329, XI 355; see Purves 2006a:184n17) or to describe the
non-fatal collapse of a fighter in boxing competition (XXIII 691). The verb is often used in similes
likening the falling body of a dying warrior to other falling objects, including trees (III 389, XIV
414, XVI 482, XXI 243), a tower (IV 462), and an ox killed in ritual sacrifice (XVII 522). The verb is
used only twice to indicate falling in a non-martial context, though with deathly implications:
the hair of Achilles' horses "falls" from either side of the yoke-pad (XVII 440), and Andromache
"falls" when she learns of the death of Hektor (XXII 467). For a fuller list of verbs meaning "to
fall" (including forms of πίπτω, ἀναπίπτω, καταπίπτω, ἐκπίπτω, ἐμπίπτω, and ἐρείπειν) in the
Iliad, see Purves 2006a:183–184 with nn10–17; for a discussion of falling and the experience of
death in the *Iliad*, see Purves 2006a, *passim*.

[89] See *Hymn to Apollo* 311–315, "Hear me, all you gods and all you goddesses, how cloud-gathering
Zeus begins to dishonor me (ἔμ' ἀτιμάζειν), when he made me his wife who knows careful ways.
And yet now apart from me (νόσφιν ἐμεῖο) he has given birth (τέκε) to bright-eyed Athena, who
is outstanding among all the blessed immortals." See also Hesiod fr. 343 M-W where the birth of
Hephaistos appears in the context of a quarrel between Hera and Zeus over the birth of Athena:
ἐκ ταύτης δ' ἔριδος ἣ μὲν τέκε φαίδιμον υἱόν | Ἥφαιστον, φιλότητος ἄτερ Διὸς αἰγιόχοιο, | ἐκ
πάντων παλάμῃσι κεκασμένον Οὐρανιώνων, "And as a result of this quarrel, she [sc. Hera] gave
birth to her glorious son Hephaistos, <u>without the love-making of aegis-bearing Zeus</u>, the most
outstanding of all the sons of Ouranos with his hands" (Hesiod fr. 343.1–3 M-W).

I quickly caught him up in my hands and threw him into the wide
    sea.

Hymn to Apollo 315–317

In the multiform preserved in the *Hymn to Apollo*, Hephaistos' lameness is not due to the effects of being thrown from heaven, but rather to a natural defect, perhaps because of Hera's attempt at parthenogenetic birth.[90] The two traditions regarding Hephaistos' birth are doublets meant to describe the god's lameness;[91] in one version, Hephaistos is born lame, and in the other, he is made lame through conflict with Zeus, father of gods and men. It is my contention that the second possibility is latent even in the *Homeric Hymn to Apollo* through the close association between the births of Hephaistos and Typhoeus/Typhaon, the final challenger to Zeus' throne.[92] As soon as Hera expresses her disappointment with Hephaistos, she delivers a second child, Typhoeus/Typhaon, to challenge Zeus' authority:[93]

κέκλυτε νῦν μοι Γαῖα καὶ Οὐρανὸς εὐρὺς ὕπερθεν,
Τιτῆνές τε θεοὶ τοὶ ὑπὸ χθονὶ ναιετάοντες
Τάρταρον ἀμφὶ μέγαν, τῶν ἐξ ἄνδρες τε θεοί τε·
αὐτοὶ νῦν μευ πάντες ἀκούσατε καὶ δότε παῖδα
νόσφι Διός, μηδέν τι βίην ἐπιδευέα κείνου·
ἀλλ' ὅ γε φέρτερος ἔστω ὅσον Κρόνου εὐρύοπα Ζεύς.
[...]

---

[90] Compare *Iliad* XVIII 394–409 for a similar version of Hephaistos' fall due to his lameness: ἥ μ' ἐσάωσ' ὅτε μ' ἄλγος ἀφίκετο τῆλε πεσόντα | μητρὸς ἐμῆς ἰότητι κυνώπιδος, ἥ μ' ἐθέλησε | κρύψαι χωλὸν ἐόντα "She [sc. Thetis] saved me when pain came upon me as I fell so far through the will of my dog-faced mother who wanted to hide me away since I was lame" (XVIII 395–397). On the association between Hera's parthenogenetic delivery and the creation of "oedipal conflict between father and son," the key element in the succession motif of early Greek theogonic/cosmological thought, see Caldwell 1978:52, 54.

[91] See Edwards 1991:192–193, Edmunds 1993:26–27 and 1997:421–422. For a reconciliation between the two narratives, see Caldwell 1978, esp. 52–58. See Braswell 1971:20–21 and Willcock 1977:44n16 for an argument that the two narratives of Hephaistos' fall are not true multiforms, but that at least one of them is non-traditional *ad hoc* invention by Homer to provide motivation for characters' actions (narrative of the first fall = *consolatio* for Hera; narrative of the second fall = motive for Hephaistos to make armor for Thetis).

[92] For a different solution, see Rinon 2008 who suggests that the two narratives in the *Iliad* in fact represent two different falls, not two different versions of the same fall. Hence, according to Rinon, Hera throws a Hephaistos already made lame (χωλὸν ἐόντα, XVIII 39) by a previous fall because "the mere presence of Hephaestus is a disgusting reflection of the goddess's failure in the quarrel with her husband, for her defeat is eternally inscribed in her son's deformed legs" (129).

[93] See Caldwell 1987:116 where he notes how Hera gives birth to Hephaistos and Typhoeus "in the same way and for the same reason" (116).

ἀλλ' ὅτε δὴ μῆνές τε καὶ ἡμέραι ἐξετελεῦντο
ἂψ περιτελλομένου ἔτεος καὶ ἐπήλυθον ὧραι,
ἡ δ' ἔτεκ' οὔτε θεοῖς ἐναλίγκιον οὔτε βροτοῖσι
δεινόν τ' ἀργαλέον τε Τυφάονα πῆμα βροτοῖσιν.

Listen to me now, Earth and wide Heaven above,
and you <u>Titans</u> who are <u>gods dwelling beneath the earth
around great Tartaros</u>, from whom come both men and gods:
You yourselves now, all of you, listen to me and grant me a son
apart from Zeus, <u>one falling short of him not at all in strength</u>,
<u>but let him be stronger by as much as far-seeing Zeus was stronger</u>
       <u>than Kronos.</u>
[...]
But indeed when the months and days were completed
as the year rolled round again and the seasons were filled,
she gave birth to one similar neither to the gods nor to mortals
but one terrible and grievous, Typhaon, a pain for mortals.

Hymn to Apollo 334–339, 349–352

Hera prays to deliver a child who will be stronger than Zeus by as much as Zeus was stronger than his father Kronos. The succession motif is overt, especially in the context of Hera's prayer to the Titans who dwell in Tartaros, the prison-house for gods who dare to challenge Zeus' authority. Richard Caldwell has persuasively argued,

> Although the *Theogony* does not mention Hera's ill-treatment of Hephaestus, and Homer in *Iliad* 18 does not mention a quarrel between Zeus and Hera, the two accounts along with the *Hymn to Apollo* seem unmistakably to represent a tradition in which Hera gave birth to Hephaestus in order to avenge herself against Zeus and in which Typhoeus and Hephaestus play similar roles. (Caldwell 1987:117)

In sum, then, Hephaistos appears to have been a rival to Zeus' throne in one mythical tradition; he was unsuccessful and was cast down to earth like Typhoeus after him.[94] Neither can be said to perish outright from their ordeals,

---

[94] It is productive to consider Prometheus, another fire god punished by Zeus, as similarly filling the role of "oedipal" challenger to Zeus' authority, after he steals fire from Zeus and gives it to mankind. For the many similarities between Prometheus and Hephaistos, including the close associations between their cults in Attica, see Caldwell 1978:44, 58nn5–13. Note that Prometheus is nearly cast into Tartaros: see Aeschylus *Prometheus Bound* 154, 1051–1052 with discussion at Detienne and Vernant 1978:81–82. See further Whitman 1970:41–42 with n11 and Fontenrose

but both are maimed and permanently reduced; although not dead, they are not quite what they once were.

A second provocative example of an "Oedipal" challenger to Zeus' authority who is nearly "killed" is Apollo. A poorly preserved fragment of Hesiod (fr. 54a M-W), partly reconstructed by Edgar Lobel, the fragment's original editor, relates a narrative in which Apollo, angered by the death of his son Asclepius at Zeus' hands, kills the Cyclopes who manufacture lightning bolts for Zeus. The account, barely legible in Hesiod, is preserved in part by Pindar (*Pythian* 3.54–58)[95] and Euripides (*Alcestis* 3–6),[96] and more fully in the later account by ps.-Apollodorus (*Library* 3.10.4):[97]

Ζεὺς δὲ φοβηθεὶς μὴ λαβόντες ἄνθρωποι θεραπείαν παρ' αὐτοῦ βοηθῶσιν ἀλλήλοις, ἐκεραύνωσεν αὐτόν. καὶ διὰ τοῦτο ὀργισθεὶς Ἀπόλλων κτείνει Κύκλωπας τοὺς τὸν κεραυνὸν Διὶ κατασκευάσαντας. Ζεὺς δὲ ἐμέλλησε ῥίπτειν αὐτὸν εἰς Τάρταρον, δεηθείσης δὲ Λητοῦς ἐκέλευσεν αὐτὸν ἐνιαυτὸν ἀνδρὶ θητεῦσαι. ὁ δὲ παραγενόμενος εἰς Φερὰς πρὸς Ἄδμητον τὸν Φέρητος τούτῳ λατρεύων ἐποίμαινε, καὶ τὰς θηλείας βόας πάσας διδυμοτόκους ἐποίησεν.

But Zeus, since he was afraid that once men acquired the healing art from him [sc. Asclepius] they would come to the rescue of one another, he struck him with a lightning bolt. Because of this, Apollo became

---

1974:539 on the connection between Hephaistos, Typhoeus, and Prometheus as fire-gods. Fontenrose argues, "This is a theme observed before, kinship and conflict between the champion and the artisan god ... it is also Zeus against Prometheus or Hephaestus or Typhon. For Typhon, we should remember, was born of Hera in the same manner of Hephaestus, and is in part a fire demon; and fire deities tend to become divine smiths and artisans" (539).

95 "But even wisdom is enthralled to gain. Gold appearing in his hands with its lordly wage prompted even him [sc. Asklepios] to bring back from death a man already carried off. But then, with a cast (ῥίψαις) from his hands, Kronos' son took the breath from both men's breasts in an instant; the flash of lightning (κεραυνός) hurled down doom (μόρον)" (trans. Race 1997).

96 "Zeus is the cause, since he killed (κατακτάς) my son Asklepios, when he struck him in the chest with a lightning bolt (φλόγα). Indeed, because I was angry at this (οὗ δὴ χολωθείς), I killed (κτείνω: historic present) the Cyclopes, the architects of Zeus' fire." Apollo goes on to explain how he was punished by being forced to become a servant of Admetus, but does not suggest that Zeus first plotted to "cast him into Tartaros" as we find in Hesiod, ps.-Apollodorus, and elsewhere.

97 See also the account by Zenobius: Διὰ γοῦν τὸ μὴ δόξαι τοῦτον παρ' ἀνθρώποις εἶναι θεὸν, ὁ Ζεὺς ἐκεραύνωσεν· Ἀπόλλων δὲ ὀργισθεὶς κτείνει Κύκλωπας τοὺς τὸν κεραυνὸν κατασκευάσαντας τῷ Διί. Ζεὺς δὲ ἐμέλλησε ῥίπτειν αὐτὸν εἰς Τάρταρον, ἀλλὰ δεηθείσης Λητοῦς ἐκέλευσεν αὐτῷ ἐνιαυτὸν ἀνδρὶ θητεῦσαι "Therefore, because he didn't think it was advisable for [Asklepios] to be a god among men, Zeus struck him with a lightning bolt. Apollo was enraged and killed the Cyclopes who fashioned the thunderbolt for Zeus. Now Zeus was about to hurl him into Tartaros, but by Leto's pleading, he ordered him to be a servant to a man for a year" (Zenobius *Epitome collectionum Lucilli Tarrhaei et Didymi* 1.18.10–15, Schneidewin and von Leutsch).

enraged and killed the Cyclopes who fashioned lightning for Zeus. Now Zeus was about to hurl him into Tartaros, but by Leto's pleading, he ordered him to be a servant to a man for a year. So he went to Admetus, son of Pheres, at Pherae, and served him as a herdsman, and caused the cows—all of them—to have twins.

Ps.-Apollodorus' account suggests that Zeus perceives Asclepius as a threat to the cosmic balance for, by means of his healing arts, men can avoid death.[98] At any rate, Zeus kills him with a lightning bolt, the same weapon by which he vanquishes Typhoeus and the Titans before him.[99] Apollo's response aims to deprive Zeus of his greatest weapon and symbol of his authority over heaven. After all, Zeus remains in control largely because of his superior strength, as he himself explains at *Iliad* VIII 19–27.

According to Hesiod, Zeus is so angered by this threat to his authority and the destruction of the source of his power that (Hesiod fr. 54a.11 M-W),

ἔνθά κεν Ἀ[πόλλωνα κατέκτανε μητίετα Ζεύς

then Zeus the counselor would have killed Apollo.

Although the verb κατέκτανε "(he would have) killed" is a reconstructed reading, the sense is likely not far off, especially when we consider that Zeus' anger is specified in terms of his desire to cast Apollo into Tartaros (as preserved in the fragment):

οὗ π[ατρός
Βρόγ[την
Ζεὺς [..]οιβρον̣τ̣[
τόν ῥα [χ]ολω[σ]άμ[ενος   ]να
ῥίψειν ἤμελ[λεν   ἀπ' Ὀλύμ]που
Τ]άρταρον ἔς, [γῆς νέρθε καὶ ἀτρυγέτοιο θα]λάσσ[ης
σκ]ληρ[ὸν] δ' ἐβ[ρόντησε καὶ ὄβριμον ἀμφὶ δὲ γ]αῖα

---

[98] Compare Pindar *Pythian* 3.54–58, cited above, and note that in Zenobius' narrative (cited in the preceding note), Zeus expresses anxiety that Asclepius is being treated like "a god among men" (τοῦτον παρ' ἀνθρώποις εἶναι θεόν).

[99] See further Hesiod frr. 51–52, 54–58.4 M-W with commentary *ad loc.*, West 1985:68, 70, and Harrell 1991:312–313, esp. 313n17. Compare also Hesiod fr. 30 M-W, ps.-Apollodorus 1.9.7, Diodorus Siculus 4.68.2, Virgil *Aeneid* 6.585–589 (with commentary by Servius), and Hyginus *Fabulae* 61 for reference to a narrative in which Zeus strikes Salmoneus, son of Aeolus, with lightning and casts him into Tartaros because Salmoneus was imitating the god and appropriating the trappings of his divine power. Sophocles wrote a Satyr-play (Σαλμωνεὺς σατυρικός) on the subject (Sophocles frr. 537–541a Radt).

κ[ι]νήθ[η
πάντες δ[᾽ ἔδδεισαν
ἀθάνατ[οι
ἔνθά κεν Ἀ[πόλλωνα κατέκτανε μητίετα Ζεύς
εἰ μὴ ἄρ᾽ [

Of his [father
Bron[tes
Zeus [
full of anger at him
was about to cast him [away from Olym]pus
into Tartaros, [beneath the earth and the barren s]ea
hard he th[undered and mightily, and on both sides the e]arth
was moved [
and all [grew afraid
the immort[als
and then he would have [killed Apollo, Zeus the counselor,
if not indeed [

Hesiod fr. 54a + 57 M-W =
P. Oxy 2495 fr. 1a + fr. 16 col. 1[100]

In spite of the damage to the papyrus, and even disregarding the supplementary readings provided by Edgar Lobel, Martin West, and Glenn Most, certain details do appear clearly, namely that Zeus was about to cast his opponent (τόν … ῥίψειν ἤμελ[λεν, 4–5) into Tartaros (Τ]άρταρον ἔς, 6) out of anger ([χ]ολω[σ] άμ[ενος, 4) over Brontes (2), one of the Cyclopes who fashions lightning for Zeus in Hesiod's *Theogony*. As we have seen, Zeus casts seditious divinities into Tartaros; that he is about to do so here emphasizes his desire to be rid of Apollo once and for all, to imprison him beneath the earth where he will remain, for all intents and purposes, dead.[101]

---

[100] I print here Hesiod fr. 54a + 57 M-W as read by Most 2007:122 as his Hesiod fr. 58.

[101] The reading of the Hesiod fragment is further corroborated by Philodemus *On Piety* 34 (= Hesiod fr. 54b M-W): Ἡσίοδος δέ καὶ Ἀκουσίλαος μέλλειν μὲν εἰς τὸν Τάρταρον ὑπὸ τοῦ Διὸς ἐμβληθῆναι "But Hesiod and Acusilaus (2 F 19) say that [Apollo] was about to be thrown into Tartaros by Zeus." For Apollo as a potential challenger to Zeus' reign, compare the opening verses of the *Homeric Hymn to Apollo* 1–9 with the analysis of Clay 1989:19–29 and Harrell 1991:312–313. On the death of Apollo at Zeus' hands, see also Fontenrose 1974:381–382.

3.2. *Coup d'état* as *Coup de theatre*: Hera, Hupnos, and Atē

Hephaistos is not the only god to be thrown from heaven.[102] Indeed, we are told that Zeus hurled Atē, the goddess of delusion, to earth (XIX 130), attempted to do the same to Hupnos, the god of sleep (XIV 258), and left Hera dangling from heaven, weighed down with anvils on both feet (XV 18–20). In all of these instances, I believe, we can see traces of the same succession motif in which Zeus casts challengers to earth; the challengers are in danger of suffering a "virtual death," for once thrown from heaven into murky Tartaros, they will never return. The three stories form a constellation of events that occurred in a pre-Iliadic tradition, when once before Hera challenged Zeus and attempted to assert her own power and authority over his, for she sought to prevent his son Herakles—a mortal child born out of wedlock to Alcmene, an Achaean woman from Argos—from becoming a powerful Greek king.[103] What ties these stories together, beside Zeus' violent response that leads to hurling gods from the heavens, is the common theme they share of deceit and political unrest as the stable rule of Zeus is threatened by Hera's machinations.

In the nineteenth Book of the *Iliad*, Agamemnon and Achilles are reconciled. The king of the Achaeans offers a formal apology to Achilles for depriving him of his war-prize, the captive Briseïs. By way of explaining his previous error in judgment, Agamemnon relates a tale that offers the *aition* of how delusion and erroneous judgment came to be among men (XIX 95–133).[104] It is because Zeus, Agamemnon explains, the father and king of the gods, was himself a victim of delusion when he was deceived by Hera into swearing a binding oath that the child born on a certain day would become lord over many:

---

[102] Willcock 1964:146 notes, "Hurling out of Olympus appears as a relatively common theme in the *Iliad*. ... The motif is common, available to the poet to use as and where he wishes."

[103] For an attempt to reconstruct this traditional story, see Lang 1983.

[104] The Greek concept Agamemnon seeks to explain here is ἄτη, personified as the goddess Atē. On the meaning and semantics of this complex term, see Dodds 1951, Dawe 1968, Wyatt Jr. 1982, Doyle 1984, Arieti 1988, Finkelberg 1995, and especially the articles in *LfgrE* by Mette (s.v. ἄτη) and Seiler (s.v. ἀάω). Agamemnon's use of this paradigm is powerful in many respects. Not only does it accomplish an obvious rhetorical comparison—surely intentional on Agamemnon's part—between Agamemnon himself, leader of the Achaeans, and Zeus, king of gods and men (on which, see the fine analysis at Edwards 1991:246 with bibliography); it also ironically undermines Agamemnon's own authority by suggesting, subversively, that his supremacy over Achilles parallels that of Eurystheus over Herakles. More importantly, however, the myth also invokes the tragic undertone of Achilles' own "delusion" in absenting himself from battle and refusing to return until it is too late and Patroklos is dead. On the ἄτη of Achilles, particularly during the embassy in *Iliad* IX, see Arieti 1988. Achilles acknowledges his own behavior as ἄτη at XIX 270–274 when he officially accepts Agamemnon's apology and agrees to return to battle. Wyatt Jr. 1982:251n8 points out that Achilles is both the first and last character in the *Iliad* to speak the word ἄτη. On tragedy in the *Iliad*, see especially Griffin 1980 and Rutherford 1982.

ψεύστης εἶς, οὐδ' αὖτε τέλος μύθῳ ἐπιθήσεις.
εἰ δ' ἄγε νῦν μοι <u>ὄμοσσον</u>, Ὀλύμπιε, <u>καρτερὸν ὅρκον</u>,
ἦ μὲν τὸν πάντεσσι περικτιόνεσσιν ἀνάξειν,
ὅς κεν ἐπ' ἤματι τῷδε πέσῃ μετὰ ποσσὶ γυναικός
τῶν ἀνδρῶν, οἳ σῆς ἐξ αἵματός εἰσι γενέθλης.
ὣς ἔφατο· Ζεὺς δ' οὔ τι <u>δολοφροσύνην</u> ἐνόησεν,
ἀλλ' <u>ὄμοσεν μέγαν ὅρκον</u>, ἔπειτα δὲ <u>πολλὸν ἀάσθη</u>.

[Hera:] "You're a liar, then, if you don't set completion upon your claim.
Come on, now, <u>swear</u> to me, Olympian, <u>a powerful oath</u>,
that this man will be lord over all those who dwell around him,
whoever on this very day falls between the feet of a woman,
born of men who are from your blood."
So she spoke. And Zeus did not at all notice her <u>deceptive intention</u>,
but <u>he swore a great oath</u>, and that's when <u>he was greatly deluded</u>.

Iliad XIX 107–113

Zeus' great delusion (πολλὸν ἀάσθη, XIX 113) is to swear an unbreakable oath that the child born on this day will become king over many, for Hera turns the oath against him. She manipulates the temporal process of the human birth cycle by slowing the childbirth of Alcmene, while simultaneously expediting that of another woman:[105]

ἣ δ' ἐκύει φίλον υἱόν, ὃ δ' ἕβδομος ἑστήκει μείς.
ἐκ δ' ἄγαγε <u>πρὸ</u> φόωσδε καὶ <u>ἠλιτόμηνον</u> ἐόντα,
Ἀλκμήνης δ' <u>ἀπέπαυσε</u> τόκον, <u>σχέθε</u> δ' Εἰλειθυίας.

[The wife of Sthenelus] was pregnant with a dear son, and this was her
        seventh month.
She lead him forth into the light <u>sooner</u>, although he was <u>premature</u>,
but <u>stopped</u> Alcmene's delivery and <u>held back</u> the Goddess of Birth-Pangs.

Iliad XIX 117–119

Hera speeds up the birth of one child so that he is born ahead of schedule (πρὸ, XIX 118) and untimely (ἠλιτόμηνον, XIX 118); but she slows down the birth of Herakles through preventing his delivery (ἀπέπαυσε; σχέθε, XIX 119). Zeus' great oath has been turned against himself, for instead of bringing about the

---

[105] On the tentative connection between Ἥρη/Ἥρᾱ and ὥρα "season," see Pötscher 1961, Householder Jr. and Nagy 1972:50–52, Adams 1987, and O'Brien 1993:5, 113–117, 137–139. A connection between the goddess and the temporality of "seasonal" events is reflected here in her power over the cycles and seasons of human sexual reproduction.

completion of his will, the unbreakable oath binds him to accept the will of another through the loophole of generalization: that man shall rule, "*whoever* (ὅς κεν) on this day falls (πέσῃ) between a woman's legs" (XIX 110).

It is instructive to study Zeus' reaction once he learns of Hera's deceit, for it demonstrates the strategic moves characteristic of his representation in Greek theogonic epic. In Hesiod's *Theogony*, Zeus establishes permanent rule through his ingestion of Metis (*Theogony* 886–891)—by swallowing the Goddess of Cunning-Intelligence, Zeus becomes quite literally endowed with her peerless intelligence and foresight (cf. West 1966:397, 401–402).[106] We find a similar move in Zeus' response to his delusion and Hera's deception in *Iliad* XIX when he swears a *second* great and unbreakable oath—namely that Atē, the Goddess of Delusion herself, will never return to Olympos.

> τὸν δ' ἄχος ὀξὺ κατὰ φρένα τύψε βαθεῖαν,
> αὐτίκα δ' εἷλ' Ἄτην κεφαλῆς λιπαροπλοκάμοιο
> χωόμενος φρεσὶν ᾗσι, καὶ <u>ὤμοσε καρτερὸν ὅρκον</u>,
> <u>μή ποτ'</u> ἐς Οὔλυμπόν τε καὶ οὐρανὸν ἀστερόεντα
> <u>αὖτις ἐλεύσεσθαι Ἄτην, ἣ πάντας ἀᾶται.</u>
> <u>ὣς εἰπὼν ἔρριψεν ἀπ' οὐρανοῦ ἀστερόεντος</u>
> χειρὶ περιστρέψας· τάχα δ' ἵκετο ἔργ' ἀνθρώπων.
> τὴν αἰεὶ στενάχεσχ', ὅθ' ἑὸν φίλον υἱὸν ὁρῷτο
> ἔργον ἀεικὲς ἔχοντα ὑπ' Εὐρυσθῆος ἀέθλων.

> But a sharp pain struck him deep in his heart,
> and straight away he seized Atē by her glossy-haired head
> while raging in his heart, and <u>he swore a powerful oath</u>,
> that "<u>Never</u> to Olympos nor to starry heaven
> <u>will Atē come again, she who deludes all men.</u>"
> <u>So he spoke and hurled her from starry heaven</u>
> after he swung her around in his hand. She soon reached men's
>   establishments.
> But he always used to bemoan her, whenever he saw his own dear son
> with the unseemly work of the tasks set him by Eurystheus.

> *Iliad* XIX 125–133

---

[106] Greek literature attributes an over-determined significance to Zeus' swallowing of Metis—not only does he thereby attain "cunning intelligence," but he also avoids a prophecy that Metis was to give birth to a child who would overthrow Zeus; by swallowing Metis while still pregnant, an act of "containing" that outdoes the similar "containment" strategies (preventing children from being born, swallowing children once they are born) of his predecessors Ouranos and Kronos, Zeus effectively ensures that the child born from Metis (Athena) will have no mother, and hence will be obedient entirely to her father's wishes.

In a move reciprocal to his ingesting of Μῆτις, the Goddess of Cunning Intelligence, so that none can outmatch Zeus with wits, Zeus deprives his enemies of that power of delusion by which he can be made into his own greatest foe. That is to say, instead of merely punishing Hera for her trickery, he deprives her of the opportunity to do so in the future again by casting Atē away from heaven and swearing a great oath that she can never return.

Most important for our investigation, however, is the connection between Zeus throwing (ἔρριψεν ἀπ᾽ οὐρανοῦ ἀστερόεντος "he <u>hurled</u> her from starry heaven," XIX 130) and the impossibility of Atē's return (μή ποτ᾽ ἐς Οὔλυμπόν τε καὶ οὐρανὸν ἀστερόεντα | <u>αὖτις ἐλεύσεσθαι Ἄτην</u> "[he swore that] 'Never to Olympos nor to starry heaven <u>will Atē come again</u>,'" XIX 128–129). For, as we have seen, the tradition relates other occasions on which Zeus "hurls" a god from heaven, and that god is also unable to return. Those gods are, specifically, the Titans and the other challengers to Zeus' authority, such as Typhoeus; Zeus hurls his challengers to the depths of Tartaros from which there is no possibility of return. The theme of falling and not returning which is implicit in the narratives of gods being hurled from the heavens into Tartaros is here made explicit in the case of Atē through the motif of the "great" and "powerful oath." In our narrative of Zeus' delusion—a veritable *Dios (ap)Atē* "story of the deception and/or delusion of Zeus"[107]—we are dealing with the convergence of three themes: Hera's deception; Zeus' wrath and violent act of throwing a god from heaven; and the inability of that god to return to Olympos/heaven ever again.

In the next case, we learn of Zeus' anger at Hupnos, "Sleep," in the prelude to the *Dios apatē* (*Iliad* XIV 263–348), the narrative of Hera's seduction and deception of her husband Zeus in which she arms herself with the seductive gear of the sex-goddess Aphrodite and distracts Zeus' attention from the battle at Troy long enough for the tide to change in favor of the Achaeans. One of Hera's preparations is to enlist the help of Hupnos so that he may cast "sleep" down upon Zeus. However, Hupnos is at first unwilling to take part in Hera's scheme. Once before, he explains, he participated in just such a plot to distract Zeus while Hera attempted to thwart his plans. The results were nearly disastrous:

Ἥρη πρέσβα θεὰ θύγατερ μεγάλοιο Κρόνοιο,
ἄλλον μέν κεν ἔγωγε θεῶν αἰειγενετάων
<u>ῥεῖα κατευνήσαιμι</u>, <u>καὶ ἂν ποταμοῖο ῥέεθρα</u>
<u>Ὠκεανοῦ</u>, ὅς περ γένεσις πάντεσσι τέτυκται·
Ζηνὸς δ᾽ οὐκ ἂν ἔγωγε Κρονίονος ἆσσον ἱκοίμην

---

[107] On the association between ἄτη "delusion" and ἀπάτη "deception," see Dawe 1968:100–101 who argues, "There is no doubt that the Greeks, rightly or wrongly, considered ἄτη and ἀπάτη as etymologically related concepts."

οὐδὲ κατευνήσαιμ', ὅτε μὴ αὐτός γε κελεύοι.
ἤδη γάρ με καὶ †ἄλλο τεῇ ἐπίνυσσεν ἐφετμῇ†,[108]
ἤματι τῷ, ὅτε κεῖνος ὑπέρθυμος Διὸς υἱός
ἔπλεεν Ἰλιόθεν Τρώων πόλιν ἐξαλαπάξας·
ἤτοι ἐγὼ μὲν ἔλεξα Διὸς νόον αἰγιόχοιο
νήδυμος ἀμφιχυθείς, σὺ δέ οἱ κακὰ μήσαο θυμῷ,
ὄρσασ' ἀργαλέων ἀνέμων ἐπὶ πόντον ἀήτας,
καί μιν ἔπειτα Κόωνδ' εὖ ναιομένην ἀπένεικας
νόσφι φίλων πάντων. ὃ δ' ἐπεγρόμενος χαλέπαινεν,
ῥιπτάζων κατὰ δῶμα θεούς, ἐμὲ δ' ἔξοχα πάντων
ζήτει· καί κέ μ' ἄϊστον ἀπ' αἰθέρος ἔμβαλε πόντῳ,
εἰ μὴ Νὺξ δμήτειρα θεῶν ἐσάωσε καὶ ἀνδρῶν.
τὴν ἱκόμην φεύγων, ὃ δ' ἐπαύσατο χωόμενός περ·
ἄζετο γάρ, μὴ Νυκτὶ θοῇ ἀποθύμια ἔρδοι.
νῦν αὖ τοῦτό μ' ἄνωγας ἀμήχανον ἄλλο τελέσσαι.

Hera, reverend goddess, daughter of great Kronos,
any other one of the gods who always are I for my part
could easily put to sleep, even the streams of the river
Okeanos, the very one who brought about creation for all things.
But I would not come near Zeus, son of Kronos,
nor would I put him to sleep, unless he himself should so command me.
For already your behest taught me another thing too,[109]
on the day when that excessively spirited son of Zeus [= Herakles]
was sailing from Ilion after he utterly sacked the city of the Trojans.
Then, I tell you, I put to sleep the mind of Zeus who holds the aegis
when I, sweet Sleep, was poured all around him; but you devised evil
        things in your heart,
when you raised up blasts of grievous winds upon the sea,
and then you carried [Herakles] away towards the well-founded city Kos
apart from all his friends. But [Zeus] was enraged when he awakened,
hurling about gods throughout his home, and he was searching
for me beyond all the rest. Now he would have cast me away from the
        bright sky and out of sight into the sea,
if Nux ["Night"], the subduer of gods and men, hadn't saved me.

---

[108] On the textual and interpretative difficulties of this verse, see the *apparatus criticus* in West *ad loc.* and Janko 1994:190–191. Janko proposes reading of the line as ἄλλοθ' ἐὴ ἐπένυσσεν ἐφετμὴ "at another occasion your command pricked me on."

[109] I translate here the line as printed with daggers in West's text, following the interpretation of Monro 1893:290, but see Janko's interpretation (1994:190–191) in the preceeding note.

I reached her in my flight, and [Zeus], although he was angry, let me be.
For he withdrew lest he do anything displeasing to Nux.
Now again you are asking me to accomplish this thing which is impossible.

Iliad XIV 243–262

Hupnos recalls a former occasion, for already once before (ἤδη, XIV 249), Hupnos cast sleep over Zeus (ἔλεξα Διὸς νόον αἰγιόχοιο, XIV 252) in order to assist Hera in a plot against Zeus' son Herakles. Zeus became enraged (ἐπεγρόμενος χαλέπαινεν, XIV 256) and began "hurling gods throughout his house" (ῥιπτάζων κατὰ δῶμα θεούς, XIV 257). The reference to Zeus "hurling" gods activates the thematic context of divine challenger cast into the depths whence return is not possible.

In this context, consider Hupnos' comment that Zeus "would have cast me away from the bright sky and out of sight into the sea" (καί κέ μ' ἄϊστον ἀπ' αἰθέρος ἔμβαλε πόντῳ, XIV 258). Zeus would have rendered Hupnos ἄϊστος, literally "in-visible."[110] To render someone ἄϊστος "invisible" in Homeric epic is to destroy them. Compare Penelope's wish that she might die before she is forced to marry one of the suitors:

ὣς ἔμ' ἀϊστώσειαν Ὀλύμπια δώματ' ἔχοντες,
ἠέ μ' ἐϋπλόκαμος βάλοι Ἄρτεμις, ὄφρ' Ὀδυσῆα
ὀσσομένη καὶ γαῖαν ὕπο στυγερὴν ἀφικοίμην,
μηδέ τι χείρονος ἀνδρὸς ἐϋφραίνοιμι νόημα.

Would that those who possess Olympian homes render me invisible,
or that lovely-braided Artemis strike me, so that while looking out for
        Odysseus
I might also arrive beneath the hateful earth,
and that I might not gladden the mind of a lesser man.

Odyssey xx 79–82

Penelope prays that the gods "render me invisible" (ἔμ' ἀϊστώσειαν, xx 79).[111] The association between "rendering someone invisible" and "killing" them becomes

---

[110] ἄϊστος is the verbal adjective in *-το- from the zero-grade root of οἶδα / *ιδ- "to see." On the form, see Chantrain 1968–1980:779, s.v. οἶδα B3. See also Ebeling 1963:I.57, s.v. ἄϊστος, citing the gloss on the line offered by Scholia BL *ad loc.*: ἔμβαλεν ὥστε ἀϊστωθῆναι "he threw [me] so that [I] become invisible."

[111] The verb ἀϊστόω is cognate with the adjective ἄϊστος following the regular formation for denominative verbs in -οω from o-stem nouns and adjectives: see Risch 1974:329–330 (§114a). As Risch points out, such verbs are generally factitive in meaning, such that ἀϊστόω means "to make invisible."

patent through the connection of thoughts in Penelope's prayer: being made invisible (ἔμ' ἀϊστώσειαν, xx 79), being shot by Artemis (μ' … βάλοι Ἄρτεμις, xx 80), and reaching the hateful land below (γαῖαν ὕπο στυγερὴν ἀφικοίμην, xx 81). In Hupnos' case, then, when Zeus was eagerly searching for him (ἐμὲ δ' ἔξοχα πάντων | ζήτει, *Iliad* XIV 57–58), Hupnos' own life was very much at stake. Zeus would have made him "invisible"; he would have effectively brought about the god's death.[112] In other words, even though Hupnos does not explicitly say so, the very semantics of verse XIV 248 and the connection between "throwing" and "rendering invisible/destroying" in the claim that κέ μ' ἄϊστον ἀπ' αἰθέρος ἔμβαλε πόντῳ, "he would have cast me away from heaven and out of sight into the sea" (XIV 258), effectively evokes the unmentioned throw and deathly fall into the murky darkness of Tartaros. Bruce Braswell (1971:21–22) and Malcolm Willcock (1977:44n16) have argued that Zeus' threat to cast Hupnos from heaven is likely an "invented" (Braswell) "reflection" (Willcock) of Zeus casting Hephaistos from heaven. Along these lines, one may note that Hera's conversation with Hupnos takes place in Lemnos, a location well known for its active cult of Hephaistos, and that Hera's promise that Hupnos can marry one of the Graces finds a double in Hephaistos' wife—a Grace—at *Iliad* XVIII 382–383. Nevertheless, even this "*ad hoc* interpretation" draws upon theogonic myth and themes of succession, rebellion, and the maintenance of cosmic order, both in Hera's expressed purpose for borrowing Aphrodite's sexual talisman for the purpose of reconciling the estranged primeval pair of Okeanos and Tethys (XIV 200–207), as well as in Hupnos' claim that he only escaped Zeus' wrath by running to Nux (Night), his mother, for help, for even Zeus is afraid to upset that primal entity (XIV 259–261).[113]

Let us consider some further implications of Hera's role in the so-called Διὸς ἀπάτη "the narrative about the deception of Zeus." Hera's purpose in seducing Zeus, as presented in the *Iliad*, is to keep the far-seeing god's attention diverted while Poseidon rouses the Achaeans into battle once more after their demoralizing losses and injuries in Books XI–XIII (cf. XIV 153–165). Hera's plan (βουλή, XIV 161) consists of seducing the attention of the god, and then putting him into a heavy slumber:

ἧδε δέ οἱ κατὰ θυμὸν ἀρίστη φαίνετο <u>βουλή</u>,
ἐλθεῖν εἰς Ἴδην εὖ ἐντύνασαν ἓ' αὐτήν,
εἴ πως <u>ἱμείραιτο παραδραθέειν φιλότητι</u>

---

[112] Leaf comments: "ἄϊστον 'put out of sight,' i.e. sent to perdition"; Leaf also notes the adjective ἀΐδηλος "destroying" (Leaf 1900–1902:II.85).

[113] See Janko 1994:180–182 for discussion (with further bibliography) of the theogony alluded to here and the threat of order overthrown into chaos.

ᾗ χροιῇ, τῷ δ' ὕπνον ἀπήμονά τε λιαρόν τε
χεύῃ ἐπὶ βλεφάροισιν ἰδὲ φρεσὶ πευκαλίμῃσι.

And this plan appeared best to her in her heart,
to array herself prettily and go to Ida,
if perhaps [Zeus] might be seized with desire to lay down
        in love
beside her flesh, and she would shed upon him an innocent and
        balmy sleep
upon his eyelids and upon his shrewd wits.

Iliad XIV 161–165

Because Hera's intrigue is, strictly speaking, unnecessary to account for Zeus' failure to notice Poseidon assisting the Achaeans,[114] it is productive to look beyond the structural significance of the episode to its other implications. Hera's βουλή "plan" to seduce Zeus' attention explicitly presents itself as a challenge to the βουλὴ Διός "plan of Zeus" which functions essentially as the "plot of the *Iliad*" as well. Hera's βουλή counters Zeus' βουλή; instead of continual Trojan victory up to the point when Patroklos enters the fray and dies in battle, Hera wants the Trojans to perish. She seduces Zeus to divert his attention and seduces the plot of the *Iliad* along with him (cf. Bergren 1980). That is to say, Hera poses a challenge to Zeus and his "plan," one that has undertones of the succession motif with all its entailed violence and destruction.

That Hera intends to overpower Zeus may be seen in her careful preparations. The "plan that appears to her in her heart to be the best one" (οἱ κατὰ θυμὸν ἀρίστη φαίνετο βουλή, XIV 161) is to array herself in finery (εὖ ἐντύνασαν ἕ' αὐτήν, XIV 162) and then set off to see Zeus. Beyond her elaborate bathing and dressing (XIV 166–186), however, Hera seeks the services of two special assistants—Aphrodite and, as we have already seen, Hupnos. From Aphrodite Hera acquires "loveliness and desire" (φιλότητα καὶ ἵμερον, XIV 198), so that Zeus "might be seized with desire" (ἱμείραιτο, XIV 163) to lay down with her. When Hera asks Aphrodite to borrow her sexual talismans, she specifically notes their power in unambiguous terms:

δὸς νῦν μοι φιλότητα καὶ ἵμερον, ᾧ τε σὺ πάντας
δαμνᾷ ἀθανάτους ἠδὲ θνητοὺς ἀνθρώπους.

---

[114] See Edwards 1987:247 and Janko 1994:168. See also the careful analysis of Bergren 1980:27, who notes that Poseidon's re-entry is itself "wholly gratuitous" at this point, since the Greek generals have already decided to marshal their troops themselves; hence, the two activities—Poseidon's re-entry and Hera's deception—are interdependent and mutually self-motivating.

Now give to me loveliness and desire, <u>with which</u> you
always <u>conquer</u> immortals and mortal men alike—all of them.

Iliad XIV 198–199

Aphrodite's talismans are the means by which the sex-goddess "conquers" or
"overcomes" (δαμνᾷ, XIV 199) men and gods;[115] the epic τε indicates the general
truth of Aphrodite's power, and further the emphatic placement of the adjective πάντας "all of them" at the end of verse XIV 198 is an index of the scope of
Aphrodite's power.[116] The verb δαμνάω, typically used to describe Aphrodite's
power over gods, men, and animals (compare ἐδαμάσσατο, *Hymn to Aphrodite* 3),
typically describes three spheres of activity: "breaking" or "taming" an animal
(e.g. *Iliad* XXIII 655), "subduing" a woman sexually to a husband (e.g. *Iliad* XVIII
432), and "conquering" an enemy (e.g. *Odyssey* ix 59).[117] When Hera borrows
Aphrodite's "loveliness and desire," she does so with the intention of overcoming Zeus, both in what might be considered a sexual and political conquest.

Zeus' reaction to Hera's seditious behavior confirms our reading of the Διὸς
ἀπάτη as part of the succession-motif. For upon awakening (XV 4) and seeing
what has happened on the battlefield (XV 6–11), he speaks threatening words
to Hera:

<u>δεινὰ δ' ὑπόδρα ἰδὼν</u> Ἥρην πρὸς μῦθον ἔειπεν·
"ἦ μάλα δὴ κακότεχνος, ἀμήχανε, σὸς δόλος, Ἥρη,
Ἕκτορα δῖον ἔπαυσε μάχης, ἐφόβησε δὲ λαούς.
οὐ μὰν οἶδ', εἰ αὖτε κακορραφίης ἀλεγεινῆς
πρώτη ἐπαύρηαι καί <u>σε πληγῇσιν ἱμάσσω</u>.
ἦ οὐ μέμνη', ὅτε τε <u>κρέμα' ὑψόθεν</u>, ἐκ δὲ ποδοῖιν
<u>ἄκμονας ἧκα δύω</u>, <u>περὶ χερσὶ δὲ δεσμὸν ἴηλα</u>
<u>χρύσεον ἄρρηκτον</u>; σὺ δ' ἐν αἰθέρι καὶ νεφέλῃσιν
<u>ἐκρέμα</u>'· ἠλάστεον δὲ θεοὶ κατὰ μακρὸν Ὄλυμπον,
λῦσαι δ' οὐκ ἐδύναντο παρασταδόν· <u>ὃν δὲ λάβοιμι</u>,
<u>ῥίπτασκον τεταγὼν ἀπὸ βηλοῦ</u>, ὄφρ' ἂν ἵκηται
<u>γῆν ὀλιγηπελέων</u>.

---

[115] See Janko 1994:180 on the formation of δαμνᾷ (with this accentuation) contracted from
*δαμνάε(σ)αι, the second person singular middle indicative form of δαμνάομαι. Aristarchus
(preserved in Scholia T *ad loc.*) accented δάμνα contracted from *δάμνα(σ)αι.

[116] Compare Hera's honorific address to Hupnos which speaks of his power of "all": Ὕπνε, ἄναξ
<u>πάντων</u> τε θεῶν <u>πάντων</u> τ' ἀνθρώπων "Hupnos, lord of <u>all</u> gods and of <u>all</u> men" (XIV 233). Like
Aphrodite's charms with which she can "conquer immortals and mortal men alike—all of them
(πάντας)" (XIV 198–199), Hupnos too has power over "all."

[117] See Calame 1977:I.411–420 and Bergren 1989:4, "The verb δαμνάω denotes the power of men
to 'break' wild creatures into civilized form—beasts through domestication, children through
education, and virgins through marriage."

[...]
τῶν σ’ αὖτις μνήσω, ἵν’ ἀπολλήξῃς ἀπατάων,
ὄφρα ἴδῃ’ ἤν τοι χραίσμῃ φιλότης τε καὶ εὐνή,
ἣν ἐμίγης ἐλθοῦσα θεῶν ἄπο καί μ’ ἀπάτησας.”

While glowering terribly he spoke a word to Hera:
“Ah, yes, it was your evilly-devised trick, Hera, unmanageable one,
that stopped brilliant Hektor from battle, and put his people to flight.
I don’t know whether once again you will be first to profit from
your troublesome scheming and I may lash you with strokes.[118]
Indeed, don’t you remember when you were hanging from on high, and
        from your feet
I let fall two anvils, and about your hands I flung a bond
made of gold and unbreakable? And you in the bright sky and clouds
were hanging there; the gods throughout tall Olympos couldn’t stand it,
but they weren’t able to free you as they stood about. And if I caught one,
grabbing hold, I would throw him from the threshold, until he reached
the earth, barely able to move.
[...]
Am I to remind you of these things again that you may give up your
        deceptions,
and that you may see whether your love-making and your bed are of help
        to you,
how you came from the gods and had intercourse with me and deceived
        me.”

Iliad XV 13–24, 31–33

While “glowering terribly” (ὑπόδρα ἰδών, XV 13),[119] Zeus threatens to beat Hera
(σε πληγῇσιν ἱμάσσω, XV 17), and reminds her of a prior time when he also

---

[118] ἱμάσσω is aorist subjunctive: see Leaf 1900–1902:II.106 and Janko 1994:229.

[119] The phrase ὑπόδρα ἰδών “glowering” occurs 26 times in Homer: *Iliad* I 148, II 245, IV 349, 411, V 251, 888, X 466, XII 320, XIV 82, XV 13, XVII 141, 169, XVIII 284, XX 428, XXII 260, 344, XXIV 559; *Odyssey* viii 165, xvii 459, xviii 14, 337, 388, xix 70, xxii 34, 60, 320. The phrase δεινὰ ὑπόδρα ἰδών occurs only here in the *Iliad*, but is found also at ps.-Hesiod *Shield of Herakles* 445 and *Homeric Hymn to Dionysus* 7.48. On the semantics and usage of ὑπόδρα ἰδών, see Holoka 1983. I analyze the data somewhat differently than Holoka, however, and provide here some different conclusions that emphasize Zeus’ potentially murderous rage in *Iliad* XIV. The phrase is restricted to two primary senses: first, it always indicates *the anger of a character speaking in response to a perceived threat of loss or diminishment of his own honor* (cf. Diomedes to Sthenelos at V 251, Hektor to Poulydamas at XII 230 and XVIII 284, and Odysseus to Agamemnon at XIV 82); *or the honor of his group* (cf. Odysseus to Thersites about Agamemnon at II 245, Diomedes to Sthenelos about Agamemnon at IV 349, Glaukos to Hektor about Sarpedon at XVII 141); *and hence points to behavior or speech which is considered improper*; and second, it *indicates an intense feeling of hatred and*

beat her for deceiving him. He reminds her how she hung from heaven (κρέμα' ὑψόθεν, XV 18) bound by her wrists (περὶ χερσὶ δὲ δεσμὸν ἴηλα, XV 19) with two anvils attached to her feet, pulling her ever downward (ἐκ δὲ ποδοῖιν | ἄκμονας ἧκα δύω, XV 18–19). Zeus asks, "Am I to remind you of these things <u>again</u>?" (τῶν σ' αὖτις μνήσω, XV 31), implying that he will repeat the same punishment.[120]

I wish to emphasize two details in Zeus' speech which point to an interpretation of the Διὸς ἀπάτη as a potential *coup d'état*. First, his punishment of Hera entails "lashing" her (πληγῇσιν ἱμάσσω, XV 17). An ancient scholion at *Iliad* XV 17d (Erbse) explains the image of "lashing" as indicating that Zeus would "strike" Hera with "lightning":

ἱμάσσω … τροπικῶς δὲ νῦν κεραυνώσω· μάστιγα γὰρ Διὸς τὸν κεραυνόν φησι.

"I'll lash you" is now being used figuratively for "I will strike you with lightning." For he [sc. Homer] says the lightning bolt is Zeus' whip.[121]

If the scholiast's interpretation is correct that Zeus is threatening Hera with lightning, then his response itself becomes an indication of the severity of Hera's offense; for Zeus does not strike just anyone with lightning—he reserves it, as we have seen, for his would-be-challengers who strive to overcome him and take his place as divine ruler.[122]

Second, when Zeus speaks of how he once dangled Hera between heaven and earth with anvils (ἄκμονας, XV 19) attached to her feet and weighing her down—and threatens that he may do so again—we find yet another suggestion of the succession motif. The term ἄκμων "anvil," which seems an odd detail in a story of domestic violence,[123] makes sense when we compare Hesiod *Theogony* 720–725 where an ἄκμων "anvil" dropping from heaven appears again, this time in context of measuring the distance between Ouranos (heaven) and Tartaros.

---

accompanies blame-speeches and threats of physical violence (cf. Achilles to Hektor at XX 428, XXII 260, and XXII 344; Achilles to Priam about Hektor at XXIV 559; and Zeus to Ares at V 888).

[120] I follow Janko 1994:232 on the interpretation of αὖτις (*pace* Leaf 1900–1902:II.106).

[121] See also Scholia D at *Iliad* II 782, van Thiel: ἱμήσσῃ· μαστίξῃ, πλήξῃ, ὅ ἐστιν κεραυνοῖς βάλῃ "he lashes: 'he whips,' 'he strikes,' that is 'he hits with lightning.'" See further Whitman 1970:38.

[122] On Zeus' lightning as the tool by which he retains his sovereignty, see especially Detienne and Vernant 1978:75, "Through [lightning] Zeus can 'tame' his divine enemies by hurling them to the ground, paralyzing their strength and pinning them down. To strike a god with his thunderbolt is, for the Master of Heaven, to bind him, to chain him up, depriving him of the vital force that previously animated him, and to relegate him, forever paralyzed, to the frontiers of the world, far from the dwelling of the gods where he used to exercise his power."

[123] See Whitman 1970, Janko 1994:229–231, and Beckwith 1998 for provocative analyses of what we may call the pre-history of Homer's narrative, itself a distant reflection of a cosmological struggle between a Proto-Indo-European Sky god and a Proto-Indo-European Earth goddess.

τόσσον ἔνερθ' ὑπὸ γῆς ὅσον οὐρανός ἐστ' ἀπὸ γαίης·
τόσσον γάρ τ' ἀπὸ γῆς ἐς τάρταρον ἠερόεντα.
ἐννέα γὰρ νύκτας τε καὶ ἤματα χάλκεος ἄκμων
οὐρανόθεν κατιών, δεκάτῃ κ' ἐς γαῖαν ἵκοιτο·
[ἶσον δ' αὖτ' ἀπὸ γῆς ἐς τάρταρον ἠερόεντα·]
ἐννέα δ' αὖ νύκτας τε καὶ ἤματα χάλκεος <u>ἄκμων</u>
ἐκ γαίης κατιών, δεκάτῃ κ' ἐς τάρταρον ἵκοι.

As far beneath under the earth, so far is heaven away from the earth;
that's how far it is from the earth to misty Tartaros.
For nine nights and days a bronze anvil going down
from heaven would reach the earth on the tenth day;
[And equally, in turn, from earth to misty Tartaros.]
And in turn for nine nights and days a bronze <u>anvil</u>
going down from earth would reach Tartaros on the tenth day.

Theogony 720–725

These lines describe rather clearly a tripartite organization of the universe arranged by a vertical hierarchy: Ouranos, Gaia, and Tartaros are conceived of as separate realms equally spaced along a vertical axis. The distance between the realms is equal, as indicated first by the correlative adverbs ὅσον and τόσσον (720–721), and secondly through the proto-scientific concept that space can be measured by the (presumably) uniform motion of falling bodies within a measured amount of time: a bronze anvil dropped from heaven (οὐρανόθεν) falls nine days and reaches the earth on the tenth; likewise, an anvil dropped from earth reaches the depths of Tartaros on the tenth day (722–725).[124] The juxtaposition of the two images of falling anvils—Hesiod's anvil free-falling from heaven into Tartaros (ἐς τάρταρον, 725) and Homer's anvils suspended from Hera's dangling feet—suggests that, like Hesiod's anvils, Hera herself may fall into Tartaros. In this context, consider *Iliad* VIII 477–483 where Zeus tells an angry Hera,

σέθεν δ' ἐγὼ οὐκ ἀλεγίζω
χωομένης, οὐδ' εἴ κε τὰ νείατα πείραθ' ἵκηαι

---

[124] That it was understood that a bronze anvil would fall an equivalent distance in an equivalent period of time (for nine days and nights, arriving on the tenth day: see *Theogony* 722–723, 724–725) is indicated by verse 723a with its emphatic ἶσον δ' αὖτ' "and equally in turn." Concepts of the distance between heaven, earth, and Tartaros in early Greek thought are complex, however. In *Iliad* I 591–592 it took Hephaistos a single day to fall from heaven to Lemnos; at *Theogony* 740–743, it would take someone an entire year to fall through the empty space (*khasma*) between earth and Tartaros. See West 1966:359, 364 for discussion.

γαίης καὶ πόντοιο, ἵν' Ἰάπετός τε Κρόνος τε
ἥμενοι οὔτ' αὐγῆς Ὑπερίονος Ἠελίοιο
τέρποντ' οὔτ' ἀνέμοισι, βαθὺς δέ τε Τάρταρος ἀμφίς·
οὐδ' ἢν ἔνθ' ἀφίκηαι ἀλωμένη, οὔ σευ ἐγώ γε
σκυζομένης ἀλέγω, ἐπεὶ οὐ σέο κύντερον ἄλλο.

As for you and your anger, I don't care;
not if you stray apart to the undermost limits
of earth and sea, where both Iapetos and Kronos
seated have no shining of the sun god Huperion
to delight them nor delight of winds, but Tartaros stands deeply about
        them;
not even if you reach that place in your wandering shall I care
for your sulking, since there is nothing more shameless than you are.

Iliad VIII 477–483

Zeus speaks explicitly to Hera about "Tartaros," and it is implied that her "wandering" to Tartaros may be construed as being thrown there by Zeus, as indeed he threatened to throw any god who disobeys him (VIII 12–16).[125]

4. The Possible Impossibility of Divine Mortality: The Death of Ares

The manifold self-contradictions in Greek ideas and phrasing about death are not errors. They are styles of imagining the unimaginable and are responsive both to personal needs and to old conventions. The same conflicts surge up in many cultures. They are necessary ambiguities in a realm of thinking where thinking cannot really be done, and where there is no experience.

—Emily Vermeule[126]

So far in our investigation into the theme of "dying gods" and "divine mortality," we have seen that although Homer does not explicitly represent the death of a god, he does point to what must be considered the functional equivalent of death for gods. First, we have looked at instances in which gods come to experience human temporality through suffering physical pain inflicted by mortal weapons, and second, instances in which gods are struck by lightning, cast to earth, and imprisoned in Tartaros. Once a god "endures" (τλῆ) mortal pain or suffering and becomes ensnared within mortal temporality, his or her recovery from the state of "virtual death" caused by these experiences is not guaranteed: although Hades

---

[125] On this interpretation, see Kirk 1990:334.
[126] Vermeule 1979:118.

is "cured" of his pains, Hera is seized by an "incurable" pain, Hephaistos' injury from his fall is permanent, and for those imprisoned in Tartaros, "there is no way out for them" (τοῖς οὐκ ἐξιτόν ἐστι, Hesiod *Theogony* 732).

In this section we now turn to one specific figure, Ares, the god of war, for whom Homer does not merely point to possible "equivalent" deaths, but explicitly raises the specter of death itself for the war god. As we will see, Ares is described as being felled on the battlefield three times, in each instance mimicking the death of a mortal both in action and in traditional poetic diction (cf. Purves 2006a:201–203). He is presented as enmeshed in mortal temporality both through physical pains as well as through emotional suffering over the death of his son which drives him to embrace the possibility of his own death (cf. Lowenstam 1981:43–45, 73–77, 83–87, 119–125, 140–143, 167–168, and 172). And finally, he is represented as bound and incarcerated in a bronze jar until he very nearly dies, an image, as I will argue, meant to evoke Tartaros itself.

4.1. Ares among the Dead (*Iliad* V 886, XV 118, XXI 406)

In the height of his *aristeia* when he is "equal to a god" (δαίμονι ἶσος, V 884), Diomedes is driven by Athena to attack the war god Ares himself. The two come upon Ares as he is stripping the armor off a fallen soldier.[127] Athena lends her strength to Diomedes' spear thrust and, together, they stab Ares deep in the belly:

δεύτερος αὖθ' ὡρμᾶτο βοὴν ἀγαθὸς Διομήδης
ἔγχεϊ χαλκείῳ· ἐπέρεισε δὲ Παλλὰς Ἀθήνη
<u>νείατον ἐς κενεῶνα</u>, ὅθι ζωνύσκετο μίτρην.

---

[127] *Iliad* V 842–844: ἤτοι ὃ μὲν Περίφαντα πελώριον <u>ἐξενάριζεν</u>, | Αἰτωλῶν ὄχ' ἄριστον, Ὀχησίου ἀγλαὸν υἱόν· | τὸν μὲν Ἄρης ἐνάριζε μιαιφόνος "Indeed, I tell you, [Ares] <u>was stripping</u> huge Periphas, by far the best of the Aetolians, the shining son of Ochesius. <u>Blood-stained Ares was stripping him</u>." The representation of a god stripping the armor off a dead human is unique in Homer (cf. Andersen 1981:325). What is particularly significant is the characterization of Ares here by his epithet μιαιφόνος "blood-stained" (cf. V 31 = V 455, XXI 402), a term combining root words indicating "staining" and "blood, gore" (μιαιφόνος < μιαίνω + φόνος). It is at the very moment when Ares is "stained" or even "polluted" (cf. μίασμα "pollution": see Parker 1993, Attridge 2004, and Johnston 2004:507–509 with further bibliography) with human blood that he becomes vulnerable to human weapons. As Kirk (1990) notes, "Other gods kill from afar, so are not directly polluted by blood" (147). On the connection between a god becoming "stained" and their experience of human temporality through physical or emotional suffering, compare Achilles' horses whose manes become "stained" (ἐμιαίνετο χαίτη "their hair was stained," XVII 439) when they leaned their heads to the ground (οὔδει ἐνισκίμψαντε καρήατα "the two leaned their heads upon the ground," XVII 437) in mourning for Patroklos, and Achilles' divine helmet which is also "stained" with blood and dust when it falls from Patroklos' head and hits the ground (μιάνθησαν δὲ ἔθειραι | αἵματι καὶ κονίῃσι "the horse-hair crests were stained with blood and dust," XVI 795–796; μιαίνεσθαι κονίῃσιν "they were stained with dust," XVI 797).

τῇ ῥά μιν οὖτα τυχών, διὰ δὲ χρόα καλὸν ἔδαψεν,
ἐκ δὲ δόρυ σπάσεν αὖτις. ὃ δ' ἔβραχε χάλκεος Ἄρης,
ὅσσόν τ' ἐννεάχειλοι ἐπίαχον ἢ δεκάχειλοι
ἀνέρες ἐν πολέμῳ ἔριδα ξυνάγοντες ἄρηος·
τοὺς δ' ἄρ' ὑπὸ τρόμος εἷλεν Ἀχαιούς τε Τρῶάς τε
δείσαντας· τόσον ἔβραχ' Ἄρης ἇτος πολέμοιο.

Second in turn Diomedes of the great war-cry drove forward
with his bronze spear; and Pallas Athena put her weight upon it,
right into his lower flank, where he was girded with his war belt.
Yes, in this place she struck and stabbed him, and ripped through his
        beautiful flesh,
and drew the spear out again. But bronze Ares was shrieking,
as much as nine-thousand shouting out, or ten thousand
men who in war drive together the strife of Ares.
And, indeed, trembling seized both Achaeans and Trojans from beneath,
and they were afraid; that's how much Ares insatiate of war was shrieking.

Iliad V 855–863

Diomedes and Athena stab Ares deep in his κενεών, the hollow area beneath
the ribs; mortal warriors stabbed in this place always die.[128] Ares survives, but
is obviously in pain as he cries out—the imperfect tense of the verb ἔβραχε "he
was shrieking" indicates the durative quality to his crying. He does not shriek
once and for all, but continually. As Egbert Bakker (2005) says of the implication
of the imperfect tense in Homer, "It can be thought of as extending beyond its
actual description: in other words, language was not able to 'grasp' the event in
its entirety. ... [The event is] somehow larger than language, escaping in part its
verbalization" (162, 173). It is an event that cannot be comprehended, but only
gestured at: nine or ten thousand men in battle would shout out (ἐπίαχον, V 860)
as loud as Ares does.

    Ares makes his way to Olympos where he complains of his rough treatment
by Diomedes and Athena. Note in particular the temporality associated with his
suffering:

αὐτὰρ ἔπειτ' αὐτῷ μοι ἐπέσσυτο δαίμονι ἶσος.
ἀλλά μ' ὑπήνεικαν ταχέες πόδες· ἦ τέ κε δηρόν

[128] Hektor stabs Patroklos νείατον ἐς κενεῶνα "deep into his flank" (XVI 821), and Telemachus stabs
Leocritus μέσον κενεῶνα "in the middle of his flank" (xxii 295). Further, at *Iliad* V 284 and XI 381
one fighter *thinks* he has stabbed another in his κενεών and boasts, only to discover that he has
actually missed his mark. The implication is that a wound to one's κενεών is fatal. On this point,
see Jouanna and Demont 1981:200n13 and Loraux 1986:467, 649n5.

αὐτοῦ πήματ᾽ ἔπασχον ἐν αἰνῇσιν νεκάδεσσιν.
ἤ κε ζὼς ἀμενηνὸς ἔα χαλκοῖο τυπῇσι.

But then against me myself he rushed, equal to a god.
But my swift feet carried me out from under, otherwise <u>for a long time</u>
<u>I would be suffering pains there among the dread piles of corpses,</u>[129]
<u>or, though still alive, I would be without strength</u> from the blows of the
      bronze.

Iliad V 884–887

Ares explains how Diomedes came upon him "like a god" and would have killed him—or at least that appears to be the implication of the alternatives Ares would be suffering "for a long time" (δηρόν, V 885) had his swift feet not been able to bear him away from beneath the blow (ἀλλά μ᾽ ὑπήνεικαν ταχέες πόδες, V 885). Otherwise, Ares emphatically asserts (ἦ τε, V 885),[130] he would either be suffering pains (πήματ᾽ ἔπασχον, V 886) or be rendered without *menos* "strength, might" (ἀ-μενηνὸς ἔα, V 887).[131] The entire passage, though presented in the form of a present contrafactual ("if my swift feet *hadn't* carried me out from under Diomedes' attack, I *would now* be suffering or *would now* be without strength"), nevertheless opens the possibility that the outcome, although it didn't happen, *could* have happened. That is to say, Ares' death—his lying among the dead or being rendered without strength—though unaccomplished, remains within the realm of the possible.[132]

There are several details that deserve attention in this passage. First, let us examine more closely the precise connotation of Ares' alternative possibilities. Either Ares would have suffered pains (κε ... πήματ᾽ ἔπασχον, V 885–886) there on the battlefield (αὐτοῦ, V 886) among the awful piles of corpses (ἐν αἰνῇσιν νεκάδεσσιν, V 886), or he would have been rendered weak (κε ... ἀμενηνὸς ἔα, V 887) but would be alive (ζώς, V 887).[133] It has been argued that the contrast

---

[129] I translate following Kirk (1990) on νεκάδεσσιν as "more graphic" than the common νεκύεσσιν, "since it probably adds the idea of *piles* of corpses" (151).

[130] See Denniston 1950:532 on the use of ἦ τε in emphatic assertions in Homer.

[131] On ἀμενηνός (ἀ- privative + μένος), a denominative adjective in -ηνος, see Risch 1974:100 (§35d).

[132] See Loraux 1986:470–471: "À l'horizon de la vie immortelle d'Arès, il y a donc la mort. Une mort très singulière, certes impossible et qu'on ne saurait penser que sur le mode de l'irréel, mais dont la potentialité se rouvre sans fin" ["On the horizon of Ares' immortal life, there is death. It is a very unique death, certainly impossible and one which could not be thought except in the mode of the contrafactual, but of which the potentiality reopens without limit"].

[133] ζώς is a contraction of ζωιός, a phenomenon within the diachronic development of the epic language which Kirk (1990) attributes to "the latest stage" and considers to be a sign of interpolation here (152). Nevertheless, the contracted form is paralleled by ζών in XVI 445, a well-attested verse describing Sarpedon.

213

between alternatives requires verse V 886 to signify Ares' death in some real way, such that his being rendered weak yet remaining alive offers a real contrast.[134] In this case, we are faced with interpretative difficulties, for although the phrase ἐν αἰνῇσιν νεκάδεσσιν "among the dread piles of the dead" might imply that Ares would be in the land of the dead, such a reading is contradicted by the spatial adverb αὐτοῦ "there," apparently indicating the battlefield.[135] My own reading emphasizes the similarity between the two possibilities rather than contrast between them. Indeed, when Ares claims he would have been ἀμενηνός "without *menos*," the term—a *hapax legomenon* in the *Iliad*—recalls the fact that the souls of dead men in Hades are regularly described as "without *menos*" in the *Odyssey*: they are the νεκύων ἀμενηνὰ κάρηνα "<u>strengthless</u> heads of the dead" (x 521, 536, xi 29, 49).[136] That is to say, *both* possibilities imply a kind of death for the god: suffering among the dead or the reduction of his vital force until he is like one of the dead. But perhaps most informative is the association of both of these possible outcomes—suffering and being rendered without strength—with the temporal adverb δηρόν "for a long time." It is precisely the experience of pain that gives weight to the passing of time for Ares; once stabbed and made to feel physical pain, Ares feels the drag of time.

As we noted above, *Iliad* V 885–887 expresses a mere possibility. Ares *could have* been left to suffer among the dead or rendered as weak as the dead, but neither outcome has in fact occurred. Ares returns to Olympos and is freed from

---

[134] Seymour 1903:143 notes the contrast: "Although the god Ares could not die, yet he assumes that he might have lain as dead. Hence the contrast with ζώς." It is interesting to note that the bT Scholia at *Iliad* V 885b (Erbse) is disturbed not so much by the logic of a "dying god," but rather by the logic that a god who has died (apparently construing ἐν αἰνῇσιν νεκάδεσσιν as meaning "dead") would still be suffering pains (πήματ' ἔπασχον). For, the scholiast argues, "death is the loosening of terrible things" (λύσις γὰρ τῶν δεινῶν ὁ θάνατος). Accordingly, the bT scholia offers a gloss of the sense of *Iliad* V 885–887b: "And the sense is: 'I would be suffering terrible things while lying among the corpses, if while living I was weak because of my wound'" (καὶ ὁ λόγος γίνεται· δεινὰ ἂν ἔπασχον ἐν τοῖς νετροῖς κείμενος, εἰ ζῶν ἀσθενὴς διὰ τὸ τραῦμα ἦν).

[135] So Kirk (1990) while discussing the "clumsiness" of verse V 887 (on which see also Leaf 1900–1902:254, who finds ζώς "highly suspicious"); Kirk concludes "either this god is thoroughly confused as Leaf suggested, or the composer of this [verse] must have taken ἐν αἰνῇσιν νεκάδεσσιν to imply 'among the dead in Hades' *vel sim.*, cf. e.g. 397—but that is specifically excluded by 886 αὐτοῦ. In either case inept rhapsodic or later embellishment is distinctly possible" (152). Willcock 1978–1984:I.241 also finds the choice difficult: "Ares' alternatives are a little confused. As he was immortal, death would not have been possible; he therefore makes an artificial distinction between a long period of pain, lying among the corpses, and total loss of strength as a result of the beating he might have received (though still remaining alive)." *Iliad* V 887 has long been the center of debate. See Leaf 1900–1902:I.254, Crosby 1922, Kirk 1990:152, West 1998–2000:I.178 (*apparatus criticus*), and West 2001:12 with n28 for arguments why V 887 should be considered an interpolated verse; see Loraux 1986:468–469 for an argument against excising the verse.

[136] On the νεκύων ἀμενηνὰ κάρηνα as a reference to the ψυχαί "souls" of dead mortals in Hades, see Heubeck 1989:71n521.

his pains by the divine healer Paieon who sprinkles ὀδυνήφατα φάρμακα "pain-killing drugs" upon his wound:

ὣς φάτο, καὶ Παιήον' ἀνώγειν <u>ἰήσασθαι·</u>
τῷ δ' ἐπὶ Παιήων <u>ὀδυνήφατα φάρμακα</u> πάσσων
<u>ἠκέσατ'·</u> οὐ μὲν γάρ τι καταθνητός γ' ἐτέτυκτο.[137]
ὡς δ' ὅτ' ὀπὸς γάλα λευκὸν ἐπειγόμενος <u>συνέπηξεν</u>
<u>ὑγρὸν ἐόν</u>, μάλα δ' ὦκα <u>περιτρέφεται</u> κυκόωντι,
ὣς ἄρα καρπαλίμως <u>ἰήσατο</u> θοῦρον Ἄρηα.
τὸν δ' Ἥβη <u>λοῦσεν</u>, χαρίεντα δὲ εἵματα ἕσσεν·
πὰρ δὲ Διὶ Κρονίωνι καθέζετο κύδεϊ γαίων.

So [Zeus] spoke, and ordered Paieon <u>to heal him</u>.
And Paieon, by sprinkling <u>pain-killing drugs</u> upon him,
<u>cured him</u>. For he was not at all made to be mortal.
And just as when fig juice rapidly <u>causes</u> white milk <u>to curdle</u>
<u>although it is a liquid</u>, and very swiftly <u>it grows thick</u> all around for one
            who is stirring it,
indeed, just so did he quickly <u>heal</u> furious Ares.
And Hebe <u>washed</u> him, and dressed him in graceful clothing.
And he sat down beside the son of Kronos, rejoicing in his glory.

Iliad V 899–906

Like Hades before him, Ares is "cured" of his pains by Paieon. He reenters the company of the gods and takes his place <u>beside</u> his father (πὰρ δὲ Διὶ Κρονίωνι καθέζετο, V 906), but only after Hebe "cleanses" him (λοῦσεν, V 905) of the stain of mortal time and dresses him once again in the clothing of the gods. Homer's simile of milk transformed from a liquid (ὑγρὸν ἐόν, V 903) into a solid (συνέπηξεν, V 902; περιτρέφεται, V 903) nicely represents the *change of state* Ares likewise undergoes as he is essentially transformed from one struggling under the effects of mortal temporality into a god free from the effects of mortal time, for the simile implies more than the clotting of Ares' own *ikhōr*. Milk, a liquid

---

[137] I read verse V 901 and πάσσων for πάσσεν in V.900 against West's deletion of V 901: West's apparatus indicates that V 901 was apparently unknown to Aristarchus and ignored by the scholiasts and, moreover, is missing from several manuscripts, and West 2001:192 discusses the possibility of V 899–904 being an interpolation based on Hades' injury and treatment by Paieon at V 398–402. In my opinion, however, it is a mistake to excise the later passage. Both passages appear in context of a god being wounded by a mortal and healed by Paieon, the divine *iatros* who provides pain killers to relieve the gods of the pains inflicted upon them by a mortal's weapons. The phrase is equally applicable in each instance, and seeks to reaffirm the gods' immortality at the very moment when they appear most mortal and subject to death. See further Loraux 1986:469 and my discussion above.

highly prone to decay, is transformed by fig juice (ὀπός, V 902) into cheese, a substance more resistant to the decaying effects of time. Just so, Paieon's "pain-killing drug" seems to render Ares more resilient to time's wasting effects. After being returned to his god-like status by Paieon's magical drugs, Ares is described as doing what only a god can do in Homer—namely, "rejoicing in his glory" (κύδεϊ γαίων, V 906).[138]

Ares' virtual re-deification is temporary at best, however, for he soon faces death once again. In *Iliad* VIII 12–14, Zeus issues a stern warning that he will blast any god who disobeys his order to hold back from aiding either the Trojans or the Achaeans:

ὃν δ' ἂν ἐγὼν ἀπάνευθε θεῶν ἐθέλοντα νοήσω
ἐλθόντ' ἢ Τρώεσσιν ἀρηγέμεν ἢ Δαναοῖσιν,
<u>πληγεὶς οὐ κατὰ κόσμον ἐλεύσεται Οὔλυμπόνδε,</u>
ἤ μιν ἑλὼν <u>ῥίψω ἐς Τάρταρον ἠερόεντα,</u>
<u>τῆλε μάλ',</u> ἧχι βάθιστον ὑπὸ χθονός ἐστι βέρεθρον,
ἔνθα σιδήρειαί τε πύλαι καὶ χάλκεος οὐδός,
τόσσον ἔνερθ' Ἀΐδεω ὅσον οὐρανός ἐστ' ἀπὸ γαίης·
γνώσετ' ἔπειθ', ὅσον εἰμὶ θεῶν κάρτιστος ἁπάντων.

Whomever of the gods I shall catch sight of as he willingly
goes either to bring help to the Trojans or to the Danaäns,
<u>after he is struck, he will not return to Olympos in a good condition,</u>
or grabbing him <u>I'll hurl him into murky Tartaros,</u>
<u>very far away,</u> where is the deepest pit under the ground,
where the gates are iron and the doorstep bronze,
as far beneath the house of Hades as heaven is away from the earth.
Then he will come to know by how much I am the strongest of all the gods.

Iliad VIII 10–17

Zeus' warning establishes conditions by which he will judge a god to be a challenger who is seeking to succeed him to the throne. The threats to whip the disobedient god (πληγείς, VIII 12)—that is, to strike him with lightning[139]—or

---

[138] All four uses of the phrase κύδεϊ γαίων in Homer describe the action of gods: Briareos, the hundred-hander, sits beside Zeus "rejoicing in his glory" after rescuing Zeus from his bonds (I 405); Ares likewise sits beside Zeus "rejoicing in his glory" here in our passage (V 906); and Zeus is twice described as sitting apart from the other gods "rejoicing in his glory" as he looks upon the men fighting below (VIII 51, XI 81).

[139] See Scholia bT at *Iliad* VIII 12b (Erbse): τὸ πληγείς ... ἀντὶ τοῦ κεραυνωθείς "the 'having been struck' ... [is used] instead of 'having been blasted by lightning.'" See Scholia bT at *Iliad* XV 17d (Erbse) and Scholia D at *Iliad* II 782 (van Thiel), cited above. See Whitman 1970:38 for an approving assessment of the scholiast's interpretation. Compare VIII 455–456 where Zeus threatens

"hurl him into murky Tartaros" (ῥίψω ἐς Τάρταρον ἠερόεντα, VIII 13) indicate that the god who disobeys Zeus will be treated like a challenger to the throne and essentially "killed." Or, at very least, should the disobedient god happen to survive, he will bear the permanent marks of Zeus' punishment: "he will not return to Olympos in a good condition" (οὐ κατὰ κόσμον ἐλεύσεται Οὐλυμπόνδε, VIII 12).[140] Zeus' threat informs our comprehension of the impossible possibility of Ares' death, for in Book XV of the *Iliad* Ares learns of the death of his son Askalaphos and is driven to distraction in his sorrow. He explains to the other Olympians that he must avenge his son's death, even though he is aware that he will be acting in violation of Zeus' command and that his life will hence be forfeit:

μὴ νῦν μοι νεμεσήσετ᾽, Ὀλύμπια δώματ᾽ ἔχοντες,
τείσασθαι φόνον υἷος ἰόντ᾽ ἐπὶ νῆας Ἀχαιῶν,
εἴ πέρ μοι καὶ <u>μοῖρα</u> Διὸς πληγέντι κεραυνῷ
<u>κεῖσθαι ὁμοῦ νεκύεσσι μεθ᾽ αἵματι καὶ κονίῃσιν.</u>

Now, don't blame me, you who have your homes on Olympos,
for avenging the murder of my son by advancing against the ships of the
    Achaeans,
even if it is my <u>fate to be struck by Zeus' thunderbolt</u>
<u>and to lie together with the corpses among the blood and dust.</u>

Iliad XV 115–118

Once again, as he did at *Iliad* V 886, Ares envisions himself lying among the corpses of the dead (ὁμοῦ νεκύεσσι, XV 118). Here, the theme of death is unmistakable, for the noun μοῖρα "fate, portion, lot" also indicates "death" (cf. *Iliad* VI 488, XVII 672, *Odyssey* ii 100, xi 560), especially when paired with being struck by Zeus' lightning (Διὸς πληγέντι κεραυνῷ, xv 117) and lying among the corpses of the dead (κεῖσθαι ὁμοῦ νεκύεσσι, xv 118).[141] The two passages where Ares imagines himself lying among the corpses of dead humans (αὐτοῦ ... ἐν "there among," V 886; ὁμοῦ "together with," XV 118) are thematically linked by an

---

    Hera and Athena that had they not turned their chariot around and returned to Olympos at once, then "you two <u>would not, after being struck by a lightning bolt</u> while in your chariot, <u>have made it back to Olympos</u>, where the seat of the gods is" (οὐκ ἂν ἐφ᾽ ὑμετέρων ὀχέων <u>πληγέντε κεραυνῷ</u> | ἂψ ἐς Ὄλυμπον ἵκεσθον, ἵν᾽ ἀθανάτων ἕδος ἐστίν).

[140] Compare Scholia A at *Iliad* VIII 12a and Kirk 1990:296, "οὐ κατὰ κόσμον, a sinister understatement, is to be taken closely with ἐλεύσεται." For οὐ κατὰ κόσμον as characterizing the poor organization of speech, compare *Iliad* II 214 where Odysseus criticizes Thersites.

[141] See Ebeling 1963:I.1113–1115 and Liddell, Scott, and Jones 1996:1140–1141, s.v. μοῖρα III.2. for discussion and further citations. On the concept of *moira* in Greek literature, see Greene 1944 and Dietrich 1967.

adverb that locates the god on the battlefield. Further, the two passages are linked in terms of their representation of Ares caught up in mortal temporality, for at V 885 Ares lies suffering "for a long time" (δηρόν), and at XV 118 Ares lies "together with" (ὁμοῦ) the dead, an adverb that has temporal implications as well as spatial ones, as Alex Purves (2006a) has argued: "In Ares' case, it is important to note that he lies not only (ἐν) among them, but also—if we expand our reading of ὁμοῦ to include all its definitions—*at the same time* as them" (203).[142] As is confirmed through the similarity between the two passages, Ares experiences mortal temporality through his physical suffering. And yet, at XV 117–118 Ares realizes the consequences of transgressing Zeus' command and freely accepts his own death. He chooses to become irrevocably tainted by the stain of mortal temporality, to be polluted by filth "among the blood and the dust" (μεθ' αἵματι καὶ κονίῃσιν, XV 118).[143]

When Ares learns of the death of his son Askalaphos, he "slaps his thighs with down-turned hands."

αὖταρ Ἄρης θαλερὼ πεπλήγετο μηρὼ
χερσὶ καταπρηνέσσ', ὀλυφυρόμενος δ' ἔπος ηὔδα.

But Ares struck his blossoming thighs
with down-turned hands, and while lamenting, spoke a word.

Iliad XV 113–114

In his remarkable study of the gesture of slapping one's thighs in Homeric epic, Steven Lowenstam (1981) has demonstrated that the gesture of thigh-slapping points to an ancient inherited Anatolian sacrificial practice in which the sacrificial animal is first stunned by a blow, followed by the fatal stroke delivered from an unseen position. When a character in Homer's epic strikes his thighs, then, he essentially becomes marked for death, and in fact soon dies by an unseen blow. Therefore, Lowenstam argues, when Ares slaps his own thighs here, he does so "in acknowledgment of his readiness to suffer what amounts to a divine death. ... He embraces his own death" (44, 121). If Lowenstam's analysis is correct, then not only do we see Ares verbally acknowledge and accept death at Zeus' hands in response to his violation of divine command not to interfere in the human battle, but we see him acknowledge and accept death by gesture as well.

---

[142] For adverbial ὁμοῦ with not merely spatial but also temporal implications, consider *Iliad* I 61, IV 122, XI 127, XVII 362, XVII 745, XX 499. For ὁμοῦ with a dative expressing spatial and temporal "togetherness," consider *Iliad* V 867 and *Odyssey* iv 723.

[143] Compare Achilles' immortal horses whose manes are "polluted" (ἐμαίνετο χαίτη, XVII 439) by dust as they mourn for Patroklos and for Achilles' divine helmet which is "polluted" (μιάνθησαν δὲ ἔθειραι | αἵματι καὶ κονίῃσι, XVI 795–796; μιαίνεσθαι κονίῃσιν, XVI 797) with blood and dust when it falls from Patroklos' head and hits the ground.

That Ares is planning to face his own death is explicitly acknowledged by his divine audience within the narrative as well. For as soon as Ares finishes his speech, Athena leaps up and persuades him *not* to go:

μαινόμενε, φρένας ἠλέ, διέφθορας. ἦ νύ τοι αὔτως
οὔατ' ἀκουέμεν ἐστί, νόος δ' ἀπόλωλε καὶ αἰδώς.

Madman, crazed in your wits, you are ruined. Yes, now as ever
it's possible for your ears to hear, but your *noos* has perished along with
your sense of shame.

Iliad XV 128–129

For Ares to even think what he has just said is an indication that he is already marked for death (διέφθορας = an intransitive perfect indicative < δια-φθείρω).[144] His νόος "mind, intelligence" has perished, and along with it any chance for his νόστος "return to light and life."[145]

Once again, however, Ares avoids death—Athena convinces him to sit down and accept Zeus' authority. As we have seen, then, the god narrowly avoids two "virtual deaths" in which he would have remained lying on the battlefield for a long time (δηρόν), along with and sharing the same physical space and temporal experience (ὁμοῦ) as the human corpses. He would have been diminished from his ontological status as a divinity to something less, something that feels the duration of lived time through pain and suffering. Although ready to submit to death by Zeus' stroke of lightning (μοῖρα Διὸς πληγέντι κεραυνῷ), although marked for death (διέφθορας), and despite having lost his mind and any possibility for return (νόος/νόστος), Ares does not die. Ares' two "virtual deaths" remain only within the realm of the possible.

Ares' two "virtual deaths" within the *Iliad* are matched by a third actual "death."[146] In Book XXI the gods reenter the battlefield and begin to fight with one another. Ares, still angry about his earlier wounding by Athena and Diomedes, rushes against the goddess. She, in turn, picks up a large stone and "kills" Ares with it:

---

[144] Liddell, Scott, and Jones 1996:418, s.v. διαφθείρω (III) identifies the perfect form διέφθορα as intransitive, but then cites *Iliad* XV 128 and translates "to have lost one's wits," as if reading φρένας as the object of διέφθορας, "you have destroyed your wits." For this interpretation, compare Cunliffe 1963:93, s.v. διαφθείρω (2). Instead, I read φρένας as an accusative of respect with ἠλέ (φρένας ἠλέ "crazed in your wits"), following the interpretation of Janko 1994:242 and the punctuation of West 1998–2000.

[145] On the etymological and conceptual connection between νόος and νόστος, both cognates from the Proto-Indo-European verbal root *nes-, see Frame 1978 and Lowenstam 1981:44–45.

[146] See Purves 2006a:202, "As it turns out, these two virtual falls are just trial runs for his actual fall in Book 21."

τῷ βάλε θοῦρον Ἄρηα κατ' αὐχένα, λῦσε δὲ γυῖα.
ἑπτὰ δ' ἐπέσχε πέλεθρα <u>πεσών</u>, ἐκόνισε δὲ <u>χαίτας</u>,
<u>τεύχεά τ' ἀμφαράβησε·</u>

With it she struck furious Ares on the neck, and <u>she loosened
        his limbs.</u>
And he stretched out over seven *pelethra* <u>when he fell</u>, and <u>got dust
        in his</u> hair,
and <u>his armor clattered about him.</u>

Iliad XXI 406–408

The poetic diction in the passage points to the god's death, for nearly the entire passage is made up of formulae traditionally used to describe the death of mortal warriors in battle. For instance, one fighter striking another with a large stone plucked from the ground is a repeated battle motif,[147] as is one fighter striking another in his neck.[148] Further, the formula λῦσε δὲ γυῖα always indicates the death of a mortal in battle,[149] and the verb πίπτειν "to fall" is regularly used in descriptions of the death of warriors.[150] Even those elements of the description which are, strictly speaking, non-formulaic—ἐκόνισε δὲ χαίτας "he got dust in his hair" (XXI 407) and τεύχεά τ' ἀμφαράβησε "his armor clattered about him" (XXI 408; cf. Purves 2006a:203n70)—still operate within a system of traditional expressions, for the defilement of a hero's hair with blood and dust is a common motif in death scenes (Fenik 1968:163, Lowenstam 1981:85), even if it

---

[147] See, for instance, *Iliad* V 305: τῷ βάλεν Αἰνείαο κατ' ἰσχίον "with it [Diomedes] struck Aeneas in the hip." See further Friedrich 2003:74–75, comparing XXI 403–406 (Athena strikes Ares with a stone) with VII 264–272 (Hektor and Ajax strikes each other with stones).

[148] Compare *Iliad* XI 240: τὸν δ' ἄορι πλῆξ' αὐνέχα, λῦσε δὲ γυῖα "[Agamemnon] struck him in the neck with his sword and loosened his limbs."

[149] For other uses of λύσε δὲ γυῖα "he loosened his limbs," see IV 469, XI 240, 260, XVI 312, 400, XVI 465, 805. Compare the formulaic γυῖα λέλυνται "his limbs were loosened" which also typically indicates death: *Iliad* VII 6, XIII 85, *Odyssey* xviii 238; however, at viii 233 Odysseus explains that he cannot race because "his limbs have been loosened" by his long voyage at sea, and at xviii 242 Irus' "limbs have been loosened" through excess drink. That is, the effects of age or physical weariness and excessive drink can bring about the effects of physical unsteadiness on the human body similar to death itself. Further, consider the instances of ὑπέλυσε ... γυῖα "he loosened his limbs beneath him" which indicate death at *Iliad* VI 27 and XV 581; however, at XXIII 726 the expression describes Odysseus and Ajax wrestling, such that their fall is a non-fatal one. Although the fall in the wrestling competition is non-fatal, it certainly has sinister implications, for it foreshadows the contest between the two over Achilles' armor and the disastrous outcome of that contest. On λῦσε δὲ γυῖα and related formulas and the implication of death, see Lowenstam 1981:85 with n29, Kirk 1990 68 (comment at *Iliad* V 122), and Purves 2006a:180 with n1.

[150] For "falling" as a regular attribute of descriptions of the deaths of warriors in the *Iliad*, see the excellent treatment by Purves 2006a:183–185 with nn9–17.

is usually worded differently in Homeric epic.[151] Similarly, although the phrase τεύχεά τ' ἀμφαράβησε "and his <u>armor</u> <u>clattered</u> about him" is unique, it is a modification of a common formula which always describes the death of a mortal in battle: ἀράβησε δὲ τεύχε' ἐπ' αὐτῷ "and <u>it clattered</u>, his <u>armor</u> did, upon him."[152] In short, then, when Athena strikes Ares in the neck with a stone and unstrings his limbs so that he falls to the ground and his armor clatters about him, Ares undergoes what for any mortal chracter would be certain death. The thunderous crash of Ares' huge body as it hits the ground joins the percussive tempo of death in the *Iliad*—he falls *in time* with the epic's mortal characters, for through his suffering, he has come to participate in mortal time. His screams and crashing armor occur within the epic's regular rhythm of death.

4.2. Binding a God: Ares' Bronze Jar (*Iliad* V 385–391)

When Dione comforts her wounded daughter Aphrodite with the stories of other immortals injured at the hands of reckless mortals, she cites an incident in which Ares suffered at the hands of two mortals, Ephialtes and Otos.[153] The identity of these figures is given at *Odyssey* xi 305–320 as Odysseus explains how he caught sight of their mother, Iphimedia, in Hades. Iphimedia was the wife of Aloeus, but she claimed that her children were the sons of Poseidon. They grew to giant size and strength, and threatened war against the immortals: Ὄσσαν ἐπ' Οὐλύμπῳ μέμασαν θέμεν, αὐτὰρ ἐπ' Ὄσσῃ | Πήλιον εἰνοσίφυλλον, ἵν' οὐρανὸς ἀμβατὸς εἴη, "They were eager to place Mt. Ossa on top of Mt. Olympos, and then Mt. Pelion with its shaking leaves upon Mt. Ossa, so that heaven might be reached by climbing" (xi 315–316). But Apollo killed the two before they could bring war to Olympos (cf. ps.-Apollodorus 1.7.4). Ephialtes and Otos, then, appear to function in a role similar to the Titans and Typhoeus, monsters of enormous size and strength who seek to wage war against the gods and overthrow Zeus. In Dione's tale, Ephialtes and Otos imprisoned the

---

[151] Compare *Iliad* XVII 50–51 (cited by Lowenstam 1981:85) where Euphorbos falls and "his hair, like to the Graces', was covered with blood" (αἵματί οἱ δεύοντο κόμαι Χαρίτεσσιν ὁμοῖαι).

[152] *Iliad* IV 504, V 42, 58, 294, 540, VIII 260, XIII 187, XVII 50, 311, *Odyssey* xxiv 525, with discussion at Muellner 1976:24–25. On modifications of the Homeric formula, see Parry 1971:68–74, 175–180, Russo 1963, 1966, and 1997, Hoekstra 1964, Hainsworth 1968, Ingalls 1970 and 1976, and M. Edwards 1986 and 1988.

[153] The Greek mythopoetic tradition seems to have been influenced by the Near Eastern tradition of monsters threatening the supreme deity, especially Ullikummi in the Hurrian-Hittite mythological tradition. On Near Eastern influences on early Greek cultural production, see Barnett 1945, Burkert 1983a, 1983b, 1987, 1991, 1992, J. W. de Jong 1985, Güterbock 1948, Morris 1989, 1995, 1997, Koenen 1994, Penglase 1994, Walcot 1966, West 1966:18–31, 106–107, and West 1997.

war god in a bronze cauldron for thirteen months until he was at the point of death:[154]

τλῆ μὲν Ἄρης, ὅτε μιν Ὦτος κρατερός τ' Ἐφιάλτης,
παῖδες Ἀλωῆος, δῆσαν κρατερῷ ἐνὶ δεσμῷ·
χαλκέῳ δ' ἐν κεράμῳ δέδετο τρισκαίδεκα μῆνας.
καί νύ κεν ἔνθ' ἀπόλοιτο Ἄρης ἆτος πολέμοιο,
εἰ μὴ μητρυιή, περικαλλὴς Ἠερίβοια,
Ἑρμέᾳ ἐξήγγειλεν· ὃ δ' ἐξέκλεψεν Ἄρηα
ἤδη τειρόμενον, χαλεπὸς δέ ἑ δεσμὸς ἐδάμνα.

Ares endured when Otos and powerful Ephialtes,
the children of Aloeus, bound him in a powerful bond.
And he was within a bronze jar for thirteen months.
And now he might have died, Ares insatiate of war,
if their stepmother, the very beautiful Eëriboia
had not announced it to Hermes. But he stole Ares away
who was already worn out, and the hard bondage conquered him.

Iliad V 385–391

Once again, Ares endures a virtual death: he is overcome and bound by Otos and Ephialtes. The passage achieves emphasis through verbal repetition, first of the adjective "powerful" (κρατερός ... κρατερῷ, V 385–386) in the same metrical position, once describing Ephialtes and the second describing the bonds in which Ares is subdued, and second with the *figura etymologica* as Ares' attackers "bind" him "in a bond" (δῆσαν ... ἐνὶ δεσμῷ, V 386).[155] According to Dione's story, Ares "might have perished" (κεν ... ἀπόλοιτο, V 388) had Hermes not stolen him from the jar. By the time Hermes comes, Ares is already worn out (ἤδη τειρόμενον, V 391), overcome by his thirteen month-long incarceration (χαλεπὸς δέ ἑ δεσμὸς ἐδάμνα, "the hard bondage conquered him" V 391). Although Ares' death is presented in a contrary-to-fact conditional sentence, we cannot dismiss that Homer posits the god's death as a radical possibility.[156]

---

[154] The scholia remark that the Aloadae bind Ares because he killed Adonis, whom Aphrodite had left in their care (Scholia bT at *Iliad* V 385b, Erbse).

[155] The noun δεσμός "bond, means of binding" is etymologically cognate with the verb δέω "to bind": see Chantraine 1968–1980:269–270 and Frisk 1973–1979:374–375, s.v. δέω. On the formation of δεσμός and other Greek nouns with a stem in -σμος/-σμη, see Risch 1974:45–46 (§19d).

[156] See Loraux 1986:466 for a serious assessment of the possibility of the god's death implied by the conditional: "Qu'entendre dans cet apóloito, qui déjà intriguait les scholiastes d'Homère, sinon l'énoncé de ce qu'Arès a bel et bien été au bord de la mort? Ou, plus exactement, qu'il eût péri sans l'intervention conjuguée d'une mortelle et du dieu aux liens. 'Il serait mort si ...': Arès d'est pas mort, mais, quand Hermès l'a libéré, il ne valait pas cher. Avec cet apóloito, la mort apparaît

Hermes rescues Ares from the jar, but the contrafactual narrative points out, once again, the concept of a "dying god."

If *Iliad* V 385–391 explicitly signals the death of a god with its indication that καί νύ κεν ἔνθ' ἀπόλοιτο "and now [Ares] would have died," it is worth considering further what precisely constitutes the nature of this potential death. I find particularly insightful here Jean-Pierre Vernant's discussion on the qualitative differences between the mortal and immortal body:

> The human body is ephemeral. This does not merely signify that, no matter how beautiful, strong, or perfect it may appear to be, *it is still destined for decrepitude and death* [*il est voué par avance ... à la décrépitude et à la mort*]; in a more essential way, it means that since *nothing in it is immutable* [*rien en lui n'étant immuable*], the vital energies it deploys and the psychological and physical forces it puts into play *can remain only for a brief moment in a state of plenitude* [*ne peuvent demeurer qu'un bref moment dans leur état de plénitude*]. These bodies are *exhausted* [*s'épuisent*] as soon as they become active. Like a fire that consumes itself as it burns, and that must continuously be fed in order to keep from going out, *the human body functions in alternating phases of expenditure and recuperation* [*le corps humain fonctionne par phases alternées de dépense et de récupération*]. ... [W]hatever positive forces, such as vitality, energy, power, and luster, the human body may harbor, *the gods possess these forces in a pure and unlimited state* [*les dieux les possèdent, mais à l'état pur et sans restriction*]. In order to conceive of *the divine body in its plenitude and permanence* [*le corps divin dans sa plénitude et sa permanence*], it is therefore necessary *to subtract from the human body all those traits that bind it to its mortal nature and betray its transitory, precarious, and unfulfilled character* [*retrancher de celui des hommes tous les traits qui tiennent à sa nature mortelle et en dénoncent le caractère transitoire, précaire, inaccompli*]. (French=Vernant 1986:28, 33–34; English translation=Vernant 1991:32, 35; translation slightly adapted, emphases added)

According to Vernant's analysis, the human body possesses a finite source of vitality which must be constantly and repeatedly replenished, lest the human

---

pour la première fois comme virtualité à l'horizon de l'existence d'Arès" ["What are we to understand in this *apoloito*—which had already intrigued Homer's scholiasts—if not the presentation that Ares had well and truly been on the verge of death? Or, more exactly, that he would have perished without the conjoined intervention of a mortal woman and a god in his bondage? 'He would have died if ...': Ares is not dead, but when Hermes freed him, he was not worth much. With this *apoloito*, death appears for the first time as virtually on the horizon of the existence of Ares"].

body's one-sided expenditure entirely diminish and waste the body away into non-existence. The god's body, on the other hand, possesses an unlimited quantity of vitality; the god never runs out, never needs to replenish his energies or recuperate. What then are we to make of Homer's explanation that Ares' cruel bonds have "worn him down" (τειρόμενον, V 391)? Like Aphrodite who was "worn down" by her wound as we saw above, Ares too is "worn down": the implication is that through his thirteen month-long incarceration the god essentially undergoes the same sort of degeneration over time as humans when in pain, exhausted, or overcome by age. That Ares can be "worn down" implies that he no longer possesses "unlimited" resources of vitality, but that his body has itself become human in its suffering and limited through the very bonds and jar that hold him.

What is the significance of the δεσμός "bond" that holds Ares captive? Besides his experience of being worn out through time, the restrictions of that god's powers and prerogatives accomplished through "binding" him or her provide the closest analogue for that god's "death" that we have yet seen. Marcel Detienne and Jean-Pierre Vernant describe the effect of binding the divine body:

> A divine being *cannot die* [*ne saurait périr*]; it can only *be bound* [*être lié*]. What does this *binding* [*enchaînment*] mean? First, that the god loses one of his principle prerogatives: *the power of instantaneous movement* [*ce pouvoir de déplacement instantané*] from one spot to another; *the gift of ubiquity* [*ce don d'ubiquité*] which enables him to be present at any place in the world where he chooses to manifest himself ... *The chaining up* [*L'enchaînment*] of a god relegates him to the furthest confines of the cosmos or even to an inaccessible beyond such as the abyss of Tartarus whose entrance has been blocked for all time ... Even when a god *is chained up* [*se trouve enchaîné*] somewhere within the organised universe, his *immobility* [*l'immobilité*] *so utterly reduces his sphere of activity* [*réduit à rien son rayon d'action*] and *his power and being are thus so diminished* [*telle diminution de son puvoir et de son être*] that he appears as an *enfeebled* [*affaibli*], *impotent* [*inefficace*], *exhausted* [*exténué*] figure existing only in that state of quasi-death which sleep represents for the gods. (French=Detienne and Vernant 1974:113–114; English translation=Detienne and Vernant 1978:115–116; emphases added)

In his bonds, a god suffers diminution of power through the limitation of movement and reduction of the god's sphere of activity. In chains, the god becomes enfeebled (*affaibli*), impotent (*inefficace*), exhausted (*exténué*). His physical body, normally capable of moving great distances at will is now restricted to a specific point.[157] If the god's body is typically a "super-body,"[158] the bound god's body, now less mobile even than a human's or an animal's body, must be a "sub-body," as powerless as the "strengthless heads of the dead," the shades of dead men in the underworld.

There is one final observation I would like to make regarding the specific nature of Ares' bronze jar, one that has been noted by a number of scholars. In our investigation of the "succession motif" above, we saw that Zeus virtually "kills" renegade divinities by smiting them with lightning, and then casts them into the murky depths of Tartaros from which the god will never return to heaven. I believe that Ares' bronze jar is itself a figure for Tartaros, for traditional Homeric and Hesiodic accounts of Tartaros indicate that it is to be conceived of as shaped like a large storage jar with an attached lid, and moreover, that it is made of metal: bronze and iron. According to the more complete description in Hesiod's *Theogony* (to which the Homeric account at *Iliad* VIII 14–16, 478–480 bears striking similarities),[159]

τὸν πέρι χάλκεον ἕρκος ἐλήλαται· ἀμφὶ δέ μιν νὺξ
τριστοιχὶ κέχυται περὶ δειρήν· αὐτὰρ ὕπερθε

---

[157] On the limitation of a divinity through binding and the entailed notion of "control" involved in the process, see Crooke 1897 who discusses the ritual practice of "binding" idols. The practice, he argues, indicates a belief that the god becomes embodied in the image, and once embodied, "it is obviously necessary, *to prevent him from escaping, to keep him under control,* so that he may not only be always at hand to receive the prayers and offerings of his subjects, but may not abscond or be removed and *thus come under the control* of a strange and presumably hostile tribe. ... [These] are clear instances in which man imagines himself able *to constrain the gods to subserve his own ends*" (338); "Wherever we find these chained images the same explanation is given—that it is intended *to keep them under control*" (342); "When we come to the cases of gods who are actually *imprisoned or confined*, the ritual seems generally based on the idea that the image is tabu, dangerous if exhibited to its votaries, though in some instances the principle of physically detaining the god may be at the root of the matter" (344; emphases added). The limitation of the god's mobility and sphere of activity essentially brings the god under "control" and subject to being "used." Consider, for instance, the use of binding in "apotropaic" ritual contexts as discussed by Faraone 1992:74–93 (I am grateful to Professor Alex Purves for bringing this reference to my attention), and see further Eliade 1969:93–124 on the "God who binds" as the sovereign of the cosmos who maintains control over those he binds, and Priest 1964 on the concept of "binding" through oaths accompanied by ritual sacrifice.

[158] On the concept of the divine body as a "super-body," see Vernant 1991:41–45.

[159] For the conception of Tartaros, compare *Iliad* VIII 14–16 where Zeus threatens to throw disobedient gods into Tartaros "very far away, where is the deepest pit under the ground, where the gates are iron and the doorstep bronze, as far beneath the house of Hades as heaven is away from the earth." Compare VIII 478–480, "I care not, not if you stray apart to the undermost limits of earth and sea, where Iapetos and Kronos are seated and have no shining of sun god Hyperion to delight them, nor winds' delight, but Tartaros stands deeply about them."

γῆς ῥίζαι πεφύασι καὶ ἀτρυγέτοιο θαλάσσης.
ἔνθα θεοὶ Τιτῆνες ὑπὸ ζόφῳ ἠερόεντι
κεκρύφαται βουλῇσι Διὸς νεφεληγερέταο,
χώρῳ ἐν εὐρώεντι, πελώρης ἔσχατα γαίης.
τοῖς οὐκ ἐξιτόν ἐστι, θύρας δ' ἐπέθηκε Ποσειδέων
χαλκείας, τεῖχος δ' ἐπελήλαται ἀμφοτέρωθεν.
ἔνθα Γύγης Κόττος τε καὶ Ὀβριάρεως μεγάθυμος
ναίουσιν, φύλακες πιστοὶ Διὸς αἰγιόχοιο.

A <u>bronze wall</u> has been drawn around it. And on both sides
       night
has been poured three-fold around its neck. But above
the roots of earth and the fruitless sea grow.
There below in the misty darkness the Titan gods
have been hidden by the councils of cloud-gathering Zeus,
in a dank place, at the extremities of huge earth.
<u>There is no way out for them</u>; Poseidon set in <u>doors</u>,
<u>bronze ones</u>, and the wall has been drawn around on both
      sides.
There Guges, Kottos, and also great-hearted Obriareos
dwell, guards trusted by aegis-bearing Zeus.

Theogony 726–735

In this lower realm (consisting of Tartaros, Erebos, and Hades) "under the earth," there is a bronze retaining wall (726), circled by three layers of "night." Here the Titans are kept "at the furthest outposts of the huge earth."[160] The location is a perfect container, for its walls circle around in both directions (τὸν <u>πέρι</u> χάλκεον ἕρκος ἐλήλαται, 726; τεῖχος δ' ἐπελήλαται <u>ἀμφοτέρωθεν</u>, 733). Outside of the

---

[160] The passage is almost identical to Hesiod's earlier description of where the hundred-handers are located (see *Theogony* 622)—that is, at "Erebos." Liddell, Scott, and Jones 1996:684, s.v. Ἔρεβος, believe Erebos (on the strength of *Iliad* VIII 368) to be "a place of passage to and from Hades." However, Richardson 1974:264 (commentary at *Homeric Hymn to Demeter* 335) notes that there is no justification for such a claim. Richardson argues that Ἔρεβος is "the darkness" (hence its association with ζόφος, as at *Hymn to Demeter* 337, *Odyssey* xii 81, xx 356, *Theogony* 658) as opposed to the light. Note that *Theogony* 123 personifies Erebos as the son of Khaos and brother of Nux "night."

Close examination of the pertinent passages suggests that although Tartaros, Erebos, and Hades are referred to as "underworld" space, each connotes different shades of meaning. Erebos is the most general term for underworld space; Hades is the land of the dead for humans; and Tartaros functions as the holding facility for Zeus' defeated enemies (compare West 1966:338, 356, 358–359). In other words, Hades (and Erebos by metonymy: cf. West 1966:310) functions as a holding facility for dead mortals, while Tartaros contains "dead" gods.

door Guges, Kottos, and Briareos,[161] the hundred-handers, appear to stand guard to prevent any would-be escape (cf. ps.-Apollodorus 1.7, Tzetes' commentary at *Theogony* 277).[162] In this way, then, Tartaros and Hades are mutually reinforcing images of containers with monstrous guards, designed to keep the dead within confines and out of the world above.

Note especially, however, that Tartaros is represented as having bronze doors (θύρας χαλκείας) and a "neck" (δειρήν, 727) surrounded by thick night.[163] The image of a neck suggests something like a storage container—specifically, a pithos jar[164]—and tempts one to interpret the doors set into Tartaros (θύρας δ' ἐπέθηκε, 732) almost as a lid set upon a jar.[165] Pithoi jars in early Greece were commonly used within funerary contexts; they served not only as storage containers for food and wine, but also as storage containers for the burial of dead bodies. Within Homeric epic, Achilles' mortal remains were placed in a jar along with those of Patroklos (*Odyssey* xxiv 73–77, *Iliad* XXIII 91–92).[166] It is perhaps not surprising, then, that the underworld, the final resting place for the dead, is conceived of as a jar (Walcot 1966:61, Onians 1954:395–410, Poljakov 1982:309–310, Penglase 1994:210, West 1997:362–363, Purves 2004:164). An old

---

[161] Briareos appears as Obriareos at Hesiod *Theogony* 617 and 734: cf. West 1966:210 on the variation.

[162] In his commentary at *Theogony* 277, Tzetes explains, τοὺς Ἑκατόγχειρας αὐτοῖς φύλακας ἐπιστήσας, "[Zeus] set up the Hundred-handers as <u>guards</u> over them [sc. the Titans]." Likewise, ps.-Apollodorus (1.7.4–5) tells that at the end of the Theomachy, Zeus and the Olympians, aided by the Cyclopes and Hundred-handers, defeated Kronos and the Titans: κρατοῦσι Τιτάνων, καὶ καθείρξαντες αὐτοὺς ἐν τῷ Ταρτάρῳ τοὺς ἑκατόγχειρας κατέστησαν φύλακας, "they overpowered the Titans, and having confined them within Tartaros, they set up the hundred-handers as guards." On inconsistencies in the various accounts of the Theomachy and the role of Guges, Kottos, and Briareos after the defeat of the Titans, compare Hesiod *Theogony* 815–819, West 1966:210, 357–358, 363, 379, and West 2002:110–118.

[163] One interpretation reads the δειρή as the neck or throat of Tartaros itself, that is, its "gaping maw" ready to swallow its prisoners (Titans, the dead)—and compares Virgil's *fauces Orci* (*Aeneid* 6.273). On this reading, see the Scholia at Hesiod *Theogony* 727, Stokes 1962:9, West 1966:360, and Johnson 1999:14.

[164] See West 1966:360 at *Theogony* 727: "δειρήν: presumably the 'neck' formed by the top of the enclosing wall. The word implies a relatively narrow entrance, as of a jar."

[165] West 1966:364, note at *Theogony* 741, notes that Hesiod's πυλέων "gates" may indicate the "entrance" to Tartaros: "if gods can be thrown into Tartarus, there must be some way in. These are probably the μαρμάρεαι πύλαι of 811."

[166] This jar, according to Stesichorus fr. 234 PMG was a gift wrought by Hephaistos and given to Dionysus in thanks for entertaining the god on Naxos, and then was given by Dionysus to Achilles' mother Thetis in thanks for rescuing the god when he fled from the Theban king Lycurgus and plunged into the sea, as narrated at *Iliad* VI 130–140 (with scholia). See Scholia bT at *Iliad* XXIII 92 with discussion at Haslam 1991. The episode was later elaborated in Aeschylus' lost trilogy the *Lykurgia*. See also Eumelus fr. 1 Davies, ps.-Apollodorus 3.5.1, Hyginus *Fabulae* 132 and 242, Servius' commentary at *Aeneid* 3.14, Diodorus Siculus 3.65.5–6, and Nonnus *Dionysiaca* 21.166. Haslam 1991, esp. 36 with n4 has shown that *Iliad* XXIII 92, the verse which connects the σορός "coffin" in which Achilles' and Patroklos' bones are to be buried with the χρύσεον ἀμφιφορῆα "golden jar" of *Odyssey* xxiv 74 which Dionysus gave to Thetis, is an interpolated verse.

Anatolian myth about the disappearance of the storm god Telepinu describes a ritual for appeasing the god's anger by calling for his anger to be locked in a bronze jar:

> May Telipinu's anger, wrath, sin, and sullenness depart. May the house release it. May the middle ... release it. May the window release it. May the hinge <release it>. May the middle courtyard release it. May the city gate release it. May the gate complex release it. May the King's Road release it. May it not go into the fruitful field, garden, or forest. May it go the route of the Sun Goddess (of the Dark Earth). The gatekeeper opened the seven doors. He drew back the seven bars. Down in the Dark Earth stand bronze vats. Their lids are of lead. Their latches are of iron. That which goes into them doesn't come up again; it perishes therein. So may they seize Telipinu's anger, wrath, sin, and sullenness, and may they not come back (here). (Hoffner Jr. 1998:17, §26–27)[167]

The ritual language speaks of Telepinu's anger being locked within "bronze vats" (*ZABAR pal-ḫi*, "bronze *palhi*-vessels"): in a note on his translation, Harry Hoffner Jr. (1998) explains, "Hittite *palhi*-vessels were large vessels with wide mouths and metal lids" (38n4); these jars were used for storage or incarceration, not for cooking (cf. Gurney 1977:53n4).[168] The text, then, locates storage jars in the underworld, "down in the Dark Earth," from which there is no escape. János Harmatta (1968) specifically compared the bronze jar of the Hittite underworld with the bronze jar (κέραμος) in which the Aloadae lock Ares in *Iliad* V 385–387.[169] Michael Astour (1980) and F. Poljakov (1982) have adduced the further parallel of the entrance of the nether world in Ugaritic mythological and cosmological texts. In Ugaritic mythology, the entrance to the world of the dead is located at *Knkny*, a word related to the Ugaritic *knkn* and Akkadian *kankannu*, which, according to Astour, "denotes a large clay jar (for wine or oil) fixed in the ground of the cellar. Such jars could be used as coffins, as is indeed stated in a Ugaritic epic

---

[167] Compare Hoffner Jr. 1998:19, §20 for another version of the ritual to appease the god's wrath: "May the evil, anger, wrath, [sin], and sullenness go away. But may it not go into the fruitful field, the forest, or the garden. May it go on the road to the Dark Earth. Down into the Dark Earth stand iron vats. Their lids are of lead. Whatever goes into them doesn't come up again; it perishes therein. So may Telipinu's evil anger, wrath, sullenness, and sin go into them and not come up again, but perish therein."

[168] See further Güterbock and Hoffner 1997 (*CHD*, vol. P):66, s.v. (DUG)*palhi*- B, 3c for the specific use of *ZABAR pal-ḫi* in mythological texts as indicating a vessel "in the netherworld or the sea, holding evils," citing this passage (KUB 17.10 iv 15–16), and Hoffner Jr. 1968:65–66.

[169] See West 1997:153, 362–363 for discussion.

... The name of the mountain ... has thus a funerary connotation" (Astour 1980: 229).[170]

The description of Ares trapped within a bronze jar may well suggest, then, the image of the god in Tartaros itself. The god conquered and bound like the Titans and Typhoeus is incarcerated in the prison-house for criminal deities. Beyond any virtual death, Ares was in fact dead—once again, resurrected only through the further expenditure of divine power, here the boundary-crossing and thievery of Hermes.

---

[170] In the Ugaritic myth of Ba'al's contest against Mot, the Ugaritic god of death, Mot is said to dwell at the foot of Mount Knkny (*ǵr knkny*: I AB, v, 12, cited at Botterweck and Ringgren 1974–2006: III.441). See further Gaster 1944:39–40 for an argument that Mot's *ǵr knkny* (I AB, v, 12) is equivalent with the *ǵr 'nn ilm* "abode in the netherworld" (VI AB, iii, 14), an underground realm where Ba'al banishes rebellious gods (VI AB, iii, 18–21a); Gaster (1944) compares this underground abode of the god of the dead and of other defeated gods with Hesiod's description of Tartaros (30–31, 33, 40). See Vidal 2004:110 (with bibliography) for an argument Knkny, properly speaking, is a "common name" derived from the verbal root *knn "to cover, hide" attested in Arabic, such that *ǵr knkny* would indicate "the mountains of my covert," namely, the entrance point to the underworld.

Epilogue

Homeric Durability
Concluding Remarks

THROUGHOUT THIS STUDY, we have considered time and temporality—the experience of time, sometimes called "lived time" within the field of phenomenological psychology[1]—in the *Iliad*, specifically in terms of how the epic represents the "durability" of various bodies and objects. Homer continually represents bodies and objects in the process of decay. The Achaeans' ships and the bodies of the dead are in danger of decay: they weaken at the joints, corruption enters pores in their supple surfaces, and they disintegrate from the inside out. The very resolve of the army is likewise worn down by time: the soldiers grow impatient as they remain on Trojan shores, far away from loved ones (μένων ἀπὸ ἧς ἀλόχοιο | ἀσχαλάᾳ, II 292–293). The durability of these objects is represented as short lived: they can be preserved for a short while—ships can be patched up, bodies can be perserved with *nektar* and *ambrosia*, and troops can be encouraged by a fiery orator—but such recuperations are themselves temporary and only serve to emphasize the temporal nature of the bodies themselves.

Homer presents other, more stable objects—the defensive walls of the Achaeans and the Trojans as well as the various burial mounds and grave markers erected in honor of the dead. These objects are very durable, and remain in place far longer than the human bodies that built them; yet they too are temporally conditioned within the epic. The very tradition of the *Iliad* depends on the destruction of the Trojan wall and the sacking of the city. Though still standing at the end of the *Iliad*, the Trojan wall that Poseidon built "so that the city would be unbreakable" (ἤτοι ἐγὼ Τρώεσσι πόλιν πέρι τεῖχος ἔδειμα | εὐρύ τε καὶ μάλα καλόν, ἵν' ἄρρηκτος πόλις εἴη, XXI 446–447) will eventually be broken. So too

---

[1] On "lived time" see Minkowski 1970, Straus 1960, 1966, Fuchs 2001a, 2003, 2005a, 2005b, Wyllie 2005a, 2005b.

does Homer represent the eventual demise of the tombs of heroes, made to outlive their frail bodies: markers can be moved (XXI 403–406) or misinterpreted (XXIII 326–333), they can be destroyed by human hands or forces of nature (XXI 316–323, xxiv 80–84; cf. Nagy 1999:160n1, Ch. 9§16n1), or they can be forgotten altogether (II 811–814).

Homer presents all these objects as existing within time; they are of our world, and as such, they are subject to the decaying forces of time that work against the integral essences of bodies and of memory itself. But we find evidence of still another dimension of time in the *Iliad*, namely the experience of time by the various characters of the epic. In an important article first published in 1931, the German Classicist Hermann Fränkel looked at the use of the word χρόνος "time" in Homeric epic, found it to be very restricted in use, and therefore argued that Homer must be indifferent to chronology and temporal sequences.[2] Fränkel traced the usage of the word χρόνος in Homer, arguing that it is restricted in sense and usage: it always indicates "duration" as opposed to a "point in time."[3] Homer never uses χρόνος as the subject of a verb, but only in adverbial phrases like ἐπὶ χρόνον or πολὺν χρόνον "for a long time,"[4] and such expressions are often replaced by adverbs of extent, such as δήν "long" and μίνυθα "short." Based on his findings, Fränkel proposed that "Homeric man" only experienced time while "waiting."[5] In other words, Homer represents his characters as "experiencing" time, chiefly, as Fränkel argues, as duration: characters wait, and in their waiting they suffer impatience and boredom (cf. II 291–298); they must "endure" time (cf. II 299–300). Throughout this study I have tried to build on Fränkel's insight by adding other occasions when characters "experience" time—namely in the experience of physical pain and emotional distress. Recent studies on the phenomenology of physical

---

[2] Fränkel argues (1968:1), "Bei Homer finden wir eine fast völlige Indifferenz gegenüber der Zeit" ["In Homer we find an almost complete indifference with regard to time"].

[3] Fränkel 1968:1–2, "Das Wort χρόνος hat bei Homer einen genau begrentzen Sinn und Gebrauch. Es bezeichnet immer eine Dauer, nie einen Punkt; es gibt also kein 'zu dieser Zeit' oder ähnliches" ["The word *khronos* ("time") in Homer has a restricted sense and usage. It always indicates a *duration*, never a point in time; there is also no 'at this time' or the like."] However, see Smith 1969 for an argument that Greek thought actually distinguishes between these two uses of "time," and has a separate lexical unit for designating "the conception of a special temporal position," namely καιρός (Smith 1969:1).

[4] Fränkel 1968:2. The expressions in Homer containing χρόνος "time" are: χρόνον "for a period of time" (iv 599, vi 295, ix 138), δηρὸν χρόνον "for a long time" (XIV 206, 305), ἕνα χρόνον "in a single moment" (XV 511), ἐπὶ χρόνον "for a while" (II 299; xii 407, xiv 193, xv 494), ὀλίγον χρόνον "for a little while" (XXIII 418), οὐκ ὀλίγον χρόνον "not for a little while" (XIX 157), πολὺν χρόνον "for a long time" (II 343, III 157, XII 9; ii 115, iv 543, 594, 675, v 319, xi 161, xv 68, 545, xvi 267, xxi 70, xxiv 218), τόσσον χρόνον ὅσσον ... "for so long a period of time, as long as ..." (XXIV 670; xix 169, 221), χρόνιον "for a period of time" (xvii 112).

[5] Fränkel 1968:2. For discussion, see Bakker 2002:11–13.

pain[6] and emotional distress[7] have demonstrated the temporal dimension of these experiences. As Thomas Fuchs has noted on his study of the temporal experience of a body in pain, "In pain and suffering we experience the temporality of our existence in an exceptional, interesting way. One could even say that it is by unpleasant and painful experiences that time as such comes to our consciousness" (Fuchs 2003:69). Pain breaks through the continuity of our experience, and with its knife-like blow it divides our experience of the present "now" of our pain from a "no longer" when we were not in pain: we experience time as such.[8] Pain makes us feel time with its own rhythm of aches and throbs; we feel pain not merely as intensity but as duration—how long between attacks, how long an attack lasts, how long until we can be free from its oppression. Indeed, modern medical diagnostic tools, such as the McGill Pain Questionnaire, use groups of adjectives such as "flickering," "quavering," "pulsing," "throbbing," and "beating"—the very terms patients themselves often use to describe their pain—to aid caregivers in diagnosis and treatment (Scarry 1985:7–8, Toombs 1992:28): as Elaine Scarry points out, these terms "express, with varying degrees of intensity, a rhythmic on-off sensation, and thus it is also clear that one coherent dimension of the felt-experience of pain is this 'temporal dimension'" (Scarry 1985:7).

We endure pain, and in our endurance we experience the temporality of the "not yet": a possible future of being pain-free lies open to our consciousness. We are hard pressed, but we can endure, for we have hope that our afflictions will pass. But if the pains increase such that we can no longer endure them, then the future itself can seem to close off:

> The taken-for-grantedness of everyday life is disrupted, not only in the sense that routine activities and involvements are disturbed (and become "problematic"), but additionally in the sense that the usual experience of time and space undergoes a significant change. *The unavoidable preoccupation with pain, sickness, or incapacity, grounds one in the present moment. Illness truncates experiencing. The future (long or short-term) is suddenly disabled, rendered impotent and inaccessible.* (Toombs 1992:97; emphasis added)

---

[6]   See, for instance, the studies by Kestenbaum 1982, Schrag 1982, Leder 1984–1985, 1992, Scarry 1985, Toombs 1990, 1992, and Fuchs 2003 building on the work of Husserl 1962, 1981, 1991, Heidegger 1962, Sartre 1956, and Merleau-Ponty 1962.

[7]   See, for instance, the studies by Minowski 1970, Straus 1960, 1966, Fuchs 2001a, 2001b, 2005a, 2005b, Wyllie 2005a, 2005b, building on the work of Bergson 1910a, 1910b, 1990, Sartre 1956, and Merleau-Ponty 1962.

[8]   Fuchs notes that "pain plays a particular role in the constitution of reality and self-awareness. It wakes us from the dream of an undisturbed identity with our environment" (Fuchs 2003:70).

Trapped in an enduring present moment without access to a future horizon, a patient is caught up in a temporality of the "no longer"; there is only an unrecoverable pain-free past and an unendurable present of world-shattering pain.

Emotional pain—care, anxiety, fear, shame—works in a similar way. We experience emotional pain as a "desynchronization" from the rhythms and habits of the world and its manifold timings—day time, week time, schedule time, punctuality—and the social experiences they regulate.[9] As Thomas Fuchs explains, "Traumatic events and serious experiences of guilt, loss or separation persistently affect the experience of time. They *entangle* the person in his/her past, and he/she temporarily loses the lived synchrony with others" (Fuchs 2001a:181; emphasis added). Emotional pains that we can endure allow us to experience a future—our grief is *not yet* forgotten, but eventually forgettable. But some grief, sorrow, or shame may be so intense as to block the future entirely—we are desynchronized from the world and cannot return; we cannot work through our grief, so it becomes *unforgettable*. As Fuchs explains, "With the uncoupling from the external time the future is blocked, which means that *the past is fixed once and for all*; it may no more be changed or compensated by future living. ... Thus in melancholia time is continually transformed, as it were, into guilt which cannot be discharged any more" (Fuchs 2005a:117).

Drawing on the insights of such phenomenological approaches to physical and emotional pain, I investigated the most durable entities represented in Homer's *Iliad*, namely the gods and goddesses themselves who are regularly designated as "immortal and ageless for all days" (ἀθάνατος καὶ ἀγήρως ἤματα πάντα, VIII 539, v 136, vii 257, xxiii 336, cf. vii 94). Unlike men, Homer's gods generally "live easily" (ῥεία ζώοντες: VI 138, iv 805, v 122) and "exist continually" (θεοὶ αἰὲν ἐόντες: I 290, 494, XXI 518, XXIV 99; v 7, viii 306, xii 371, 377; Hesiod fr. 296.2 M-W; cf. *Hymn to Demeter* 325). Nevertheless, Homer's gods feel pain. They suffer at the hands of men and other gods, and in their suffering, they come to experience human time and dis-ease. They also suffer grief and sorrow for humans: gods grieve for their mortal children and for their devout attendants. According to Heidegger, "entanglement" is the essential human experience: we become "entangled" (*verfängt*) in our "care" (*Sorge*) for ourselves, for others (*Fürsorge*), and for being-in-the-world itself (*Besorgen*).[10] We must consider Homer's gods as essentially human, then, for the gods become entangled in their care for mankind. Zeus himself explains that mortal creatures are a "care" to him, in spite of their mortal nature (μέλουσί μοι ὀλλύμενοί περ, "they are a care to me, even though they are dying," XX 21). Though Homer's gods do

---

[9]   See especially Minkowski 1970:64–78, Straus 1960, 1966, Fuchs 2001a, 2005b, Wyllie 2005a.
[10]   See Inwood 1999:35–37 on Heidegger's *Sorge*, *Besorgen*, and *Fürsorge*.

not die, though they do not grow old, they do "endure" time in their pain, care, and grief,[11] they get "worn down" by their sufferings,[12] and they come to experience the downward drag of weight and exhaustion.[13]

What does it mean for an analysis of the *Iliad* and its representation of time and temporality that the gods themselves experience time? If Homer's gods are essentially "men" who do not die and do not age—as suggested by their formulaic epithets ἀθάνατος καὶ ἀγήρως "immortal and ageless" which posit the gods' status as the negated condition of the quintessential mortal experiences of aging and dying—then what does it mean for the gods to experience human time and suffer everything but age and death in the *Iliad*? This question, I have argued throughout this study, is of great significance for our understanding of the poetics of the *Iliad* itself, for Homer presents the project of the *Iliad* as a kind of "immortalizing" of the hero through the preservation of his fame. Achilles chooses to stay and fight in Troy, where he is guaranteed a quick death, but in compensation will have "unwithered fame" (μοι ... κλέος ἄφθιτον ἔσται, IX 413). How are we to determine the durability Homer envisions for his poetry when every other entity in his work is depicted as temporally conditioned, such that even the gods themselves appear as caught up in mortal temporality?

Throughout this study I have tried to emphasize the temporal aspect of the narrative and tie it to the temporary nature of the poetic medium itself. In spite of any tradition of "heroic fame" that Homer may have inherited, I have argued that the formulation of μοι ... κλέος ἄφθιτον ἔσται "I will have *kleos aphthiton*" (IX 413) indicates a specifically time-bound conceptualization of the poetic tradition itself. Margalit Finkelberg has drawn attention to the temporal nature of κλέος in Homeric epic:

> Note now that κλέος οὔποτ᾽ ὀλεῖται, "*kleos* will never be lost," the only Homeric formula making provision for the perpetuation of *kleos*, is actually formulated so as to exclude the idea of its imperishability: if anything, it implies that one's *kleos* is normally expected to perish. The same conclusion follows if we analyze the supplementary expression "*kleos* may be inextinguishable" (ἄσβεστον κλέος εἴη) ... In both cases,

---

[11] Compare Dione's soothing words to Aphrodite: "Endure, my child, and bear it, although you are troubled" (τέτλαθι, τέκνον ἐμόν, καὶ ἀνάσχεο κηδομένη περ, V 381). See my discussion of *τλάω "endure, suffer" in the Introduction and chapter 5 above.

[12] Compare Ares already worn out (ἤδη τειρόμενον, V 391), overcome by his thirteen month-long incarceration in an bronze jar (χαλεπὸς δέ ἑ δεσμὸς ἐδάμνα, "the hard bondage conquered him" V 391).

[13] Compare Aphrodite "weighted down by her pains" (ἀχθομένην ὀδύνῃσι, V 354), and explaining to Ares that "I am weighed down too much by my wound" (λίην ἄχθομαι ἕλκος, V 361) to return to heaven on her own.

rather than being taken for granted, the imperishability of one's *kleos* is predicated on something else: Agamemnon's *kleos* will be inextinguishable *if* Menelaus builds a tomb for him; Alkinoos's *kleos* will be inextinguishable *if* he helps Odysseus to return home—the alternative is the extinction of *kleos*, which is obviously envisaged as the norm. (Finkelberg 2007:343)

The very phraseology describing the perpetuation of "fame" indicates that, generally speaking, "fame" does not last—it is a temporal and temporary object, destined to fade over time as memory and the various mnemonic devices—graves, tombs, and the oral tradition itself—fade into oblivion. So in those cases when the durability of κλέος is emphasized—when it is claimed that it will never be lost, that it will be inextinguishable, that it will be imperishable—we can only measure that durability with the scale Homer provides elsewhere in the epic. The adjective ἄφθιτος "unwithered" in κλέος ἄφθιτον ἔσται is otherwise used for the marvelous: grapevines that do not fade in their bounty (ix 133), Zeus' divine counsels (XXIV 88), and the material craftwork of Hephaistos, including Agamemnon's σκῆπτρον "scepter" (II 46, 186), Hera's θρόνος "throne" (XIV 238), the rims of the wheels of her chariot (V 724), and the homes of Poseidon (XIII 22) and Hephaistos himself (XVIII 370). These divine objects are durable and certainly long lasting—though Homer elsewhere shows us divine craft that does break in spite of its being created to be ἄρρηκτος "unbreakable" (XXI 446–447). Hephaistos' other "immortal" craftwork—namely the armor he makes for Achilles (cf. XIX 3, 10–11)[14]—cannot preserve his life (cf. XVIII 464–467). Zeus' divine counsels are only "imperishable" so long as he remains king of the pantheon. It is worth considering the distribution of the formulaic Ζεὺς δ' ἄφθιτα εἰδῶς in early Greek poetry: it appears once in the *Iliad* (XXIV 88) when Zeus summons Thetis to talk about the return of Hektor's corpse, but three times in Hesiod's *Theogony* (545, 550, 561), significantly all in context of Zeus' struggles with Prometheus. In other words, Zeus' counsels are emphasized as ἄφθιτος only in contexts where there is a real question of whether he will be obeyed.

These arguments, which I have detailed in the pages above, have led me to emphasize the temporally bound nature of the tradition itself. Homer depicts his own poetry as possessing great durability—but that durability is not meant

---

[14] Achilles first set of armor—a wedding gift for Peleus made by Hephaistos (XVIII 83–85)—was "immortal" (ἄμβροτα τεύχεα, XVII 194, 202); presumably the second set made at Thetis' request is also "immortal." Its divine manufacture is emphasized at XIX 3, 10–11, and its fine quality is emphasized as "beautiful" (καλά: XVIII 466, XIX 11), "shimmering" and "bright" (μαρμαίροντα, XVIII 618; ἀγλαά, XIX 18), emphasizing its metallic construction.

to imply any concept of the "eternal." In his discussion of the Indo-European tradition of "heroic fame" inherited by Homer, Martin West has noted,

> The evidence is perhaps too thinly scattered to warrant the conclusion that this was an Indo-European trope, especially as parallels can be found in the Near East. But we have seen enough to establish beyond any reasonable doubt that *the idea of posthumous fame was a pervasive theme of Indo-European poetry.* Its predicates—good (or bad), great, wide, high, unfailing—may almost be said to form a formulaic system, not in the Parryist sense of being metrically complementary, but in the sense of being semantically complementary. *The hero whose feats achieved acclaim and renown in his lifetime could hope that after the death of his body his name would remain: not perhaps explicitly "to the end of the world," but indefinitely.* (West 2007:410; emphases added)

Achilles' κλέος ἄφθιτον is not "imperishable fame," for there is nothing in the world of the *Iliad* that would allow us to comprehend what "imperishable" means. Instead, we should interpret it as "unwithered fame," fame that is temporally conditioned, though projected into an indefinite future.

I have invoked Heidegger's concepts of "Being-toward-death" (*das Sein zum Tode*) and "Being-toward-the-end" (*das Zu-Ende-sein*) to help understand both Achilles' decision to stay in Troy and fight and die, as well as Homer's representation of the temporally conditioned nature of his poetry and its orientation toward its own end as encapsulated in the concept of κλέος ἄφθιτον ἔσται, a fame which has not yet, but will eventually fade. Achilles' Being-toward-death enables him truly to become the hero he is meant to be: it is only when Patroklos has died and he has acknowledged his own death (XVIII 98–116) that he can say: "But now I wish to take up noble fame" (νῦν δὲ κλέος ἐσθλὸν ἀροίμην, XVIII 121). As for the tradition itself, its claim to preserve Achilles' κλέος ἄφθιτον is likewise oriented toward the future possibility of its own end. This Being-toward-the-end is determined as its own Being-toward-decay. Within the form and semantics of the adjective ἄφθιτον the tradition signals its own end within its very being—its project of preserving Achilles' fame is itself an acknowledgment of its own mortality. Homer's poetry represents itself as being-toward-its-end: as a temporal object existing in mortal temporality, the durability of the *Iliad* itself can only last as long as the *process* of Achilles' κλέος ἄφθιτον—celebrating and listening to Achilles' fame *so that it remains unwithered*—is repeated. Like its hero, it is beautiful in its very fragility that must be the object of our continued care.

Appendix

The Semantic Field of "Decay" in Homeric Epic

HOMER MAKES USE OF SIX SEPARATE VERBAL ROOTS to describe the process of decay as the physical bodies of plants, animals, and humans undergo the degenerative effects of time. These verbs are: φθίω/φθίνω/φθίνυθω "to wither, waste away, die"; σήπω "to rot, decay"; πύθω "to cause to rot, rot, putrefy"; σκέλλω "to dry up"; κάρφω "to cause to shrivel up, dry up, parch"; and ἄζω "to dry out, parch." Each of these verbs, as I demonstrate below, is used to indicate a temporally conditioned experience of degenerative change over time.[1] Insofar as these changes are gradual, as a body slips from a pristine state into one of corruption or decay, the physical change itself becomes a material record of the passage of time and its withering effects. The value of the semantic field of "decay" in Homer extends beyond the narrative to the poetics of the *Iliad* itself, for the poetic project of the *Iliad* is nothing other than to preserve Achilles' κλέος ἄφθιτον, his fame which is characterized by being ἀ- "not (yet)" + *φθιτον "having undergone the process of (vegetal) decay." In order to fully understand the poetic project of the *Iliad*, then, we should track the precise sense of the semantic field of "decay."

The following discussion, based on a comprehensive analysis of Homer's verbs of "decay" and their cognates, argues that Homeric usage demonstrates a clear concept of time in the abstract as measured through the change in the structural integrity of physical bodies over time. I treat each verb separately, and have organized textual evidence according to an analysis of the contexts in which each term occurs.

---

[1] The ancient scholiasts noted the functional equivalence between σήπομαι "decay," πύθομαι "rot," and yet another verb, φθείρω "destroy" (cognate with the Sanskrit root *kṣar-: cf. Burrow 1959a, 1959b, Chantraine 1968–1980:1198–1200, Frisk 1973–1979:II.1013–1014, s.v. φθείρω), and gloss one word with the other. See, for example, Scholia D at *Iliad* XI 395 (van Thiel), which glosses πύθεται· σήπεται. Likewise, Scholia T glosses the words as equivalent at *Odyssey* I 161; cf. Scholia D at *Iliad* XXIII 328 (van Thiel) which equates all the three verbs: καταπύθεται· σήπεται, φθείρεται.

1. φθίω/φθίνω/φθινύθω "to wither, waste away, die"[2]

The verbal root *φθι- is the most common way to refer to the organic process of decay in Homeric epic. The verb originally describes the process of vegetal decay, as plants lose their vital force and wither away, and the diminishing of streams of water; however, as we will see, the verb has already extended beyond these specific meanings to describe a series of possibilities for how humans "waste away" through the diminishment of life or vitality—namely, through old age, illness, the lack of eating, inactivity, longing, and sorrow. Further, the verb may be used to describe how one "perishes" in battle or through trickery and deceit. The substantive use of the passive participle (οἱ φθινόμενοι) can be used to refer to the "dead" who occupy the underworld, as if implying that those beneath the ground are subject to the forces of decay brought on by the dampness of the earth itself.[3] And finally, the verb may be used as a curse when calling imprecations upon someone's head.

1.1. Vegetal Decay

The sense of φθίω describing "vegetal decay" is preserved in certain passages, such as *Iliad* XXI 462–467 where Apollo's response to Poseidon's charge that he has forgotten the rough treatment the two gods received at the hands of Laomedon draws together the imagery of mankind (βροτοί) as vegetal matter (φύλλοισιν ἐοικότες "just like leaves") which flourish and grow up to a certain fullness, but then wither and perish.

> ἐννοσίγαι᾽, οὐκ ἄν με σαόφρονα μυθήσαιο
> ἔμμεναι, εἰ δὴ σοί γε <u>βροτῶν</u> ἕνεκα πτολίξω
> <u>δειλῶν</u>, οἳ <u>φύλλοισιν ἐοικότες</u> ἄλλοτε μέν τε
> <u>ζαφλεγέες</u> τελέθουσιν <u>ἀρούρης καρπὸν ἔδοντες</u>,
> ἄλλοτε δὲ <u>φθινύθουσιν ἀκήριοι</u>.

> Earth-shaker, you would say I am not sound-of-wit,
> if indeed I should make war with you for the sake of <u>miserable
> mortals</u>, who, <u>just like leaves</u> at one time always

---

[2] For discussions of the etymology and semantics of φθίω/φθίνω/φθινύθω, see Ebeling 1963:II.425–426, Pokorny 1959, s.v. ĝʰi̯/gʷʰ, Leumann 1950:212n4, Cunliffe 1963:408, Chantraine 1968–1980:1200–1201, Frisk 1973–1979:II.1014–1016, Liddell, Scott, and Jones 1996:1928–1929, s.v. φθινύθω, φθίνω, φθίω. On the cognate Sanskrit verbal root *kṣi-, see Pokorny 1959 and Burrow 1959a, 1959b. On the relationship between the variant forms φθίνω and φθίνύθω, see Chantraine 1958:160 who notes that the two forms reflect an original *φθίνω. On the root *φθι- and decay in epic poetry, see Nagy 1974:229–261, esp. 240–255, 1999:174–189 (Ch. 10§1–19), and Bakker 2002.

[3] On this point, see the discussion of πύθομαι below.

grow warm as they flourish while <u>eating</u> the <u>fruit of the ploughed field</u>, and at another time <u>wither away, lifeless</u>.

Iliad XXI 462–466

Apollo offers a poetic image of man's mortal nature: βροτῶν < IE root *mr̥to- + δειλῶν "wretched," a term structurally opposed to the gods' "easy" and "blessed" living.[4] For the image of man compared with leaves, we may consider the comparison of the vast size of the Greek army to the number of leaves and flowers that grow "in season" (ὥρῃ, *Iliad* II 468),[5] or Glaukos' famous comparison of the generations of men to those of leaves that flourish "in season" (ὥρῃ, VI 146–149) replicated so beautifully in Mimnermus fr. 2 (West).[6] At one time both men and leaves are full of internal warmth (ζαφλεγέες, XXI 465) and they flourish; at another time they diminish, decay, and die (ἀκήριοι, XXI 466). Life consists of consuming food (ἀρούρης καρπὸν ἔδοντες, XXI 465), which in turn fuels the internal "fire" that characterizes living bodies (ζαφλεγής < ζα- + φλέγειν "to burn, blaze"); death (ἀκήριος < ἀ- + κῆρ "without heart, life"), then, implies a lack of eating and a corresponding reduction of growth, as well as a lack of the internal heat characteristic of living bodies.[7]

On the concept of "vegetal decay" and its close associations with the concept of a "cycle" of life, we may compare the description of Helios' magical cattle on Thrinakia which do not die, but do not reproduce either.

Θρινακίην δ' ἐς νῆσον ἀφίξεαι· ἔνθα δὲ πολλαὶ
βόσκοντ' Ἠελίοιο βόες καὶ ἴφια μῆλα.
ἑπτὰ βοῶν ἀγέλαι, τόσα δ' οἰῶν πώεα καλά,
πεντήκοντα δ' ἕκαστα. <u>γόνος</u> δ' οὐ γίνεται αὐτῶν,
οὐδέ ποτε <u>φθινύθουσι</u>.

Then you will reach the island Thrinakia, where are pastured
the cattle and the fat sheep of the sun god, Helios,

---

4 On the *mr̥to- root, see my discussion in chapter 2 above (with bibliography); on the structural opposition between men's "wretched" lives and gods' "easy" and "blessed" lives, see my discussion in chapter 5 above (with citations).

5 ὅσσα τε φύλλα καὶ ἄνθεα γίνεται <u>ὥρῃ</u> "as many leaves and flowers are born <u>in season</u>" (*Iliad* II 468).

6 Glaukos' simile: οἵη περ φύλλων γενεή, τοίη δὲ καὶ ἀνδρῶν. | φύλλα τὰ μέν τ' ἄνεμος χαμάδις χέει, ἄλλα δέ θ' ὕλη | τηλεθόωσα φύει, ἔαρος δ' ἐπιγίνεται <u>ὥρῃ</u> "Just as the generations of leaves, so also are the generations of men. The wind sheds the leaves upon the ground, but the tree, ever burgeoning, makes them grow when spring comes <u>in season</u>" (*Iliad* VI 146–148). On Mimnermus fr. 2, see Griffith 1975 and Bakker 2002.

7 In this context, it is useful to note that θυμός, regularly undersood as "life, spirit, passion" in Homeric diction, is etymologically cognate with Latin *fumus* "smoke" (cf. Sanskrit *dhumá*); in other words, θυμός indicates a connection between life and internal heat—the "fire in the belly."

seven herds of oxen, and as many beautiful flocks of sheep,
and fifty to each herd. There is no <u>giving birth</u> among them,
nor do they ever <u>waste away</u>.

Odyssey xii 127–131

The sun god Helios' cattle and sheep are magical animals who are apart from the
mortal effects of time. Their number is fixed: they neither reproduce (γόνος δ'
οὐ γίνεται αὐτῶν, xii 130), nor perish (οὐδέ ποτε φθινύθουσι, xii 131). They do
not decay, because they are outside of time's influence, as if that which is not
born into time does not suffer its withering effects.[8]

1.2. The Diminishment of Human Vitality through Old Age and Disease

The metaphorical step from "vegetal decay" to the physical wasting away of the
human body through old age (γῆρας) and disease (νοῦσος) is an easy one. The
human body ages and deteriorates over time just as vegetation does—both wither
away, die, and rot. Hence, we find passages such as when Odysseus reproaches
Agamemnon's suggestion that the Achaeans quit fighting and return home:

> αἴθ' ὤφελλες ἀεικελίου στρατοῦ ἄλλου
> σημαίνειν, μηδ' ἄμμιν ἀνασσέμεν, οἷσιν ἄρα Ζεύς
> <u>ἐκ νεότητος</u> ἔδωκε καὶ <u>ἐς γῆρας</u> τολυπεύειν
> ἀργαλέους πολέμους, ὄφρα <u>φθιόμεσθα</u> ἕκαστος.

> I wish that of another unseemly army
> you were the leader, and did not command us, to whom indeed Zeus
> has granted <u>from our youth</u> even <u>until old age</u> to bring to completion
> grievous wars, until we <u>waste away</u>, each one of us.

Iliad XIV 84–87

Odysseus' speech connects the verb φθίω with the concept of passing ἐκ
νεότητος "from youth" ἐς γῆρας "to old age." With age, the Achaeans will not
only accomplish their war, but will—each one of them—waste away.

---

[8] One may compare the story of how Apollo's cattle in the *Hymn to Hermes* are designated as
ἀδμῆτες (103), a word that, with its double sense of "unbroken by the plow" as well as "not yet
sexually penetrated," suggests that the cattle do not engage in sexual reproduction and are fixed
in number. However, by the end of the hymn, once Apollo and Hermes have exchanged their
essential accoutrements of lyre and cattle, the cattle begin to reproduce sexually (490–494), as if
through theft and commerce the herd has essentially moved from a divine space into a human
one. On this reading, see especially Kahn 1978:48, and on ἀδμῆτες as indicating the status of the
female *parthenos* as "not yet" sexually penetrated, see Bergren 1989:10.

Further, Laertes is described as wasting away both through grief over the absence of his son and the death of his wife, which has set upon him an untimely old age:

Λαέρτης μὲν ἔτι ζώει, Διὶ δ' εὔχεται αἰεὶ
θυμὸν ἀπὸ μελέων φθίσθαι οἷσ' ἐν μεγάροισιν·
ἐκπάγλως γὰρ παιδὸς ὀδύρεται οἰχομένοιο
κουριδίης τ' ἀλόχοιο δαΐφρονος, ἥ ἑ μάλιστα
ἤκαχ' ἀποφθιμένη καὶ ἐν ὠμῷ γήραϊ θῆκεν.

Laertes is still alive, but he prays to Zeus always
that his <u>heart</u> <u>waste away</u> from his limbs in his home.
For terribly he <u>grieves</u> for his child who is gone away
and for his wedded virtuous wife, who especially
<u>pained</u> him when she <u>died</u> and set him <u>in raw old age</u>.

Odyssey xv 353–357

The phrase "raw old age" indicates that Laertes has aged before his time;[9] the implication, then, is that the effects of old age (γῆρας, cf. xv 357) upon the body—similar to those brought on by intense grief (ἐκπάγλως ... ὀδύρεται, xv 355)—are degenerative: the body withers away (φθίσθαι, xv 354) under their influence.

As for disease, we find a description of an Achaean warrior who was fated to die in one of two ways: either to *wither away* at home under a grievous sickness, or to be killed in battle by the Trojans:

νούσῳ ὑπ' ἀργαλέῃ φθίσθαι οἷς ἐν μεγάροισιν,
ἢ μετ' Ἀχαιῶν νηυσὶν ὑπὸ Τρώεσσι δαμῆναι.

---

[9] Compare Hesiod *Works and Days* 705 in which marriage with a bad wife ὠμῷ γήραϊ δῶκεν "gives one over to raw old age"; the context of Hesiod's use of the expression securely demonstrates the sense "premature, before its time" for ὠμός. Contrast the adjective ὠμογέροντα at *Iliad* XXIII 791 which, in context, describes Odysseus as being "green for his age"—i.e., despite his age, he is nonetheless able to outrun Ajax and Antilochus in a footrace. For commentary on ὠμός, ὠμῷ γήραϊ, and ὠμογέροντα, see West 1978:329 (at Hesiod *Works and Days* 705), Hoekstra 1989:255 (at *Odyssey* xv 377), and Richardson 1993:257 (at *Iliad* XXIII 791). See further Scholia AbT at *Iliad* XXIII 791 (Erbse), a passage not mentioned in Richardson's discussion, which glosses ὠμογέροντα "raw old man" as τὸν μὴ καθηψημένον ὑπὸ τοῦ γήρως· ἡ δὲ μεταφορὰ ἀπὸ τῶν κρεῶν "the man who has not been softened (lit. "boiled down") by old age; the metaphor derives from meats." The suggestion that the description of Odysseus as essentially "still fresh" for his age derives from a metaphorical usage of an adjective proper to describing cooking meat is suggestive, for it implies a similar effect of cooking time upon man and meat. For different use of "raw" and "green" to suggest not premature old age, but youthful vigor, see Virgil *Aeneid* 6.304 where Charon is described as *iam senior, sed cruda deo viridisque senectus* "already quite old, but for the god there is a raw and green old age," and the imitation of this verse at Tacitus *Agricola* 29.4 *quibus cruda et viridis senectus.*

> [... that he would] <u>wither away</u> by a grievous <u>sickness</u> in his
>> own home,
> or that he would <u>be conquered</u> among the ships of the Achaeans
>> at the hands of the Trojans.

Iliad XIII 667–668

Pairing defeat at war (δαμῆναι, XIII 668) with the withering effects of disease (νούσῳ … φθίσθαι, XIII 667) marks the inner dynamics of heroic action in the *Iliad*—since mortals are destined to die anyway, they should seek to gain fame through their deeds in war (cf. XII 310–328). The description of a warrior being given a choice of an ignoble death at home versus a glorious death in battle reminds us of Achilles' own choice to stay and fight in Troy and die but win κλέος ἄφθιτον or to return home and live a long life in his homeland of Φθίη, but lose any chance at fame (*Iliad* IX 410–416). It is significant to note that Achilles' homeland Phthia where he would wither away in ignoble death is itself related to the *φθι- verbal stem.[10]

As we move further from "vegetal decay," the verbal root *φθι- is used to describe other "wasting" effects which are similar to old age. That is, one may "wither" or "waste away" their body (χρώς "flesh"), their heart (κῆρ, θυμός), or their life/life-force/vitality (αἰών). This kind of physical, emotional, and spiritual degeneration is brought about by means of longing (πόθος) for an absent person and sorrow (ὀδύρομαι, ὀιζυρός).

We begin with the more concrete examples, namely the physical wasting away of the body that is associated with improper eating.

1.3. The Diminishment of Human Life or Vitality through Excessive Eating or the Failure to Eat Sufficiently

As might be expected, examples connecting the *φθι- root with improper eating appear only in the *Odyssey*, the epic which treats improper eating as a key example of violated relations of *xenia*. In our first example, Laertes wastes away through a lack of eating:

αὐτὰρ νῦν, ἐξ οὗ σύ γε ᾤχεο νηῒ Πύλονδε,
οὔ πώ μίν φασιν <u>φαγέμεν</u> καὶ <u>πιέμεν</u> αὔτως,

---

[10] On the connection between Phthia and "decay," compare *Iliad* XIX 322–323 in which Achilles speaks of the prospect of learning of the *withering away* of his father (εἴ κεν τοῦ πατρὸς ἀποφθιμένοιο πυθοίμην) who is still in *Phthia*, shedding tears for his absent son (ὅς που νῦν Φθίηφι τέρεν κατὰ δάκρυον εἴβει). See also XIX 329–330 for Achilles' impossible wish that he alone would have *perished* in Troy (οἶον ἐμὲ φθείσεσθαι … | αὐτοῦ ἐνὶ Τροίῃ, XIX 329–330) and that Patroklos could have returned to *Phthia* (σὲ δέ τε <u>Φθίηνδε</u> νέεσθαι, XIX 330). See further Nagy 1999:184–85 (Ch. 10§14) and Lynn-George 1988:155.

οὐδ' ἐπὶ ἔργα ἰδεῖν, ἀλλὰ <u>στοναχῇ</u> τε <u>γόῳ</u> τε
ἧσται <u>ὀδυρόμενος</u>, <u>φθινύθει</u> δ' <u>ἀμφ' ὀστεόφι χρώς</u>.

But now, since the time when you [sc. Telemachus] went away by ship to
        Pylos,
they say [Laertes] has not yet <u>eaten</u> nor <u>drunk</u> as before,
nor looked to his farm, but in both <u>lamentation</u> and <u>mourning</u>
sits <u>grieving</u>, and <u>the flesh on his bones</u> is <u>wasting away</u>.

Odyssey xvi 142–145

Laertes' χρώς "flesh" is wasting away (φθινύθει, xvi 145) because he has neither
eaten (φαγέμεν, xvi 143) nor drunk (πιέμεν, xvi 143) anything out of his lamentation and grief. His loss of his wife, son, and even grandson while Telemachus
leaves town, drives him to self-destruction through not eating.[11] Note that the
upkeep of the body through food and drink is connected with agriculture, for in
addition to not taking care of himself, Laertes has not looked after his farm (οὐδ'
ἐπὶ ἔργα ἰδεῖν, xvi 144). The *cultus* of body and plants are likened: both require
upkeep, without which both tend towards decay.

    In a series of examples, the suitors "waste away" Odysseus' and Telemachus'
property through their uncontrolled feasting.

τόσσοι μητέρ' ἐμὴν μνῶνται, <u>τρύχουσι</u> δὲ <u>οἶκον</u>.
ἡ δ' οὔτ' ἀρνεῖται στυγερὸν γάμον οὔτε τελευτὴν
ποιῆσαι δύναται· τοὶ δὲ <u>φθινύθουσιν ἔδοντες</u>
οἶκον ἐμόν· τάχα δή με <u>διαρραίσουσι</u> καὶ αὐτόν.

So many men are wooing my mother, and they <u>wear out</u> my <u>house</u>.
And she does not refuse the hateful marriage, nor is she able
to make an end of it; and these men <u>waste away</u> my home
<u>with their eating</u>. In truth, they will quickly <u>break</u> even me myself <u>to</u>
    <u>pieces</u>.

Odyssey I 248–251
= xvi 125–128[12]

---

11 On the temporal experience of melancholia brought on by extreme grief, resulting in the physical loss of "drive, appetite, or sexuality," see Fuchs 2005a:116–118.

12 Compare *Odyssey* xiv 90–95: ὅ τ' οὐκ ἐθέλουσι δικαίως | μνᾶσθαι οὐδὲ νέεσθαι ἐπὶ σφέτερ', ἀλλὰ
ἕκηλοι | <u>κτήματα δαρδάπτουσιν ὑπέρβιον</u>, οὐδ' ἔπι φειδώ. | ὅσσαι γὰρ νύκτες τε καὶ ἡμέραι ἐκ
Διός εἰσιν, | οὔ ποθ' ἓν ἱρεύουσ' ἱερήϊον οὐδὲ δύ' οἶα· | <u>οἶνον δὲ φθινύθουσιν ὑπέρβιον ἐξαφύοντες</u>
"the fact that they [sc. the suitors] are not willing to make their suit decently, nor go home to
their own houses, but at their ease they <u>forcibly eat up his property</u>, and spare nothing. For as
many as the nights and the days from Zeus, on not one of these do they dedicate a single victim,
nor only two, and they <u>violently draw the wine and waste it away</u>."

Note in particular the association between the οἶκος "household" and Telemachus' own body: the suitors "wear out" (τρύχουσι, i 248)[13] and "waste away" (φθινύθουσιν, i 250) the property by eating and drinking, and will soon break Telemachus himself apart (διαρραίσουσι, i 251). In other words, the diminution of the household by means of depleting its supplies is likened to the diminution of the human body, here figured as being broken into pieces.

1.4. The Diminishment of Human Life or Vitality through Longing and Inactivity

We now turn to a less physical kind of "wasting away"—instead of the diminishment of one's physical body, we now investigate those passages which describe the wasting away of one's heart, life, or vitality through longing.

In our first passage, Penelope wishes for death so that she may not continue to waste away her αἰών "life, vitality" through longing for her absent husband.

> αἴθε μοι ὡς μαλακὸν θάνατον πόροι Ἄρτεμις ἀγνή
> αὐτίκα νῦν, ἵνα μηκέτ' ὀδυρομένη κατὰ θυμόν
> αἰῶνα φθινύθω, πόσιος ποθέουσα φίλοιο
> παντοίην ἀρετήν, ἐπεὶ ἔξοχος ἦεν Ἀχαιῶν.

> How I wish chaste Artemis would give me a gentle death,
> now at once, so that I may no longer grieving throughout my heart
> waste away my life, longing for my dear husband
> excellent in every virtue, since he was outstanding among the Achaeans.

> *Odyssey* xviii 202–205

Penelope wastes away her αἰών "life, life-force, vitality" (xviii 204) through the constant lamentation (ὀδυρομένη, xviii 203) that effects her in her heart (κατὰ θυμόν, xviii 203). Her sorrow comes from her "longing" (ποθέουσα, xviii 204) for her absent husband, and this very loss constitutes a diminishment of personal vitality (αἰῶνα φθινύθω, xviii 204) that results in a wish for death (αἴθε μοι ... θάνατον πόροι Ἄρτεμις, xviii 202).

Achilles likewise continually wastes away his own κῆρ "heart" through his longing to participate in battle.

[13] The verb τρύχω "to wear away" appears five times in the *Odyssey*: three times it refers to the suitors "wearing away" Odysseus'/Telemachus' οἶκος (i 248 = xvi 125, xix 133); once it refers to Telemachus himself as being "worn down" by the suitors, essentially equating Telemachus with his household (i 288); and once it refers to Odysseus' men who are "worn out" with hunger (λιμῷ) on Thrinakia (x 177). Every instance of the verb in Homer, then, is associated with an act of *eating* that wastes away a household's stores and by extension the livelihood of the owner of that household, or with a *lack of eating* that wastes away the body.

αὐτὰρ ὁ <u>μήνιε</u> νηυσὶ παρήμενος ὠκυπόροισιν
διογενὴς Πηλῆος υἱός, πόδας <u>ὠκὺς</u> Ἀχιλλεύς·
<u>οὔτέ ποτ'</u> εἰς ἀγορὴν <u>πωλέσκετο</u> κυδιάνειραν
<u>οὔτέ ποτ'</u> ἐς πόλεμον, ἀλλὰ <u>φθινύθεσκε</u> φίλον <u>κῆρ</u>
αὖθι <u>μένων</u>, <u>ποθέεσκε</u> δ' ἀϋτήν τε πτόλεμόν τε.

But he <u>was raging</u> as he sat beside the <u>swift</u>-moving ships,
the Zeus-born son of Peleus, <u>swift</u>-footed Achilles.
<u>Never</u> to the public assembly where men win glory did he
       <u>continue to go</u>,
<u>never</u> to war, but rather he <u>continually wasted away</u> his own
       heart
while <u>waiting</u> there, and he <u>continually longed</u> for both battle-cry
       and war.

Iliad I 488–492

Note the implication of wasting away through (1) longing which wears out one's heart (κῆρ), and (2) the extended temporality implicit in the anaphoric repetition of the adverb "never" (οὔτέ ποτ', I 490, 491), the repeated use of the iterative infix -σκ- which emphasizes the "continuative" and "repetitive" nature of the actions (πωλέ<u>σκ</u>ετο, I 490; φθινύ<u>σκ</u>θεσκε, I 491; ποθέεσκε, I 492), and the circumstantial participial phrases νηυσὶ παρήμενος "sitting beside the ships" (I 488) and αὖθι μένων "waiting there" (I 492). The emphasis is that Achilles is by the ships and not in battle; instead of being engaged in action where he can be most like himself—that is, where he can exhibit the characteristic behavior for which he received the epithet πόδας ὠκὺς Ἀχιλλεύς "swift-footed Achilles" (I 489)—the Greek hero is out of the action and wasting away, like the swift ships of the Achaeans dragged onto the Trojan shore. At this moment, both Achilles and Achaean ships are inactive; Homer's use of the adverb ὠκύς "swift" in the same metrical position in successive verses—once in the compound ὠκυπόροισιν "swift-moving" (I 488), a participle modifying the ships, and once as the adverb in Achilles' epithet πόδας ὠκύς "swift footed" (I 489)—strikes an ironic tone, for while both sit and wait, neither is particularly "swift." Consider further the description of the Achaean ships grounded and rotting from the long delay and their continued inactivity (II 134–135): both the Achaean ships and Achilles *decay* (σέσηπε, II 135; φθινύσθεσκε, I 491), suggesting that *inactivity* is a constitutive part of decay.[14]

---

[14] See my discussion of the decay of the Achaean ships and the disintegration of the Achaean resolve in chapter 1 above.

1.5. The Diminishment of Human Life or Vitality through Grief, Sorrow, and Weeping

Further analysis of the metaphorical use of *φθι- root verbs in which a person wastes away his or her heart, life, or vitality shows that they are used in context of grief, sorrow, and weeping only in the *Odyssey*, and express the emotions of loss felt by Penelope, Laertes, and Odysseus brought about through their physical separation from a loved one.

In our first example, which we have already investigated in another context, Laertes wastes away by not eating because of his "grief" for his absent grand-son:

> αὐτὰρ νῦν, ἐξ οὗ σύ γε ᾤχεο νηΐ Πύλονδε,
> οὔ πώ μίν φασιν φαγέμεν καὶ πιέμεν αὔτως,
> οὐδ’ ἐπὶ ἔργα ἰδεῖν, ἀλλὰ <u>στοναχῇ</u> τε <u>γόῳ</u> τε
> ἧσται <u>ὀδυρόμενος</u>, <u>φθινύθει</u> δ’ ἀμφ’ ὀστεόφι χρώς.

> But now, since you went away in the ship to Pylos,
> they say [Laertes] has not eaten in this way, nor drunk anything,
> nor looked to his farm, but always in <u>lamentation</u> and <u>mourning</u>
> sits <u>grieving</u>, and the flesh on his bones is <u>wasting away</u>.

Odyssey xvi 142–145

Laertes' failure to eat and the subsequent wearing away of his flesh (χρώς, xvi 145) is attributed to his grief, lamentation, and mourning.

One's lamentation can wear a body down physically, as in the simile describing a woman wasting away her cheeks with her tears as she cries over her dead husband and is led away into slavery.

> ὡς δὲ γυνὴ κλαίῃσι φίλον πόσιν ἀμφιπεσοῦσα,
> ὅς τε ἑῆς πρόσθεν πόλιος λαῶν τε πέσῃσιν,
> ἄστεϊ καὶ τεκέεσσιν ἀμύνων νηλεὲς ἦμαρ·
> ἡ μὲν τὸν θνήσκοντα καὶ ἀσπαίροντα ἰδοῦσα
> ἀμφ’ αὐτῷ χυμένη λίγα κωκύει· οἱ δέ τ’ ὄπισθε
> κόπτοντες δούρεσσι μετάφρενον ἠδὲ καὶ ὤμους
> εἴρερον εἰσανάγουσι, <u>πόνον</u> τ’ ἐχέμεν καὶ <u>ὀϊζύν·</u>
> τῆς δ’ ἐλεεινοτάτῳ <u>ἄχεϊ φθινύθουσι</u> παρειαί.

> As a woman weeps, having fallen upon the body of her dear
>   husband,
> who fell fighting in front of his city and people
> as he tried to beat the pitiless day from his city and children;

she sees him dying and gasping for breath,
and winding her body about him she wails shrilly; but the men
      behind her,
hitting her back and shoulders with their spears,
lead her away into slavery, to have both <u>hard work</u> and <u>wretchedness</u>,
and her cheeks are <u>worn away with the most piteous distress</u>.

                    Odyssey viii 523–530

Here, tears waste away the mourner's cheeks. The noun ὀϊζύν "wretched-ness" often appears in context of *φθι- root verbs that describe a character's emotional suffering.[15]

Elsewhere, Odysseus complains to Kirke that she must set him and his crew on their way, for his crew's constant lamenting is wearing away his heart.

ὦ Κίρκη, τέλεσόν μοι ὑπόσχεσιν, ἥν περ ὑπέστης,
οἴκαδε πεμψέμεναι· <u>θυμὸς</u> δέ μοι ἔσσυται ἤδη
ἠδ' ἄλλων ἑτάρων, οἵ μευ <u>φθινύθουσι</u> φίλον <u>κῆρ</u>
ἀμφ' ἔμ' <u>ὀδυρόμενοι</u>, ὅτε που σύ γε νόσφι γένηαι.

O Kirke, accomplish now the promise you gave me,
that you would see me home. The <u>spirit</u> within me is urgent now,
as also in the rest of my friends, who are <u>wasting away</u> my <u>heart</u>,
<u>lamenting</u> around me, when you are away.

                    Odyssey x 483–486

This passage connects θυμός and κῆρ with a *φθι- verb in the context of lamen-tation (ὀδυρόμενοι, x 486). Here, the lamentation wastes away not Odysseus' physical body (as the tears wasted away the mourning woman's cheeks in the previous example: viii 529–530), but what we might call his "emotional body": his κῆρ is worn down, such that his θυμός urges him to seek help from Kirke.

Further, when Kalypso releases Odysseus, she notes that he need not waste away his vitality (αἰών) any longer with his mourning.

<u>κάμμορε</u>, μή μοι ἔτ' ἐνθάδ' <u>ὀδύρεο</u>, μηδέ τοι <u>αἰὼν</u>
<u>φθινέτω</u>· ἤδη γάρ σε μάλα πρόφρασσ' ἀποπέμψω.

<u>Ill-fated man</u>, no longer <u>mourn</u> here beside me nor let your <u>vitality</u>
<u>waste away</u>, since now I will send you on, with a good will.

                    Odyssey v 160–161

---

[15] Compare *Odyssey* xi 182–183, xiii 337–338, and xvi 38–39 for Penelope's *wretched* days and nights (ὀϊζυραί ... νύκτες τε καὶ ἤματα) which *waste away* (φθίνουσιν) as she weeps (δάκρυ χεούσῃ).

Formerly, Odysseus wasted away his vitality (αἰών, v 160) with his lamenting. His continual sorrow marks him as one with bad fortune (κάμμορε, v 160), an adjective that calls to mind Andromache's speech to Hektor in *Iliad* VI 407–408 where she notes that Hektor's own μένος "might" will destroy him (φθίσει σε, VI 407) and she will be left behind in her bad fortune (ἔμ' ἄμμορον, VI 407).

And finally, Laertes wastes away through his grief over his absent son and dead wife.

> Λαέρτης μὲν ἔτι ζώει, Διὶ δ' εὔχεται αἰεὶ
> θυμὸν ἀπὸ μελέων <u>φθίσθαι</u> οἷσ' ἐν μεγάροισιν·
> ἐκπάγλως γὰρ παιδὸς <u>ὀδύρεται</u> οἰχομένοιο
> κουριδίης τ' ἀλόχοιο δαΐφρονος, ἥ ἑ μάλιστα
> <u>ἤκαχ' ἀποφθιμένη</u> καὶ ἐν <u>ὠμῷ γήραϊ</u> θῆκεν.

> Laertes is still alive, but he prays to Zeus always
> that his spirit <u>waste away</u> from his limbs in his houses.
> For terribly he <u>grieves</u> for his child who is gone away
> and for his wedded virtuous wife, who especially
> <u>pained</u> him when she <u>died</u> and set him <u>in raw old age</u>.

> *Odyssey* xv 353–357

We have already seen this passage in connection with the theme of old age, but it is worth considering again for its mention of "grief" (xv 355) for lost son and wife that causes Laertes' θυμός to wither away (xv 354).

1.6. The Diminishment or Passing of Time

The implication of "diminishment" implicit in φθίω carries over from vegetal and human bodies to other bodies—specifically the moon—which itself then functions as a method to measure passing time. As the moon's body appears to diminish in size, its progress is described as a *wasting away* or a *waning*. Compare *Odyssey* xiv 162, xix 307: τοῦ μὲν φθίνοντος μηνός "at the wasting/waning of the month/moon," describing the time when Odysseus is predicted to make his return and punish the suitors.[16] Compare further the description of how time passes when Odysseus and his crew are visiting with Kirke:

> ἀλλ' ὅτε τέτρατον ἦλθεν ἔτος καὶ ἐπήλυθον ὧραι,
> <u>μηνῶν φθινόντων</u>, περὶ δ' ἤματα πόλλ' ἐτελέσθη ...

---

[16] The Greek words for moon (μήνη) and month (μήν) are cognate: cf. Chantraine 1968–1980:695–696, s.v. μήν.

But when the end of a year came, and the seasons changed,
and the <u>months wasted away</u>, and the long days were accomplished, ...

Odyssey x 469–470[17]

The wasting of the month is intimately connected with the visual experience of seeing the moon *diminish* in size. However, once the verb φθίω has been applied to describe *time* (e.g. a month) instead of the *moon*, it becomes more abstract, such that it can be paired with expressions for "the end of the year coming" or "the long days were accomplished." It is with this sense that the poet describes Penelope's days and nights *wasting away* as she weeps for Odysseus:

καὶ λίην κείνη γε μένει <u>τετληότι θυμῷ</u>
σοῖσιν ἐνὶ μεγάροισιν· <u>ὀϊζυραὶ</u> δέ οἱ αἰεὶ
<u>φθίνουσιν</u> νύκτες τε καὶ ἤματα <u>δάκρυ χεούσῃ</u>.

All too much does she [i.e., Penelope] wait for you with <u>enduring spirit</u>
there in your own palace, and always do both her nights and days,
<u>wretched things</u>, <u>waste away</u> as she sheds a tear.

Odyssey xi 181–183[18]

Time itself, measured day after wretched day, seems ever to waste away for Penelope as she weeps for Odysseus, as if all days become a single day for Penelope in her sorrow, or as if time is passing her by.[19]

Finally, references to passing time may be used rhetorically to indicate the size of the poetic task at hand.

<u>πάσας</u> δ' οὐκ ἂν ἐγὼ μυθήσομαι οὐδ' ὀνομήνω,
<u>ὄσσας</u> ἡρώων ἀλόχους ἴδον ἠδὲ θύγατρας·
πρὶν γάρ κεν καὶ <u>νὺξ φθῖτ' ἄμβροτος</u>. ἀλλὰ καὶ <u>ὥρη</u>
εὕδειν.

But I could not tell or name them <u>all</u>
<u>the many</u> women I saw who were the wives and daughters of heroes,
for before that even the <u>immortal night would waste away</u>. It is now <u>time</u>
to sleep.

Odyssey xi 328–331

---

[17] *Odyssey* x 469–470 = xix 152–153 = xxiv 142–143.
[18] Compare *Odyssey* xiii 337–338 and xvi 38–39.
[19] Compare the description of the melancholic patient's experience of time as analyzed in terms of phenomenological psychology: Straus 1960, 1966, Fuchs 2001a:183–184, 2001b:236–240, 2003:73, 2005a:110, 112–114, 117, 2005b:196–197, Wyllie 2005a:180–183.

Odysseus claims that there are so many names of famous women that *immortal night would waste away*. Passing time is once again seen as "wasting," though not in sorrow, but through the labor of relating "all" the women (πάσας, xi 328), however many (ὅσσας, xi 329) wives and daughters of heroes Odysseus saw in the underworld. For a similar claim about the impossibility of delivering an extraordinarily long catalogue, compare the second invocation of the Muses in the second book of the *Iliad* (II 484–493), especially with its claim that without the Muses' aid, the poet would not be able to go through the whole catalogue,

οὐδ' εἴ μοι δέκα μὲν γλῶσσαι, δέκα δὲ στόματ' εἶεν,
φωνὴ δ' ἄρρηκτος, χάλκεον δέ μοι ἦτορ ἐνείη.

not even if I had ten tongues and ten mouths
and an unbreakable voice, and the heart within me were made of bronze.

Iliad II 489–490

In other words, the difficulty of performing a long catalogue is exaggerated as so strenuous as to wear out multiple singers, an "unbreakable voice," and bronze itself. Just so does Odysseus suggest that his performance of the catalogue of women would exhaust the resources of the night, here emphasized in terms of its durability as "immortal" (ἄμβροτος, xi 331).

1.7. Death in Battle or by Means of Deceit

The verb φθίω can be used rather colorlessly as well to mean simply "die, perish," specifically in battle contexts.[20] One example describes the death of soldiers rather generally:

αἵματι δὲ χθών
δεύετο πορφυρέῳ, τοὶ δ' ἀγχιστῖνοι ἔπιπτον
νεκροί, ὁμοῦ Τρώων καὶ ὑπερμενέων ἐπικούρων
καὶ Δαναῶν· οὐδ' οἳ γὰρ ἀναιμωτί γ' ἐμάχοντο,
παυρότεροι δὲ πολὺ φθίνυθον, μέμνηντο γὰρ αἰεί
ἀλλήλοις καθ' ὅμιλον ἀλεξέμεναι φόνον αἰπύν.

The ground was wet

with red blood, and close together were they falling,

---

[20] Compare *Iliad* VI 32–33: λαοὶ μὲν φθινύθουσι περὶ πτόλιν αἰπύ τε τεῖχος | μαρνάμενοι. Death in battle is associated with "falling" (πίπτειν), "corpses" (νεκροί), "blood" (αἷμα), and "death" (φόνος): cf. XVII 360–365.

the corpses of the Trojans, together with those of their very-mighty allies
and those of the Danaäns. For <u>not without bloodletting</u> were they fighting,
although far fewer [of the Danaäns] <u>were dying</u>, for they remembered
always
to defend one another throughout their massed formation from sheer
death.

Iliad XVII 360–365

In battle scenes, φθινύθω has basic sense of die. It is difficult to see any specific "vegetal" imagery in this passage, although the reference to the ground being wet (χθὼν | δεύετο, XVII 360–361) with blood (αἵματι, XVII 360) does suggest a kind of agricultural image of watering the earth in order to nourish plant life. Here, however, the fluid points more to wasting vitality than to nurturing it.

In another passage, Hektor chides Paris for refraining from battle when so many people are perishing (φθινύθουσι) on his account (σέο δ' εἵνεκ', VI 326–331). One may also "perish" at the hands of his enemy, as at VIII 359 which describes Hektor "perishing under the hands of the Argives in his father's country" (χερσὶν ὑπ' Ἀργείων φθίμενος ἐν πατρίδι γαίη). Alternatively, one may "perish" beneath his enemy's spear, as when Patroklos wonders whether the Achaeans will be able to hold back Hektor, under whose spear they will perish (φθίσονται, XI 820). The participle may simply indicate that someone is "dead," as at XVI 581 where Patroklos feels grief for his <u>dead</u> companion (Πατρόκλῳ δ' ἄρ' ἄχος γένετο <u>φθιμένου</u> ἑτάροιο), or at *Odyssey* xi 356–358 where Odysseus explains to Ajax how the Achaeans continually grieved for him when he was <u>dead</u> (ἀχνύμεθα <u>φθιμένοιο</u> διαμπερές). Further, a simile likening Achilles to a lion uses φθίω "to cause to wither" as a synonym for πέφνω "to kill":

ἑὲ δ' αὐτὸν ἐποτρύνει μαχέσασθαι,
γλαυκιόων δ' ἰθὺς φέρεται μένει, ἤν τινα <u>πέφνῃ</u>
ἀνδρῶν, ἢ αὐτὸς <u>φθίεται</u> πρώτῳ ἐν ὁμίλῳ.

> he rouses himself to fight,
> and with glowering eyes he is carried straight forward with
> might, if he <u>may kill</u>
> someone of the men, or is himself <u>killed</u> in the first onrush.

Iliad XX 171–173

And finally, one may be driven on to death by one's own eagerness for battle, as Andromache tells Hektor that his μένος "might" will lead to his ruin (φθίσει σε, VI 407–413)—that is, it will cause him to wither away, for he cannot hold out against so many Achaeans. It remains implicit that Hektor's death will cause Andromache to "wither away" as well through sorrow (ἄχεα).[21]

In addition to "being killed in battle," the verb φθίω may be used to describe someone being killed through deceit (δόλος), as we find once in the *Odyssey*:

> οἱ δέ τοι αὐτίκ' ἰόντι <u>κακὰ φράσσονται</u> ὀπίσσω,
> ὥς κε <u>δόλῳ φθίῃς</u>, τάδε δ' αὐτοὶ <u>πάντα δάσωνται</u>.

> But as soon as you go, these men will <u>devise evils</u> against you
>   hereafter,
> so that you may <u>perish by guile</u>, and they may <u>divide all</u>
>   <u>that is yours.</u>

> *Odyssey* ii 367–368

Athena warns Telemachus that the suitors will attempt to kill him in secret when he returns from his voyage to Pylos and Mycenae.

1.8. Reference to the Dead in the Underworld

Perhaps as an extension of the sense of φθίω to indicate "perish, die," the passive participle of φθίω (οἱ φθιμένοι) is used to refer to the inhabitants of the underworld.

> <u>λώβη</u> γὰρ τάδε γ' ἐστὶ καὶ ἐσσομένοισι πυθέσθαι,
> εἰ δὴ μὴ παίδων τε κασιγνήτων τε φονῆας
> τεισόμεθ'· οὐκ ἂν ἐμοί γε μετὰ φρεσὶν ἡδὺ γένοιτο
> ζωέμεν, ἀλλὰ τάχιστα θανὼν <u>φθιμένοισι</u> μετείην.

> For these things are a <u>shame</u> even for men of the future to learn about,
> if indeed we don't take revenge for the murder of our sons and
>   brothers.
> There would not be any sweetness in heart—for me, at least—
> to go on living, but dying quickly, I would wish to be among <u>the dead</u>.

> *Odyssey* xxiv 433–436

The families of the murdered suitors plan revenge on Odysseus and his family: failure to avenge the deaths of their sons and brothers would be so shameful that they would rather be "among the dead" (φθιμένοισι μετείην, xxiv 346).

---

[21] Compare Hektor's reply to Andromache at VI 462–463: σοὶ δ' αὖ νέον ἔσσεται <u>ἄλγος</u> | χήτεϊ τοιοῦδ' ἀνδρὸς ἀμύνειν δούλιον ἦμαρ, "you will have a new <u>grief</u>, to be the widow of such a man as could fight back your day of slavery."

The text suggests a sense in which shame itself may cause a body to *waste away*, such that a person who experiences extreme shame is reduced to the status of the dead.[22]

1.9. Curse—Let Someone Perish

The use of φθίω to mean "be dead" receives one further variation: it is used as a formula for cursing someone—literally, wishing that someone may perish.

> τούσδε δ' ἔα φθινύθειν, ἕνα καὶ δύο, τοί κεν Ἀχαιῶν
> νόσφιν βουλεύωσ'.

> Let those men perish, one and two, those men of the Achaeans
> who make plans apart.

Iliad II 346–347

In this passage, Nestor curses those one or two Achaeans, whoever they are, who foster ideas different from the group—namely, as Nestor makes clear in the following verses—those who want to return to Argos before learning whether Zeus' promise that Troy would be captured in the tenth year is true or false.[23]

1.10. Compound Cognates[24]

In addition to the simple root forms of φθίω, φθίνω, φθινύθω, there are several compound cognate nouns, adjectives, and verbs, which I list here with citations.

1. ἀποφθίω/ἀποφθινύθω < ἀπό "away" + φθίω/φθινύθω = "to waste away, perish." This compound is semantically indistinguishable from the pure root verb: compare V 643 and XVI 540 which take θυμός as the accusative of respect—one wastes away "with respect to his life."

2. ἐκφθίω < ἐκ "out of" + φθίω = "to waste away from out of," used twice in the *Odyssey* to describe the supply of wine and food on Odysseus' ships: ix 163 (the wine has not yet been wasted away from within the ships), xii 329 (the food in the ships was all wasted away).

3. καταφθίω < κατά "down, throughout, thoroughly" + φθίω = "to cause to waste away, perish," a compound which appears in the active only

---

22 See chapter 2 above (with bibliography) above on the representation of shame as devouring one's body like dogs that feast upon the corpses of the dead. On the temporal experience of shame and the awareness of one's own body as "corporeal," see Fuchs 2001b and 2005a.

23 See Kirk 1985:152 for a useful discussion of Nestor's speech here.

24 Chantraine 1968–1980:1200–1201.

once (v 341), and otherwise appears in the passive, mostly indicating simply that a person is "dead" (II 288, iii 196, xi 491).

4. φθισήνωρ < φθίω + ἀνήρ "man" = "man-destroying," used only as an epithet of πόλεμος "war": II 833, IX 604, X 78, XI 331, XIV 43.

5. φθισίμβροτος < φθίω + (μ)βροτός = "mortal-destroying," used as an epithet of μάχη "battle" at XIII 339, and as an epithet of Athene's *aegis* at xxii 297.

6. ἄφθιτος < ἀ- + φθιτος = "unwithered." The adjective formed with the alpha privative is used primarily of the works of Hephaistos' divine craftsmanship: Agamemnon's σκῆπτρον "scepter" (II 46, 186), Hera's θρόνος "throne" (XIV 238), the rims of the wheels of her chariot (V 724), Hephaistos' home (XVIII 370), and Poseidon's home (XIII 22) are all designated by the adjective ἄφθιτος, mostly with the formulaic line ending ἄφθιτον αἰεί # "continually unwithered."[25] In each of these cases, the god's craft is made of metal (gold, bronze), which is an indication of its enduring quality; his craft renders his products "beautiful," particularly because of their "starry" decorations.[26] The adjective ἄφθιτος is also used to describe the remarkably productive grapevines on the island of the Cyclopes (ἄφθιτοι ἄμπελοι εἶεν #, ix 133), Zeus' divine thoughts (Ζεὺς ἄφθιτα μήδεα εἰδώς #, XXIV 88, cf. Hesiod *Theogony* 545, 550, 561, frr. 141.26, 234.2 M-W),[27]

[25] The line-final formulaic ἄφθιτον / ἄφθιτα αἰεί # appears four times in the *Iliad*: II 46, 186, XIV 238, XIII 22. For different metrical positions of ἄφθιτος in Homeric epic, see *Iliad* XVIII 369–371: Ἡφαίστου δ' ἵκανε δόμον Θέτις ἀργυρόπεζα | ἄφθιτον ἀστερόεντα μεταπρεπέ' ἀθανάτοισι | χάλκεον, ὅν ῥ' αὐτὸς ποιήσατο κυλλοποδίων, "Thetis of the silver feet arrived at Hephaistos' house, unwithered, starry, shining among the immortals, made of bronze, which the club-footed god himself made"; and V 274–275: τῶν ἤτοι χρυσέη ἴτυς ἄφθιτος, αὐτὰρ ὕπερθεν | χάλκε' ἐπίσσωτρα προσαρηρότα, θαῦμα ἰδέσθαι, "In truth, the rim of them [i.e., the wheels of Hera's chariot] is unwithered gold, but upon it are fitted bronze tires, a wonder to behold."

[26] In the nine uses of the adjective ἀστερόεις "starry" in the *Iliad* (IV 44, V 769 = VIII 46, VI 108, XV 371, XVI 134, XVIII 370, XIX 128, 130), four in the *Odyssey* (ix 527, xi 17, xii 380, xx 113), and three in the *Homeric Hymns* (Hymn to Demeter 33, Homeric Hymn 30.17, Homeric Hymn 31.3), the adjective is regularly used in the line-final formulaic οὐρανὸν ἀστερόεντα (2x *Il.*, 3x *Od.*, 1x *h. Hom.*) preceded by εἰς or καί, but flexible enough to work in the genitive (οὐρανοῦ ἀστερόεντος, 4x *Il.*, 1x *Od.*, 2x *h. Hom.*) and dative (οὐρανῷ ἀστερόεντι, 1x *Il.*). Only twice does the adjective modify something other than οὐρανός "heaven": at *Iliad* XVIII 370 Hephaistos' δόμος "home" is said to be "starry," and at *Iliad* XVI 134, Peleus' armor is called "starry" as Patroklos puts it on to go into battle. Peleus' armor was a gift from the gods (cf. XVII 194–198, XVIII 84–85) presented on the day he married the goddess Thetis, and said to be the craftsmanship of Hephaistos (cf. Paton 1912:1 with n2, citing Eustathius). In short, then, the adjective "starry," applied only to the heavens themselves and twice to works of Hephaistos' craftsmanship, helps to define the long-lasting (ἄφθιτον, ἄμβροτα) quality of divine craft.

[27] Nagy 1974:Appendix A provides a different interpretation, suggesting the phrase Ζεὺς ἄφθιτα μήδεα εἰδώς indicates "Zeus' unfailing genitals." In other words, the tradition is here evaluating Zeus' own sexual productivity in terms of an unfailing stream.

and, of course, Achilles' "unwithered fame" (κλέος ἄφθιτον ἔσται #, IX 413). In her discussion of the distribution of ἄφθιτος in Homer, Margalit Finkelberg has noted, "Only one out of the nine cases in which ἄφθιτος is found in Homer, κλέος ἄφθιτον at *Il.* 9.413, does not belong to the sphere of divine and marvelous, and only two, κλέος ἄφθιτον again and ἄφθιτα μήδεα at 24.88, fall into the sphere of incorporeal objects" (Finkelberg 2007:346n19).

The phrase κλέος ἄφθιτον ἔσται occurs only here in Homer, though we find similar formulations in κλέος οὔποτε ὀλεῖται "fame will never be lost" (II 325, VII 91, xxiv 196) and ἄσβεστον κλέος εἴη "fame may be unquenched" (iv 584, vii 333), as well as phrases that refer to the extent of a hero's fame: κλέος οὐρανὸν ἵκει / κλέος οὐρανὸν εὐρὺν ἱκάνει "fame reaches heaven / fame reaches wide heaven" (VIII 192, viii 74, ix 20, xix 108), ὑπουράνιον κλέος "heaven-reaching fame" (X 212, ix 264.), μέγα κλέος "great fame" (VI 446, XI 21, XVII 131, i 240, ii 125, xiv 340, xvi 241, xxiv 33), and κλέος εὐρύ "wide fame" (i 344, iii 83, 204, iv 726, 816, xix 333, xxiii 137).[28] It would seem, then, that Achilles' κλέος ἄφθιτον is part of a larger traditional theme of heroic fame in Indo-European poetry— though we find traces of the theme in ancient Near Eastern literature as well.[29]

7. It is worthwhile to point out a further compound not of φθίνω "wither, fade, decay, perish," but of φθείρω "destroy": θυμοφθόρος < θυμός + φθόρος = "life-destroying": *Iliad* VI 169 (of the σῆμα "signs" in Bellerophon's tablets), *Odyssey* ii 329 (of φάρμακα "drugs"), iv 716 (of ἄχος

---

[28] For κλέος ἄφθιτον outside of Homer, see Hesiod fr. 70 M-W, Sappho fr. 44.4 L-P, Ibycus fr. 151.47–48 PMG, and Theognis fr. 245 W, with discussion by Floyd 1980 on these post-Homeric uses of the phrase. It cannot be determined whether these uses are "borrowings" of Homer or an epic tradition, or independent uses of the phrase within non-epic poetic genres.

[29] See Nagy 1974 (following Kuhn, who identified an equivalent of the "formula" κλέος ἄφθιτον in the Vedic *śrávaḥ ... ákṣitam*) on κλέος ἄφθιτον as an Indo-European formula, such that the other uses outside of Homer are explained by the common tradition and not by any specific contact or knowledge of the Homeric epics. See also Schmidt 1967:61–102, esp. 61–70, Watkins 1995:173–178, and West 2007:396–410 on the theme of "undying fame" in Indo-European poetry. Finkelberg (1986) argued to the contrary that κλέος ἄφθιτον ἔσται is not a proper "formula" nor an Indo-European borrowing, but an *"ad hoc* innovation" by the poet (5) based on two established formulae: κλέος οὔποτ' ὀλεῖται # (3x), and u u ἄφθιτον αἰεί # (4x) (Finkelberg 1986:4–5, 2007:344–349). Finkelberg's arguments have been accepted by Olson 1995:224–227, but effectively refuted by A. Edwards 1988, Nagy 1990a:122n3, 1990b:244n126, and, most recently, Volk 2002— although see Finkelberg 2007 for a strengthened restatement of her 1986 article. Finkelberg 1986, 2007 and Volk 2002 provide citations of earlier literature on the topic. Important also is Risch's demonstration of compound names in *-kleos* in Linear B, including perhaps a shortened form of *Akᵂhthitoklewejja, which Risch understands as a compound of ἄφθιτον and κλέος (Risch 1987:10–11): here we perhaps have another attestation of *kleos aphthiton* attested in Mycenaean Greek, suggesting the continuity of a traditional Indo-European heroic epic. On "heroic fame" in Near Eastern poetry, see West 1997:514–515.

"grief"), x 363 (of κάματον "work, labor"). The verb φθείρω is cognate with Sanskrit root *kṣar- "flow, melt away, perish" (as opposed to Sanskrit *kṣi- "perish," which is cognate with φθίνω), but the semantics of φθείρω and φθίνω (related to *kṣar- and *kṣi-, respectively) are close, and some scholars have suggested that they are in fact related (cf. Burrow 1959b:262).

The compounds of φθίω all exhibit the same characteristics as the simple verb root itself. Organic matter withers away under the effect of pain, grief, work, and perhaps also poisonous drugs. The single adjective which attempts to negate the effect of this wasting—ἄφθιτος—deals mostly with works which are not, or no longer, organic, such as Agamemnon's σκῆπτρον which has been cut from a tree and covered in gold so that it can no longer grow or shrink (cf. *Iliad* I 234–237).[30] The metallic composition of Hephaistos' craftwork suggests the characteristic perdurative nature of these items, yet does not guarantee that they are themselves everlasting and beyond any temporal measure.[31] As I show in chapter 3 above, the *Iliad* represents other material works (the Trojan defensive walls) made by the gods (Poseidon, Apollo) as durable, but eventually breakable, even though they were constructed to be ἄρρηκτος. I argue that Homer's use of ἄρρηκτος in the context of the Trojan Wall does not imply not the actual *unbreakability* of the Trojan wall, but rather the wall's temporal condition of remaining *unbroken*, but only for the time being; although it does not collapse within the narrative bounds of the *Iliad*, the very tradition to which the *Iliad* belongs necessitates its collapse. So too, I suggest, does the adjective ἄφθιτον describe Zeus' counsels and Achilles' fame—that is to say, they have the same temporally conditioned status as Hephaistos' works of art. Zeus' counsels are unfailing only because they have not yet failed; Achilles fame is unwithering only because it has not yet withered (cf. Benveniste 1975:166, quoted in the Introduction above). They have so far survived the temporal degeneration implied by the *φθι- verbal root, but their survival is itself temporally conditioned. It is long lasting, to be sure, but not permanent.

---

[30] See the seminal discussion of Agamemnon's σκῆπτρον and its characterization as ἄφθιτον in Nagy 1999:179–180 (Ch. 10§8).

[31] Compare Floyd 1980, arguing that the objects modified by the compound adjectival root *a-kṣi- in Sanskrit (cognate with Greek *ἀ-φθι-) do not in fact appear to be "everlasting." See further Nagy's reply (1981).

2. σήπω "to rot, decay"[32]

In comparison with φθίω/φθίνω/φθινύθω, the verb σήπω is far more restricted in usage. It appears only three times in Homeric epic, and on each occasion describes the decay of organic bodies—the wooden planks of the Achaeans' ships, and the bodies of Patroklos and Hektor. In the first passage describing the rotting of the ship's wooden planks, Homer emphasizes the passage of time (nine years) during which the timber and the cables that hold the planks together have become ruined.

ἐννέα δὴ βεβάασι Διὸς μεγάλου ἐνιαυτοί,
καὶ δὴ δοῦρα σέσηπε νεῶν καὶ σπάρτα λέλυνται.

Indeed, nine years of great Zeus have gone by,
and indeed the wooden planks of our ships have rotted and the cables are
destroyed.

Iliad II 134–135

The implication of the rotting of wood and cables—as I have argued at length in chapter 1 above—is that the ships have begun to fall apart at their joints. The cohesion between the separate elements of the compound bodies of ship and rope has weakened, and the ships are literally disintegrating before the Achaeans' eyes.

In the two remaining Homeric uses of σήπω to describe the decay of the bodies of fallen heroes, we find a similar implication of a body that is no longer intact and can no longer maintain its pristine integrity. First, Achilles explains his reasons for hesitating to return to battle at once—he fears for the body of his companion Patroklos, lest it be defiled by maggots that enter the wounds:

νῦν δ' ἤτοι μὲν ἐγὼ θωρήξομαι· ἀλλὰ μάλ' αἰνῶς
δείδω, μή μοι τόφρα Μενοιτίου ἄλκιμον υἱόν
μυῖαι καδδῦσαι κατὰ χαλκοτύπους ὠτειλάς
εὐλὰς ἐγγείνωνται, ἀεικίσσωσι δὲ νεκρόν—
ἐκ δ' αἰὼν πέφαται—κατὰ δὲ χρόα πάντα σαπήῃ.

And now, in truth, I tell you, I will arm myself. But very terribly
am I afraid lest in the meantime the flies enter

---

[32] See Ebeling 1963:II.275, s.v. σήπω ("*putrefacio*"), Frisk 1973–1979:II.696–697 ("'*verfaulen, faul werden*'; *Akt. 'faulen machen*'"), Chantraine 1968–1980:998–99 ("*être pourri, corrompu*"), and Liddell, Scott, and Jones 1996:1594. The etymology of this verb is obscure.

Menoitios' strong son, <u>down through the wounds beaten into him by
    bronze,</u>
and breed <u>maggots</u>, and do unbefitting things to the <u>corpse—</u>
now that <u>his life has been slain</u> out of him—and that all <u>his flesh may
    completely</u> <u>rot</u>.

Iliad XIX 23–27

Here, Achilles speaks to Thetis about his fears that the body of Patroklos will
rot while Achilles dons his armor and fights Hektor. There is a stark contrast
between the immortal armor that Achilles is to put on and the pathetic state
of Patroklos' very mortal body which is now open to the flies to become a
breeding ground for maggots. For Patroklos' body has been penetrated by
bronze weapons: flies may now enter his καλκοτύπους ὠτειλάς "bronze-struck
wounds" (XIX 25). It is through these openings that corruption would enter, if
Thetis did not artificially—through the application of *nektar* and *ambrosia*—close
the corpse's openings (XIX 29–39).[33] We find the same situation in the case of
Hektor, as Hermes describes the status of the corpse to Priam:

δυωδεκάτη δέ οἱ ἠώς
κειμένῳ, οὐδέ τί οἱ <u>χρὼς σήπεται</u>, οὐδέ μιν <u>εὐλαί</u>
ἔσθουσ', αἵ ῥά τε φῶτας ἀρηϊφάτους κατέδουσιν.
[...]
    θηοῖό κεν αὐτὸς ἐπελθών,
οἷον ἐερσήεις κεῖται, περὶ δ' αἷμα νένιπται,
  οὐδέ ποθι μιαρός· <u>σὺν δ' ἕλκεα πάντα μέμυκεν,</u>
ὅσσ' <u>ἐτύπη</u>· πολέες γὰρ ἐν αὐτῷ <u>χαλκὸν</u> ἔλασσαν.

    But it is the twelfth dawn for him
lying there, but neither is his <u>flesh rotted</u> at all, nor do <u>maggots</u>
eat him, which indeed always devour mortals slain in battle.
[...]
    You yourself can look in wonder when you go there,
how he lies fresh with dew, and the blood all around has been washed
    from him,
nor is he defiled anywhere. <u>All the wounds have closed up</u>
where he was <u>struck</u>; for many drove <u>bronze</u> into him.

Iliad XXIV 412–415, 418–421

---

[33] See my discussion at chapter 2 above.

The εὐλαί "maggots" have *not yet* entered the body and begun to devour it, for Hektor's wounds—struck (ἐτύπη, XXIV 421) into him when many drove their bronze weapons (χαλκόν, XXIV 421) into him (compare Patroklos' καλκοτύπους "bronze-struck" wounds, XIX 25)—have been magically *closed* (σὺν ... μέμυκεν, XXIV 420) by the *ambrosia* Aphrodite instilled into his body (XXIII 185–187).[34]

In short, then, the natural process of decay indicated by the verb σήπω appears to lead to the disintegration of organic bodies by attacking those bodies at joints and openings—the places where life-force must be expended to maintain strict cohesion of parts and an intact surface. Once that surface has been broken and those joints weakened, however, corruption slips inside and causes the deterioration of the body from within. In the case of the mortal bodies of Patroklos and Hektor, it is only the divine interference of the gods and their application of immortal and immortalizing products—*nektar* and *ambrosia*—that virtually seal the body from decay for a given period of time.

3. πύθω "cause to rot, rot, putrefy"[35]

The verb πύθω occurs four times in Homer, always describing the physical decay of human remains, often associated with the purification of a body in the damp earth or other wet environment. The first three uses all describe the rotting of human bones (ὀστέα). In the first passage, Agamemnon laments that Menelaus, whom he believes to be mortally wounded by Pandarus's arrow (IV 148–149), will perish and his bones will be left behind to rot in Troy, while the war will now be given up to Agamemnon's shame.

> καί κεν ἐλέγχιστος πολυδίψιον Ἄργος ἱκοίμην.
> αὐτίκα γὰρ μνήσονται Ἀχαιοὶ πατρίδος αἴης,
> κὰδ δέ κεν εὐχωλὴν Πριάμῳ καὶ Τρωσὶ λίποιμεν
> Ἀργείην Ἑλένην· <u>σέο δ' ὀστέα πύσει ἄρουρα</u>
> κειμένου ἐν Τροίῃ ἀτελευτήτῳ ἐπὶ ἔργῳ.

> And I would return most blameworthy to very thirsty Argos.
> For at once the Achaeans will remember the land of their fathers,
> and we would leave behind Argive Helen for Priam and the Trojans
> to be their triumph. <u>But the ploughland will rot your bones</u>
> as you lie dead in Troy with your task unaccomplished.[36]

Iliad IV 171–175

---

[34] See my discussion at chapter 2 above.

[35] See Ebeling 1963:II.248, Pokorny 1959, s.v. pŭ-/peu̯ə-, Frisk 1973–1979:II.621–622, Chantraine 1968–1980:952–953, Cunliffe 1963:352, Liddell, Scott, and Jones 1996:1551–1552, s.v. πύθομαι.

[36] I translate ἀτελευτήτῳ ἐπὶ ἔργῳ following Cunliffe 1963:143, s.v. ἐπί II (f).

The collocation of πύθω with the term for plowed fields (ἄρουρα, IV 174) may suggest a cognitive link between physical decay and the natural pattern of vegetal life, especially that cultivated through agriculture: crops grow, diminish, and eventually decay. But most significant for our study here is the implication that if the Achaeans leave, there will be none left to care for the dead; the Argives will remember (μνήσονται, IV 172) their own homelands, not Menelaus and his unaccomplished labors (ἀτελευτήτῳ ἐπὶ ἔργῳ).

Mention of "plowland" (ἄρουρα, IV 174) seems to imply the dampness of the earth which aids in the putrefaction of the bones, as is also implied in a passage from the pseudo-Hesiodic *Shield of Herakles*:

τῶν καὶ ψυχαὶ μὲν χθόνα δύνουσ' Ἄιδος εἴσω
αὐτῶν, ὀστέα δέ σφι περὶ ῥινοῖο <u>σαπείσης</u>
Σειρίου ἀζαλέοιο κελαινῇ <u>πύθεται</u> αἴῃ.

The souls of these men [sc. men who wage war against Zeus] go down
        beneath the earth into the house of Hades
and when the flesh <u>has rotted</u> all around, their bones
<u>putrefy</u> in the dark earth with parching Sirius above.

Shield of Herakles 151–153, Most

The souls (ψυχαι, 151) of the dead enter Hades, but their bodies are left behind to rot: their skin rots away (ῥινοῖο σαπείσης, 152) and their bones putrefy (ὀστέα ... πύθεται, 152–153) within the "dark earth" (μαλαίνη ... αἴῃ, 153). I interpret the reference to "parching Sirius" (Σειρίου ἀζαλέοιο, 153) to mean that we are to imagine that the earth itself is warm from the Dog Star's heat. Note that that the underworld (Tartaros, Hades) is regularly represented as "moldy" and "damp" in Greek epic; it is a place dark, damp, and full of mold and decay, as noted by the epithets εὐρώεις "moldy, full of decay"[37] and ἠερόεις "misty."[38] The combination

---

[37] For Hades described as εὐρώεις "moldy, full of decay," see *Iliad* XX 65, *Odyssey* x 512, xxiii 322, xxiv 10, Hesiod *Works and Days* 153. For Tartaros described as εὐρώεις "moldy, full of decay," see Hesiod *Theogony* 731, 739 = 810, with commentary by West 1966:361, noting the underworld "as a place of physical decay." Compare *Odyssey* xxiv 10 for the "moldy path" (εὐρώεντα κέλευθα), a euphemism for death, and *Hymn to Demeter* 482 "under the dank darkness" (ὑπὸ ζόφῳ εὐρώεντι). See further Chantraine 1968–1980:388, s.v. εὐρώς, and Liddell, Scott, and Jones 1996:731, s.v. εὐρώεις. Edwards 1991:295 (at *Iliad* XX 65–66) notes that "εὐρώεις (etc.) is used in archaic epic only of the Underworld"; Heubeck 1989:70 (at *Odyssey* x 512) glosses εὐρώεντα as "abounding in mold, decay."

[38] For Tartaros described as ἠερόεις "misty," see *Iliad* VIII 13, Hesiod *Theogony* 119. Compare *Iliad* XV 191 for the "gloominess of the underworld" (ζόφος); *Odyssey* xx 64 for the "misty path" (ἠερόεντα κέλευθα), a euphemism for death. See Chantraine 1968–1980:26–27, s.v. ἀήρ, Liddell, Scott, and Jones 1996:766, s.v. ἠερόεις.

of heat and damp provided in *Shield of Herakles* 152–153 provides the perfect condition for decay.[39] In sum, πύθομαι appears to be associated particularly with damp or wet aspects of decay: hence, "to induce putrefaction."

In another passage, Telemachus complains to his visitor (Athena in disguise) that the suitors are eating up the livelihood of his father who has died and whose bones are rotting in the rain or the sea:

τούτοισιν μὲν ταῦτα μέλει, κίθαρις καὶ ἀοιδή,
ῥεῖ᾽, ἐπεὶ ἀλλότριον βίοτον νήποινον ἔδουσιν,
ἀνέρος, οὗ δή που <u>λεύκ᾽ ὀστέα πύθεται ὄμβρῳ</u>
κείμεν᾽ ἐπ᾽ ἠπείρου, ἢ <u>εἰν ἁλὶ κῦμα</u> κυλίνδει.

For these things are an easy care to them, the lyre and epic
       poetry,
since they are eating up the livelihood of another with impunity,
of a man whose <u>white bones</u>, I suppose, <u>are putrefying in the rain</u>
as they lie on the shore, or a <u>wave</u> rolls them about <u>in the salt sea</u>.

Odyssey i 159–162

Telemachus imagines his father's white bones rotting in the rain, or being rolled about in the sea—both images involve his father's mortal remains exposed and lacking proper burial, and hence subject to the elements. Note especially the association with water, both rain (ὄμβρῳ, i 161) and sea (ἁλί, i 162), once again indicating that the verb πύθω "rot" is intimately connected with liquid and liquefaction.[40]

Elsewhere Kirke warns Odysseus about sailing too near to the Sirens in terms of the death and decay that await those who listen to their song.

Σειρῆνας μὲν πρῶτον ἀφίξεαι, αἵ ῥά τε πάντας
ἀνθρώπους θέλγουσιν, ὅ τίς σφεας εἰσαφίκηται.
ὅς τις ἀϊδρείῃ πελάσῃ καὶ φθόγγον ἀκούσῃ
Σειρήνων, τῷ δ᾽ οὔ τι γυνὴ καὶ νήπια τέκνα
οἴκαδε νοστήσαντι παρίσταται οὐδὲ γάνυνται,
ἀλλά τε Σειρῆνες λιγυρῇ θέλγουσιν ἀοιδῇ,

---

[39] Consider the Scholia vetera to Hesiod *Works and Days* 782a2–3 (Pertusi) which explains that "The sixteenth day of the month is not favorable for plants, for the light of the moon, <u>since it is warm, is septic</u> [i.e., causes them to rot]" (ἡ ἑκκαιδεκάτη οὐκ ἐπιτηδεία τοῖς φυτοῖς· τὸ γὰρ τῆς σελήνης φῶς <u>χλιαρὸν</u> ὂν σηπτικόν ἐστι). The combination of warmth and dampness proves destructive for organic bodies.

[40] Compare Hesiod *Works and Days* for the advice that during the rainy winter, one should haul a ship onto dry land (νῆα δ᾽ ἐπ᾽ ἠπείρου ἐρύσαι, 624) and draw out the ship's bilge plug (χείμαρον ἐξερύσας, 626) so that rain doesn't cause it to putrefy (ἵνα μὴ πύθη Διὸς ὄμβρος, 626).

ἥμεναι ἐν λειμῶνι· πολὺς δ' ἀμφ' <u>ὀστεόφιν</u> θίς
ἀνδρῶν <u>πυθομένων</u>, περὶ δὲ <u>ῥινοὶ μινύθουσιν</u>.

First, you will reach the Sirens, who indeed always enchant
all men, whoever comes upon them.
Whoever without knowing draws near and listens to the voice
of the Sirens, for that man not at all do his wife and his helpless children
stand about him as he returns home nor are they gladdened by him,
but the Sirens enchant him with their high-pitched epic poetry,
while they sit on their meadow. And there is a great heap all about with
       the <u>bones</u>
of <u>rotting</u> men, and their <u>skins shrink</u> around them.

Odyssey xii 39–46

The Sirens' song enchants men to stop their voyage and listen to their song, but the wait is deadly. Men perish, and the meadow all around the Sirens is littered with piles of the bones of their rotting corpses. Once again we find rotting connected with ὄστεα "bones"—here, a great pile of bones (πολὺς ... ὀστεόφιν θίς, xii 45). Further, Homer offers an image of human skin growing smaller in size (μινύθουσιν, xii 46); it is no longer big enough to cover the bones. The dead lack burial—they are lost to the world, forgotten and uncared for by loved ones, for their loved ones will no longer surround them and offer them care (τῷ δ' οὔ τι ... παρίσταται, xii 43); they will no loner return home (τῷ δ' οὔ τι ... οἴκαδε νοστήσαντι, xii 42–43).

In our last passage, Diomedes verbally attacks Paris who has just wounded him with an arrow in his foot. Diomedes claims that Paris' arrow has only "scratched" (ἐπιγράψας) his foot, whereas Diomedes' spear kills a man outright:

καὶ εἴ κ' ὀλίγον περ ἐπαύρῃ,
ὀξὺ βέλος πέλεται, καὶ <u>ἀκήριον</u> αἶψα τίθησι.
τοῦ δὲ γυναικὸς μέν τ' ἀμφίδρυφοί εἰσι παρειαί,
παῖδες δ' ὀρφανικοί· ὃ δέ θ' <u>αἵματι γαῖαν ἐρεύθων</u>
<u>πύθεται</u>, <u>οἰωνοὶ</u> δὲ περὶ πλέες ἠὲ γυναῖκες.

even if it touches him only a little,
the missile is sharp, and at once renders him <u>lifeless</u>.
And the cheeks of his wife are torn on both sides in mourning,
and his children are orphans, and he, while <u>reddening the earth with his blood</u>,
<u>putrefies</u>, and there are more <u>birds</u> around him than women.

Iliad XI 391–395

Here Diomedes indicates a connection between the blood pouring from a life-less body and the process of decay: here too we find a reference to liquid in the form of blood that reddens the earth (αἵματι γαῖαν ἐρεύθων, XI 394). As in the previous passage, rotting is connected with a lack of proper burial rites: instead of women standing around the body ready to care for the dead (περί, XI 395), there are vultures ready to devour his corpse (οἰωνοὶ δὲ περὶ πλέες, XI 395).[41]

The four Homeric uses of πύθω all point to the fear of the fate of the human body if left uncared for and unburied/unburned. The body ceases to be what it was—solid, supple, intact—and rots away into nothing but tatters of flesh, a meal for scavengers, and bones bleached white in the sun. I believe the emphasis on "purification" may be especially significant in this context, for, as I argue in chapter 4 above, the funeral rites performed for the dead—cremation followed by a secondary burial of the bones and the erection of a mound of earth (τύμβος) and gravemarker (στήλη)—are represented as a means by which to reduce the mortal part of man's body into something more durable. The passages which describe the "putrefaction" of bones, then—the process of the corruption of bones as solid body itself molders and loses its physical rigidity, more liquid now than solid, or the shrinking of skin from around bones—points to the very fear of temporal vulnerability that underlies both the attempt to stabilize human remains through long-lasting architectural constructions and memorializing poetic compositions.

4. σκέλλω "to dry up"[42]

The verb σκέλλω appears once in the Homeric corpus, when Homer describes how Apollo protects Hektor's corpse from being "dried out" by the sun by positioning a dark cloud overhead.

> ὣς φάτ' ἀπειλήσας· τὸν δ' οὐ κύνες ἀμφεπένοντο,
> ἀλλὰ κύνας μὲν ἄλαλκε Διὸς θυγάτηρ Ἀφροδίτη
> ἤματα καὶ νύκτας, ῥοδόεντι δὲ χρῖεν ἐλαίῳ
> ἀμβροσίῳ, ἵνα μή μιν ἀποδρύφοι ἑλκυστάζων.
> τῷ δ' ἐπὶ <u>κυάνεον νέφος</u> ἤγαγε Φοῖβος Ἀπόλλων
> οὐρανόθεν πεδίον δέ, <u>κάλυψε</u> δὲ χῶρον ἅπαντα

---

[41] See Vermeule 1979:103–109 with figures 21–23 on the Iliadic imagery of birds and dogs devouring dead, unburied men.

[42] See Ebeling 1963:II.280, Liddell, Scott, and Jones 1996:1606, s.v. σκέλλω, Frisk 1973–1979:II.722–723, Chantraine 1968–1980:1012–1013, s.v. σκέλλομαι. Compare ἐνσκέλλω "to dry or wither up" used of wood/timber ("to be dry, seasoned") by Apollonius of Rhodes *Argonautica* III 1251. See Liddell, Scott, and Jones 1996:573, s.v. ἐνσκέλλω for further citations.

ὅσσον ἐπεῖχε νέκυς, μὴ πρὶν μένος ἠελίοιο
σκήλει᾽ ἀμφὶ περὶ χρόα ἴνεσιν ἠδὲ μέλεσσιν.

Thus he spoke, threatening. But the dogs did not gather about him,
but rather Aphrodite, Zeus' daughter, warded off the dogs
throughout days and nights, and she anointed him with a rosy,
ambrosial oil, so [Achilles] might not tear his flesh by continually dragging
    it.
And upon him Phoibos Apollo led a dark cloud
from heaven to the ground, and covered the entire space,
however much the corpse was taking up, lest too soon the might of the sun
might wither his flesh all around on his sinews and limbs.

Iliad XXIII 184–191

The verb takes as object Hektor's χρόα "flesh," and indicates how the force of
the sun (μένος ἠελίοιο, XXIII 190), if not filtered by Apollo's dark cloud (κυάνεον
νέφος, XXIII 188), would dry out the body. Scholia A at *Iliad* XXIII 191b (Erbse)
glosses the Homer's σκήλει(ε) as σκληροποιήσειεν "make hard, harden."[43]

    The passage indicates the fate of a body left unburied and lying in the sun.
However, unlike πύθω (as we saw above), the verb σκέλλω does not speak of
decay as a *wet* process, but rather as a *dry* process. Indeed, Apollo's divine care
preserves Hektor's body such that both Hermes and Hecuba describe it as dewy
fresh (ἐερσήεις, *Iliad* XXIV 419, 757).[44]

5. κάρφω "cause to shrivel up, dry out, parch"[45]

The verb κάρφω appears twice in the thirteenth book of Homer's *Odyssey*, both
passages in which Athena disguises Odysseus so that he may return to Ithaca

---

[43] See see Liddell, Scott, and Jones 1996:1612, s.v. σκληροποιέω. Similarly, Scholia D at *Iliad* XXIII
191: σκήλῃ· σκληρύνῃ. ξηράνῃ, ὅθεν καὶ σκελετὸς ὁ ξηρός "Make hard. Parch, from which also
the word σκελετός 'dried up.'" Compare Hesychius: σκελοῦνται· σκελετισθήσονται. Note that
Apollonius of Rhodes follows Homer in using σκέλλω to describe the "drying" of human flesh
(χρὼς | ἐσκλήκει, *Argonautica* II 200–201) when he describes how Phineus, worn down and trem-
bling in his limbs from old age (τρέμε δ᾽ ἅψεα νισσομένοιο | ἀδρανίη γήραΐ τε, II 199–200), makes
his way on withered feet (ῥικνοῖς ποσὶν, II 198) to Jason and the Argonauts to request aid against
the Harpies who continually snatch away and befoul his food.

[44] The dew on Hektor's body accords with the cloud cover provided by Apollo to safeguard the
body from decay (XXIII 184–191), as noted by Richardson (1993:315). "Dewy" is also used to
describe the λωτός flower that springs up beneath Zeus as he, bewitched by Aphrodite's *zōnē*,
takes Hera in his arms and covers the two of them with a golden cloud raining dew on the grass
below (XIV 346–351). See my discussion at chapter 2 above.

[45] See Ebeling 1963:I.657, Frisk 1973–1979:I.795, Chantraine 1968–1980:501–502, and Liddell, Scott,
and Jones 1996:881, s.v. κάρφω.

without being recognized by the suitors. In order that he not be recognized (ἄγνωστον, xiii 397), she "shrivels up" his flesh:

ἀλλ' ἄγε σ' ἄγνωστον τεύξω πάντεσσι βροτοῖσι·
κάρψω μὲν χρόα καλὸν ἐνὶ γναμπτοῖσι μέλεσσι,
ξανθὰς δ' ἐκ κεφαλῆς ὀλέσω τρίχας, ἀμφὶ δὲ λαῖφος
ἕσσω, ὅ κεν στυγέῃσιν ἰδὼν ἄνθρωπος ἔχοντα,
κνυζώσω δέ τοι ὄσσε πάρος περικαλλέ' ἐόντε,
ὡς ἂν ἀεικέλιος πᾶσι μνηστῆρσι φανήῃς
σῇ τ' ἀλόχῳ καὶ παιδί, τὸν ἐν μεγάροισιν ἔλειπες.

But come, let me make you <u>unrecognizable</u> to all mortals.
<u>I will shrivel up</u> the <u>beautiful flesh</u> upon your flexible limbs;
<u>I'll destroy</u> the sandy <u>hair</u> on your head; and about you a tattered garment
I will dress, one which a man will loathe you when he sees you with it.
And <u>I will dim your two eyes</u> which were formerly <u>very lovely</u>,
so you will appear <u>unprepossessing</u> to all the suitors
and to your wife and child, whom you left behind in your palace.

Odyssey xiii 397–403

and,

ὣς ἄρα μιν φαμένη ῥάβδῳ ἐπεμάσσατ' Ἀθήνη.
κάρψε μέν οἱ χρόα καλὸν ἐνὶ γναμπτοῖσι μέλεσσι.

So speaking, with her wand Athena tapped him.
<u>She shriveled up</u> his <u>beautiful flesh</u> upon his flexible limbs.

Odyssey xiii 429–430

In both passages, Athena brings about, step by step, the physical degeneration of Odysseus' body as if by old age. She causes Odysseus' χρόα καλόν "beautiful flesh" (xiii 398, 430) to shrivel up (κάρψω, xiii 398; κάρψε, xiii 430), she destroys (ὀλέσω, xiii 399) his "sandy hair" (ξανθὰς... τρίχας, xiii 399), and she dims (κνυζώσω, xiii 401) his "eyes which were formerly very lovely" (ὄσσε πάρος περικαλλέ' ἐόντε, xiii 401). In each instance, Odysseus' body, formerly beautiful and youthful, undergoes a magical process of instantaneous aging, so that he appears old and decrepit, "unrecognizable" to all mortals—even his own wife and child.

The sense of κάρφω as a *drying* agent is preserved in the ancient scholastic tradition. In his discussion of the verses of the *Odyssey* just cited, Eustathius writes,

267

κάρψαι δέ ἐστι τὸ ξηρᾶναι καὶ συσπάσαι, ἐκ τοῦ κάρφω. ἀφ' οὗ καὶ τὸ κάρφος. κάρφεται δὲ χροῦς ὁ τοῦ γέροντος, ὡς δηλοῖ τὸ, ἀμφὶ δὲ δέρμα πᾶσι μέλεσσι παλαιοῦ θῆκε γέροντος. ταυτὸν γὰρ εἰπεῖν κάρψε χρόα, καὶ δέρμα γέροντος ἔθετο. (Eustathius *Commentarii ad Homeri Odysseam*, ed. Stallbaum, II.54, 2–3)

"κάρψαι" is "to dry" and "to shrivel," from the verb κάρφω, from which is also the noun κάρφος "a dry thing." κάρφεται is used of the flesh of an old man, as this verse makes clear, that "she placed the skin of an old man about all his limbs." For κάρψε χρόα "she shriveled his flesh" means the same thing as δέρμα γέροντος ἔθετο "she placed the skin of an old man upon him."

What is particularly interesting in Eustathius' discussion is his emphasis on the association between "drying out" with old age itself in the passage from the *Odyssey*. Old age is essentially a "drying up" of youthful vitality, as though youthful vigor is itself a fluid that is evaporated by the withering effects of time and the continual exposure to drying agents, like the sun and the wind.

The verb κάρφω also appears in both Hesiod and Archilochus in passages describing the "shriveling up" of χρώς "flesh." These passages are instructive for our understanding of the semantics of κάρφω, so I include analysis of them here.

φεύγειν δὲ σκιεροὺς θώκους καὶ ἐπ' ἠῶ κοῖτον
ὥρη ἐν ἀμήτου, ὅτε τ' ἠέλιος χρόα κάρφει·
τημοῦτος σπεύδειν καὶ οἴκαδε καρπὸν ἀγινεῖν
ὄρθρου ἀνιστάμενος, ἵνα τοι βίος ἄρκιος εἴη.

But avoid shady seats and staying in bed until dawn
in the season of reaping, when the sun shrivels up the flesh.
At that time be serious and bring home the fruit
after waking up early, so that your livelihood may be sure.

Hesiod Works and Days 574–577

Hesiod connects "shriveling" with age of a different sort—namely, with the maturation of agricultural produce in the proper season. During the "season of reaping" (ὥρη ἐν ἀμήτου, 575) when the fruit (καρπόν, 576) is ripe, the sun (ἠέλιος, 575) causes one's flesh to shrivel up (χρόα κάρφει, 575), and so, Hesiod advises, one should begin work early. Hesiod may be suggesting an etymological connection between κάρφω and καρπός, perhaps implying that mortal flesh and vegetal matter are similar insofar as they both undergo processes of maturation and shrivel up once past their prime.[46]

In Archilochus fr. 188 W, the poet likewise indicates an association between "shriveling up" and old age, and, like Hesiod, employs terms suggesting agriculture:

οὐκέθ' ὁμῶς θάλλεις ἁπαλὸν <u>χρόα</u>· κάρφεται γὰρ ἤδη
    ὄγμος· κακοῦ δὲ <u>γήραος</u> καθαιρεῖ
. . . . .] ἀφ' ἱμερτοῦ δὲ θορὼν γλυκὺς ἵμερος π[ροσώπου
    . . . . .]κεν· ἦ γὰρ πολλὰ δή σ' ἐπῆιξεν
πνεύμ]ατα χειμερίων ἀνέμων, μάλα πολλάκις δ' ε[

No longer as before does your tender <u>flesh</u> <u>blossom</u>; for already
    <u>your furrow</u>[47] is shriveled up. The . . . . . of evil <u>old age</u>
is destroying, and sweet desire rushing . . . . . from your desirable face.
    Yes, for indeed many a blast of winters' winds
has attacked you, and very often ...

Archilochus fr. 188 W

Archilochus speaks, presumably, to a woman whose "blossom" of youth has begun to fade—the metaphorical use of θάλλεις "blossom, bloom" and ὄγμος "furrow," both terms properly belonging to agriculture, implies an association between "shriveling" and the natural vegetal cycle of growth followed by diminishment and decay. As Christopher Brown has argued,

> The vegetative imagery implicit in ὄγμος ["furrow"] is anticipated
> by the use of the verb θάλλω ["blossom, flourish"], which suggests

---

[46] Ebeling 1963:I.657 suggests a connection between κάρφω and καρπός, identifying them as both from a root *καρπ- and compares the Latin *carpere* "to pluck, harvest," though neither Chantraine (1968–1980) nor Frisk (1973–1979) draw a connection between the terms. Even if κάρφω and καρπός are not etymologically related, it may well be the case that Hesiod suggests a connection with them here by folk-etymology, such as that offered by Eustathius *Commentarii ad Homeri Odysseam* (Stallbaum), II.54, 10–11: δοκεῖ δὲ τοῦ κάρφω μέσος παρακείμενος εἶναι κέκαρπα, καὶ ἐξ αὐτοῦ καρπός, ὡς οἱ παλαιοί φασι καὶ αὐτό, "it seems that the root (μέσος) of the verb κάρφω ("to cause to shrivel") is closely connected with κέκαρπα ("I have produced fruit"), and from it comes καρπός ("fruit"), as the ancients say it also."

[47] I read ὄγμος in verse 2 instead of Snell's conjectured ὄγμοις (Snell 1944). Brown and Gerber (1993) (cf. further Brown 1995, Gerber 1999) have argued convincingly (*pace* Slings 1995, cf. Bremer, van Erp Taalman Kip, and Slings 1987) that ὄγμος here refers to the "sexual vitality of youth" (Gerber 1999:203)—or more specifically, to a "woman's procreative capability," which is said to be "drying up" (Brown and Gerber 1993:196). In other words, κάρφεται ... ὄγμος provides "a powerful image for fading sexual allure and diminishing fertility" (Brown 1995:34).

luxuriant, flourishing vegetation ... The reason for this loss of softness is explained in the γάρ-clause by an image that makes the more general point that the ὥρα ["season"] has passed, that the fertile vigor of youth is drying up with the passage of time. (Brown 1995:33)

Evil old age destroys youth and its attendant "sweet sexual desire" (γλυκὺς ἵμερος). It shrivels the flesh (χρόα), once tender (ἁπαλόν). Old age *dries* up youth, like one blasted repeatedly by gusts of winter wind. In this context, I find very attractive Brown's suggestion that the poem further suggests the passing of time through references to a cycle of seasons: "θάλλεις evokes spring, the parched furrow summer ... , the loss of desire may imply autumn, and then there is a clear reference to the winter in [verse] 5" (Brown 1995:33n19). Although the fragmentary condition of the poem prevents this reading from being secure, it does not seem controversial to say that Archilochus here presents the human life in terms of a vegetative cycle in which a "springtime" of youthful, flour-ishing growth is followed by a "summertime" and "autumn" of the diminish-ment and drying out of age.

In an important article Steven Lowenstam (1979) argued that the primary sense of Greek θάλλω and its cognates (from Indo-European root *dhal-) is not specific to the vegetal or agricultural process of "blooming" or "growing,"[48] but rather indicates a more general act of "spring[ing] forth or emerg[ing] with or from moisture" (Lowenstam 1979:132, 135). I accept Lowenstam's argument, but wish to note that the collocation of θάλλω with ὄγμος "furrow" in Archilochus' fragment points to a specifically "vegetal" sense of the verb in this context. I do find particularly significant Lowenstam's finding that in those cases where θάλλω refers to plants, "there is an association, often explicit, always implicit, between water and a bush or tree which is healthy or growing" (Lowenstam 1979:131). In other words, there is a connection between *growing, blooming, youth,* and *vitality* with water or wetness. The corollary—that is, that *withering, shriveling, old age,* and *dying* are associated with dryness—is to be found precisely in the semantics of the use of κάρφω with its basic sense of drying out and causing to shrivel up.[49]

---

[48] Lowenstam 1979, *pace* Pokorny 1959:234, Frisk 1973–1979:I.649, and Chantraine 1968–1980:420.

[49] On the association between life, youth, and vitality with liquid, and old age, decrepitude, and death with dryness, see Onians 1951:200–228 with bibliography and extensive citations of Greek and Roman literature.

6. ἄζω "dry out, parch"[50]

Besides κάρφω, we may compare ἄζω "dry out, parch" which appears at Hesiod *Theogony* 99 in the context of a person's life force being "dried out" through tears and sorrow (ἄζηται κραδίην ἀκαχήμενος, "he dries out his heart with sorrow").[51] The "drying out" of experienced in moments of duress recalls the Homeric usage discussed above of a person's heart being "withered" by grief (e.g. φθινύθεσκε φίλον κῆρ, *Iliad* I 491; ἤτοι ὁ τῆς ἀχέων φρένας ἔφθιεν, XVIII 446): one's liquid vitality becomes sapped away, like a plant withering away.[52]

Hesiod uses the verb ἄζω again at *Works and Days* 578 to desribe the effect of the dog star Sirius on men as it "dries out their head and knees" (ἐπεὶ κεφαλὴν καὶ γούνατα Σείριος ἄζει). The appearance of Sirius in the morning sky heralds a period of summer that offers dangers to the unwary farmer: the summer heat causes plants to wilt, men to grow weak, and women to become sexually aroused. Onians (1951) argued that drying out one's "head and knees" (κεφαλὴν καὶ γούνατα) suggests the weakening of the male's sexual procreative capabilities, again as vital fluid leaves the body.[53]

A passage from the *Homeric Hymn to Aphrodite* connects "drying" (ἀζάνεσθαι) and "withering away" (ἀμφιπεριφθινύθειν). Aphrodite discusses the life of the nymphs who will raise her son Aeneas, explaining that these creatures will perish when their trees dry up and wither away:

ἀλλ' ὅτε κεν δὴ μοῖρα παρεστήκῃ θανάτοιο
<u>ἀζάνεται</u> μὲν πρῶτον ἐπὶ χθονὶ δένδρεα καλά,

---

[50] On ἄζω, see Pokorny 1959, s.v. *ās- "*brennen, glühen*," and *azd- "*dörre, trocke*"; according to Frisk (1973–1979:I.25–26, s.v. ἄζω) the nearest cognates are the Old Polish ozd "dried malt," Slovenian ozdíti "to dry malt." Benveniste (1955:39) suggests a connection between ἄζω and Hittite verb ḫāt- "dry," with its present tense ḫāteš- "dry out" and ḫātnu- "cause to dry out, wither." Beekes (2010:I.26–27) posits an Indo-European root *$h_2$ed-ie/o- based on the apparent Hittite cognates, but notes a possible "extension of the same root" in *h_2eh_1s-, apparently the root of Latin āreō "to be dry," āra "altar (āsa in old Latin), and Hittite ḫašša- "hearth," and perhaps Sanskrit āsa "ashes, dust."

[51] The ancient scholia at *Theogony* 99 glosses the passage: ἀναξηραίνει γὰρ ἡ λύπη, ὅθεν καὶ ἄϋπνον τίθησι, "Pain dries out, because it makes one sleepless." Indeed, the scholiast at *Iliad* XIV 253, explaining why sleep is described as being "poured" around someone (ἀμφιχυθείς), notes that "sleep is wet" (ὑγρὸς γὰρ ὁ ὕπνος); the implication is that those worries that prevent one from sleeping would have a drying effect. See West 1966:187–188 for discussion and further citations connecting pain with dryness (e.g. ξηρόν ... λύπαις at Euripides *Electra* 239–240).

[52] See Onians 1951:48, "When a man is in trouble or pines away, he may be said to 'melt', 'dissolve' (τήκειν) his θυμός, or to 'waste it away' (ἀποφθινύθειν) ... Elsewhere in similar circumstances the organs of consciousness, the heart or the lungs (φρένες) that contain the θυμός, are said to be 'eaten' or 'wasted' ('diminished')."

[53] Onians 1951:175–186, esp. 177–178. See West 1978:305 for further bibliography.

φλοιὸς δ' ἀμφιπεριφθινύθει, πίπτουσι δ' ἄπ' ὄζοι,
τῶν δέ χ' ὁμοῦ ψυχὴ λείποι φάος ἠελίοιο.

But indeed whenever their fated death stands beside them,
first the beautiful trees <u>dry out</u> upon the ground,
and their bark <u>withers away all around on either side</u>, and their branches
       fall,
and at the same time their soul departs the light of the sun.

Hymn to Aphrodite 269–272

The nymphs who will raise Aeneas eat the "immortal food" of the gods (ἄμβροτον εἶδαρ ἔδουσιν, 260), though are not themselves immortal; rather, they live for a long time (δηρὸν μὲν ζώουσι, 260)—as long as the trees that grow when they are born (264–265). But when these trees themselves "dry out" (ἀζάνεται, 270) and their bark "withers away all around on either side" (ἀμφιπεριφθινύθει, 271), then the nymphs themselves perish. We may compare a description of a fallen tree drying out as it lies by the bank of a river at *Iliad* IV 487 (ἡ μέν τ' ἀζομένη κεῖται ποταμοῖο παρ' ὄχθας) in a simile describing the warrior Simoeisios as he lies dead, cut down by Ajax.

The family of words related to ἄζω "dry out, parch" includes the adjective ἀζαλέος "dry," used to describe "a mountain" (οὔρεος, *Iliad* XX 491); "wood" (ὕλη, *Odyssey* ix 234); "a dry bull's-hide" (βῶν ἀζαλέην, *Iliad* VII 239). The substantive ἄζα "dryness, heat" attested in Hellenistic poets is perhaps the same word found at *Odyssey* xxii 184 (ἄζη), traditionally interpreted as "mildew" or "rust."[54] In all these cases we may detect a temporal dimension as what was once vital, supple, and moist dries out and withers.

---

[54] Chantraine 1968–1980:25, s.v. ἄζομαι, notes *"Il s'agit probablement de poussière et peut-être de cuir desséché et racorni"* ["This is probably dust and perhaps shriveled leather"]. Compare Scholia HQ at *Odyssey* xxii 184: πεπαλαγμένον ἄζῃ· μεμολυσμένον τῇ ξηρότητι, "it has become stained with dryness."

Works Cited

Adams, D. Q. 1987. "Ἥρως and Ἥρα: Of Men and Heroes in Greek and Indo-European." *Glotta* 65:171–178.

Adams, M. J. 1977. "Style in Southeast Asian Materials Processing: Some Implications for Ritual and Art." In *Material Culture: Studies, Organization, and Dynamics of Technology* (ed. M. H. Lechtman and R. Merrill) 21–52. St. Paul.

Adkins, A. W. H. 1960. *Merit and Responsibility*. Oxford.

———. 1971. "Homeric Values and Homeric Society." *Journal of Hellenic Studies* 91:1–14.

———. 1972. "Homeric Gods and the Values of Homeric Society." *Journal of Hellenic Studies* 92:1–19.

———. 1982. "Values, Goals, and Emotions in the *Iliad*." *Classical Philology* 77:292–326.

Alden, M. J. 2000. *Homer beside Himself: Para-Narratives in the Iliad*. Oxford.

Alexiou, M. 1974. *The Ritual Lament in Greek Tradition*. Cambridge.

Allen, T. W., ed. 1912. *Homeri Opera V*. Oxford.

———, ed. 1931. *Homeri Ilias*. Oxford.

Allen, T. W., W. R. Halliday, and E. E. Sikes, eds. 1980. *The Homeric Hymns*. Amsterdam. Orig. pub. 1936.

Almeida, J. A. 2003. *Justice as an Aspect of the Polis Idea in Solon's Political Poems: A Reading of the Fragments in Light of the Researches of New Classical Archaeology*. Leiden.

Ameis, K. F., K. Hentze, and P. Cauer, eds. 1965. *Ilias: Für den Schulgebrauch*. Amsterdam.

Anderson, J. K. 1970–1971. "The Trojan Horse Again." *Classical Journal* 66:22–25.

Andersen, Ø. 1981. "A Note on the 'Mortality' of Gods in Homer." *Greek, Roman, and Byzantine Studies* 22:323–327.

———. 1987. "Myth, Paradigm, and 'Spatial Form' in the *Iliad*." In Bremer, de Jong, and Kalff 1987:1–13.

———. 1990. "The Making of the Past in the *Iliad*." *Harvard Studies in Classical Philology* 93:25–45.

Andrews, P. B. S. 1965. "The Falls of Troy in Greek Tradition." *Greece and Rome* 12: 28–37.

Antonaccio, C. M. 1994. "Contesting the Past: Hero Cult, Tomb Cult, and Epic in Early Greece." *American Journal of Archaeology* 98:389–410.

Arieti, J. A. 1988. "Homer's *Litae* and *Atē*." *Classical Journal* 84:1–12.

Arthur, M. B. 1982. "Cultural Strategies in Hesiod's *Theogony*: Law, Family, Society." *Arethusa* 15:63–82.

———. 1983. "The Dream of a World without Women: Poetics and Circles of Order in the *Theogony* Prooemium." *Arethusa* 16:97–116.

Astour, M. C. 1980. "The Nether World and Its Denizens at Ugarit." In *Death in Mesopotamia* (ed. B. Alster) 227–238. Copenhagen.

Attridge, H. W. 2004. "Pollution, Sin, Atonement, Salvation." In *Religions of the Ancient World: A Guide* (ed. S. I. Johnston) 71–83. Cambridge, MA.

Austin, N. 1966. "The Function of Digressions in the *Iliad*." *Greek, Roman, and Byzantine Studies* 7:295–312.

Bachelard, G. 2000. *The Dialectic of Duration.* Trans. M. M. Jones. Manchester. Orig. pub. 1950.

Bader, F. 2002. "L'Immortalité des morts dans l'*Iliade*: Autour de grec ΤΑΡΧΥΩ." In *Donum grammaticum: Studies in Latin and Celtic Linguistics in Honour of Hannah Rosén* (ed. L. Sawicki and D. Shalev) 11–28. Leuven.

Bakker, E. J. 1993. "Discourse and Performance: Involvement, Visualization, and 'Presence' in Homeric Poetry." *Classical Antiquity* 12:1–29.

———. 1997. *Poetry in Speech: Orality and Homeric Discourse, Myth, and Poetics.* Ithaca.

———. 1999. "Homeric ΟΥΤΟΣ and the Poetics of Deixis." *Classical Philology* 94: 1–19.

———. 2002. "*Khrónos, Kléos*, and Ideology from Herodotus to Homer." In Reichel and Rengakos 2002:11–30.

———. 2005. *Pointing to the Past: From Formula to Performance in Homeric Poetics.* Hellenic Studies 12. Washington, DC.

Barnett, R. D. 1945. "The Epic of Kumarbi and the *Theogony* of Hesiod." *Journal of Hellenic Studies* 65:100–101.

Bassett, S. E. 1922. "The Three Threads of Plot in the *Iliad*." *Transactions of the American Philological Association* 53:52–62.

———. 1927. "The Single Combat between Hector and Aias." *American Journal of Philology* 48:148–156.

———. 1933. "Achilles' Treatment of Hector's Body." *Transactions of the American Philological Association* 64:41–65.

Bassi, K. 2005. "Things of the Past: Objects and Time in Greek Narrative." *Arethusa* 38:1–32.

Beckwith, M. C. 1998. "The 'Hanging of Hera' and the Meaning of Greek ἄκμων." *Harvard Studies in Classical Philology* 98:91–102.

Beekes, R. S. P. 1969. *The Development of the Proto-Indo-European Laryngeals in Greek*. Trans. T. S. Preston. The Hague.

———. 2010. *Etymological Dictionary of Greek*. 2 vols. Leiden.

Bell, A. A., Jr. 1975. "Three Again." *Classical Journal* 70:40–41.

Benveniste, E. 1935. *Origines de la formation des noms en indo-européen*. Paris.

———. 1937. "Expression indo-européenne de l'éternité." *Bulletin de la Société de Linguistique de Paris* 38:103–112.

———. 1955. "Études hittites et indo-européennes." *Bulletin de la Société de Linguistique de Paris* 50:29–43.

———. 1969. *Le vocabulaire des institutions indo-européennes*. 2 vols. Paris.

———. 1975. *Noms d'agent et noms d'action en indo-européen*. Paris.

Bergren, A. L. T. 1980. "Helen's Web: Time and Tableau in the *Iliad*." *Helios* 7:19–34.

———. 1989. "*The Homeric Hymn to Aphrodite*: Tradition and Rhetoric, Praise and Blame." *Classical Antiquity* 8:1–40.

———. 1992. "Architecture Gender Philosophy." In *Strategies in Architectural Thinking* (ed. J. Whiteman, J. Kipnis, and R. Burdett) 8–46. Cambridge, MA.

———. 1995. "The (Re)Marriage of Penelope and Odysseus." In Carter and Morris 1995:205–220.

———. 2008. *Weaving Truth: Essays on Language and the Female in Greek Thought*. Hellenic Studies 19. Washington, DC.

Bergson, H. 1910a. *Time and Free Will: An Essay on the Immediate Data of Consciousness*. Trans. F. L. Pogson. London. Orig. pub. 1889.

———. 1910b. *Creative Evolution*. Trans. A. Mitchell. New York. Orig. pub. 1907.

———. 1990. *Matter and Memory*. Trans. N. M Paul and W. S. Palmer. New York. Orig. pub. 1896.

Bernabé, A., ed. 1987. *Poetarum epicorum Graecorum: Testimonia et fragmenta*. Leipzig.

Bernal, M. 2006. *Black Athena: The Afroasiatic Roots of Classical Civilization*, vol. III: *The Linguistic Evidence*. New Brunswick.

Bettini, M. 1991. *Anthropology and Roman Culture: Kinship, Time, Images of the Soul*. Baltimore.

Beye, C. R. 1966. *The Iliad, the Odyssey, and the Epic Tradition*. Garden City.

———. 1993. *Ancient Epic Poetry: Homer, Apollonius, Virgil*. Ithaca.

Bloch, M. 1982. "Death, Women, and Power." In Bloch and Parry 1982:211–230.

Bloch, M., and J. Parry, eds. 1982. *Death and the Regeneration of Life*. Cambridge.

Blümel, R. 1927. "Homerisch ταρχύω." *Glotta* 15:78–84.

Boardman, J. 1974. *Athenian Black Figure Vases*. London.

———. 1998. *Early Greek Vase Painting*. London.

Boedeker, D. 1984. *Descent from Heaven: Images of Dew in Greek Poetry and Religion*. Chico.

Boisacq, É. 1950. *Dictionnaire étymologique de la langue grecque: Étudiée dans sense rapports avec les autres langues indo-européennes*. 4th ed. Heidelberg.

Boisvert, R. D. 2006. "Clock Time/Stomach Time." *Gastronomica: The Journal of Food and Culture* 6:40–46.

Bolling, G. M. 1945. "The Etymology of IXΩP." *Language* 21:49–54.

Botterweck, J., and H. Ringgren, eds. 1974–2006. *Theological Dictionary of the Old Testament*. 15 vols. Trans. J. T. Willis, D. E. Green, and D. W. Stott. Grand Rapids.

Bowra, C. M. 1930. *Tradition and Design in the Iliad*. Oxford.

Braswell, B. K. 1971. "Mythological Innovation in the *Iliad*." *Classical Quarterly* 21: 16–21.

Bremer, J. M., A. M. van Erp, T. Kip, and S. R. Slings. 1987. *Some Recently Found Greek Poems: Text and Commentary*. Leiden.

Bremer, J. M., I. J. F. de Jong, and J. Kalff, eds. 1987. *Homer, beyond Oral Poetry: Recent Trends in Homeric Interpretation*. Amsterdam.

Brommer, F. 1978. *Hephaistos: Der Schmiedegott in der antiken Kunst*. Mainz am Rhein.

Brown, C. G. 1995. "The Parched Furrow and the Loss of Youth: Archilochus fr. 188 West." *Quaderni urbinati di cultura classica* 50:29–35.

Brown, C. G., and D. E. Gerber. 1993. "The Parched Furrow: Archilochus fr. 188, 1–2 W." In *Tradizione e innovazione nella cultura greca da Omera all' età ellenistica* (ed. B. Bentili and R. Pretagostini) 195–197. Rome.

Bryce, T. 1986. *The Lycians in Literary and Epigraphic Sources*. Copenhagen.

Buchan, M. 2001. "Food for Thought: Achilles and the Cyclops." In *Eating Their Words: Cannibalism and the Boundaries of Cultural Identity* (ed. K. Guest) 11–34. New York.

———. 2004. *The Limits of Heroism: Homer and the Ethics of Reading*. Ann Arbor.

Buck, C. D. 1933. *Comparative Grammar of Greek and Latin*. Chicago.

Burgess, J. S. 1996. "The Non-Homeric *Cypria*." *Transactions of the American Philological Association* 126:77–99.

———. 2001. *The Tradition of the Trojan War in Homer and the Epic Cycle*. Baltimore.

———. 2004. "Performance and the Epic Cycle." *Classical Journal* 100:1–23.

———. 2009. *The Death and Afterlife of Achilles*. Baltimore.

Burkert, W. 1983a. "Itinerant Diviners and Magicians: A Neglected Element in Cultural Contacts." In Hägg 1983:115–120.

———. 1983b. "Oriental Myth and Literature in the *Iliad*." In Hägg 1983:51–56.

———. 1985. *Greek Religion*. Trans. J. Raffan. Cambridge, MA.

———. 1987. "Oriental and Greek Mythology: The Meeting of Parallels." In *Interpretations of Greek Mythology* (ed. J. N. Bremmer) 10–40. London.

———. 1991. "Homerstudien und Orient." In *Zweihundert Jahre Homer-Forschung: Rückblick und Ausblick* (ed. J. Latacz) 155–181. Stuttgart.

———. 1992. *The Orientalizing Revolution: Near Eastern Influence on Greek Culture in the Early Archaic Age*. Trans. M. E. Pinder and W. Burkert. Cambridge, MA.

Burrow, T. 1959a. "On the Phonological History of Sanskrit *KṢÁM-* 'Earth,' *ṚKṢA* 'Bear,' and *LIKṢĀ* 'Nit'." *Journal of the American Oriental Society* 7:85–90.

———. 1959b. "Sanskrit *kṣi-*: Greek φθίνω." *Journal of the American Oriental Society* 79:255–262.

Burton, D. 2001. "The Death of Gods in Greek Succession Myths." In *Homer, Tragedy, and Beyond: Essays in Honour of P. E. Easterling* (ed. F. Budelmann and P. Michelakis) 43–56. London.

Calame, C. 1977. *Les choeurs de jeunes filles en Grèce archaïque*. 2 vols. Rome.

Caldwell, R. S. 1978. "Hephaestus: A Psychological Study." *Helios* 6:43–59.

———. 1987. *Hesiod's Theogony: Translated with Introduction, Commentary, and Interpretive Essay*. Cambridge, MA.

Carroll, J. B., ed. 1956. *Language, Thought, and Reality: Selected Writings of Benjamin Whorf*. Cambridge.

Carter, J. B., and S. P. Morris, eds. 1995. *The Ages of Homer*. Austin.

Cassin, E. 1981. "The Death of the Gods." In Humphreys and King 1981:317–325.

Caswell, C. P. 1990. *A Study of Thumos in Early Greek Epic*. Leiden.

Chantraine, P. 1958. *Grammaire homérique*, vol. I: *Phonétique et morphologie*. Paris.

———. 1961. *Morphologie historique du grec*. 2nd ed. Paris.

———. 1968–1980. *Dictionnaire étymologique de la langue grecque: Histoire des mots*. Paris.

Clackson, J. 2007. *Indo-European Linguistics: An Introduction*. Cambridge.

Clark, Matthew. 1986. "Neoanalysis: A Bibliographic Review." *Classical World* 79: 379–394.

Clarke, Michael J. 1999. *Flesh and Spirit in the Songs of Homer: A Study of Words and Myths*. Oxford.

Clay, J. 1982. "Immortal and Ageless Forever." *Classical Journal* 77:112–117.

———. 1983. *The Wrath of Athena: Gods and Men in the Odyssey*. Princeton.

———. 1989. *The Politics of Olympus: Form and Meaning in the Major Homeric Hymns*. Princeton.

———. 1994. "The Dais of Death." *Transactions of the American Philological Association* 124:35–40.

———. 1999. "The Whip and Will of Zeus." *Literary Imagination* 1:40–60.

Coldstream, J. N. 1976. "Hero-Cults in the Age of Homer." *Journal of Hellenic Studies* 96:8–17.

Collins, D. 1998. *Immortal Armor: The Concept of Alkē in Archaic Greek Poetry*. Lanham.

Combellack, F. M. 1981. "The Wish without Desire." *American Journal of Philology* 102:115–119.

Cook, E. 2003. "Agamemnon's Test of the Army in *Iliad* Book 2 and the Function of Homeric *Akhos*." *American Journal of Philology* 124:165–198.

Cook, R. M. 1954–1955. "Thucydides I, 11, 1." *Proceedings of the Cambridge Philological Society* 3:3.

Coope, U. 2005. *Time for Aristotle: Physics IV.10-14*. Oxford.

Corbeill, A. 2009. "Weeping Statues, Weeping Gods, and Prodigies from Republican to Early Christian Rome." In *Tears in the Graeco-Roman World* (ed. T. Fögen) 297–310. Berlin.

Crooke, W. 1897. "The Binding of a God: A Study in the Basis of Idolatry." *Folklore* 8:325–355.

Crosby, N. E. 1922. "*Iliad* V.885–87." *Classical Philology* 17:142–143.

Cunliffe, R. J. 1963. *A Lexicon of the Homeric Dialect*. New ed. Norman. Orig. pub. 1924.

Curry, B. 2005. *Pindar and the Cult of Heroes*. Oxford.

Dastur, Françoise. 1998. *Heidegger and the Question of Time*. Trans. F. Raffoul and D. Pettigrew. New Jersey.

Davies, A. M. 1977. "Epic τε (Review of Ruijgh 1971)." *Classical Review* 27:55–58.

Davies, M. 1986. "Nestor's Advice in *Iliad* 7." *Eranos* 84:69–76.

———, ed. 1988. *Epicorum Graecorum fragmenta*. Göttingen.

———. 1989. *The Greek Epic Cycle*. 2nd ed. Bristol.

Davison, J. A. 1965. "Thucydides, Homer, and the 'Achaean Wall.'" *Greek, Roman, and Byzantine Studies* 6:5–28.

Dawe, R. D. 1968. "Some Reflections on ATH and HAMAPTIA." *Harvard Studies in Classical Philology* 72:89–123.

de Jong, I. J. F. 1985. "Eurykleia and Odysseus' Scar: *Odyssey* 19.393–466." *Classical Quarterly* 35:517–518.

———. 1987. *Narrators and Focalizers in the Iliad*. Amsterdam.

———. 1997. "Homer and Narratology." In Morris and Powell 1997:305–325.

———. 2001. *A Narratological Commentary on the Odyssey*. Cambridge.

———. 2002. "Developments in Narrative Technique in the *Odyssey*." In Reichel and Rengakos 2002:77–91.

de Jong, J. W. 1985. "The Over-Burdened Earth in India and Greece." *Journal of the American Oriental Society* 105:397–400.

Denniston, J. D. 1950. *The Greek Particles*. 2nd ed. Indianapolis.

Detienne, M. 1994. *The Gardens of Adonis: Spices in Greek Mythology.* 2nd ed. Trans. J. Lloyd. Princeton.

———. 1996. *The Masters of Truth in Archaic Greece.* Trans. J. Lloyd. New York.

Detienne, M., and J.-P. Vernant. 1974. *Les ruses de l'intelligence: La mètis des Grecs.* Paris.

———. 1978. *Cunning Intelligence in Greek Culture and Society.* Trans. J. Lloyd. Atlantic Highlands.

Dickson, K. 1992. "Kalkhas and Nestor: Two Narrative Strategies in *Iliad* 1." *Arethusa* 25:327–358.

———. 1995. *Nestor: Poetic Memory in Greek Epic.* New York.

Dietrich, B. C. 1967. *Death, Fate, and the Gods: The Development of a Religious Idea in Greek Popular Belief and Homer.* London.

———. 1979. "Views of Homeric Gods and Religion." *Numen* 26:129–151.

Dittrich, E. 1895. "Zu Thukydides." *Jahrbücher für classischen Philologie* 151:180–182.

D-K = Diels, H., and W. Kranz, eds. 1974. *Die Fragmenta der Versokratiker.* 3 vols. 6th ed. Zurich. Orig. pub. 1903.

Dodds, E. R. 1951. *The Greeks and the Irrational.* Berkeley.

———. 1968. "Homer." In *Fifty Years (and Twelve) of Classical Scholarship* (ed. M. Platnauer) 1–49. Oxford.

Dolin, E. 1983. "Thucydides on the Trojan War: A Critique of the Text of 1.11.1." *Harvard Studies in Classical Philology* 87:119–149.

Dougherty, C. 2001. *The Raft of Odysseus: The Ethnographic Imagination of Homer's Odyssey.* Oxford.

Dowden, K. 1996. "Homer's Sense of Text." *Journal of Hellenic Studies* 116:47–61.

———. 2004. "The Epic Tradition in Greece." In *The Cambridge Companion to Homer* (ed. R. Fowler) 188–205. Cambridge.

Doyle, R. E. 1984. *ATH: A Study in the Greek Poetic Tradition from Homer to Euripides.* New York.

Dreyfus, H. L. 1991. *Being-in-the-World: A Commentary on Heidegger's Being in Time, Division I.* Cambridge, MA.

———. 2005. "Foreword." In White 2005:ix–xxxvi.

Drinka, B. 2009. "The *-to-/-no-* Construction of Indo-European: Verbal Adjective or Passive Participle?" In *Grammatical Change in Indo-European Linguistics* (ed. V. Bubenik, J. Hewson, and S. Rose) 141–158. Amsterdam.

Duckworth, G. E. 1933. *Foreshadowing and Suspense in the Epics of Homer, Apollonius, and Vergil.* Princeton.

Dué, C. 2002. *Homeric Variations on a Lament by Briseis.* Lanham, MD.

Dunkel, G. E. 1982–1983. "πρόσσω καὶ ὀπίσσω." *Zeitschrift für vergleichende Sprachforschung* 96:66–87.

Dunn, F. M. 1996. *Tragedy's End: Closure and Innovation in Euripidean Drama.* Oxford.

Ebeling, H., ed. 1963. *Lexicon Homericum.* 2 vols. Hildesheim. Orig. pub. 1885.

Edmunds, L. 1993. *Myth in Homer: A Handbook.* 2nd ed. Highland Park.

———. 1997. "Myth in Homer." In Morris and Powell 1997:415–441.

Edmunds, S. T. 1990. *Homeric Nēpios.* New York.

Edwards, A. T. 1988. "Κλέος ἄφθιτον and Oral Theory." *Classical Quarterly* 38:25–30.

Edwards, M. W. 1980. "Convention and Individuality in *Iliad* I." *Harvard Studies in Classical Philology* 84:1–28.

———. 1986. "Homer and Oral Tradition: The Formula, Part I." *Oral Tradition* 1:171–230.

———. 1987. *Homer, Poet of the Iliad.* Baltimore.

———. 1988. "Homer and Oral Tradition: The Formula, Part II." *Oral Tradition* 3:11–60.

———. 1991. *The Iliad: A Commentary, Volume V (Books 17–20).* Ed. G. Kirk. Cambridge.

Einstein, A. 1961. *Relativity: The Special and General Theory, A Popular Exposition.* New York.

Einstein, A., et al. 1952. *The Principle of Relativity: A Collection of Original Memoirs on the Special and General Theory of Relativity.* New York.

Eliade, M. 1969. *Images and Symbols: Studies in Religious Symbolism.* Trans. P. Mairet. New York.

Elmer, D. 2008. "*Epikoinos*: The Ball Game *Episkuros* and *Iliad* 12.421–23." *Classical Philology* 103:414–423.

Erbse, H., ed. 1969–1988. *Scholia Graeca in Homeri Iliadem (Scholia vetera).* 7 vols. Berolini.

Ervin, M. 1963. "A Relief Pithos from Mykonos." *Deltion* 18:37–75.

Evans, G. B., ed. 1997. *The Riverside Shakespeare.* Boston.

Fagles, R., trans. 1990. *The Iliad.* New York.

Faraone, C. A. 1992. *Talismans and Trojan Horses.* Oxford.

Fehling, D. 1991. *Die ursprüngliche Geschichte vom Fall Trojas; oder: Interpretationen zur Troja-Geschichte.* Innsbruck.

Fenik, B. 1968. *Typical Battle Scenes in the Iliad: Studies in the Narrative Technique of Homeric Battle Descriptions.* Weisbaden.

———. 1977. "Review of Nagler 1974." *Classical Philology* 72:60–65.

———, ed. 1978. *Homer: Tradition and Invention.* Leiden.

———. 1978. "Stylization and Variety: Four Monologues in the *Iliad*." In Fenik 1978:68–90.

Fenno, J. 2005. "'A Great Wave Against the Stream': Water Imagery in Iliadic Battle Scenes." *American Journal of Philology* 126:475–504.

FGrHist = Jacoby, F., ed. 1923–1958. *Die Fragmente der griechischen Historiker*. Leiden.

Fineberg, S. 2009. "Hephaestus on Foot in the Ceramicus." *Transactions of the American Philological Association* 139:275–324.

Finkel, D. 2009. *The Good Soldiers*. New York.

Finkelberg, M. 1986. "Is κλέος ἄφθιτον a Homeric Formula?" *Classical Quarterly* 36:1–5.

———. 1995. "Patterns of Error in Homer." *Journal of Hellenic Studies* 115:15–28.

———. 1998. "*Timē* and *Aretē* in Homer." *Classical Quarterly* 48:14–28.

———. 2007. "More on ΚΛΕΟΣ ΑΦΘΙΤΟΝ." *Classical Quarterly* 57:341–350.

Floyd, E. D. 1980. "*Kleos Aphthiton*: An Indo-European Perspective on Early Greek Poetry." *Glotta* 58:133–157.

Foley, H. P., ed. 1994. *The Homeric Hymn to Demeter: Translation, Commentary, and Interpretive Essays*. Princeton.

Foley, J. M. 1988. *The Theory of Oral Composition*. Bloomington.

———. 1991. *Immanent Art: From Structure to Meaning in Traditional Oral Epic*. Bloomington.

———. 1995. *The Singer of Tales in Performance*. Bloomington.

———. 1999. *Homer's Traditional Art*. University Park.

Fontenrose, J. 1974. *Python: A Study of Delphic Myth and Its Origins*. Repr. ed. New York. Orig. pub. 1959.

———. 1983. "The Building of the City Walls: Troy and Asgard." *Journal of American Folklore* 96:53–63.

Ford, A. L. 1992. *Homer: The Poetry of the Past*. Ithaca.

Foster, B. O. 1914. "The Duration of the Trojan War." *American Journal of Philology* 35:294–308.

Fraenkel, E., ed. 1962. *Aeschylus: Agamemnon*. 3 vols. Corrected ed. Oxford.

Frame, D. 1978. *The Myth of Return in Early Greek Epic*. New Haven.

Frank, R. 1963. *The Widening Gyre: Crisis and Mastery in Modern Literature*. New Brunswick.

———. 1977. "Spatial Form: An Answer to Critics." *Critical Inquiry* 4:231–252.

———. 1978. "Spatial Form: Some Further Reflections." *Critical Inquiry* 5:275–290.

———. 1981. "Spatial Form: Thirty Years After." In Smitten and Dhagistany 1981: 202–243.

Fränkel, H. F. 1946. "Man's *ephemeros* Nature According to Pindar and Others." *Transactions and Proceedings of the American Philological Association* 77:131–145.

Fränkel, H. F. 1968. "Die Zeitauffassung in der frühgriechischen Literatur." In *Wege und Formen frühgriechischen Denkens*, 3rd ed. (ed. F. Tietze) 1–22. Munich. Orig. pub. 1931.

———. 1975. *Early Greek Poetry and Philosophy: A History of Greek Epic, Lyric, and Prose to the Middle of the Fifth Century*. Trans. M. Hadas and J. Willis. New York.

Friis, J. K. 1967. *The Iliad in Early Greek Art*. Copenhagen.

Frisk, H. 1973–1979. *Griechisches etymologisches Wörterbuch*. 3 vols. 2nd ed. Heidelberg.

Fuchs, T. 2001a. "Melancholia as a Desynchronisation." *Psychopathology* 34:179–186.

———. 2001b. "The Phenomenology of Shame, Guilt, and the Body in Dysmorphic Disorder and Depression." *Journal of Phenomenological Psychology* 33:223–243.

———. 2003. "The Temporality of Pain and Suffering." In *Phénoménologie des sentiments corporels. T. 1: Douleur, souffrance, depression* (ed. B. Granger and G. Charbonneau) 69–75. Argenteuil.

———. 2005a. "The Phenomenology of Body, Space, and Time in Depression." *Comprendre* 15:108–121.

———. 2005b. "Implicit and Explicit Temporality." *Philosophy, Psychiatry, and Psychology* 12:195–198.

Gantz, T. 1993. *Early Greek Myth*. 2 vols. Baltimore.

Garcia, L. F., Jr. 2007. *Homeric Temporalities: Simultaneity, Sequence, and Durability in the Iliad*. Ph.D. diss., University of California, Los Angeles.

Garland, R. S. 1981. "The Causation of Death in the *Iliad*: A Theological and Biological Investigation." *British Institute of Classical Studies* 28:43–60.

———. 1982. "*Geras Thanontōn*: An Investigation into the Claims of the Homeric Dead." *Bulletin of the Institute of Classical Studies* 29:69–80.

———. 2001. *The Greek Way of Death*. 2nd ed. Ithaca.

Gaster, T. H. 1944. "Folklore Motifs in Canaanite Myth." *Journal of the Royal Asiatic Society of Great Britain and Ireland* 1:30–51.

Gentili, B., and G. Paioni, eds. 1977. *Il mito greco*. Rome.

Gerber, D. E. 1999. *Greek Iambic Poetry*. Cambridge, MA.

Göbel, F. 1935. *Formen und Formeln der epischen Dreiheit in der griechischen Dichtung*. Stuttgart.

Goodwin, W. W. 1893. *Syntax of the Moods and Tenses of the Greek Verb*. Rewritten and enlarged ed. Boston.

Gottschall, J. 2001. "Homer's Human Animal: Ritual Combat in the *Iliad*." *Philosophy and Literature* 25:278–294.

Grassmann, H. 1964. *Wörterbuch zum Rig-Veda*. Wiesbaden. Orig. pub. 1872.

Greene, W. C. 1944. *Moira: Fate, Good, and Evil in Greek Thought.* Cambridge, MA.

Grethlein, J. 2008. "Memory and Material Objects in the *Iliad* and *Odyssey.*" *Journal of Hellenic Studies* 128:27–51.

Griffin, J. 1976. "Homeric Pathos and Objectivity." *Classical Quarterly* 26:161–187.

———. 1977. "The Epic Cycle and the Uniqueness of Homer." *Journal of Hellenic Studies* 97:39–53.

———. 1978. "The Divine Audience and Religion of the *Iliad.*" *Classical Quarterly* 28:1–22.

———. 1980. *Homer on Life and Death.* Oxford.

Griffith, M. W. 1975. "Man and Leaves: A Study of Mimnermus fr. 2." *California Studies in Classical Antiquity* 8:73–88.

Griffith, R. D. 1994. "Nektar and Nitron." *Glotta* 72:20–23.

Guignon, C. 1984. "Heidegger's 'Authenticity' Revisited." *Review of Metaphysics* 38:321–339.

———. 1993. "Authenticity, Moral Values, and Psychotherapy." In *The Cambridge Companion to Heidegger* (ed. C. Guignon) 268–292. Cambridge.

———. 2000. "Philosophy and Authenticity: Heidegger's Search for a Ground for Philosophizing." In *Heidegger, Authenticity, and Modernity: Essays in Honor of Hubert L. Dreyfus, vol. I* (ed. M. A. Wrathall and J. Malpas) 79–101. Cambridge, MA.

Güntert, H. 1919. *Kalypso: Bedeutungsgeschichtliche Untersuchungen auf dem Gebiet der indogermanischen Sprachen.* Halle.

Gurney, O. R. 1977. *Some Aspects of Hittite Religion.* Oxford.

Güterbock, H. G. 1948. "The Hittite Version of the Hurrian Kumbari Myths: Oriental Forerunners of Hesiod." *American Journal of Archaeology* 52:123–134.

Güterbock, H. G., and H. A. Hoffner, eds. 1997. *The Hittite Dictionary of the Oriental Institute of the University of Chicago,* Vol. P. Chicago.

Hägg, R., ed. 1983. *The Greek Renaissance of the Eighth Century B.C.: Tradition and Innovation.* Stockholm.

Hainsworth, J. B. 1968. *The Flexibility of the Homeric Formula.* Oxford.

———. 1970. "The Criticism of an Oral Homer." *Journal of Hellenic Studies* 90:90–98.

———. 1988. "Homer *Odyssey*: Books v–viii." In Heubeck, West, and Hainsworth 1988:247–385.

———. 1993. *The Iliad: A Commentary, Volume III (Books 9–12).* Ed. G. Kirk. Cambridge.

Hampe, R. 1936. *Frühe griechische Sagenbilder in Böotien.* Athens.

Hansen, P. A., ed. 1983. *Carmina epigraphica graeca saeculorum VIII–V A. CHR. N.* Berlin.

Hansen, W. F. 1976. "Three and Third Time." *Classical Journal* 71:253–254.

Harmatta, J. 1968. "Zu den kleinasiatischen Beziehungen der griechischen Mythologie." *Acta Antiqua* 16:57–76.

Harrell, S. E. 1991. "Apollo's Fraternal Threats: Language of Succession and Domination in the *Homeric Hymn to Hermes*." *Greek, Roman, and Byzantine Studies* 32:307–329.

Haslam, M. 1991. "Kleitias, Stesichoros, and the Jar of Dionysos." *Transactions of the American Philological Association* 121:35–45.

Haupt, P. 1922. "Manna, Nectar, and Ambrosia." *Proceedings of the American Philological Association* 61:227–236.

Heidegger, M. 1962. *Being and Time*. Trans. J. Macquarrie and E. Robinson. New York.

——. 1979. *Prolegomena zur Geschichte des Zeitbegriffs. Gasamtausgabe, Band 20: Marburger Vorlesung Sommersemester 1925*. Ed. P. Jaeger. Frankfurt am Main.

——. 1985. *History of the Concept of Time*. Trans. T. Kisiel. Bloomington.

——. 1992. *The Concept of Time*. Trans. W. McNeill. Oxford.

——. 2006. *Sein und Zeit*. 19th ed. Ed. E. Husserl. Tübingen. Orig. pub. 1927.

Heiden, B. 1991. "Shifting Contexts in the *Iliad*." *Eranos* 89:1–12.

Hendel, R. S. 1987. "Of Demigods and the Deluge: Toward an Interpretation of Genesis 6:1–4." *Journal of Biblical Literature* 106:13–26.

Henderson, J. 1991. *The Maculate Muse: Obscene Language in Attic Comedy*. Oxford. Orig. pub. 1975.

Hertz, R. 1960. *Death and the Right Hand*. Trans. R. Needham and C. Needham. Glencoe. Orig. pub. 1907.

Heubeck, A. 1984. "Die homerische Göttersprache." In *Kleine Schriften zur griechischen Sprache und Literatur* (ed. B. Forssman, S. Koster, and E. Pöhlmann) 94–115. Erlangen.

Heubeck, A., and A. Hoekstra, eds. 1989. *A Commentary on Homer's Odyssey*, vol. 2: *Books ix–xvi*. Oxford.

——. 1989. "Homer *Odyssey*: Books ix–xii." In Heubeck and Hoekstra 1989:1–143.

Heubeck, A., S. West, and J. B. Hainsworth, eds. 1988. *A Commentary on Homer's Odyssey*, vol. 1: *Books i–viii*. Oxford.

Heyne, C. G., ed. 1821. *Homeri Ilias cum brevi annotatione*. 2 vols. Oxford.

Himmelmann, N. 1998. *Reading Greek Art*. Ed. W. Childs and H. Meyer. Princeton.

Hocart, A. M. 1922. "Myths in the Making." *Folklore* 33:57–71.

Hoekstra, A. 1964. *Homeric Modifications of Formulaic Prototypes: Studies in the Development of Greek Epic Diction*. Amsterdam.

——. 1989. "Homer *Odyssey*: Books xiii–xvi." In Heubeck and Hoekstra 1989:147–287.

Hoffner, H. A., Jr. 1968. "Hittite *TARPIŠ* and Hebrew *TERĀPHÎM*." *Journal of Near Eastern Studies* 27:61–68.

———. 1998. *Hittite Myths*. 2nd ed. Ed. G. M. Beckmann. Atlanta.

Hogan, J. C., and D. J. Schenker. 2001. "Challenging Otherness: A Reassessment of Early Greek Attitudes toward the Divine." In *Ancient Journeys: A Festschrift in Honor of Eugene Numa Lane*. Ed. C. Callaway. http://www.stoa.org/lane/.

Holoka, J. P. 1983. "'Looking Darkly' (ὑπόδρα ἰδών): Reflections on Status and Decorum in Homer." *Transactions of the American Philological Association* 113: 1–16.

Holt, P. 1992. "Ajax's Burial in Early Greek Epic." *American Journal of Philology* 113: 319–333.

Hooker, J. T. 1987. "Homeric Society: A Shame Culture?" *Greece and Rome* 34:121–125.

Horrocks, G. 1997. "Homer's Dialect." In Morris and Powell 1997:193–217.

Householder, F. W., Jr., and G. Nagy 1972. *Greek: A Survey of Recent Work*. The Hague.

Howie, J. G. 1995. "The *Iliad* as Exemplum." In *Homer's World: Fiction, Tradition, Reality* (ed. Ø. Andersen and M. Dickie) 141–173. Bergen.

Humphreys, S. C. 1981. "Death and Time." In Humphreys and King 1981:261–283.

Humphreys, S. C., and H. King, eds. 1981. *Mortality and Immortality: The Anthropology and Archaeology of Death*. London.

Hunter, V. 1981. "Classics and Anthropology." *Phoenix* 35:145–155.

Huntington, R., and P. Metcalf. 1991. *Celebrations of Death: The Anthropology of Mortuary Ritual*. 2nd ed. Cambridge.

Husserl, E. 1962. *Ideas: General Introduction to Pure Phenomenology*. Trans. W. R. Boyce Gibson. New York. Orig. pub. 1913.

———. 1981. *Husserl: Shorter Works*. Ed. P. McCormick and F. A. Elliston. Notre Dame.

———. 1991. *On the Phenomenology of the Consciousness of Internal Time (1893-1917): Edmund Husserl, Collected Works*, vol. 4. Ed. R. Bernet. Trans. J. B. Brough. Dordrecht. Orig. pub. 1928.

Huxley, G. L. 1969. *Greek Epic Poetry from Eumelos to Panyassis*. London.

Ingalls, W. B. 1970. "The Structure of the Homeric Hexameter: A Review." *Phoenix* 24:1–24.

———. 1976. "The Analogical Formula in Homer." *Transactions of the American Philological Association* 106:211–226.

Inwood, M. 1999. *A Heidegger Dictionary*. Oxford.

Jacoby, F. 1944. "*Patrios Nomos*: State Burial in Athens and the Public Cemetery in the Kerameikos." *Journal of Hellenic Studies* 64:37–66.

Janda, M. 1996. "Das Einsperren der Totengeister: Homerisch ταρχύω." *Die Sprache: Zeitschrift für Sprachwissenschaft* 38:76–86.

Janko, R. 1981. "ΑΘΑΝΑΤΟΣ ΚΑΙ ΑΓΗΡΩΣ: The Genealogy of a Formula." *Mnemosyne* 34:382–385.

Janko, R. 1982. *Homer, Hesiod, and the Hymns: Diachronic Development in Epic Diction.* Cambridge.

———. 1994. *The Iliad: A Commentary,* vol. 4: *Books 13-16.* Ed. G. Kirk. Cambridge.

Johnson, D. M. 1999. "Hesiod's Descriptions of Tartarus ('*Theogony*' 721–819)." *Phoenix* 53:8–28.

Jones, P. V., and G. M. Wright, eds. 1997. *Homer: German Scholarship in Translation.* Oxford.

Jouanna, J., and P. Demont. 1981. "Le sens d' ἰχώρ chez Homère (*Iliade* V, v. 340 et 416) et Eschyle (*Agamemnon*, v. 1480) en relation avec les emplois du mot dans la Collection *hippocratique*." *Revue des études anciennes* 83:197–209.

Kahane, A. 2005. *Diachronic Dialogues: Authority and Continuity in Homer and the Homeric Tradition.* Lanham.

Kahn, L. 1978. *Hermès passe; ou, Les ambiguïtés de la communication.* Paris.

Kahn-Lyotard, L. 1977. "Le récit d'un passage et ses points nodaux (Le vol et le sacrifice des boeufs d'Apollon par Hermès)." In Gentili and Paioni 1977: 107–117.

Kakridis, J. 1971. *Homer Revisited.* Lund.

Kassian, A., A. Korolëv, and A. Sidel'tsev. 2002. *Hittite Funerary Ritual: šališ waštaiš.* Ed. M. Dietrich and O. Loretz. Münster.

Katz, J. 2005. "The Indo-European Context." In *A Companion to Ancient Epic* (ed. J. M. Foley) 20–30. Oxford.

Kesenbaum, V. 1982. "Introduction: The Experience of Illness." In Kesenbaum 1982:3–38.

Kestenbaum, V., ed. 1982. *The Humanity of the Ill: Phenomenological Perspectives.* Knoxville.

King, H. 1986. "Tithonos and the Tettix." *Arethusa* 19:15–35.

King, K. C. 1987. *Achilles: Paradigms of the War Hero from Homer through to the Middle Ages.* Berkeley.

Kirk, G. S. 1962. *The Songs of Homer.* Cambridge.

———. 1964. *The Language and Background of Homer.* Cambridge.

———. 1985. *The Iliad: A Commentary,* vol. I: *Books 1-4.* Ed. G. Kirk. Cambridge.

———. 1990. *The Iliad: A Commentary,* vol. II: *Books 5-8.* Ed. G. Kirk. Cambridge.

Kitts, M. 1994. "Two Expressions for Human Mortality in the Epics of Homer." *History of Religions* 34:132–151.

———. 2005. *Sanctified Violence in Homeric Society: Oath-Making Rituals and Narratives in the Iliad.* Cambridge.

Kleinlogel, A. 1981. "Götterblut und Unsterblichkeit: Homerische Sprachreflexion und die Probleme epischer Forchungsparadigmata." *Poetica* 13:252–279.

Knox, P., and J. A. Russo. 1989. "Agamemnon's Text: *Iliad* 2.73–75." *Classical Antiquity* 8:351–358.

Koenen, L. 1994. "Greece, the Near East, and Egypt: Cyclic Destruction in Hesiod and the Catalogue of Women." *Transactions of the American Philological Association* 124:1–34.

Koller, H. 1967. "Αἷμα." *Glotta* 45:149–155.

Krell, D. F. 1993. "Where Deathless Horses Weep." In *Reading Heidegger: Commemorations* (ed. J. Sallis) 95–106. Bloomington.

Kretschmer, P. 1940. "Die Stellung der lykischen Sprache." *Glotta* 18:101–116.

———. 1947. "NEKTAR." *Anzeiger der österreichischen Akademie der Wissenschaften* 84:13–26.

Krischer, T. 1971. *Formale Konventionen der homerischen Epik*. Munich.

Kühner, R., and G. Gerth. 1963. *Ausführliche Grammatik der griechischen Sprache, Zweiter Teil (Satzlehre), Zweiter Band*. 3rd ed. Munich. Orig. pub. 1904.

Kullmann, W. 1960. *Die Quellen der Iliad (troischer Sagenkreis)*. Weisbaden.

———. 1984. "Oral Poetry Theory and Neoanalysis in Homeric Research." *Greek, Roman, and Byzantine Studies* 25:307–323.

———. 2001. "Past and Future in the *Iliad*." In *Oxford Readings in Homer's Iliad* (ed. D. L. Cairns) 385–408. Oxford.

Kurtz, D. C., and J. Boardman. 1971. *Greek Burial Customs*. London.

Laneri, N., ed. 2007. *Performing Death: Social Analyses of Funerary Traditions in the Ancient Near East and Mediterranean*. Chicago.

Lang, A., W. Leaf, and E. Myers, trans. 1950. *The Iliad*. Repr. ed. New York. Orig. pub. 1883.

Lang, M. L. 1983. "Reverberation and Mythology in the *Iliad*." In Rubino and Shelmerdine 1983:140–164.

———. 1989. "Unreal Conditions in Homeric Narrative." *Greek, Roman, and Byzantine Studies* 30:5–26.

Lateiner, D. 2002. "Pouring Bloody Drops (*Iliad* 16.459): The Grief of Zeus." *Colby Quarterly* 38:42–61.

Lattimore, R., trans. 1951. *The Iliad of Homer*. Chicago.

Leach, E. R. 1961. *Rethinking Anthropology*. London.

Leaf, W., ed. 1900–1902. *The Iliad*. 2 vols. 2nd ed. London.

Leder, D. 1984–1985. "Towards a Phenomenology of Pain." *Review of Existential Psychology and Psychiatry* 19:255–266.

———. 1992. "The Experience of Pain and Its Clinical Implications." In *The Ethics of Diagnosis* (ed. J. L. Peset and D. Garcia) 95–105. Dordrecht.

Lesky, A. 1956. "Peleus und Thetis im frühen Epos." *Studi italiani di filologia classica* 27/28:216–226.

———. 1996. *A History of Greek Literature*. Trans. C. de Heer and J. Willis. 2nd repr. Indianapolis. Orig. pub. 1966.

Leumann, M. 1950. *Homerische Wörter*. Basel.

Levin, S. 1971. "The Etymology of NEKTAR: Exotic Scents in Early Greece." *Studi micenei ed egeo-anatolici* 13:31–50.

Levy, H. L. 1979. "Homer's Gods: A Comment on Their Immortality." *Greek, Roman, and Byzantine Studies* 20:215–218.

LfgrE = Snell, Bruno, ed. 1955–2010. *Lexikon des frühgriechischen Epos*. Göttingen.

Liddell, H. G., R. Scott, and H. S. Jones, eds. 1996. *A Greek-English Lexicon, with Revised Supplement*. Oxford.

Lincoln, B. 1991. *Death, War, and Sacrifice: Studies in Ideology and Practice*. Chicago.

Lombardo, S., trans. 1997. *Homer: Iliad*. Indianapolis.

Long, A. 1970. "Morals and Values in Homer." *Journal of Hellenic Studies* 90:121–139.

Loraux, N. 1986. "Le corps vulnérable d'Arès." In Malamoud and Vernant 1986:465–492.

———. 1998. *Mothers in Mourning*. Trans. C. Pache. Ithaca.

Lord, A. B. 2000. *The Singer of Tales*. 2nd ed. Cambridge, MA. Orig. pub. 1960.

Lorimer, H. L. 1950. *Homer and the Monuments*. London.

Louden, B. 1993. "Pivotal Contrafactuals in Homeric Epic." *Classical Antiquity* 12:181–198.

———. 1995. "Categories of Homeric Wordplay." *Transactions of the American Philological Association* 125:27–46.

Lowenstam, S. 1979. "The Meaning of IE *dhal-*." *Transactions of the American Philological Association* 109:125–135.

———. 1981. *The Death of Patroklos: A Study in Typology*. Königstein.

L-P = Lobel, E., and D. Page, eds. 1955. *Poetarum Lesbiorum Fragmenta*. Oxford.

Luce, J. V. 1975. *Homer and the Heroic Age*. New York.

Lynn-George, M. 1988. *Epos: Word, Narrative, and the Iliad*. Atlantic Highlands.

———. 1996. "Structures of Care in the *Iliad*." *Classical Quarterly* 46:1–26.

Mackie, C. J. 1997. "Achilles' Teachers: Chiron and Phoenix in the *Iliad*." *Greece and Rome* 44:1–10.

———. 1998. "Achilles in Fire." *Classical Quarterly* 48:329–338.

Macleod, C. W., ed. 1982. *Homer: Iliad Book XXIV*. Cambridge.

Maitland, J. 1999. "Poseidon, Walls, and Narrative Complexity in the Homeric *Iliad*." *Classical Quarterly* 49:1–13.

Malamoud, C., and J.-P. Vernant, eds. 1986. *Corps des dieux*. Paris.

Martin, R. 1989. *The Language of Heroes: Speech and Performance in the Iliad*. Ithaca.

Mayo, M. E. 1973. "The Gesture of '*Anakalypsis*.'" *American Journal of Archaeology* 77:220.

McGowan, E. P. 1995. "Tomb Marker and Turning Post: Funerary Columns in the Archaic Period." *American Journal of Archaeology* 99:615–632.

Meier-Brügger, M. 2003. *Indo-European Linguistics*. 8th ed. Trans. C. Gertmenian. Berlin.

Meillet, A. 1929. "Les adjectifs grecs en –τος." In *Donum Natalicum Schrijnen* (ed. J. Schrijnen) 635–639. Nijmegen-Utrecht.

Meissner, T. 2006. *S-Stem Nouns and Adjectives in Greek and Proto-Indo-European: A Diachronic Study in Word Formation.* Oxford.

Merleau-Ponty, M. 1962. *Phenomenology of Perception.* Trans. C. Smith. London.

Minkowski, E. 1970. *Lived Time: Phenomenological and Psychopathological Studies.* Trans. N. Metzel. Evanston. Orig. pub. 1933.

Mitchell W. J. T. 1980. "Spatial Form in Literature: Towards a General Theory." In *The Language of Images* (ed. W. J. T. Mitchell) 271–300. Chicago.

———. 1984. "The Politics of Genre: Space and Time in Lessing's *Laocoön*." *Representations* 6:98–115.

———. 1989. "Space, Ideology, and Literary Representation." *Poetics Today* 10:91–102.

Molyneux, J. H. 1972. "Two Problems Concerning Heracles in Pindar *Olympian* 9.28–41." *Transactions of the American Philological Association* 103:301–327.

Monro, D. B., ed. 1893. *Homer: Iliad, Books XIII-XXIV.* 3rd rev. ed. Oxford.

Moore, C. H. 1921. "Prophecy in the Ancient Epic." *Harvard Studies in Classical Philology* 32:99–175.

Morpurgo, A. 1963. *Mycenaeae Graecitatis Lexicon.* Rome.

Morris, I. 1987. *Burial and Society: The Rise of the Greek City-State.* Cambridge.

———. 1989. "Attitudes toward Death in Archaic Greece." *Classical Antiquity* 8:296–320.

Morris, I., and B. Powell, eds. 1997. *A New Companion to Homer.* Leiden.

Morris, S. P. 1989. "Daidalos and Kadmos: Classicism and 'Orientalism.'" *Arethusa* 22:39–54.

———. 1992. *Daidalos and the Origins of Greek Art.* Princeton.

———. 1995. "The Sacrifice of Astyanax: Near Eastern Contributions to the Siege of Troy." In Carter and Morris 1995:221–245.

———. 1997. "Homer and the Near East." In Morris and Powell 1997:599–623.

Morrison, J. V. 1992. "Alternatives to the Epic Tradition: Homer's Challenges in the *Iliad*." *Transactions of the American Philological Association* 122:61–71.

———. 1994. "Thematic Inversion in the *Iliad*: The Greeks Under Siege." *Greek, Roman, and Byzantine Studies* 35:209–227.

———. 1997. "*Kerostasia*, the Dictates of Fate, and the Will of Zeus in the *Iliad*." *Arethusa* 30:273–296.

Most, G. W. 1987. "Alcman's 'Cosmogonic' Fragment (fr. 5 Page, 81 Calame)." *Classical Quarterly* 37:1–19.

———. 2007. *Hesiod: The Shield, Catalogue of Women, and Other Fragments.* Cambridge, MA.

Motto, A. L., and J. R. Clark. 1969. "*Isē Dais*: The Honor of Achilles." *Arethusa* 2: 109–125.

Muellner, L. 1976. *The Meaning of Homeric εὔχομαι through Its Formulas*. Innsbruck.

———. 1996. *The Anger of Achilles: Mēnis in Greek Epic*. Ithaca.

Munn, N. D. 1992. "The Cultural Anthropology of Time: A Critical Essay." *Annual Review of Anthropology* 21:93–123.

Murnaghan, S. 1992. "Maternity and Mortality in Homeric Poetry." *Classical Antiquity* 11:242–264.

———. 1997. "Equal Honor and Future Glory: The Plan of Zeus in the *Iliad*." In *Classical Closure: Reading the End in Greek and Latin Literature* (ed. D. H. Roberts, F. M. Dunn, and D. Fowler) 23–42. Princeton.

Murray, A. T. 1988. *Homer: The Iliad*. Reprint edition. Cambridge, MA. Orig. pub. 1924.

M-W = Merkelbach, R. and M. L. West, eds. 1967. *Fragmenta Hesiodea*. Oxford.

Myloans, G. E. 1948. "Homeric and Mycenaean Burial Customs." *American Journal of Archaeology* 52:56–81.

Nagler, M. 1967. "Towards a Generative View of the Oral Formula." *Transactions of the American Philological Association* 98:269–311.

———. 1974. *Spontaneity and Tradition: A Study in the Oral Art of Homer*. Berkeley.

Nagy, G. 1974. *Comparative Studies in Greek and Indic Meter*. Cambridge, MA.

———. 1981. "Another Look at *kléos áphthiton*." *Wurzburger Jahrbucher für die Altertumswissenschaft* 7:113–116.

———. 1983. "On the Death of Sarpedon." In Rubino and Shelmerdine 1983. 189–217.

———. 1990a. *Greek Mythology and Poetics*. Ithaca.

———. 1990b. *Pindar's Homer: The Lyric Possession of an Epic Past*. Baltimore.

———. 1992. "Mythological Exemplum in Homer." In *Innovations of Antiquity* (ed. R. Hexter and D. Selden) 311–331. London.

———. 1996. *Homeric Questions*. Austin.

———. 1999. *The Best of the Achaeans: Concepts of the Hero in Archaic Greek Poetry*. Revised edition. Baltimore. Orig. pub. 1979.

———. 2000. "Distortion diachronique dans l'art homérique: quelques précisions." In *Constructions du temps dans le monde ancien* (ed. C. Darbo-Peschanski) 417–426. Paris.

———. 2010. "The Origins of Greek Poetic Language (Review of West 2007)." *Classical Review* 60:333–338.

Nehring, A. 1947. "Homer's Descriptions of Syncopes." *Classical Philology* 42: 106–121.

Northrup, M. 1979. "Tartarus Revisited: A Reconsideration of *Theogony* 711–819." *Weiner Studien* 13:22–36.

Oakley, J. H. 1982. "The Anakalupteria." *Archäologischer Anzeiger* 8a:113–118.

———. 1995. "Nuptial Nuances: Wedding Images in Non-Wedding Scenes in Myth." In Reeder 1995:63–73.

Oakley, J. H., and R. H. Sinos. 1993. *The Wedding in Ancient Athens*. Madison.

O'Brien, J. V. 1993. *The Transformation of Hera: A Study of Ritual, Hero, and the Goddess in the Iliad*. Lanham.

Olson, D. 1995. *Blood and Iron: Stories and Storytelling in Homer's Odyssey*. Leiden.

Onians, R. B. 1954. *The Origin of European Thought: About the Body, the Mind, the World, Time, and Fate*. Cambridge.

Otten, H. 1958. *Hethitische Totenrituale*. Berlin.

Page, D. 1959. *History and the Homeric Iliad*. Berkeley.

Palmer, L. R. 1963. *The Interpretation of Mycenaean Greek Texts*. Oxford.

———. 1996. *The Greek Language*. Norman. Orig. pub. 1980.

Parker, R. 1993. *Miasma: Pollution and Purification in Early Greek Religion*. Oxford.

Parker Pearson, M. 2000. *The Archaeology of Death and Burial*. College Station.

Parry, A. 1956. "The Language of Achilles." *Transactions of the American Philological Association* 87:1–7.

Parry, M. 1971. *The Making of Homeric Verse: The Collected Papers of Milman Parry*. Ed. A. Parry. Oxford.

Patton, W. R. 1912. "The Armor of Achilles." *Classical Review* 26:1–4.

———. 1913. "The Dragging of Hector." *Classical Review* 27:45–47.

Pavlou, M. 2008. "Metapoetics, Poetic Tradition, and Praise in Pindar *Olympian* 9." *Mnemosyne* 61:533–567.

Peek, W. 1955. *Griechische Vers-Inschriften*. Berlin.

Penglase, C. 1994. *Greek Myths and Mesopotamia: Parallels and Influence in the Homeric Hymns and Hesiod*. London.

Peradotto, J. 1990. *Man in the Middle Voice: Name and Narration in the Odyssey*. Princeton.

Perry, C. D. 1972. "The Tyranny of Three." *Classical Journal* 68:144–148.

Pertusi, A., ed. 1955. *Scholia vetera in Hesiodi Opera et dies*. Milan.

Petropoulou, A. 1988. "The Interment of Patroklos (*Iliad* 23.252–57)." *American Journal of Philology* 109:482–495.

Philippides, S. N. 1983. "Narrative Strategies and Ideology in Livy's 'Rape of Lucretia.'" *Helios* 10:113–119.

PMG = Page, D., ed. 1962. *Poetae melici Graeci*. Oxford.

Pokorny, J. 1959. *Indogermanisches etymologisches Wörterbuch*. 3 vols. Bern.

Poljakov, F. 1982. "Miscellanea Hellenosemitica 2: The Jar and the Underworld." *Ugarit-Forschungen: Internationales Jahrbuch für die Altertumskunde Syrien-Palästinas* 14:309–310.

Pötscher, W. 1961. "Hera und Heros." *Rheinisches Museum für Philologie* 104:302–355.

Priest, J. F. 1964. "ΌΡΚΙΑ in the *Iliad* and Consideration of a Recent Theory." *Journal of Near Eastern Studies* 23:48–56.

Pritchard, J. B., ed. 1969. *Ancient Near Eastern Texts Relating to the Old Testament*. 3rd ed. Princeton.

Pugliese Carratelli, G. 1954. "Ταρχύω." *Archivo glottologico italino* 39:79–82.

Puhvel, J. 1953. "Indo-European Negative Composition." *Language* 29:14–25.

———. 1954. "Greek Etymologies." *Language* 30:454–457.

———. 1991. *Homer and Hittite*. Innsbruck.

Purves, A. 2004. "Topographies of Time in Hesiod." In *Time and Temporality in the Ancient World* (ed. R. M. Rosen) 147–168. Philadelphia.

———. 2006a. "Falling into Time in Homer's *Iliad*." *Classical Antiquity* 25:179–209.

———. 2006b. "Unmarked Space: Odysseus and the Inland Journey." *Arethusa* 39:1–20.

Rabel, R. 1997. *Plot and Point of View in the Iliad*. Ann Arbor.

Race, W. H. 1997. *Pindar*. 2 vols. Cambridge, MA.

Radin, A. P. 1988. "Sunrise, Sunset: ἦμος in Homeric Epic." *American Journal of Philology* 109:293–307.

Reckford, K. J. 1964. "Helen in the *Iliad*." *Greek, Roman, and Byzantine Studies* 5:5–20.

Redfield, J. 1975. *Nature and Culture in the Iliad*. Chicago.

———. 1979. "The Proem of the *Iliad* and Homer's Art." *Classical Philology* 74:95–110.

Reece, S. 2009. *Homer's Winged Words: The Evolution of Early Greek Diction in Light of Oral Theory*. Leiden.

Reeder, E. D., ed. 1995. *Pandora: Women in Classical Greece*. Baltimore.

———. 1995. "The Catalogue, Section One: Representing Women." In Reeder 1995:123–193.

Reichel, M., and A. Rengakos, eds. 2002. *Epea pteroenta: Beiträge zur Homerforschung. Festschrift für Wolfgang Kullmann zum 75 Geburstag*. Stuttgart.

Richardson, N. J., ed. 1974. *The Homeric Hymn to Demeter*. Oxford.

———. 1993. *The Iliad: A Commentary*, vol. 6: *Books 21–24*. Ed. G. Kirk. Cambridge.

Richardson, S. 1990. *The Homeric Narrator*. Nashville.

Ricoeur, P. 1979. "The Human Experience of Time and Narrative." *Research in Phenomenology* 9:17–34.

———. 1980. "Narrative Time." *Critical Inquiry* 7:169–190.

———. 1984–1988. *Time and Narrative*. 3 vols. Chicago.

Rinon, Y. 2008. *Homer and the Dual Mode of the Tragic*. Ann Arbor.

Risch, E. 1974. *Wortbildung der homerischen Sprache.* 2nd ed. Berlin.

———. 1987. "Die ältesten Zeugnisse für κλέος ἄφθιτον." *Zeitschrift für vergleichende Sprachforschung* 100:3–11.

Robb, J. 2007. "Burial Treatment as Transformations of Bodily Ideology." In Laneri 2007:287–297.

Robertson, D. S. 1924. "Thucydides and the Greek Wall at Troy." *Classical Review* 38:7.

Rohde, E. 1925. *Psyche: The Cult of Souls and Belief in Immortality among the Greeks.* Trans. W. B. Hillis. 8th ed. Chicago.

Rouman, J. C., and W. H. Held. 1972. "More Still on the Trojan Horse." *Classical Journal* 67:327–330.

Rowe, C. J. 1983. "Archaic Thought in Hesiod." *Journal of Hellenic Studies* 103:124–135.

Rubino, C. A. 1979. "'A Thousand Shapes of Death': Heroic Immortality in the *Iliad*." In *Arktouros: Hellenic Studies Presented to B. M. W. Knox on the Occasion of His 65th Birthday* (ed. G. W. Bowersock, W. Burkert, and M. C. J. Putnam) 12–18. Berlin.

Rubino, C. A., and C. W. Shelmerdine, eds. 1983. *Approaches to Homer.* Austin.

Ruijgh, C. J. 1971. *Autour de 'τε épique': Études sur la syntaxe grecque.* Amsterdam.

Rundin, J. 1996. "A Politics of Eating: Feasting in Early Greek Society." *American Journal of Philology* 117:179–215.

Russo, J. A. 1963. "A Closer Look at Homeric Formulas." *Transactions of the American Philological Association* 94:235–247.

———. 1966. "The Structural Formula in Homeric Verse." *Yale Classical Studies* 20:219–240.

———. 1968. "Homer Against His Tradition." *Arion* 7:275–295.

———. 1997. "The Formula." In Morris and Powell 1997:238–260.

Rutherford, I. 2007. "Achilles and the *Sallis Wastais* Ritual: Performing Death in Greece and Anatolia." In Laneri 2007:223–236.

Rutherford, R. B. 1982. "Tragic Forma and Feeling in the *Iliad*." *Journal of Hellenic Studies* 102:145–160.

Rykwert, J. 1981. *On Adam's House in Paradise: The Idea of the Primitive Hut in Architectural History.* 2nd ed. Cambridge, MA.

Saïd, S. 1979. "Les crimes des prétendants, la maison d'Ulysse, et les festins de l'Odyssée." In *Études de littérature ancienne* (ed. S. Saïd, F. Desbordes, J. Bouffartigue, and A. Moreau) 9–49. Paris.

Sartre, J.-P. 1956. *Being and Nothingness: An Essay on Phenomenological Ontology.* Trans. H. E. Barnes. New York.

Scarry, E. 1985. *The Body in Pain: The Making and Unmaking of the World.* Oxford.

Schadewaldt, W. 1965. *Von Homers Welt und Werk.* 4th ed. Stuttgart.

Schein, S. L. 1984. *The Moral Hero: An Introduction to Homer's Iliad.* Berkeley.

———. 2002. "The Horses of Achilles in Book 17 of the *Iliad.*" In Reichel and Rengakos 2002:193–205.

Schmitt, R. 1961. "Nektar." *Zeitschrift für vergleichende Sprachforschung* 77:88.

———. 1967. *Dichtung und Dichtersprache in indogermanischer Zeit.* Wiesbaden.

———, ed. 1968. *Indogermanische Dichtersprache.* Darmstadt.

Schneidewin, F. G., and E. L. von Leutsch, eds. 1965. *Corpus paroemiographororum Graecorum.* Repr. ed. Hildesheim. Orig. pub. 1889.

Schrag, C. O. 1982. "Being in Pain." In Kestenbaum 1982:101–124.

Schwyzer, E. 1950–1971. *Griechische Grammatik, auf der Grundlage von Karl Brugmanns Griechischer Grammatik.* 4 vols. Munich.

Scodel, R. 1982. "The Achaean Wall and the Myth of Destruction." *Harvard Studies in Classical Philology* 86:33–50.

———. 1997. "Pseudo-Intimacy and the Prior Knowledge of the Homeric Audience." *Arethusa* 30:201–219.

Scott, J. A. 1913. "The Assumed Duration of the War of the *Iliad.*" *Classical Philology* 8:445–446.

Scott, W. C. 1974. *The Oral Nature of the Homeric Simile.* Leiden.

Scully, S. 1990. *Homer and the Sacred City.* Ithaca.

Segal, C. 1971. *The Theme of the Mutilation of the Corpse in the Iliad.* Leiden.

Severyns, A. 1928. *Le cycle épique dans l'école d'Aristarque.* Paris.

Seymour, T. D. 1903. *The First Six Books of Homer's Iliad.* Rev. ed. Boston. Orig. pub. 1890.

Sheppard, J. T. 1922. *The Pattern of the Iliad.* London.

Shive, D. 1996. "ΟΜΗΡΟΝ ΕΞ ΑΙΣΧΥΛΟΥ ΣΑΦΗΝΙΖΕΙΝ: *Iliad* 7.332–338 and *Agamemnon* 433–455." *Phoenix* 50:189–196.

Sihler, A. L. 1995. *New Comparative Grammar of Greek and Latin.* Oxford.

Singor, H. W. 1992. "The Achaean Wall and the Seven Gates of Thebes." *Hermes* 120:401–411.

Sinos, D. S. 1980. *Achilles, Patroklos, and the Meaning of Philos.* Innsbruck.

Sissa, G., and M. Detienne. 2000. *The Daily Life of the Greek Gods.* Trans. J. Lloyd. Stanford.

Slatkin, L. 1986. "The Wrath of Thetis." *Transactions of the American Philological Association* 116:1–24.

———. 1991. *The Power of Thetis: Allusion and Interpretation in the Iliad.* Berkeley.

Slings, S. R. 1995. "Archilochus, fr. 188, 1–2." *Zeitschrift für Papyrologie und Epigraphik* 106:1–2.

Smith, J. 1969. "Time, Times, and the 'Right Time': *Chronos* and *Kairos.*" *Monist* 53: 1–13.

Smith, P. 1981. *Nursling of Mortality: A Study of the Homeric Hymn to Aphrodite*. Frank-furt.

Smitten, J. R. 1981. "Introduction: Spatial Form and Narrative Theory." In Smitten and Daghistany 1981:15–34.

Smitten, J. R., and A. Dhagistany, eds. 1981. *Spatial Form in Narrative*. Ithaca.

Snell, B. 1944. "Zu den Fragmenten der griechischen Lyriker, 2. Archilochos fr. 113 u. 114 Diehl." *Philologus* 96:283–284.

Sourvinou-Inwood, C. 1981. "To Die and Enter the House of Hades: Homer, Before and After." In *Studies in the Social History of Death* (ed. J. Whaley) 15–39. London.

———. 1995. *"Reading" Greek Death: To the End of the Classical Period*. Oxford.

Spanos, W. V. 1970. "Modern Literary Criticism and the Spatialization of Time: An Existential Critique." *Journal of Aesthetics of Art Criticism* 29:87–104.

Sparkes, B. A. 1975. "The Trojan Horse in Classical Art." *Greece and Rome* 18:54–70.

Stanford, W. B., ed. 1967. *The Odyssey of Homer*. 2 vols. 2nd ed. London.

Staten, H. 1993. "The Circulation of Bodies in the *Iliad*." *New Literary History* 24: 339–361.

Steiner, D. 1986. *The Crown of Song: Metaphor in Pindar*. Oxford.

Stewart, A. 1995. "Rape?" In Reeder 1995:74–90.

Stokes, M. C. 1962. "Hesiodic and Milesian Cosmogonies—I." *Phronesis* 7:1–37.

Straus, E. 1960. "Das Zeiterlebnis in der endogenen Depression und in der psycho-pathischen Verstimmung." In *Psychologie der menschlichen Welt: Gesammelte Schriften* (ed. E. Strauss) 126–140. Berlin. Orig. pub. 1928.

———. 1966. "Disorders of Personal Time in Depressive States." In *Phenomeno-logical Psychology* (ed. E. Strauss) 290–295. New York. Orig. pub. 1947.

Stubbs, H. W. 1959. "Troy, Asgard, and Armageddon." *Folklore* 70:440–459.

Taplin, O. 1992. *Homeric Soundings: The Shaping of the Iliad*. Oxford.

Thalmann, W. G. 1984. *Conventions of Form and Thought in Early Greek Poetry*. Balti-more.

Thesleff, H. 1985. "Notes on the Name of Homer and the Homeric Question." In *Studia in honorem Iiro Kajanto* 293–314. Helsinki.

Thieme, P. 1952. *Studien zur indogermanischen Wortkunde und Religionsgeschichte*. Berlin.

Toombs, S. K. 1990. "The Temporality of Illness: Four Levels of Experience." *Theore-tical Medicine* 11:227–241.

———. 1992. *The Meaning of Illness: A Phenomenological Account of the Different Per-spectives of Physician and Patient*. Dordrecht.

Tsagarakis, O. 1969. "The Achaean Wall and the Homeric Question." *Hermes* 97:129–135.

Tsymbursky, V. L. 2007. "The Greek Verb ΤΑΡΧΥΩ 'To Bury' and the Asia-Minor Myth of the Defeated God [in Russian]." *Vestnik drevnej istorii* 260:152–169.

van Brock, N. 1959. "Substitution rituelle." *Revue hittite et asianique* 65:117–146.

van den Hout, T. P. J. 1994. "Death as a Privilege: The Hittite Royal Funerary Ritual." In *Hidden Futures: Death and Immortality in Ancient Egypt, Anatolia, the Classical, Biblical, and Arabic-Islamic World* (ed. J. M. Bremer, T. P. J. van den Hout, and R. Peters) 37–75. Amsterdam.

van der Valk, M. H. A. L. H. 1963–1964. *Researches on the Text and Scholia of the Iliad.* 2 vols. Leiden.

van Gennep, A. 1961. *The Rites of Passage.* Trans. M. B. Visedon and G. L. Caffee. Chicago. Orig. pub. 1909.

van Leeuwen, J. 1911. *Commentationes Homericae.* Leiden.

van Thiel, Helmut. 2000a. "Die D-scholien der *Iliad* in den Handschriften." *Zeitschrift für Papyrologie und Epigraphik* 132:1–62.

———, ed. 2000b. *Scholia D in Iliadem (Proecdosis 2000).* http://kups.ub.uni-koeln.de/volltexte/2006/1810/pdf/Scholia_D_Gesamt.pdf.

Ventris, M., and J. Chadwick. 1953. "Evidence for Greek Dialect in the Mycenaean Archives." *Journal of Hellenic Studies* 73:84–103.

Verdenius, W. J. 1985. *A Commentary on Hesiod, Works and Days, vv. 1-382.* Leiden.

Vermeule, E. 1979. *Aspects of Death in Early Greek Art.* Berkeley.

Vernant, J. 1977. "Le mythe 'Prométhéen' chez Hésiode: *Thégonie*, 535–616, *Travaux*, 42–105." In Gentili and Paioni 1977:91–106.

———. 1981. "Death with Two Faces." In Humphreys and King 1981:285–291.

———. 1986. "Corps obscur, corps éclatant." In Malamoud and Vernant 1986:19–45.

———. 1989. "At Man's Table: Hesiod's Foundation Myth of Sacrifice." In *The Cuisine of Sacrifice among the Greeks* (ed. M. Detienne and J.-P. Vernant) 21–86. Chicago

———. 1991. *Mortals and Immortals: Collected Essays.* Ed. F. I. Zeitlin. Princeton.

Vidal, J. 2004. "Geografía del Infierno Ugarítico según el ciclo mitológico de Ba'al." *Historiae* 1:108–115.

Vivante, P. 1970. *The Homeric Imagination.* Bloomington.

Volk, K. 2002. "ΚΛΕΟΣ ΑΦΘΙΤΟΝ Revisited." *Classical Philology* 97:61–68.

von der Mühl, P., ed. 1984. *Homeri Odyssea.* 3rd ed. Stuttgart. Orig. pub. 1962.

Wackernagel, J. 1943. "Indogermanische Dichtersprache." *Philologus* 95:1–19.

Walcot, P. 1961. "Pandora's Jar: *Erga* 83–105." *Hermes* 89:249–251.

———. 1966. *Hesiod and the Near East.* Cardiff.

Ward, D. 1968. *The Divine Twins: An Indo-European Myth in Germanic Tradition.* Berkeley.

Watkins, C. 1995. *How to Kill a Dragon: Aspects of Indo-European Poetics.* Oxford.

———. 1998. "Homer and Hittite Revisited." In *Style and Tradition: Studies in Honor of Wendell Clausen* (ed. P. Knox and C. Foss) 201–211. Stuttgart.

Welker, F. G. 1835–1847. *Der epische Cyclus oder die homerischen Dichter*. Bonn.

West, M. L., ed. 1966. *Hesiod: Theogony*. Oxford.

———. 1969. "The Achaean Wall." *Classical Review* 19:255–260.

———, ed. 1978. *Hesiod: Works and Days*. Oxford.

———. 1985. *The Hesiodic Catalogue of Women: Its Nature, Structure, and Origins*. Oxford.

———. 1988. "The Rise of Greek Epic." *Journal of Hellenic Studies* 108:151–172.

———. 1997. *The East Face of Helicon: West Asiatic Elements in Greek Poetry and Myth*. Oxford.

———, ed. 1998–2000. *Homeri Ilias*. 2 vols. Stuttgart.

———. 1999. "The Invention of Homer." *Classical Quarterly* 49:364–382.

———. 2001. *Studies in the Text and Transmission of the Iliad*. Munich.

———. 2002. "'Eumelos': A Corinthian Epic Cycle?" *Journal of Hellenic Studies* 122: 109–133.

———. 2003. "*Iliad* and *Aethiopis*." *Classical Quarterly* 53:1–14.

———. 2007. *Indo-European Poetry and Myth*. Oxford.

West, S. 1988. "Homer *Odyssey*: Books i–iv." In Heubeck, West, and Hainsworth 1988:49–245.

Wexler, R. D. 1993. *The Concepts of Mortality and Immortality in Ancient Mesopotamia*. PhD diss., University of California, Los Angeles.

Wheeler, B. J. 1889. "Linguistic Studies by John and Theodore Baunack." *Classical Review* 3:130–131.

White, C. J. 2005. *Time and Death in Heidegger's Analysis of Finitude*. Ed. M. Ralkowski. Aldershot.

Whitehead, O. 1984. "The Funeral of Achilles: An Epilogue to the '*Iliad*' in Book 24 of the '*Odyssey*.'" *Greece and Rome* 31:119–125.

Whitley, J. 1988. "Early States and Hero Cults: A Re-Appraisal." *Journal of Hellenic Studies* 108:173–182.

Whitman, C. H. 1958. *Homer and the Heroic Tradition*. Cambridge, MA.

———. 1970. "Hera's Anvils." *Harvard Studies in Classical Philology* 74:37–42.

———. 1982. *The Heroic Paradox: Essays on Homer, Sophocles, and Aristophanes*. Ithaca.

Whorf, B. L. 1956a. "An American Indian Model of the Universe." In Carroll 1956: 57–64.

———. 1956b. "The Relation of Habitual Thought and Behavior to Language." In Carroll 1956:134–159.

Willcock, M. M. 1964. "Mythological Paradeigma in the *Iliad*." *Classical Quarterly* 14:141–154.

Willcock, M. M. 1970. "Some Aspects of the Gods in the *Iliad.*" *Bulletin of the Institute of Classical Studies* 17:1–10.

———. 1976. *A Companion to the Iliad: Based on the Translation by Richmond Lattimore*. Chicago.

———. 1977. "Ad hoc Invention in the *Iliad.*" *Harvard Studies in Classical Philology* 81:41–53.

———, ed. 1978–1984. *The Iliad of Homer*. 2 vols. London.

———. 1997. "Neoanalysis." In Morris and Powell 1997:174–189.

Williams, B. 1993. *Shame and Necessity*. Berkeley.

Williams, H. 2004. "Death Warmed Up: The Agency of Bodies and Bones in Early Anglo-Saxon Cremation Rites." *Journal of Material Culture* 9:263–291.

Williams, R. D. 1972. *The Aeneid of Vergil*. 2 vols. London.

Wright, F. A. 1917. "The Food of the Gods." *Classical Review* 31:4–6.

Wyatt, W. F., Jr. 1982. "Homeric ATH." *American Journal of Philology* 103:247–276.

Wyllie, M. 2005a. "Lived Time and Psychopathology." *Philosophy, Psychiatry, and Psychology* 12:173–185.

———. 2005b. "Body-Subjects." *Philosophy, Psychiatry, and Psychology* 12:209–214.

Zannini Quirini, B. 1983. "ΙΧΩΡ 'il sangue' degli dèi." *Orpheus: Rivista di umanità classica e cristiana* 4:355–363.

Index Verborum

Greek

ἀγήρως "ageless", 161–162, 162nn8–9

ἀγχίθεοι "close to the gods", 171 and n35, 172n36

ἀδμήτη "untamed", 11–12, 242n8. *See also* δαμνάω/δαμνάζω

ἄζω "dry out, parch", 239, 271–272

αἷμα "blood", 176–178

ἄϊστος "invisible", 203–204 and nn110–112

αἰσχρός, 60–61, 61n23

ἀκήριος "without life/spirit", 167n21, 241

ἄκος "cure": 30n78, 184, 184n67; ἀκέεσθαι "to cure", 186. *See also* ἀνήκεστος

ἄλαστον "unforgettable/not yet forgotten", 36 and n89

ἀλέξω "ward off, defend", 77–78, 78nn40–41

ἄμβροτος "immortal, undying", 176

ἀμβροσία "food/drink of the gods, immortalizing substance", 22–23, 66, 71–74 and nn14–15, nn18–29. *See also* βροτός, βρότος

ἀμενός "strengthless", 213–214 and n131, n136

ἀμφιγυήεις "with crooked limbs on both sides", 189, 191–192. *See also* γυιώσω

anakalupteria "unveiling" (of bride to husband on wedding day), 128

ἀνήκεστος "incurable/not yet cured", 30 and n78, 184, 186 and n72

ἀντιτορέω "gouge through", 175 and n43

ἀπάτη "deception", 201 and n107. *See also* Διὸς ἀπάτη

ἄπρηκτον "unaccomplished", 50–51

ἀριστεία "experience of being the best of one's kind", 65, 120, 163–164

ἄρρηκτος "unbreakable/unbroken", 13–14, 42, 113–116

ἄσβεστος "inextinguishable/not yet extinguished", 146–147

ἀσχαλάω "grow impatient, suffer from boredom", 59–60, 231

ἄτη "delusion, blindness", 198n104, 201 and n107

ἄφθιτος "unwithering", 3, 5, 8n12, 11, 13, 19–20 and nn43–46, 41–42, 64, 66, 73, 94, 143, 235–237. *See also* κλέος ἄφθιτον

ἄχθος "burden, load", 179 and n59

ἄχθομαι "be weighed down", 179–180

βουλυτόνδε "to the position in the sky at which herders generally loosen their oxen", 24–25 and nn55–56

βροτός "mortal", 178 and n48

βρότος "blood, gore", 178 and n49

γέρας "prize, privilege, gift as manifestation of one's honor", 68 and nn3–4, 133–136 and nn4–8, n11

γέρας θανόντων "the honorable portion due the dead", 68, 133–139

γέρων "old man", 133, 136n11

γῆρας "old age", 68 and nn3–4, 133–134 and nn4–5, n8, 136 and n11

γυιόωσω "make lame", 189 and n79, 191–192. *See also* ἀμφιγυήεις

δαίμονι ἶσος "equal to a god", 164–166 and nn17–18, 211

δαίομαι "divide", 133 and n6

δαίς "feast", 133 and n6

δαμνάω/δαμνάζω "conquer, tame, subdue (sexually)", 129n71, 205–206 and n115, n117. *See also* ἀδμήτη

δάπτω "devour", 135n10

δεσμός "bond", 222 and n155, 224

δέω "bind", 222 and n155

Διὸς ἀπάτη "deception of Zeus", 93n75, 201 and n107, 204, 208

Διὸς βουλή "plan of Zeus", 47 and n4, 121 and n48, 205

duskleos "dishonored, without *kleos*", 50–51, 55

ἔμπεδος "in place, fixed in/on the ground", 78–80 and n43, 82; of the camp wall of the Achaeans, 78–80, 107; of the city wall of the Trojans, 130; of human resources (strength, youth, life), 71n17, 78–79 and n43, n45, 80, 162n9; of Odysseus' bed, 79 and n44; of tombs, 79n44, 151–152

ἐρείπω "throw down, fall", 108n16, 192n88

ἔχω "hold, protect", 124 and n54

ἤματα πάντα διαμπερές "throughout all days", 134–135

ἥρως "hero", 23n50, 167–168 and nn23–24, 199n105

θάλλω "flourish", 168n26, 269–270

θάπτω "bury, cremate", 137–138 and n17

θεράπων "henchman, ritual substitute", 104n15

ἰχώρ "divine blood", 40n95, 176–178 and n45

καλός "beautiful", 110n27

κάπετος "trench", 108n17

κῆδος "care, distress", 36–37, 38–39 and n98, 92, 181

κλέος ἄφθιτον "unwithered fame", 3–5 and nn3–5, 7–9 and n12, 14 and n28, 19–20 and nn44–45, 41–43, 46, 64, 66–67, 94, 132, 143, 148, 153, 157, 161, 257 and n29

κρήδεμνον "head covering", 126–127

κυλλός "crooked", 189n80

κυλλοποδίων "little twisted-foot", 189 and n80

λύω "loosen, destroy", 53

λῦσε δὲ γυῖα "he loosened his limbs", 220 and nn148–149; cf. γυῖα λέλυνται "his limbs were loosened", 220n149; cf. ὑπέλυσε ... γυῖα, "he loosened his limbs beneath him", 220n149

μασχαλισμός "the ritual desecration of a corpse", 75n32
μένος "strength, might, force", 79–80, 250; cf. μένος ἠελίοιο "might of the sun", 266. *See also* ἀμενός
μῆνις "rage", 134n8, 166
μῆτις "cunning intelligence", 190n83, 201
μιαιφόνος "blood-stained", 211n127
μίασμα "stain, pollution", 211n127
μίγνυμι "mix", 129n71
μοῖρα "fate, lot, portion", 217 and n141
μύω "close (eyes, mouth, wound)", 92n73–74

νέκταρ "food/drink of the gods, immortalizing substance", 23, 80–84 and nn46–48, 163 and n11
νήδυμος "sweet", 46n1
νήπιος "foolish, unreliable in speech", 58n19, 59n20
νόστος "return home", 4, 55, 99n4, 219
nympheutria "bridal attendant", 128

ὁμοῦ "together, at the same time", 218 and n142
ὄνειδος "blame, reproach", 134–136
ὄργυια "fathom", 150n33
οὐκ ἔτι "no longer", 47–49, 51, 106–107
οὔ πω "not yet", 50, 92–93
οὐρός "launching channel", 54n14
οὖρος "boundary marker", 148, 149n32

παίνομαι "to grow fat", 135n10
πίπτω "fall", 220 and n150, 252n20
πύθω "to rot", 53, 239, 261–264

σβέννυμι "to put out, quench", 146
σῆμα, σήματα "sign, tomb", 68n4, 131, 143, 150–151, 154–155
σήπω/σήπεσθαι "to decay (of organic material)", 53, 77, 92, 239, 259–261
σκέλλω "to dry up", 87n61, 239, 265–266
στήλη "tombstone, grave marker", 68, 143, 145

ταρχύειν "to provide with funeral rites", 68–69 and nn6–11
τε (epic), 167n20
τείρω "wear down, use up", 179 and nn52–57
τιμή "honor", 133–134 and n7
*τλάω "endure, suffer", 29–30, 181, 185 and n71
τύμβος/τύμβοι "tomb", 68, 132, 143–147
τυμβοχοέω "heap up a tomb", 143n26

ὑπόδρα ἰδών "glowering", 207–208 and n119

φθί(ν)ω/φθινύθω "to decay, rot", 5 and n5, 53, 239, 240–258

χάρις "grace", 93–94 and n77
χρόνος "time", 62, 232 and nn2–4

ὥρη "season", 167–168 and nn23–26

Proto-Indo-European

*ǵer-, 136n11

*nes-, 99n4, 219n145

*n̥-mr̥to-, 71, 73n29

*tr̥h₂-, 69, 80–81

Sanskrit

ákṣiti śrávas "fame imperishable", 13–14 and n28, 19–20 and nn44–45

śrávas ... ákṣitam "fame imperishable", 13–14 and n28, 19–20 and nn44–45

Index Locorum

Claudius Aelianus
  Varia historia 2.26, 172n36
Aeschylus
  Agamemnon 928–929, 32n84
  Libation Bearers 23–31, 91n69;
    423–428, 91n69; 439, 75n32
  Lykurgia (F 124–126 *TrGF*), 227n166
  Persians 1054–1065, 91n69
  Prometheus Bound 154, 194n94;
    1051–1052, 194n94
  Suppliants 134–135, 57n18
Anacreon fr. 46 PMG, 126n62
ps.-Apollodorus
  Library 1.6, 191n87; 1.7, 221, 227 and
    n162; 1.9, 196n99; 2.5, 114n35;
    2.6, 182 and n61; 2.7, 184–185n64;
    3.5, 227n166; 3.10, 195–196; 5.7,
    138
Apollonius of Rhodes
  Argonautica II 198–201, 266n43; IV
    869–872, 163n11
Archilochus fr. 13 W, 30; fr. 188 W,
    269–270
Aristotle
  History of Animals 580a18, 172n36
  Metaphysics III 4.12: 1000a5–17,
    71–72n17
  Nicomachean Ethics I 5: 1095b23–24,
    134n7

Physics IV 10–14, 24n53
Poetics XXIII 1459a35–37 Kassel,
    48n6; fr. 147 Rose, 48n6; fr. 167
    Rose, 92–93n74
Artemon
  FGrHist 443 F 2, 117n42

The Bible
  Deuteronomy 4:28, 185n70
  Genesis 6:1–4, 109n20, 170–171n31
  Habukkuk 2:18–19, 185n70
  Hosea 11:8, 185n70
  Jeremiah 8:21, 185n70; 9:1, 185n70;
    9:17, 185n70; 9:18, 185n70; 10:14,
    185n70; 10:19, 185n70; 10:20,
    185n70; 42:12, 185n70; 42:15,
    185n70; 42:17, 185n70; 51:17,
    185n70
  Joshua 6:1–27, 16n34

Certamen Homeri et Hesiodi 265–270,
    156n43.
Cicero
  On the Nature of Gods 3.42, 182n61;
    3.57, 172n36

Dicaearchus fr. 49.3 Wehrli, 170.
Diodorus Siculus
  Library 2.47, 172n36; 3.65, 227n166;
    4.68, 196n99

Diogenes Laertes
  Lives of Greek Philosophers 1.6,
    156n43
Epic Cycle
  Kypria fr. 1 Davies, 121n48, 123n52,
    126n60; fr. 3 Davies, 170–171n31
  Little Iliad fr. 3 Davies, 138
  Thebaid fr. 5 Davies, 84–85n57
Eumelus fr. 1 Davies, 227n166
Euphorion fr. 58 M, 117n41
Euripides
  Alcestis 3–6, 195; 86–92, 91n69;
    98–104, 91n69
  Andromache 100–102, 32n84;
    825–835, 91n69
  Children of Heracles 865–866,
    32n84
  Electra 239–240, 271n51; 954–956,
    32n84
  Hecuba 910, 126n62
  Helen 108, 110n24
  Phoenician Women 1485–1492,
    91n69
  Rhesus 166, 124; 821, 124
  Suppliant Women 71, 91n69; 826–
    827, 91n69; 977–979, 91n69; 1160,
    91n69
  Trojan Women 509–510, 32n84; 784,
    126n62
Eustathius
  Commentary on Homer's Iliad 852.35,
    167n21; 1245.49, 114n36
  Commentary at Homer's Odyssey II 54
    2–3, 268; II 54 10–11, 269n46

Hellanicus
  FGrHist 4 F 26a, 114n35; 4 F 26b,
    114n35; 4 F 32a, 117n42
Heraclides Ponticus fr. 172 Wehrli,
    48n6
Heraclitus B 62 D-K, 174

Herodotus
  Histories 1.29–33, 32; 1.93, 149n32;
    2.86, 69n10; 4.32, 172n36; 9.120,
    69n10
Hesiod
  Theogony 21, 162n10; 33, 162n10;
    99, 271; 105, 162n10; 119, 262n38;
    123, 226n160; 277, 162n8; 305,
    162n8; 535, 172; 545, 236, 256;
    550, 236, 256; 561, 236, 256; 622,
    226n160; 640, 72n18; 642, 72n18;
    658, 226n160; 717–719, 191;
    720–725, 209 and n124; 726–735,
    225–227; 731, 262n37; 739,
    262n37; 740–743, 209n124; 801,
    162n10; 810, 262n37; 815–819,
    227n162; 820, 191; 857–858,
    191–192; 886–891, 200; 924–929,
    192; 949, 162n8; 955, 162n8,
    184–185, 185n68; 978, 126n62
  Works and Days 3, 13n24; 90–92,
    169–170; 106–201, 109n22, 168;
    108, 168; 112–115, 169; 116,
    172–173n37; 153, 262n37; 283,
    184; 574–577, 268; 578, 271;
    624–626, 263n40; 705, 243n9;
    718, 162n10
  Catalogue of Women fr. 1.1–7 M-W,
    170; fr. 1.8–13 M-W, 173n39;
    fr. 23a.21–24 M-W, 71n17, 162n8;
    fr. 25.28 M-W, 162n8; fr. 30 M-W,
    196n99; fr. 35.6–9 M-W, 182; fr.
    51–52 M-W, 196n99; fr. 54–58.4
    M-W, 196n99; fr. 54a M-W, 196;
    fr. 54b M-W, 197n101; fr. 54a +
    57 M-W = fr. 58 Most, 196–197;
    fr. 70 M-W = fr. 41 Most, 155n42,
    257n28; fr. 141.26, 256; fr.
    204.87–89 M-W, 186–187n74; fr.
    229.8 M-W, 162n8; fr. 234.2, 256;
    fr. 296.2 M-W, 162n10, 234; fr. 298
    M-W, 179n55; fr. 343 M-W, 192n89

ps.-Hesiod

 Shield of Heracles 105, 126n62;
  151–153, 262; 359–367, 182n61,
  183–184n64; 367, 178n49

Homer

 Epigram 3, 156n43; 13.1, 126n62

 Iliad

  I 4–5, 47, 85n58, 121n48; I
   61, 218n142; I 228, 30n75;
   I 234–237, 258; I 250–252,
   150n35; I 266, 163n13; I 290,
   162n10, 234; I 352, 7n10, 66n2;
   I 393–412, 47, 114n35, 161n6,
   163, 216n138; I 416, 7n10,
   66n2; I 423–424, 171n34;
   I 488–492, 247, 271; I 494,
   162n10, 234; I 505–510, 47; I
   529, 72n23; I 590–593, 40n95,
   78n40, 188–189, 209n124; I
   599–600, 40n95, 146, 190; I
   607, 189

  II 1–6, 46, 47 and n2; II 12–15,
   48–49; II 19, 72n21; II 20, 51; II
   29–33, 47–48; II 46, 236, 256,
   256n25; II 57, 72n20; II 66–70,
   48–49; II 73, 49; II 110–122,
   49–50, 51–52; II 123–128, 49n8;
   II 134–141, 21, 51, 52–53, 55,
   247, 259; II 149–154, 50, 54,
   55; II 186, 236, 256, 256n25; II
   214, 217n140; II 217, 189n81;
   II 245, 207n119; II 272–274, 11;
   II 284–290, 58, 256; II 291–298,
   30, 59–60, 231, 232; II 299–308,
   30, 61–63, 122, 122n50, 232,
   232n4; II 325, 155n42, 257; II
   337–341, 58n19; II 343, 232n4; II
   346–347, 255; II 350–353, 24n54,
   122; II 354–356, 128n70; II 393,
   85n58; II 447, 162n8; II 458,
   55; II 467–468, 6, 168 and n25,
   241; II 484–493, 62n25, 252; II

  594–600, 137n15, 165n17; II
   604, 143 and n26; II 743, 24n54;
   II 755, 72n18; II 793, 143 and
   n26; II 809–810, 108–109n19; II
   811–814, 151, 223; II 833, 256

  III 9, 78n40; III 74, 97n2; III 94,
   97n2; III 103–104, 97n2; III 145,
   111n28; III 153–154, 110n26;
   III 157, 232n4; III 189, 24n54,
   152n38; III 250, 111n31; III
   298–301, 97n2; III 303, 111n31;
   III 383–447, 97; III 389, 192n88

  IV 8, 78n40; IV 27, 40n95; IV
   34–36, 84n57, 110n25; IV 44,
   256n26; IV 45, 163; IV 58, 168;
   IV 75–77, 179; IV 105–126,
   97 and n1, 218n142; IV 127,
   163; IV 148–149, 261; IV 152,
   188–189n76; IV 157–168, 97n2,
   122; IV 171–175, 261; IV 177,
   143n26; IV 178–179, 83n54; IV
   234–239, 97n2, 122, 128n70; IV
   309, 192n88; IV 313–316, 83n54,
   179n57; IV 349, 207n119; IV
   401, 186; IV 462, 192n88; IV
   469, 220n149; IV 482, 6; IV 493,
   192n88; IV 504, 221n152

  V 31, 211n172; V 42, 221n152; V
   47, 108n16, 192n88; V 57–58,
   108n16, 192n88, 221n152;
   V 68, 192n88; V 75, 192n88;
   V 127–128, 174n41; V 159,
   111n31; V 210, 24n54; V 251,
   207n119; V 254, 79; V 284,
   212n128; V 294, 192n88,
   221n152; V 302–310, 108n16,
   148n31, 220n147; V 330–343,
   40n95, 41n96, 72n18, 72n25,
   174–176, 175–178, 177n45; V
   352–354, 179, 180, 235n13; V
   357, 40n95, 192n88; V 359–362,
   180, 235n13; V 369, 72n18;

Homer

Iliad

V (*cont.*) 381, 235n11; V 382–391,
29, 40n95, 41n96, 161, 181, 186,
222–223, 224, 228, 234n12; V
392–404, 29, 161, 181–182, 183
and n62, 183–184n64, 186–187,
186n74, 215n137; V 416–417,
176; V 433–442, 164–165,
166n18; V 455, 211n127; V
459, 164, 166n18; V 473–474,
124; V 540, 221n152; V 560,
6; V 640–642, 114n37; V 643,
255; V 646, 183–184n64; V
648–651, 114n37; V 697, 70n13;
V 724–725, 236, 256, 245n25;
V 757–759, 97; V 769, 256n26;
V 777, 72n18; V 779, 78n40; V
788–791, 103–104n13; V 796,
179n56; V 812, 167n21; V 817,
167n21; V 842–844, 211n127; V
855–863, 40n95, 176, 211–212;
V 867, 218n142; V 870, 40n95,
176; V 884–887, 30, 40n95, 164,
166n18, 211, 212–214, 214n135,
217; V 888, 207–208n119; V
890, 163; V 899–906, 186 and
n74, 187, 215–216, 215n137,
216n138; V 908, 78n40

VI 27, 220n149; VI 32–33, 252n20;
VI 100, 167n21; VI 108, 256n26;
VI 130–140, 227n166; VI 136,
38n91; VI 137, 40n95; VI
138, 163, 234; VI 142, 162; VI
145–211, 25; VI 146–149, 5, 168
and n26, 241; VI 169, 257; VI
237, 111n28; VI 326–331, 110
and n25, 253; VI 345, 24n54; VI
386, 110n26; VI 388, 110n25; VI
403, 124 and n53; VI 407–413,
250, 253; VI 416–419, 135n9;
VI 431–432, 110n26, 124; VI
433–439, 110n25, 116n39;

VI 446, 257; VI 454–465,
124, 128n70, 154–155n40; VI
480, 178n49; VI 488, 217; VI
500–502, 124

VII 1, 108–109n19; VII 6,
220n149; VII 17–42, 97; VII
69–72, 122–123; VII 73–91,
69, 74, 137n16, 146n30,
153–155, 155n42, 257; VII 157,
79; VII 164–166, 110n26; VII
219, 16n30; VII 239, 272; VII
264–272, 148n31, 220n147;
VII 307, 111n28; VII 327–343,
98–99, 103, 143n26; VII
350–353, 97n2, 123; VII 366,
111n31; VII 392, 111n28; VII
400–402, 97n2, 122; VII 402,
129; VII 408–411, 99; VII 425,
178n49; VII 433–441, 100–101,
101n7, 143n26; VII 446–450,
99 and n4, 101n7; VII 451–453,
112, 113n33; VII 461, 101n7;
VII 463, 101n7; VII 480, 30n75;
VII 518–519, 110n26; VII 533,
110n25

VIII 10–17, 210, 216–217,
225 and n159, 262n38; VIII
19–27, 196; VIII 46, 256n26;
VIII 51, 216n138; VIII 58–59,
108–109n19; 111n28; VIII 69,
30n74; VIII 122, 192n88; VIII
177, 101n7; VIII 184, 126n60;
VIII 192, 257; VIII 260, 192n88,
221n152; VIII 314, 192n88; VIII
329, 192n88; VIII 359, 253; VIII
368, 226n160; VIII 379–380,
85n58; VIII 402, 189 and n79;
VIII 416, 189 and n79; VIII
434, 72n18; VIII 439, 171; VIII
455–456, 216–217n139; VIII
470–483, 24n54, 120, 209–210,
225 and n159; VIII 538–541,
83n54, 162n8, 234

IX 67, 101n7; IX 87, 101n7; IX
186–189, 144n27; IX 232, 101n7;
IX 251, 78n40; IX 253, 24n54;
IX 312, 184n64; IX 327, 128n69;
IX 347, 78n40; IX 348–354,
101n7, 103, 110n25, 111n28; IX
406–409, 3; IX 410–416, 4, 55,
66n2, 244; IX 413, 21, 135, 146,
155n42, 235, 257; IX 439, 24n54;
IX 524, 144n27; IX 535, 171n31;
IX 550–552, 103–104n13; IX
558, 163n13; IX 604, 256; IX
605, 78n40; IX 670, 78n40

X 2, 47, 47n2; X 41, 72n20; X 78,
91n69, 256; X 142, 72n20; X 187,
46n1; X 212, 257; X 267, 175n43;
X 415, 143; X 406, 91n69

XI 10–14, 55n16; XI 21, 257; XI
50, 146; XI 81, 216n138; XI
127, 218n142; XI 162, 85n58;
XI 166–168, 143; XI 181, 110
and n25; XI 236, 175n43; XI
240, 220n148, 220n149; XI
260, 220n149; XI 331, 256; XI
355, 192n88; XI 369–372, 143
and n26; XI 381, 212n128; XI
385–395, 58n19, 85n58, 167n21,
264; XI 453–454, 85n58; XI
560–561, 58n19; XI 690–693,
182; XI 743, 192n88; XI 766,
24n54; XI 818, 85n58; XI 820,
253; XI 830–831, 186–187n74;
XI 846–848, 186–187n74

XII 2–37, 101n7, 104–107,
109–110; XII 9, 78, 232n4; XII
10–18, 14; XII 64, 101n7; XII
90, 101n7; XII 121, 111n29; XII
137, 101n7; XII 143, 101n7;
XII 177, 101n7; XII 195, 111;
XII 198, 101n7; XII 216–229,
101n7, 122; XII 230, 207n119;
XII 257–258, 101n7, 108n16,
110n27; XII 261–264, 101n7,

110n27; XII 289, 101n7; XII
291, 101n7; XII 308, 101n7,
110n27; XII 310–328, 244; XII
323, 162n8; XII 338, 55; XII 352,
101n7; XII 374–375, 101n7,
110n27; XII 380–383, 101n7,
110n27, 148n31; XII 388, 101n7;
XII 390, 101n7; XII 397, 110n27;
XII 399, 101n7; XII 406, 101n27;
XII 416, 101n7; XII 417–424,
101n7, 149n32; XII 424, 101n27;
XII 430, 101n27; XII 433, 30n74;
XII 438, 101n7; XII 440, 101n7;
XII 443, 101n7; XII 445–449,
148n31; XII 453, 111n29; XII
461, 111n29; XII 468–469,
101n7; XII 470, 108–109n19

XIII 22, 236, 256 and n25; XIII
35, 72n18; XIII 50, 101n7; XIII
85, 220n149; XIII 87, 101n7;
XIII 105–110, 103–104n13; XIII
169, 146; XIII 178, 6; XIII 187,
221n152; XIII 224, 167n21; XIII
339, 256; XIII 355, 24n54; XIII
376, 111n31; XIII 470, 58n19;
XIII 475, 78n40; XIII 518–525,
174n40; XIII 527–539, 175n42;
XIII 540, 146; XIII 663–670,
66n2, 243–244; XIII 679, 101n7;
XIII 683–684, 101n7, 116n39;
XIII 764, 110n25; XIII 831–832,
85n58; XIII 825–828, 83n54

XIV 7, 178n49; XIV 15, 101n7,
108n16; XIV 32, 101n7; XIV 43,
256; XIV 55–56, 14, 101n7, 115;
XIV 66–68, 101n7, 115; XIV 82,
207n119; XIV 84–87, 242; XIV
143, 163; XIV 153–165, 204; XIV
161–165, 204–205; XIV 166–186,
205; XIV 170, 72n19; XIV 172,
72n25; XIV 177, 72n23; XIV 178,
72n25; XIV 198–199, 205–206,
206n117; XIV 200–207,

Homer

Iliad

XIV (*cont.*) 204, 232n4; XIV 233, 206n116; XIV 238, 236, 256 and n25; XIV 239, 189; XIV 242, 46n1; XIV 243–262, 201–203; XIV 250–256, 24n54, 114n37; XIV 257–258, 204; XIV 258, 198; XIV 259–261, 204; XIV 263–348, 201; XIV 279, 191n85; XIV 305, 232n4; XIV 346–351, 93n75, 266n44; XIV 354, 46n1; XIV 414, 192n88; XIV 509, 178n49

XV 1–11, 206; XV 13–33, 179n52, 198, 206–208; XV 59–71, 120–121, 137n15; XV 76, 24n54; XV 80–83, 179; XV 100–148, 174n40; XV 113–114, 218; XV 115–118, 217–218; XV 128–129, 219; XV 170–173, 179; XV 191, 262n38; XV 240, 188–189n76; XV 350, 137n16; XV 354, 101n7; XV 355–366, 101n7, 107–109, 108n16; XV 360, 108–109n19; XV 361, 101n7, 108n16; XV 371, 256n26; XV 384, 101n7; XV 391, 101n7; XV 395, 101n7; XV 452, 192n88; XV 511, 232n4; XV 565, 78n40; XV 581, 220n149; XV 721–723, 103–104n13; XV 736, 101n7

XVI 46–47, 121n48; XVI 97–100, 126n62, 127; XVI 123, 146; XVI 134, 256n26; XVI 249–252, 121n48; XVI 312, 220n149; XVI 319, 192n88; XVI 344, 192n88; XVI 397, 101n7; XVI 381, 82n52, 176n44; XVI 400, 220n149; XVI 433, 39n94; XVI 435–438, 39n94; XVI 440–449, 40n94; XVI 440–442, 450–457, 39n94; XVI 445, 213n133; XVI 450, 39n94; XVI 450–457, 67–68, 133, 143n26; XVI 458–461, 16, 39n94; XVI 465, 220n149; XVI 479–491, 65; XVI 482, 6, 192n88; XVI 498–501, 134–135; XVI 510, 179n53; XVI 512, 101n7; XVI 540, 255; XVI 558, 101n7; XVI 562, 78n40; XVI 581, 253; XVI 667–675, 70–71, 73n26 and n28, 133, 143n26; XVI 680, 73n26 and n28; XVI 684–693, 121n48; XVI 700, 110n26; XVI 702–704, 110, 110n25, 116n39; XVI 705, 164, 166n18; XVI 712, 111n28; XVI 714, 110n25; XVI 722, 83n54; XVI 786, 164, 166n18; XVI 795–797, 211n127, 218n143; XVI 805, 220n149; XVI 818–829, 65, 212n128; XVI 836, 85n58; XVI 851–854, 65n1, 122n49; XVI 867, 82n52, 176n44

XVII 50–51, 221n151 and n152; XVII 53–60, 6; XVII 89, 146; XVII 125–127, 75n32; XVII 131, 257; XVII 141, 207n119; XVII 153, 78n41; XVII 194–198, 82n52, 83n53, 176n44, 236n14, 256n26; XVII 202, 82n52, 83n53, 176n44, 236n14; XVII 205–206, 83n53; XVII 241, 85n58; XVII 311, 221n152; XVII 356, 78n40; XVII 360–365, 218n142, 252–253, 252n20; XVII 401–409, 66n2, 110n25; XVII 426–428 and 434–447, 34–35; XVII 432–440, 143n26, 185n70, 192n88, 211n127, 218n143; XVII 443–447, 162n8, 163; XVII 457, 185n70; XVII 497–498, 177; XVII 522, 192n88; XVII 556–559, 85n58, 110n25, 135; XVII 619, 192n88; XVII 672, 217; XVII 745, 179n56, 218n142

XVIII 25, 73n26; XVIII 37–60,

66n2; XVIII 39, 193n92; XVIII
52–60, 7; XVIII 83–85, 24n54,
82n52, 176n44, 236n14,
256n26; XVIII 95–126, 38 and
n90, 42, 66n2, 77n38, 237;
XVIII 175–177, 75n32; XVIII
179–191, 85–86; XVIII 203–204,
75; XVIII 205–214, 75; XVIII
215, 101n7; XVIII 217–221,
75; XVIII 228–231, 75n33;
XVIII 256, 110n25; XVIII 265,
128n69; XVIII 267–268, 72n20;
XVIII 271, 85n58; XVIII 274,
110n26; XVIII 275, 111 and
n28; XVIII 279, 110n25; XVIII
284, 207n119; XVIII 329–332,
66n2; XVIII 333–337, 75, 86n59;
XVIII 345, 178n49; XVIII 365,
78n40; XVIII 369–371, 189, 236,
256, 256n25 and n26; XVIII
372, 40n95; XVIII 378–394, 75;
XVIII 382–383, 126n60, 189,
204; XVIII 387, 190n84; XVIII
393, 189; XVIII 394–409, 38n91,
40n95, 189, 193n90; XVIII
411, 190n84; XVIII 417–421,
190n84; XVIII 428–443, 37–39,
206; XVIII 446, 271; XVIII 462,
189; XVIII 464–467, 82n50, 83,
236, 236n14; XVIII 472, 40n95;
XVIII 564, 108n17; XVIII 587,
189; XVIII 590, 189; XVIII 614,
189; XVIII 618, 82n50, 236n14
XIX 3, 82n49, 236 and n14;
XIX 10–11, 82n49, 82n50,
236 and n14; XIX 13, 82n51;
XIX 18, 82n50, 236n14; XIX
19, 82n51; XIX 21–39, 53n12,
73n28, 76–78, 79–80, 81–82, 87,
259–260, 261; XIX 60, 24n54;
XIX 89, 24n54; XIX 95–133, 198;
XIX 98, 24n54; XIX 99, 126n62;
XIX 107–113, 199; XIX 117–119,
199–200; XIX 125–133, 200–201,
256n26; XIX 155–170, 22,
73n27, 232n4; XIX 178, 72n25;
XIX 205–214, 73n27; XIX 223,
30n74; XIX 225–233, 22, 77n39;
XIX 270–274, 198n104; XIX
284–285, 91n69; XIX 322–323,
244n10; XIX 325, 189n81; XIX
329–330, 244n10; XIX 347–348,
73n27, 80, 163n11; XIX
352–354, 22, 73n27, 163n11;
XIX 404–423, 16; XIX 416–417,
66n2
XX 21, 40, 234; XX 30, 19n42,
78n41, 110n25; XX 54–66, 163,
186n73, 262n37; XX 145–148,
110n25, 114n37; XX 168–181,
40n94, 254; XX 236, 111n31; XX
270, 189; XX 285–287, 148n31;
XX 299, 163; XX 315, 78n40; XX
336, 19n42; XX 369, 78n40; XX
428, 207–208n119; XX 443–444,
166n18; XX 447, 164, 166n18;
XX 491, 272; XX 493, 164,
166n18; XX 499, 218n142
XXI 6, 108–109n19; XXI 8,
108–109n19; XXI 18, 164,
166n18; XXI 27–32, 86n59; XXI
34, 111n31; XXI 49, 101n7; XXI
77, 24n54; XXI 108–113, 66n2;
XXI 138, 72n40; XXI 150, 30n75,
78n40; XXI 227, 164, 166n18;
XXI 243, 192n88; XXI 257–264,
108–109n19; XXI 277–278,
66n2, 110n25; XXI 295, 110n25;
XXI 299, 110n25; XXI 316–323,
109, 223; XXI 331, 189; XXI 374,
78n40; XXI 392, 175n43; XXI
402, 211n127; XXI 403–408,
148 and n31, 220 and n147,
223; XXI 417, 188–189n76; XXI
441–457, 14, 25 and n58, 42,
110n25, 112–114, 231, 236;

Homer
  Iliad
    XXI (*cont.*) 462–467, 110n25,
      162, 166–167, 168, 240–241;
      XXI 489–496, 40n95; XXI 507,
      72n25; XXI 516–517, 19n42,
      110n25; XXI 518, 162n10, 234;
      XXI 526, 110n26; XXI 530–536,
      110n25, 111, 116n39; XXI
      537–543, 78n40, 110n25, 111
      and n28; XXI 557, 110n25;
      XXI 608, 110n25; XXI 610,
      108–109n19
    XXII 3–4, 110 and n25 and n27,
      111; XXII 12, 108–109n19; XXII
      16, 110n25; XXII 56, 110n25;
      XXII 59–76, 124; XXII 79–83,
      163n11; XXII 85–89, 85n58,
      110n25, 124; XXII 96, 146;
      XXII 99, 110n25, 111n28; XXII
      112, 110n25; XXII 144, 110n25;
      XXII 146, 110n25; XXII 168,
      110n25; XXII 169–170, 40n94;
      XXII 195–196, 78n40, 110 and
      n26; XXII 208, 16n34; XXII
      209, 30n74; XXII 237, 110n25;
      XXII 242, 179n54; XXII 260,
      207–208n119; XXII 273–277,
      16n34; XXII 325–363, 65;
      XXII 330, 192n88; XXII 335–336,
      85n58; XXII 342–343, 137n16;
      XXII 344, 207–208n119;
      XXII 345–354, 78n41, 83n54,
      84, 86n59, 85n58, 111n31; XXII
      358–360, 24n54, 66, 122n49;
      XXII 361, 75n35; XXII 378–
      394, 75; XXII 405–407, 38; XXII
      408–411, 125 and n58; XXII
      466–474, 24n54, 125, 126n60,
      192n88; XXII 475, 188–189n76;
      XXII 507, 110n25, 124 and
      n53; XXII 508–510, 85 and
      n58

    XXIII 9, 136; XXIII 19–23,
      86n59; XXIII 41, 178n49; XXIII
      65–76, 76, 137, 183–184n64;
      XXIII 80–81, 66n2, 110n25,
      122n49; XXIII 87, 24n54; XXIII
      91–92, 227 and n166; XXIII
      108–227, 136; XXIII 179–191,
      73n28, 78n41, 85n58, 85–87,
      87–88n63, 90 and n68, 92n72,
      93n75, 261, 265–266, 266n45;
      XXIII 205–207, 171n34; XXIII
      229–897, 136; XXIII 231–234,
      93n76; XXIII 245, 143n26;
      XXIII 250, 147; XXIII 283–284,
      185n70; XXIII 326–333,
      149–150, 223; XXIII 349, 143;
      XXIII 418, 232n4; XXIII 420,
      108–109n19; XXIII 655, 206;
      XXIII 691, 192n88; XXIII 726,
      220n149; XXIII 791, 243n9
    XXIV 3–21, 87–90, 92n72; XXIV
      23, 163; XXIV 31, 90; XXIV 35,
      30n75; XXIV 85, 163n11; XXIV
      88, 236, 256; XXIV 90–91, 36,
      38; XXIV 99, 162n10, 163, 234;
      XXIV 104–105, 36, 38; XXIV
      107–108, 90; XXIV 128–132,
      93n76; XXIV 134–135, 40n94;
      XXIV 152, 40n94; XXIV 171,
      111n31; XXIV 210–211, 85;
      XXIV 212–214, 84n57; XXIV
      220, 163n13; XXIV 243–246,
      125; XXIV 340–341, 72n24;
      XXIV 354, 111n31; XXIV
      411–423, 53n12, 90n66, 91–93,
      93n75, 163, 260–261, 266;
      XXIV 475–476, 93n76; XXIV
      505, 30n75; XXIV 519, 30n75;
      XXIV 522–526, 38–39; XXIV
      559, 207–208n119; XXIV
      602–609, 165n17; XXIV 629,
      111n31; XXIV 631, 111n31;
      XXIV 635–642, 92n73, 93n76;

XXIV 661, 94n77; XXIV
662, 108–109n19; XXIV 665,
127n64; XXIV 666, 143n26;
XXIV 675–676, 93n76, 232n4;
XXIV 678, 47 and n2; XXIV
711, 91n69; XXIV 719–804,
136; XXIV 747–760, 38, 40n94,
93n75, 266; XXIV 797–798,
108n17; XXIV 800, 87n62, 94

Odyssey

i 22–26, 171n34; i 67, 163; i
97, 72n24; i 159–162, 263; i
167, 163; i 239–241, 143n26,
146, 257; i 248–251, 245–246,
246n13; i 263, 162n10; i 288,
246n13; i 344, 257; i 378,
162n10

ii 14, 171; ii 26, 171; ii 100, 217;
ii 115, 232n4; ii 125, 257; ii 143,
162n10; ii 329, 257; ii 367–368,
254; ii 357, 254

iii 3, 163; iii 83, 257; iii 147,
162n10; iii 196, 256; iii 203–204,
146n30, 257; iii 392, 126n61

iv 32, 58n19; iv 197–198, 136;
iv 232, 186; iv 271–289, 118;
iv 378, 163; iv 427, 72n20; iv
445, 72n19; iv 543, 232n4; iv
583–584, 143n26, 146 and n30,
162n10, 257; iv 594, 232n4; iv
599, 232n4; iv 623, 126n60; iv
675, 232n4; iv 716, 257; iv 723,
218n142; iv 726, 257; iv 793,
46n1; iv 805, 163, 234; iv 816,
257

v 7, 162n10, 234; v 35, 171n35;
v 93, 72n18; v 122, 163, 234;
v 136, 162n8, 234; v 160–161,
249–250; v 167, 163; v 199,
72n18; v 218, 162n8; v 309,
24n54; v 319, 232n4; v 341, 256;
v 346, 126n60; v 351, 126n60; v
373, 126n60; v 458, 188–189n76;

v 459, 126n60; v 574, 72n20

vi 100, 126n60; vi 150, 163; vi
153, 163; vi 240, 163; vi 243,
163; vi 240, 163; vi 295, 232n4

vii 94, 162n8, 234; vii 201–206,
171–172; vii 209, 163; vii 257,
162n8, 234; vii 260, 73n26; vii
283, 72n20, 188–189n76; vii
333, 146, 257

viii 74, 257; viii 222, 162; viii
224–227, 165n17; viii 233,
220n149; viii 300, 189; viii 306,
162n10, 234; viii 308, 189n79;
viii 326, 146; viii 332, 189n79;
viii 349, 189; viii 357, 189; viii
492–495, 118; viii 511–515, 118;
viii 523–530, 248–249; viii 635,
162n10

ix 19–20, 55–56, 257; ix 58–59,
24–25n55, 206; ix 82–84, 10; ix
89, 162; ix 133, 256; ix 163, 255;
ix 199, 72n20; ix 133, 236, 256;
ix 138, 232n4; ix 234, 272; ix
264, 257; ix 289, 84n57; ix 325,
150n33; ix 357, 72n18; ix 527,
256n26

x 101, 162; x 114, 84n57; x 167,
150n33; x 177, 246n13; x 363,
258; x 469–470, 250–251; x
483–486, 249; x 512, 262n37; x
514, 72n18; x 521, 214; x 536,
214

xi 17, 256n26; xi 25, 150n33;
xi 29, 214; xi 41, 178n49; xi 49,
214; xi 71–78, 74n30, 135n9,
137–138, 143–144, 143n26,
146n30; xi 126–127, 145n29;
xi 161, 232n4; xi 181–183,
249n15, 251; xi 245, 128n67;
xi 305–320, 221; xi 328–331,
251–252; xi 356–358, 253; xi
491, 256; xi 523–537, 118; xi
560, 217

Homer

 Odyssey (cont.)

  xii 8–15, 74n30, 144–145, 143n26; xii 39–46, 263–264; xii 81, 226n160; xii 127–131, 241–242; xii 329, 255; xii 311, 46n1; xii 337, 163; xii 344, 163; xii 371, 162n10, 234; xii 377, 162n10, 234; xii 380, 256n26; xii 386, 163; xii 407, 232n4

  xiii 55, 163; xiii 337–338, 249n15; xiii 386–388, 126–127, 126n62; xiii 397–403, 267; xiii 429–430, 267

  xiv 90–95, 245n12; xiv 162, 250; xiv 193, 232n4; xiv 340, 257; xiv 369–370, 143n26, 146n30; xiv 394, 163

  xv 8, 72n20; xv 68, 232n4; xv 71, 118; xv 353–357, 243, 250; xv 494, 232n4; xv 545, 232n4

  xvi 38–39, 249n15; xvi 125–128, 245, 246n13; xvi 142–145, 244–245, 248; xvi 183, 163; xvi 211, 163; xvi 241, 257; xvi 267, 232n4

  xvii 112, 232n4; xvii 115, 163n13; xvii 484–487, 114n36

  xviii 136, 163; xviii 149–150, 177; xviii 180, 163; xviii 191, 82n52, 176n44; xviii 193, 72n19; xviii 202–205, 246; xviii 238, 220n149; xviii 242, 220n149

  xix 43, 163; xix 108, 257; xix 133, 246n13; xix 169, 232n4; xix 221, 232n4; xix 279, 171n35; xix 307, 250; xix 333, 257; xix 593, 163

  xx 19, 24n54; xx 64, 262n38; xx 79–82, 203–204; xx 113, 256n26; xx 346, 146; xx 356, 226n160.

  xxi 70, 232n4; xxi 282, 58n19

  xxii 39, 163; xxii 65, 163; xxii 184, 272; xxii 295, 212n128; xxii 297, 256; xxii 414, 163

  xxiii 137, 257; xxiii 203, 79; xxiii 206, 79n44; xxiii 252, 24n54; xxiii 322, 262; xxiii 336, 162n8, 234

  xxiv 10, 262n37; xxiv 32, 143n26; xxiv 33, 257; xxiv 43–84, 136; xxiv 59, 73n26; xxiv 73–77, 227 and n166; xxiv 80–84, 74n30, 109–110, 143n26, 146n30, 147, 223; xxiv 85–93, 136; xxiv 189, 178n49; xxiv 190, 136; xxiv 196–202, 146n30, 155n42, 163n13, 257; xxiv 218, 232n4; xxiv 292–296, 136; xxiv 349, 188–189n76; xxiv 433–436, 245; xxiv 525, 221n152; xxiv 531–532, 177

 Homeric Hymn to Aphrodite 3, 206; 12, 163n13; 62, 162n10; 63, 72n25; 81–83, 11–12; 135, 168; 164, 128n67; 200–201, 172n36; 214, 162n8; 269–272, 271–272

 Homeric Hymn to Apollo 1–9, 197n101; 69, 163; 151, 162n8; 156, 155n42; 279, 163n12; 305–358, 192; 311–315, 192n89; 315–317, 189n81, 192–193; 334–339 and 349–352, 193–194; 442, 55; 498, 163; 512, 163

 Homeric Hymn to Demeter 25, 126n60; 33, 256n26; 41, 72n22, 126n60; 49, 72n18; 152–152, 126n62; 237–238, 71–72n17, 72n19, 73n28; 242, 73n28, 162n8; 260, 162n8; 325, 162n10, 234; 335, 226n160; 337, 226n160; 438, 126n60; 459, 126n60; 482, 262n37

 Homeric Hymn to Dionysus 37, 72n19

Homeric Hymn to Hermes 103, 242n8; 119, 175n43; 130–136, 167n19; 178, 175n43; 283, 175n43; 324, 30n74; 490–494, 242n8; 548, 162n10

Homeric Hymn 6.2, 126n62; 6.6, 73n26

Homeric Hymn 30.17, 256n26

Homeric Hymn 31.3, 256n26

Hyginus
   Fabulae 61, 196n99; 89.1–2, 114n35; 132, 242, 227n166

Iamblichus
   De mysteriis 5.12, 71–72n17

Ibycus fr. 151.47–48 PMG, 257n28

Isocrates
   Archidamus 19, 182

KN Ap 639.12, 21n46

KN Ra 1540, 16n30

Lucian
   On Sacrifices 4, 114n35
   Jupiter confutatus 8, 114n35

Lycophron
   Alexandria 39–40, 182n61

Megasthenes
   FHG 30.30, 172n36

Metrodorus
   FGrHist 43 F 2 = 70 B 4 D-K, 114n36

Mimnermus fr. 2 W, 7n10, 241

MY Oe 103, 21n46

Mythographi Vatacani I 136, II 193, 114n35

Ovid
   Metamorphoses XI 194–210, 114n35

Nonnus
   Dionysiaca 1.481–512, 191n87; 21.166, 227n166

Palatine Anthology 7.153, 156n43

Panyassis frr. 6A-6C Davies, 183

Pausanius
   Description of Greece 1.18.5, 172n36; 1.23.8, 118n45; 3.21.8, 182n61; 3.26.8, 182; 5.3.1, 182; 6.25.2, 183–184n64; 10.13.7, 182n61

Pherecydes of Athens
   FGrHist 3 F 145, 70n13

Philodemus
   On Pity 34, 197n101

Pindar
   Isthmian 6.23, 172n36; 8.46–47, 171n31
   Nemian 3.43–53, 186–187n74; 4.65–68, 170–171n31; 5.22–39, 170–171n31; 6.1–6, 169n29.
   Olympian 1.59–63, 73; 8.30–46, 114n35; 8.32–36, 117n41, 126n62; 9.28–35, 183; 9.33, 183–184n64
   Pythian 3.54–58, 195 and n95, 196n98; 3.86–96, 170–171n31; 6.21–23, 186–187n74; 8.95–96, 7n11; 10.34–40, 172n36; 10.41–44, 172n36
   Paean 8.63, 172n36

Plato
   Phaedo 80c, 69n10; 89b, 91n69
   Phaedrus 264c–d, 156n43

Pliny the Elder
   Natural History 7.202, 118n45; 24.65, 57n18

Plutarch
   de E Delphico 3, 156n43
   Moralia 378d, 182n61

Porphyry
   De abstinentia 4.2, 170

Proclus
   epitome *Aethiopis* 18–21, 76n36
   epitome *Little Iliad*, 117

PY An 657.3, 21n46

PY Eb 416.1, 133n4

Rig Veda 1.40.4b, 14, 19; 1.9.7bc, 14, 19, 19–20n45; 8.103.5b, 14, 19; 9.66.7c, 14, 19

Sappho
   fr. 44.4 L-P, 257n28
   fr. 140a L-P, 91n69
   fr. 142 L-P, 173n38
Scholia at Aeschylus *Suppliant Women* 134–135, Smith, 57n18
Scholia at Apollonius of Rhodes *Argonautica* I 211c, 70n13
Scholia at Hesiod *Theogony* 727 Pertusi, 227n163; 782a2–3 Pertusi, 263n39
Scholia at Homer *Iliad*: bT at *Iliad* I 1b Erbse, 104; bT at *Iliad* I 5c Erbse, 121n48; A at *Iliad* I 400 Erbse, 114n35; bT at *Iliad* I 584b1 Erbse, 190; D at *Iliad* I 593 van Thiel, 188n76; A at *Iliad* II 60–71 Erbse, 48n5; bT at *Iliad* II 135 Erbse, 53; D at *Iliad* II 135 van Thiel, 53; bT at *Iliad* II 153b Erbse, 54; D at *Iliad* II 153 van Thiel, 54n14; D at *Iliad* II 782 van Thiel, 208n121, 216n139; D at *Iliad* II 814 van Thiel, 152n38; Gen. at *Iliad* V 126 Nicole, 84–85n57; bT at *Iliad* V 385b Erbse, 222n154; bT at *Iliad* V 392–394 Erbse, 182, 183–184n64; bT at *Iliad* V 395–397 Erbse, 182n61; T at *Iliad* V 397 Erbse, 183–184n64; bT at *Iliad* V 885b Erbse, 214n134; bT at *Iliad* V 885–887b Erbse, 214n134; A at *Iliad* VII 334 Erbse, 101n8; A at *Iliad* VII 443–464 Erbse, 112n32; A at *Iliad* VIII 12a Erbse, 217n140; bT at *Iliad* VIII 12b Erbse, 216n139; bT at *Iliad* IX 352–353 Erbse, 104; D at *Iliad* XI 395 van Thiel, 239n1; A at *Iliad* XI 690 Erbse, 183–184n64; bT at *Iliad* XI 690 Erbse, 182; T at *Iliad* XI 690 Erbse, 182; T at *Iliad* XII 29d1 Erbse, 104; T at XIV 199 Erbse, 206n115; bT at *Iliad* XV 17d Erbse, 208, 216n139; A at *Iliad* XVI 100 Erbse, 127; A at *Iliad* XX 146 Erbse, 114n35; D at *Iliad* XXI 392 van Thiel, 175n43; AbT at *Iliad* XXI 392 Erbse, 175n43; Gen. at *Iliad* XXI 444c Nicole, 114nn35–36; T at *Iliad* XXI 444d Erbse, 114nn35–36; bT at *Iliad* XXIII 92 Erbse, 227n166; A at *Iliad* XXIII 191b Erbse, 266; D at *Iliad* XXIII 191 van Thiel, 266n43; D at *Iliad* XXIII 328 van Thiel, 239n1; AbT at *Iliad* 791 Erbse, 243n9; T at *Iliad* XXIV 420b Erbse, 92–93n74

Scholia at Homer *Odyssey*: T at *Odyssey* i 161 Dindorf, 239n1; QV at *Odyssey* ix 58 Dindorf, 24–15n55; H at *Odyssey* xiii 388 Dindorf, 127; HQ at *Odyssey* xxii 184 Dindorf, 272n54; T at *Odyssey* xxiv 80–81 Dindorf, 101n8
Scholia at Lycophron *Alexandria* 39–40 Scheer, 182n61
Scholia at Pindar *Olympian Odes*, Drachmann 8.31/41, 114n35, 117n41; 8.33/44b, 116–117; 9.33, 184n64; 9.43 and 9.44a and 9.48, 182n61
Scholia at Statius *Thebaid* 4.106, 182n61
Scholia at Thucydides *History of the Peloponnesian War* 1.11.1, 102n10

Servius
  Commentary at Virgil's Aeneid 2.15,
    118n45; 3.14, 227n166; 6.585,
    196n99
Shakespeare, William
  Hamlet V.i.41–59, 131
  The Rape of Lucrece 463–469,
    129n71
Simonides fr. 76 PMG, 156–157; fr. 570
    PMG, 172n36; fr. 581 PMG, 156n43
Solon fr. 36 W, 149n32
Sophocles
  Ajax, 138
  Antigone 122, 126n62; 832, 173n38
  Electra 89–91, 91n69; 445, 75n32
  Oedipus the King 1528–1530, 32n84
  Salmoneus (F 537–541a *TrGF*),
    196n99
  Troilos (F 623 *TrGF*), 75n32
  Tyndareus (F 646 *TrGF*), 32n84
  Tyro (F 662 *TrGF*), 32n84
  Women of Trachis 1–5, 32n84
Stesichorus fr. 234 PMG, 227n166
Strabo
  Geography 11.5.4 and 12.8.6 and
    13.3.6 and 14.1.4, 152n38; 15.57,
    172n36

Tacitus
  Agricola 29.4, 243n9
Tertullian
  Ad nationes 1.10.38, 40–41; 1.10.39,
    41n96
Theognis
  fr. 245 W, 257n28
  fr. 867 W, 155n42
Theopompus of Chios
  FGrHist 115 F 351, 53
Thucydides
  History of the Peloponnesian War
    1.11.1, 101–102

Tzetzes
  Commentary at Hesiod's Theogony
    277, 227 and n162
  Scholia at Lycophron 34, 114n35

Varro
  apud Aulus Gellius *Attic Nights* 17.3,
    57n18
Virgil
  Aeneid 2.185–187, 118 and 43; 2.234,
    118; 2.604–606, 174n41; 6.273,
    227n163; 6.304, 243n9; 6.585–589,
    196n99
Vita Homeri Herodotea 135–140, 156n43

Xenophon
  Anabasis 5.24.28, 69n10

Zenobius
  *Epitome collectionum Lucilli Tarrhaei
    et Didymi* 1.18.10–15, Schneidewin
    and von Leutsch, 195n97

General Index

abuse: of the dead, 75n32, 85n58; mutilation of corpses by dogs and birds, 78, 85 and n58, 135–136; of self in mourning, 90–91, 91n69

Achilles: armor of Achilles, 73n26, 77, 82 and nn49–52, 175–176, 176n44; *atē* of Achilles, 198n104 (*see also* Index Verborum, s.v. ἄτη); choice of Achilles, 4; death of Achilles, 66n2, 110; fame of Achilles (see *kleos aphthiton*); fasting of Achilles, 73n27; heroism of Achilles, 42, 163–168, 23; horses of Achilles, 33–36, 185n70; like a corpse in sorrow, 89, 90–91 and 91n71; like a dog in anger at Hektor, 87–88; temporal experience of Achilles in mourning, 89–91; tomb of Achilles, 109–110, 136, 147

Agamemnon: *atē* of Agamemnon, 198–199 (*see also* Index Verborum, s.v. ἄτη); fame of Agamemnon, 146–147; Agamemnon's rhetoric of time, 49–56; tomb of Agamemnon, 146

Ajax. *See under* burial

ambrosia, 22–23, 43n97, 71–73, 81–82, 131, 163 and n11, 177; immortalizing agent, 43n97, 73 and nn28–29, 81–82, 131. *See also* Index Verborum, s.v. ἀμβροσία

Andromache: diadem of Andromache, 125–129; foretells Hektor's death, 124, 250; imagines Hektor's corpse, 85–86

Aphrodite: defends Hektor's corpse, 86–87; temporal experience when weighed down by pain, 180; temporal experience when worn down by pain, 179; temporal experience when wounded by Diomedes, 178–181

Apollo: antagonism with Greek heroes, 163–165; antagonism with Poseidon, 166–167; builder of Trojan wall with Poseidon, 112–114; challenger of Zeus, 195–197; preserves Hektor's corpse, 87; preserves Sarpedon's corpse, 70–71

aristeia: hero becomes like a god, 163–164, 165 and n17, 166n18; logic of *aristeia*, 65–66, 163–166; three times vs. four times, 164–166 and 166n15. *See also* Index Verborum, s.vv. ἀριστεία *and* δαίμονι ἶσος

Astyanax, 124 and n56

Atē, goddess of delusion, 160, 198–201

Being-in-the-world, 31 and n79, 185n70; and human temporality, 31–32, 31n78 and n81, 32n82, 185n70. *See also under* phenomenology: Heidegger; temporality: body subject

Being-toward-death, 32n84, 33, 42, 237. *See also under* phenomenology: Heidegger

Being-toward-the-end, 32n84, 42, 237. *See also under* phenomenology: Heidegger

binding, 161n6, 173n37, 191, 222–225, 225n157

blame speech, 135; biting its victim like a dog eating a corpse, 135–136, 135n10. *See also* Index Verborum, s.v. ὄνειδος

body-subject/body in the world. *See under* Being-in-the-world; phenomenology: Heidegger; temporality

boredom. *See under* temporality; Index Verborum, s.v. ἀσχαλάω

boundary divisions: and the game *episkuros*, 149n32; and property dividers, 149. *See also* Index Verborum, s.v. οὖρος

Briseïs, 3, 47, 93 and n76, 128, 134, 198

burial: as product driven ritual, 140–141; as rites due to the dead (γέρας θανόντων), 133–137; as rite of passage for the dead, 139–140; of Achilles, 136–137, 147; of Ajax, 138; of Elpenor, 143–145; of Hektor, 93–94, 136–137; of Patroclus, 136–137, 137n14; of Sarpedon, 67–74; primary burial (as "purification"), 140; secondary burial (as "joining the ancestors"), 140. *See also* cremation; funerary ritual;

tomb; Index Verborum, s.v. γέρας θανόντων

cannibalism, 84n57

Cleobulus, 155–157

clock time: objective means for measuring time, 23–24, 27, 42, 55; decaying Achaean ships as clocks, 23, 52–54; clotted launching channels as clocks, 54–55; decay of human body as clock, 23, 27, chapter 2 *passim*

cremation: as acceleration of physical decay, 140–142, 141n23; as *sine qua non* of Homeric burial, 137–139, 141; as strategy of commemorating the dead, 140–142, 142n23 and n25. *See also* burial, tomb

dactylic hexameter. *See under* epic

death: Being-towards-death, 32n84, 33, 42, 237; of the gods, 43n97, chapter 5 *passim*

decay: and time, 21–23, 45, 52, 56–57, 60; and temporality, 21–23, 55, 89–94; Being-towards-decay, 41–42, 237; of the bodies of the dead, 21, chapter 2 *passim*; of the epic tradition, 41–42, 148–157, 235–237; of the ships of the Achaeans, 21, 52–55; semantic field of decay (*see* Appendix)

deixis and immediacy, 63 and n26

desynchronization. *See under* temporality

Dios apatē "deception of Zeus", 93n75, 201 and n107, 204, 208. *See also* Index Verborum, s.v. Διὸς ἀπάτη

Dios boulē "plan of Zeus", 19n42, 47 and n4, 121 and n48, 205. *See also* Index Verborum, s.v. Διὸς βουλή

divine twins, 170n30

dogs. *See under* abuse; Achilles; blame speech
durability, 2, 4–5, 13–14, 21, 23, 29, 30; of communal memory, 150–155; of defensive walls, 13–14, 23, 42, 95, 106–107, 118–119; of divine craft, 82–83, 111–116, 236, 256–257; of human bodies/vitality, 5–8, 21–23, 79–80, 82, 84, 90–93, 179, 242–244; of *kleos aphthiton*, 2, 4–5, 7–9, 12–14, 19–20, 21, 30, 109, 150–155, 236, 256–257; of ships/wood, 21, 23, 52–55; of tombs and architectural memorials, 23, 131–132, 141–142, 143, 146–147, 149–150, 152–153, 157; of vegetal life, 5–8. *See also* clock time; decay; epic; *kleos*; *kleos aphthiton*; memory; temporality (endurance); tomb

epic: as cultural strategy of commemoration, 41–42, 45–46, 66, 148, 152–153; epic cycle, 16, 117n42; flexibility and modification of formulae, 18n38, 90n67, 220–221 and nn148–152; innovation in oral epic poetic tradition, 17–21 and nn38–40 and n42 and n45; meter/dactylic hexameter, 16, 18, 90; oral epic poetic tradition, 15–21 and n42 and nn44–46, 117, 119n47. *See also kleos aphthiton*
Ephialtes and Otos, 221–222

flexibility and modification of formulae. *See under* epic
funerary ritual: *Šalliš waštaiš* ritual, 137n14. *See also* burial; cremation; *kleos*; Index Verborum, s.v. γέρας θανόντων

Hades: temporal experience when wounded by Herakles, 186–187
Hektor: corpse preserved by Aphrodite and Apollo, 86–88, 90, 92–93; defender of Troy, 124–125; serial abuse of corpse by Achilles, 88–89
Heidegger, Martin. *See under* phenomenology
Hephaistos: and human temporality, 83n55; god of divine craftwork, 82–83, 111–116, 236, 256–257; lame god, 188–190; rival of Zeus, 188–195
Hera: hatred of Trojans, 84n57; and the hero, 167–168, 167n23; and time/seasons, 167–168, 167n23; rival of Zeus, 204–210; temporal experience when wounded by Herakles, 181–182, 184–185
Hupnos, god of sleep: power over all creatures, 206n116; rival of Zeus, 160, 201–204
Husserl, Edmund. *See under* phenomenology

Indo-European: inherited vocabulary, 68; phraseology, 13–14, 19–21 and nn44–45; poetics, 19n45

kleos "fame", 5; and hero's tomb, 74 and n30, 109, 131–132, 139, 141–147; of the camp wall of the Achaeans, 110, 112, 114n37; vs. *nostos* "return home", 55
kleos aphthiton "unwithered fame", 3–5 and nn3–5, 7–9, 8n12, 14 and n28, 19–20 and nn44–45, 41–43, 46, 64, 66–67, 94, 132, 143, 148, 153, 157, 161, 257 and n29

lightning, 160, 195–196, 196n99, 207–208 and nn121–122

memory: and performance, 63; as force preserving objects against decay, 45, 62–63. *See also* epic, *kleos*, tomb

mourning. *See under* Achilles; temporality; Thetis; Zeus

narrative spatialization, 89n65

nektar, 23, 80–84 and nn46–48, 163 and n11. *See also* Index Verborum, s.v. νέκταρ

no longer, 4, 9, 23, 24, 29–30, 34–36, 45, 49–52, 57, 61, 89, 107, 149, 151, 224, 233–234. *See also* Index Verborum, s.v. οὐκ ἔτι.

nostos "return", 4, 55, 59, 99n4, 219; vs. *kleos* "fame", 4, 55. *See also* Index Verborum, s.v. νόστος

not yet, 2–5, 9, 11–12, 22–23, 24, 30, 35, 36, 50–52, 61, 74, 92–93, 94, 96, 107, 113, 132, 153, 159, 184, 233. *See also* still perfectly; Index Verborum, s.v. οὔ πω.

Odysseus: rhetoric of time, 57–64; vivid recollection, 62–63

oral poetry. *See* epic

ordinal numbers, 10–11

pain. *See under* Aphrodite; temporality: emotional pain *and* physical pain; Thetis

Patroklos: burial of Patroklos, 75–76; foretells Hektor's death, 65n1; ghost of, 75–76, 76n37; killed by Hektor, 65; kills Sarpedon, 65; preservation of Patroklos' corpse by Thetis, 76–82

phenomenology, 5, 26–29, 31–33; anxiety (*Angst*), 31; authenticity, 33n85; Being-in-the-world, 33; Being-there (*Dasein*), 31; Being-toward-death, 33, 42, 237; Being-

toward-the-end, 42, 237; care (*Sorge*), 31, 41, 234–235; death, 32–33; entangled (*verfängt*), 31, 234; fragility, 42, 110, 237; Heidegger, Martin, 24nn52–53, 26, 31–33, 185n70; Husserl, Edmund, 26–27, 29; lived-body, 28n69, 178n51; pain (*see under* temporality: emotional pain *and* physical pain); protension, 27; retention, 27; temporal objects, 26–27. *See also* temporality

primary burial. *See under* burial

protension. *See under* phenomenology

retention. *See under* phenomenology

Sarpedon. *See under* Apollo; burial; Zeus

secondary burial. *See under* burial

shame: and blame speech, 135–136, 135n10; and failure to defend a companion from abuse at enemy's hands, 134–135; and failure to meet social obligation, 58, 60–61

Simonides, 155–157

still perfectly, 1–2, 4, 9, 12, 43, 94. *See also* not yet

superlative adjectives, 10–11, 10n18

Tartaros, 208–210; as prison of challengers, 160, 191 and n86, 210; as bronze jar, 225–227; and underworld in Near Eastern mythology, 227–229

temporality, 26 (*see also under* phenomenology: Heidegger *and* Husserl); acceleration of time (boredom), 60 and n22, 232 (*see also* under temporality: impatience); body-subject/body in the world, 27–29, 84n56; decelera-

tion of time (depression), 35 and
n87, 91 and n71; desynchronization, 22, 28n68, 60n22, 94n78,
234; endurance, 29–30, 36, 62,
107, 161, 174–187; explicit and
implicit temporality, 27–29 and
nn67–69; impatience, 60 and n22,
232 (*see also under* temporality:
acceleration of time); lived time,
27–28 and nn67–68, 178n51;
resynchronization, 93n76, 94n78;
and anxiety, 22, 31 and nn80–81,
40, 42, 68, 160, 179, 234; and
desire, 22, 28n69, 179n55; and
hunger, 21–22, 21n47, 28nn68–69,
35n86, 73n27, 167n19, 177n47;
and emotional pain, 33–40,
174n40, 179n54, 185n70; and
exertion/exhaustion, 40n95,
179, 188–189, 222, 224; and
illness, 29, 173 and n39, 233; and
mourning, 90–91, 91n70, 93n76;
and old age, 79, 173, 179n57; and
perception ("temporal objects"),
26–27; and physical pain, 27–30,
35n86, 40n95, 178–181, 178n51,
184–185, 185n70; human vs.
divine experience of time, 29–30,
33–39, 39n93, 40n95, 41n96, 52,
84, 90–91, 93, 162, 166–167, 173,
178–180, 184–185, 185nn69–70,
222–224, 225n158, 234
Thetis: as mother figure, 7, 37–38,
38n91; defender of Patroclus'
corpse, 77–78, 87; mourning and
emotional pain, 36–38, 174n40
time, 62, 232; as force of decay, 52,
56–57, 60, 231–232; made visible/
manifest through clock, (*see* clock
time); human experience of time
vs. divine experience of time
(*see under* temporality); rhetoric
of time (*see under* Agamemnon;

Odysseus). *See also* Index
Verborum, s.v. χρόνος
Titans: gods of former generation,
191n85; incarcerated in Tartaros,
194
tomb, tombstone: as index of buried
dead, 143; as identifying trait of
dead, 145; as means to preserve
memory and fame of dead (see
under *kleos*); as physical counterpart of verbal *kleos* (see under
kleos); of Achilles, 109–110,
136–137, 147; of Aiputos, 143; of
Aisuetes, 131, 143; of Dardanus,
131; of Elpenor, 143–145; of Ilus,
131, 143; of Myrina, 151–152.
See also burial, cremation, *kleos*;
Index Verborum, s.vv. τύμβος,
σῆμα, στήλη
Typhon/Typhoeus, challenger of
Zeus, 191–195

walls: as substitutes for heroes,
102–104, 104n15; as unbreakable/
unbroken, 113, 115–119 (*see also*
Index Verborum, s.v. ἄρρηκτος);
of the Achaeans, 97–110; of the
Trojans, 110–119

Zeus: *atē* of Zeus, 198–201; care for
humans, 234; challengers (see
Apollo, Atē, Hera, Hephaistos,
Hupnos, lightning, Typhon);
mourns Hektor, 39–40n94;
mourns Sarpedon, 39–40n94 ;
plan of Zeus and plot of *Iliad* (see
Dios boulē); potentially unstable
rule of, 40, 160, 187–210. See also
Dios apatē, Dios boulē